Lecture Notes in Computer Science   16145

Founding Editors

Gerhard Goos
Juris Hartmanis

Editorial Board Members

Elisa Bertino, *Purdue University, West Lafayette, IN, USA*
Wen Gao, *Peking University, Beijing, China*
Bernhard Steffen, *TU Dortmund University, Dortmund, Germany*
Moti Yung, *Columbia University, New York, NY, USA*

The series Lecture Notes in Computer Science (LNCS), including its subseries Lecture Notes in Artificial Intelligence (LNAI) and Lecture Notes in Bioinformatics (LNBI), has established itself as a medium for the publication of new developments in computer science and information technology research, teaching, and education.

LNCS enjoys close cooperation with the computer science R & D community, the series counts many renowned academics among its volume editors and paper authors, and collaborates with prestigious societies. Its mission is to serve this international community by providing an invaluable service, mainly focused on the publication of conference and workshop proceedings and postproceedings. LNCS commenced publication in 1973.

Meenakshi D'Souza · Raghavan Komondoor ·
B. Srivathsan
Editors

Automated Technology for Verification and Analysis

23rd International Symposium, ATVA 2025
Bengaluru, India, October 27–31, 2025
Proceedings

Springer

Editors
Meenakshi D'Souza
IIIT Bangalore
Bengaluru, Karnataka, India

Raghavan Komondoor
Indian Institute of Science
Bengaluru, Karnataka, India

B. Srivathsan
Chennai Mathematical Institute
Kelambakkam, Tamil Nadu, India

ISSN 0302-9743 ISSN 1611-3349 (electronic)
Lecture Notes in Computer Science
ISBN 978-3-032-08706-5 ISBN 978-3-032-08707-2 (eBook)
https://doi.org/10.1007/978-3-032-08707-2

© The Editor(s) (if applicable) and The Author(s), under exclusive license to Springer Nature Switzerland AG 2026

This work is subject to copyright. All rights are solely and exclusively licensed by the Publisher, whether the whole or part of the material is concerned, specifically the rights of translation, reprinting, reuse of illustrations, recitation, broadcasting, reproduction on microfilms or in any other physical way, and transmission or information storage and retrieval, electronic adaptation, computer software, or by similar or dissimilar methodology now known or hereafter developed.
The use of general descriptive names, registered names, trademarks, service marks, etc. in this publication does not imply, even in the absence of a specific statement, that such names are exempt from the relevant protective laws and regulations and therefore free for general use.
The publisher, the authors and the editors are safe to assume that the advice and information in this book are believed to be true and accurate at the date of publication. Neither the publisher nor the authors or the editors give a warranty, expressed or implied, with respect to the material contained herein or for any errors or omissions that may have been made. The publisher remains neutral with regard to jurisdictional claims in published maps and institutional affiliations.

This Springer imprint is published by the registered company Springer Nature Switzerland AG
The registered company address is: Gewerbestrasse 11, 6330 Cham, Switzerland

If disposing of this product, please recycle the paper.

Preface

We are pleased to present the volume of regular and tool papers that were accepted to the 23rd International Symposium on Automated Technology for Verification and Analysis (ATVA 2025). ATVA 2025 was held in Bengaluru, India from the 27th to the 31st of October, 2025. ATVA is dedicated to the presentation of research results pertaining to theoretical and practical aspects of automated analysis, verification, and synthesis of formal structures as well as programs. ATVA seeks to enhance interactions between worldwide researchers, academics, students, and industry, and is frequently held in Asia and surrounding regions.

ATVA 2025 sought paper submissions in two categories – research and tool. Fifty-nine submissions were originally received, of which 48 were reviewed (11 were desk rejected due to non-alignment with the conference topics). These consisted of 39 research paper submissions and 9 tool paper submissions. Reviews were double blind, and each submission was reviewed by at least three program committee members. There was an artifact evaluation process as well, which was mandatory for all tool paper submissions and optional for accepted research papers. The review process was rigorous, with substantive online discussions among reviewers. In the end, 17 research papers and 4 tool papers were accepted.

The conference program was highlighted by three invited talks, delivered by renowned researchers, covering important ideas and results on three diverse topics:

- Aarti Gupta, from Princeton University, USA, delivered a talk titled "Network Abstractions for Modularity and Performance Verification".
- Peter Müller, from ETH Zurich, Switzerland, delivered a talk titled "15 Years of Viper: Building and Evolving a Verification Infrastructure".
- Rahul Sharma, from Microsoft Research, India, delivered a talk titled "LLMs meet Program Synthesis".

Continuing the tradition from previous years' ATVAs, the program this year included two in-depth tutorials, each two hours long, given by renowned experts in the respective areas:

- Benjamin Kaminski, from Saarland University, Germany, gave a tutorial on Quantitative and Probabilistic Verification using Quantitative Predicate Transformers.
- Kartik Nagar, from IIT Madras, India, gave a tutorial on Specification and Verification of Replicated Data Types.

The last day of the program was devoted to a workshop titled "Milestones and Motifs in Automata and Concurrency". The workshop featured internationally renowned invited speakers giving talks on automata, concurrency and timed systems, with a focus on recent advances in these areas. The invited speakers were Ahmed Bouajjani from IRIF, Université Paris Cité, France, Pavithra Prabhakar from Kansas State University, USA, P.S. Thiagarajan from University of North Carolina, USA, and Pascal Weil from LIPN,

CNRS, France. We thank the organizers of the workshop, S. Akshay from IIT Bombay, Kumar Madhukar from IIT Delhi, and C. Aiswarya from Chennai Mathematical Institute, India, for having organized this workshop, which served as an added opportunity for the conference attendees.

We thank the program committee and the external reviewers for their rigorous reviews and discussions, which formed the backbone of the efforts towards selecting good papers and forming a good program. The program committee consisted of 56 members, who were leading researchers in various areas of relevance to the conference, residing in different regions of the world. The vast majority of papers were reviewed by three members, while a handful of papers received four reviews. Initial reviews were sent out to authors, and then they were given an opportunity to turn in a response to the reviews. An online discussion then took place for each paper, where reviewers took into account the authors' responses, and discussed and came to a consensus. For papers that had an extensive online discussion with many points brought out by the reviewers, a meta review was written by a PC Chair or by a PC member to summarize the discussion for the benefit of the authors. The meta reviews were meant as additional feedback to authors of rejected papers, and contained suggestions for improvements in the camera-ready versions to authors of accepted papers. About a third of the paper submissions received such meta reviews. The EasyChair system was used for entering reviews, for discussions, and to convey decisions. At the time of this writing, a process whereby the PC members could select a small number of distinguished papers from among the accepted papers was being put into place.

Continuing the practice introduced in ATVA 2024, this edition of ATVA also featured an artifact evaluation process. There was a separate artifact evaluation committee, headed by Jie An, from ISCAS, Beijing, China and Priyanka Golia from IIT Delhi, India. The Committee consisted of 17 researchers with interest and expertise in practical techniques and tools and their evaluation. There were two rounds of artifact evaluation. The first round ran concurrently with the paper reviews. In this round, it was mandatory for authors of each tool paper submission to also make an artifact submission. There was an initial "smoke test", where any minor technical issues with running the artifacts were identified, and authors were given an opportunity to clarify these matters. Each artifact was evaluated by two to three reviewers, who then discussed among themselves, and awarded one of the following combination of badges: Available, Available and Functional, or Available, Functional, and Reusable. For a tool paper to be accepted, it had to be accepted by the PC members reviewing the paper, and had to be awarded the Functional badge by the artifact evaluation committee. In the second round of artifact evaluation, authors of accepted research papers were invited to (optionally) submit their artifacts. Authors of 11 of the accepted research papers (out of a total of 17) submitted artifacts, and these were evaluated and granted badges in a similar way as in the first round. All told, of the 20 artifacts submitted, 10 earned all three badges, 5 earned the Available and Functional badges, while 5 earned the Available badge. The EasyChair system was used to receive artifact submissions, for discussions, and for returning the corresponding reviews and badge award decisions as well.

We thank the International Institute of Information Technology (IIIT) Bangalore for stepping forward to host the conference. We thank the General Chair, Deepak D'Souza, from IISc, Bangalore and the Organizing Chair, Sujit Kumar Chakrabarti, from IIIT Bangalore, and the entire organizing team, for the entire work behind hosting the conference, the venue logistics, accommodation and local transportation, and taking care of the finances. We are grateful to Springer for publishing the proceedings and for sponsoring the awards, and to Microsoft for being a sponsor.

October 2025

Meenakshi D'Souza
Raghavan Komondoor
B. Srivathsan
Jie An
Priyanka Golia

Organization

General Chair

Deepak D'Souza   Indian Institute of Science, India

Program Committee Chairs

Meenakshi D'Souza   IIIT Bangalore, India
Raghavan Komondoor   Indian Institute of Science, India
B. Srivathsan   Chennai Mathematical Institute, India

Artifact Evaluation Committee Chairs

Jie An   ISCAS, China
Priyanka Golia   IIT Delhi, India

Local Organization Chair

Sujit K. Chakrabarti   IIIT Bangalore, India

Program Committee

S. Akshay   IIT Bombay, India
Étienne André   Université Sorbonne Paris Nord, France
Guy Avni   University of Haifa, Israel
Gogul Balakrishnan   Google, USA
A. R. Balasubramanian   Technical University of Munich, Germany
Ansuman Banerjee   ISI Kolkata, India
Suguman Bansal   Georgia Institute of Technology, USA
Dirk Beyer   LMU Munich, Germany
Mingshuai Chen   Zhejiang University, China
Yu-Fang Chen   Academia Sinica, Taiwan
Yunja Choi   Kyungpook National University, South Korea
Christoph Csallner   University of Texas at Arlington, USA

Rayna Dimitrova	CISPA, Germany
Susanna Donatelli	Università degli Studi di Torino, Italy
Grigory Fedyukovich	Florida State University, USA
Hongfei Fu	Shanghai Jiao Tong University, China
Orna Grumberg	Technion - Israel Institute of Technology, Israel
Shibashis Guha	Tata Institute of Fundamental Research, India
Ashutosh Gupta	Tata Institute of Fundamental Research, India
Ichiro Hasuo	National Institute of Informatics, Japan
Frédéric Herbreteau	University of Bordeaux, France
Jie-Hong Roland Jiang	National Taiwan University, Taiwan
S. Krishna	IIT Bombay, India
Orna Kupferman	Hebrew University, Israel
Milan Lopuhaä-Zwakenberg	University of Twente, Netherlands
Kumar Madhukar	IIT Delhi, India
Shahar Maoz	Tel Aviv University, Israel
Umang Mathur	National University of Singapore, Singapore
Ashish Mishra	IIT Hyderabad, India
Benjamin Monmege	Aix-Marseille Université, France
Sergio Mover	École Polytechnique, France
Kartik Nagar	IIT Madras, India
Daniel Neider	Technical University of Dortmund, Germany
Youssouf Oualhadj	Université Paris-Est Créteil, France
Andreas Pavlogiannis	Aarhus University, Denmark
Doron Peled	Bar-Ilan University, Israel
Lauren Pick	Chinese University of Hong Kong, China
Sumanth Prabhu	TCS Research, India
M. Praveen	Chennai Mathematical Institute, India
Xiaokang Qiu	Purdue University, USA
Murali Krishna Ramanathan	AWS AI Labs, USA
Subhajit Roy	IIT Kanpur, India
Prakash Saivasan	Institute of Mathematical Sciences, India
Sriram Sankaranarayanan	University of Colorado at Boulder, USA
Anne-Kathrin Schmuck	MPI Software Systems, Germany
Arpit Sharma	IISER Bhopal, India
Quentin Stiévenart	Université du Québec à Montréal, Canada
Vaishnavi Sundararajan	IIT Delhi, India
Nathalie Sznajder	Sorbonne Université, France
Aditya V. Thakur	University of California, Davis, USA
Yakir Vizel	Technion - Israel Institute of Technology, Israel
Masaki Waga	Kyoto University, Japan
Zhilin Wu	ISCAS, China

Artifact Evaluation Committee

Burak Ekici	University of Oxford, UK
Chiao Hsieh	Kyoto University, Japan
Mehrdad Karrabi	ISTA, Austria
Sumit Lahiri	IIT Kanpur, India
Deyun Lyu	National Institute of Informatics, Japan
Enrico Magnago	Amazon Web Services, Germany
Awanish Pandey	IIT Roorkee, India
Frédéric Recoules	CEA - LIST, France
Hans-Jörg Schurr	University of Iowa, USA
Arijit Shaw	Chennai Mathematical Institute, India
Han Su	ISCAS, China
Yican Sun	Peking University, China
Aalok Thakkar	Ashoka University, India
Yedi Zhang	National University of Singapore, Singapore
Xindi Zhang	ISCAS, China

Local Organization Committee

Meenakshi D'Souza	IIIT Bangalore, India
Saumya Shankar	IIIT Bangalore, India

Steering Committee

Yu-Fang Chen	Academia Sinica, Taiwan
Yunja Choi	Kyungpook National University, South Korea
Ichiro Hasuo	National Institute of Informatics, Japan
Jie-Hong Roland Jiang	National Taiwan University, Taiwan
Doron A. Peled	Bar-Ilan University, Israel

Advisory Committee

Teruo Higashino	Osaka University, Japan
Oscar H. Ibarra	University of California, Santa Barbara, USA
Insup Lee	University of Pennsylvania, USA
Farn Wang	National Taiwan University, Taiwan
Hsu-Chun Yen	National Taiwan University, Taiwan

Additional Reviewers

Benedikt Bollig
Jan Corazza
Long-Hin Fung
Aline Goeminne
Sipeng Sun
Anantha Padmanabha
Yu-Hung Pan
Mohammad Afzal
Benjamin Bordais
Kwan Shun Quinson Hon

Yu-Hsuan Wu
Daniel Baier
Prantik Chatterjee
Soumyajit Paul
Boris Wu
Tian-Fu Chen
Jean-Marc Talbot
Marian Lingsch-Rosenfeld
Himadri Sekhar Paul
Pranshu Gaba

Contents

Automata and Temporal Logic

Componentwise Automata Learning for System Integration 3
  *Hiroya Fujinami, Masaki Waga, Jie An, Kohei Suenaga,
  Nayuta Yanagisawa, Hiroki Iseri, and Ichiro Hasuo*

Learning Event-Recording Automata Passively 27
  Anirban Majumdar, Sayan Mukherjee, and Jean-François Raskin

TAPAAL HyperLTL: A Tool for Checking Hyperproperties of Petri Nets 49
  *Bruno Maria René Gonzalez, Peter Gjøl Jensen, Stefan Schmid,
  Jiří Srba, and Martin Zimmermann*

Games and Controller Synthesis

Quantitative Strategy Templates 65
  *Ashwani Anand, Satya Prakash Nayak, Ritam Raha, Irmak Sağlam,
  and Anne-Kathrin Schmuck*

Energy Games with Weight Uncertainty 87
  Orna Kupferman and Naama Shamash Halevy

Widest Path Games and Maximality Inheritance in Bounded Value
Iteration for Stochastic Games 109
  Kittiphon Phalakarn, Yun Chen Tsai, and Ichiro Hasuo

Monitoring and Runtime Verification

Prompt Runtime Enforcement 135
  *Ayush Anand, Loïc Germerie Guizouarn, Thierry Jéron,
  Sayan Mukherjee, Srinivas Pinisetty, and Ocan Sankur*

Efficient Dynamic Shielding for Parametric Safety Specifications 157
  Davide Corsi, Kaushik Mallik, Andoni Rodríguez, and César Sánchez

Learning Verified Monitors for Hidden Markov Models 180
  Luko van der Maas and Sebastian Junges

Probabilistic Verification and Quantum Computing

Generalized Parameter Lifting: Finer Abstractions for Parametric Markov Chains 207
    Linus Heck, Tim Quatmann, Jip Spel, Joost-Pieter Katoen, and Sebastian Junges

Towards Unified Probabilistic Verification and Validation of Vision-Based Autonomy 231
    Jordan Peper, Yan Miao, Sayan Mitra, and Ivan Ruchkin

Q-Sylvan: A Parallel Decision Diagram Package for Quantum Computing 260
    Sebastiaan Brand and Alfons Laarman

Learning

Inductive Generalization in Reinforcement Learning from Specifications 277
    Vignesh Subramanian, Rohit Kushwah, Subhajit Roy, and Suguman Bansal

Solution-Aware Vs Global ReLU Selection: Partial MILP Strikes Back for DNN Verification 299
    Yuke Liao, Blaise Genest, Kuldeep Meel, and Shaan Aryaman

Locally Pareto-Optimal Interpretations for Black-Box Machine Learning Models 321
    Aniruddha Joshi, Supratik Chakraborty, S. Akshay, Shetal Shah, Hazem Torfah, and Sanjit Seshia

Hybrid and Dynamical Systems

Evaluation, Reduction, and Approximation of Dynamical Systems and Networks with ERODE 345
    Luca Cardelli, Giuseppe Squillace, Mirco Tribastone, Max Tschaikowski, and Andrea Vandin

Deriving Liveness Properties of Hybrid Systems from Reachable Sets and Lyapunov-Like Certificates 363
    Ludovico Battista and Stefano Tonetta

Control Closure Certificates 387
    Vishnu Murali, Mohammed Adib Oumer, and Majid Zamani

Verification

POLYQENT: A Polynomial Quantified Entailment Solver 411
*Krishnendu Chatterjee, Amir Kafshdar Goharshady,
Ehsan Kafshdar Goharshady, Mehrdad Karrabi, Milad Saadat,
Maximilian Seeliger, and Đorđe Žikelić*

Data Structures for Finite Downsets of Natural Vectors: Theory and Practice ... 425
Michaël Cadilhac, Vanessa Flügel, Guillermo A. Pérez, and Shrisha Rao

Antarbhukti: Verifying Correctness of PLC Software During System
Evolution 447
Soumyadip Bandyopadhyay and Santonu Sarkar

Author Index 473

Automata and Temporal Logic

Componentwise Automata Learning for System Integration

Hiroya Fujinami[1,5(✉)], Masaki Waga[1,2], Jie An[3], Kohei Suenaga[1,2], Nayuta Yanagisawa[4], Hiroki Iseri[4], and Ichiro Hasuo[1,5,6]

[1] National Institute of Informatics, Tokyo, Japan
{makenowjust,hasuo}@nii.ac.jp
[2] Kyoto University, Kyoto, Japan
{mwaga,ksuenaga}@fos.kuis.kyoto-u.ac.jp
[3] Institute of Software, Chinese Academy of Sciences, Beijing, China
anjie@iscas.ac.cn
[4] Toyota Motor Corporation, Tokyo, Japan
{nayuta_yanagisawa,hiroki_iseri}@mail.toyota.co.jp
[5] SOKENDAI (The Graduate University for Advanced Studies), Kanagawa, Japan
[6] Imiron Co., Ltd., Tokyo, Japan

Abstract. *Compositional automata learning* is attracting attention as an analysis technique for complex black-box systems. It exploits a target system's internal compositional structure to reduce complexity. In this paper, we identify *system integration*—the process of building a new system as a composite of potentially third-party and black-box components—as a new application domain of compositional automata learning. Accordingly, we propose a new problem setting, where the learner has direct access to black-box components. This is in contrast with the usual problem settings of compositional learning, where the target is a legacy black-box system and queries can only be made to the whole system (but not to components). We call our problem *componentwise automata learning* for distinction. We identify a challenge there called *component redundancies*: some parts of components may not contribute to system-level behaviors, and learning them incurs unnecessary effort. We introduce a *contextual componentwise learning* algorithm that systematically removes such redundancies. We experimentally evaluate our proposal and show its practical relevance.

Keywords: automata learning · compositional automata learning · systems engineering · Moore machine

---

J. An—Technical contribution was made when at National Institute of Informatics, Tokyo, Japan.
N. Yanagisawa—Theoretical investigation independent of testing procedures at industry-affiliated institutions.
H. Iseri—Additional contribution to the study.

© The Author(s), under exclusive license to Springer Nature Switzerland AG 2026
M. D'Souza et al. (Eds.): ATVA 2025, LNCS 16145, pp. 3–26, 2026.
https://doi.org/10.1007/978-3-032-08707-2_1

1 Introduction

Automata Learning. *(Active) automata learning* is a problem to infer an automaton recognizing the target language $\mathcal{L}_{\mathrm{tgt}} \subseteq \Sigma^*$ via a finite number of queries to an oracle. The L* algorithm [2], the best known active automata learning algorithm by Angluin, infers the minimum DFA recognizing the target regular language $\mathcal{L}_{\mathrm{tgt}}$ via two kinds of queries: *membership* and *equivalence* queries.

- In a membership query, the learner asks if a word $w \in \Sigma^*$ is in $\mathcal{L}_{\mathrm{tgt}}$. (For machines with output (e.g. Mealy and Moore), membership queries are called *output queries*, a term we will be using in this paper.) The answers to those membership/output queries are recorded in an *(observation) table*; once the table is *closed* it induces a *hypothesis DFA*.
- In an equivalence query, the learner asks if a hypothesis DFA $\mathcal{A}_{\mathrm{hyp}}$ recognizes $\mathcal{L}_{\mathrm{tgt}}$. If not, the oracle returns a *counterexample* $\mathit{cex} \in \mathcal{L}_{\mathrm{tgt}} \triangle \mathcal{L}(\mathcal{A}_{\mathrm{hyp}})$ that witnesses the deviation of $\mathcal{A}_{\mathrm{hyp}}$'s language from $\mathcal{L}_{\mathrm{tgt}}$.

A target of automata learning is commonly called a *system under learning (SUL)*.

After the seminal work [2], various algorithms have been proposed, for example, to improve the efficiency [12,26,29] and to learn other classes of automata (e.g. Mealy machines [22], weighted automata [11,19], symbolic automata [3,5,7], and visibly pushdown automata [1]). The LearnLib library offers an open source framework for automata learning [13]. Many real-world applications of automata learning have been reported, too. See e.g. [4,6].

In the context of verification and testing, active automata learning is used to approximate *black-box* systems and obtain a surrogate model amenable to whitebox analysis. For example, automata learning of Moore or Mealy machines has been applied for model checking [20,24,27] and controller synthesis [30].

Compositional Automata Learning. Recently, algorithms for *compositional automata learning* are attracting attention [6,8,15,16,21]. Assuming that the SUL M is a composition of some subsystems $M_1, \ldots, M_n$ (called *components*), those algorithms try to learn individual components M_i and construct a model of M as their composition, rather than *monolithically* learning the SUL M itself.

A major benefit of such compositional approaches is *complexity*: if each M_i has k_i states, the SUL has $k_1 \times \cdots \times k_n$ states and the monolithic learning has to learn these, while the compositional learning has to learn only $k_1 + \cdots + k_n$ states in total. Since many real-world systems are constructed using components, compositional automata learning is a promising approach to scalable learning.

It is important to note that different compositional automata learning algorithms assume very different problem settings. The differences lie in the type of automata to learn, how they are composed, the learning interface, etc. We will make a detailed comparison later; its summary is in Table 1.

In most existing works including [6,8,15,16,21], the learner has no access to individual components to make queries. It thus tries to learn components indirectly via system-level queries. A typical application scenario is where the SUL

M is a *legacy* black-box system: M's compositional structure may be known, e.g. via old documentation; yet M's components are buried in the black-box system M and their interface is not exposed. In this case, the technical challenge is *how to throw component-level queries indirectly*, that is, to translate component-level queries (that the learner wants to ask) to system-level queries (that the learner can ask in reality). The works [6,8,15,16,21] propose different solutions to this challenge, specializing in each problem setting.

Our problem setting—we call it *componentwise learning* for distinction—is very different from the above; so is the main technical challenge there. We first motivate our problem setting with *system integration* as application.

Motivation: System Integration with Black-Box Components. *System integration (SI)* in ICT industry refers to "the process of creating a complex information system that may include designing or building a customized architecture or application, integrating it with new or existing hardware, packaged and custom software, and communications."[1] SI is nowadays a norm in various layers of ICT system development:

- Large-scale ICT systems for banks, e-commerce, and other business processes are products of SI where different software components, typically developed by different parties, get integrated.
- Smaller software pieces also rely on existing software components offered as libraries (e.g. `pip` for Python). They can be thus seen as products of SI.

SI is not unique to ICT. In fact, our original motivation comes from the automotive industry, where various systems (a car, an engine, control software, etc.) get built by assembling parts that are often manufactured by other parties.

In this paper, a body that conducts SI is called a *system integrator (SIer)*. SIers have to make sure that the composite system behaves as expected. This is not easy, however, since components that constitute the composite system are usually black-box systems. This situation thus makes SI a natural target of automata learning. Moreover, *compositional* automata learning can be used, since an SIer knows the compositional structure that combines black-box components.

Contribution: Contextual Componentwise Automata Learning. In SI, the learner (an SIer) is building a *new* composite system. The learner has (raw) component in its hands, and thus has direct interface for component-level queries. This is in stark contrast with other works [6,8,15,16,21] where the target is an *old* (legacy) system and the main challenge is indirect component-level queries. To highlight this difference, we use the term *componentwise automata learning* for compositional learning where direct component-level queries are available.

---

[1] Gartner Information Technology Glossary, https://www.gartner.com/en/information-technology/glossary/system-integration.

A new challenge that we face in componentwise automata learning is *component redundancies*. In an SI scenario (no matter if it is ICT or automotive), components are rarely *lean*, meaning that most of the time they come with more functionalities than an SIer needs for the composite system. Learning those *rich* components holistically, including redundancies, is costly and wasteful.

This problem of redundancy is practically relevant. It is widely recognized in software engineering, resulting in active research on *dead code identification* and *elimination* (see e.g. [18]). As a specific example, in our MQTT_Lighting benchmark (§5), there is a component that can handle many different modes of a communication protocol, but the composite system uses only one mode.

Towards the goal of eliminating component redundancies, we devise a *contextual* componentwise automata learning algorithm, where observation tables for automata learning are pruned to system-level relevant behaviors.

To describe how our algorithm works, we first introduce our system model.

Formalization by Moore Machine Networks. In this paper, we model each component as a Moore machine (MM), and their composition as what we call a *Moore machine network (MMN)*. The latter arranges Moore machine components as nodes of a graph, and edges of the graph designate either system-level or inter-component input/output. An example is in Example 1.1, where two component MMs operate, driven by system-level input words. The component M_{c_1} passes its output to M_{c_2}, and M_{c_2} produces system-level output.

Components of an MMN operate in a fully synchronized manner. They share the same clock, and at each tick of it, each component M_c produces an output character a_e at each outgoing edge e from M_c. In case the edge e points to another component $M_{c'}$, the character a_e becomes (the e-component of) the input character to $M_{c'}$ at that tick. System-level input/output characters are consumed/produced synchronously, too. (The choice of Moore machines over Mealy machines is crucial for this operational semantics; see [10, Appendix D.1].)

Therefore our formalism models *structured*, *synchronized* and *dense* composition of components. This is suited for system integration, where 1) the learner (the SIer) arranges components with explicit interconnections, and 2) many components continuously receive signals from, and send signals to, other components (as is the case with many automotive, cyber-physical, web, and other systems).

This formalization of ours is in contrast with *flat*, (mostly) *interleaving* and *sparse* composition of components in other compositional works [6,15,16,21]. This difference mirrors different target applications. See Table 1.

Context Analysis by Reachability Analysis in a Product. Based on the MMN formalization, we shall sketch our technique for eliminating component redundancies. Component redundancy gets formalized as the fact that *system-level input words do not necessarily induce all component-level input words.* To see which input character a component M_c can receive at its state q_c, it suffices to know at which state $q_{c'}$ every other component $M_{c'}$ can be at the same time.

We conduct this *context analysis (CA)* using the hypothesis automata learned so far for the components. Identifying all state tuples $(q_c, (q_{c'})_{c'})$ which can be simultaneously active is done by the reachability analysis in the product automaton of the hypotheses. This can be costly; we therefore introduce two *context analysis parameters (CA-parameters)*, namely $\mathcal{E}$ (for abstracting contexts by quotienting hypothesis automata) and $\mathcal{R}$ (for limiting reachability analysis).

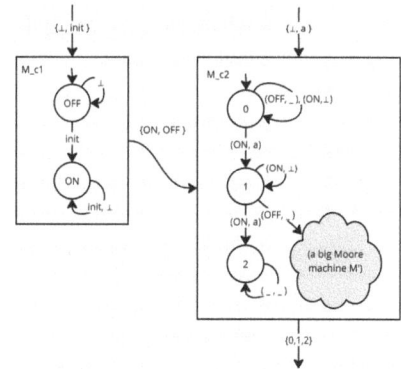

Fig. 1. an MMN example, a counter with initialization.

These parameters give us flexibility in the cost-benefit trade-off of context analysis. This kind of flexibility is important in automata learning since different application scenarios have different cost models. Specifically, running the SUL can be costly—processing one input character can take some milliseconds (in an embedded system) or even seconds (in a hardware-in-the-loop simulation (HILS) setting). In this case, extensive CA on the learner side (that can use a fast laptop) will pay off. In other cases where the SUL is fast, the cost of CA can be a bottleneck, and we might choose a cheaper and coarser CA-parameters.

We evaluated our contextual componentwise learning algorithm (called CCwL*) with experiments. Comparison is against two baselines: 1) *monolithic L* (MnL*)* that learns the whole SUL, 2) (naive) *componentwise L* (CwL*)* that learns each component individually (without CA and thus component redundancies). We used a few realistic benchmarks, including one inspired by robotics application, together with some toy benchmarks. We also evaluated the effect of different CA-parameters $(\mathcal{E}, \mathcal{R})$. Overall, the experiment results indicate the value of our algorithm in application scenarios of system integration.

Example 1.1 (counter with initialization). The MMN in Fig. 1 consists of two component MMs (M_{c_1} and M_{c_2}). Each has a system-level input edge with the designated alphabet, and M_{c_2} has a system-level output edge. The output of M_{c_1} is plugged in as input of M_{c_2}, too.

This example exhibits component redundancies: the M' part of M_{c_2} is irrelevant to system-level behaviors. Indeed, M' is never activated—once M_{c_1} moves to the ON state, it never goes back to OFF. Our contextual componentwise learn-

Table 1. comparison of compositional automata learning frameworks, settings and challenges. Shading is made to signify the span of combined cells

	current work	[16]	[21]	[6]	[15]	[8]
typical application	system integration	analysis of legacy systems				learning beyond regular
querying interface	system- & component-level	system-level only				
target systems	Moore machine networks	Mealy machines	LTSs	LTSs	Mealy machines	SPAs
component interaction	structured, synchronized, dense	flat, (mostly) interleaving, sparse				procedure calls
challenge	eliminating component redundancies	querying components via system-level queries				

ing algorithm detects and exploits this fact; it learns M_{c_1} and M_{c_2} separately, but in the latter it prunes the unreachable part M'.

Contributions. Our contributions are summarized as follows.

- We identify *system integration* as a new application domain of compositional automata learning. There, component-level queries are fully available; we use the term *componentwise automata learning* for distinction.
- We formalize the problem using *Moore machine networks* and identify the main challenge to be eliminating component redundancies.
- We introduce a *contextual* componentwise learning algorithm. It eliminates component redundancies by pruning observation tables using reachability analysis in the product of (hypothesis automata for) the components.
- We show its practical values through experiments.

Related Work. Many works on automata learning in general have been already discussed; here we focus on compositional approaches. A comparison of works on compositional automata learning is summarized in Table 1. All works but ours allow only system-level queries, and many are aimed at learning a *legacy* black-box system. In contrast, in our system integration applications, we are usually building a *new* system.

The compositional algorithm in [16] assumes that the SUL is a parallel composition of Mealy machines $M_1, \ldots, M_n$ whose input alphabets $\Sigma_1, \ldots, \Sigma_n$ are disjoint. The components operate in the interleaved manner, where each component M_i takes care of those input characters in Σ_i. The partition $\Sigma = \Sigma_1 \sqcup \cdots \sqcup \Sigma_n$ as well as the number n of components is not known to the learner, and the challenge is to find them. Their algorithm first assumes the finest partition ($n = |\Sigma|$ and each Σ_i is a singleton), and merges them in a counterexample-guided manner, when it is found that some input characters must be correlated.

The algorithm in [21] relies on more specific assumptions, namely that 1) the SUL is a parallel composition of LTSs which can synchronize by shared input characters, and 2) the output/observation to input words is whether the system gets stuck (i.e. there is no outgoing transition). The challenge here is that, when the SUL gets stuck for an input word w and w contains characters shared by different components, the learner may not know which component to blame. Their solution consists of 1) constructing an "access word" w' that extends w and localizes the blame, and 2) allowing "unknown" in observation tables in case there is no such w'. Unlike in [16], the number of components and their input alphabets must be known. The work [21] shows that some Petri nets yield such combinations of LTSs; it is not clear how other types of systems (such as Mealy machines) can be learned by this algorithm.

The works [6,15] can be thought of as variations of [16] with similar problem settings. In [6], the disjointness assumption in [16] is relaxed, and they give some graph-theoretic conditions that enable compositional learning. These conditions, however, are detailed and the learner has to somehow know that they hold in the SUL. In [6], dually to [16], they separate components according to output. It is yet to be identified what SULs are suited for this algorithm.

The work [8] has a different flavor from others. It is in the line of work on learning more expressive formalisms than (usual) automata and regular languages, such as (visibly) pushdown automata. Indeed, their target systems (system of procedural automata, SPA) are described much like context-free grammars. They assume that the invocation of nonterminals (*procedure calls* in the SPA terminology) is observable; this enables application of automata learning. Otherwise the setting is similar to those in [6,15,16,21]; in particular, the challenge is the same, namely to query components via system-level queries.

Besides the works compared in Table 1, *distributed reactive synthesis* [25] and *synthesis from component libraries* [17] are related to our work in their emphasis on compositionality. These works target at *synthesis* of automata from given logical specifications, a goal different from ours or the works in Table 1 (namely active automata learning).

Notations. $X \sqcup Y$ denotes the disjoint union of sets X and Y. The powerset of X is denoted by 2^X. The set of all partial functions from X to Y is denoted by $X \rightharpoonup Y$. For $f\colon X \rightharpoonup Y$ and $x \in X$, we write $f(x)\!\downarrow$ if $f(x)$ is defined, and $f(x)\!\uparrow$ otherwise.

Given an equivalence relation $\sim\, \subseteq X \times X$, equivalence classes are denoted by $[x]_\sim$ using $x \in X$, and the quotient set is denoted by $X/\!\sim$, as usual.

2 Problem Formalization by Moore Machine Networks

We start by some basic definitions. Let X be a nonempty finite set. X^* denotes the set of finite strings (also called words) over X; ε denotes the empty string;

$|s|$ denotes the length of $s \in X^*$; and $s_1 \cdot s_2$ (or simply $s_1 s_2$) denotes the concatenation of strings $s_1, s_2 \in X^*$.

In this paper, we use the 0-based indexing for strings. For a string $s \in X^*$ and an integer $i \in [0, |s|)$, $s_{[i]}$ denotes the $(i+1)$-th character of s (thus $s = s_{[0]} s_{[1]} \cdots s_{[|s|-1]}$); for $i, j \in [0, |s|]$ such that $i \leq j$, $s_{[i,j)}$ denotes the substring $s_{[i]} s_{[i+1]} \cdots s_{[j-1]}$. Note that $s_{[i,i)} = \varepsilon$ for each i.

Let $(X_k)_{k \in K}$ be a (K-indexed) family of sets. Its product is denoted by $\prod_{k \in K} X_k$, with its element denoted by a tuple $(x_k)_{k \in K}$ (here $x_k \in X_k$).

The restriction of a tuple $t = (x_k)_{k \in K} \in \prod_{k \in K} X_k$ to a subset $K' \subseteq K$, denoted by $t|_{K'}$, is $(x_k)_{k \in K'} \in \prod_{k \in K'} X_k$. This restriction of tuples t along $K' \subseteq K$ is extended, in a natural pointwise manner, to subsets $S \subseteq \prod_{k \in K} X_k$ and sequences $s \in (\prod_{k \in K} X_k)^*$, resulting in the notations $S|_{K'}$ and $s|_{K'}$.

2.1 Moore Machines

Our algorithm learns the following (deterministic) Moore machines (MMs).

Definition 2.1 (Moore machine). A *Moore machine (MM)* is a tuple $M = (Q, q_0, I, O, \Delta, \lambda)$, where

- Q is a finite set of states, $q_0 \in Q$ is an initial state,
- I is an input alphabet, O is an output alphabet,
- $\Delta \colon Q \times I \rightharpoonup Q$ is a transition (partial) function, and
- $\lambda \colon Q \to O$ is an output function that assigns an output symbol to each state.

A Moore machine is *complete* if $\delta(q, i)\downarrow$ for all $q \in Q$ and $i \in I$; otherwise, it is called *partial*.

We will also use *nondeterministic* MMs, later in §4, but only for the purpose of approximate context analysis (CA). It is emphasized that we do *not* learn nondeterministic MMs. The theory of nondeterministic MMs (their definition, semantics, etc.) is obtained in a straightforward manner; it is in [10, Appendix A.1].

As usual, the transition function Δ can be extended to an input string $w \in I^*$. Precisely, $\Delta(q, \varepsilon) = q$ and $\Delta(q, wi) = \Delta(\Delta(q, w), i)$. Similarly, the output function is extended by $\lambda(q, w) = \lambda(\Delta(q, w))$. When starting from the initial state q_0, often we simply write $\Delta(w) = \Delta(q_0, w)$ and $\lambda(w) = \lambda(q_0, w)$.

Given a Moore machine $M = (Q, q_0, I, O, \Delta, \lambda)$ and a state $q \in Q$, the *semantics* of M, denoted by $[\![M]\!]_q \colon I^* \to O^*$ and defined below, represents the behavior of the machine when starting from q. For each $w \in I^*$,

$$[\![M]\!]_q(w) = \lambda(q, w_{[0,0)}) \, \lambda(q, w_{[0,1)}) \cdots \lambda(q, w_{[0,k)}), \qquad (1)$$

where k is the smallest number such that $\lambda(q, w_{[0,k+1)})$ is undefined, or $|w|$ if no such k exists. Note that $[\![M]\!]_q \colon I^* \to O^*$ is a *total* function: even if Δ gets stuck (making $\lambda(q, w_{[0,k+1)})$ undefined), it does not make $[\![M]\!]_q(w)$ undefined, while it does make $[\![M]\!]_q(w)$ shorter. When starting from the initial state q_0, we write $[\![M]\!](w)$ for $[\![M]\!]_{q_0}(w)$ (much like for Δ and λ).

Using this semantics, we define the equivalence of Moore machines.

Definition 2.2 (equivalence of Moore machines). *Two Moore machines M_1 and M_2 are said to be equivalent if and only if $[\![M_1]\!] = [\![M_2]\!]$.*

2.2 Moore Machine Networks

A *directed graph* is a tuple $G = (V, E)$ of a finite set V of nodes (or vertices) and a set $E \subseteq V \times V$ of (directed) edges.

Let $G = (V, E)$ be a directed graph. Let E_v^{in} denote the set of *incoming edges* for a node $v \in V$, i.e. $E_v^{\text{in}} = \{(u,v) \in E \mid u \in V\}$. Similarly, E_v^{out} denotes the set of *outgoing edges* ($E_v^{\text{out}} = \{(v,u) \in E \mid u \in V\}$). For a set $U \subseteq V$ of nodes, we define $E_U^{\text{in}} = \bigcup_{u \in U} E_u^{\text{in}}$ and $E_U^{\text{out}} = \bigcup_{u \in U} E_u^{\text{out}}$.

Towards our definition of MMNs (Definition 2.3; see also Fig. 1), we introduce the following classification of nodes: a node $v \in V$ is 1) a *system-level input node* if $E_v^{\text{in}} = \emptyset$, 2) a *system-level output node* if $E_v^{\text{out}} = \emptyset$, and 3) a *component node* otherwise. We denote the sets of input, output, and component nodes by $V^{\text{in}}, V^{\text{out}}$, and V^{c}, respectively. We impose the condition on $G = (V, E)$ that $V = V^{\text{in}} \sqcup V^{\text{out}} \sqcup V^{\text{c}}$ is a disjoint union of three nonempty sets. (See Fig. 1, where system-level input and output nodes are implicit.)

An edge $e = (v, v') \in E$ is called a *system-level input edge* if $v \in V^{\text{in}}$, and a *system-level output edge* if $v' \in V^{\text{out}}$. The set of system-level input and output edges of $G = (V, E)$ are denoted by E^{in} and E^{out}, respectively, and are given by $E^{\text{in}} = E_{V^{\text{in}}}^{\text{out}}$ and $E^{\text{out}} = E_{V^{\text{out}}}^{\text{in}}$.

A *Moore machine network (MMN)* is a directed graph, with a Moore machine associated with each component node $c \in V^{\text{c}}$. Here we present a deterministic definition. Later in Sect. 4 we also use a nondeterministic version (not to learn, but for CA); this is an easy adaptation. See [10, Appendix A.2] for explicit definitions.

Definition 2.3 (Moore machine network). *A (deterministic) Moore machine network (MMN) is a tuple $\mathcal{M} = (G, (\Sigma_e)_{e \in E}, (M_c)_{c \in V^c})$, where*

- $G = (V, E)$ *is a directed graph representing the network structure,*
- Σ_e *is an alphabet associated with each edge $e \in E$, and*
- M_c *is a (deterministic) Moore machine associated with a component $c \in V^c$.*

On each component Moore machine $M_c = (Q_c, q_{0,c}, \Sigma_c^{\text{in}}, \Sigma_c^{\text{out}}, \Delta_c, \lambda_c)$, we require that its input and output alphabets are in accordance with the edge alphabets Σ_e. Specifically, we require $\Sigma_c^{\text{in}} = \prod_{e \in E_c^{\text{in}}} \Sigma_e$ (the product of the alphabets of all incoming edges) and, similarly, $\Sigma_c^{\text{out}} = \prod_{e \in E_c^{\text{out}}} \Sigma_e$.

For an MMN $\mathcal{M}$, we define three *system-wide alphabets*: 1) $\Sigma^{\text{in}} = \prod_{e \in E^{\text{in}}} \Sigma_e$ is the *system-level input alphabet*, 2) $\Sigma^{\text{out}} = \prod_{e \in E^{\text{out}}} \Sigma_e$ is the *system-level output alphabet*, and 3) $\overline{\Sigma} = \prod_{e \in E \setminus E^{\text{in}}} \Sigma_e = \prod_{c \in V^c} \Sigma_c^{\text{out}}$ is the *total output alphabet*. Note that $\overline{\Sigma}$ collects also those characters sent from a component to another.

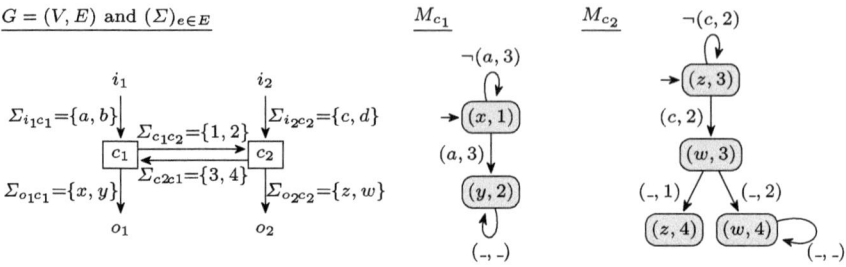

Fig. 2. an example MMN $\mathcal{M}_{\mathrm{ex}}$. On the left we show its network $G = (V, E)$ and the alphabets $(\Sigma_e)_{e \in E}$ for edges. The component MMs are shown on the right, where state labels designate output. In the transition labels, $\neg i$ stands for all characters other than i, and the symbol _ matches any character.

Example 2.4. An example of MMN is in Fig. 2. Its detailed formalization is in [10, Appendix D.2].

We move on to define the semantics of MMNs. It is via a translation of an MMN $\mathcal{M}$ to an MM $[\mathcal{M}]$; in the translation, the component MMs in $\mathcal{M}$ operate in a fully synchronized manner. The definition is intuitively straightforward, although its precise description below involves somewhat heavy notations.

The set of *(system-level) configurations* of $\mathcal{M}$, denoted by $\mathbf{Q}$, is defined by $\mathbf{Q} = \prod_{c \in V^c} Q_c$. The *initial configuration* is $\mathbf{q}_0 = (q_{0,c})_{c \in V^c}$.

Given a configuration $\mathbf{q} = (q_c)_{c \in V^c} \in \mathbf{Q}$, the *total output* of $\mathcal{M}$ at $\mathbf{q}$, denoted by $\overline{\lambda}(\mathbf{q}) \in \overline{\Sigma}$, is defined by $\overline{\lambda}(\mathbf{q}) = (\lambda_c(q_c))_{c \in V^c}$. Similarly, the *system-level output* of $\mathcal{M}$ at $\mathbf{q}$ is defined by $\lambda(\mathbf{q}) = \overline{\lambda}(\mathbf{q})|_{E^{\mathrm{out}}} \in \Sigma^{\mathrm{out}}$. (Recall the restriction operation | from Sect. 2.)

Given a configuration $\mathbf{q} = (q_c)_{c \in V^c} \in \mathbf{Q}$ and a system-level input character $\mathbf{i} \in \Sigma^{\mathrm{in}}$, we define Δ, the *system-level transition function* of $\mathcal{M}$, by $\Delta(\mathbf{q}, \mathbf{i}) = \left(\Delta_c \left(q_c, (\mathbf{i}, \overline{\lambda}(\mathbf{q}))|_{E_c^{\mathrm{in}}} \right) \right)_{c \in V^c}$. Intuitively: the tuple $\overline{\lambda}(\mathbf{q})$ of characters is output from the current states $\mathbf{q} = (q_c)_{c \in V^c}$; it is combined with the system-level input $\mathbf{i}$ and fed to each component's transition function Δ_c.

We formalize the following definition, using the above constructions.

Definition 2.5 (Moore machine $[\mathcal{M}]$). Let $\mathcal{M}$ be an MMN. The *Moore machine* $[\mathcal{M}]$ *induced by* $\mathcal{M}$ is $[\mathcal{M}] = (\mathbf{Q}, \mathbf{q}_0, \Sigma^{\mathrm{in}}, \Sigma^{\mathrm{out}}, \Delta, \lambda)$.

The semantics of $\mathcal{M}$ is defined by $[\![\mathcal{M}]\!]_{\mathbf{q}} = [\![[\mathcal{M}]]\!]_{\mathbf{q}}$ for any $\mathbf{q} \in \mathbf{Q}$.

When we turn to completeness of MMs (Definition 2.1), the completeness of $[\mathcal{M}]$ does not necessarily imply that of each component MM M_c. This is obvious from Example 1.1—it does not matter even if some transitions are not defined in M', since M' is never invoked. This is an implication of component redundancies (Sect. 1).

3 An L*-Style Algorithm

We review the classic L* algorithm from [2]. We formulate it in such a way that it easily adapts to our componentwise and contextual algorithm in Sect. 4. Consequently, the algorithm we present (Algorithm 1) differs slightly from the original L*; nevertheless, for simplicity, we call it L* throughout the paper.

We start with formulating the problem.

Proposition 3.1 (Moore machine learning).

Input: the problem takes two alphabets I, O and two oracles OQ, EQ as inputs: 1) I and O are input and output alphabets, respectively; 2) the *output query* oracle OQ, given an input string $w \in I^*$, returns a string $\text{OQ}(w) \in O^*$; and 3) the *equivalence query* oracle EQ, given a (hypothesis) Moore machine H, returns "yes" or a *counterexample* sequence $w \in I^*$.
Output: a Moore machine M.

Here, OQ and EQ form an abstraction of a black-box SUL, and the goal is to learn M that behaves the same as the SUL.

Our L*-style algorithm (Algorithm 1), henceforth simply called L*, uses an *observation table* (S, R, E, T). Here

- $S \subseteq I^*$ is a set of *prefixes*,
- $R \subseteq (S \cdot I) \setminus S$ is a set of *1-step extensions* of S,
- $E \subseteq I^*$ is a set of *suffixes*, and
- $T: (S \cup R) \cdot E \to O$ is the *entry map*, where $(S \cup R) \cdot E$ collects all concatenations of strings from $S \cup R$ and those from E.

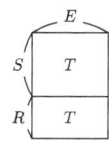

Fig. 3. an observation table.

See Fig. 3. We initialize an observation table as $(\{\varepsilon\}, \emptyset, \{\varepsilon\}, (\varepsilon \mapsto \text{OQ}(\varepsilon)))$, and both S and E will always contain the empty string ε. We write row(s) for the row of s in the observation table, i.e. row(s) : $e \in E \mapsto T(s \cdot e)$. An observation table is *closed* if every $r \in R$ has some $s \in S$ such that row(r) = row(s).

From a closed observation table (S, R, E, T), we can construct a deterministic Moore machine $H = (Q, q_0, I, O, \delta, \lambda)$ with $Q = \{\text{row}(s) \mid s \in S\}$, $q_0 = \text{row}(\varepsilon)$, $\delta(\text{row}(s), i) = \text{row}(s \cdot i)$ for $s \cdot i \in R$, and $\lambda(\text{row}(s)) = T(s)$. This MM is called the *hypothesis Moore machine* from the observation table (S, R, E, T).

The L* algorithm Algorithm 1 works by initializing an observation table, growing it using OQ till it is closed, making a hypothesis MM H, checking if H is good using EQ, and if H is not good, using the counterexample to further grow the table. When OQ and EQ are based on some MM M, Algorithm 1 terminates and returns a MM equivalent to M.

The differences between Algorithm 1 and the original L* [2] are as follows.

1. L* grows an observation table by 1) "extending input words" by picking $s \in S$ and $i \in I$ and adding $s \cdot i$ to R (Lines 8–12), and 2) "closing the table" by moving rows from R to S (Lines 4–6). We parameterize the first part with a function 1Ext^{L^*}. This parameter is set in the usual L* manner in Algorithm 1 (namely $1\text{Ext}^{L^*}(H) = \{(s, i) \mid \text{row}(s) \in Q_H \wedge i \in I\}$ where Q_H is the state space of H). Changing this parameter will be central in the next section.

Algorithm 1. an L*-style Moore machine learning algorithm (simply called L*)

```
 1: procedure L*(I, O, OQ, EQ)
 2:     S ← {ε}, R ← ∅, E ← {ε}, and T(ε) ← OQ(ε)
 3:     repeat
 4:         while (S, R, E, T) is not closed do
 5:             Find s · i ∈ R s.t. row(s · i) ≠ row(t) for all t ∈ S
 6:             S ← S ∪ {s · i} and R ← R \ {s · i}
 7:         Let H be the hypothesis Moore machine constructed from (S, R, E, T)
 8:         D ← {(s, i) ∈ 1EXT^{L*}(H) | s · i ∉ S ∪ R}          ▷ 1EXT^{L*} is defined in the main text
 9:         if D ≠ ∅ then
10:             for (s, i) ∈ D do
11:                 R ← R ∪ {s · i} and T(s · i · e) ← OQ(s · i · e) for each e ∈ E
12:             continue
13:         if EQ(H) ≠ true then
14:             Let w be a counterexample reported by EQ(H)
15:             ANALYZECEX^{L*}(H, w)
16:     until EQ(H) = true

17: procedure ANALYZECEX^{L*}(H, w)
18:     Find the decomposition (s, i, d) of the counterexample w s.t. s · i · d = w and
            OQ(t · i · d) ≠ OQ(t' · d) where row(t) = δ_H(s) and row(t') = δ_H(s · i)
19:     E ← E ∪ {d} and T(s · d) ← OQ(s · d) for each s ∈ S ∪ R
```

2. In the original L* [2], all the prefixes of the counterexample are added to S, but this can break a property called consistency. We, instead, add to E a suffix d that satisfies the condition in Line 18. This maintains consistency. This is a well-known technique; see e.g. [14].

An appropriate suffix d in Line 18 is effectively searched by the binary search [14,26]; this leads to the following complexity bounds.

Theorem 3.2 (OQ and EQ complexities of L* (Algorithm 1)). *Assume that OQ and EQ are implemented using an MM M. Then Algorithm 1 can correctly infer M with at most $O(\ell n^2 + n \log m)$ output queries and $O(n)$ equivalence queries, where n is the number of states of M, m is the maximal length of counterexamples, and ℓ is the input alphabet size.*

4 Our Contextual Componentwise Learning Algorithm

We introduce our main contribution, a *contextual componentwise L* algorithm* CCwL*. Two baselines are *monolithic L** (MnL*) and *componentwise L** (CwL*).

Problem. We formulate the problem. As discussed in Sect. 1, it is tailored to system integration applications where the learner has more access to the SUL.

Proposition 4.1 (componentwise automata learning).

Input: the problem takes the following inputs: 1) a directed graph $G = (V, E)$; 2) alphabets $(\Sigma_e)_{e \in E}$; 3) system-level oracles OQ and EQ; 4) component-level oracles OQ_c and EQ_c for each $c \in V^c$

Output: a Moore machine M

Typically, all the oracles are implemented by a black-box MMN $\mathcal{M}$, and the goal is to learn an MM M that is equivalent to $[\mathcal{M}]$.

Two Baselines. The monolithic L* (MnL*) simply applies L* (Algorithm 1) to OQ and EQ, ignoring the network structure G and the component-level oracles. This way one has to learn a large MM, as discussed in §1.

The (naive) componentwise L* (CwL*), in contrast, runs L* (Algorithm 1) with the component-level oracles OQ_c and EQ_c, and learns each component MM M_c separately. Once it is done, it combines the learned MMs along the graph G, gets an MMN $\mathcal{H}$. This can exploit compositionality and decrease the states to learn; yet it may still suffer from *component redundancies* (the cost of learning parts of components that are not relevant system-level). See Sect. 1.

Our Algorithm CCwL*. Our contextual algorithm CCwL* is shown in Algorithm 2; it aims to alleviate component redundancies. We list its core features.

1. CCwL* learns components separately. This is much like CwL*. Therefore it keeps an observation table (S_c, R_c, E_c, T_c) for each component $c \in V^c$.
2. CCwL* only uses (component-level) OQ_c and (system-level) EQ. This is unlike CwL* that uses only component-level OQ_c and EQ_c.
3. Learning each component c is much like L* (Algorithm 1), but CCwL* uses different procedure/function there (namely, $1\text{E{\sc xt}}_{\mathcal{E},\mathcal{R}}$ and $\text{A{\sc nalyze}C{\sc ex}}^C$ in Lines 9 and 15). Notably, these $1\text{E{\sc xt}}_{\mathcal{E},\mathcal{R}}$ and $\text{A{\sc nalyze}C{\sc ex}}^C$ are *contextual*— they depend not only on the component c but also on the other components.

The oracle $\overline{\mathsf{OQ}} \colon (\Sigma^{\text{in}})^* \to \overline{\Sigma}^*$ in Line 27 is for *total output queries*: it answers what strings are observed *at all edges* (including system-level output and inter-component edges), given an input string. The learner can compute it using component-level output query oracles $(\mathsf{OQ}_c)_{c \in V^c}$ in a natural way.

On AnalyzeCex^C. Overall, Algorithm 2 mirrors the structure of Alg. 1, with differences only in $1\text{E{\sc xt}}_{\mathcal{E},\mathcal{R}}$ and $\text{A{\sc nalyze}C{\sc ex}}^C$ (Lines 9 and 15)). To motivate the latter, recall that CCwL* uses only system-level EQs—using component-level EQs means we try to learn everything about a component and thus goes against our goal of eliminating component redundancies. Therefore the counterexamples obtained from EQs are system-level input strings $\mathbf{w}$. The procedure $\text{A{\sc nalyze}C{\sc ex}}^C$ in Algorithm 2 lets such $\mathbf{w}$ generate a component-level input string $\mathbf{w}'$ for c in Line 27, and passes it to the analysis routine in Algorithm 1 (namely $\text{A{\sc nalyze}C{\sc ex}}^{L^*}$).

On 1Ext$_{\mathcal{E},\mathcal{R}}$. On the other difference from L* ($1\text{E{\sc xt}}_{\mathcal{E},\mathcal{R}}$ in Line 9), we note that the function $1\text{E{\sc xt}}_{\mathcal{E},\mathcal{R}}$ has two parameters $\mathcal{E}$ (called *component abstraction*) and $\mathcal{R}$ (called *reachability analysis bound (RA bound)*). Combined, they are called *context analysis parameters (CA-parameters)*. We start with some intuitions.

Algorithm 2. our contextual componentwise L* algorithm CCwL*

```
 1: procedure CCwL*((V, E), (Σₑ)ₑ∈E, OQ, EQ, (OQc)c∈Vc, (EQc)c∈Vc)
 2:    for c ∈ Vc do
 3:        Sc ← {ε}, Rc ← ∅, Ec ← {ε}, and Tc(ε) ← OQc(ε)
 4:    repeat
 5:        while (Sc, Rc, Ec, Tc) is not closed for some c ∈ Vc do
 6:            Find s · i ∈ Rc s.t. rowc(s · i) ≠ rowc(t) for all t ∈ Sc
 7:            Sc ← Sc ∪ {s · i} and Rc ← Rc \ {s · i}
 8:        Let H be the hypothesis MMN constructed from (Sc, Rc, Ec, Tc)c∈Vc
 9:        D ← {(c, s, î) ∈ 1EXTε,R(H) | s · î ∉ Sc ∪ Rc}
10:        if D ≠ ∅ then
11:            for (c, s, î) ∈ D do
12:              ⌊ Rc ← Rc ∪ {s · î} and Tc(s · î · e) ← OQc(s · î · e) for each e ∈ Ec
               continue
13:        if EQ(H) ≠ true then
14:            Let w be a counterexample reported by EQ(H)
15:            ANALYZECEXᶜ(H, w)
16:    until EQ(H) = true

17: function 1EXTε,R(H)
18:    H̃ ← the quotient MMN H/ε ([10, Thm. A.3]) with respect to (ε(c))c∈Vc
19:    D ← ∅
20:    for q̃ = ([row(sc)]ε(c))c∈Vc ∈ R(H̃) do
21:        for i ∈ Σⁱⁿ, c ∈ Vc, ō ∈ λ̄(q̃), and row(s′) ∈ [row(sc)]ε(c) do
22:            Let î be a possible input character to c in H on q and i, i.e., î = (i, ō)|Eᶜⁱⁿ
23:          ⌊ D ← D ∪ {(c, s′, î)}
24:    return D

25: procedure ANALYZECEXᶜ(H, w)
26:    ▷ this ANALYZECEXᶜ is for sound (ε, R); otherwise ext. is needed ([10, Appendix D.4])  ◁
27:    Find a component c ∈ Vc that produces an incorrect output,
       that is, OQ̄(w)|Eᶜᵒᵘᵗ ≠ [H](w)|Eᶜᵒᵘᵗ     ▷ the oracle OQ̄ is described in the main text
28:    Construct an input ŵ to the component c from the system-level input w
       where ŵ[k] = (w[k], OQ̄(w)[k])|Eᶜⁱⁿ for each k ∈ [0, |w|)
29:  ⌊ Apply ANALYZECEXᴸ*(Hc, ŵ)     ▷ ANALYZECEXᴸ* is from Alg. 1
```

Firstly, the goal of $1\text{EXT}_{\mathcal{E},\mathcal{R}}$ is to find out *what input character* **i** *a component c can receive, when c runs in the MMN $\mathcal{M}$ and c's current state is (represented by the prefix)* **s**′. It adds all such tuples $(c, \mathbf{s}', \hat{\mathbf{i}})$ to D (Line 23).

In principle, it does so via the reachability analysis $\mathcal{R}$ of the current hypothesis MMN $\mathcal{H}$. Specifically, $1\text{EXT}_{\mathcal{E},\mathcal{R}}$ identifies all the combinations $\tilde{\mathbf{q}}$ of component states that $\mathcal{H}$ can encounter (Line 20), collects all output characters $\bar{\mathbf{o}}$ given by such component states $\tilde{\mathbf{q}}$ (Line 21), and combines this $\bar{\mathbf{o}}$ with system-level input **i** to find a possible input character $\hat{\mathbf{i}}$ to c (Line 22).

This baseline behavior of $1\text{EXT}_{\mathcal{E},\mathcal{R}}$ is what happens with the most fine-grained CA-parameters ($\mathcal{E} = \text{Eq}, \mathcal{R} = \text{D}_\infty$). We present this special case in [10, Appendix D.3] for illustration.

CA-Parameters $\mathcal{E}, \mathcal{R}$. However, this full reachability analysis can be very expensive; the CA-parameters $\mathcal{E}, \mathcal{R}$ are there to relieve it. The basic idea here is that we quotient hypothesis MMNs in order to ease reachability analysis. Those quotients naturally come with nondeterminism; thus we need the notions of nondeterministic MM and MMN (see [10, Appendix A]).

The *component abstraction* $\mathcal{E}$ specifies how we quotient the components in the hypothesis MMN $\mathcal{H}$ (Line 18). Note that it is used only within $1\text{Ext}_{\mathcal{E},\mathcal{R}}$ (i.e. for context analysis); in particular, it is not directly used in observation tables.

- $\mathcal{E} = \mathsf{Eq}$ (*equality*) means no quotienting.
- $\mathcal{E} = \mathsf{Eq}_k$ (*k-equivalence*), with $k \in \mathbb{N}$, is $\mathsf{Eq}_k = \{(s,t) \mid \lambda(s \cdot w) = \lambda(t \cdot w) \text{ for all strings } w \text{ with } |w| \leq k\}$. In particular, $\mathsf{Eq}_0 = \{(s,t) \mid \lambda(s) = \lambda(t)\}$.
- $\mathcal{E} = \mathsf{Uni}$ (*universal*) is given by $Q_c \times Q_c$ and collapses each component MM to a single state.

We define quotients of MMs (see [10, Thm A.3]) so that quotienting always leads to an *overapproximation* of output behaviors. Therefore, a possible input character $\hat{\mathsf{i}}$ (Line 23) is never missed. Such a choice of CA-parameters is said to be *sound*.

The *RA bound* $\mathcal{R}$ specifies how complete our reachability analysis should be (for finding $\tilde{\mathsf{q}}$, Line 20). We do so by limiting the depth of breadth-first search.

- $\mathcal{R} = \mathsf{D}_\infty$ means we set no bound and run full breadth-first search.
- $\mathcal{R} = \mathsf{D}_d$ means we set the limit of depth $d \in \mathbb{N}$.

Here, unlike with $\mathcal{E}$, the use of $\mathcal{R} \neq \mathsf{D}_\infty$ may lead to missing some $\tilde{\mathsf{q}}$ and thus some possible input $\hat{\mathsf{i}}$. Such a choice of CA-parameters is said to be *unsound*.

On AnalyzeCex^C, Again. In case unsound CA-parameters are chosen (i.e. $\mathcal{R} \neq \mathsf{D}_\infty$), a counterexample can arise not only in the usual L* way (wrong output), but also by finding out that the hypothesis MM for a component c is not prepared for some input character $\hat{\mathsf{i}}$, missing a transition for $\hat{\mathsf{i}}$. Therefore AnalyzeCex^C must be extended to handle such counterexamples. Doing so is not hard, and the extension is shown in [10, Appendix D.4]. The extension subsumes the one in Algorithm 2; one can use the extension regardless of soundness of CA-parameters.

Query Complexities. We state the following result.

Theorem 4.2 (OQ and EQ complexities of CCwL*). *Assume that $\mathcal{E}, \mathcal{R}$ is sound (i.e. $\mathcal{R} = \mathsf{D}_\infty$). The CCwL* algorithm (Algorithm 2), assuming that all oracles are implemented using an MMN $\mathcal{M}$, can correctly infer $\mathcal{M}$ with at most $O(\ell n^2 + n|V^c| \log m)$ component-level output queries and $O(n)$ system-level equivalence queries. Here n is the sum of the numbers of states of component Moore machines in $\mathcal{M}$, m is the maximal length of counterexamples, and ℓ is the system-level input alphabet size.*

If $\mathcal{E}, \mathcal{R}$ is unsound, then the number of component-level OQs is bounded by $O(\ell n^2 + n|V^c| \log m + \ell n|V^c|)$, and that of system-level EQs is $O(n + \ell n)$.

Here is a proof sketch. The sound case adapts Theorem 3.2; the extra $|V^c|$ factor comes from the use of total output queries $\overline{\mathsf{OQ}}(w)$ in AnalyzeCex^C. For the unsound case, EQs may also increase transitions (besides states, as in L*); this increase the bound for EQs. The bound for OQs grows because calls of AnalyzeCex^C increase and OQs are used there.

5 Implementation and Experiments

The code of the implementations, as well as all experiment scripts, is available [9].

Implementation. We implemented our proposal CCwL*, together with two baselines MnL* and CwL*, in Scala. It takes an MMN as input, which is treated as a black-box teacher and used only for answering queries. Equivalence queries (EQs) are implemented through testing by randomly generated input words.

Benchmarks. We used two families: *random* benchmarks where random components are arranged in a fixed network, and *realistic* benchmarks.

The random benchmarks Rand(nwk, comp) use the following parameters.

- The parameter nwk specifies the network topology. We use three families of network topologies: Compl(k) (a complete graph of k components), Star(k) (a "frontend" component interconnected with k "backend" components), and Path(k) (k components serially connected). See Fig. 4a.
- The parameter comp ∈ {LeanComp, RichComp} specifies how each component is randomly generated. When comp = LeanComp, each component is a Moore machine whose number of states is chosen from the normal distribution $N(10,1)$. For each (inter-component) edge, its alphabet size is picked from the uniform distribution over $\{2,3,4,5\}$.

  When comp = RichComp, we augment each component in such a way that roughly a half of it is redundant. Specifically, 1) each component is the interleaving product $M_c^\circ \times M_c^\bullet$ of two Moore machines generated in the above way (for LeanComp); 2) the two machines $M_c^\circ, M_c^\bullet$ have disjoint input and output alphabets; 3) therefore the alphabet for each edge in the MMN is bigger than for LeanComp; 4) nevertheless, the system-level input alphabets as well as component output alphabets are chosen so that only the first machine M_c° is invoked. This way we force the redundancy of $M_c^\bullet$.

Our realistic benchmarks are MQTT_Lighting and BinaryCounter(k). The latter models a k-bit counter; its details are in [10, Appendix B.2]. In what follows, we describe MQTT_Lighting in some detail (further details are in [10, Appendix B.1]).

The MMN MQTT_Lighting models a lighting system in which two sensors and one light communicate (Fig. 4b). Notably, it uses the *MQTT protocol* [23]—a protocol commonly used for IoT applications—and thus has a component called an *(MQTT) broker*. In this system, (1) the brightness sensor uses *QoS 1* of MQTT—meaning that, for each sensing data, four messages Connect, ConnAck, Publish, PubAck are exchanged; and (2) the motion sensor uses *QoS 2* of MQTT. It uses six messages: Connect, ConnAck, Publish, PubRec, PubRel, and PubComp. Different QoS levels provide different guarantees; see e.g. [23]. Our Moore machine model for the broker,[2] without knowing who uses which QoS, prepares for both

---
[2] Our broker model is adapted from Automata Wiki https://automata.cs.ru.nl/BenchmarkMQTT-TapplerEtAl2017/Description. It is originally from [28].

QoS levels for each client. This redundancy (e.g. QoS 2 for brightness) is what we would like to eliminate via context analysis.

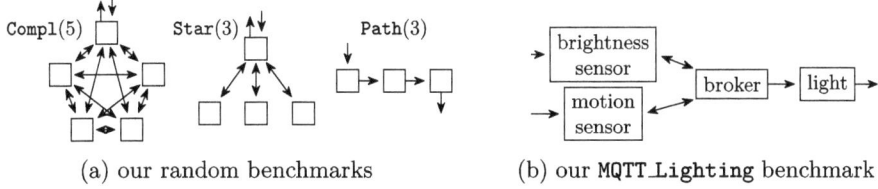

(a) our random benchmarks

(b) our MQTT_Lighting benchmark

Fig. 4. network topologies for our random and MQTT_Lighting benchmarks.

Experiment Settings. We conducted experiments on AWS EC2 r7i.2xlarge instances, with 3.2 GHz Intel Xeon Scalable (Sapphire Rapids), 8 virtual cores, and 64 GB RAM, with OpenJDK 23 (OpenJDK 64-Bit Server VM Temurin-23.0.2+7). Both the learner and an SUL were executed in the same machine. We set a timeout of 3600 s for the whole learning process; it returns once a system-level equivalence query succeeds.

After a successful return, we ran extra *validation* where, unlike equivalence queries during learning (these are by random-word testing), rigorous system-level equivalence verification is conducted between the learned system and the SUL. Note that this validation time is not included in the aforementioned timeout.

For random benchmarks Rand(nwk, comp), we generated 10 instances for each parameter value (nwk, comp), and we report the average.

In evaluation, noting that the speed of SUL execution can vary greatly in different applications (cf. Sect. 1), we are not so interested in the total execution time as in the number of queries. Following [16], we report

- the number of *steps* (i.e. the number of input characters, but we use the word "step" since our input character can be a tuple $(a_e)_e$ in our setting), and
- the number of *resets* (resets can be much more costly than steps, see [16]).

We report these numbers separately for OQs and EQs. This is because the numbers for EQs depend heavily on how we choose to implement EQs, namely which method to use (random testing, conformance testing, black-box checking etc.), how many and how long words, etc.[3]

Results and Discussions. We report the results in Tables 2 and 3. We discuss them along some research questions (RQs).

---

[3] We can imagine application scenarios where we need a more refined view, separating the numbers of resets and steps for system-level queries and component-level ones. This is the case, for example, when a component-level interface is well-developed and fast (since a component is a commodity) but a system-level interface is slow (since it is a system under development). This data is not shown due to limited space.

Table 2. experiment results I. The rows are for different algorithms: two baselines (MnL*, CwL*) and our proposal (CCwL*) with different CA-parameters (Sect. 4). In the columns, $st.$ is the number of learned states, $tr.$ is that of learned transitions, $OQ\ reset$ is the number of resets caused by output queries (it coincides with the number of OQs), $OQ\ step$ is the number of steps caused by output queries, EQ is the number of equivalence queries, $EQ\ reset$ and $EQ\ step$ are the numbers of resets and steps caused by EQs, respectively (an EQ conducts testing and thus uses many input words), and $L.\ time$ ("Learner time") is the time (seconds) spent for the tasks on the learner's side (context analysis, counterexample analysis, building observation tables, etc.), and $valid?$ reports the numbers of instances of "result validated," "result found incorrect," and "timeout." Note that we used 10 instances for each random benchmark.

Rand(Compl(5),LeanComp)

algo.	st.	tr.	OQ reset	OQ step	EQs	EQ reset	EQ step	L. time	valid?
MnL*	27K	53K	591K	18M	15.0	129	32K	1.0K	0/1/9
CwL*	46.9	12K	15K	32K	6.20	501	137K	0.86	10/0/0
CCwL*(Eq,D_∞)	46.9	9.0K	11K	35K	2.00	101	27K	30.8	10/0/0
CCwL*(Eq,D_0)	46.9	8.3K	16K	911K	5.4K	133K	33M	1.4K	0/10/0
CCwL*(Eq$_0$,D_∞)	46.9	9.0K	11K	35K	2.00	101	27K	30.4	10/0/0
CCwL*(Eq$_0$,D_0)	46.9	8.3K	16K	911K	5.4K	133K	33M	1.3K	0/10/0
CCwL*(Uni,D_0)	46.9	9.0K	11K	29K	2.20	101	27K	93.0	10/0/0

Rand(Star(5),LeanComp)

algo.	st.	tr.	OQ reset	OQ step	EQs	EQ reset	EQ step	L. time	valid?
MnL*	26K	53K	917K	33M	23.5	417	105K	1.0K	0/2/8
CwL*	55.6	26K	26K	51K	17.6	613	165K	1.14	10/0/0
CCwL*(Eq,D_∞)	54.8	18K	18K	46K	7.30	107	28K	188	10/0/0
CCwL*(Eq,D_0)	54.3	7.0K	14K	1.2M	6.8K	231K	59M	1.6K	0/9/1
CCwL*(Eq$_0$,D_∞)	54.8	18K	18K	47K	7.10	107	28K	24.0	10/0/0
CCwL*(Eq$_0$,D_0)	54.3	7.0K	14K	1.2M	6.8K	231K	59M	1.6K	0/9/1
CCwL*(Uni,D_0)	54.8	19K	19K	47K	7.10	107	28K	32.5	10/0/0

Rand(Path(5),LeanComp)

algo.	st.	tr.	OQ reset	OQ step	EQs	EQ reset	EQ step	L. time	valid?
MnL*	21K	496K	15M	19.7	223	54K	221	1/8/1
CwL*	166	570	2.8K	17.9	513	137K	0.53	10/0/0
CCwL*(Eq,D_∞)	140	457	2.5K	6.70	110	29K	6.43	10/0/0
CCwL*(Eq,D_0)	133	490	6.6K	64.3	203	41K	1.35	7/3/0
CCwL*(Eq$_0$,D_∞)	151	501	2.8K	6.60	110	29K	2.01	10/0/0
CCwL*(Eq$_0$,D_0)	134	490	6.2K	58.0	191	39K	1.37	7/3/0
CCwL*(Uni,D_0)	152	506	2.7K	6.60	110	28K	2.06	10/0/0

Rand(Compl(5),RichComp)

algo.	st.	tr.	OQ reset	OQ step	EQs	EQ reset	EQ step	L. time	valid?
MnL*	—	—	—	—	—	—	—	—	0/0/10
CwL*	747	239K	1.3M	8.4K	23.6	519	138K	20.7	10/0/0
CCwL*(Eq,D_∞)	47.3	9.4K	10K	31K	1.90	101	27K	23.4	10/0/0
CCwL*(Eq,D_0)	47.2	7.8K	14K	838K	5.0K	120K	30M	1.2K	0/9/1
CCwL*(Eq$_0$,D_∞)	47.3	9.4K	10K	31K	1.90	101	27K	22.4	10/0/0
CCwL*(Eq$_0$,D_0)	47.2	7.8K	14K	838K	5.0K	120K	30M	1.2K	0/9/1
CCwL*(Uni,D_0)	47.3	9.4K	11K	26K	1.90	101	27K	74.3	10/0/0

Rand(Star(5),RichComp)

algo.	st.	tr.	OQ reset	OQ step	EQs	EQ reset	EQ step	L. time	valid?
MnL*	41K	82K	1.0M	31M	22.0	272	67K	2.0K	0/1/9
CwL*	910	22K	70K	5833K	40.1	637	167K	1.96	10/0/0
CCwL*(Eq,D_∞)	56.7	11K	11K	29K	8.00	107	28K	190	10/0/0
CCwL*(Eq,D_0)	56.7	11K	12K	991K	5.8K	187K	48M	1.3K	0/10/0
CCwL*(Eq$_0$,D_∞)	56.7	11K	11K	29K	8.00	107	28K	16.1	10/0/0
CCwL*(Eq$_0$,D_0)	56.7	6.0K	12K	991K	5.8K	187K	48M	1.4K	0/10/0
CCwL*(Uni,D_0)	56.7	11K	11K	28K	8.20	108	28K	20.5	10/0/0

Rand(Path(5),RichComp)

algo.	st.	tr.	OQ reset	OQ step	EQs	EQ reset	EQ step	L. time	valid?
MnL*	26K	6.8K	26K	732K	23M	22.1	301	75K	361	1/9/0
CwL*	681	4.8K	39K	404K	36.4	536	139K	1.33	10/0/0
CCwL*(Eq,D_∞)	138	462	2.6K	7.10	106	28K	6.76	8/2/0
CCwL*(Eq,D_0)	136	512	7.7K	68.4	216	44K	1.54	6/4/0
CCwL*(Eq$_0$,D_∞)	145	482	2.7K	7.00	106	28K	1.89	8/2/0
CCwL*(Eq$_0$,D_0)	137	505	7.0K	59.2	202	43K	1.47	6/4/0
CCwL*(Uni,D_0)	147	488	2.7K	7.10	106	28K	1.99	9/1/0

MQTT_Lighting

algo.	st.	tr.	OQ reset	OQ step	EQs	EQ reset	EQ step	L. time	valid?
MnL*	169	1.5K	47K	1.4M	10.9	238	59K	17.6	0/10/0
CwL*	39.0	2.5K	12K	61K	11.8	412	105K	0.76	10/0/0
CCwL*(Eq,D_∞)	27.0	130	348	2.4K	4.40	112	28K	1.36	10/0/0
CCwL*(Eq,D_0)	27.0	129	412	7.4K	72.5	292	59K	1.94	10/0/0
CCwL*(Eq$_0$,D_∞)	27.0	129	348	4.60	116	29K	1.21	10/0/0
CCwL*(Eq$_0$,D_0)	27.0	134	362	2.8K	4.60	116	29K	1.96	9/1/0
CCwL*(Uni,D_0)	27.0	129	413	7.6K	71.5	311	64K	2.54	10/0/0

BinaryCounter(5)

algo.	st.	tr.	OQ reset	OQ step	EQs	EQ reset	EQ step	L. time	valid?
MnL*	70.0	140	212	5.9K	2.00	101	26K	0.76	10/0/0
CwL*	15.0	39.1	80.6	6.00	501	129K	0.41	10/0/0
CCwL*(Eq,D_∞)	14.0	30.0	45.0	1.00	100	26K	0.88	10/0/0
CCwL*(Eq,D_0)	14.0	25.0	44.4	357	15.4	115	28K	0.88	10/0/0
CCwL*(Eq$_0$,D_∞)	14.0	25.0	30.0	45.0	1.00	100	26K	0.87	10/0/0
CCwL*(Eq$_0$,D_0)	14.0	25.0	44.4	357	15.4	115	28K	0.87	10/0/0
CCwL*(Uni,D_0)	14.0	28.0	33.0	54.0	1.00	100	26K	0.87	10/0/0

BinaryCounter(10)

algo.	st.	tr.	OQ reset	OQ step	EQs	EQ reset	EQ step	L. time	valid?
MnL*	—	—	—	—	—	—	—	—	0/0/10
CwL*	30.0	60.0	74.1	141	11.0	1.0K	258K	0.72	10/0/0
CCwL*(Eq,D_∞)	50.0	60.0	90.0	1.00	100	26K	2.27	10/0/0
CCwL*(Eq,D_0)	25.0	41.0	73.4	2.0K	23.4	128	28K	1.73	0/10/0
CCwL*(Eq$_0$,D_∞)	29.0	50.0	60.0	90.0	1.00	100	26K	2.27	10/0/0
CCwL*(Eq$_0$,D_0)	25.0	41.0	73.4	2.0K	23.4	128	28K	1.78	0/10/0
CCwL*(Uni,D_0)	29.0	58.0	68.0	114	1.00	100	26K	9.73	10/0/0

Table 3. experiment results II. The legend is the same as Table 2

algo.			Rand(Star(3),LeanComp)								Rand(Star(7),LeanComp)					
	st.	tr.	OQ reset	OQ step	EQ reset	EQ step	EQ time	L.	valid?	st.	tr.	OQ reset	OQ step	EQs	EQ reset	EQ step	L. time	valid?
MnL*	3.3K	13K	347K	6.8M	26.8	474	119K	89.1	1/9/0	—	—	—	—	—	—	—	—	0/0/10
CwL*	38.4	1.7K	2.6K	6.9K	12.9	409	110K	0.50	10/0/0	74.7	280K	280K	534K	26.6	819	220K	5.01	10/0/0
CCwL*(Eq,D_∞)	38.4	1.3K	2.0K	6.5K	6.80	106	28K	3.57	10/0/0	66.0	9.4K	10K	27K	9.00	108	28K	1.1K	1/0/9
CCwL*(Eq,D_0)	38.4	1.1K	2.7K	160K	1.0K	16K	3.9M	79.8	2/8/0	66.0	6.4K	13K	1.0M	6.2K	200K	51M	1.9K	0/1/9
CCwL*(Eq_0,D_∞)	38.4	1.3K	2.1K	6.6K	6.90	106	28K	1.65	10/0/0	74.5	179K	179K	447K	10.0	109	28K	646	10/0/0
CCwL*(Eq_0,D_0)	38.4	1.1K	2.7K	160K	1.0K	16K	3.9M	77.9	2/8/0	66.0	6.4K	13K	1.0M	6.2K	200K	51M	2.0K	0/1/9
CCwL*(Uni,D_0)	38.4	1.4K	2.2K	6.8K	6.40	106	28K	1.98	10/0/0	74.5	183K	183K	415K	9.50	109	28K	693	10/0/0

algo.			Rand(Star(3),RichComp)								Rand(Star(7),RichComp)					
	st.	tr.	OQ reset	OQ step	EQs	EQ reset	EQ step	L. time	valid?	st.	tr.	OQ reset	OQ step	EQs	EQ reset	EQ step	L. time	valid?
MnL*	3.2K	12K	238K	4.1M	22.1	298	74K	56.0	1/9/0	—	—	—	—	—	—	—	—	0/0/10
CwL*	540	5.6K	37K	360K	27.4	430	112K	1.21	10/0/0	1.2K	471K	535K	1.6M	57.2	851	222K	9.01	10/0/0
CCwL*(Eq,D_∞)	37.4	1.3K	2.2K	7.0K	4.90	104	28K	2.76	10/0/0	73.5	100K	101K	279K	10.5	110	28K	2.3K	4/0/6
CCwL*(Eq,D_0)	37.4	1.2K	3.0K	163K	1.1K	16K	4.0M	85.4	1/9/0	75.0	8.3K	17K	1.4M	8.1K	297K	76M	3.5K	0/1/9
CCwL*(Eq_0,D_∞)	37.4	1.3K	2.3K	7.5K	5.30	105	28K	1.54	10/0/0	74.1	204K	204K	520K	9.50	108	28K	616	10/0/0
CCwL*(Eq_0,D_0)	37.4	1.2K	3.0K	163K	1.1K	16K	4.0M	83.4	1/9/0	75.0	8.3K	17K	1.4M	8.1K	297K	76M	3.0K	0/1/9
CCwL*(Uni,D_0)	37.4	1.4K	2.4K	7.6K	5.00	104	28K	1.73	10/0/0	74.2	214K	215K	487K	9.80	109	28K	676	10/0/0

RQ1: Is the flexibility of CA-parameters useful? Which parameter to use?

A natural theoretical expectation of benefit, and also the learner's computational cost ($L.\ time$), is $\mathsf{Eq} > \mathsf{Eq}_0 > \mathsf{Uni}$ (on $\mathcal{E}$) and $\mathsf{D}_\infty > \mathsf{D}_0$ (on $\mathcal{R}$). The experimental results confirm that this expectation is largely correct.

On benefit, indeed, finer-grained CA (e.g. $(\mathsf{Eq}, \mathsf{D}_\infty)$) yielded smaller automata with fewer resets and steps. This is more notable in $\mathcal{R}$ than in $\mathcal{E}$.

As an anomaly, $(\mathsf{Uni}, \mathsf{D}_0)$ performed pretty well on Rand(_,RichComp). But it did not on MQTT_Lighting. This is natural: the redundancy in Rand(_,RichComp) is non-temporal (some input characters are never used) and even coarse-grained $(\mathsf{Uni}, \mathsf{D}_0)$ could detect it; but the redundancy in MQTT_Lighting is temporal (what input characters are not used changes over time) and finding it was harder.

On the learner's cost ($L.\ time$), the above expectation is not always correct: coarser CA often led to explosion of queries, which incurred the learner's bookkeeping cost. That said, the coarsest $\mathcal{E} = \mathsf{Uni}$ did not suffer from this problem.

Overall, these observations suggest the following. There are different classes of SULs: in one class (e.g. MQTT_Lighting), component redundancies are temporal, and only fine-grained CA e.g. with $(\mathsf{Eq}, \mathsf{D}_\infty)$ can detect them; in another class (e.g. Rand(_,RichComp)), redundancies are totally not temporal, and coarse-grained CA with e.g. $(\mathsf{Uni}, \mathsf{D}_0)$ can detect them without much overhead. This will guide a choice of CA-parameters when the nature of an SUL is known (which class it belongs to?). When an SUL's nature is unknown, one can try some intermediate CA-parameters; in [10, Appendix D.5], we introduce three such ($\mathcal{R} = \mathsf{D}_{\mathsf{sum}}, \mathsf{D}_{\mathsf{max}}, \mathsf{D}_{\mathsf{min}}$) and evaluate them.

RQ2: How does CCwL*'s performance compare with that of CwL* or MnL*?

Henceforth, we follow the suggestion in RQ1 and focus on the CA-parameters CCwL*(Eq,D_∞) and CCwL*(Uni, D_0).

The advantages of CwL* and CCwL*—both are componentwise—over monolithic MnL* are observed in general. This is as expected (cf. §1).

In the comparison of CCwL* and (naive) CwL*, we observe that our goal (CA for eliminating component redundancies) is fulfilled: in the benchmarks with such redundancies (Rand(_,RichComp), MQTT_Lighting, BinaryCounter(k)), CCwL* clearly outperformed CwL* in terms of automata size, resets and steps.

On the other benchmarks (namely Rand(_, LeanComp)), we still observe that 1) CCwL* and CwL* perform similarly, and 2) CCwL* can reduce the cost of EQs. The latter is because EQs in CCwL* are system-level, unlike component-level EQs in CwL*; a counterexample from the former can be reused for multiple components and suggest many new states.

RQ3: What is the cost of context analysis? Is it tolerable?

The additional cost for context analysis is part of *L. time*. This cost is on the learner's side and can often be discounted (an SUL is usually slower and is more likely to be a bottleneck); still we want to confirm that the cost is tolerable.

Indeed, *L. time* is often much larger for CCwL* than for CwL*: in a large benchmark Rand(Star(7), LeanComp), a few seconds for CwL* but hundreds of seconds for CCwL*. Whether this cost is tolerable depends on the cost model. For example, in embedded or HILS applications, taking 1 sec. for a reset and 10 ms. for a step is a norm. The gap of *L. time* then becomes ignorable.

RQ4: How does CCwL* scale to complex SULs? What SULs are suited?

CCwL* is designed to exploit redundancy of components. We have seen that, indeed, it performs well with benchmarks with redundancy.

The scalability question can be interpreted in two ways. One is *whether CCwL* can extract a small essence from a seemingly complex system*; then the answer is yes. For example, on MQTT_Lighting and Rand(Star(7), LeanComp), it learned much smaller automata than MnL* and CwL* did.

The other possible question is *whether CCwL* can extract an essence even if it is large* and our experiments do not allow us to answer yes. The largest MMN learned by CCwL* so far is of dozens of states, not more. The challenge here is the alphabet size—it grows exponentially with respect to the number of incoming edges—and the cost of CA that is impacted by it. As future work, we plan to work on deal with such large alphabets, e.g. by abstracting alphabets.

Summarizing the above discussions along RQ1–4, we conclude that 1) we are yet to investigate in-depth the practical scalability of our redundancy elimination methods, but 2) with the experimental results that show the efficiency of CCwL* for several benchmarks, the current work definitely opens promising avenues for future research. Regarding the first point, the main difficulty is that there are no existing benchmarks suited for our purpose, namely large real-world compositional systems whose network structures are known and formalized. We are currently mining IoT and robotics applications for such benchmarks.

6 Conclusions and Future Work

For compositional automata learning, we identified a new application domain of *system integration*, formalized its problem setting using *Moore machine networks*, and presented a novel *contextual componentwise learning* algorithm CCwL*. It assumes that both system-level and component-level queries are available; to cope with the challenge of complexities due to redundancies in components (some parts do not contribute to the whole system), CCwL* performs *context analysis*. Our experimental evaluation shows its practical relevance.

One important future direction is to deal with large alphabets, as mentioned in Sect. 5. For example, in those applications where inter-component interactions are *sparse*—the characters transmitted are $\bot$ ("do nothing") most of the time— a theoretical framework that exploits this sparseness will be useful. We are also considering abstraction using *symbolic automata* [5].

References

1. Alur, R., Madhusudan, P.: Visibly pushdown languages. In: Babai, L. (ed.) Proceedings of the 36th Annual ACM Symposium on Theory of Computing, Chicago, IL, USA, 13–16 June 2004, pp. 202–211. ACM (2004). https://doi.org/10.1145/1007352.1007390
2. Angluin, D.: Learning regular sets from queries and counterexamples. Inf. Comput. **75**(2), 87–106 (1987). https://doi.org/10.1016/0890-5401(87)90052-6
3. Argyros, G., D'Antoni, L.: The learnability of symbolic automata. In: Chockler, H., Weissenbacher, G. (eds.) CAV 2018. LNCS, vol. 10981, pp. 427–445. Springer, Cham (2018). https://doi.org/10.1007/978-3-319-96145-3_23

4. Bainczyk, A., Schieweck, A., Steffen, B., Howar, F.: Model-based testing without models: the TodoMVC case study. In: Katoen, J.-P., Langerak, R., Rensink, A. (eds.) ModelEd, TestEd, TrustEd. LNCS, vol. 10500, pp. 125–144. Springer, Cham (2017). https://doi.org/10.1007/978-3-319-68270-9_7
5. Drews, S., D'Antoni, L.: Learning symbolic automata. In: Legay, A., Margaria, T. (eds.) TACAS 2017. LNCS, vol. 10205, pp. 173–189. Springer, Heidelberg (2017). https://doi.org/10.1007/978-3-662-54577-5_10
6. al Duhaiby, O., Groote, J.F.: Active learning of decomposable systems. In: Bae, K., Bianculli, D., Gnesi, S., Plat, N. (eds.) FormaliSE@ICSE 2020: 8th International Conference on Formal Methods in Software Engineering, Seoul, Republic of Korea, 13 July 2020, pp. 1–10. ACM (2020). https://doi.org/10.1145/3372020.3391560
7. Fisman, D., Frenkel, H., Zilles, S.: Inferring symbolic automata. Log. Methods Comput. Sci. **19**(2) (2023). https://doi.org/10.46298/LMCS-19(2:5)2023
8. Frohme, M., Steffen, B.: Compositional learning of mutually recursive procedural systems. Int. J. Softw. Tools Technol. Transf. **23**(4), 521–543 (2021). https://doi.org/10.1007/S10009-021-00634-Y
9. Fujinami, H., Waga, M., Hasuo, I.: Artifact archive for "componentwise automata learning for system integration" (2025). https://doi.org/10.5281/zenodo.15846781
10. Fujinami, H., et al.: Componentwise automata learning for system integration (extended version) (2025). https://arxiv.org/abs/2508.04458
11. Heerdt, G., Kupke, C., Rot, J., Silva, A.: Learning weighted automata over principal ideal domains. In: FoSSaCS 2020. LNCS, vol. 12077, pp. 602–621. Springer, Cham (2020). https://doi.org/10.1007/978-3-030-45231-5_31
12. Isberner, M., Howar, F., Steffen, B.: The TTT algorithm: a redundancy-free approach to active automata learning. In: Bonakdarpour, B., Smolka, S.A. (eds.) RV 2014. LNCS, vol. 8734, pp. 307–322. Springer, Cham (2014). https://doi.org/10.1007/978-3-319-11164-3_26
13. Isberner, M., Howar, F., Steffen, B.: The open-source LearnLib. In: Kroening, D., Păsăreanu, C.S. (eds.) CAV 2015. LNCS, vol. 9206, pp. 487–495. Springer, Cham (2015). https://doi.org/10.1007/978-3-319-21690-4_32
14. Isberner, M., Steffen, B.: An abstract framework for counterexample analysis in active automata learning. In: Clark, A., Kanazawa, M., Yoshinaka, R. (eds.) Proceedings of the 12th International Conference on Grammatical Inference, ICGI 2014, Kyoto, Japan, 17–19 September 2014. JMLR Workshop and Conference Proceedings, vol. 34, pp. 79–93. JMLR.org (2014). http://proceedings.mlr.press/v34/isberner14a.html
15. Koenders, R., Moerman, J.: Output-decomposed learning of mealy machines. CoRR arxiv:2405.08647 (2024). https://doi.org/10.48550/ARXIV.2405.08647
16. Labbaf, F., Groote, J.F., Hojjat, H., Mousavi, M.R.: Compositional learning for interleaving parallel automata. In: Kupferman, O., Sobocinski, P. (eds.) Foundations of Software Science and Computation Structures - 26th International Conference, FoSSaCS 2023, Held as Part of the European Joint Conferences on Theory and Practice of Software, ETAPS 2023, Paris, France, 22–27 April 2023, Proceedings. Lecture Notes in Computer Science, vol. 13992, pp. 413–435. Springer, Heidelberg (2023). https://doi.org/10.1007/978-3-031-30829-1_20
17. Lustig, Y., Vardi, M.Y.: Synthesis from component libraries. Int. J. Softw. Tools Technol. Transf. **15**(5–6), 603–618 (2013). https://doi.org/10.1007/S10009-012-0236-Z

18. Malavolta, I., et al.: Javascript dead code identification, elimination, and empirical assessment. IEEE Trans. Softw. Eng. **49**(7), 3692–3714 (2023). https://doi.org/10.1109/TSE.2023.3267848
19. Maletti, A. (ed.): CAI 2015. LNCS, vol. 9270. Springer, Cham (2015). https://doi.org/10.1007/978-3-319-23021-4
20. Meijer, J., van de Pol, J.: Sound black-box checking in the learnlib. Innov. Syst. Softw. Eng. **15**(3-4), 267–287 (2019). https://doi.org/10.1007/s11334-019-00342-6
21. Neele, T., Sammartino, M.: Compositional automata learning of synchronous systems. In: Lambers, L., Uchitel, S. (eds.) Fundamental Approaches to Software Engineering - 26th International Conference, FASE 2023, Held as Part of the European Joint Conferences on Theory and Practice of Software, ETAPS 2023, Paris, France, 22–27 April 2023, Proceedings. Lecture Notes in Computer Science, vol. 13991, pp. 47–66. Springer, Heidelberg (2023). https://doi.org/10.1007/978-3-031-30826-0_3
22. Niese, O.: An integrated approach to testing complex systems. Ph.D. thesis, Technical University of Dortmund, Germany (2003). http://eldorado.uni-dortmund.de:8080/0x81d98002_0x0007b62b
23. OASIS: MQTT Version 5 (2019). https://docs.oasis-open.org/mqtt/mqtt/v5.0/mqtt-v5.0.pdf
24. Peled, D.A., Vardi, M.Y., Yannakakis, M.: Black box checking. In: Wu, J., Chanson, S.T., Gao, Q. (eds.) Formal Methods for Protocol Engineering and Distributed Systems, FORTE XII / PSTV XIX'99, IFIP TC6 WG6.1 Joint International Conference on Formal Description Techniques for Distributed Systems and Communication Protocols (FORTE XII) and Protocol Specification, Testing and Verification (PSTV XIX), Beijing, China, 5–8 October 1999. IFIP Conference Proceedings, vol. 156, pp. 225–240. Kluwer (1999)
25. Pnueli, A., Rosner, R.: Distributed reactive systems are hard to synthesize. In: 31st Annual Symposium on Foundations of Computer Science, St. Louis, Missouri, USA, 22–24 October 1990, vol. II, pp. 746–757. IEEE Computer Society (1990). https://doi.org/10.1109/FSCS.1990.89597
26. Rivest, R.L., Schapire, R.E.: Inference of finite automata using homing sequences. Inf. Comput. **103**(2), 299–347 (1993). https://doi.org/10.1006/INCO.1993.1021
27. Shijubo, J., Waga, M., Suenaga, K.: Probabilistic black-box checking via active MDP learning. ACM Trans. Embed. Comput. Syst. **22**(5s), 148:1–148:26 (2023). https://doi.org/10.1145/3609127
28. Tappler, M., Aichernig, B.K., Bloem, R.: Model-based testing iot communication via active automata learning. In: 2017 IEEE International Conference on Software Testing, Verification and Validation, ICST 2017, Tokyo, Japan, 13–17 March 2017, pp. 276–287. IEEE Computer Society (2017). https://doi.org/10.1109/ICST.2017.32

29. Vaandrager, F., Garhewal, B., Rot, J., Wißmann, T.: A new approach for active automata learning based on apartness. In: TACAS 2022. LNCS, vol. 13243, pp. 223–243. Springer, Cham (2022). https://doi.org/10.1007/978-3-030-99524-9_12
30. Zhang, H., Feng, L., Li, Z.: Control of black-box embedded systems by integrating automaton learning and supervisory control theory of discrete-event systems. IEEE Trans. Autom. Sci. Eng. **17**(1), 361–374 (2020). https://doi.org/10.1109/TASE.2019.2929563

Learning Event-Recording Automata Passively

Anirban Majumdar[1], Sayan Mukherjee[2(✉)], and Jean-François Raskin[3]

[1] Independent Researcher, Kolkata, India
[2] Univ Rennes, Inria, CNRS, IRISA, Rennes, France
sayan.mukherjee@irisa.fr
[3] Université Libre de Bruxelles, Brussels, Belgium

Abstract. This paper presents a state-merging algorithm for learning timed languages definable by Event-Recording Automata (ERA) using positive and negative samples in the form of symbolic timed words. Our algorithm, LEAP (Learning Event-recording Automata Passively), constructs a possibly nondeterministic ERA from such samples based on merging techniques. We prove that determining whether two ERA states can be merged while preserving sample consistency is an NP-complete problem, and address this with a practical SMT-based solution. Our implementation demonstrates the algorithm's effectiveness through examples. We also show that every ERA-definable language can be inferred using our algorithm with a suitable sample.

1 Introduction

Formal modeling is essential in fields like requirements engineering and computer-aided verification, where it supports the analysis of complex systems. However, creating formal models is labor-intensive and prone to error. Learning algorithms can streamline this process by deriving models from execution scenario descriptions [26]. When the set of possible behaviors of a system aligns with a regular language, it can be represented by a finite state automaton, and passive and active learning algorithms and efficient implementations are available to derive the minimal Deterministic Finite Automaton (DFA) describing this language. In contrast, learning timed languages remains underdeveloped. In this paper, we contribute to this line of research by providing a passive learning algorithm, and an implementation, that transforms sets of positive and negative *symbolic timed words* into *Event-Recording Automata* (ERA, for short) [4].

The class of Event-Recording Automata (ERA) is a subclass of Timed Automata (TA) [2], where each clock x_σ is linked to an event $\sigma \in \Sigma$ and records

---

Professor Jean-François Raskin receives support from the PDR Weave project FORM-LEARN-POMDP funded by FNRS and DFG, and from the Fondation ULB. Most of this work was done when both Dr. Anirban Majumdar and Dr. Sayan Mukherjee were post-doctoral researchers at ULB, they were funded by a grant from Fondation ULB during that time.

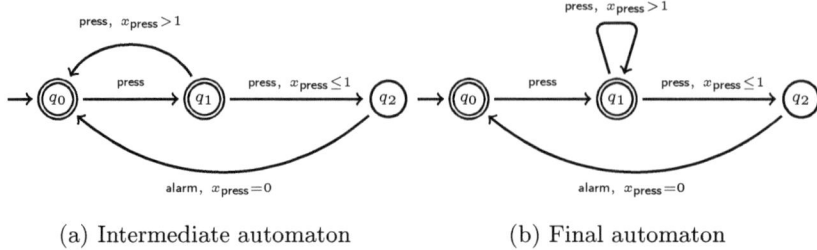

(a) Intermediate automaton (b) Final automaton

Fig. 1. Motivation for choosing symbolic words as specification

the time since its last occurrence. ERA offer key advantages over TA: they are determinizable and complementable, making them suitable for specification in verification tasks, as inclusion checking is decidable for ERA but not for TA. Additionally, clocks in ERA are directly tied to events and reset automatically with each event occurrence, enhancing *interpretability* compared to TA and making ERA appealing for learning applications where trust is important. Further, it is a folklore result that ERA combined with homomorphism is equally expressive as TA. This means, every system that can be modelled as a timed automaton can also be modelled as an ERA, by increasing the alphabet.

Before detailing our contributions, let us consider an example that illustrates how formal specifications, in the form of ERA, can be learned from *symbolic scenarios*, as advocated in [16], and expressed here as *symbolic timed words*.

Learning ERA from Symbolic Timed Words. Let us consider the task for a *requirement engineer* (RE) to write a formal model in the form of an ERA, for the following informal requirement: *whenever a (button)* press *is followed by another (button)* press *within 1 time unit, then an* alarm *must happen immediately.*

We demonstrate how the RE can use our learning algorithm to obtain the corresponding ERA. The RE must provide positive and negative examples in the form of scenarios. Instead of requiring explicit timed words, i.e., $(\sigma_1, t_1)(\sigma_2, t_2) \ldots (\sigma_n, t_n)$, which are sequences of events (e.g., press or alarm) with timestamps $t_i \in \mathbb{R}_{\geq 0}$, we allow more abstract examples in the form of *symbolic timed words*. These are sequences of the form $(\sigma_1, g_1)(\sigma_2, g_2) \ldots (\sigma_n, g_n)$, where σ_i are events and g_i are conjunctions of constraints of the form $x_{\sigma_i} \in I$. Here, x_{σ_i} is the event-recording clock associated with σ_i, and I is an interval with non-negative integer bounds. Symbolic timed words provide higher-level information, which is natural for requirements elicitation.

Consider a positive example: a press occurs, followed by another press within 1 time unit, and then an alarm happens immediately. This translates into the symbolic timed word (press, $\top$)(press, $x_{\text{press}} \leq 1$)(alarm, $x_{\text{press}} = 0$). A second example is: if a press occurs followed by another press after 1 time unit, and nothing happens afterwards, it is acceptable. This is represented as (press, $\top$)(press, $x_{\text{press}} > 1$). Additionally, trivial scenarios include: if nothing happens, it is acceptable (i.e., ε is a positive example), and if a **press** occurs followed by nothing, that is also fine (i.e., (**press**, $\top$) is a positive example).

The RE must also provide some *undesired* scenarios as negative samples to avoid the learning algorithm producing a one-state universal automaton that allows all scenarios. A first negative example could be: a **press** followed by another **press** after 1 time unit and then an **alarm** happens. This is specified as (**press**, $\top$)(**press**, $x_{\mathsf{press}} > 1$)(**alarm**, $x_{\mathsf{press}} \geq 0$). Another negative example is a **press** followed by another **press** within 1 time unit and no **alarm** afterward, formalized by (**press**, $\top$)(**press**, $x_{\mathsf{press}} \leq 1$). Also, an **alarm** should not occur immediately after the first **press**, which can be specified by (**press**, $\top$)(**alarm**, $x_{\mathsf{press}} \geq 0$).

Using these samples, our algorithm will generate the ERA in Fig. 1a. By inspecting this ERA, the RE may discover that the model allows a scenario where a **press** is followed by another **press** after 1 time unit, then followed by a **press** immediately, which is not desired. This can be provided as a negative word (**press**, $\top$)(**press**, $x_{\mathsf{press}} > 1$)(**press**, $x_{\mathsf{press}} = 0$). The algorithm will then compute the ERA in Fig. 1b, which correctly models the target specification.

This example demonstrates that using symbolic timed words, and not plain timed words, is natural in the process of *requirements elicitation* and that our learning algorithm effectively helps the RE generalize natural scenarios that are easy to formulate.

Context and Contributions. This paper focuses on passive learning from positive and negative examples, a concept pioneered by Gold [11,12], who defined conditions under which a language from a given class can be identified based on sample data. Building on Gold's insights, the *Regular Positive and Negative Inference* (RPNI) algorithm [21] emerged as a key technique for identifying regular languages from examples, using state-merging techniques. RPNI starts with positive and negative examples, treating each positive prefix as a distinct state, then progressively merges states that are compatible with the samples. For regular languages, this approach ensures the result is a DFA consistent with the examples and converges to the correct language given enough data. Passive learning has applications in synthesis, such as serving as a subroutine in frameworks like SyGuS [1] or allowing users to provide guiding examples to simplify synthesis outputs, as suggested in [6].

Our main technical contributions are threefold. First, we propose an algorithm to infer Event-Recording Automata (ERA) compatible with specific sets of positive and negative symbolic timed words (Sect. 3), providing a new algorithm for passive learning for timed systems from high level symbolic examples, and not from plain timed words. However, this requires addressing a computational challenge: as a second contribution, we establish that determining whether a symbolic timed word intersects the language of an ERA, even if deterministic, is an NP-complete problem (Sect. 4). This problem is essential to our state-merging algorithm for deciding permissible state merges, and we address this complexity issue using a reduction to SMT. Our third contribution proves that LEAP is *complete*: for every ERA-recognizable language, there exist finite characteristic sets of positive and negative examples such that our algorithm returns an ERA accurately representing the language (Sect. 5). We achieve this via a novel language-theoretic approach, showing that the final automaton's language aligns with the target language, a method potentially extendable to other models without unique minimal automata. We have implemented LEAP in a PYTHON prototype, demonstrating its effectiveness on various examples (Sect. 6). Definitions and notations appear in Sect. 2.

Related Works. Several methods have been proposed for inferring ERA in different frameworks. Works such as [13,14,18] introduce *active* learning algorithms for ERA-recognizable languages, while a recent contribution [19] adapts a separability-based algorithm to infer ERA with a minimal number of control states. Other efforts target more expressive models: for example, [15] infers automata from an extended ERA class, while [25,32] learn the full class of Deterministic Timed Automata. Additional algorithms target subclasses of automata, such as One-clock Timed Automata [30,33], Real-time Automata [5], and Mealy Machines with Timers [7,27]. Being in the active learning framework, all these algorithms assume access to a teacher, who answers queries that progressively refine the target automaton. For instance, algorithms in [14,15] use state-merging with tree-based data structures that represent membership queries. They apply restricted merging criteria requiring that the tree is complete up to a certain depth to cover the target language. Also, all those techniques maintain trees and automata that are deterministic. In contrast, our approach addresses a fixed sample of words and allows more flexible merging, yielding potentially smaller non-deterministic automata. Similarly, $L^\#$ [28], an active learning algorithm for regular languages, merges states based on apartness but relies on sufficient data about the target language, making it not directly applicable to passive learning.

In the *passive* learning framework, fewer works exist [9,22,31], where subclasses of TA are inferred from *timed words*. Also, the models that are considered are different. Of these, [9,31] target Deterministic Real-time Automata, a weaker model than ERA, while [9,22] only consider positive data, with [31] incorporating both positive and negative samples. These works model systems from logs, typically in the form of timed words, with [23] proposing a Genetic programming approach for TA. An SMT-based algorithm for inferring TA has also been studied in [24]. While timed words are well-suited for learning from execution logs and extracting models from software treated as a black box, they are less appealing for our intended use case. Here, a requirements engineer (RE) aims to craft an ERA based on scenarios. Our approach uses symbolic words (positive and negative) as input, enabling the RE to provide a compact set of scenarios and construct smaller automata (see Sect. 6 for empirical evidence of this).

The missing proofs in this article can be found in the extended version [20].

2 Preliminaries

Timed Words and Timed Languages. A *timed word* over an alphabet Σ is a finite sequence $(\sigma_1, t_1)(\sigma_2, t_2)\ldots(\sigma_n, t_n)$ where each $\sigma_i \in \Sigma$ and $t_i \in \mathbb{R}_{\geq 0}$, for all

$1 \leq i \leq n$, and for all $1 \leq i < j \leq n$, $t_i \leq t_j$ (time is monotonically increasing). We use $\mathsf{TW}(\Sigma)$ to denote the set of all timed words over the alphabet Σ.

A *timed language* is a (possibly infinite) set of timed words. Timed Automata (TA) [2] extend deterministic finite-state automata with *clocks*. In what follows, we will use a subclass of TA, where clocks have a pre-assigned semantics and are not reset arbitrarily. This class is known as Event-recording Automata (ERA) [4]. We now define the necessary vocabulary and notations for their definition.

Constraints. A *clock* is a non-negative real valued variable, that is, a variable ranging over $\mathbb{R}_{\geq 0}$. Let K be a positive integer. A K-*atomic constraint* over a clock x, is an expression of the form $x = c$, $x \in (c, d)$ or $x > K$ where $c, d \in \mathbb{N} \cap [0, K]$. We also consider a *trivial* K-atomic constraint $\top$. A K-*constraint* over a set of clocks X is a conjunction of K-atomic constraints over clocks in X.

A K-*elementary constraint* over a clock x, is an atomic constraint where the interval is restricted to unit intervals; more formally, it is an expression of the form $x = c$, $x \in (c, c+1)$ or $x > K$ where $c, c+1 \in \mathbb{N} \cap [0, K]$. A K-*simple constraint* over X is a conjunction of K-elementary constraints over clocks in X, where each variable $x \in X$ appears exactly in one conjunct. The definition of simple constraints also appear in earlier works [13].

For example, let $X = \{x_1, x_2, x_3\}$ be a set of clocks, and let $K = 2$. Then, $0 < x_1 < 2$ (that is, $x_1 \in (0, 2)$) is a K-atomic constraint, but not a K-elementary constraint since the interval is not a unit interval; $1 < x_1 < 2$ (that is, $x_1 \in (1, 2)$) is an example of a K-elementary constraint; $x_1 > 2 \wedge 1 < x_3 < 2$ is a K-constraint, but not a K-simple constraint since the clock x_2 does not appear in this constraint; $x_1 > 2 \wedge 1 < x_3 < 2 \wedge x_2 = 2$ is a K-simple constraint.

Valuation and Satisfaction of Constraints. A *valuation* for a set of clocks X is a function $v \colon X \to \mathbb{R}_{\geq 0}$. A valuation v for X satisfies a K-atomic constraint ψ, written as $v \models \psi$, if: when every clock x appearing in ψ is replaced with its value $v(x)$, the expression evaluates to True. Every valuation satisfies $\top$.

A valuation v satisfies a K-constraint over X if v satisfies all its conjuncts. Given a K-constraint ψ, $[\![\psi]\!]$ will denote the set of all valuations v such that $v \models \psi$. It is easy to verify that for any K-simple constraint r and any K-elementary constraint ψ, either $[\![r]\!] \cap [\![\psi]\!] = \emptyset$ or $[\![r]\!] \subseteq [\![\psi]\!]$. W.l.o.g., in this work, we will only consider K-constraints g s.t. $[\![g]\!] \neq \emptyset$.

Lemma 1. *Let K be a positive integer. Then for any two K-simple constraints r_1 and r_2, either $[\![r_1]\!] = [\![r_2]\!]$ or $[\![r_1]\!] \cap [\![r_2]\!] = \emptyset$.*

Let $\Sigma = \{\sigma_1, \sigma_2, \ldots, \sigma_k\}$ be a finite *alphabet*. The set of all *event-recording clocks* associated with Σ is denoted by $X_\Sigma = \{x_\sigma \mid \sigma \in \Sigma\}$. We denote by $\mathsf{C}(\Sigma, K)$ the set of all K-constraints over the set of clocks X_Σ and we use $\mathsf{SC}(\Sigma, K)$ to denote the set of all K-simple constraints over the clocks in X_Σ. Since K-simple constraints are also K-constraints, we have that $\mathsf{SC}(\Sigma, K) \subset$

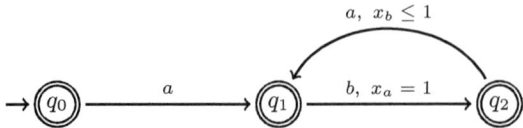

Fig. 2. A deterministic ERA describing the timed language, where every a is followed by a b after exactly 1 time unit and every b is followed by an a within 1 time unit. Here and in the successive figures, we do not write the guard $\top$.

$C(\Sigma, K)$. We will omit K when not important, or if it is clear from context, and denote the above sets by $\mathsf{SC}(\Sigma)$ and $\mathsf{C}(\Sigma)$, respectively.

Event-Recording Automata. A K-Event-recording Automaton (K-ERA) $\mathcal{A}$ is a tuple $(Q, q_{\text{init}}, \Sigma, E, F)$ where Q is a (non-empty) finite set of states, $q_{\text{init}} \in Q$ is the initial state, Σ is a finite alphabet, $E \subseteq Q \times \Sigma \times \mathsf{C}(\Sigma, K) \times Q$ is the set of transitions, and $F \subseteq Q$ is the set of accepting states. Each transition in $\mathcal{A}$ is a tuple (q, σ, g, q'), where $q, q' \in Q$, $\sigma \in \Sigma$ and $g \in \mathsf{C}(\Sigma, K)$, g is called the *guard* of the transition. $\mathcal{A}$ is called a K-*deterministic*-ERA (K-DERA) if for every state $q \in Q$ and every letter σ, if there exist two transitions (q, σ, g_1, q_1) and (q, σ, g_2, q_2) then $[\![g_1]\!] \cap [\![g_2]\!] = \emptyset$. Again, we will not mention K unless necessary.

For the semantics, initially, all the clocks of an ERA start with the value 0 and then they all increase with rate 1. For every transition on a letter σ, once the transition is taken, its corresponding recording clock x_σ gets reset to the value 0.

Clocked Words. Given a timed word $\mathsf{tw} = (\sigma_1, t_1)(\sigma_2, t_2) \ldots (\sigma_n, t_n)$ over Σ, we associate with it a *clocked word* $\mathsf{cw}(\mathsf{tw}) = (\sigma_1, v_1)(\sigma_2, v_2) \ldots (\sigma_n, v_n)$ where each $v_i : X_\Sigma \to \mathbb{R}_{\geq 0}$ maps each clock of X_Σ to a real value as follows: $v_i(x_\sigma) = t_i - t_j$ where $j = \max\{1 \leq l < i \mid \sigma_l = \sigma\}$, with the convention that $\max(\emptyset) = 0$ and $t_0 = 0$. In words, the value $v_i(x_\sigma)$ is the amount of time elapsed since the last occurrence of σ in tw; which is why we call the clocks x_σ 'recording' clocks. So, as mentioned earlier, even though not explicitly, each clock is implicitly reset immediately after every occurrence of its associated event.

The Timed Language of a K-ERA. A timed word $\mathsf{tw} = (\sigma_1, t_1)(\sigma_2, t_2) \ldots (\sigma_n, t_n)$, with its clocked word $\mathsf{cw}(\mathsf{tw}) = (\sigma_1, v_1)(\sigma_2, v_2) \ldots (\sigma_n, v_n)$, is *accepted* by $\mathcal{A}$ if there exists a sequence of states $q_0 q_1 \ldots q_n$ of $\mathcal{A}$ such that $q_0 = q_{\text{init}}$, $q_n \in F$, and for all $1 \leq i \leq n$, there exists $e = (q_{i-1}, \sigma, \psi, q_i) \in E$ such that $\sigma_i = \sigma$, and $v_i \models \psi$. The set of all timed words accepted by $\mathcal{A}$ is called the *timed language* of $\mathcal{A}$, and will be denoted by $\mathsf{L}(\mathcal{A})$.

For example, the automaton $\mathcal{A}$ depicted in Fig. 2, accepts all the timed words where every a is followed by a b after exactly 1 time-unit and every b is followed by an a within 1 time unit. In particular, $\mathcal{A}$ accepts $(a, 2.3)(b, 3.3)(a, 3.4)$, but rejects $(a, 2.3)(b, 3.4)(a, 3.4)$.

A timed language L is K-ERA-definable if there exists a K-ERA $\mathcal{A}$ such that $\mathsf{L}(\mathcal{A}) = L$. Lemma 2 implies that a timed language L is K-ERA-definable iff it is also K-DERA-definable.

Lemma 2 ([4]). *For every K-ERA $\mathcal{A}$, there exists a K-DERA $\mathcal{A}'$ such that the two automata have the same timed language, i.e. $\mathsf{L}(\mathcal{A}) = \mathsf{L}(\mathcal{A}')$.*

Symbolic timed words over (Σ, K) are finite sequences $(\sigma_1, g_1)(\sigma_2, g_2) \ldots (\sigma_n, g_n)$ where each $\sigma_i \in \Sigma$ and $g_i \in \mathsf{C}(\Sigma, K)$, for all $1 \leq i \leq n$. Similarly, a *region word* over (Σ, K) is a finite sequence $(\sigma_1, r_1)(\sigma_2, r_2) \ldots (\sigma_n, r_n)$ where each $\sigma_i \in \Sigma$ and $r_i \in \mathsf{SC}(\Sigma, K)^1$, for all $1 \leq i \leq n$. We will use $\mathsf{SW}(\Sigma, K)$ and $\mathsf{RW}(\Sigma, K)$ to denote the sets of all symbolic timed words and all region words over an alphabet (Σ, K), respectively.

We are now equipped to define when a timed word tw is compatible with a symbolic timed word sw. Let $\mathsf{tw} = (\sigma_1, t_1)(\sigma_2, t_2) \ldots (\sigma_n, t_n)$ be a timed word and $\mathsf{sw} = (\sigma_1', g_1)(\sigma_2', g_2) \ldots (\sigma_m', g_m)$ be a symbolic timed word. We say that tw is compatible with sw, noted $\mathsf{tw} \models \mathsf{sw}$ if we have that: (*i*) $n = m$, i.e., both words have the same length, (*ii*) $\sigma_i = \sigma_i'$ and (*iii*) $v_i \models g_i$, for all i, $1 \leq i \leq n$. We use $[\![\mathsf{sw}]\!]$ to denote the set of all timed words that are compatible with sw, that is, $[\![\mathsf{sw}]\!] = \{\mathsf{tw} \in \mathsf{TW}(\Sigma) \mid \mathsf{tw} \models \mathsf{sw}\}$. We say that a symbolic timed word sw is *consistent* if $[\![\mathsf{sw}]\!] \neq \emptyset$, and *inconsistent* otherwise.

3 A Passive Learning Algorithm for ERA

In this section, we propose a *state-merging algorithm* – we call it LEAP (Learning Event-recording Automata Passively) – that can be seen as an adaptation of the classical state-merging algorithm RPNI [21] for regular inference, into the timed setting. Typically, in a passive learning framework, a pair of sets of words $\mathsf{S} = (\mathsf{S}_+, \mathsf{S}_-)$, called the *sample set*, is given as input, and the objective is to construct an automaton $\mathcal{A}$ (an ERA in our case) that is *consistent* with S. Here consistency means, $\mathcal{A}$ accepts all the words in S_+ and rejects all the words in S_-. It is important to note here that no two words, one from S_+ and one from S_-, should have a non-empty intersection. Here we assume that the alphabet Σ of the target ERA is given as an input, and that, the sample sets contain symbolic timed words over the alphabet Σ.

Order Between Symbolic Timed Words. The set of all symbolic timed words can be ordered using a *total order* '$\prec$'. This order will be used later in this section for merging states in LEAP, and also in Sect. 5 to prove the completeness result. However, we will not delve into the specifics of this order relation here; only its existence is relevant. The details of this order relation are in [20].

An Overview of the Algorithm LEAP. LEAP initially constructs a tree, called the *prefix tree*, denoted PT, from the positive set S_+ and then tries to

---
[1] since simple constraints are similar (but not equal) to the standard notion of 'regions' as defined in [2], we refer to this kind of symbolic timed words as region words.

Algorithm 1. Pseudo-code for algorithm LEAP

Input: An alphabet Σ, and a *consistent* sample set (S_+, S_-)
Output: An ERA that accepts (resp. rejects) all timed words in S_+ (resp. S_-)
1: $T \leftarrow PT(S_+)$
2: RED $= \{q_\varepsilon\}$
3: BLUE $= \{q_u \mid q_u$ is a successor of $q_\varepsilon\}$ // always sorted wrt a total order
4: **while** BLUE is not empty **do**
5:     pop q_v where v is the minimum element wrt $\prec$ in $\{v' \mid q_{v'} \in$ BLUE$\}$
6:     **for** every node $q_u \in$ RED **do**
7:         **if** merge(q_u, q_v) is possible **then**
8:             add the successors of q_u ($\notin$ BLUE) to BLUE   // keeping BLUE sorted
9:             go to the next iteration of the **while** loop
10:        **end if**
11:    **end for**
12:    **if** no merge was possible **then**
13:        add q_v to RED
14:        add the successors of q_v to BLUE   // keeping BLUE sorted
15:    **end if**
16: **end while**

merge nodes from the tree keeping the resulting automaton *consistent* with the sample. During the procedure, we maintain a coloring of nodes in the tree – red and blue – where the red nodes represent the nodes that will be the states in the target automaton, and at each iteration of the algorithm, a blue node will either be merged with one of the red nodes, or be promoted to a red node. A pseudo-code of LEAP is presented in Algorithm 1. The algorithm consists of two main steps:

In the first step LEAP constructs a prefix tree T from S_+ (line 1). We can formally define the prefix tree as an ERA $PT(S_+) = (Q, q_\varepsilon, \Sigma, E, F)$ where the set of states $Q = \{q_u \mid u \in Pr(S_+)\}$ is the set of prefixes of words in S_+ (denoted by $Pr(S_+)$), the initial state is the state corresponding to the empty string ε, the set of edges E is defined as follows: for $(a,g) \in \Sigma \times C(\Sigma)$, and $u, u.(a,g) \in Pr(S_+)$, the transition $(q_u, a, g, q_{u.(a,g)}) \in E$; and finally, the set of accepting states $F = \{q_u \mid u \in S_+\}$ is the set of all words in S_+, *i.e.*, the prefix tree accepts exactly the words in S_+.

Note that there may exist states from which there are more than one transition on the same letter σ but with different guards g, g' that intersect. As a consequence, a prefix tree can be non-deterministic. However, note that, when all words in the sample set are region words, the PT will be deterministic (cf. Lemma 1).

In the second step the algorithm initializes a set RED that contains the initial node q_ε (line 2), and maintains a *sorted list* BLUE containing the successors of q_ε in the PT (line 3). The list BLUE is sorted according to the order $\prec$ defined between symbolic timed words mentioned earlier in this section, the lowest element in the order being at the beginning of the list. Then, it iteratively does the following until BLUE becomes empty: at every iteration i, the algorithm pops the first node q_v from BLUE (line 5), and executes the procedure merge that checks if a merge is possible between q_v and one of the nodes in RED (line 6-11): a merge is possible if the resulting automaton after the merge remains *consistent* with the sample – that is, if the merged automaton does not intersect with any word in S_-; otherwise, the merge is discarded. When a merge is successful, RED and BLUE are updated accordingly (line 8). If no merge is possible, q_v is *promoted* to a red state, i.e., RED := RED $\uplus \{q_v\}$, and all successors of q_v are appended to BLUE according to the order $\prec$ (line 12-15).

Procedure Merge: The procedure takes as input an ERA $\mathcal{A}$, a node q_u from RED and a node q_v from BLUE. Note that, every node in BLUE has a *unique* predecessor node, and this node is always in RED. Let q_w be the unique predecessor of the blue node q_v, i.e., there exists a transition $t = q_w \xrightarrow{(\sigma,g)} q_v$ in $\mathcal{A}$. Then construct an ERA $\mathcal{A}'$ as follows: delete the transition t from $\mathcal{A}$, and add the transition $q_w \xrightarrow{(\sigma,g)} q_u$ (if it does not already exist in $\mathcal{A}$), and then recursively *fold* the subtree of q_v into q_u. Here, *fold* means after merging q_u and q_v, if these nodes have successors q'_u and q'_v on transitions labelled with the *same* letter σ and the *same* guard g, respectively, then we also merge q'_u and q'_v, and repeat this process. Notice that, the automaton $\mathcal{A}'$ can, in general, be non-deterministic.

Checking Consistency with the Sample: A merge between two states is allowed in LEAP only if the resulting automaton does not intersect with any negative sample. We now provide an SMT-based algorithm for checking if an ERA intersects a symbolic word. Thus, this algorithm can be used inside LEAP to determine when a merge is allowed: each time two states are merged during an iteration of LEAP, say $\mathcal{A}$ is the resulting automaton due to the merge, then the following algorithm can be used to check if for every $w \in S_-$, $L(\mathcal{A}) \cap [\![w]\!] \neq \emptyset$ or not. Such an encoding of this problem into an SMT formula is justified, since in the next section (in Lemma 4) we will show that deciding this problem is, in fact, NP-complete.

We reduce the afore-mentioned problem in the theory of (quantifier-free) Linear Real Arithmetic (LRA) with Boolean variables, for which checking satisfiability is also known to be NP-complete. Assume w be the symbolic word $(\sigma_1, g_1)(\sigma_2, g_2)\ldots(\sigma_p, g_p)$. We want to find a timed word (as a certificate) $w_t = (\sigma_1, t_1)(\sigma_2, t_2)\ldots(\sigma_p, t_p)$, where $t_i \in \mathbb{R}_{\geq 0}$ and $t_i \leq t_j$ for every $1 \leq i < j \leq p$, such that $w_t \in [\![w]\!] \cap L(\mathcal{A})$. For this, we construct a formula ϕ over p real variables $t_1, t_2, \ldots, t_p$ such that, a model $w_t \models \phi$ iff $w_t \in [\![w]\!] \cap L(\mathcal{A})$. The formula ϕ is constructed as a conjunction of ϕ_w and $\phi_\mathcal{A}$, as described below.

First, we encode the constraints present in w. Consider the i-th position in w, suppose the constraint in this position is g_i. Now, let $x_\sigma \sim c$ be an elementary constraint present as a conjunct in g_i. Now, let $0 \leq j < i$ be the largest position in w such that $\sigma_j = \sigma$. Then, g_i will be satisfied by the timed word w_t only if $t_i - t_j \sim c$. For every constraint g_i in w, we construct the formula ϕ_{g_i} where each clock x_σ is replaced with $t_i - t_j$. Then define $\phi_w := \bigwedge_{1 \leq i \leq n} \phi_{g_i}$.

We now describe the formula $\phi_{\mathcal{A}}$. We encode the underlying transition system $\mathcal{A}$ in a fairly standard way. Assuming $\mathcal{A}$ contains n states, we use $\log(n)$-many Boolean variables to denote the states of the automaton. For each state q of $\mathcal{A}$ we have the following formula: $\phi_q := \ell_1 \wedge \ell_2 \wedge \ldots \wedge \ell_k$, where $k = \log(n)$ and $\ell_j \in \{p_j, \neg p_j\}, 1 \leq j \leq k$. The formula for the initial state is $\phi_I := \phi_{q_{\text{init}}}$, and the formula for the final states is: $\phi_F := \bigvee_{q_f \in F} \phi_{q_f}$. We now encode the transitions of $\mathcal{A}$. Suppose $e = (q, \sigma, g, q')$ be a transition of $\mathcal{A}$, where $\sigma \in \Sigma$ and the guard g is a constraint $\bigwedge_m x_m \sim c$. To encode the guards, we use the same technique as we used when encoding a symbolic word. We then get the formula for a transition: $\phi_e := \phi_q \wedge \phi_g \wedge \phi_{q'}$. For the set of all transitions E with event σ of $\mathcal{A}$, noted $E|\sigma$, we use the formula $\phi_{E|\sigma} := \bigvee_{e=(q,\sigma,g,q') \in E} \phi_e$.

We will use superscripts on the state-variables (ℓ_i's) to denote the state of the automaton after m steps in a run; for instance, $\phi_{q_i}^m := \ell_1^m \wedge \ell_2^m \wedge \ldots \wedge \ell_k^m$ will encode the fact that the automaton is in q_i at the m-th step of a run. Further, the m-th transition in a run will be represented by $\phi_e^m := \phi_{q_i}^m \wedge \phi_{g_i} \wedge \phi_{q_j}^{m+1}$. Similarly, we use $\phi_{E|\sigma}^m := \bigvee_{e=(q,\sigma,g,q') \in E} \phi_e^m$. To represent the set of all p-length paths in $\mathcal{A}$ on w, we use the following formula:

$$\phi_{\mathcal{A}} := \phi_I^1 \wedge \phi_{E|\sigma_1}^1 \wedge \phi_{E|\sigma_2}^2 \ldots \wedge \phi_{E|\sigma_p}^p \wedge \phi_F^p$$

Note that, every satisfying model of $\phi_{\mathcal{A}}$ is a timed word w_t that has a run in $\mathcal{A}$ along w, and further it starts from the initial state and ends at a final state after p steps; i.e. w_t has an *accepting* run in $\mathcal{A}$.

Then the final formula is $\phi := \phi_w \wedge \phi_{\mathcal{A}}$.

Lemma 3. ϕ *is satisfiable iff* $[\![w]\!] \cap \mathsf{L}(\mathcal{A}) \neq \emptyset$.

This concludes the description of the SMT encoding. Then one can show the correctness of LEAP:

Theorem 1 (Correctness). *Given a sample set* $\mathsf{S} = (\mathsf{S}_+, \mathsf{S}_-)$ *of symbolic timed words as input, (1) LEAP terminates, and (2) LEAP returns a possibly nondeterministic automaton* $\mathcal{A}$ *such that for every* $w \in \mathsf{S}_+$, $[\![w]\!] \subseteq \mathsf{L}(\mathcal{A})$ *and for every* $w \in \mathsf{S}_-$, $[\![w]\!] \cap \mathsf{L}(\mathcal{A}) \neq \emptyset$.

We will now illustrate the execution of LEAP on an example.

Example 1. Let $\mathsf{S} = (\mathsf{S}_+, \mathsf{S}_-)$ be a sample set, where S_+ is the set $\{\varepsilon, (a, x_a = 1)(b, x_a = 1), (a, \top)(b, x_a = 1)(a, x_b \leq 1)\}$ and S_- is $\{(a, \top)(a, \top), (a, \top)(b, x_a = 1)(a, x_b = 2)(b, x_a = 1), (a, \top)(b, x_a = 1)(b, x_a = 1), (a, \top)(b, x_a = 1)(a, x_b = 1)(a, \top)(b, x_a = 1)\}$. With this sample as input, in the first step, the algorithm computes the prefix tree depicted in Fig. 3a. The algorithm starts by putting q_0 in RED and q_1 and q_3 in BLUE according to the order $\prec$, mentioned earlier in this section. It picks q_1 and tries to merge this state with q_0, the merged automaton is depicted in Fig. 3b, but the merge fails since it accepts the negative word $(a, \top)(a, \top)$. Since q_0 is the only state in RED, q_1 gets promoted to RED, and q_2 is added to BLUE, keeping the list sorted. The algorithm then

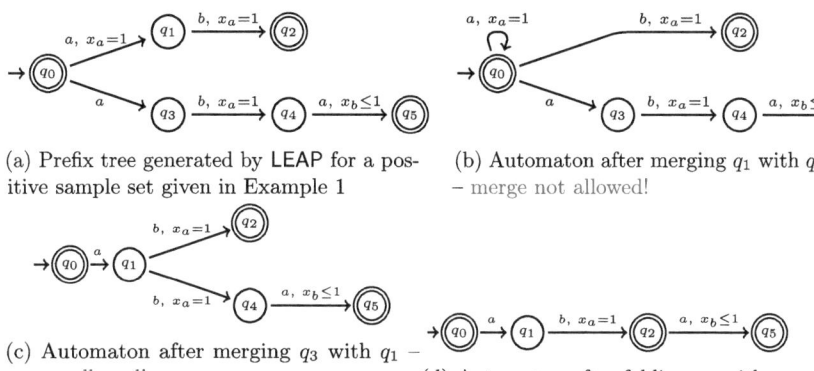

Fig. 3. Different steps of the algorithm LEAP. In the prefix tree, we associate each state with the word that leads to that state as described in Sect. 3, for example, q_2 corresponds to $(a, x_a = 1)(b, x_a = 1)$, and q_3 to $(a, \top)$, etc.

picks q_3; the merge of q_3 with q_0 fails, but, the merge of q_3 with q_1 succeeds. The automaton computed after this merge is depicted in Fig. 3c. After this, the algorithm *folds* q_2 and q_4 (since the incoming transitions to these two states are both from q_1 with the same event and guard) and gets the automaton in Fig. 3d. At this point, the only state in BLUE is q_2. Both merges of q_2 with q_0 and q_2 with q_1 fail, and therefore, q_2 is promoted to RED, and q_5 to BLUE. Finally, the algorithm tries to merge q_5 with q_0, which fails due to the negative word $(a, \top)(b, x_a = 1)(a, x_b = 1)(a, \top)(b, x_a = 1)$. The merge of q_5 with q_1 succeeds, the algorithm computes the automaton in Fig. 2.

The above example demonstrates that our algorithm LEAP does not need to maintain deterministic structure during merging, and the result of the merging phase can be a non-deterministic ERA. This is in sharp contrast to RPNI. Other differences with RPNI and other merging techniques that we are aware of, are explained in more details in [20] and evaluated experimentally in Sect. 6.

4 Complexity Results

In this section, we will first show that given an ERA $\mathcal{A}$ and a symbolic timed word w, checking whether the language accepted by $\mathcal{A}$ *is not disjoint from* w, i.e. whether $\mathsf{L}(\mathcal{A}) \cap [\![w]\!] \neq \emptyset$, is NP-complete. Consequently, deciding if a merge is allowed in any iteration of LEAP is also NP-complete. Later, we will discuss the overall complexity of the LEAP algorithm.

Given an ERA $\mathcal{A}$ and a symbolic timed word w, we study the complexity of the following decision problem:

INTERSECTION NON-EMPTINESS PROBLEM
Input: An ERA $\mathcal{A}$, and a symbolic timed word w.
Output: Yes if $\mathsf{L}(\mathcal{A}) \cap [\![w]\!] \neq \emptyset$, and No otherwise.

We show that the above problem is NP-complete, even for DERA. We prove the hardness by providing a polynomial time reduction from 3-SAT.

Lemma 4. *The* INTERSECTION NON-EMPTINESS *problem for DERA is NP-hard.*

Proof. The proof of NP-hardness is established via a polynomial-time reduction from 3-SAT, which is known to be NP-complete [8]. Given a 3-CNF instance φ, we construct a DERA $\mathcal{A}_\varphi$ and a symbolic timed word w_φ such that φ is satisfiable if and only if $\mathsf{L}(\mathcal{A}_\varphi) \cap [\![w_\varphi]\!]$ is non-empty.

The high-level idea is as follows: the automaton $\mathcal{A}_\varphi$ consists of two parts. The first part includes a block of states for each propositional variable in φ, ensuring that every run of $\mathcal{A}_\varphi$ corresponds to an assignment of these variables. The second part ensures that if a run of $\mathcal{A}_\varphi$ completes the first part, the corresponding assignment must make at least one literal in each clause of φ true. Together, they ensure that every run of $\mathcal{A}_\varphi$ corresponds to a satisfying assignment for φ. Then we construct w_φ in such a way that, for every timed word w_t that has an accepting run in $\mathcal{A}_\varphi$, we will have $w_t \in [\![w_\varphi]\!]$. This in turn will imply that φ is satisfiable if and only if $\mathsf{L}(\mathcal{A}_\varphi) \cap [\![w_\varphi]\!] \neq \emptyset$. We formalize this idea below. An example of the construction of $\mathcal{A}_\varphi$ is depicted in Fig. 4.

We first fix some notations: let φ be the 3-CNF formula $C_1 \wedge C_2 \wedge \ldots \wedge C_m$, where each C_h is of the form $\ell_{h,1} \vee \ell_{h,2} \vee \ell_{h,3}$. We call each C_h a *clause* and each $\ell_{h,j}$ a *literal*. We assume $p_1, p_2, \ldots, p_n$ are all the propositional variables present in φ. W.l.o.g., the order on the variables is fixed throughout the construction. A literal is then either a propositional variable or the negation of a propositional variable, i.e., for every $1 \leq j \leq 3$, $\ell_{h,j} \in \{p_i, \neg p_i \mid 1 \leq i \leq n\}$.

The Automaton $\mathcal{A}_\varphi$. The alphabet Σ of $\mathcal{A}_\varphi$ consists of p_i for every $1 \leq i \leq n$ and two special letters $\oplus$ and $\checkmark$. Since $\mathcal{A}_\varphi$ is an ERA, we have a clock x_σ for every $\sigma \in \Sigma$. Intuitively, the amount of delay required before taking the transitions labelled with p_i's will be used to determine the values of the propositions, the transitions on $\oplus$ will maintain the time elapsed during an execution, and the transitions on $\checkmark$ will be used to ensure that every clause evaluates to True.

Formally, $\mathcal{A}_\varphi = (Q, \Sigma, q_0, \Delta, F)$, where: $Q = \{q_0\} \cup \{v_i \mid 0 \leq i \leq n\} \cup \{q_i, \bar{q}_i \mid 1 \leq i \leq n\} \cup \{C_h \mid 1 \leq h \leq m+1\}$; $\Sigma = \{p_i \mid 1 \leq i \leq n\} \cup \{\oplus\} \cup \{\checkmark\}$; and $q_0 \in Q$ is the initial state. Recall here that n is the number of propositional variables and m is the number of clauses present in φ. The transition relation Δ is defined as follows. For every $i \in \{1, 2, \ldots, n\}$, from the state v_{i-1}, we keep two outgoing transitions, one to q_i and the other to $\bar{q}_i$, which denotes the fact that the proposition p_i has been set to True and False, respectively. From each of q_i and $\bar{q}_i$, there is a transition to v_{i+1}. The guards on these transitions ensure that v_{i+1} is reached exactly after 3 time units from v_i. Formally,

$$v_{i-1} \xrightarrow[x_\oplus = 1]{p_i} q_i \xrightarrow[x_{p_i} = 2]{\oplus} v_i, \quad v_{i-1} \xrightarrow[x_\oplus = 2]{p_i} \bar{q}_i \xrightarrow[x_{p_i} = 1]{\oplus} v_i, \text{ for every } 1 \leq i \leq n.$$

Notice that each run of $\mathcal{A}_\varphi$ can take only one of these paths for each i, since the guards on the transitions on p_i's are disjoint. A run of $\mathcal{A}_\varphi$, from v_0 to v_n,

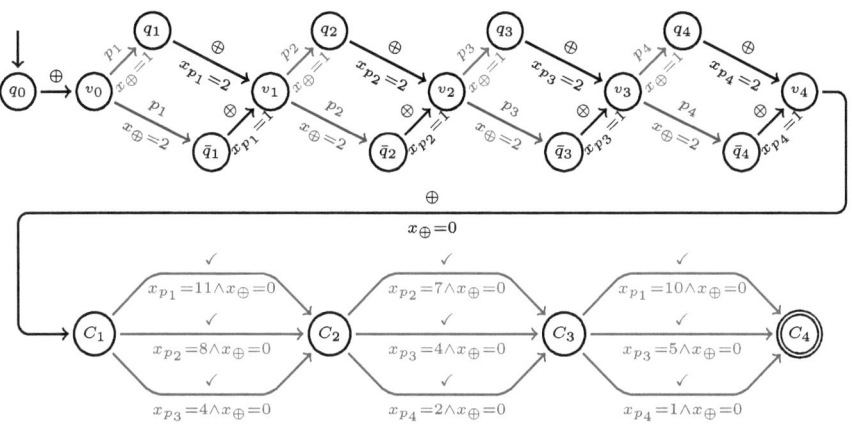

Fig. 4. The automaton $\mathcal{A}_\varphi$ corresponding to the formula $\varphi = (p_1 \vee p_2 \vee \neg p_3) \wedge (\neg p_2 \vee \neg p_3 \vee p_4) \wedge (\neg p_1 \vee p_3 \vee \neg p_4)$. The corresponding symbolic timed word is $w_\varphi = (\oplus, \top)(p_1, \top)(\oplus, \top)(p_2, \top)(\oplus, \top)(p_3, \top)(\oplus, \top)(p_4, \top)(\oplus, \top)(\checkmark, \top)^3$.

will determine the values of the propositions p_i's: if the path through q_i is taken, we assign p_i to True and when the other path (through $\bar{q}_i$) is taken, we assign p_i to False. Additionally, we add the following transition from the initial state q_0 that resets the clock $x_\oplus$: $q_0 \xrightarrow{\oplus}_{\top} v_0$.

The second phase begins from C_1. In this phase, we ensure that the automaton cannot elapse time at any of the states. We, for the sake of readability, keep a (dummy) transition between the two phases on the letter $\oplus$, that resets the clock $x_\oplus$, and we keep the guard in such a way that no time can elapse at v_n: $v_n \xrightarrow[x_\oplus = 0]{\oplus} C_1$. We then *sequentially* check whether, for every $h \in \{1, 2, \ldots, m\}$, a literal in C_h is made True by the valuation chosen in the first phase. This is achieved using appropriate guards on the transitions: for every $1 \leq j \leq 3$, if $\ell_{h,j} = p_i$ for some p_i, then we add: $C_h \xrightarrow[x_{p_i} = 3 \times (n-i)+2 \wedge x_\oplus = 0]{\checkmark} C_{h+1}$, and if $\ell_{h,j} = \neg p_i$ for some p_i, then we add: $C_h \xrightarrow[x_{p_i} = 3 \times (n-i)+1 \wedge x_\oplus = 0]{\checkmark} C_{h+1}$. These transitions are depicted in green in Fig. 4. However, each of them actually represent sets of transitions. For example, the transition $(C_1, \checkmark, x_{p_1} = 11 \wedge x_\oplus = 0, C_2)$ denotes the set of transitions $\{(C_1, \checkmark, \psi, C_2) \mid \psi \in \bigcup_{d_2 \in \{7,8\}, d_3 \in \{4,5\}, d_4 \in \{1,2\}} \{x_{p_1} = 11 \wedge x_{p_2} = d_2 \wedge x_{p_3} = d_3 \wedge x_{p_4} = d_4\}\}$. Now note that, although the automaton in Fig. 4 is non-deterministic as it is presented, if the green edges are replaced with the set of edges it represents as described above (removing redundant edges, if present), then the resulting automaton will indeed be deterministic. Finally, we make C_{m+1} the unique final state of the automaton: $F = \{C_{m+1}\}$.

To illustrate the assignments to propositions, consider the following example. Suppose, $\ell_{h,2} = p_i$ for some h. Then, if a run of $\mathcal{A}_\varphi$ has visited the state q_i, it means p_i has been set to True, and so is $\ell_{h,2}$. Note that this can be checked using

the guard $x_{p_i} = 3 \times (n-i) + 2$, where the value of x_{p_i} is the time elapsed since q_i. On the other hand, if the run had visited the state $\bar{q}_i$, then p_i would be False, and so is $\ell_{h,2}$, which can again be checked using the guard $x_{p_i} = 3 \times (n-i) + 1$.
The symbolic timed word w_φ is defined in a way so that $[\![w_\varphi]\!]$ is the set of all timed words whose untimed projection is $\oplus \; p_1 \oplus \; p_2 \oplus \; p_n \oplus \; \oplus \; \checkmark^m$. Note that, this untimed word is visited in every accepting run in $\mathcal{A}_\varphi$.

$$w_\varphi := (\oplus, \top)(p_1, \top) \ldots (\oplus, \top)(p_n, \top)(\oplus, \top) \; (\oplus, \top) \; (\checkmark, \top) \ldots (\checkmark, \top).$$

The above reduction ensures the following equivalence.

Lemma 5. *Given a 3-CNF formula φ, φ is satisfiable iff* $\mathsf{L}(\mathcal{A}_\varphi) \cap [\![w_\varphi]\!] \neq \emptyset$.

This concludes the proof of Lemma 4. □

We can also show that the INTERSECTION NON-EMPTINESS problem for (possibly non-deterministic) ERA is in NP. Then the following theorem follows.

Theorem 2. *The* INTERSECTION NON-EMPTINESS PROBLEM *is* NP-*complete, both for ERA and DERA.*

Proof (sketch). We have established hardness in Lemma 4. NP membership follows from the following: once we guess a run of an ERA, whether there exists a timed word satisfying both this run and also the symbolic timed word w can be decided by solving a linear program. □

However, if the sample set only contains region words and the ERA is deterministic, then the INTERSECTION NON-EMPTINESS PROBLEM is in P.

Lemma 6. *Given any DERA $\mathcal{A}$ and any symbolic timed word w s.t. all guards in $\mathcal{A}$ and all guards in w are K-simple constraints, for some $K \in \mathbb{N}$, then the* INTERSECTION NON-EMPTINESS *problem can be solved in polynomial time.*

Proof. Without loss of any generality, we can assume that $\mathcal{A}$ is complete, *i.e.*, for every state q, every letter $\sigma \in \Sigma$, and every K-simple constraint r, there exists exactly one outgoing transition from q on (σ, r). Now, since the guards present in w are also K-simple constraints, one can just syntactically trace the path corresponding to w in $\mathcal{A}$ (it always exists, since $\mathcal{A}$ is complete). Then, it only remains to check if this path can indeed be taken by the automaton. This can be determined by checking whether $[\![w]\!] \neq \emptyset$ or not, which can be checked by solving a linear program. □

Note that, having to solve an NP-complete problem for every merge (unlike the case in RPNI for regular languages) is somewhat expected, as we deal with sequences of constraints over clocks. Even PSPACE-completeness is common in analyzing Timed Automata, yet tools like UPPAAL [17] remain useful in practice.

Complexity of LEAP. The size of the PT constructed by LEAP is *linear* in the size of S_+. The rest of the algorithm tries to merge states of this PT to get smaller models at each iteration, the total number of merges performed by the algorithm is *polynomial* in the size of the PT. Now, in the most general case, when the sample contains symbolic timed words, at each iteration, the algorithm uses an NP oracle (the algorithm for INTERSECTION NON-EMPTINESS PROBLEM) to determine whether the merge is allowed or not. Therefore, the overall complexity of LEAP is P^{NP}. Whereas, if the sample sets only contain region words, since INTERSECTION NON-EMPTINESS PROBLEM is in P (Lemma 6), LEAP also is in P.

Theorem 3. *LEAP executes in polynomial time when the sample sets contain only region words, and executes with a polynomial number of calls to an NP-oracle when the sample sets contain symbolic words in general.*

Symbolic timed words vs region words. From any input sample set S containing symbolic timed words, one can construct a sample set S^{rw} containing only region words, and apply LEAP on S^{rw}. Since LEAP runs in polynomial time in the size of S^{rw} (Lemma 6), and S^{rw} contains at most exponentially many samples than in S, the worst case complexities of the procedures are indeed similar. However, as also witnessed in the theory of TA, dealing with *zones* is often more efficient than dealing with *regions* in practice. We will see in Sect. 6 that this is indeed also the case for LEAP, *i.e.*, handling symbolic timed words directly is often more efficient in practice.

5 Completeness of LEAP

In this section, we will provide a completeness result for the algorithm LEAP. We will define the notion of *characteristic sets* for ERA-recognizable languages. Intuitively, these are sample sets that contain necessary information for the learning algorithm to infer the correct language. We show that, given an ERA-recognizable language L, there exist characteristic sets S_L such that, when S_L is given as input to LEAP, it will return an ERA recognizing L.

In our construction, the characteristic sets only contain region words. In the worst case, the size of these sets can be *exponential* in the size of the alphabet Σ and also in the size of a minimal DERA $\mathcal{A}$ recognizing L. However, one can show that the exponential blowup in the size of the characteristic sets (containing only region words) is necessary. The reason being the class of ERA is not polynomially learnable, as shown in Theorem 1 of [29]. Even though the original result in [29] was shown for the class of DTA, the same proof also holds for the class of ERA, by relabeling the transitions of the TA in Figure 2 of [29] to form an ERA.

Lemma 7 ([29]). *The class of ERA is not polynomially learnable.*

Now, notice that, thanks to Theorem 3, if a sample set only contains region words, then LEAP runs in polynomial time in the size of such a set. Therefore, if for every ERA-recognizable language L there would exist a polynomial size characteristic set containing only region words, then that would contradict Lemma 7. Thus, we conclude the following corollary.

Table 1. $|S| = |S_+| + |S_-|$; #queries for tLsep is the number of membership and inclusion queries; for LearnTA, this is the number of membership and equivalence queries. Times are reported in seconds; 'TO' denotes a timeout of 900 s.

Model	LEAP(zones)			LEAP(regions)[a]			tLsep [19]			LearnTA [32]		
	$\|S\|$	$\|Q\|$	time	$\|S\|$	$\|Q\|$	time	#queries	$\|Q\|$	time	#queries	$\|Q\|$	time
Fig. 1b	8	3	0.10	75	3	87.29	339	6	6.43	131	3	0.01
Fig. 2	7	3	0.13	56	2	49.21	106	2	1.66	268	3	0.01
Fig. 5	8	3	0.16	24	3	4.53	31	3	0.22	45	3	0.01
Unbalanced-1	16	4	0.13	–	–	TO	438	9	10.64	2400	8	0.04
Unbalanced-2	16	4	0.12	–	–	TO	1122	14	47.12	13671	12	0.17
Unbalanced-3	16	4	0.12	–	–	TO	2124	18	343.34	46220	16	1.120
PC	176	19	147.85	–	–	TO	–	–	TO	1613401	38	607.45
L_2	10	4	0.20	–	–	TO	246	6	1.51	513	5	0.01
L_4	16	6	0.90	–	–	TO	778	18	17.60	3739	17	0.15
L_8	28	10	12.39	–	–	TO	–	–	TO	141635	257	100.57

[a] the samples for LEAP(region) are constructed from the samples of LEAP(zones) by *systematically* breaking each symbolic timed word into all its included region words

Corollary 1. *There exist ERA-recognizable languages for which there cannot exist polynomial size characteristic sets for LEAP containing only region words.*

However, for every ERA-recognizable language L, one can construct characteristic sets containing only region words, for which LEAP returns a DERA recognizing L. This is formalized in the following theorem.

Theorem 4. *For every K-ERA recognizable language L, there exist characteristic sets S, such that, when provided as input to LEAP, it returns a DERA $\mathcal{A}$ with $L(\mathcal{A}) = L$.*

The characteristic sets that we construct (as stated in Theorem 4) consist only of region words, and the size of these sets can be exponential in the worst case w.r.t. the size of a minimal K-DERA recognizing L, as justified in Corollary 1. Due to the large number of samples present in these characteristic sets, it is not practical to use LEAP on such sets, but it is still interesting (from a theoretical point of view) to prove that LEAP would indeed terminate and return the correct language. The construction of characteristic sets is similar to the regular case [21], however, the proof of the fact that LEAP indeed returns an automaton with the correct language when provided with a characteristic set is novel and non-trivial, it can be found in [20]. On the other hand, notice that Corollary 1 does not rule out the possibility of the existence of characteristic sets of polynomial size containing general symbolic timed words. We plan on exploring this possibility in the future. Indeed, this possibility is substantiated by the empirical evidence provided in Sect. 6, where we will demonstrate that, in prac-

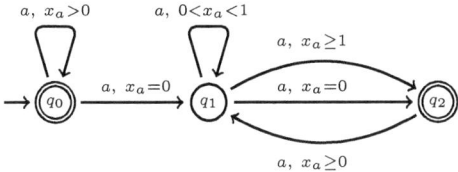

Fig. 5. Example ERA

tice, one can often construct reasonably small sample sets for ERA-recognizable languages, containing general symbolic words, that are correct for LEAP.

6 Empirical Evaluation

We have implemented a prototype[2] of LEAP in PYTHON. The steps shown in Figs. 1b and 3 are outputs from this implementation. Here, we empirically compare LEAP's performance with the implementations of other learning algorithms applicable to the class of ERA.

Existing passive learning approaches differ significantly from ours. Works such as [9,22,31] learn from plain timed words rather than *symbolic timed words* as we do; [9,22] use only positive data, and [9,31] infer automata from a weaker class. A merging based algorithm was proposed in [14], however, it requires examples that meet certain completeness criteria, which our method does not, and moreover, implementation of their algorithm is not available. These differences make a direct comparison of these algorithms with LEAP inappropriate. On the other hand, as remarked in the introduction of this article, LEAP can be used interactively, with the requirement engineer providing additional symbolic timed words representing unmet requirements, which LEAP then incorporates. This resembles an active learning approach where the user acts as the teacher and LEAP as the learner. Recent works propose active learning frameworks for ERA [19] and Deterministic Timed Automata (DTA) [25,32]. To the best of our knowledge, the implementation in [25] is not available. Therefore, we compare our algorithm with following three methods: (1) a version of LEAP restricted to region words (reported in the column "LEAP(regions)" in Table 1), highlighting the advantage of working with general symbolic (zone) words (the column "LEAP(zones)" in Table 1); (2) tLsep [19], a recent active learning tool for ERA; and (3) LearnTA [32], an active learning tool for deterministic TA. We use the number of samples (all the reported algorithms operate on symbolic words) as the metric for comparison: for active learning, it is the number of queries, while for passive learning, it is $|S_+| + |S_-|$.

Table 1 summarizes the experimental results. The first two rows in the table represent timed languages recognized by the ERA in Figs. 1b and 2, respectively. The third model corresponds to the language of the automaton in Fig. 5, while

---

[2] The source code of LEAP is available at: https://github.com/anirban11/leap.

Unbalanced-k and PC are all DTA models (ERA, after clock renaming) used as benchmarks for LearnTA. The last three examples are instances of a family of languages L_n that showcases the compactness of nondeterministic ERA over equivalent DERA, which is formally defined as follows. Let $\Sigma = \{a, b\}$; then L_n is a timed language over $\Sigma_\# := \Sigma \cup \{\#\}$ that accepts timed words satisfying the conditions: (i) they begin with the symbol $\#$, (ii) $\#$ does not reappear, and (iii) the n-th last letter is a which occurs exactly 1 time unit after reading $\#$.

We now illustrate the main advantages of LEAP witnessed by our experiments.

1. Small number of samples. As we can observe in Table 1, "LEAP(zones)" requires significantly fewer symbolic words as input compared to the number of queries needed by tLsep and LearnTA. This difference arises because the symbolic zone words used as input for LEAP are based on specific intuitions from the informal requirements, that a requirements engineer (RE) can provide, delivering rich information about the target language. In contrast, active learning algorithms like tLsep and LearnTA must derive all aspects of the target language through *systematic* membership and equivalence queries. While we do not claim that LEAP is universally superior to active learning algorithms, it is better suited for helping an RE craft an ERA from scenarios, as it avoids the need for the RE to respond to numerous membership queries, as required in active learning setups.

2. Insensitivity to the maximal constant. Another advantage of being able to handle symbolic timed words directly is demonstrated by the two Unbalanced examples – the two models here are identical, except the maximum constant being 1 and 3, respectively. Since symbolic timed words are not dependent on this maximum constant, the sample size required by LEAP remains the same, while the performances of the active learning algorithms take a considerable hit, due to their sensitivity to this constant.

3. Advantages of zone words. In Sect. 5, we showed that for every ERA-recognizable language, there exists characteristic sets for which LEAP returns the correct automaton, however, these sets contain only region words and can be prohibitively large. Even though handling region words is computationally easier than handling general symbolic timed words (Theorem 3), the smaller values in the column "LEAP(zones)" compared to the ones in "LEAP(regions)" showcase the advantages of working with symbolic timed words. Splitting them into region words can very quickly result in an enormous blowup in the number of samples, as evidenced by the models Unbalanced-k and L_n's in the table. Symbolic timed words can usually represent large sets of region words at once. The example PC is seemingly the largest (in terms of number of states) practical benchmark as mentioned in [32]. Due to the conciseness of zone words, LEAP manages to learn the automaton for this example, showing its ability to scale.

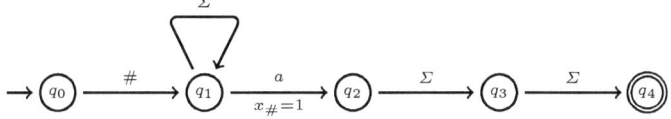

Fig. 6. An ERA recognizing the language L_3.

4. Advantages of maintaining nondeterminism. As noted earlier, each step in LEAP produces a possibly non-deterministic ERA, allowing it to learn smaller models for a given language compared to existing algorithms in the literature, which target deterministic models [13,19,32]. With standard techniques, one can show that any DERA recognizing L_n defined earlier requires at least $O(2^n)$ states (also witnessed in the outputs of tLSep and LearnTA), while there exists non-deterministic ERA A_n recognizing L_n with only $n+2$ states (e.g., A_3 in Fig. 6 recognizes L_3). To learn L_n, we construct a sample set S_n of size linear in n, containing symbolic words, which when provided to LEAP, yields A_n. Table 1 compares the size of S_n with the number of queries required by tLSep and LearnTA for various values of n.

Note that, the values reported for the tool LearnTA on the benchmarks taken from [32] are different from the ones reported in [32]. This is because, these are modelled as DTAs in [32], whereas here we model these as ERAs. The ERA models are larger in size and hence LearnTA takes more time.

7 Discussion and Future Works

In this work, we introduced a merging-based passive learning algorithm for ERA-definable languages. We proved that determining if a merge is possible is an NP-complete problem, and we have provided an SMT-based solution for this problem. As shown in our experiments, LEAP successfully learns ERA from small sets of symbolic timed words as positive and negative samples. We established the completeness of LEAP using a characteristic sample set, that is guaranteed to exist for all ERA-recognizable languages.

As demonstrated, LEAP is well-suited to scenarios where a user guides the learning process, making symbolic timed words a natural input format. However, LEAP can also be readily applied to timed words (obtained from logs for instance). With a known maximal constant K and a fixed granularity for atomic constraints, a timed word can be converted to a region word by constructing its corresponding clocked word and replacing each valuation with its unique K-simple constraint. LEAP can then be applied to these transformed samples.

In future we aim to define characteristic sets that include symbolic words. As noted in Sect. 5, polynomial size characteristic sets containing symbolic words may still exist for ERA recognizable languages. Secondly, we would like to explore the possibility of generating the examples using LLMs instead of handcrafting. This is because, handcrafting many symbolic timed words (for instance, 176 in the PC example), some being relatively long, may not be practical for a requirement engineer. However, this opens up an interesting potential application of Large Language Models (LLM), where, instead of handcrafting the examples, the requirement engineer may specify the requirement in natural language and ask the LLM to produce examples and only verify the validity of each of the examples before providing them to LEAP. While asking to turn a natural language specification into a fully-fledged ERA is out of reach of LLMs, it appears that generating positive and negative examples in the form of symbolic timed words is feasible even with off-the-shelf LLMs. Further, an incremental approach to learning ERA, where the sample is presented one word at a time instead of all at once in the beginning, similar to the work in [10] for regular languages, would be an interesting direction to explore.

In [6], a framework combines reactive synthesis from LTL specifications with example-based learning to produce a Mealy machine that satisfies an LTL formula and aligns with specified execution traces, independent of environmental behavior. Our merging algorithm for timed languages suggests a natural extension of this approach to real-time settings, where the input can be a real-time formula (say, in MITL [3]), along with symbolic words as *hints* that our algorithm could process.

References

1. Alur, R., et al.: Syntax-guided synthesis. In: Formal Methods in Computer-Aided Design, FMCAD 2013, Portland, OR, USA, 20–23 October 2013, pp. 1–8. IEEE (2013). https://ieeexplore.ieee.org/document/6679385/
2. Alur, R., Dill, D.L.: A theory of timed automata. Theor. Comput. Sci. **126**(2), 183–235 (1994)
3. Alur, R., Feder, T., Henzinger, T.A.: The benefits of relaxing punctuality. J. ACM **43**(1), 116–146 (1996)
4. Alur, R., Fix, L., Henzinger, T.A.: Event-clock automata: a determinizable class of timed automata. Theor. Comput. Sci. **211**(1–2), 253–273 (1999)
5. An, J., Wang, L., Zhan, B., Zhan, N., Zhang, M.: Learning real-time automata. Sci. China Inf. Sci. **64**(9), 1–17 (2021). https://doi.org/10.1007/s11432-019-2767-4
6. Balachander, M., Filiot, E., Raskin, J.: LTL reactive synthesis with a few hints. In: TACAS (2). Lecture Notes in Computer Science, vol. 13994, pp. 309–328. Springer, Heidelberg (2023). https://doi.org/10.1007/978-3-031-30820-8_20
7. Bruyère, V., Garhewal, B., Pérez, G.A., Staquet, G., Vaandrager, F.W.: Active learning of mealy machines with timers. CoRR arxiv:2403.02019 (2024)
8. Cook, S.A.: The complexity of theorem-proving procedures. In: STOC, pp. 151–158. ACM (1971)
9. Cornanguer, L., Largouët, C., Rozé, L., Termier, A.: TAG: learning timed automata from logs. In: AAAI, pp. 3949–3958. AAAI Press (2022)
10. Dupont, P.: Incremental regular inference. In: ICGI. Lecture Notes in Computer Science, vol. 1147, pp. 222–237. Springer, Heidelberg (1996). https://doi.org/10.1007/978-3-031-30820-8_20
11. Gold, E.M.: Language identification in the limit. Inf. Control. **10**(5), 447–474 (1967). https://doi.org/10.1016/S0019-9958(67)91165-5

12. Gold, E.M.: Complexity of automaton identification from given data. Inf. Control. **37**(3), 302–320 (1978). https://doi.org/10.1016/S0019-9958(78)90562-4
13. Grinchtein, O., Jonsson, B., Leucker, M.: Learning of event-recording automata. Theor. Comput. Sci. **411**(47), 4029–4054 (2010)
14. Grinchtein, O., Jonsson, B., Pettersson, P.: Inference of event-recording automata using timed decision trees. In: Baier, C., Hermanns, H. (eds.) CONCUR 2006. LNCS, vol. 4137, pp. 435–449. Springer, Heidelberg (2006). https://doi.org/10.1007/11817949_29
15. Henry, L., Jéron, T., Markey, N.: Active learning of timed automata with unobservable resets. In: Bertrand, N., Jansen, N. (eds.) FORMATS 2020. LNCS, vol. 12288, pp. 144–160. Springer, Cham (2020). https://doi.org/10.1007/978-3-030-57628-8_9
16. Holbrook, H.: A scenario-based methodology for conducting requirements elicitation. ACM SIGSOFT Softw. Eng. Notes **15**(1), 95–104 (1990)
17. Larsen, K.G., Pettersson, P., Yi, W.: UPPAAL in a nutshell. Int. J. Softw. Tools Technol. Transf. **1**(1–2), 134–152 (1997)
18. Lin, S.-W., André, É., Dong, J.S., Sun, J., Liu, Y.: An efficient algorithm for learning event-recording automata. In: Bultan, T., Hsiung, P.-A. (eds.) ATVA 2011. LNCS, vol. 6996, pp. 463–472. Springer, Heidelberg (2011). https://doi.org/10.1007/978-3-642-24372-1_35
19. Majumdar, A., Mukherjee, S., Raskin, J.: Greybox learning of languages recognizable by event-recording automata. In: ATVA. Lecture Notes in Computer Science, vol. 15054, pp. 235–256. Springer, Heidelberg (2024). https://doi.org/10.1007/978-3-031-78709-6_12
20. Majumdar, A., Mukherjee, S., Raskin, J.F.: Learning event-recording automata passively (2025). https://arxiv.org/abs/2508.03627
21. Oncina, J., Garcia, P.: Inferring regular languages in polynomial updated time. In: Pattern Recognition and Image Analysis: Selected Papers from the IVth Spanish Symposium, pp. 49–61. World Scientific (1992)
22. Pastore, F., Micucci, D., Mariani, L.: Timed k-tail: automatic inference of timed automata. In: ICST, pp. 401–411. IEEE Computer Society (2017)
23. Tappler, M., Aichernig, B.K., Larsen, K.G., Lorber, F.: Time to learn - learning timed automata from tests. In: FORMATS. Lecture Notes in Computer Science, vol. 11750, pp. 216–235. Springer, Heidelberg (2019). https://doi.org/10.1007/978-3-030-29662-9_13
24. Tappler, M., Aichernig, B.K., Lorber, F.: Timed automata learning via SMT solving. In: NFM. Lecture Notes in Computer Science, vol. 13260, pp. 489–507. Springer, Heidelberg (2022). https://doi.org/10.1007/978-3-031-06773-0_26
25. Teng, Y., Zhang, M., An, J.: Learning deterministic multi-clock timed automata. In: HSCC, pp. 6:1–6:11. ACM (2024)
26. Vaandrager, F.W.: Model learning. Commun. ACM **60**(2), 86–95 (2017). https://doi.org/10.1145/2967606
27. Vaandrager, F.W., Ebrahimi, M., Bloem, R.: Learning mealy machines with one timer. Inf. Comput. **295**(Part B), 105013 (2023)
28. Vaandrager, F.W., Garhewal, B., Rot, J., Wißmann, T.: A new approach for active automata learning based on apartness. In: TACAS (1). Lecture Notes in Computer Science, vol. 13243, pp. 223–243. Springer, Heidelberg (2022). https://doi.org/10.1007/978-3-030-99524-9_12

29. Verwer, S., Weerdt, M., Witteveen, C.: Polynomial distinguishability of timed automata. In: Clark, A., Coste, F., Miclet, L. (eds.) ICGI 2008. LNCS (LNAI), vol. 5278, pp. 238–251. Springer, Heidelberg (2008). https://doi.org/10.1007/978-3-540-88009-7_19
30. Verwer, S., Weerdt, M., Witteveen, C.: One-clock deterministic timed automata are efficiently identifiable in the limit. In: Dediu, A.H., Ionescu, A.M., Martín-Vide, C. (eds.) LATA 2009. LNCS, vol. 5457, pp. 740–751. Springer, Heidelberg (2009). https://doi.org/10.1007/978-3-642-00982-2_63
31. Verwer, S., Weerdt, M., Witteveen, C.: A likelihood-ratio test for identifying probabilistic deterministic real-time automata from positive data. In: Sempere, J.M., García, P. (eds.) ICGI 2010. LNCS (LNAI), vol. 6339, pp. 203–216. Springer, Heidelberg (2010). https://doi.org/10.1007/978-3-642-15488-1_17
32. Waga, M.: Active learning of deterministic timed automata with myhill-nerode style characterization. In: CAV (1). Lecture Notes in Computer Science, vol. 13964, pp. 3–26. Springer, Heidelberg (2023). https://doi.org/10.1007/978-3-031-37706-8_1
33. Xu, R., An, J., Zhan, B.: Active learning of one-clock timed automata using constraint solving. In: ATVA. Lecture Notes in Computer Science, vol. 13505, pp. 249–265. Springer, Heidelberg (2022). https://doi.org/10.1007/978-3-031-19992-9_16

TAPAAL HyperLTL: A Tool for Checking Hyperproperties of Petri Nets

Bruno Maria René Gonzalez[1], Peter Gjøl Jensen[2], Stefan Schmid[1], Jiří Srba[2], and Martin Zimmermann[2(✉)]

[1] TU Berlin, Berlin, Germany
[2] Aalborg University, Aalborg, Denmark
mzi@cs.aau.dk

Abstract. Petri nets are a modeling formalism capable of describing complex distributed systems and there exists a large number of both academic and industrial tools that enable automatic verification of model properties. Typical questions include reachability analysis and model checking against logics like LTL and CTL. However, these logics fall short when describing properties like non-interference and observational determinism that require simultaneous reasoning about multiple traces of the model and can thus only be expressed as hyperproperties. We introduce, to the best of our knowledge, the first HyperLTL model checker for Petri nets. The tool is fully integrated into the verification framework TAPAAL and we describe the semantics of the hyperlogic, present the tool's architecture and GUI, and evaluate the performance of the HyperLTL verification engine on a benchmark of problems originating from the computer networking domain.

Keywords: Petri nets · Model checking · HyperLTL · Tool

1 Introduction

Many important properties of systems inherently relate multiple execution traces of a system, e.g., security and information-flow properties [1, 23, 33, 39, 40, 42] as well as network properties like congestion [10, 24]. These are not expressible in classical specification languages like LTL [35], CTL [12], and CTL* [21], as those are restricted to reasoning about one trace at a time. Clarkson and Schneider termed properties relating multiple traces *hyperproperties* and initiated their rigorous investigation [14]. Technically speaking, a hyperproperty is a set of sets of traces, just like a trace property is a set of traces. Their study received considerable attention after the introduction of specification languages for hyperproperties, which enabled the specification, analysis, and verification of hyperproperties. The two most important ones are HyperLTL and HyperCTL* which extend LTL and CTL* by quantification over traces [13]. These logics are able to express many important hyperproperties from security like non-interference, non-inference, observational determinism, etc. [22]. On the other hand, they are

© The Author(s), under exclusive license to Springer Nature Switzerland AG 2026
M. D'Souza et al. (Eds.): ATVA 2025, LNCS 16145, pp. 49–61, 2026.
https://doi.org/10.1007/978-3-032-08707-2_3

also able to express properties about paths in graphs, e.g., networks, like the existence of several disjoint paths between a source and a target node. This allows us to formalize quantitative aspects like congestion using HyperLTL as a requirement on the maximal number of flows that can traverse any given edge.

Petri nets [34] are widely used to represent concurrent and distributed systems due to their expressive power and an intuitive graphical representation. Despite the versatility of Petri nets, no prior HyperLTL verification tool has provided user-friendly support for designing and verifying Petri net models. Existing approaches often rely on textual specifications or lack intuitive interfaces.

To address this challenge, we introduce TAPAAL HyperLTL, a novel HyperLTL model checker integrated into the TAPAAL [17] verification suite, specifically designed to verify complex temporal properties of distributed systems modeled as Petri nets. Our implementation is the first to bring HyperLTL verification to Petri nets, offering a robust verification engine coupled with an intuitive user interface for modeling as well as debugging purposes.

To evaluate our tool, we conduct an extensive case study showing the applicability of HyperLTL for the analysis of congestion in a computer networking setting. Our results show that our HyperLTL engine outperforms the baseline approach based on self-composition [2,39] and achieves competitive performance compared to state-of-the-art tools like MCHyper [22].

Related Work. HyperLTL and its branching-time companion HyperCTL* have been introduced and their model-checking problems have been shown decidable in the seminal work of Clarkson et al. [13]. In general, model checking of HyperLTL is TOWER-complete [32,36] in the number of quantifier alternations. Hence, almost all tool development has been concerned with the alternation-free fragment, although recently the first tools tackling (a small number of) alternations have been presented.

For example, the tool MCHyper models the system using And-Inverter Graphs (AIGs) and has originally been restricted to alternation-free formulae [22] (like our tool), where it relies on the ABC [9] backend. More recently, it has been extended to handle one alternation using a game-based approach [15]. On the other hand, the tool AutoHyper handles quantifier alternations [5] by implementing an automata-theoretic model checking algorithm, relying on efficient automata inclusion checking.

Another approach for handling the inherent complexity of HyperLTL model checking is to consider incomplete methods like bounded model checking, which searches for counterexamples of bounded size. Hsu et al. [26,27] implemented this in their tool HyperQube using a reduction to QBF.

Finally, model checking asynchronous extensions of HyperLTL has been studied by Baumeister et al. [3] and probabilistic extensions by Dode et al. [18]. Most recently, the game-based approach mentioned above has been generalized [4,41] and planning-based [6] algorithms and implementations have been presented.

None of the existing tools mentioned above can handle Petri nets natively. Thus, our tool offers an alternative modeling language based on Petri nets, which naturally support concurrency, while existing tools use NuSMV [11] models (like HyperQube) or VHDL [37] and VeriLog [38] models (like MCHyper).

2 Modeling Formalism and HyperLTL Logic

We shall now semi-formally introduce the Petri net model as well as the syntax and semantics of the variant of HyperLTL that is supported by our tool and tailored to express properties of Petri nets.

2.1 Petri Nets

Our tool uses the classical Petri net (PN) model [34] with weighted and inhibitor arcs. It also supports colored Petri nets, following the PNML syntax used in the annual Model Checking Contest (MCC) [31]. The colored PNs are unfolded into classical P/T (place/transition) nets, after which the HyperLTL model checking is executed.

Figure 1b shows an example of a P/T net where places from the set $P = \{v_0, \ldots, v_3, a(t_0), a(t'_0), \ldots, a(t_4), a(t'_4)\}$ are drawn as circles, transitions from the set $T = \{t_1, t'_1, \ldots, t_4, t'_4, v_1^{deliver}, v_2^{deliver}\}$ are drawn as rectangles, and arcs are the directed edges connecting either places to transitions or transitions to places. Unless otherwise stated, the default weight of all arcs is 1.

A *marking* $M: P \to \mathbb{N}^0$ is a function that represents the placement of tokens (denoted as dots) across the places in the net. A transition t is *enabled* in a marking M if there are enough tokens in all of the input places to the transition. An enabled transition t can *fire* and produce the new marking M', written as $M[t\rangle M'$, by (i) removing as many tokens from the input places as is the weight of the corresponding arc, and (ii) producing new tokens to every output place of the transition, again according to the weights of the output arcs. For example, firing the transition t_1 in Fig. 1b removes the tokens from v_0 and $a(t_1)$ and adds a token to v_2. All other tokens are unchanged.

The Petri net in Fig. 1b models all possible routing sequences for the computer network depicted in Fig. 1a where a packet (token) starts at the node v_0 and the aim is to reach the node v_1 or v_2. Moreover, every link in the network corresponds to some transition t in the Petri net and once this transition fires, the token in the place $a(t)$ is consumed, representing the fact that the corresponding link is now occupied.

A *trace* (run) in a Petri net is an infinite sequence $\rho = M_0 M_1 M_2 \cdots$ of markings such that for every $n \geq 0$ either (i) $M_n[t_n\rangle M_{n+1}$ for some transition $t_n \in T$, or (ii) $M_{n+1} = M_n$ in case that M_n is a deadlock, i.e., if M_n does not enable any transition. As HyperLTL is interpreted over infinite traces, we introduce the stuttering to prolong possibly deadlocked traces into infinite ones (as it is e.g., assumed in the MCC [31]). Given a trace $\rho = M_0 M_1 M_2 \cdots$, we denote the n'th marking M_n in the trace by ρ^n.

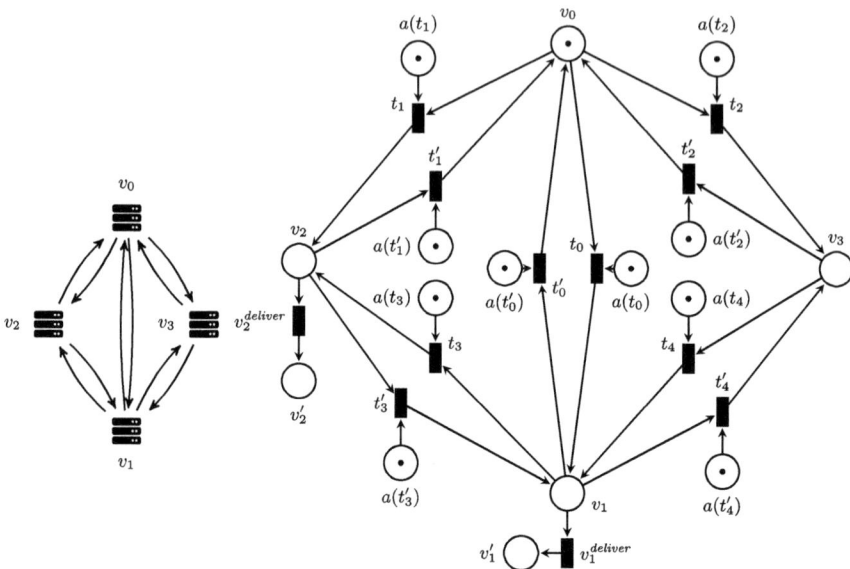

(a) A comp. network   (b) A Petri net N modeling the computer network

$\varphi_1 \equiv \exists \pi_1.\ \exists \pi_2.\ (\mathbf{F}\ \pi_1.v'_1 = 1) \wedge (\mathbf{F}\ \pi_2.v'_1 = 1) \wedge \mathbf{G}\ noCongestion2$
$\varphi_2 \equiv \exists \pi_1.\ \exists \pi_2.\ \exists \pi_3.\ (\mathbf{F}\ \pi_1.v'_1 = 1) \wedge (\mathbf{F}\ \pi_2.v'_1 = 1) \wedge (\mathbf{F}\ \pi_3.v'_1 = 1) \wedge \mathbf{G}\ noCongestion3$
$\varphi_3 \equiv \exists \pi_1.\ \exists \pi_2.\ (\mathbf{F}\ \pi_1.v'_2 = 1) \wedge (\mathbf{F}\ \pi_2.v'_2 = 1) \wedge \mathbf{G}\ noCongestion2$
$\varphi_4 \equiv \exists \pi_1.\ \exists \pi_2.\ \exists \pi_3.\ (\mathbf{F}\ \pi_1.v'_2 = 1) \wedge (\mathbf{F}\ \pi_2.v'_2 = 1) \wedge (\mathbf{F}\ \pi_3.v'_2 = 1) \wedge \mathbf{G}\ noCongestion3$

where

$noCongestion2 \equiv \bigwedge_{t \in T \setminus \{v_1^{deliver}, v_2^{deliver}\}} (\pi_1.a(t) + \pi_2.a(t) \geq 1)$
$noCongestion3 \equiv \bigwedge_{t \in T \setminus \{v_1^{deliver}, v_2^{deliver}\}} (\pi_1.a(t) + \pi_2.a(t) + \pi_3.a(t) \geq 2)$

(c) Examples of HyperLTL formulae where $N \models \varphi_1$, $N \models \varphi_2$, $N \models \varphi_3$ and $N \not\models \varphi_4$

Fig. 1. Example of a Petri net and HyperLTL formulae

2.2 HyperLTL

HyperLTL [13] extends LTL [35] (which is evaluated over single traces) by quantification over multiple traces, and is therefore evaluated over sets of traces. Our tool supports an alternation-free hyperlogic specifically tailored to Petri nets.

Figure 1c shows example formulae in the logic where the π_i are trace variables ranging over infinite traces of a Petri net. Every formula starts with either existential or universal quantification over a list of trace variables $\pi_1, \ldots, \pi_m$. Thus, quantification assigns traces of the Petri net to the trace variables. This is followed by a formula composed of the standard LTL temporal operators that is (synchronously) evaluated over the quantified traces:

- **X** φ stating that φ holds at the next position,
- **F** φ stating that φ holds at some future position,
- **G** φ stating that φ holds at all future positions, and
- ψ **U** φ stating that φ holds at some future position and ψ holds at all intermediate positions.

Finally, we consider two types of atomic propositions:

- for every variable π and every transition t there is a proposition $\pi.\mathsf{en}_t$, and
- we allow linear (in)equalities of the form $\sum_\ell c_\ell \cdot \pi_{i_\ell}.p_\ell \bowtie b$ where the c_ℓ and b are integer constants, the π_{i_ℓ} are trace variables, and the p_ℓ are places of the net, and where $\bowtie\, \in \{<, \leq, =, \geq, >\}$ is a comparison operator.

Now, assuming that the trace ρ_i is assigned to the variable π_i for each i, we evaluate atomic propositions at position n as follows:

- $\pi_i.\mathsf{en}_t$ is satisfied if t is enabled in the n'th marking ρ_i^n, and
- $\sum_\ell c_\ell \cdot \pi_{i_\ell}.p_\ell \bowtie b$ is satisfied if the inequality obtained by replacing each $\pi_{i_\ell}.p_\ell$ with the number of tokens in the marking $\rho_{i_\ell}^n$, i.e., the value $\rho_{i_\ell}^n(p_\ell)$, is valid.

For a formal definition of the syntax and semantics of HyperLTL, see, e.g., [13].

Coming back to our example in Fig. 1, the formula φ_1 (resp. φ_3) from Fig. 1c expresses that there are two traces that both eventually (but possibly at different positions) receive a token in v_1' (resp. v_2') and each transition t is fired in at most one of the traces (hence there must be a token in $a(t)$ in at least one of the two traces). In other words, φ_1 and φ_3 express that there are two disjoint paths in the graph in Fig. 1a, starting at v_0 and leading to v_1 resp. v_2. Analogously, φ_2 and φ_4 express similar properties, but requiring the existence of three disjoint paths. Hence, φ_1, φ_2, and φ_3 are satisfied by the example net N, but not φ_4.

The reason for introducing the places v_1' and v_2' is that once the token initially in v_0 arrives to one of them, the corresponding trace gets stuck and the last reached marking is allowed to stutter and hence does not use any of the remaining link capacities. This is important as the existentially quantified traces may be of different lengths before reaching the goal place, and such traces must globally synchronize.

3 Tool Implementation and Graphical User Interface

The verification engine of our tool is implemented in C++ and extends the existing LTL verification engine that is part of the `verifypn` command line tool [28]. The HyperLTL engine supports nets described in PNML [7] and, for universal formulae φ, constructs in an on-the-fly manner the vector of markings currently reached in all the considered traces and explores its product with the Büchi automaton representing the negation of the LTL property obtained by dropping the quantifiers of φ. On this product Büchi automaton, we perform a classical search for a reachable accepting loop using the nested DFS search strategy [16]. If such a loop is found, the engine returns the verification answer

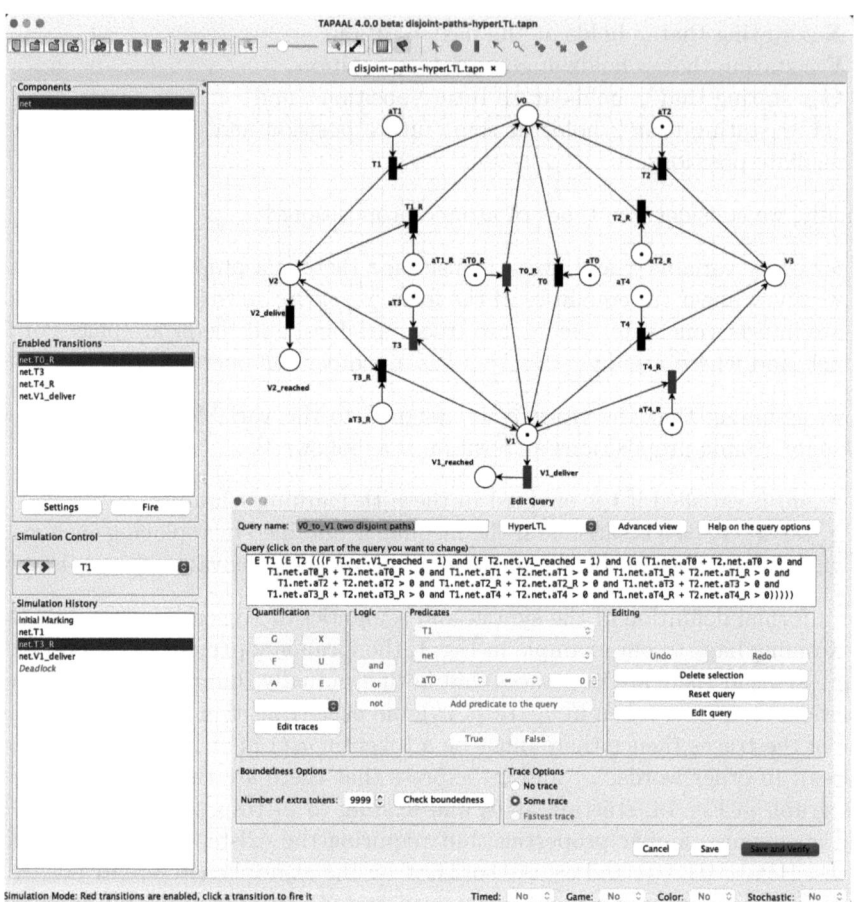

Fig. 2. TAPAAL HyperLTL screenshot (simulator mode with a query dialog)

together with the set of traces (in an XML format) that form such a loop. In the case where no counter-example exists, the tool reports that the property is satisfied together with statistics about the explored state-space. Existential quantification is handled by negating the formula and swapping the results the tool reports.

The HyperLTL engine is directly called from the tool TAPAAL [17] that has been extended with a graphical way to construct HyperLTL queries as well as a simulator that allows to replay multiple traces returned by the engine. Figure 2 displays a screenshot of the TAPAAL HyperLTL interface. The GUI is in simulation mode where the user can select the traces returned by the verification engine (currently, trace T1 is selected) and simulate the traces in the GUI. A graphical dialog for creating HyperLTL queries is shown as overlay. The tool is available at http://www.tapaal.net/downloads, including a complete reproducibility package [25].

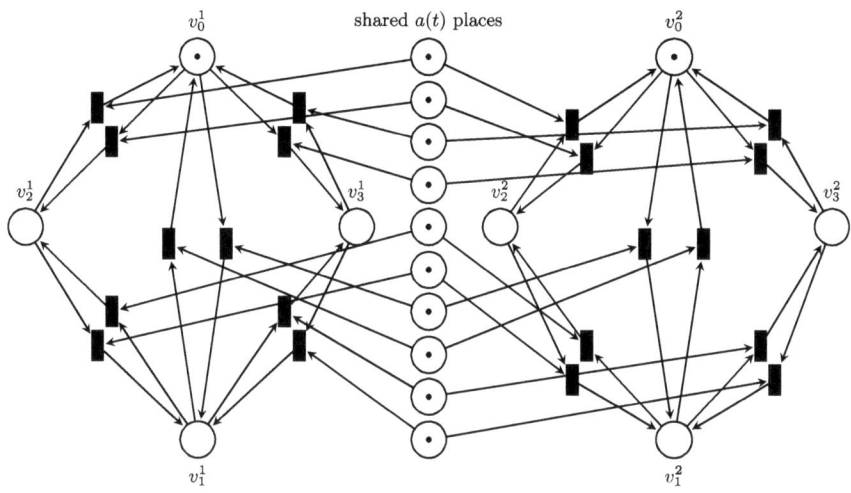

Fig. 3. Self-composition with the LTL query $(\mathbf{F}\, v_1^1 = 1) \wedge (\mathbf{F}\, v_1^2 = 1)$

4 Performance Evaluation and Case Study

We evaluate the performance of our HyperLTL model checker on a case study inspired by routing problems from computer networking [19]. For given source and destination nodes s and t, and for a given network (directed graph), we want to find k directed paths from s to t such that these paths do not cause congestion on any of the links (edges) in the network. In our simplified scenario, we say that an edge is congested if there are strictly more than ℓ paths from s to t that use the given edge; hence ℓ indirectly models edge capacities. The introductory example in Fig. 1b shows how this problem can be modeled as a Petri net. The formulae for $k = 2, 3$ and $\ell = 1$ are depicted in Fig. 1c as φ_1 and φ_3 for the target node v_1 and as φ_2 and φ_4 for the target node v_2.

Our benchmark contains 3900 HyperLTL formulae, evaluated on Petri net models of 260 real-world network topologies from the Topology Zoo dataset [30]. We consider three (k, ℓ) problem variants for $(2, 1)$, $(3, 1)$ and $(4, 2)$, where for each network topology we generate five HyperLTL queries for randomly selected pairs of source and target nodes. To balance the number of true and false queries in the benchmark, the source is selected to be a random high-degree node. The experiments are executed on an AMD EPYC 7551 processor running at 1996 MHz, with 900 s timeout. TAPAAL additionally had a 2 GB memory limit.

First, we compare our HyperLTL implementation (referred to as TAPAAL) with a self-composition approach [2,39] that creates a copy of the composed model for each trace and adds a synchronization mechanism to the model in order to guarantee that we iteratively perform one step in each copy of the model before we evaluate the predicates and continue with another single step in each copy. This allows us to reduce the HyperLTL formula into a normal LTL formula where instead of each trace we now refer to the respective copy of

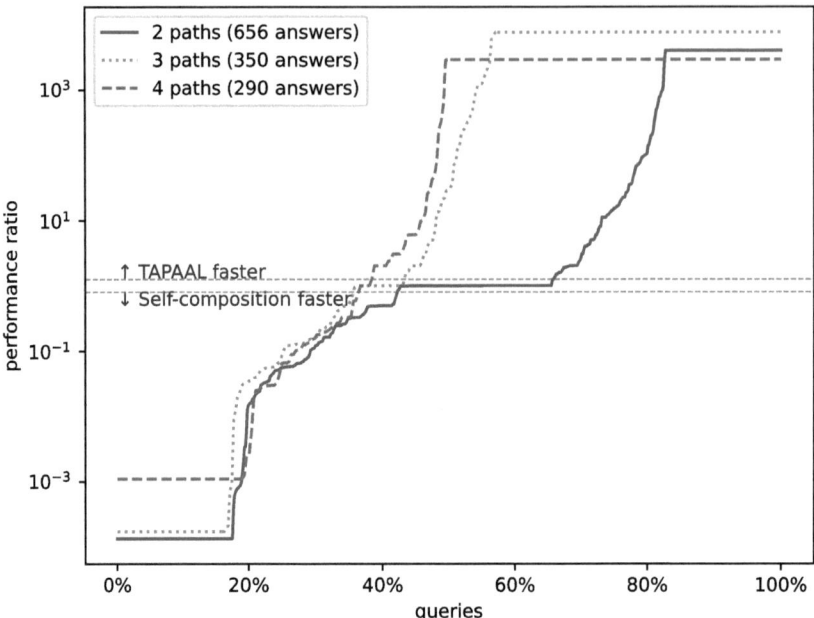

Fig. 4. Ratio plot of TAPAAL HyperLTL vs. Self-composition

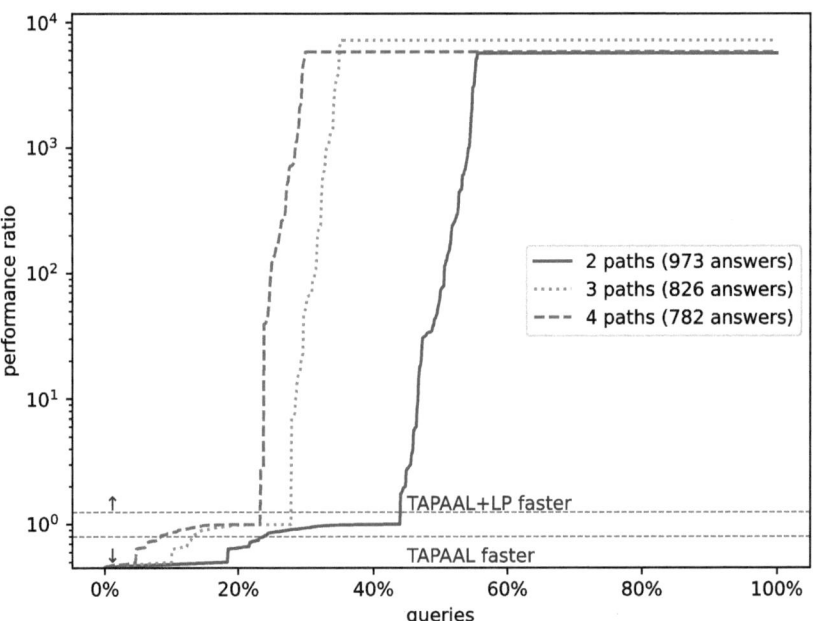

Fig. 5. Ratio plot of TAPAAL HyperLTL with and without LP Check

the model. However, this is at the expense of creating a possibly complicated model that explodes with the number of traces and additionally implements a synchronization mechanism in order to keep all copies synchronized.

In our concrete example, the self-composition does not require such a complicated synchronization mechanism as for each quantified trace we can create a copy of the net that can run completely concurrently (avoiding the lock-step synchronization), while checking for the congestion using the shared places $a(t)$ that contain as many tokens as is the edge capacity. Figure 3 shows our simplified self-composition for our running example as well as a classical LTL query that expresses the same property as the HyperLTL formula φ_1 from Fig. 1c. To verify the classical LTL formula on the self-composed system, we benchmark our tool against the LTL engine of TAPAAL [29], the winner in the 2025 Model Checking Contest [31] in the LTL category. A ratio plot is depicted in Fig. 4 where the x-axis contains all queries solved by at least one of the methods, sorted by the ratio of self-composition running time divided by TAPAAL running time. We remark that because the plot contains three different problem instances where the tools solve different number of queries (the numbers of answers in the parenthesis show the total number of solved problems by at least one of the methods), we use the percentage scale on the x-axis instead of the absolute count. For two disjoint paths, both methods are comparable, however, for 3 and 4 paths there is a clear advantage of using our new HyperLTL implementation. For example, for 4 paths, the self-composition timeouts (depicted by the straight horizontal line) on more than 50% of all queries that the HyperLTL implementation managed to solve. This is in particular true for queries with positive answers, as the on-the-fly method that we implemented in TAPAAL is more efficient than self-composition, where the net size explodes with number of trace variables in the HyperLTL formula.

In order to further improve the performance of our tool on negative queries, we employ an over-approximation method based on state-equations and linear programming [8] (we refer to this method as TAPAAL+LP). We create the self-composition net and apply the fast LP check that can in many cases show that a HyperLTL query is not satisfied, notably without performing any state-space search. If the LP check is inconclusive, we run our HyperLTL engine to perform the state-space exploration using nested depth-first search. Figure 5 shows the ratio plot of TAPAAL vs. TAPAAL+LP. Most of the additionally answered queries are negative ones that are solved using this LP check. Even though the LP check is in general often beneficial, the tool allows the user to skip it and proceed directly to the state-space search if needed.

Finally, we compare our HyperLTL engine with the LP check against MCHyper [15] which is a state-of-the-art model checker for HyperLTL properties. MCHyper operates by encoding the system, described as an AIG circuit, and the formula into a new compact circuit of linear size w.r.t. to the size of the model and the formula [22]. While Petri nets can naturally represent nonnegative integers as a number of tokens in places, in MCHyper these numbers have to be encoded into Boolean variables. To this end, we translated all 260 network topologies in

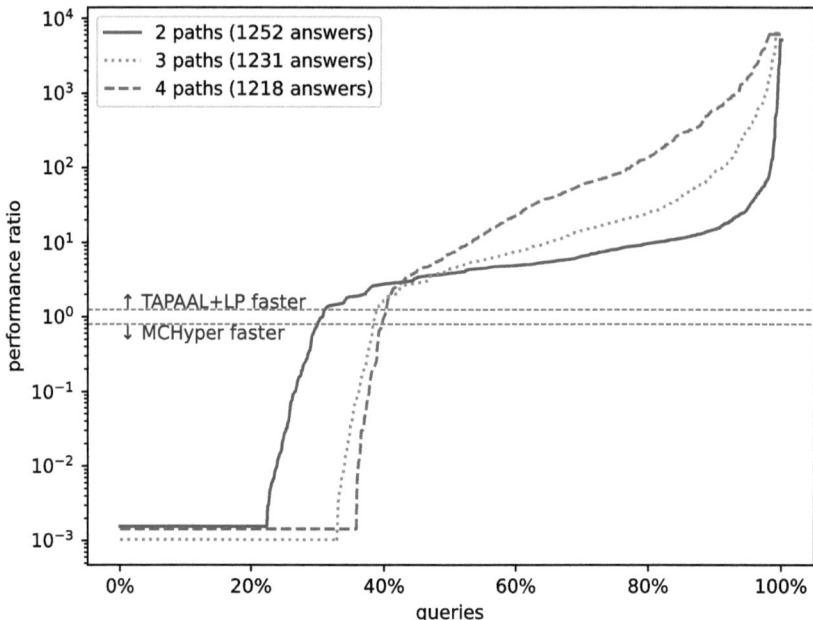

Fig. 6. Ratio plot of TAPAAL HyperLTL+LP vs. MCHyper

our benchmark into AIG circuits, using a unary encoding for the nodes of the topologies. The transitions of the system are modeled as a simple state machine, where each transition t additionally requires a latch, representing the token in the $a(t)$ place, to be enabled. To allow traces of differing lengths, the circuit cannot leave the target state after entering it (similarly to the Petri net encoding). The formula is translated into the MCHyper format. For a given problem with parameters (k, ℓ), we encode the sum by simply enumerating the $\binom{k}{\ell}$ terms, as the values are sufficiently small. The comparison of TAPAAL HyperLTL+LP vs. MCHyper is provided in Fig. 6. It shows that our tool is faster on about 60% of all queries, however, MCHyper solves a significant number of queries where our tool timeouts. This is caused by the fact that for alternation-free formulae (like in our benchmarks), the encoding of MCHyper allows the property to be verified by a simpler reachability query on the circuit. This enables it to rely on the specialized verification tool ABC [9], which implements state-of-the-art SAT-solvers including PDR (property-directed reachability heuristics) [20].

5 Conclusion

We presented the first HyperLTL verification engine for Petri nets, implemented a GUI that allows the user to visually design Petri net models as well as HyperLTL queries and provides debugging feedback as the traces discovered by our engine can be simulated in the TAPAAL GUI. We showed that our HyperLTL engine is more efficient than an alternative self-composition approach and that it is competitive with the state-of-the-art HyperLTL model checker MCHyper. In future work, we plan to transfer the techniques that enable MCHyper to quickly answer positive HyperLTL queries, in particular property-directed search heuristics, into TAPAAL, in order to further improve its performance.

Acknowledgements. Research supported by the German Research Foundation (DFG), project ReNO (SPP 2378), 2023–2027, and by DIREC—Digital Research Centre Denmark.

References

1. Abadi, M., Lamport, L.: Composing specifications. ACM Trans. Program. Lang. Syst. **15**(1), 73–132 (1993)
2. Barthe, G., D'Argenio, P.R., Rezk, T.: Secure information flow by self-composition. Math. Struct. Comput. Sci. **21**(6), 1207–1252 (2011)
3. Baumeister, J., Coenen, N., Bonakdarpour, B., Finkbeiner, B., Sánchez, C.: A temporal logic for asynchronous hyperproperties. In: Silva, A., Leino, K.R.M. (eds.) CAV 2021. LNCS, vol. 12759, pp. 694–717. Springer, Cham (2021). https://doi.org/10.1007/978-3-030-81685-8_33
4. Beutner, R., Finkbeiner, B.: Prophecy variables for hyperproperty verification. In: CSF 2022, pp. 471–485. IEEE (2022)
5. Beutner, R., Finkbeiner, B.: AutoHyper: explicit-state model checking for HyperLTL. In: TACAS 2023, Part I. LNCS, vol. 13993, pp. 145–163. Springer (2023)
6. Beutner, R., Finkbeiner, B.: Non-deterministic planning for hyperproperty verification. In: ICAPS 2024, pp. 25–30. AAAI Press (2024)
7. Billington, J., et al.: The Petri Net markup language: concepts, technology, and tools. In: van der Aalst, W.M.P., Best, E. (eds.) ICATPN 2003. LNCS, vol. 2679, pp. 483–505. Springer, Heidelberg (2003). https://doi.org/10.1007/3-540-44919-1_31
8. Bønneland, F., Dyhr, J., Jensen, P.G., Johannsen, M., Srba, J.: Simplification of CTL formulae for efficient model checking of Petri nets. In: Khomenko, V., Roux, O.H. (eds.) PETRI NETS 2018. LNCS, vol. 10877, pp. 143–163. Springer, Cham (2018). https://doi.org/10.1007/978-3-319-91268-4_8
9. Brayton, R., Mishchenko, A.: ABC: an academic industrial-strength verification tool. In: Touili, T., Cook, B., Jackson, P. (eds.) CAV 2010. LNCS, vol. 6174, pp. 24–40. Springer, Heidelberg (2010). https://doi.org/10.1007/978-3-642-14295-6_5
10. Chiesa, M., Kindler, G., Schapira, M.: Traffic engineering with equal-cost-multipath: an algorithmic perspective. IEEE/ACM Trans. Netw. **25**(2), 779–792 (2017)
11. Cimatti, A., et al.: NuSMV 2: an OpenSource tool for symbolic model checking. In: Brinksma, E., Larsen, K.G. (eds.) CAV 2002. LNCS, vol. 2404, pp. 359–364. Springer, Heidelberg (2002). https://doi.org/10.1007/3-540-45657-0_29
12. Clarke, E.M., Emerson, E.A.: Design and synthesis of synchronization skeletons using branching time temporal logic. In: Kozen, D. (ed.) Logic of Programs 1981. LNCS, vol. 131, pp. 52–71. Springer, Heidelberg (1982). https://doi.org/10.1007/BFb0025774

13. Clarkson, M.R., Finkbeiner, B., Koleini, M., Micinski, K.K., Rabe, M.N., Sánchez, C.: Temporal logics for hyperproperties. In: Abadi, M., Kremer, S. (eds.) POST 2014. LNCS, vol. 8414, pp. 265–284. Springer, Heidelberg (2014). https://doi.org/10.1007/978-3-642-54792-8_15
14. Clarkson, M.R., Schneider, F.B.: Hyperproperties. J. Comput. Secur. **18**(6), 1157–1210 (2010)
15. Coenen, N., Finkbeiner, B., Sánchez, C., Tentrup, L.: Verifying hyperliveness. In: Dillig, I., Tasiran, S. (eds.) CAV 2019, Part I. LNCS, vol. 11561, pp. 121–139. Springer, Cham (2019). https://doi.org/10.1007/978-3-030-25540-4_7
16. Courcoubetis, C., Vardi, M.Y., Wolper, P., Yannakakis, M.: Memory-efficient algorithms for the verification of temporal properties. Formal Methods Syst. Des. **1**(2/3), 275–288 (1992)
17. David, A., Jacobsen, L., Jacobsen, M., Jørgensen, K.Y., Møller, M.H., Srba, J.: TAPAAL 2.0: integrated development environment for timed-arc Petri nets. In: Flanagan, C., König, B. (eds.) TACAS 2012. LNCS, vol. 7214, pp. 492–497. Springer, Heidelberg (2012). https://doi.org/10.1007/978-3-642-28756-5_36
18. Dobe, O., Ábrahám, E., Bartocci, E., Bonakdarpour, B.: HYPERPROB: a model checker for probabilistic hyperproperties. In: Huisman, M., Păsăreanu, C., Zhan, N. (eds.) FM 2021. LNCS, vol. 13047, pp. 657–666. Springer, Cham (2021). https://doi.org/10.1007/978-3-030-90870-6_35
19. Dunn, D.A., Grover, W.D., MacGregor, M.H.: Comparison of k-shortest paths and maximum flow routing for network facility restoration. IEEE J. Sel. Areas Commun. **12**(1), 88–99 (1994)
20. Eén, N., Mishchenko, A., Brayton, R.K.: Efficient implementation of property directed reachability. In: FMCAD 2011, pp. 125–134. FMCAD Inc. (2011)
21. Emerson, E.A., Halpern, J.Y.: "Sometimes" and "Not Never" revisited: on branching versus linear time temporal logic. J. ACM **33**(1), 151–178 (1986)
22. Finkbeiner, B., Rabe, M.N., Sánchez, C.: Algorithms for model checking HyperLTL and HyperCTL*. In: Kroening, D., Păsăreanu, C.S. (eds.) CAV 2015, Part I. Algorithms for model checking HyperLTL and HyperCTL, vol. 9206, pp. 30–48. Springer, Cham (2015). https://doi.org/10.1007/978-3-319-21690-4_3
23. Focardi, R., Gorrieri, R.: Classification of security properties. In: Focardi, R., Gorrieri, R. (eds.) FOSAD 2000. LNCS, vol. 2171, pp. 331–396. Springer, Heidelberg (2001). https://doi.org/10.1007/3-540-45608-2_6
24. Fortz, B., Thorup, M.: Internet traffic engineering by optimizing OSPF weights. In: INFOCOM 2000, pp. 519–528. IEEE Computer Society (2000)
25. Gonzalez, B.M.R., Jensen, P.G., Schmid, S., Srba, J., Zimmermann, M.: Reproducibility package for "TAPAAL HyperLTL: a tool for checking hyperproperties of Petri net, July 2025. https://doi.org/10.5281/zenodo.15854993
26. Hsu, T.-H., Bonakdarpour, B., Finkbeiner, B., Sánchez, C.: Bounded model checking for asynchronous hyperproperties. In: TACAS 2023, Part I. LNCS, vol. 13993, pp. 29–46. Springer (2023)
27. Hsu, T.-H., Sánchez, C., Bonakdarpour, B.: Bounded model checking for hyperproperties. In: TACAS 2021, Part I. LNCS, vol. 12651, pp. 94–112. Springer, Cham (2021). https://doi.org/10.1007/978-3-030-72016-2_6
28. Jensen, J.F., Nielsen, T., Oestergaard, L.K., Srba, J.: TAPAAL and reachability analysis of P/T nets. Trans. Petri Nets Other Model. Concurr. **11**, 307–318 (2016)
29. Jensen, P.G., Srba, J., Ulrik, N.J., Virenfeldt, S.M.: Automata-driven partial order reduction and guided search for LTL model checking. In: Proceedings of the 23rd International Conference on Verification, Model Checking, and Abstract Interpretation (VMCAI 2022). LNCS, vol. 13182, pp. 151–173. Springer (2022)

30. Knight, S., Nguyen, H.X., Falkner, N., Bowden, R., Roughan, M.: The internet topology zoo. IEEE J. Sel. Areas Commun. **29**(9), 1765–1775 (2011)
31. Kordon, F., et al.: Complete Results for the 2025 Edition of the Model Checking Contest (2025). https://mcc.lip6.fr/2025/results.php
32. Mascle, C., Zimmermann, M.: The keys to decidable HyperLTL satisfiability: small models or very simple formulas. In: CSL 2020. LIPIcs, vol. 152, pp. 29:1–29:16. Schloss Dagstuhl - Leibniz-Zentrum für Informatik (2020)
33. McLean, J.: A general theory of composition for a class of "possibilistic" properties. IEEE Trans. Software Eng. **22**(1), 53–67 (1996)
34. Petri, C.A.: Kommunikation mit Automaten. Ph.D. thesis, Darmstadt (1962)
35. Pnueli, A.: The temporal logic of programs. In: FOCS 1977, pp. 46–57. IEEE (1977)
36. Rabe, M.N.: A temporal logic approach to Information-flow control. Ph.D. thesis, Saarland University (2016)
37. IEEE Computer Society: IEEE standard VHDL language reference manual. IEEE Std 1076–1987, pp. 1–218 (1988)
38. IEEE Computer Society: IEEE standard for Verilog hardware description language. IEEE Std 1364-2005 (Revision of IEEE Std 1364-2001), pp. 1–590 (2006)
39. Terauchi, T., Aiken, A.: Secure information flow as a safety problem. In: Hankin, C., Siveroni, I. (eds.) SAS 2005. LNCS, vol. 3672, pp. 352–367. Springer, Heidelberg (2005). https://doi.org/10.1007/11547662_24
40. Volpano, D.: Safety versus Secrecy. In: Cortesi, A., Filé, G. (eds.) SAS 1999. LNCS, vol. 1694, pp. 303–311. Springer, Heidelberg (1999). https://doi.org/10.1007/3-540-48294-6_20
41. Winter, S., Zimmermann, M.: Prophecies all the way: game-based model-checking for HyperQPTL beyond $\forall^*\exists^*$. arXiv:2504.08575 (2025). Accepted for publication at CONCUR 2025
42. Zakinthinos, A., Lee, E.S.: A general theory of security properties. In: SCP 1997, pp. 94–102. IEEE Computer Society (1997)

Games and Controller Synthesis

Quantitative Strategy Templates

Ashwani Anand, Satya Prakash Nayak(✉), Ritam Raha,
Irmak Sağlam, and Anne-Kathrin Schmuck

Max Planck Institute for Software Systems, Kaiserslautern, Germany
{ashwani,sanayak,rraha,isaglam,akschmuck}@mpi-sws.org

Abstract. This paper presents (permissive) *Quantitative Strategy Templates* (QaSTels) to succinctly represent infinitely many winning strategies in two-player energy and mean-payoff games. This transfers the recently introduced concept of *Permissive (qualitative) Strategy Templates* (PeSTels) for ω-regular games to games with quantitative objectives. We provide the theoretical and algorithmic foundations of (i) QaSTel synthesis, and (ii) their (incremental) combination with PeSTels for games with mixed quantitative and qualitative objectives. Using a prototype implementation, we demonstrate empirically that QaSTels extend the advantageous properties of strategy templates over single winning strategies – known from PeSTels – to games with (additional) quantitative objectives. This includes (i) the enhanced robustness of strategies due to their runtime-adaptability, and (ii) the compositionality of templates w.r.t. incrementally arriving objectives. We use control-inspired examples to illustrate these superior properties of QaSTels for CPS design.

1 Introduction

Two player games on finite graphs provide a powerful abstraction for modeling the strategic interactions between reactive systems and their environment. In this context, game-based abstractions are often enriched with quantitative information to model aspects like energy consumption, cost minimization, or maintaining system performance thresholds under varying conditions. As a result, games with quantitative objectives, such as energy [8] or mean-payoff [28] have gained significant attention in recent years. These games have been applied to a wide range of cyber-physical systems (CPS), such as energy management in electric vehicles [8], optimizing resource-constrained task management in autonomous robots [18,22], embedded systems [11], and dynamic resource allocations [6].

In practical CPS applications, strategic control decisions (i.e., the moves of the controller player in the abstract game) are typically implemented via low-level actuators. For instance, a robot's strategic decision to move to a different room involves motion control integrated with LiDAR-based obstacle avoidance.

All authors are partially supported by the DFG project 89792660 as part of TRR 248-CPEC, and by the Emmy Noether Grant SCHM 3541/1-1.

However, due to unmodeled dynamics of the physical environment that become observable only at runtime, strategic adaptations may be necessary [17,26]. For example, if the robot detects that an entrance is obstructed by obstacles (e.g., humans), it should dynamically adjust its strategy and navigate through an alternative door instead. Therefore, synthesized (high-level) control strategies must not only be correct-by-design, but also flexible enough to accommodate runtime adaptations. This control-inspired property of strategies has recently been formalized via permissive strategy templates (PeSTels) [3], which are similar to classical strategies but contain a vast set of strategies in a succinct and simple data structure. Intuitively, PeSTels *localize* required progress towards ω-regular objectives by classifying outgoing edges of a control-player vertex as unsafe, co-live and live – indicating edges to be taken never, finitely often and infinitely often, respectively, in case the source vertex of the edge is visited infinitely often.

Inspired by PeSTels and driven by the need to capture quantitative objectives in CPS design, this paper introduces *Quantitative Strategy Templates* (QaSTels) for games with energy and mean-payoff objectives. n the context of the previously discussed robot example, such games model scenarios where a robot with limited battery must make informed re-routing decisions at runtime, ensuring that its remaining energy suffices for the required tasks. Similar to PeSTels, QaSTels localize necessary information about the *future* of the game. In contrast to PeSTels, which localize *liveness* requirements induced by a *qualitative* objective, QaSTels consider *quantitative* objectives and thereby localize the required energy loss and gain through local edge annotations. Knowing the current energy level at runtime, the control player can select from all edges that remain feasible given the available energy. This contrasts with standard game-solving approaches, which typically store only a single (optimal) action per node.

Concretely, our contributions are as follows: (i) We formalize QaSTels for energy and mean-payoff objectives, and present algorithms to extract winning strategies from them. (ii) We introduce an edge-based value iteration algorithm to compute winning QaSTels and show that QaSTels are *permissive*, i.e., they capture all winning strategies for energy objectives and all finite-memory winning strategies for mean-payoff objectives. (iii) We combine QaSTels with a bounded version of PeSTels, and propose an *efficient incremental algorithm* for updating templates and strategies under newly arriving qualitative and quantitative objectives. (iv) We highlight the advantages of strategy templates for games with quantitative and qualitative objectives, via extensive experiments on benchmarks derived from the SYNTCOMP benchmark suite. Detailed proofs for all claims are provided in the full version of the paper [2].

Related Work. The computation of permissive strategies has received significant attention over the past decade, particularly for qualitative objectives [7,9,20,25]. A key development in this area is the introduction of permissive strategy templates (PeSTels) by Anand et al. [1,3], which capture a strictly broader class of winning strategies while maintaining the same worst-case computational complexity as standard game-solving techniques. This paper extends the idea behind PeSTels to quantitative games.

When only 'classical' synthesis algorithms are available, achieving the adaptability of strategies that motivate PeSTels requires recomputing a new strategy from scratch whenever moves become unavailable at runtime or additional objectives arise. For the objectives considered in this paper, this entails using 'classical' synthesis algorithms for energy objectives [8], mean-payoff objectives [10,28], multi mean-payoff objectives [27], and mean-payoff co-Büchi objectives [12,13]. However, since these approaches recompute strategies from scratch at each iteration, they are computationally expensive. Our benchmark experiments demonstrate that QaSTel-based adaptations offer a more efficient alternative for the applications considered.

2 Preliminaries

In this section, we introduce the basic notations used throughout the paper. We denote $\mathbb{Z}$ as the set of integers, $\mathbb{Q}$ as the set of rational numbers, $\mathbb{N}$ as the set of natural numbers including 0, and $\mathbb{N}_{>0}$ as the set of positive integers. Let $\mathbb{N}_\infty = \mathbb{N} \cup \{\infty\}$ and $\mathbb{Z}_\infty = \mathbb{Z} \cup \{\infty, -\infty\}$. The interval $[a;b)$ represents the set $\{a, a+1, \cdots, b-1\}$ and $[a;b]$ represents $\{a, a+1, \cdots, b\}$.

Two-Player Games. A two-player game graph is a pair $G = (V, E)$, where $V = V_0 \uplus V_1$ is a finite set of nodes, and $E \subseteq V \times V$ is a set of edges. The nodes are partitioned into two sets, V_0 and V_1, where V_i represents the set of nodes controlled by Player i for $i \in \{0,1\}$. We write E_i to denote the set of edges originating from nodes in V_i, i.e., $E_i = E \cap (V_i \times V)$. Given a node v, we write $E(v)$ to denote the set $\{e \in E \mid e = (v, v')$ for $v' \in V\}$ of all edges from v.

Value Functions. For a set of nodes V, and a set of edges E let $\mathcal{F}_V$ denote $\{f \mid f : V \to \mathbb{N}_\infty\}$, and $\mathcal{F}_E$ denote $\{f \mid f : E \to \mathbb{N}_\infty\}$.

Plays. A *play* $\rho = v_0 v_1 \ldots \in V^\omega$ on G is an infinite sequence of nodes starting from v_0 such that, $(v_i, v_{i+1}) \in E$ for each i. We denote the ith node v_i of ρ as $\rho[i]$ and use the notations $\rho[0; i] = v_0 \ldots v_i$, $\rho[i; j] = v_i \ldots v_j$, and $\rho[i; \infty] = v_i \ldots$ to denote a *prefix*, *infix*, and (infinite) *suffix* of ρ, respectively. We write $v \in \rho$ (resp. $e \in \rho$) to denote that the node v (resp. the edge e) appears in ρ. Furthermore, we write $v \in \texttt{Inf}(\rho)$ (resp. $e \in \texttt{Inf}(\rho)$) to denote that node v (resp. edge e) appears infinitely often in the play ρ. We denote by $\texttt{plays}(G)$ the set of all plays on G, by $\texttt{plays}(G, v)$ denote the set of all plays starting from node v.

Strategies. A *strategy* π for Player i, where $i \in \{0,1\}$ (or, a Player i-strategy) is a function $\pi : V^* \cdot V_i \to E$ such that for all $H \cdot v \in V^* \cdot V_i$, we have $\pi(H \cdot v) \in E(v)$. A play $\rho = v_0 v_1 \ldots$ is called a π-play if it follows π, i.e., for all $j \in \mathbb{N}$, whenever $v_j \in V_i$ it holds that $\pi(v_0 \ldots v_j) = (v_j, v_{j+1})$. Given a strategy π, we write $\texttt{plays}_\pi(G, v)$ to denote the set of all π-plays starting from node v and $\texttt{plays}_\pi(G)$ to denote the set of all π-plays in G. For an edge e, we write $\texttt{plays}_\pi(G, e)$ to denote the set of plays that start with e and follows π, i.e., a play $\rho \in \texttt{plays}_\pi(G, e)$ iff $(\rho[0], \rho[1]) = e$ and $\rho[1; \infty] \in \texttt{plays}_\pi(G, \rho[1])$.

Let M be a *memory* set. A Player i-strategy π with memory M is represented as a tuple (M, m_0, α, β), where $m_0 \in M$ is the initial memory value, $\alpha : M \times$

$V \to M$ is the memory update function, and $\beta : M \times V_i \to V$ is the state transition function. Intuitively, if the current node is a Player i node v and the current memory value is m, the strategy π selects the next node $v' = \beta(m, v)$ and updates the memory to $\alpha(m, v)$. If M is finite, we call π a *finite-memory strategy*; otherwise, it is an *infinite-memory strategy*. Formally, given a history $H \cdot v \in V^* \cdot V_i$, the strategy is defined as $\pi(H \cdot v) = \beta(\hat{\alpha}(m_0, H), v)$, where $\hat{\alpha}$ is the canonical extension of α to sequences of nodes. A strategy is called *memoryless* or *positional* if $|M| = 1$. For a memoryless strategy π, it holds that $\pi(H_1 \cdot v) = \pi(H_2 \cdot v)$ for every history $H_1, H_2 \in V^*$. For convenience, we write $\pi(v)$ instead of $\pi(H \cdot v)$ for such strategies.

For a game graph $G = (V, E)$ with a finite-memory strategy $\pi = (M, m_0, \alpha, \beta)$, we denote by $G_\pi = (V', E')$ the product of G and π, that is, $V_0' = V_0 \times M$, $V_1' = V_1 \times M$, and $E' = \{((v, m), (v', m')) \mid (v, v') \in E, m' = \alpha(m, v)\}$. With slight abuse of terminology, we say that a state v is *reachable from* q in G_π if there exists a tuple (v, m') reachable from (q, m_0) in G_π. Similarly, we say that a sequence $v_0 v_1 \ldots$ is a play in G_π if there exists a corresponding play $(v_0, m_0)(v_1, m_1) \ldots$ in G_π.

Games and Objectives. A *game* is a tuple (G, φ), where G is a game graph and $\varphi \subseteq V^\omega$ is an *objective* for Player 0. A play ρ is considered *winning* if $\rho \in \varphi$. A Player 0 strategy π is *winning from a node* v, if all π-plays starting from v are winning. Similarly, π is winning from $V' \subseteq V$ if it is winning from all nodes in V'. We define the *winning region* $\mathcal{W}(G, \varphi)$ as the set of nodes from which Player 0 has a winning strategy in (G, φ). A Player 0 strategy is *winning* if it is winning from $\mathcal{W}(G, \varphi)$.

We define a *weight function* $w : E \to [-W; W]$ for some $W \in \mathbb{N}_{>0}$, which assigns an integer weight to each edge in G. This function extends naturally to finite infixes of plays, i.e., $w(v_0 v_1 \ldots v_k) = \sum_{i=0}^{k-1} w(v_i, v_{i+1})$. Furthermore, we define the average weight of a finite prefix $v_0 v_1 \ldots v_k$ as $\mathtt{avg}(v_0 v_1 \ldots v_k) = \frac{1}{k} \sum_{i=0}^{k-1} w(v_i, v_{i+1})$. With this, we consider the following objectives in games:

▷ *(Quantitative) Energy Objectives.* Given a weight function w and an initial credit $c \in \mathbb{N}$, the *energy objective* is defined as $En_c(w) = \{\rho \in V^\omega \mid c + w(\rho[0; i]) \geq 0, \forall i \in \mathbb{N}\}$. Intuitively, the energy objective ensures that the total weight ('energy level') remains non-negative along a play.
▷ *(Quantitative) Mean-Payoff Objectives.* Given a weight function w, the *mean-payoff objective* is defined as[1] $MP(w) = \{\rho \in V^\omega \mid \limsup_{n \to \infty} \mathtt{avg}(\rho[0; n]) \geq 0\}$ and ensures that the limit average weight of play is non-negative.
▷ *(Qualitative) Parity Objectives.* Given a *priority labeling* $\mathbb{L}_P : V \to [0; d]$ with $d \in \mathbb{N}_{>0}$, which assigns a priority to each node, the *parity objective* is defined as $Parity(\mathbb{L}_P) = \{\rho \in V^\omega \mid \max_{v \in \mathtt{Inf}(\rho)} \mathbb{L}_P(v) \text{ is even}\}$ and ensures that the highest priority seen infinitely often along a play is even.

---

[1] We note that mean-payoff objectives can also be defined via the *limit-inferior* function i.e., $\{\rho \in V^\omega \mid \liminf_{n \to \infty} \mathtt{avg}(\rho[0; n]) \geq 0\}$. However, it has been shown that games with either definition are equivalent [15, Corollary 8].

We refer to a game with a mean-payoff, energy, or parity objective as a *mean-payoff game*, *energy game*, and *parity game*, respectively. A game is called *mixed* if it is equipped with a conjunction of quantitative and qualitative objectives. Further, we call G weighted, if it is annotated with a weight function w, denoted by G_w. Consequently, energy and mean-payoff are referred to as weighted games.

Fixed and Unknown Initial Credit Problem. We consider the following game variants for energy objectives. **(1)** Given an initial credit c, the *energy game with fixed initial credit* c is defined as the game $(G, En_c(w))$. **(2)** A game $(G, En(w))$ with *unknown initial credit* asks Player 0 to ensure the objective $En_c(w)$ for some finite initial credit c.

In an energy game $(G = (V, E), En(w))$, there exists an optimal initial credit $\mathsf{opt}(v) \in \mathbb{Z}_\infty$ for each node v, where $\mathsf{opt}(v)$ is the minimal value (in $\mathbb{N}_\infty$) such that for every initial credit $c \geq \mathsf{opt}(v)$, there exists a winning strategy from v in the game $(G, En_c(w))$. We use $\mathsf{opt} \in \mathcal{F}_V$ to denote this *optimal value function* which assigns the optimal initial credit to each node in the game graph. It is well-known that for winning nodes, the optimal initial credit is upper bounded by $c^* = W \cdot |V|$, where W is the maximum weight in the weight function w. Hence, for any initial credit $c \geq c^*$, the winning region for $(G, En(w))$ with unknown initial credit is the same as the winning region for $(G, En_c(w))$. Moreover, every winning strategy in $(G, En_c(w))$ is also winning in $(G, En(w))$.

3 Quantitative Strategy Templates (QaSTels)

In this section, we first define a quantitative strategy template (QaSTel) for weighted games and show how it can be used to represent the set of strategies in a weighted game. We then define winning and maximally permissive QaSTels.

Definition 1 (Quantitative Strategy Template (QaSTel)). *Given a game graph $G = (V, E)$, a QaSTel for Player 0 is a function $\Pi : V_0 \times \mathbb{N}_\infty \to 2^E$ that maps a Player 0 node u and the current credit c to a subset of outgoing edges of u in G that are activated by c s.t. $\Pi(u, c) \subseteq \Pi(u, c')$ for all $c' \geq c$.*

We also use a QaSTel Π as a function $V_0 \times \mathbb{Z}_\infty \to 2^E$ by extending it to negative credits as follows: $\Pi(v, c) = \emptyset$ for all $c < 0$. If $\Pi(u, i) = \Pi(u, i + 1) = \cdots = \Pi(u, j) = E'$, then for notational simplicity, we will write $\Pi(u, [i; j]) = E'$. This naturally defines the *activation function* for an edge e, denoted by $act_\Pi(e)$, as the smallest value k such that $e \in \Pi(u, [k; \infty])$.

Given a weighted game G_w with a QaSTel Π and a weight $c \in \mathbb{N}$, a play $\rho = v_0 v_1 \cdots$ is said to be a (Π, c)-play if there exists a $k \in \mathbb{N}_\infty$ such that for all $i \in [0; k]$ with $v_i \in V_0$, $(v_i, v_{i+1}) \in \Pi(v_i, c + w(\rho[0; i]))$ and if $k \neq \infty$, then whenever $v_{k+1} \in V_0$ it holds that $\Pi(v_{k+1}, c + w(\rho[0; k+1])) = \emptyset$. Intuitively, either the play only uses the active edges from the QaSTel forever, or it reaches a node where no edge is active in the QaSTel and then the play continues with arbitrary edges. We collect all (Π, c)-plays in G from a node v in the set $\mathtt{plays}_\Pi(G, c, v)$. Similarly, we write $\mathtt{plays}_\Pi(G, c)$ to denote the set of all (Π, c)-plays in G.

Similar to PeSTels, a QaSTels define a set of (Player 0) strategies in a weighted game which *follow it*, as formalized next.

Definition 2. *Given an energy game $(G, En_c(w))$ with initial credit $c \in \mathbb{N}$, a strategy π is said to follow a QaSTel Π, denoted by $(G, \pi) \vDash_c \Pi$ (or simply $\pi \vDash_c \Pi$ when G is clear from the context), if $\text{plays}_\pi(G) \subseteq \text{plays}_\Pi(G, c)$. Similarly, for a mean-payoff game $(G, MP(w))$, a strategy π is said to follow a QaSTel Π if $(G, \pi) \vDash_c \Pi$ for some $c \geq W \cdot |V|$.*

For mean-payoff games, the previous definition chooses the initial credit c to be at least the upper bound on the optimal credit, i.e., $c \geq W \cdot |V|$. This is motivated by the fact that mean-payoff games are equivalent to energy games with unknown initial credit [10]. Therefore, winning strategies of mean-payoff games can be captured by winning strategies of energy games with credit above the upper bound on the optimal credit. Now we formally define wining QaSTels.

Definition 3 (Winning QaSTel). *Given a weighted game, a QaSTel Π is said to be winning from a node v (resp. a set V' of nodes) if every strategy following Π is also winning from v (resp. V'). Furthermore, a QaSTel Π is said to be winning if it is winning from the winning region.*

A winning QaSTel is *maximally permissive* if it includes all winning strategies. This is formalized as follows.

Definition 4 (Maximal Permissiveness). *Given a weighted game, a QaSTel Π is said to be maximally permissive if every winning strategy follows Π. Furthermore, a QaSTel Π is said to be f-maximally permissive if every winning strategy with finite memory follows Π.*

Given the simple and local structure of QaSTels, one can easily extract a positional strategy for Player 0 following the QaSTel by picking the edge with the smallest activation value at every node. This clearly results in a winning strategy if the QaSTel is winning.

Proposition 1. *Given a weighted game graph G_w s.t. $G = (V, E)$ with a QaSTel Π, a positional strategy π following Π can be extracted in time[2] $\mathcal{O}(|E|)$. Let $\text{EXTRACTSTRAT}(G, w, \Pi)$ be the procedure extracting this strategy.*

This result implies that a winning strategy can be obtained by extracting it from a winning QaSTel.

Proposition 2. *Given a weighted game with game graph G_w and a winning QaSTel Π, the strategy $\text{EXTRACTSTRAT}(G, w, \Pi)$ is winning.*

---

[2] The complexity also depends on how the QaSTel Π is defined, however, we state the complexity results assuming the activation function act_Π is given as an input.

4 Synthesizing QaSTels

We now discuss the synthesis of QaSTels over weighted games. As QaSTels are defined on edges, we first introduce an edge-optimal value function and an edge-based value iteration algorithm for weighted games. Then, we show how to extract *optimal* QaSTels from the edge-optimal value function. Finally, we show that optimal QaSTels are winning and permissive.

Edge-Based Value Iteration. It is known that both energy games and mean-payoff games (with threshold 0 as considered in objective $MP(w)$) have the same value iteration algorithm [10]. To simplify the presentation we therefore restrict the discussion to energy games.

Recall that in energy games, $\mathtt{opt}(v)$ is the minimal credit required to win the game from node v. We extend this notion to $\mathtt{optE}(e)$ such that $\mathtt{optE}(e)$ is the minimal credit required to take the edge e and win the energy game from the source node of e. Formally, for some edge $e = (u, v)$, $\mathtt{optE}(e)$ is the minimal value (in $\mathbb{N}_\infty$) such that for any initial credit $c \geq \mathtt{optE}(e)$, there exists a Player 0 strategy π with $\mathtt{plays}_\pi(G, e) \subseteq En_c(w)$. To compute $\mathtt{optE}$, we extend the standard value iteration algorithm to an edge-based value iteration algorithm.

Given a weighted game graph G_w, the standard value iteration algorithm computes the least fixed point of the operator $\mathbb{O}_V : \mathcal{F}_V \to \mathcal{F}_V$ defined as:

$$\mathbb{O}_V(\mu)(u) = \begin{cases} \min\{(\mu(v) \ominus w(e)) : e = (u,v) \in E\}, & \text{if } u \in V_0 \\ \max\{(\mu(v) \ominus w(e)) : e = (u,v) \in E\}, & \text{if } u \in V_1 \end{cases} \quad (1)$$

where $l \ominus w = \max(l - w, 0)$. This fixed-point computation is initialized with an initial function $\mu_{in} : V \to \mathbb{Z}$, and each value is upper bounded by $|V| \cdot W$, i.e., once a value reaches $|V| \cdot W + 1$, we replace it by ∞. Let us denote this procedure of fixed-point computation of an operator $\mathbb{O}$ starting from an initial function μ_{in} as $\text{FixPoint}(G, w, \mathbb{O}, \mu_{in})$. Then, the optimal value function $\mathtt{opt}$ can be obtained by $\text{FixPoint}(G, w, \mathbb{O}_V, \mu_0)$ where $\mu_0(v) = 0$ for all $v \in V$.

To compute the edge-optimal value function $\mathtt{optE}$, we modify the value iteration algorithm by extending the operator $\mathbb{O}_V$ from functions over vertices to functions over edges. Hence, we define $\mathbb{O}_E : \mathcal{F}_E \to \mathcal{F}_E$ for an edge $e = (u, v)$ as:

$$\mathbb{O}_E(\mu)(e) = \begin{cases} \min\{\mu(e') \ominus w(e) : e' \in E(v)\}, & \text{if } v \in V_0 \\ \max\{\mu(e') \ominus w(e) : e' \in E(v)\}, & \text{if } v \in V_1. \end{cases} \quad (2)$$

Remark 1. It is not hard to see that the operators $\mathbb{O}_E$ and $\mathbb{O}_V$ are closely related. In particular, if $\mu_i^V \in \mathcal{F}_V$ and $\mu_i^E \in \mathcal{F}_E$ are the corresponding value functions obtained in the i-th iteration of $\mathbb{O}_V$ and $\mathbb{O}_E$ respectively, then $\mu_i^E(e) = \mu_i^V(v) \ominus w(e)$ for every edge $e = (u, v)$. This leads to a similar relation between $\mathtt{opt}$ and $\mathtt{optE}$, and hence, one can also obtain the optimal QaSTel using the standard node-based value iteration algorithm. However, our choice of presenting the edge-based approach allows us to explain our idea better, at no additional cost.

With Remark 1, the following theorem directly follows from the properties of the standard value iteration algorithm.

Theorem 1. *Given a game graph $G = (V, E)$ and weight function $w : E \to [-W, W]$, the fixed-point $\text{FIXPOINT}(G, w, \mathbb{O}_E, \mu_0)$ is the edge-optimal value function* optE *and can be computed in time $\mathcal{O}(|V| \cdot |E| \cdot W)$.*

Given a weighted game graph G_w, the winning region $\mathcal{W}$ for both mean-payoff and energy games with unknown initial credit can be extracted from the edge-optimal value function $\mu = \text{optE}$ as

$$\mathcal{W} := \{v \in V_0 \mid \exists e \in E(v). \ \mu(e) \neq \infty\} \cup \{v \in V_1 \mid \forall e \in E(v). \ \mu(e) \neq \infty\}. \quad (3a)$$

Furthermore, for energy games with initial credit c we obtain the winning region

$$\mathcal{W}_c := \{v \in V_0 \mid \exists e \in E(v). \ \mu(e) \leq c\} \cup \{v \in V_1 \mid \forall e \in E(v). \ \mu(e) \leq c\}. \quad (3b)$$

QaSTel Extraction. Given an edge function $\mu \in \mathcal{F}_E$, we can extract a QaSTel Π from μ as follows. For every node $u \in V$ and credit $k \in \mathbb{N}_\infty$, $\Pi(u, k)$ defines the set of edges that can be taken from u with credit k, i.e.,

$$\Pi(u, k) := \{e \in E(u) \mid k \geq \mu(e)\}. \quad (4)$$

Intuitively, in an energy game, the QaSTel in (4) allows taking an edge e whenever it's feasible w.r.t. edge function μ, i.e., the current energy is more than the edge value $\mu(e)$. We call the QaSTel in (4) *optimal* for the weighted game graph G_w if μ is the edge-optimal value function optE. Given an initial edge function μ_{in}, we write $\text{COMPUTEQASTEL}(G, w, \mu_{in})$ to denote the procedure that computes the fixed-point $\mu = \text{FIXPOINT}(G, w, \mathbb{O}_E, \mu_{in})$ and returns the corresponding winning region (as in (3)) and the corresponding QaSTel obtained from the μ (as in (4)). This means, the optimal QaSTel can be obtained by the procedure $\text{COMPUTEQASTEL}(G, w, \mu_0)$ (where μ_0 is the zero function on edges). An example of the computation of the optimal QaSTel is shown in Fig. 1.

Winning and Maximally Permissive QaSTels. We now show that optimal QaSTels are winning for weighted games, and (f-)maximally permissive for (mean-payoff) energy games. As a play defined by an optimal QaSTel only takes an edge if the credit is higher than its edge-optimal value, it is winning in the energy game. Furthermore, the equivalence of energy and mean-payoff games gives the following result.

Theorem 2. *Given a weighted game graph G_w, the optimal QaSTel Π is winning in both the mean-payoff game $(G, MP(w))$ and the energy game $(G, En_c(w))$ for every initial credit $c \in \mathbb{N}$.*

As an optimal QaSTel allows every edge ensuring positive energy w.r.t. the current credit, it is maximally permissive in an energy game.

Theorem 3. *Given a weighted game graph G_w, the optimal QaSTel Π is maximally permissive in the energy game $(G, En_c(w))$ for every $c \in \mathbb{N}$.*

Edge-based Value Iteration								
-	e_1	e_2	e_3	e_4	e_5	e_6	e_7	e_8
μ_0	0	0	0	0	0	0	0	0
μ_1	0	2	5	2	0	0	0	1
μ_2	0	2	5	2	0	1	0	2
μ_3	0	2	5	2	0	2	0	3
μ_4	0	2	5	2	0	3	0	4
				$\vdots$				
μ_{15}	0	2	5	2	0	14	0	15
μ_{16}	0	2	5	2	0	15	0	∞
μ_{17}	0	2	5	2	0	∞	0	∞

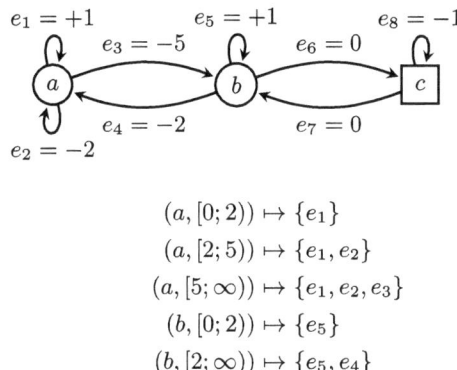

$(a, [0; 2)) \mapsto \{e_1\}$
$(a, [2; 5)) \mapsto \{e_1, e_2\}$
$(a, [5; \infty)) \mapsto \{e_1, e_2, e_3\}$
$(b, [0; 2)) \mapsto \{e_5\}$
$(b, [2; \infty)) \mapsto \{e_5, e_4\}$

Fig. 1. Example of an energy game (right top) with the computation for the edge-based value iteration (left) and the optimal QaSTel (right bottom).

Unlike in energy games, the optimal QaSTels are *not* maximally permissive in mean-payoff games. This is because there can exist infinite memory winning strategies in mean-payoff games that are not captured by any QaSTels as the energy level during a play can go arbitrarily negative. For instance, consider a mean-payoff game with one cycle of negative weight and one cycle of zero weight (e.g., the game shown in Fig. 3, restricted to the vertices $\{b, c\}$). In this case, one winning strategy is to alternate between the two cycles, gradually increasing the number of repetitions: once for the negative cycle, then once for the zero cycle, then twice for the negative cycle, then twice for the zero cycle, and so on. With this strategy, the energy level can go arbitrarily negative, and hence it cannot be captured by QaSTels. However, the optimal QaSTel can still capture all winning strategies with finite memory, i.e., it is f-maximally permissive. To show this, we use the following property of finite memory winning strategies in mean-payoff games.

Lemma 1. *Let $(G, MP(w))$ be a mean-payoff game with finite memory winning strategy π. Then there exists a weight bound $\mathsf{B}_\pi \in \mathbb{N}$ such that for every π-play ρ from a node $v \in \mathcal{W}(G, MP(w))$, it holds that $w(\rho[0; i]) \geq -\mathsf{B}_\pi$ for all $i \in \mathbb{N}$.*

With the above lemma, one can see that every winning strategy π in the mean-payoff game is a winning strategy in the energy game with initial credit $c = \max\{\mathsf{B}_\pi, W \cdot |V|\}$. Combining this with Theorem 3, we get the following result.

Theorem 4. *Given a weighted game graph G_w, the optimal QaSTel Π is f-maximally permissive in the mean-payoff game $(G, MP(w))$.*

This shows that a winning and permissive QaSTel can be obtained by the procedure COMPUTEQASTEL(G, w, μ_0), giving us the following result.

Corollary 1. *Given a weighted game graph G_w, a winning and maximally permissive QaSTel for the energy game $(G, En_c(w))$ can be computed in time $\mathcal{O}(|V| \cdot |E| \cdot W)$. Similarly, a winning and f-maximally permissive QaSTel for the mean-payoff game $(G, MP(w))$ can be computed in time $\mathcal{O}(|V| \cdot |E| \cdot W)$.*

5 Applications of QaSTels

As discussed in the introduction, our study of QaSTels is inspired by the advantages that their qualitative counterparts – permissive strategy templates (PeSTels) for parity games introduced in [3] – possess over classical strategies in control-inspired applications. In particular, PeSTels allow (i) to adapt winning strategies at runtime [3,23], and (ii) to compose different templates into new ones leading to novel iterative and compositional synthesis techniques [4,5,24]. This section investigates whether QaSTels possess similar runtime adaptability (Sect. 5.1) and compositional (Sect. 5.2) properties.

5.1 Dynamic Strategy Extraction from QaSTels

We first consider scenarios where the runtime operation of the controlled system, e.g. a robot, is supplied with local preferences over moves that can only be determined at runtime. As an example, consider a mobile robot in a smart factory operating in the presence of (non-modeled) human operators. Here, the robot might be equipped with a perception module which predicts the probability of the successful completion of an action (e.g. reaching a certain work station) within these (dynamic) obstacles. In this case, the logical control strategy can choose the activated move from the QaSTel with the highest success probability. More generally, given a weighted game (G, φ) with optimal QaSTel Π and a dynamic preference function $\mathsf{pref}_t : E_0 \to [0,1]$ for every $t \in \mathbb{N}_0$, we define the Player 0 strategy π_0 *online* (after obtaining pref_t in time step t) s.t.

$$\pi_0(v_0 \ldots v_t) := \arg\max\{\mathsf{pref}_t(e) \mid e \in \Pi(v_t, c_t)\}, \tag{5}$$

where c_t is the credit value at time-step t. It follows directly from the correctness of optimal QaSTels that π_0 is winning for (G, φ).

A slightly more involved scenario occurs if edges with low preference values cannot be taken by the controlled system. This can for example be due to a static obstacle persistently blocking a mobile robot in one direction, an actuation failure, e.g., a faulty motor in a quad rotor preventing the execution of certain maneuvers, or due to a high risk level associated with an action at runtime preventing its execution. By assuming that the corresponding Player 0 moves in the game abstraction are annotated with preference 0, (5) then changes to

$$\pi_0(v_0 \ldots v_t) := \arg\max\{\mathsf{pref}_t(e) > \epsilon \mid e \in \Pi(v_t, c_t)\}, \tag{6}$$

for some given $\epsilon > 0$. Unfortunately, if $\pi_0(v_0 \ldots v_t)$ becomes empty, we cannot continue to control the system with the current template. However, due to the permissiveness of optimal QaSTels (see Theorem 3 and 4), such scenarios cannot occur if at least one edge with the minimal activation energy is always retained. Formally, we have the following observation.

Proposition 3. *Given a weighted game graph $(G = (V, E), w)$ with an optimal QaSTel Π, let $E_t^* := \{e \in E_0 \mid \mathsf{pref}_t(e) < \epsilon\}$ for some $t \in \mathbb{N}_0$. If there exists no $v \in V$ s.t. $\mathtt{minEdges}(v) \subseteq E_t^*$, where*

$$\mathtt{minEdges}(v) := \arg\min\{act_\Pi(e) \mid e \in E(v)\}, \qquad (7)$$

then $\Pi = \textsc{computeQaSTel}(G', w, \mu_0)$ is the optimal QaSTel for $G' = G \setminus E_t^*$.

It follows from Proposition 3 that whenever there exists no $v \in V$ s.t. $\mathtt{minEdges}(v) \subseteq E_t^*$ for all $t \in \mathbb{N}_0$, the Player 0 strategy in (6) is winning in the original weighted game (G, φ). Furthermore, if this condition is violated at some time point t, a re-computation of QaSTels can be triggered. As an obvious corollary (see [2, Corollary 2]) of the known monotonicity properties of the value iteration algorithm, this re-computation can be hot-started from the current optimal value over G, i.e.,

$$\Pi' := \textsc{computeQaSTel}(G', w, \mu_0) = \textsc{computeQaSTel}(G', w, act_\Pi). \qquad (8)$$

It should be noted that this dynamic re-computation of QaSTels might return an empty winning region at some time step, in which case the dynamically adapted strategy from (6) returns a finite play which is not winning anymore. Intuitively, such scenarios occur when preferences and QaSTels do not interact favorably. If preferences are due to unmodeled disturbances, such as dynamic obstacles, there is not much one can do to prevent such blocking situations. If additional objectives are, however, known and can be modeled as additional quantitative or qualitative objectives over the given game graph G, one should incorporate them into template synthesis as soon as they are available. This then leads to compositional synthesis approaches as discussed next.

5.2 Composing QaSTels

The previous section has outlined the advantages of QaSTels for the local adaptation of strategies at runtime, which is in close analogy to the properties of PeSTels [3]. Unfortunately, this section shows that QaSTels – in contrast to PeSTels – are not composable in a straightforward manner. That is, given a QaSTel Π for a weighted game graph (G, φ) and a QaSTel Π' for a different weighted game (G, φ') over the same graph, we cannot easily combine Π and Π' into a QaSTel which is winning for the combined game $(G, \varphi \wedge \varphi')$. This is due to the fact that a winning strategy for $(G, \varphi \wedge \varphi')$ might require infinite memory [27].

Nevertheless, we can still extract a single (infinite-memory) winning strategy from multiple QaSTels over mean-payoff games. The resulting algorithm, given in Algorithm 1, uses the function Combine to combine winning strategies of all games extracted from QaSTels following the procedure given in [27, Lemma 8] and results in a winning strategy for the conjunction of mean-payoff objectives.

Theorem 5. *Given a game graph $G = (V, E)$ with multiple mean-payoff objectives $\{MP(w_i)\}_{i \in [1;k]}$, COMBINEQASTEL($G, \{MP(w_i)\}_{i \in [1;k]}$) returns a winning strategy for the game $(G, \bigwedge_{i \in [1;k]} MP(w_i))$. Furthermore, the procedure terminates in time $\mathcal{O}(k \cdot |V| \cdot |E| \cdot W)$, where W is the maximal weight in the game.*

It should be noted that COMBINEQASTEL can also be used for iterative synthesis, i.e., if a mean-payoff objective arrives, a new combined strategy can be derived by hot-starting COMBINEQASTEL.

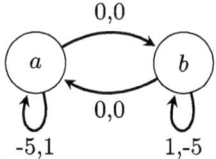

Fig. 2. A multi-energy game.

We remark that the compositionality of QaSTels cannot be extended to energy games. This is due to the fact that, even if the winning regions coincide, it is not always possible to combine local winning strategies for multiple energy objectives into a single winning strategy for the combined game. For example, in the multi-energy game shown in Fig. 2, the local optimal winning strategies for each energy objective (i.e., to eventually always loop in b or a) cannot be combined into a single winning strategy for the multi-energy game.

Remark 2. It is known that parity objectives can be reduced to mean-payoff objectives with threshold 0 over the same game graph in polynomial time [15, Theorem 40]. This also suggests that the procedure COMBINEQASTEL can be applied to synthesize strategies for (multi-objective) mean-payoff parity games.

Algorithm 1. COMBINEQASTEL

Input: Game graph $G = (V, E)$ with $\{MP(w_i)\}_{i \in [1;k]}$
Output: Winning strategy π for $(G, \bigwedge_{i \in [1;k]} MP(w_i))$
1: $\mathcal{W} = V$; $act_{\Pi_i} = \mu_0$ for all $i \in [1; k]$
2: $(\mathcal{W}_i, \Pi_i) \leftarrow$ COMPUTEQASTEL(G, w_i, act_{Π_i})
3: $\mathcal{W}' \leftarrow \bigcap \mathcal{W}_i$
4: **while** $\mathcal{W} \neq \mathcal{W}'$ **do**
5:     **for all** $e \in \mathcal{W}' \times (\mathcal{W} \setminus \mathcal{W}')$ **do** $\Pi(e) = \infty$
6:     $(\mathcal{W}_i, \Pi_i) \leftarrow$ COMPUTEQASTEL(G, w_i, act_{Π_i})
7:     $\mathcal{W} \leftarrow \mathcal{W}'$; $\mathcal{W}' \leftarrow \bigcap \mathcal{W}_i$
8: $\pi_i =$ EXTRACTSTRAT(Π_i), for all $i \in [1; k]$
9: **return** COMBINE($\{\pi_i\}_{i \in [1;k]}$)

6 Combining QaSTels with (Bounded) PeSTels

While the previous section discussed control-inspired applications of QaSTels for runtime-adaptability and composition of templates for purely *quantitative* objectives, this section considers the construction of strategy templates for games with both *quantitative and qualitative* objectives. As Remark 2 already shows that the most general combination, i.e., mean-payoff-Parity games, require infinite strategies in general, we cannot hope for the construction of winning templates which are maximal for the full class of parity, and hence, ω-regular objectives over the weighted game graphs G_w. Instead, we propose to start with qualitative strategy templates which under-approximate the set of winning strategies for any parity objective, but allow for a straight forward combination with QaSTels, and hence for efficient incremental synthesis. These restricted qualitative templates are based on PeSTels from [3], which we recall in Sect. 6.1 before formalizing their composition with QaSTels in Sect. 6.2. Section 6.3 then discusses control-inspired mixed specifications where this class of templates ensure to capture a huge class of relevant strategies. We test the completeness and efficiency of the resulting algorithms in Sect. 7.

6.1 Bounded PeSTels

Given a game graph $G = (V, E)$, PeSTels (as defined in [3]) contain three types of edge templates: (i) *unsafe* edges $S \subseteq E_0$, (ii) *co-live* edges $D \subseteq E_0$ and (iii) *live* groups $H_\ell \subseteq 2_0^E$. Their combination $\Gamma = (S, D, H_\ell)$ is called a PeSTel, which represents the objective $\text{plays}_\Gamma(G) = \{\rho \in V^\omega \mid \forall e \in S : e \notin \rho \text{ and } \forall e \in D : e \notin \text{Inf}(\rho) \text{ and } \forall H \in H_\ell : src(H) \cap \text{Inf}(\rho) \neq \emptyset \Rightarrow H \cap \text{Inf}(\rho) \neq \emptyset\}$, where $src(H)$ denotes the source nodes of the edges in H.

We say a strategy π (for Player 0) *follows* Γ, denoted by $(G, \pi) \models \Gamma$ (or simply $\pi \models \Gamma$ when G is clear from the context), if $\text{plays}_\pi(G) \subseteq \text{plays}_\Gamma(G)$. Intuitively, π follows Γ if every π-play (i) never uses the unsafe edges in S, and (ii) stops using the co-live edges in D eventually, and (iii) if ρ visits source nodes of a live group $H \in H_\ell$ infinitely often, then it also visits at least one edge of H infinitely often. In a qualitative game (G, Φ), a PeSTel Γ is *winning* from a node v if every strategy following Γ is also winning from v.

Within this paper, we restrict our attention to PeSTels which only consist of safety & co-live templates and call such PeSTels *bounded* as constraint edges can never be taken unboundedly.

Given a qualitative objective Φ which can be modelled as a parity objective over G, one can compute a bounded PeSTel $\Gamma = (S, D)$ for (G, Φ) by using the algorithm PARITYTEMPLATE from [3, Alg.3] to compute a (full) PeSTel $\widetilde{\Gamma} = (S, D, H_\ell)$ first. This PeSTel $\widetilde{\Gamma}$ can then be *bounded* into a bounded template Γ by adding all non-live outgoing edges of a live-group node, i.e. $\{(q, q') \notin H \cup S \mid (q, \cdot) \in H\}$ to D, and then setting $H_\ell := \emptyset$. We refer to the combined synthesis algorithm as COMPUTEPESTEL.

Remark 3. We note that COMPUTEPESTEL usually under-approximates the set of winning plays for (G, Φ). It is however known that for co-Büchi games no additional winning strategies can be captured by live-group templates, naturally leading to bounded templates. Notably, the algorithms for computing winning PeSTels in co-Büchi games, presented in [3], exhibit the same worst-case computation time as standard methods for solving such (finite-state) games.

6.2 Mixed Strategy Templates (MiSTels)

Following the previous discussion, this section introduces MiSTels $\Lambda = (S, D, \Pi)$ as a combination of a (bounded) PeSTel $\Gamma = (S, D)$ with a QaSTel Π defined over the same weighted game graph G_w. Thereby, MiSTels concisely represent a set of winning strategies for *mixed games* $(G, \varphi \wedge \Phi)$ which contain a quantitative objective φ and a qualitative objective Φ. A Player 0 strategy π is said to follow the MiSTel Λ over G_w if it follows both Γ and Π over G_w.

Conflict-Free MiSTels. Given any combination of PeSTels and QaSTels, their direct combination might result in a MiSTel for which no strategy exists that follows it. As an example consider the discussion from Sect. 5.1 on the runtime adaptation of a strategy which follows a QaSTel but at the same time avoids taking unavailable edges. Given a PeSTel (S, D), the edge set S can directly be interpreted as the set of unavailable edges, which – in contrast to the case discussed in Sect. 5.1 – does not change and is known a priori. Similarly, the set of D collects all edges that eventually become unavailable. Following Proposition 3, we obtain the existence of a strategy following a MiSTel if $\mathtt{minEdges}(v) \not\subseteq S \cup D$ for all $v \in V$. If a MiSTel has this property, we call it *conflict free*. Similar to Proposition 1, one can extract a strategy following a conflict-free MiSTel by picking an unconstrained edge (i.e. $e \notin S \cup D$) with the smallest activation value at every node.

Proposition 4. *Given a weighted game graph G_w with a conflict-free MiSTel $\Lambda = (S, D, \Pi)$, a positional strategy following Λ can be extracted in time $\mathcal{O}(|E|)$.*

Winning MiSTels. We say that the MiSTel Λ is *winning* in the *mixed game* $(G, \varphi \wedge \Phi)$ from a node v if all strategies π that follow Λ are winning from v in both the quantitative game (G, φ) and the qualitative game (G, Φ). In order to synthesize a winning MiSTel for a given mixed game $(G = (V, E), \varphi \wedge \Phi)$, we can therefore iteratively construct winning QaSTels and PeSTels and remove all conflicts from their joint winning region. An efficient way to do so is formalized in Algorithm 2. After QaSTel synthesis is initialized with μ_0, winning PeSTels and QaSTels are computed (Line 9 and 10) and conflicts in their joint winning region are detected (Line 12). If no conflict is detected, the algorithm directly terminates. Otherwise, conflicts are resolved by (i) adding an additional safety requirement to the qualitative specification Φ (Line 4), and (ii) increasing the edge-weight of conflicting edges, i.e., edges in $\mathtt{minEdges}(v) \subseteq S \cup D$, to ∞ (Line 5). After this, PeSTels and QaSTels are recomputed to resolve conflicts,

Algorithm 2. COMPUTEMISTEL(G, w, φ, Φ)

Input: Mixed game $(G = (V, E), \varphi \wedge \Phi)$ with $\varphi = MP(w)$ or $En(w)$
Output: winning region $\mathcal{W}$, winning conflict-free MiSTel Λ
1: $act_\Pi = \mu_0$
2: $(\mathcal{W}, \mathcal{C}, \Lambda) \leftarrow$ FINDCONF(G, w, φ, Φ, Π)
3: **while** $\mathcal{C} \neq \emptyset$ **do**
4: $\quad \Phi \leftarrow \Phi \wedge Safety(\mathcal{W})$
5: $\quad$ **for all** $e \in \mathcal{C}$ **do** $\Pi(e) = \infty$
6: $\quad (\mathcal{W}, \mathcal{C}, \Lambda) \leftarrow$ FINDCONF(G, w, φ, Φ, Π)
7: **return** $(\mathcal{W}, \Lambda)$

8: **procedure** FINDCONF(G, w, φ, Φ, Π)
9: $\quad (\mathcal{W}_\Phi, (S, D)) \leftarrow$ COMPUTEPESTEL(G, Φ)
10: $\quad (\mathcal{W}_\varphi, \Pi) \leftarrow$ COMPUTEQASTEL(G, w, act_Π)
11: $\quad \mathcal{W} \leftarrow \mathcal{W}_\Phi \cap \mathcal{W}_\varphi$
12: $\quad \mathcal{C} = \cup_{v \in \mathcal{W}} \{\texttt{minEdges}(v) \mid \texttt{minEdges}(v) \subseteq S \cup D\}$
13: $\quad$ **return** $(\mathcal{W}, \mathcal{C}, (S, D, \Pi))$

which might result in new ones. If no more conflicts are generated, the algorithm terminates. The resulting MiSTel is winning and conflict free, as formalized next.

Theorem 6. *Let $\mathcal{G} = (G, \varphi \wedge \Phi)$ be a mixed game with $\varphi = MP(w)$ or $En(w)$ and Φ a qualitative objective. Then, if $(\mathcal{W}, \Lambda) =$ COMPUTEMISTEL(G, w, φ, Φ), it holds that Λ is a conflict-free winning MiSTel from $\mathcal{W}$.*

Remark 4. We note that the iterative computation of PeSTels and QaSTels in Algorithm 2 can be hot-started, which makes COMPUTEMISTEL more efficient. For QaSTels, the correctness of hot-starting follows from Eq. 8. Notably, COMPUTEPESTEL can also be hot-started if specifications are added [3, Alg.4].

Incremental MiSTel Synthesis. Surprisingly, Algorithm 2 can directly be extended to incremental MiSTel synthesis. That is, given an already computed winning MiSTel $\Lambda = (S, D, \Pi)$ with winning region $\mathcal{W}$ for the mixed game $\mathcal{G} = (G, \varphi \wedge \Phi)$, Λ can be refined to a new winning MiSTel $\Lambda' = (S', D', \Pi')$ for the mixed game $\mathcal{G} = (G, \varphi \wedge \Phi \wedge \Phi')$ with winning region $\mathcal{W}' \subseteq \mathcal{W}$ if a new quantitative objective Φ' arrives. For this, one would use Algorithm 2 for the combined quantitative objective $\Phi \wedge \Phi'$ and hot-starts both COMPUTEPESTEL and COMPUTEQASTEL with (S, D) and Π from the already existing MiSTel Λ.

Remark 5. We recall from Sect. 5.2 that adding additional *quantitative* objectives only allows to extract new winning *strategies* (and no templates) if all quantitative objectives are mean-payoff objectives. Nevertheless, this clearly can also be incorporated in an iterative version of Algorithm 2.

6.3 Applications of MiSTels

While MiSTels can be applied to any mixed game, the class of winning strategies they capture might be a quite restricted (possibly empty) subset of all available strategies. This can (i) downgrade the adaptability of strategy choices during runtime and (ii) might lead to an empty winning region in incremental or compositional synthesis approaches. MiSTels therefore have a higher potential whenever they capture a large set of winning strategies. One such example are co-Büchi games, where it is known that PeSTels are naturally bounded. After discussing how specifications commonly used in CPS applications reduce to co-Büchi games in this section, we investigate this instance further in Sect. 6.4.

LTL$_f$ Specifications. LTL$_f$ is a fragment of linear temporal logic (LTL) where system properties are evaluated over finite traces only, which has gained popularity in robotic applications over the last decade [14]. Specifications given in LTL$_f$ can be translated into deterministic finite automata which can be composed with a weighted game, adding a reachability objective to it. The resulting reachability objective can then be translated into a co-Büchi objective by removing all outgoing transitions from target states, adding self-loops to them and adding all states which are not a target state into the co-Büchi region.

Uniform Attractivity. If one manipulates the graph as outlined before, one can show that for every winning strategy π exists a time bound $k \in \mathbb{N}$ s.t. all plays ρ compliant with π will never leave the set of target states again after k time steps, i.e., $\forall i \geq k. \, \rho[i] \in T^3$. Such specifications are called uniform attractivity specifications and are used to translate classical stability objectives into formal specifications. Formally, the computation of winning strategies for general uniform attractivity games (without manipulating the game graph) are solved by first computing the winning set of the safety objective $\mathcal{W}_{safe} := Safety(T)$ and then solving the co-Büchi game $(G, co\text{-}Büchi(\mathcal{W}_{safe}))$. It is therefore not hard to see, that PeSTels for uniform attractivity games are also naturally bounded.

Adding Quantitative Objectives. Due to the fact that every winning strategy comes with a uniform bound on when the target set is reached, the above instances of co-Büchi games are naturally combined with qualitative energy objectives with fixed initial credit. This is in contrast to 'classical' co-Büchi objectives which are more naturally combined with mean-payoff objectives, ensuring that strategies are optimal in the limit even if they deviate for finite time duration.

6.4 Mean-Payoff co-Büchi Games

This section restricts attention to scenarios where the qualitative objective is a co-Büchi condition. This allows us to utilize the (bounded) PeSTel synthesis algorithm specialized for co-Büchi games called COBÜCHITEMP from [3,

---

[3] For classical co-Büchi games, such a uniform bound over all plays does in general not exist (see [16] for an example).

Alg. 2] for MiSTel synthesis in this section. As Mean-payoff co-Büchi games have been already studied in [12], we benchmark our prototype implementation of COBÜCHITEMP-based MiSTel synthesis, called QuanTemplate, against the (state-of-the-art) algorithm from [12], called MPCoBuechi, in Sect. 7.

We note that the results of this section directly apply to the control-inspired applications of MiSTels discussed in Sect. 6.3, as (i) QaSTel synthesis coincides for energy and mean-payoff objectives (see Sect. 3), and (ii) reachability and uniform attractivity objectives (possibly resulting from LTL_f objectives) can be translated into co-Büchi objectives (see Sect. 6.3).

Complexity. Using COBÜCHITEMP from [3, Alg. 2] instead of COMPUTEPESTEL in COMPUTEMISTEL (Algorithm 2), the complexity of MiSTel synthesis for mean-payoff co-Büchi games reduces to $\mathcal{O}(n^2m + nmW)$, where $n = |V|$, $m = |E|$, and W is the maximum weight in w (see [2, Corollary 3]). In comparison, the worst-case computation time of MPCoBuechi is $\mathcal{O}(nmW)$ [12, Theorem 5] and, hence, lower. We however note that we achieve the same worst-case complexity when $W \geq n$, which is very often the case.

Completeness. We note that COMPUTEMISTEL is not complete. First of all, the bounded PeSTel computed by COBÜCHITEMP does not capture winning strategies for instances in which Player 1 (unexpectedly) helps Player 0 and is therefore already incomplete (see [3] for details). In addition, conflicts with co-Büchi nodes are removed immediately for conflict resolution in COMPUTEMISTEL, while they could be used by a strategy finitely often. This leads to a further potential under-approximation of the winning region, as illustrated in the example game depicted in Fig. 3. Here, COBÜCHITEMP outputs the co-live edges denoted by orange dashed lines. Further, the activation energy of the edges (a, b) and (a, a) are 0 and 1 respectively, and hence, the edge (a, b) is a conflict by definition. Hence, in Algorithm 2, the edge (a, b) will be assigned the value ∞ while resolving the conflict, making the node a losing in the next iteration. However, we observe that all the nodes are winning for Player 0.

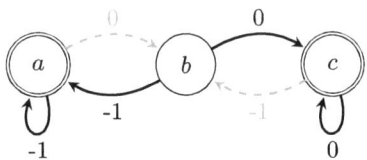

Fig. 3. Mean-payoff co-Büchi game with $co\text{-}Büchi(\{a, c\})$ and colive edges shown as orange dashed lines.

We note that the state-of-the-art algorithm for mean-payoff-co-Büchi games by Chatterjee et al. [12] is instead complete. Our experimental results presented in Sect. 7 however show that the winning region computed by QuanTemplate coincides with the full winning region computed by MPCoBuechi for more then 90% of the considered benchmark instances.

7 Empirical Evaluations

This section aims to highlight the advantages of strategy templates for games with qualitative (and quantitative) objectives. However, benchmarking QaSTel (and MiSTel) synthesis as well as their adaptability and compositional properties is difficult for two reasons. First, to the best of our knowledge, there are no benchmark suites that include real-world applications with combined quantitative and qualitative objectives. Second, while there exist algorithms for mean-payoff parity games, we are not aware of any implementation or benchmark-based evaluation of these algorithms. To address this, we build new benchmark suites based on the SYNTCOMP benchmark [19] and implement the MPCoBuechi algorithm from [12] (discussed in Sect. 6.4) to benchmark our Java-based prototype implementation QuanTemplate of COMPUTEMISTEL against it.

Experimental Setup. We built a new benchmark suite from the SYNTCOMP benchmark [19] by (a) translating SYNTCOMP parity games into mean-payoff games using standard techniques [21], and (b) adding co-Büchi objectives to the qualitative games from (a) by randomly choosing avoidance regions (i.e., the set of co-Büchi nodes which a play is not allowed to visit infinitely often). For practical reasons, we imposed limits of 5×10^5 nodes and 10^5 energy values on the edges. As a result, our benchmark suite comprises 245 mean-payoff game graphs. All experiments were executed on a 32-core Debian machine equipped with an Intel Xeon E5-V2 CPU (3.3 GHz) and up to 256 GB of RAM.

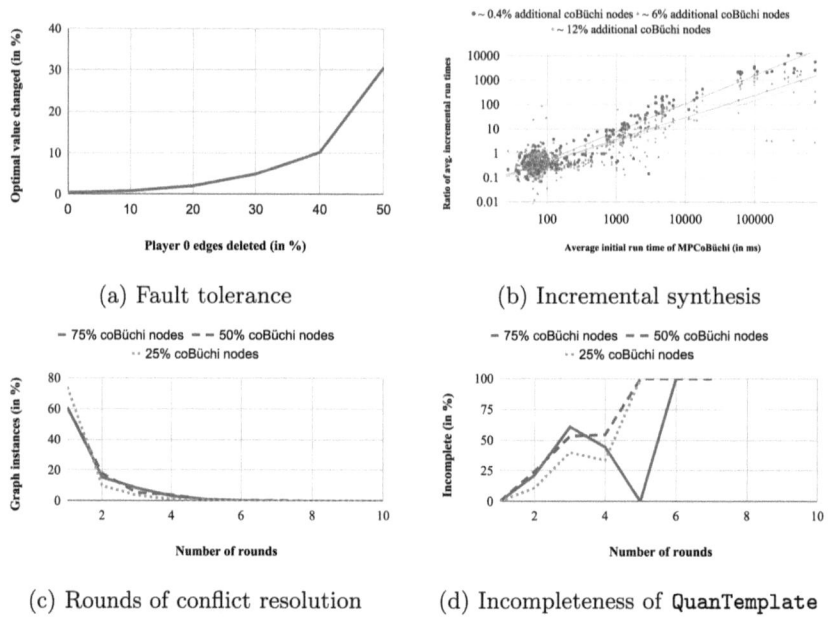

(a) Fault tolerance (b) Incremental synthesis

(c) Rounds of conflict resolution (d) Incompleteness of QuanTemplate

Fig. 4. Plots summarizing the experimental evaluations.

Dynamic Strategy Adaptation. We evaluated the robustness of QaSTels to the unavailability of edges due to additional edge preferences used for dynamic strategy extraction at runtime. As discussed in Sect. 5.1, QaSTels need no adaptation if the edges with minimum activation energy are still available. To assess how often re-computation is needed, we randomly removed edges from the game graphs and measured the average number of deletions required until a minimum activation edge was removed for any node. We ran `QuanTemplate` on each graph, incrementally deleting random edges until an optimal value changed, repeating this process 10 times per graph and averaging the results. Figure 4a illustrates the trend between the proportion of game graphs in which the optimal value changes against the proportion of Player 0 edges removed from them. The trend clearly shows that in practice, it is very unlikely that minimum activation edges are deleted even after removing a significant number of edges from the graph. This establishes the efficiency of QaSTels to produce robust strategies.

Incremental Synthesis. We have benchmarked our prototype implementation `QuanTemplate` of ComputeMiSTel for mean-payoff co-Büchi games against our implementation of the `MPCoBuechi` algorithm [12]. The experiment starts by providing both algorithms only with a mean-payoff game from our benchmark suite. We then add 5 co-Büchi objectives incrementally. To evaluate the dependence of runtimes on the co-Büchi objectives, we run this experiment thrice, with varying amounts of additional nodes added to the avoidance region in every incremental step: (i) 0.4% (blue circles in Fig. 4b), (ii) 6% (red triangles in Fig. 4b) and (iii) 12% (green stars in Fig. 4b) leading to (i) 2%, (ii) 30% and (iii) 60% avoidance region in the final iteration of incremental synthesis. To compare the performance of `QuanTemplate` and `MPCoBuechi`, Fig. 4b shows (i) the ratio of average runtimes of `MPCoBuechi` vs `QuanTemplate` to complete the 5 incremental synthesis steps outlined above (y-axis in Fig. 4b), against (ii) the running times of `MPCoBuechi` over the original mean-payoff game without co-Büchi objectives (x-axis in Fig. 4b).

The plot shows that when the instances are very simple (resulting in a low initial runtime of `MPCoBuechi`), `QuanTemplate` may be slow in the re-computation on additional co-Büchi objectives. However, as the graphs get more complex, `QuanTemplate` is magnitudes faster than `MPCoBuechi` in recomputing the winning regions on the fly. In fact, we see that `QuanTemplate` is around 10000 times faster on the most complex instances. This demonstrates the utility of our approach avoiding the need of re-computations from scratch.

Completeness. We conducted experiments to quantify the loss of completeness (in terms of the size of the winning region) of ComputeMiSTel compared to `MPCoBuechi`. For each of the 245 mean-payoff game graphs in our benchmark suite, we randomly selected (i) 25%, (ii) 50%, and (iii) 75% of the nodes and defined them as the avoidance region in the respective mean-payoff co-Büchi game. `QuanTemplate` could *not* compute the *complete* winning region in (i) 10, (ii) 30 and (iii) 28 instances of games, respectively. This shows that `QuanTemplate` computes the full winning region for over 90% of the considered games.

To further investigate the root cause of incompleteness, we evaluated the number of rounds of conflict resolutions required by `QuanTemplate` for each instance. In Fig. 4c, we plot the percentage of instances requiring a certain number of conflict resolution rounds. In Fig. 4d, we plot the percentage of incomplete instances against the number of conflict resolution rounds required to solve the respective instance. Together the two plots present the relationship between the number of game graphs for which `QuanTemplate` was unable to synthesize a winning strategy and the number of iterations required to resolve conflicts. Figure 4d indicates a clear trend: as the number of iterations increases, the likelihood of failure to synthesize a winning strategy also increases. However, as noted in Fig. 4c, the number of iterations required in practice remains low. This observation explains the low number of incomplete instances (less than 10%, as noted above), and supports the claim that while our algorithm may be incomplete in the worst case, it is able to synthesize winning strategies in most scenarios.

References

1. Anand, A., Mallik, K., Nayak, S.P., Schmuck, A.K.: Computing adequately permissive assumptions for synthesis. In: Tools and Algorithms for the Construction and Analysis of Systems (2023)
2. Anand, A., Nayak, S.P., Raha, R., Sağlam, I., Schmuck, A.K.: Quantitative strategy templates (2025). https://arxiv.org/abs/2504.16528
3. Anand, A., Nayak, S.P., Schmuck, A.K.: Synthesizing permissive winning strategy templates for parity games. In: Computer Aided Verification - 35th International Conference, CAV 2023, Paris, France, 17-22 July 2023, Proceedings, Part I. LNCS. (2023). https://doi.org/10.1007/978-3-031-37706-8_22
4. Anand, A., Nayak, S.P., Schmuck, A.: Strategy templates - robust certified interfaces for interacting systems. In: ATVA. LNCS, vol. 15054, pp. 22–41. Springer (2024).https://doi.org/10.1007/978-3-031-78709-6_2
5. Anand, A., Schmuck, A.K., Prakash Nayak, S.: Contract-based distributed logical controller synthesis. In: Proceedings of the 27th ACM International Conference on Hybrid Systems: Computation and Control, HSCC 2024 (May 2024).https://doi.org/10.1145/3641513.3650123
6. Avni, G., Henzinger, T.A., Kupferman, O.: Dynamic resource allocation games. Theoretical Comput. Sci. **807**, 42–55 (2020). https://doi.org/10.1016/j.tcs.2019.06.031,inmemoryofMauriceNivat,afoundingfatherofTheoreticalComputerScience-PartII
7. Bernet, J., Janin, D., Walukiewicz, I.: Permissive strategies: from parity games to safety games. RAIRO Theor. Inform. Appl. **36**(3), 261–275 (2002). https://doi.org/10.1051/ita:2002013
8. Bouyer, P., Fahrenberg, U., Larsen, K.G., Markey, N., Srba, J.: Infinite Runs in Weighted Timed Automata with Energy Constraints. In: Cassez, F., Jard, C. (eds.) FORMATS 2008. LNCS, vol. 5215, pp. 33–47. Springer, Heidelberg (2008). https://doi.org/10.1007/978-3-540-85778-5_4
9. Bouyer, P., Markey, N., Olschewski, J., Ummels, M.: Measuring Permissiveness in Parity Games: Mean-Payoff Parity Games Revisited. In: Bultan, T., Hsiung, P.-A. (eds.) ATVA 2011. LNCS, vol. 6996, pp. 135–149. Springer, Heidelberg (2011). https://doi.org/10.1007/978-3-642-24372-1_11

10. Brim, L., Chaloupka, J., Doyen, L., Gentilini, R., Raskin, J.: Faster algorithms for mean-payoff games. Formal Methods Syst. Des. **38**(2), 97–118 (2011). https://doi.org/10.1007/S10703-010-0105-X
11. Chakrabarti, A., de Alfaro, L., Henzinger, T.A., Stoelinga, M.: Resource Interfaces. In: Alur, R., Lee, I. (eds.) EMSOFT 2003. LNCS, vol. 2855, pp. 117–133. Springer, Heidelberg (2003). https://doi.org/10.1007/978-3-540-45212-6_9
12. Chatterjee, K., Henzinger, M., Svozil, A.: Faster algorithms for mean-payoff parity games. In: Larsen, K.G., Bodlaender, H.L., Raskin, J. (eds.) 42nd International Symposium on Mathematical Foundations of Computer Science, MFCS 2017, 21-25 August 2017 - Aalborg, Denmark. LIPIcs, vol. 83, pp. 39:1–39:14. Schloss Dagstuhl - Leibniz-Zentrum für Informatik (2017).https://doi.org/10.4230/LIPICS.MFCS.2017.39
13. Chatterjee, K., Henzinger, T.A., Jurdzinski, M.: Mean-payoff parity games. In: 20th IEEE Symposium on Logic in Computer Science (LICS 2005), 26-29 June 2005, Chicago, IL, USA, Proceedings, pp. 178–187. IEEE Computer Society (2005). https://doi.org/10.1109/LICS.2005.26
14. De Giacomo, G., Vardi, M.Y., et al.: Synthesis for ltl and ldl on finite traces. In: Proceedings of the Twenty-Fourth International Joint Conference on Artificial Intelligence, IJCAI 2015, pp. 1558–1564. AAAI Press (2015)
15. Fijalkow, N., et al.: Games on graphs. CoRR abs/ arxiv **2305**, 10546 (2023)
16. Girard, A., Eqtami, A.: Least-violating symbolic controller synthesis for safety, reachability and attractivity specifications. Automatica **127**, 109543 (2021)
17. Gittis, A., Vin, E., Fremont, D.J.: Randomized synthesis for diversity and cost constraints with control improvisation. In: CAV (2). LNCS, vol. 13372, pp. 526–546. Springer (2022). https://doi.org/10.1007/978-3-031-13188-2_26
18. He, K., Lahijanian, M., Kavraki, L.E., Vardi, M.Y.: Reactive synthesis for finite tasks under resource constraints. In: 2017 IEEE/RSJ International Conference on Intelligent Robots and Systems (IROS), pp. 5326–5332 (2017).https://doi.org/10.1109/IROS.2017.8206426
19. Jacobs, S., Perez, G., Schlehuber-Caissier, P.: Data, scripts, and results from syntcomp 2023 (2023). https://doi.org/10.5281/zenodo.8112518
20. Klein, J., Baier, C., Klüppelholz, S.: Compositional construction of most general controllers. Acta Informatica , 443–482 (2015). https://doi.org/10.1007/s00236-015-0239-9
21. Meyer, P.J., Luttenberger, M.: Solving mean-payoff games on the gpu. In: Artho, C., Legay, A., Peled, D. (eds.) Automated Technology for Verification and Analysis, pp. 262–267. Springer International Publishing, Cham (2016)
22. Muvvala, K., Lahijanian, M.: Efficient symbolic approaches for quantitative reactive synthesis with finite tasks. In: 2023 IEEE/RSJ International Conference on Intelligent Robots and Systems (IROS), pp. 8666–8672 (2023). https://doi.org/10.1109/IROS55552.2023.10342496
23. Nayak, S.P., Egidio, L.N., Della Rossa, M., Schmuck, A.K., Jungers, R.M.: Context-triggered abstraction-based control design. IEEE Open J. Control Syst. **2**, 277–296 (2023). https://doi.org/10.1109/OJCSYS.2023.3305835
24. Nayak, S.P., Schmuck, A.: Most general winning secure equilibria synthesis in graph games. In: Finkbeiner, B., Kovács, L. (eds.) Tools and Algorithms for the Construction and Analysis of Systems - 30th International Conference, TACAS 2024, Held as Part of the European Joint Conferences on Theory and Practice of Software, ETAPS 2024, Luxembourg City, Luxembourg, April 6-11, 2024, Proceedings, Part III. Lecture Notes in Computer Science, vol. 14572, pp. 173–193. Springer (2024). https://doi.org/10.1007/978-3-031-57256-2_9

25. Neider, D., Rabinovich, R., Zimmermann, M.: Down the borel hierarchy: solving muller games via safety games. Theor. Comput. Sci. **560**, 219–234 (2014). https://doi.org/10.1016/j.tcs.2014.01.017
26. Vazquez-Chanlatte, M., Junges, S., Fremont, D.J., Seshia, S.: Entropy-guided control improvisation. Robot. Sci, Syst (2021)
27. Velner, Y., Chatterjee, K., Doyen, L., Henzinger, T.A., Rabinovich, A., Raskin, J.F.: The complexity of multi-mean-payoff and multi-energy games. Inform. Comput. **241**, 177–196 (2015)
28. Zwick, U., Paterson, M.: The complexity of mean payoff games on graphs. Theor. Comput. Sci. **158**(1&2), 343–359 (1996). https://doi.org/10.1016/0304-3975(95)00188-3

Energy Games with Weight Uncertainty

Orna Kupferman and Naama Shamash Halevy(✉)

The Hebrew University, Jerusalem, Israel
orna@cs.huji.ac.il , naama.shamashhal@mail.huji.ac.il

Abstract. An *energy game* is played between two players, modeling a resource-bounded system and its environment. The players take turns moving a token along a finite graph. Each edge of the graph is labeled by an integer, describing how its traversal affects the energy level of the system. The system wins if it never runs out of energy.

We introduce and study *energy games with weight uncertainty* (EGWUs), where the exact updates to the energy level are not a-priori known to the system. Instead, an EGWU specifies, for some subsets of edges, upper and lower bounds for their joint weight. EGWUs thus model settings in which there is only an estimation of the effect of some actions or sets of actions on the energy level, for example due to uncertainty about road conditions for an autonomous car or about the location of docking stations for a robot patrolling a warehouse. The system wins an EGWU if it has a strategy to never run out of energy, no matter what the weights are, as long as they respect the bounds. The environment wins if there are weights that respect the bounds with which it can cause the system to run out of energy.

Unlike uncertainty about the exact location of the token, which persists during the interaction, the weight of an edge is revealed upon its traversal. The fact the system learns the weights during the interaction makes EGWUs interesting, and we study the memory required to the players, determinacy of the game, and the possibility of coping with uncertainty by a larger initial energy. We give tight complexity bounds to the problems of deciding whether the system or the environment wins, and we study the effect of parameters like the richness of the function estimating the weights, or the distribution of control along the interaction.

1 Introduction

A reactive system interacts with its environment and should behave correctly in all environments. Synthesis of a reactive system thus corresponds to finding a winning strategy in a *two-player game* between the system and the environment [3]. The game is played on a graph whose vertices are partitioned between the players. Starting from some initial vertex, the players take turns moving a token along the graph. In each turn, the player that owns the current vertex decides which action to take, which amounts to choosing an edge along which the token moves to the next vertex. Together, the players generate an infinite path in the game graph.

The winning condition in the game is induced by the specification for the system. For example, using ω-regular winning conditions, one can synthesize systems that have desired on-going behaviors in all environments [18]. Adding weights to the edges of the game graph enables the winning condition to express also quantitative specifications, referring, for example, to the limit sum or average of the weights along the graph [13]. Then, a winning strategy for the system, namely a mechanism that directs it how to move the token in a way that ensures the satisfaction of the winning condition, corresponds to a system that satisfies its specification in all environments.

In *energy games* (EGs), we are interested in the ability of a *resource-bounded* system to maintain an interaction with the environment without running out of resources. Each edge of the game graph is labeled by an integer, describing its *weight* – the update to the energy level of the system that occurs whenever the edge is traversed. The game starts in some initial vertex with the system having some initial energy level. When the players move the token, the energy level of the system is updated according the weights of the edges traversed. The system wins if it never runs out of energy in the generated path. The term "energy" may refer to a wide range of applications: an actual energy level, where actions involve consumption or charging of energy; storage, where actions involve using or freeing of disc space; money, where actions involve costs and rewards to a budget of some economic entity, and more [10]. It is shown in [16] that EGs are determined, thus the system or the environment have a winning strategy, and, assuming weights given in unary, the game can be decided in polynomial time.

Different applications have led to extensions of basic EGs. For example, addressing a combination of bounded resources with behavioral requirements, researchers have studied *energy parity games*, whose winning conditions combine quantitative and qualitative conditions [1,7]. Then, addressing systems with several bounded resources, researchers have studied *generalized energy games*, in which the system player has a multi-dimensional energy level, the updates along the edges are vectors of integers, and the system wins if it does not run out of energy in any of its resources [9]. Finally, for settings in which the environment is also resource bounded, actions in *both-bounded energy games* change the (multi-dimensional) energy level of both the system and the environment [14].

Sometimes, the system may observe only a subset of the variables that participate in the interaction. For example, in a game modeling a robot that navigates a warehouse, the robot may not be able to observe the precise location of other moving objects, such as human workers or other robots, and should still fulfill its mission while avoiding collisions. This has led to extensive studies of two-player games with *incomplete information* [15,19]. The system wins a game with incomplete information if it has a strategy (that obviously depends only on the observable variables) such that no matter how the environment behaves and what the missing information is, the generated path satisfies the winning condition. From a technical point of view, incomplete information as above leads to uncertainty about the location of the token in the game graph. Consequently, algorithms for games with incomplete information maintain sets of indistinguishable vertices, making them (typically, exponentially) more complex than games with full information, and causing the synthesized systems to be larger [2,8,12].

In [11], the authors studied energy games with incomplete information. There, uncertainty makes the problem much harder: deciding the winner is Ackerman-complete [17], and determining whether there is some initial energy that is sufficient for the system to win is undecidable [11].

We introduce and study *energy games with weight uncertainty* (EGWUs), where the incomplete information concerns the updates to the energy level, rather than the location of the token. Consider again the robot that navigates an area. Factors like the type of terrain, the surface condition, and elevation gain or loss induce some estimation on the energy consumption of the robot along some routes, but the exact consumption may not be known. The estimations may refer to segments of routes or their combination, for example when we have an estimated location for a docking station or for the height difference between certain locations. Accordingly, while an EG includes a weight function $w : E \to \mathbb{Z}$ that maps each edge of the game graph to the change in the system's energy when the edge is traversed, in an EGWU we have instead a partial function $\tau : 2^E \to \mathbb{Z} \times \mathbb{Z}$ that specifies, for some subsets of edges, in particular for all singletons, upper and lower bounds on the sum of their weights. The system wins an EGWU if it has a strategy to win against all environments, and no matter which weights are used, as long as they respect the bounds. The environment wins if there are weights that respect the bounds with which it can cause the system to run out of energy. Note that since the weights are part of the setting and are only not known to the system, their choice is done offline, before the game starts.

We argue that EGWU capture realistic settings. In addition to the example above of planning in unknown environments, our work is motivated by *dynamic cloud environments*, where the cost of executing a task (e.g., in terms of CPU or memory) may only be known once the task has run, due to shared infrastructure and workload fluctuations. Then, in *energy-aware mobile apps*, apps often rely on estimated energy usage (e.g., for network or GPS access), but actual energy costs depend on background processes or current hardware state. The cost is only revealed upon execution, and systems must adapt. Note that while the cost of a certain action may not be fixed, its cost in a particular context is fixed, and corresponds to a single edge in an EGWU whose state space models the different contexts.

Unlike uncertainty about the exact location of the token, which persists during the game, the weight of an edge is revealed upon its traversal. Thus, during the interaction, the system learns the weight of traversed edges. This suggests that a system may need memory in order to win an EGWU. This is in contrast with EGs, where memoryless strategies, namely ones that only depend on the current location of the token, are sufficient for the system to win [4,5]. We show that indeed, each EGWU G with state space S induces an EG learn(G) with state space $S \times \mathcal{W}_\tau$, where $\mathcal{W}_\tau$ is the set of *learned weights functions* that respects τ, namely partial weight functions that can be extended to complete ones that respect τ. The size of $\mathcal{W}_\tau$ is exponential in G, implying the system may need an exponential memory in order to with G, which we show to be tight.

While the state space of learn(G) is exponential in G, its diameter is only polynomial, which leads to a PSPACE algorithm for deciding whether the system can win G, which we show to be tight. By bounding the initial energy that may be required to Player 1 in order to win G, we get a PSPACE algorithm also for the problem of deciding whether such a finite initial energy exists. We also study cases in which weight uncertainty can be compensated by extra initial energy. Intuitively, the initial energy enables the systems to learn the weights, but in order for this to always succeed, the game should include no traps for the system. As for the environment, we show that memoryless strategies are sufficient for it, making the problem of deciding whether the environment wins NP-complete. This is also the complexity of deciding whether Player 2 can win the game whatever the initial energy is. We show that our lower bounds apply also for simple classes of EGWUs, for example when the system controls all the vertices of the game or when τ involves only one global estimation on the set of all edges. We also study a variant of EGWUs in which the missing weights are determined in an online manner, thus weights may be assigned in a hostile manner that depends on the history of the game so far. We show that unlike usual (offline) EGWUs, the online variant is determined.

Due to the lack of space, some proofs are missing and can be found in the full version, in the authors' URLs.

2 Preliminaries

2.1 Energy Games

An *energy game* (EG, for short) is a two-player game $G = \langle S_1, S_2, s_0, E, b, w \rangle$, where S_1 and S_2 are disjoint sets of vertices, controlled by Player 1 and Player 2, respectively, and we let $S = S_1 \cup S_2$. Then, $s_0 \in S$ is an initial vertex, and $E \subseteq S \times S$ is a total edge relation, thus for every $s \in S$, there is $s' \in S$ such that $\langle s, s' \rangle \in E$. For $j \in \{1, 2\}$, let $E_j = E \cap (S_j \times S)$ be the set of edges that leave vertices controlled by Player j. If $S = S_j$, we say that G is j-controlled. The value $b \in \mathbb{N}$ is the *initial energy* of Player 1, and $w : E \to \mathbb{Z}$ is a weight function, with $w(e)$ describing the change to the energy level of Player 1 whenever an edge $e \in E$ is traversed. We extend w to sets of edges in the expected way, thus for $A \subseteq E$, we define $w(A) = \sum_{e \in A} w(e)$. Also, for an edge $\langle s_1, s_2 \rangle \in E$, we sometimes abuse notations and write $w(s_1, s_2)$ rather than $w(\langle s_1, s_2 \rangle)$. We define the *size* of G, denoted $|G|$, to be the size required for storing the cost function w, that is $|G| = |E| \cdot m$, where m is the largest integer in the image of w. Note that the definition corresponds to the integers in the range of w being given in unary.

In the beginning of a play in the game, a token is placed on s_0, and the energy level of Player 1 is b. Then, in each turn, the player that controls the vertex s that hosts the token chooses a successor vertex s' and moves the token along the edge $\langle s, s' \rangle$, making s' the new vertex that hosts the token. Together, the players generate a *play* $\rho = s_0, s_1, s_2, \ldots \in S^\omega$ in G, namely an infinite path that starts in s_0 and respects E: for all $i \geq 0$, we have that $\langle s_i, s_{i+1} \rangle \in E$.

Traversing an edge e updates to the energy level of Player 1 by $w(e)$. In particular, $w(e) > 0$ means that traversing e charges Player 1 with energy, and $w(e) < 0$ consumes energy. Formally, for a play ρ and an index $n \geq 0$, we define the *energy level* of ρ after n rounds, denoted $\mathcal{E}(\rho, n)$, as $b + \sum_{i=0}^{n-1} w(s_i, s_{i+1})$. Note that if an edge is traversed in ρ several times, its weight contributes to the energy level after each traversal. For a finite infix $p = s_k, s_{k+1}, \ldots, s_{k+n}$ of a play, we define the *energy change* along p by $\mathcal{E}_\Delta(p) = \sum_{i=0}^{n-1} w(s_{k+i}, s_{k+i+1})$. The goal of Player 1 is not to run out of energy; that is, keep the energy level non-negative throughout the play. The goal of Player 2 is dual, namely to make Player 1 eventually run out of energy. Formally, a play ρ is winning for Player 1 if for all $n \geq 0$, it holds that $\mathcal{E}(\rho, n) \geq 0$. Otherwise, ρ is winning for Player 2.

For $j \in \{1, 2\}$, a *strategy* for Player j directs him how to move the token in vertices he controls. The direction may depend on the history of the game so far. Thus, a strategy is a function $f_j : S^* \cdot S_j \to S$ that maps prefixes of plays that end in a vertex that is controlled by Player j to possible extensions in a way that respects E. That is, for every $\rho \in S^*$ and $s \in S_j$, we have that $\langle s, f_j(\rho \cdot s) \rangle \in E$.

A *profile* is a pair $\pi = \langle f_1, f_2 \rangle$ of strategies, one for each player. The *outcome* of a profile $\pi = \langle f_1, f_2 \rangle$ is the play obtained when the players follow their strategies in π. Formally, outcome$(\pi) = s_0, s_1, s_2 \ldots \in S^\omega$ is such that for all $i \geq 0$, we have that $s_{i+1} = f_j(s_0, s_1, \ldots, s_i)$, where $j \in \{1, 2\}$ is such that $s_i \in S_j$. A strategy f_1 for Player 1 is *winning* if for every strategy f_2 for Player 2, the play outcome(f_1, f_2) is winning for Player 1. Likewise, a strategy f_2 for Player 2 is winning if for every strategy f_1 for Player 1, the play outcome(f_1, f_2) is winning for Player 2. A player wins a game if he has a winning strategy.

For an EG $G = \langle S_1, S_2, s_0, E, b, w \rangle$, the *diameter* of G is the length of the longest simple path in G. By definition, if a prefix of a play in G is longer than its diameter, then this prefix includes a cycle.

2.2 Energy Games with Weight Uncertainty

In an *energy game with weight uncertainty* (EGWU, for short), the weight function is only estimated, and the exact weights are revealed during the play. Formally, rather than a weight function, an EGWU includes a partial function $\tau : 2^E \to \mathbb{Z} \times \mathbb{Z}$ that specifies for some subsets of edges, in particular for all singletons, lower and upper bounds for the sum of their weights. We call τ an *estimated weight function*, and we say that τ is *pervasive* if $\tau(\{e\})$ is defined for all edges $e \in E$. For simplicity, for an edge $e = \langle s, s' \rangle$, we sometimes write $\tau(e)$ or $\tau(s, s')$ rather than $\tau(\{e\})$ or $\tau(\{\langle s, s' \rangle\})$, respectively. Note that possibly $\tau(e) = \langle c, c \rangle$, for some $c \in \mathbb{Z}$, in which case we say that (the energy change along) e is *known* and write $\tau(e) = c$.

Formally, an EGWU is $G = \langle S_1, S_2, s_0, E, b, \tau \rangle$, where S_1, S_2, s_0, E, and b are as in EGs, and $\tau : 2^E \to \mathbb{Z} \times \mathbb{Z}$ is a pervasive estimated weight function. Let l_G be the minimal sufficient energy to traverse a single edge in G when the weight function respects τ. Formally, $l_G = \max_{e \in E}\{-c_1 : \tau(e) = \langle c_1, c_2 \rangle\}$. Note that in order for a G to be interesting, some lower bounds c_1 need to be negative. Thus, l_G is typically positive. Then, let m_G be the largest absolute value of an integer in the image of τ. Formally, $m_G = \max_{A \subseteq E}\{|c_1|, |c_2| : \tau(A) = \langle c_1, c_2 \rangle\}$. We define the *size* of G, denoted $|G|$, as the size required for storing τ; that is $|G| = 2 \cdot k \cdot m_G$, where k is the number of sets $A \subseteq E$ for which $\tau(A)$ is defined.

A weight function $w : E \to \mathbb{Z}$ *respects* an estimated weight function τ if for every set of edges $A \subseteq E$ for which $\tau(A) = \langle c_1, c_2 \rangle$ is defined, we have that $c_1 \leq w(A) \leq c_2$. We say that τ is satisfiable iff there is at least one weight function that respects it.

For an EGWU $G = \langle S_1, S_2, s_0, E, b, \tau \rangle$ and a weight function w, let G_w denote the EG with the structure of G and weight function w. That is, $G_w = \langle S_1, S_2, s_0, E, b, w \rangle$. One natural candidate for defining the semantics of EGWU is to say that Player 1 wins G if he has a strategy that is winning in all EGs G_w, for every weight function w that respects τ. Such a semantics, however, ignores the fact that Player 1 views his energy level, and thus learns the weight of edges traversed during the play. Below we define a semantics that models a setting with such a learning.

We start with the definitions of strategies for the players. A strategy for Player 1 in an EGWU is $f_1 : (S \times \mathbb{Z})^* \cdot S_1 \to S$ that respects E. Thus, for every $\rho \in (S \times \mathbb{Z})^*$ and $s \in S_1$, we have that $\langle s, f_j(\rho \cdot s) \rangle \in E$. Note that since Player 1 learns the weight of traversed edges, the strategy depends not only on the sequence of the vertices visited so far, but also on the weights on the edges traversed.

As for Player 2, since a strategy for Player 1 is winning iff it is winning against the most hostile weight function that respects τ, we start a play by letting Player 2 choose such a function. In addition, Player 2 moves the token in vertices he controls. Thus, a strategy for Player 2 is a pair $\langle w, f_2 \rangle$, where $w : E \to \mathbb{Z}$ is a weight function that respects τ and $f_2 : (S \times \mathbb{Z})^* \cdot S_2 \to S$ respects E. We sometimes refer to w and f_2 as the *weight* and *token* components of the strategy, respectively. Note that when τ is not satisfiable, Player 2 has no strategy, and Player 1 wins the game. We thus assume that in all EGWUs, the estimated weight function is satisfiable. Note also that since w is known to Player 2, we could have defined f_2 to have only S^* in its domain, but we preferred to have f_1 and f_2 with the same types.

In order to take into an account the learned weights, we define a *play* in an EGWU as a sequence in $(S \times \mathbb{Z})^\omega$ rather than a sequence in S^ω. For a profile $\pi = \langle f_1, \langle w, f_2 \rangle \rangle$ of strategies for the players, we define outcome(π) to be the infinite play $\rho = \langle s_0, w(s_0, s_1) \rangle, \langle s_1, w(s_1, s_2) \rangle, \langle s_2, w(s_2, s_3) \rangle \ldots \in (S \times \mathbb{Z})^\omega$ such that for all $i \geq 0$, we have that $s_{i+1} = f_j(\langle s_0, w(s_0, s_1) \rangle, \langle s_1, w(s_1, s_2) \rangle, \ldots, \langle s_{i-1}, w(s_{i-1}, s_i) \rangle, s_i)$, where $j \in \{1, 2\}$ is such that $s_i \in S_j$. For $n \geq 0$, the energy level of ρ after n rounds, denoted $\mathcal{E}(\rho, n)$ is defined as in EGs. Thus, $\mathcal{E}(\rho, n) = $

$b + \sum_{i=0}^{n-1} w(s_i, s_{i+1})$. Likewise, for a finite infix $p = \langle s_k, c_k \rangle, \langle s_{k+1}, c_{k+1} \rangle, \ldots,$ $\langle s_{k+n+1}, c_{k+n+1} \rangle$ of a play, we define the *energy change* along p as the sum of the weights of the edges traversed from s_k to s_{k+n}, thus $\mathcal{E}_\Delta(p) = \sum_{i=0}^{n} c_{k+i}$. Finally, winning plays and strategies for Player 1 and Player 2 are defined as in EGs.

Example 1. Consider the EGWU $G = \langle S_1, S_2, v_0, E, b, \tau \rangle$ appearing in Fig. 1. Drawing EGWUs, we describe vertices in S_1 and S_2 by circles and squares, respectively. The initial vertex v_0 is marked by an incoming edge labeled by the initial energy b. Each edge e is labeled by $\tau(e)$. Additional sets for which τ is defined are listed. In the example here, τ is defined also for the set E, with $\tau(E) = \langle -1, 0 \rangle$.

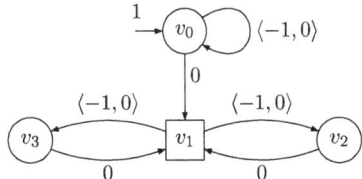

Fig. 1. The EGWU G.

Note that the three edges $\langle v_0, v_1 \rangle$, $\langle v_2, v_1 \rangle$, and $\langle v_3, v_1 \rangle$ all may have weight 0 or -1, yet $\tau(E) = \langle -1, 0 \rangle$ implies that at most one of them has weight -1, and the rest have weight 0.

We argue that Player 1 wins G. Indeed, a winning strategy f_1 of Player 1 can first take the loop on v_0. If the learned weight for it is 0, then f_1 directs Player 1 to loop in v_0 forever, keeping his energy level 1 forever. If the learned weight is -1, the energy level of Player 1 drops to 0, and f_1 directs him to move to v_1. Since the weights of both edges $\langle v_2, v_1 \rangle$ and $\langle v_3, v_1 \rangle$ must be 0, the energy level of Player 1 stays 0 forever no matter how Player 2 proceeds. □

Recall that the estimated weight function $\tau : 2^E \to \mathbb{Z} \times \mathbb{Z}$ has to be pervasive, thus specify an estimation on all sets of single edges. Note that an EGWU whose estimated weight function is defined only for single edges is not too interesting. Indeed, for such an estimated weight function there is a single *most hostile* weight function that respects it. Formally, if τ is defined only for single edges and $G = \langle S_1, S_2, s_0, E, b, \tau \rangle$, then Player 1 wins G iff Player 1 wins $G_w = \langle S_1, S_2, s_0, E, b, w \rangle$ for the weight function $w : E \to \mathbb{Z}$ in which for every edge e with $\tau(e) = \langle c_1, c_2 \rangle$, we have that $w(e) = c_1$. Accordingly, such EGWUs have the same properties as EGs.

Defining τ also with respect to sets of edges enables the specification of richer estimations on the weights. As we shall show, this richness changes the theoretical and computational properties of EGs. It is interesting to analyze these properties also with respect to different classes of estimated weight functions. In particular, we study the following two special cases, where the width of τ is $|E|+1$ and $2 \cdot |E|$, respectively. Consider an EGWU $G = \langle S_1, S_2, s_0, E, b, \tau \rangle$.

- G is *global* if τ is defined only for singletons and the set E.
- G is *flat* if each edge appears in at most two sets for which τ is defined (that is, in one set in addition to the singleton for it). Note that a global estimated weight function is flat.

For an estimated weight function τ, let $\mathcal{W}_\tau$ denote the set of functions $g : E \to \mathbb{Z} \cup \{\bot\}$ that can be extended to a function that respects τ. One can view g as a partial function from E to $\mathbb{Z}$, with $g(e) = \bot$ indicating that $g(e)$ is undefined. Intuitively, in the beginning of a play in an EGWU, Player 1 has no knowledge about the weights of the edges beyond the estimated weights induced from τ; thus Player 1 starts the game with a *learned function* g_0 such that $g_0(e) = \bot$ for all $e \in E$. Then, when the current learned function is g and the token traverses an edge e, it may be the case that the play has already used the edge e, in which case $g(e) \in \mathbb{Z}$, or this is the first traversal of e, in which case Player 1 can update his learned function to one that takes the energy change caused by the traversal. Formally, for $g \in \mathcal{W}_\tau$, $e \in E$ and $c \in \mathbb{Z}$, we define $\mathsf{update}(g, e, c)$ to be the function g' such that:

- If $g(e) \neq \bot$ then $g' = g$.
- Otherwise, g' agrees with g on all edges but e, which now has weight c. That is, $g'(e) = c$ and $g'(e') = g(e')$ for all $e' \neq e$.

Let $k = \max_{e \in E} \{|c_2 - c_1| : \tau(e) = \langle c_1, c_2 \rangle\}$ be the largest uncertainty that τ imposes for a single edge. Note that since τ is pervasive, k is well defined. Also, as all the functions in $\mathcal{W}_\tau$ can be extended to functions that respect τ, we have that $|\mathcal{W}_\tau| \leq (k+1)^{|E|}$. Thus, $\mathcal{W}_\tau$ is of size at most exponential in $|G|$.

For two learned functions $g, g' \in \mathcal{W}_\tau$, we say that g' *extends* g, denoted $g \preceq g'$, if g' is obtained from g by assigning values in $\mathbb{Z}$ to edges that are assigned $\bot$ in g. Formally, $g \preceq g'$ iff for all edges $e \in E$, if $g'(e) = \bot$ then $g(e) = \bot$, and if $g(e) \in \mathbb{Z}$ then $g'(e) = g(e)$. Clearly, the relation $\preceq$ is reflexive and transitive. Also, for every $g \in \mathcal{W}_\tau$, edge $e \in E$, and value $c \in \mathbb{Z}$ for which $\mathsf{update}(g, e, c)$ is in $\mathcal{W}_\tau$, we have that $g \preceq \mathsf{update}(g, e, z)$.

3 Theoretical Properties of EGWUs

In this section we study the theoretical properties of EGWUs. We first examine the effect of learning the weights during the interaction, and show that it can be captured by augmenting the vertices with learned weight functions. We then study the requirement to fix the weight function before the interaction starts. We show that it makes EGWUs undetermined, and that allowing Player 2 to fix the weights in an online manner makes the game determined.

3.1 From EGWUs to EGs

For an EGWU $G = \langle S_1, S_2, s_0, E, b, \tau \rangle$, we define the *EG induced from G*, denoted $\mathsf{learn}(G)$, as the EG induced from G when Player 1 maintains the weights learned during the interaction. As we shall see in Lemma 1, Player 1 wins the EGWU G iff he wins the EG $\mathsf{learn}(G)$. An analysis of $\mathsf{learn}(G)$ then provides helpful properties on the strategies required for Player 1 to win G.

Formally, $\mathsf{learn}(G) = \langle V_1, V_2, v_0, E', b, w \rangle$, where

- $V_1 = S_1 \times \mathcal{W}_\tau$. Thus, Player 1 controls vertices that correspond to vertices in G, augmented by learned weight functions.
- $V_2 = (S_2 \cup E_1) \times \mathcal{W}_\tau$. Thus, Player 2 controls two types of vertices. Vertices in $S_2 \times \mathcal{W}_\tau$, which correspond to vertices in G augmented by learned weight functions, and vertices in $E_1 \times \mathcal{W}_\tau$, which serve as intermediate vertices that enable Player 2 to decide the weight of edges in G that leave vertices in S_1 (recall that $E_1 = E \cap (S_1 \times S)$).
  Let $V = V_1 \cup V_2$. For a vertex in V of the form $(s, g) \in S \times \mathcal{W}_\tau$, we refer to s and g as the S-component and the $\mathcal{W}_\tau$-component of (s, g).
- $v_0 = (s_0, g_0)$.
- The set E' of edges is induced by these of G, and their weight is induced from the way Player 2 chooses to update the learned weight function. Formally, we define E' and the weight function $w : E' \to \mathbb{Z}$ as follows.
  - For every vertex $(s, g) \in V_1$ and edge $\langle s, s' \rangle \in E$, we add to E' an edge with weight 0 from (s, g) to $(\langle s, s' \rangle, g)$. The edge corresponds to Player 1 choosing the successor s' of s when the token is in s and the learned weights so far agree with g.
  - For every vertex $(\langle s, s' \rangle, g) \in V_2$ and for every $c \in \mathbb{Z}$ for which the function $g' = \mathsf{update}(g, \langle s, s' \rangle, c)$ is in $\mathcal{W}_\tau$, we add to E' an edge with weight $g'(s, s')$ from $(\langle s, s' \rangle, g)$ to (s', g'). The edge corresponds to Player 2 choosing c as the weight of the edge $\langle s, s' \rangle$. Note that if Player 2 has already chosen this weight, then $(\langle s, s' \rangle, g)$ has a single succesor, which is (s', g). Indeed, by the definition of $\mathsf{update}(g, \langle s, s' \rangle, c)$, if $g(s, s') \neq \bot$, then for all $c \in \mathbb{Z}$, we have that $\mathsf{update}(g, \langle s, s' \rangle, c) = g$.
  - For every vertex $(s, g) \in V_2$, edge $\langle s, s' \rangle \in E$, and $c \in \mathbb{Z}$ for which the function $g' = \mathsf{update}(g, \langle s, s' \rangle, c)$ is in $\mathcal{W}_\tau$, we add to E' an edge with weight $g'(s, s')$ from (s, g) to (s', g'). The edge corresponds to Player 2 choosing both the successor s' of s and the weight of the edge $\langle s, s' \rangle$. As in the case above, if $g(s, s') \neq \bot$, then $g' = g$, in which case the only successor of (s, g) with S-component s' is (s', g).

We now relate G and $\mathsf{learn}(G)$. A *history* in G is a prefix $h \in (S \times \mathbb{Z})^* \cdot S$ of a play in G with the last pair contributing only the vertex element. A *history* in $\mathsf{learn}(G)$ is a prefix $h' \in V^* \cdot (S \times \mathcal{W}_\tau)$ of a play in $\mathsf{learn}(G)$ that ends in a vertex in $(S \times \mathcal{W}_\tau)$.

For a history $h = \langle s_0, c_0 \rangle, \langle s_1, c_1 \rangle, \ldots, \langle s_k, c_k \rangle, s_{k+1}$ in G, let $g_h \in \mathcal{W}_\tau$ be the learned weight function that corresponds to h. That is, g_h is defined for exactly all edges that are traversed in h, and it maps these edges to the weights revealed during h. Formally, for all $0 \leq i \leq k$, we have that $g_h(s_i, s_{i+1}) = c_i$. Since h is a prefix of a play, it is guaranteed that an edge that is traversed several times is assigned the same weight in all its traversals, thus g_h is well defined.

We define a relation $\approx$ between histories in G and learn(G). The definition of $\approx$ proceeds by induction on the length of the histories, with $s_0 \approx \langle s_0, g_0 \rangle$ serving as the base, described formally in the full version. For all histories h and h', and vertices s and $\langle s', g \rangle$, in G and learn(G), respectively, the definition maintains the following three invariants: $h \cdot s \approx h' \cdot \langle s', g \rangle$ implies $s = s'$, $g_{h \cdot s} = g$, and $\mathcal{E}_\Delta(h) = \mathcal{E}_\Delta(h')$. For plays $\rho \in (S \times \mathbb{Z})^\omega$ in G and $\rho' \in V^\omega$ in learn(G), we say that $\rho \approx \rho'$ if for every finite history h in ρ, there is a finite history h' in ρ' such that $h \approx h'$. By the invariant about the energy update, if $\rho \approx \rho'$, then ρ is winning for Player 1 iff ρ' is winning for Player 1.

Lemma 1. *Consider an EGWU G and the EG learn(G). Player 1 wins G iff he wins learn(G).*

Proof. Assume first that Player 1 wins G. Let $f_1 : (S \times \mathbb{Z})^* \cdot S_1 \to S$ be a winning strategy for Player 1 in G. Consider the strategy $f_1' : V^* \cdot V_1 \to V$ such that for every history $h' \cdot \langle s, g \rangle \in V^* \cdot V_1$, we have that $f_1'(h', \langle s, g \rangle) = \langle (s, f_1(h \cdot s)), g \rangle$, where h is the single history in G such that $h \approx h'$. That is, f_1' chooses the successor that f_1 chooses in the corresponding history. In the full version, we prove that f_1' is winning for Player 1 in learn(G). Essentially, it follows from the fact that every strategy f_2' for Player 2 in learn(G) induces a strategy $\langle w, f_2 \rangle$ for Player 2 in G such that outcome$(f_1', f_2') \approx$ outcome$(f_1, \langle w, f_2 \rangle)$.

Assume now that Player 1 wins learn(G). Let $f_1' : V_1 \to V$ be a memoryless winning strategy for Player 1 in learn(G). Since learn(G) is an EG, such a strategy exists [4,5]. Consider the strategy $f_1 : (S \times \mathbb{Z})^* \cdot S_1 \to S$ such that for every history $h \cdot s \in (S \times \mathbb{Z})^* \cdot S_1$, we have that $f_1(h \cdot s) = s'$, where s' is such that $f_1'(\langle s, g_{h \cdot s} \rangle) = \langle (s, s'), g_{h \cdot s} \rangle$. That is, f_1 chooses the successor that f_1' chooses when s is paired with the learned weight function that corresponds to $h \cdot s$. In the full version, we prove that f_1 is winning for Player 1 in G. Essentially, it follows from the fact that every strategy $\langle w, f_2 \rangle$ for Player 2 in G induces a strategy f_2' for Player 2 in learn(G) such that outcome$(f_1', f_2') \approx$ outcome$(f_1, \langle w, f_2 \rangle)$. □

3.2 Determinacy: Online and Offline Weight Functions

A two-player game is *determined* if for every instance G of the game, either Player 1 or Player 2 wins in G. Since energy objectives are closed sets, EGs are determined [16]. We show that this is not the case for EGWUs, and argue that undeterminacy is caused by the fact Player 2 chooses the weights in advance, rather than in an online manner. Formally, we show that a variant of EGWUs in which the weights are chosen online is determined.

Theorem 1. *EGWUs need not be determined. Undeterminacy holds already for 1-controlled and global EGWUs.*

Proof. Consider the EGWU $G_{undet} = \langle S_1, S_2, s_0, E, b, \tau \rangle$ described in Fig. 2. In addition to the estimated weights labeling the edges in the figure, we have that $\tau(E) = \langle 0, 0 \rangle$. Note that since $S_2 = \emptyset$, a strategy for Player 2 consists only of a weight function that respects τ.

In the full version, we prove that neither Player 1 nor Player 2 wins G_{undet}. □

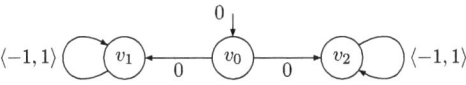

Fig. 2. The EGWU G_{undet}.

Remark 1. [**Online EGWUs**]. In an *online EGWU*, we let Player 2 choose, for each edge e, the weight $w(e)$ in the first traversal of e. Since a strategy of Player 1 is winning if it wins against all strategies of Player 2 (in particular these that happen to agree with some online strategy), then from the point of view of Player 1, usual (offline) and online EGWUs coincide.

As for Player 2, the ability to choose the weights in an online manner is helpful. For example, Player 2 has a winning strategy in the online variant of the EGWU G_{undet} described in Theorem 1. Indeed, after Player 1 chooses a loop, Player 2 can assign it a weight of -1. Moreover, the reasoning in the proof of Lemma 1 implies that Player 2 wins an online EGWU G iff he wins the EG learn(G). Thus, as EGs are determined, so are online EGWUs. □

4 Using Initial Energy for Learning

In this section we show that in some cases, incomplete information can be compensated by extra initial energy. Intuitively, the initial energy enables Player 1 to learn the weights, but in order for this to always succeed, the game should include no traps for Player 1.

Consider an EGWU $G = \langle S_1, S_2, s_0, E, b, \tau \rangle$. We say that Player 1 can *reset* G if, ignoring energy constraints, Player 1 has a strategy to reach s_0 from all vertices $s \in S$. We say that Player 1 *wins G with complete information* if for every weight function w that respects τ, Player 1 wins the EG G_w. Clearly, if Player 1 wins G, then Player 1 also wins G with full information. The other direction, however, is not true. For example, the undetermined EGWU G_{undet} presented in the proof of Theorem 1 is such that Player 1 wins G_{undet} with complete information, yet does not win G_{undet}.

It is not surprising that an extra initial energy enables Player 1 to learn the weight function in an EGWU he can reset. Below we analyze the exact extra energy needed and a strategy for Player 1 to use it.

Recall that l_G is the minimal sufficient energy to traverse a single edge in G when the weight function respects τ. If $l_G \leq 0$, then all edges have non-negative weights, and Player 1 wins G with an arbitrary strategy and with no extra initial energy. Otherwise, we have the following.

Theorem 2. *Consider an EGWU $G = \langle S_1, S_2, s_0, E, b, \tau \rangle$. If Player 1 can reset G and wins G with complete information, then there is $\Delta_G \leq 2 \cdot l_G \cdot |E|^2$ such that Player 1 wins in G with initial energy $b + \Delta_G$. The bound on Δ_G is tight, even for 1-controlled and global EGWUs.*

Proof. Assume that Player 1 can reset G and wins G with complete information. Let $w_1, w_2, \ldots, w_n$ be an order on the weight functions that respect τ. Since Player 1 wins G with complete information, then for every $1 \leq i \leq n$, there is a winning strategy f'_i for Player 1 in G_{w_i}. Since EGs are memoryless, we assume that f'_i is memoryless. Also, as Player 1 can reset G, then for every vertex $s \in S$, there is a memoryless strategy f_s for Player 1 to reach s_0. Note that since f_s is memoryless, s_0 is reached along a simple path (indeed, if Player 2 can force a cycle, he can prevent Player 1 from reaching s_0).

A winning strategy f_1 for Player 1 in G with initial energy $b + 2 \cdot l_G \cdot |E|^2$ then proceeds as follows: Let $i = 1$. (∗) Apply f'_i from s_0. If at some point an edge $\langle s, s' \rangle$ is traversed and its weight is not $w_i(s, s')$, then apply from s' the strategy $f_{s'}$ to reach s_0, increase i to the minimal index $j > i$ such that w_j agrees with the weights revealed so far, and return to (∗).

In the full version, we prove that f_1 is winning. Essentially, it follows from the fact that we are guaranteed to reach, within $|E|$ iterations, each consuming energy at most $2 \cdot l_G \cdot |E|$, an iteration i in which all edges traversed agree with the weight function w_i, and in which an initial energy of b suffices.

While the bound on Δ_G can be tightened for specific EGWUs, taking into account the bounds that τ defines for sets of edges and the structure of the game graph, in some cases an extra energy of $O(l_G \cdot |E|^2)$ is needed. Below we present a family of EGWUs that attains the bound. Given $n, l \geq 1$, let $c = \sum_{i=1}^{n} i$, and consider the EGWU $G_{n,l}$ described in Fig. 3. In addition to the definition of τ for single edges in the figure, we have that $\tau(E) = (l \cdot (c - n)) - (n - 1)$. Note that $l_{G_{n,l}} = l$ and that G is 1-controlled and global.

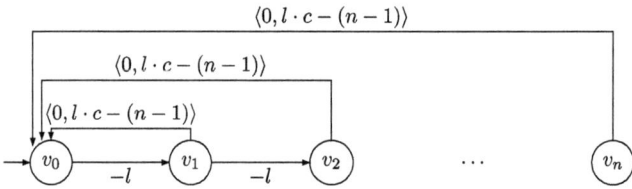

Fig. 3. The EGWU $G_{n,l}$.

In the full version, we prove that for every weight function w that respects τ, there is $1 \leq i \leq n$ such that $w(v_i, v_0) \geq l \cdot i$, that the latter implies that Player 1 wins G with complete information with the initial energy of $l \cdot n$. On the other hand, when Player 1 has uncertainty about the weights, then for every strategy f_1 of Player 1, there is a weight strategy w_{f_1} for Player 2 such that Player 1 runs out of energy in outcome(f_1, w_{f_1}) unless his initial energy is at least $l \cdot c$. Thus, $\Delta_G = l \cdot (c - n)$, which is $O(l \cdot n^2)$. □

The key to the learning performed in the proof of Theorem 2 is the ability of Player 1 to avoid cycles that may be negative. Below we formalize this intuition further, and show that it is tight. Consider an EGWU $G = \langle S_1, S_2, s_0, E, b, \tau \rangle$. We say that G is *permissive* if $\tau(A) \geq 0$, for every $A \subseteq E$ such that there is path in G that visits exactly all edges in A, and these are the only sets for which τ is defined. In particular, τ is not pervasive. Thus, as long as Player 1 avoids traversing the same edge twice, his energy level is guaranteed to be non-negative. As we state below (see proof in the full version), not only the lack of traps enables Player 1 to maintain his energy non-negative, traps enable Player 2 to win.

Theorem 3. *Permissive EGWUs are determined. Player 1 wins a permissive EGWU iff he has a strategy to visit its initial vertex infinitely often.*

5 Memory Requirements in EGWU

Traditional EGs are memoryless: a player that has a winning strategy also has one that does not depend on the history of the play so far [4,5]. As demonstrated in Example 1, this is not the case for EGWUs. Indeed, the described winning strategy f_1 of Player 1 may direct the token to different successors in different visits to v_0, according to the learned weight of $\langle v_0, v_0 \rangle$, and it is not hard to see that a strategy that is independent of the learned weight does not win. In this section we study the memory requirements of winning strategies in EGWUs.

Consider an EGWU $G = \langle S_1, S_2, s_0, E, b, \tau \rangle$. A finite-memory structure for G is $\mathcal{M} = \langle M, m_0, \delta \rangle$, where M is a finite set of memory states, $m_0 \in M$ is an initial memory state, and $\delta : M \times (E \times \mathbb{Z}) \to M$ is a memory-update function. A memory structure is similar to an automaton with alphabet $E \times \mathbb{Z}$ that is executed in parallel to the game: it starts at m_0 and reads the edges traversed by the token, together with their learned weight: when the current memory state is m and the token traverses an edge e and the energy is updated by c, the new memory state is $\delta(m, \langle e, c \rangle)$.

A strategy for Player j that relies on $\mathcal{M}$ replaces the dependency on the history of the play by dependency on the current memory state of $\mathcal{M}$. In addition, the strategy depends on the current vertex of the game. Formally, a strategy for Player j is a function $f_j : M \times S_j \to S$. Then, when the current memory state is m and the token is in vertex $s \in S_j$, Player j moves the token to $s' = f_j(m, s)$. The strategy f_j is *memoryless* if it relies on a memory structure with a single memory state. A memoryless strategy for Player j is thus given by $f_j : S_j \to S$.

The outcome of strategies that rely on finite memory structures can be defined via the induced strategies that are defined with respect to histories.

Here, we give a direct definition for the case the strategy of Player 2 is memoryless. Let $\pi = \langle f_1, \langle w, f_2 \rangle \rangle$ be a profile of strategies for Player 1 and Player 2, where f_1 relies on a memory structure $\mathcal{M} = \langle M, m_0, \delta \rangle$, thus $f_1 : M \times S_1 \to S$, and $f_2 : S_2 \to S$ is memoryless. Then, outcome(π) is the infinite play $\rho = s_0, w(s_0, s_1), s_1, w(s_1, s_2), s_2, \ldots \in S^\omega$ such that there is a sequences $\eta = m_0, m_1, m_2, \ldots \in M^\omega$ such that for all $i \geq 0$, if $s_i \in S_1$, then $s_{i+1} = f_1(m_i, s_i)$, and if $s_i \in S_2$, then $s_{i+1} = f_2(s_i)$. Also, $m_{i+1} = \delta(m_i, \langle (s_i, s_{i+1}), w(s_i, s_{i+1}) \rangle)$.

We can now analyse the memory required for the players in en EGWU. We start with Player 2, where things are easy (see proof in the full version).

Lemma 2. *Player 2 wins an EGWU G iff there is a weight function w that respects τ such that Player 2 wins G_w.*

Since for EGs, memoryless strategies are sufficient, Lemma 2 implies the following (see proof in the full version).

Theorem 4. *Player 2 wins an EGWU iff he has a memoryless winning strategy.*

We continue to Player 1, where things are more involved.

Theorem 5. *Player 1 wins an EGWU G iff he has a winning strategy with a memory of size exponential in G. The bound is tight and is required already in 1-controlled and flat EGWUs.*

Proof. We start with the upper bound. Consider an EGWU G and assume Player 1 wins G. By Lemma 1, he wins the EG learn(G), and can do so with a memoryless strategy. We show how a memoryless winning strategy for Player 1 in learn(G) induces a winning strategy for Player 1 in G that relies on a memory structure with state space $\mathcal{W}_\tau$. Since $|\mathcal{W}_\tau|$ is exponential in $|G|$, we are done.

Let $f_1' : V_1 \to V$ be a memoryless winning strategy for Player 1 in learn(G). Consider the memory structure $\mathcal{M} = \langle \mathcal{W}_\tau, g_0, \delta \rangle$, where for all $g \in \mathcal{W}_\tau$, $e \in E$, and $z \in \mathbb{Z}$, we define $\delta(g, \langle e, z \rangle) = \text{update}(g, e, z)$. Now, consider the finite-memory strategy $f_1'' : \mathcal{W}_\tau \times S_1 \to S$ that relies on $\mathcal{M}$ and is defined, for every $g \in \mathcal{W}_\tau$ and $s \in S_1$, by $f_1''(g, s) = s'$, where the vertex $s' \in S$ is such that $f_1'(\langle s, g \rangle) = (\langle s, s' \rangle, g)$. In the full version, we prove that f_1'' is winning in G.

We proceed to the lower bound and describe a family of EGWUs $G_1, G_2, \ldots$ such that for all $n \geq 1$, the game G_n is of size $O(n)$, all whose vertices are controlled by Player 1, it has a flat estimated weight function, Player 1 wins in G_n, yet needs a memory with at least 2^n memory states in order to win.

The EGWU $G_n = \langle S_1, S_2, v_0, E, n, \tau \rangle$ is described in Fig. 4. In addition to the weight estimation of the edges in the figure, we have, for every $0 \leq i \leq n-1$, that $\tau(\{\langle v_i, a_i \rangle, \langle v_i, b_i \rangle\}) = \langle -1, 0 \rangle$. Clearly, τ is flat. For a weight function $w : E \to \mathbb{Z}$ and $0 \leq i \leq n-1$, we say that w *blocks* a_i if $w(v_i, a_i) = -1$, and similarly for b_i. By the definition of τ, every weight function w that respects τ blocks at most one of a_i or b_i, and so there is an *open cycle* $C_w \subseteq E$, namely a cycle from v_0 back to itself all whose edges have weight 0.

A winning strategy for Player 1 that is based on this observation first "scans" G_n in order to find an open cycle, and then traverses this cycle forever. Such a

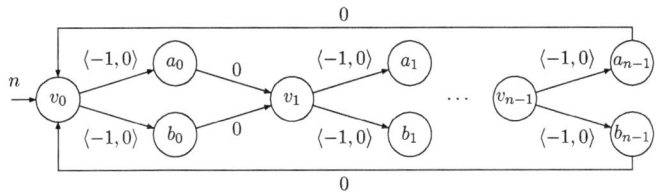

Fig. 4. The game graph G_n.

strategy has to remember for each $0 \leq i \leq n-1$, whether a_i is blocked, and thus requires space 2^n. In the full version, we describe the strategy formally, show that it is indeed winning, and that every winning strategy for Player 1 in G_n requires memory of size at least 2^n. □

6 Deciding Whether Player 1 Wins an EGWU

Let $G = \langle S_1, S_2, s_0, E, b, \tau \rangle$ be an EGWU. As proved in Lemma 1, Player 1 wins G iff he wins the EG learn(G). Since the size of learn(G) is exponential in $|G|$ and EGs can be decided in polynomial time, this gives us an exponential upper bound for the problem of deciding whether Player 1 wins G. In this section, we show that we can do better and the problem of deciding whether Player 1 wins an EGWU is PSPACE-complete.

Our upper bound is based on the connection between G and learn(G). We first bound the diameter of learn(G) and then claim that the diameter is the computational bottleneck in the complexity of deciding EGs.

Lemma 3. *Consider an EGWU $G = \langle S_1, S_2, s_0, E, b, \tau \rangle$. The diameter of learn($G$) is at most $2 \cdot |S| \cdot |E|$.*

Proof. Consider a simple path $p = v_0, v_1, \ldots v_n$ in learn(G), and let $p' = \langle s_0, g_0 \rangle$, $\langle s_1, g_1 \rangle, \ldots, \langle s_k, g_k \rangle \in (S \times \mathcal{W}_\tau)^*$ be the sequence obtained from p by removing vertices in $E_1 \times \mathcal{W}_\tau$. By the definition of the transitions of learn(G), for all $i \geq 1$ we have that $g_{i+1} = \mathsf{update}(g_i, e, c)$ for some $e \in E$ and $c \in \mathbb{Z}$. Thus, $g_i \preceq g_{i+1}$. Hence, for every edge $e \in E$, once a weight for e is defined in a learned function that appears in p', it is fixed in all the successive learned functions. Formally, for every $i \geq 0$, if $g_i(e) \in \mathbb{Z}$, then $g_j(e) = g_i(e)$ for all $j \geq i$. Hence, at most $|E|$ different learned functions in $\mathcal{W}_\tau$ participate in p', and so $|p'| \leq |S| \cdot |E|$. Since vertices in $E_1 \times \mathcal{W}_\tau$ cannot be successive in p, it must be that $|p| \leq 2 \cdot |p'|$, and we are done. □

Theorem 6. *Let G be an EG of size exponential in n and diameter polynomial in n. Then, G can be decided in space polynomial in n.*

Proof. We describe an alternating Turing machine (ATM, see a definition in the full version) that decides G in time polynomial in n. Since alternating polynomial time can be simulated in polynomial space [6], the bound follows.

Let $G = \langle S_1, S_2, s_0, E, b, w \rangle$. A *configuration* of G is a pair $\langle s, k \rangle \in (S \times \mathbb{N})^*$, describing a vertex in the game and the (non-negative) energy level of Player 1. The initial configuration is $\langle s_0, b \rangle$. Let d be the diameter of G. Recall that Player 1 wins G iff he has a strategy that guarantees that every outcome ρ satisfies $\mathcal{E}(\rho, n) \geq 0$, for all $n \geq 0$. Since Player 1 wins G iff he has a memoryless strategy that is winning in G, we can assume that for every outcome ρ of a winning strategy of Player 1, every cycle in ρ has a non-negative weight. Indeed, if a negative cycle is formed, Player 2 can force looping in it forever, which makes Player 1 lose.

We describe an ATM $\mathcal{T}$ that decides whether Player 1 wins G. The idea is that $\mathcal{T}$ simulates the game for d rounds. It does so by maintaining on its tape the number i of rounds taken so far, and the sequence $\langle s_0, k_0 \rangle \cdot \langle s_1, k_1 \rangle \cdot \ldots \langle s_i, k_i \rangle \in (S \times \mathbb{N})^*$ of configurations of the game so far.

As long as $i < d$, the ATM $\mathcal{T}$ proceeds as follows. Let $\langle s, k \rangle$ be the last configuration on the tape. If $s \in S_1$, the ATM $\mathcal{T}$ is in an existential configuration: it guesses a successor s' of s in G, and adds the configuration $\langle s', k' \rangle$ to the tape, with $k' = k + w(s, s')$. Then, $\mathcal{T}$ checks whether $k' < 0$, and if so, it rejects. Otherwise, it checks for every configuration $\langle s'', k'' \rangle$ on the tape whether $s' = s''$. If so, it accepts if $k' \geq k''$, and rejects otherwise. If s' has not been visited before, it increases i to $i+1$ and moves to the next simulation step. If $s \in S_2$, the ATM proceeds similarly, except that now it is in a universal configuration, and thus the check is performed for every successor s' of s in G.

Since the diameter of G is d, all the computations of $\mathcal{T}$ terminate before i reaches d. Also, the length of the sequence of configurations that need to be checked is bounded by d, and since G is of size exponential in n, the description of each configuration is of polynomial length.

Since $\mathcal{T}$ accepts G iff Player 1 has a strategy that induces only non-negative cycles, while maintaining the energy above 0, it accepts G iff Player 1 wins. □

Theorem 7. *Deciding whether Player 1 wins a given EGWU is PSPACE-complete. PSPACE hardness holds already for flat EGWUs.*

Proof. We start with the upper bound. By Lemmas 1 and 3, deciding Player 1 wins a given EGWU G can be reduced to deciding an EG with of size exponential in $|G|$ and diameter polynomial in $|G|$. By Theorem 6, the latter can be decided in PSPACE.

For the lower bound, we describe a reduction from TQBF – the problem of determining the truth of quantified Boolean formulas. Let $X = \{x_1, \ldots, x_n\}$ and $Y = \{y_1, \ldots, y_n\}$ be sets of Boolean variables, and let φ be a Boolean propositional formula over the variables in $X \cup Y$. Also, let $\overline{X} = \{\overline{x_1}, \ldots, \overline{x_n}\}$, $\overline{Y} = \{\overline{y_1}, \ldots, \overline{y_n}\}$, and $L = X \cup \overline{X} \cup Y \cup \overline{Y}$. We assume that φ is in 3CNF. That is, $\varphi = C_1 \wedge C_2 \wedge \ldots \wedge C_m$, where for all $1 \leq i \leq m$, it holds that $C_i = l_i^1 \vee l_i^2 \vee l_i^3$ for $l_i^1, l_i^2, l_i^3 \in L$. Finally, let $\theta = \exists x_1 \forall y_1 \exists x_2 \forall y_2 \ldots \exists x_n \forall y_n \varphi$. By [20], deciding whether θ is valid is PSPACE-hard.

Given θ, we define an EGWU $\mathcal{G}_\theta$ such that θ is valid iff Player 1 wins $\mathcal{G}_\theta$. The idea of the reduction is as follows. A play in $\mathcal{G}_\theta$ starts in an *assignment part*, where the players choose assignment to the variables: Player 1 to the variables in X, and Player 2 to the variables in Y. Then, the play moves to a *check part*, where Player 2 challenges the assignment induced form the outcome in the assignment part: Player 2 chooses a clause C_i, for $1 \leq i \leq m$, and Player 1 wins if it can respond with a literal in $\{l_i^1, l_i^2, l_i^3\}$ that was assigned T in the assignment part. The challenging part in the reduction is to define the estimated weight function such that Player 1 can indeed respond only with literals that were assigned T.

We now explain the reduction in detail. In Fig. 5, we describe the assignment part of $\mathcal{G}_\theta$. In the figures for both parts, black (undashed) edges are known to have weight 0 and dashed edges e have $\tau(e) = \langle -1, 0 \rangle$, and thus can be assigned either -1 or 0. Additional constraints by τ are defined below.

Note that a strategy for Player 1 and a token strategy for Player 2 induce an assignment to the variables in $X \cup Y$: traversing the edge $\langle a_i, a_i^+ \rangle$ (respectively, $\langle a_i, a_i^- \rangle$) corresponds to assigning T (respectively, F) to the variable x_i, and similarly for the edges leaving the vertex b_i and the variable y_i.

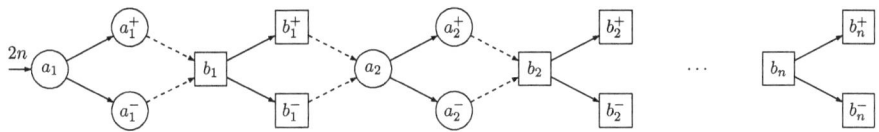

Fig. 5. The assignment part of $\mathcal{G}_\theta$.

Note that since the initial energy is $2 \cdot n$ and no matter how the players proceed the token traverses $2 \cdot n$ dashed edges, namely ones that can get weight -1, then for every strategy of Player 1, there is a strategy of Player 2 such that the energy level of Player 1 after the play completes the assignment part is 0.

In Fig. 6, we describe the check part of $\mathcal{G}_\theta$. The figure corresponds to the case $C_1 = x_1 \vee \overline{y_1} \vee \overline{x_2}$, $C_2 = \overline{x_1} \vee y_1 \vee \overline{x_2}$, and $C_m = \overline{y_1} \vee x_2 \vee \overline{y_n}$. Black edges are known with weight 0, while other edges are labeled with $\langle -1, 0 \rangle$. Note that the vertices b_n^+ and b_n^- appear in both figures, thus a play enters the check part immediately after the players fix an assignment to the variables.

In the check part, Player 2 challenges this assignment by choosing a clause C_i, for $1 \leq i \leq m$. He does so by moving the token to the *clause vertex* c_i. Then, Player 1 responds by moving the token to a *literal vertex* s_l, for a literal l that appears in C_i. From s_l, the token continues to the sink, where it can loop for free. The edge from s_l to the sink may have weight -1, and so, keeping in mind that Player 1 may have already spent his initial energy in the check part, his goal is to choose a literal l for which a weight function that respects τ cannot assign -1 to the edge $\langle s_l, \text{sink} \rangle$.

The definition of τ guarantees that Player 1 can do so iff θ is valid: For each literal $l \in L$, let E_l be the following set of two edges: the edge that is

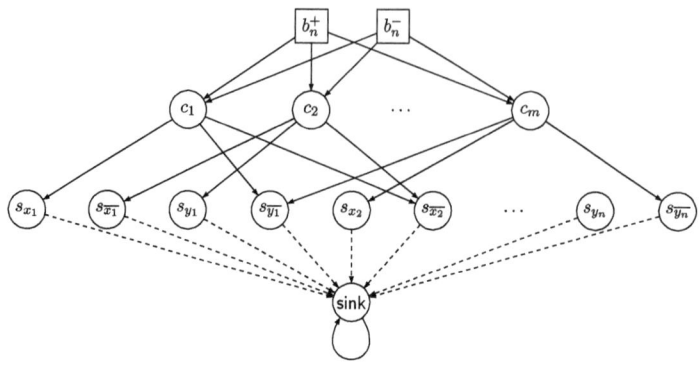

Fig. 6. The check part of G_θ.

traversed when l is assigned T in the assignment part, and the edge from s_l to the sink in the check part. For example, $E_{x_1} = \{\langle a_1, a_1^+\rangle, \langle s_{x_1}, \mathsf{sink}\rangle\}$ and $E_{\overline{y_2}} = \{\langle b_2, b_2^-\rangle, \langle s_{\overline{y_2}}, \mathsf{sink}\rangle\}$. By adding the requirement $\tau(E_l) = \langle -1, 0\rangle$, it is guaranteed that the weight of at least one of the edges is 0. Intuitively, these requirements imply that Player 1 can traverse the edge from s_l to the sink for free iff Player 1 has already spent energy on assigning T to l in the check part, which is possible iff θ is valid. Note that G_θ is flat.

In the full version, we prove that θ is valid iff Player 1 wins G_θ. □

In the *unknown initial-energy* problem we ask, given an EGWU $G = \langle S_1, S_2, s_0, E, b', \tau\rangle$, whether there is an initial energy b such that Player 1 wins in $G_b = \langle S_1, S_2, s_0, E, b, \tau\rangle$. Thus, rather than checking whether Player 1 wins an EGWU with a given initial energy, we ask for the existence of a finite initial energy with which Player 1 can win, and we seek to find a minimal such initial energy.

By Lemma 1, Player 1 wins an EGWU G iff he wins the EG $\mathsf{learn}(G)$. Moreover, the proof shows that winning G and $\mathsf{learn}(G)$ can be done with the same initial energy. Thus, solving the unknown initial-energy problem for G can be reduced to solving it for $\mathsf{learn}(G)$. By [5], the minimal energy required for winning an EG G' is at most $-\sum_{e \in E'} \min\{0, w(e)\}$, where E' and w are the edges and weight function of G'. This gives us a bound polynomial in the size of $\mathsf{learn}(G)$, which is exponential in $|G|$. As we shall see below, a tighter analysis leads to a bound that is only polynomial in $|G|$. Essentially (see full proof in the full version), the bound follows from the fact winning strategies of Player 1 avoid negative cycles. Thus, the important parameter is not the size of $\mathsf{learn}(G)$ but its diameter.

Lemma 4. *Consider an EGWU $G = \langle S_1, S_2, s_0, E, b', \tau\rangle$. There is $b \in \mathbb{N}$ such that Player 1 wins G_b iff Player 1 wins $G_{\hat{b}}$, for $\hat{b} = 2 \cdot |S| \cdot |E| \cdot l_G$. The bound on $\hat{b}$ is tight.*

By Lemma 4, we can solve the unknown initial-energy problem for an EGWU G by checking whether Player 1 wins $G_{\hat{b}}$, for $\hat{b} = 2 \cdot |S| \cdot |E| \cdot l_G$. Moreover, a minimal sufficient initial energy can be searched, and so both the decision and optimization problems can be solved in PSPACE.

7 Deciding Whether Player 2 Wins an EGWU

Theorem 8. *Deciding whether Player 2 wins a given EGWU is NP-complete. Hardness in NP holds already for 1-controlled and global EGWUs.*

Proof. For the upper bound, consider a non-deterministic Turing machine that given an EGWU $G = \langle S_1, S_2, s_0, E, b, \tau \rangle$, guesses a weight function w that respects τ, and accepts iff Player 2 has a winning strategy in G_w. By Lemma 2, this machine decides whether Player 2 wins G. Since traditional energy games can be decided in polynomial time when weights are given in unary [5], we are done.

For the lower bound, we describe a reduction from the Vertex-Cover problem. Given an undirected graph $G = \langle V, E \rangle$ and $k \in \mathbb{N}$, we construct an EGWU G' such that G has a vertex cover of size at most k iff Player 2 wins G'. The reduction is illustrated in Fig. 7. In the figure, dashed edges e have $\tau(e) = \langle -1, 0 \rangle$ and black edges are known with weight 0. An additional vertex s_0 has black edges to all vertices of the form v_{in}, which we omit from clarity.

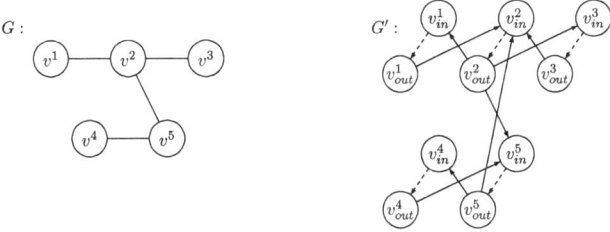

Fig. 7. The graph G has a vertex cover of size k iff Player 2 wins G'.

We define $G' = \langle S_1, \varnothing, s_0, E, 0, \tau \rangle$ as follows. First, $S_1 = \{v_{in}, v_{out} : v \in V\} \cup \{s_0\}$. Thus, each vertex in G has two copies in S_1: an entry copy and an exit copy. The exit copy is going to be reachable from the entry copy via an *internal edge* that may have a negative weight -1. Also, each edge $\langle v, u \rangle$ in G induces a cycle that involves the two internal edges of v and u, and is reachable from the initial vertex s_0. The estimated weight function τ restricts Player 2 to allocate a negative weight only to k internal edges. Since all cycles are reachable from s_0, Player 2 can prevent all the strategies of Player 1 from finding a non-negative cycle iff for all edges $\langle v, u \rangle$ in G, at least one of the internal edges of v and u have weight -1, which is possible iff G has a vertex cover of size k.

Formally, $E' = E_{init} \cup E_{internal} \cup E_{orig}$, where $E_{init} = \{\langle s_0, v_{in}\rangle : v \in V\}$ connects s_0 to all the entry copies, $E_{internal} = \{\langle v_{in}, v_{out}\rangle : v \in V\}$ connects each entry copy to the corresponding exit copy, and $E_{orig} = \{\langle v_{out}, u_{in}\rangle : \{v, u\} \in E\}$ causes each edge $\langle v, u\rangle \in E$ to induce a cycle $(v_{in}, v_{out}, u_{in}, u_{out})$ in G'.

The function τ is such that for all $e \in E_{internal}$, we have that $\tau(e) = \langle -1, 0\rangle$. All other edges e have $\tau(e) = 0$. Finally, $\tau(E) = \langle -k, 0\rangle$. Note that G' is global.

In the full version, we prove that G has a vertex cover of size at most k iff Player 2 wins G'. Essentially, a vertex cover of size at most k induces a weight function w that assigns -1 to at least one internal edge in every pair of successive internal edges, causing all plays to run out of energy. On the other hand, if no vertex cover of size at most k exists, then every strategy for Player 2, namely a weight function w that respects τ, leaves in G' at least one cycle of weight 0. Then, a play that reaches the cycle and loops in it forever is winning for Player 1, and so Player 1 has a strategy that wins against w. □

Recall the unknown initial-energy problem, where we ask whether Player 1 can win an EGWU with some initial value. In the dual problem we ask, given $G = \langle S_1, S_2, s_0, E, b', \tau\rangle$, whether there is a strategy for Player 2 that is winning in G_b for all $b \in \mathbb{N}$. It is not hard to see that such a strategy exists iff there is a weight function w that respects τ and a token strategy f_2 that forces a cycle with a negative weight in the EG G_w, where we can restrict attention to memoryless token strategies. Given w and a memoryless strategy f_2 in G_w, consider the weighted graph $G_w^{f_2} = \langle S, E_{f_2}, w\rangle$ obtained by applying $\langle w, f_2\rangle$ to G. That is, edges are labeled according to w, and each vertex $s \in S_2$ has a single successor, which is $f_2(s)$. The paths in $G_w^{f_2}$ correspond to all the possible outcomes of a play in G when Player 2 uses the strategy $\langle w, f_2\rangle$. Thus, the latter is a solution to the dual unknown initial-energy problem iff all cycles in $G_w^{f_2}$ are negative. Hence, the problem can be solved in NP by guessing w and f_2 and then checking, in polynomial time, whether $G_w^{f_2}$ has a non-negative cycle. Since the EGWU G' described in the proof of Theorem 8 is such that Player 1 does not win G' iff he does not win G'_b for all $b \in \mathbb{N}$, the reduction from the vertex-cover problem applies also here, and so the dual problem is NP-complete.

8 Discussion

We introduced and studied a new type of uncertainty in qualitative games: energy games with uncertainty about weights. As elaborated in Sect. 1, EGWU can model a variety of applications in which the exact cost of actions is only estimated. Unlike uncertainty about location, information about weights is fixed in an offline manner and is revealed during the play. This makes weight uncertainty very different from location uncertainty, and we study their theoretical properties and the complexity of decision problems for EGWU.

Possible directions for future research include conceptual as well as technical extensions. Conceptual extensions involve variants of the model, and require further research. Such variants include, for example, uncertainty about both location and weights, bounds on the memory of the system (and hence, bound on the learning that can be performed), a stochastic setting and randomized strategies (which also enable a more informative competitive analysis of the price of uncertainty), and a setting with energy constraints, possibly with uncertainty, also for the environment.

On the more technical side, an interesting extension is to EGWU with *parity* winning conditions. Each parity condition α defines a subset of S^ω, namely the set of plays that satisfy α. In order to win an EG augmented with a parity condition α, Player 1 has to generate an outcome that satisfies α and does not run out of energy. Clearly, all our negative results for EGWUs apply also to parity EGWUs. Also, it is not hard to see that our construction of learn(G) from G applies also to parity EGWUs, with $\alpha' = \alpha \times \mathcal{W}_\tau$. Thus, Player 1 wins a parity-EGWU G iff he wins the parity-EG learn(G). Since the learning performed in the proof of Theorem 2 is along a finite prefix, it applies also to parity EGWUs. As for decision problems, deciding whether Player 1 wins a parity-EGWU G can be reduced to deciding the parity EG learn(G), and deciding whether Player 2 wins can be reduced to solving the parity-EG G_w for a guessed weight function w. Beyond the complexity of deciding parity-EGs ([7] solved the unknown initial-energy variant), it may well be that a naive application of the above reductions is not optimal. Indeed, for EGWUs we were able to improve it, for example by an analysis that based on the diameter of learn(G) rather than it size. Thus, the exact complexity of solving parity-EGWUs requires further research.

References

1. Amram, G., Maoz, S., Pistiner, O., Ringert, J.O.: Efficient algorithms for omega-regular energy games. In: Huisman, M., Păsăreanu, C., Zhan, N. (eds.) FM 2021. LNCS, vol. 13047, pp. 163–181. Springer, Cham (2021). https://doi.org/10.1007/978-3-030-90870-6_9
2. Berwanger, D., Chatterjee, K., De Wulf, M., Doyen, L., Henzinger, T.A.: Strategy construction for parity games with imperfect information. Inf. Comput. **208**(10), 1206–1220 (2010)
3. Bloem, R., Chatterjee, K., Jobstmann, B.: Graph games and reactive synthesis. In: Handbook of Model Checking, pp. 921–962. Springer, Cham (2018). https://doi.org/10.1007/978-3-319-10575-8_27
4. Bouyer, P., Fahrenberg, U., Larsen, K.G., Markey, N., Srba, J.: Infinite runs in weighted timed automata with energy constraints. In: Cassez, F., Jard, C. (eds.) FORMATS 2008. LNCS, vol. 5215, pp. 33–47. Springer, Heidelberg (2008). https://doi.org/10.1007/978-3-540-85778-5_4
5. Chakrabarti, A., Alfaro, L., Henzinger, T.A., Stoelinga, M.: Resource interfaces. In: Alur, R., Lee, I. (eds.) EMSOFT 2003. LNCS, vol. 2855, pp. 117–133. Springer, Heidelberg (2003). https://doi.org/10.1007/978-3-540-45212-6_9
6. Chandra, A.K., Kozen, D.C., Stockmeyer, L.J.: Alternation. J. Associat. Comput. Mach. **28**(1), 114–133 (1981)
7. Chatterjee, K., Doyen, L.: Energy parity games. Theoret. Comput. Sci. **458**, 49–60 (2012)

8. Chatterjee, K., Doyen, L., Henzinger, T.A., Raskin, J.-F.: Algorithms for omega-regular games with imperfect information. In: Ésik, Z. (ed.) CSL 2006. LNCS, vol. 4207, pp. 287–302. Springer, Heidelberg (2006). https://doi.org/10.1007/11874683_19
9. Chatterjee, K., Doyen, L., Henzinger, T.A., Raskin, J-F.: Generalized mean-payoff and energy games. In: Proceedings of 30th Conference on Foundations of Software Technology and Theoretical Computer Science, volume 8 of LIPIcs, pp. 505–516. Schloss Dagstuhl - Leibniz-Zentrum für Informatik (2010)
10. Chatterjee, K., Goharshady, A.K., Velner, Y.: Quantitative analysis of smart contracts. In: Ahmed, A. (ed.) ESOP 2018. LNCS, vol. 10801, pp. 739–767. Springer, Cham (2018). https://doi.org/10.1007/978-3-319-89884-1_26
11. Degorre, A., Doyen, L., Gentilini, R., Raskin, J., Torunczyk, S.: Energy and mean-payoff games with imperfect information. In: Proceedings of 19th Annual Conference of the European Association for Computer Science Logic, pp. 260–274 (2010)
12. Doyen, L., Raskin, J-F.: Games with imperfect information: theory and algorithms. Lectures in Game Theory for Computer Scientists, vol. 10 (2011)
13. Henzinger, T.A.: From Boolean to quantitative notions of correctness. In: Proceedings of 37th ACM Symp. on Principles of Programming Languages, pp. 157–158 (2010)
14. Kupferman, O., Shenwald, N.: Games with trading of control. In: Proceedings of 34th International Conference on Concurrency Theory, vol. 279 of Leibniz International Proceedings in Informatics (LIPIcs), pp. 19:1–19:17. Schloss Dagstuhl – Leibniz-Zentrum für Informatik (2023)
15. Kupferman, O., Vardi, M.Y.: Synthesis with incomplete information. In: Advances in Temporal Logic, pp. 109–127. Kluwer Academic Publishers (2000)
16. Martin, D.A.: Borel determinacy. Ann. Math. **65**, 363–371 (1975)
17. Pérez, G.A.: The fixed initial credit problem for partial-observation energy games is ack-complete. Inf. Process. Lett. **118**, 91–99 (2017)
18. Pnueli, A., Rosner, R.: On the synthesis of a reactive module. In: Proceedings of 16th ACM Symposium on Principles of Programming Languages, pp. 179–190 (1989)
19. Reif, J.H.: The complexity of two-player games of incomplete information. J. Comput. Syst. Sci. **29**, 274–301 (1984)
20. Stockmeyer, L.J., Meyer, A.R.: Word problems requiring exponential time. In: Proceedings of the 5th ACM Symp. on Theory of Computing, pp. 1–9 (1973)

Widest Path Games and Maximality Inheritance in Bounded Value Iteration for Stochastic Games

Kittiphon Phalakarn[1(✉)], Yun Chen Tsai[1,2], and Ichiro Hasuo[1,2,3]

[1] National Institute of Informatics, Tokyo, Japan
{kphalakarn,yctsai,hasuo}@nii.ac.jp
[2] SOKENDAI (The Graduate University for Advanced Studies), Kanagawa, Japan
[3] Imiron Co., Ltd., Tokyo, Japan

Abstract. For model checking stochastic games (SGs), *bounded value iteration (BVI)* algorithms have gained attention as efficient approximate methods with rigorous precision guarantees. However, BVI may not terminate or converge when the target SG contains end components. Most existing approaches address this issue by explicitly detecting and processing end components—a process that is often computationally expensive. An exception is the *widest path-based BVI* approach previously studied by Phalakarn et al., which we refer to as *1WP-BVI*. The method performs particularly well in the presence of numerous end components. Nonetheless, its theoretical foundations remain somewhat ad hoc. In this paper, we identify and formalize the core principles underlying the widest path-based BVI approach by (i) presenting *2WP-BVI*, a clean BVI algorithm based on *(2-player) widest path games*, and (ii) proving its correctness using what we call the *maximality inheritance principle*—a proof principle previously employed in a well-known result in probabilistic model checking. Our experimental results demonstrate the practical relevance and potential of our proposed 2WP-BVI algorithm.

Keywords: stochastic game · probabilistic model checking · bounded value iteration · fixed point

1 Introduction

Stochastic Games. Stochastic games (SGs) are two-player games played on probabilistic transition systems (also called 2.5-player games). On each player's turn, the player chooses an *action* available in the current state, aiming to achieve their *objectives*. The chosen action induces a transition to a successor state, determined by a predefined probabilistic distribution.

When considering the *reachability objective*, the two main players are Maximizer (denoted by △) and Minimizer (denoted by ▽). The Maximizer's goal is to maximize the probability of reaching a designated target set from the current state, while the Minimizer's objective is to minimize this probability.

Stochastic games have been studied across various areas of computer science. On the theoretical side, several problems—such as solving games with parity and mean-payoff objectives—have been reduced to SGs [1,10]. While the problem of solving SGs under the reachability objective remains without a known polynomial-time algorithm, its complexity class is known to be **UP ∩ coUP** [22].

On the practical side, SGs are used to model and analyze control systems under probabilistic uncertainties. These include cyber-physical systems, networked systems, probabilistic programs, and applications in computer security [36].

Bounded Value Iteration. A central goal in the study of SGs is to compute the *optimal* reachability probability—that is, the probability achieved when both Maximizer and Minimizer always take optimal actions. Several techniques exist for this purpose, including quadratic programming (QP), strategy iteration (SI), and value iteration (VI). In practice, when approximate results are acceptable, VI is often preferred due to its performance [19].

VI follows a simple fixed-point principle, i.e., Kleene's theorem (Theorem 2.7). In brief, VI starts with a function that assigns zero to all states and repeatedly applies the *(reachability) Bellman operator* (Definition 2.10). This produces a sequence of functions—called the *under-approximation sequence*—that converges to the (optimal) reachability probability from below.

However, a drawback of standard VI is that it offers no indication of how close the approximation is to the true value [18], and therefore provides no guarantee of precision. To address this, *bounded* VI (BVI) has been introduced, where an *over-approximation sequence* is constructed alongside the under-approximation. When the two sequences converge within 2ε, their average differs from the true value by at most ε.

Several BVI approaches have been proposed (see related work in §6). The main challenge, however, is that the two sequences may fail to converge due to a theoretical gap between the least and greatest fixed points of the Bellman operator. To ensure convergence, it is often necessary to enforce uniqueness of the fixed point—typically by handling *end components*, i.e., sets of states where players can remain indefinitely.

The Previous Widest Path Approach 1WP-BVI: via MDPs. We are interested in the *widest path-based BVI approach* proposed in [33] (referred to in this paper as *1WP-BVI*), which offers an alternative means of enforcing fixed-point uniqueness. This approach constructs the over-approximation sequence by computing the *widest path width* of a certain weighted directed graph derived from the SG. Notably, it does not rely on end-component analysis—a particularly significant advantage in the context of SGs (as opposed to Markov decision processes (MDPs)), since end components in SGs cannot be identified solely through graph-based analysis. Indeed, the algorithm demonstrates superior performance, especially in SGs with many end components [33].

However, both the algorithm and the correctness proof of 1WP-BVI are rather intricate. This is somewhat unsatisfying, especially given that VI is based on a simple fixed-point principle. As our goal is to establish another simple fixed-point property—i.e., uniqueness—it is natural to seek a corresponding mathematical principle that clearly explains why the widest path-based BVI works.

Moreover, although not explicitly stated, 1WP-BVI is primarily designed for MDPs rather than SGs. For SGs, the approach requires an additional mechanism referred to as *player reduction* (§5.2), which depends on the outcome of the under-approximation sequence. This dependency makes the over-approximation sequence non-standalone and contributes to the complication of the correctness proof. Due to the use of player reduction in [33], which reduces the number of players from two to *one*, we refer to their algorithm as 1WP-BVI (with "1").

Identifying the Principle Behind Widest Path-Based BVI, and a New Algorithm 2WP-BVI. Our main contribution is to identify the mathematical principle underlying the widest path-based BVI approach and to refine both the algorithm and its theoretical foundations. Specifically:

1. We present a cleaner and more streamlined algorithm (called *2WP-BVI* (Algorithm 2)), based on a construct we call the *(2-player) widest path game*, which avoids the use of player reduction; and
2. For its correctness proof (§5.1), we identify and apply a proof principle that we call the *maximality inheritance principle*, presented in §3.

Regarding the first key ingredient—(2-player) widest path games (WPGs)—we find that their close structural similarity to SGs naturally leads to the use of the maximality inheritance principle. Furthermore, we show that WPGs can be solved not only using fixed-point methods (such as Kleene iteration or the Bellman–Ford algorithm), but also via an enhanced Dijkstra-like algorithm. Isolating this game structure gives 2WP-BVI theoretical advantages over 1WP-BVI.

Regarding the second key ingredient—the maximality inheritance principle—it is inspired by a classical result in probabilistic model checking [5, Thm. 10.19]: in a Markov chain (MC), one can enforce the uniqueness of fixed points of the Bellman operator by "removing" states with reachability probability 0.

The proof of [5, Thm. 10.19] proceeds by contradiction, and is outlined as follows (with a detailed version provided in §3). Assuming a gap exists between the least and the greatest fixed points, we select a *gap maximizer*—a state where the gap is maximal. (The finiteness of the state space is really needed here; a separating example is in Rem. 5.7.) We then observe that *maximality* (i.e., being a gap maximizer) *is inherited* by successor states, leading to the conclusion that all reachable states from a gap maximizer are also gap maximizers. This yields a contradiction: a gap maximizer, by definition, cannot be a target state; thus the above argument implies that it must have reachability probability 0; but such a state must have been removed by assumption.

In §5.1, we apply this maximality inheritance principle to prove the correctness of our algorithm 2WP-BVI (Algorithm 2). We highlight a clear similarity between our proof and the one for [5, Thm. 10.19].

Contributions. Our technical contributions are summarized as follows:

1. We present 2WP-BVI, a clean BVI algorithm for stochastic games (SGs) based on the concept of widest path width. The algorithm is formalized using a construct called *(2-player) widest path games*.
2. We formulate the *maximality inheritance principle* and demonstrate its application both in a classical result [5, Thm. 10.19] and in the correctness proof of 2WP-BVI. This provides a principled foundation that improves upon the ad hoc 1WP-BVI [33].
3. We evaluate 2WP-BVI via experiments (§7). As expected, it performs particularly well on SGs with many end components. Also, it significantly outperforms other tools on a class of benchmarks. This confirms the relevance and potential of 2WP-BVI.

1WP-BVI vs. 2WP-BVI. Three main differences between 1WP-BVI and 2WP-BVI are highlighted below. A detailed comparison is provided in §5.2.

1. *Computation of the over-approximation sequence.* 2WP-BVI constructs this sequence by solving (2-player) widest path games (Algorithm 1), whereas 1WP-BVI applies player reduction and then computes (1-player) widest path widths.
2. *Underlying principle for the convergence proof.* The fixed-point uniqueness of 2WP-BVI is by the maximality inheritance principle, but the proof of 1WP-BVI in [33] is by the infinitary pigeonhole principle and is non-constructive.
3. *Dependency between under- and over-approximations.* 2WP-BVI does not have such dependency, unlike 1WP-BVI.

Organization. The paper is organized as follows: §2 reviews some backgrounds. The maximality inheritance principle is introduced in §3, using [5, Thm. 10.19] as a showcase. In §4, we define (2-player) widest path games and present a Dijkstra-type algorithm to solve them. Building on these key ingredients, we describe our 2WP-BVI algorithm in §5 and prove its correctness and convergence. Related works are reviewed in §6. The experimental results are in §7; in §8 we conclude.

2 Preliminaries

Notation 2.1. For a finite set S, the set of all functions from S to $[0,1]$ is denoted by $[0,1]^S$. The set of all discrete probability distributions on S is denoted by $\text{DIST}(S) := \{d \in [0,1]^S : \sum_{s \in S} d(s) = 1\}$.

2.1 Stochastic Games

Definition 2.2 (stochastic game $\mathcal{G}$). A *stochastic game (SG)* is $\mathcal{G} = (S, S_\triangle, S_\triangledown, s_{\text{init}}, A, \text{Av}, \delta, T)$, where $S = S_\triangle \uplus S_\triangledown$ is a finite set of *states* partitioned into *Maximizer's* ($S_\triangle$) and *Minimizer's* ($S_\triangledown$) states, $s_{\text{init}} \in S$ is an *initial* state, A is a finite set of *actions*, $\text{Av} : S \to 2^A \setminus \{\emptyset\}$ defines *available* actions at each state, $\delta : S \times A \to \text{DIST}(S)$ is a *transition function*, and $T \subseteq S$ is a *target* set.

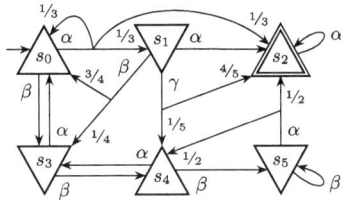 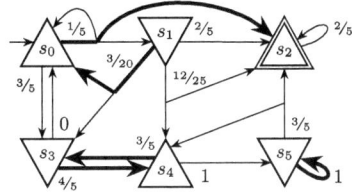

Fig. 1. Left: an example of SG. The labels 1 for $\delta(s,a,s') = 1$ are omitted. Right: the WPG constructed from the SG and $u : s_i \mapsto i/5$ for $0 \leq i \leq 5$. Each (s,a) is labeled by its width $\phi_u(s,a)$. Players' optimal strategies for the widest path objective are in bold.

The semantics of SGs [23] is summarized as follows. Let $\text{POST}(s,a) := \{s' : \delta(s,a,s') > 0\}$. An *infinite path* is $\rho = s_0 a_0 s_1 a_1 \ldots \in (S \times A)^\omega$ where $a_i \in \text{Av}(s_i)$ and $s_{i+1} \in \text{POST}(s_i, a_i)$ for $i \in \mathbb{N}$. A *strategy for Maximizer* is $\sigma_\triangle : S_\triangle \to A$ such that $\sigma_\triangle(s) \in \text{Av}(s)$ for $s \in S_\triangle$. A *strategy for Minimizer* $\sigma_\triangledown : S_\triangledown \to A$ is similarly defined. We only consider strategies of this form (i.e., memoryless pure strategies) as they are complete for finite SGs with the reachability objective [14].

Given an SG $\mathcal{G}$, a pair of strategies $(\sigma_\triangle, \sigma_\triangledown)$ induces a Markov chain $\mathcal{G}^{(\sigma_\triangle, \sigma_\triangledown)}$ with a transition function $\delta^{(\sigma_\triangle, \sigma_\triangledown)} : S \to \text{DIST}(S)$ such that $\delta^{(\sigma_\triangle, \sigma_\triangledown)}(s, s') = \delta(s, \sigma_\triangle(s), s')$ if $s \in S_\triangle$ and $\delta(s, \sigma_\triangledown(s), s')$ if $s \in S_\triangledown$. The Markov chain assigns to each $s \in S$ a probability distribution $\mathcal{P}_s^{(\sigma_\triangle, \sigma_\triangledown)}$ over S^ω. For each measurable subset $X \subseteq S^\omega$, $\mathcal{P}_s^{(\sigma_\triangle, \sigma_\triangledown)}(X)$ is the probability that, when starting at s, the Markov chain generates an infinite path which belongs to X.

For the *reachability objective* with a target set $T \subseteq S$, we consider the measurable subset of infinite paths which contain a state in T, denoted by $\Diamond T$. We are interested in $\mathcal{P}_s^{(\sigma_\triangle, \sigma_\triangledown)}(\Diamond T)$ when both players play optimally, defined in the following definition as the *(reachability) value function*. Informally, Maximizer aims to maximize the reachability probability to T while Minimizer aims to minimize it. As proved in [14], the player order of choosing a strategy is irrelevant.

Definition 2.3 ((reachability) value function V). Let $\mathcal{G}$ be an SG as in Definition 2.2. The *(reachability) value function* is the function $V : S \to [0,1]$ defined by $V(s) := \max_{\sigma_\triangle} \min_{\sigma_\triangledown} \mathcal{P}_s^{(\sigma_\triangle, \sigma_\triangledown)}(\Diamond T) = \min_{\sigma_\triangledown} \max_{\sigma_\triangle} \mathcal{P}_s^{(\sigma_\triangle, \sigma_\triangledown)}(\Diamond T)$.

Example 2.4. Figure 1 (left) shows an example of SG with $T = \{s_2\}$. Its (reachability) value function is $V : s_0 \mapsto 4/5 \mid s_1 \mapsto 3/5 \mid s_2 \mapsto 1 \mid s_3, s_4, s_5 \mapsto 0$ under a pair of optimal strategies $(\sigma_\triangle, \sigma_\triangledown)$ where $\sigma_\triangle(\cdot) = \alpha$ and $\sigma_\triangledown(\cdot) = \beta$.

2.2 Fixed Points in a Complete Lattice

We recall some backgrounds on lattices. Although their usages are not limited to probabilistic model checking, we use SGs here for intuitions and illustrations.

Our focus in this paper is the complete lattice $(L = [0,1]^S, \preccurlyeq)$ where $f \preccurlyeq f'$ iff $f(s) \leq f'(s)$ for all $s \in S$. Its least element is $\bot : S \to [0,1]$ with $\bot(s) = 0$

and its greatest element is $\top : S \to [0,1]$ with $\top(s) = 1$ for all $s \in S$. A function $\Gamma : L \to L$ is *monotone* if $f \preccurlyeq f'$ implies $\Gamma f \preccurlyeq \Gamma f'$. Also, $f \in L$ is a *fixed point* of $\Gamma : L \to L$ if $f = \Gamma f$. Below we state two well-known theorems on fixed points.

Definition 2.5 (Cousot–Cousot sequence). Let $(L, \preccurlyeq)$ be a complete lattice and $\Gamma : L \to L$ be a monotone function. The *bottom-up Cousot–Cousot sequence* and the *top-down Cousot–Cousot sequence* are the (transfinite) sequences

$$\bot \preccurlyeq \Gamma\bot \preccurlyeq \Gamma^2\bot \preccurlyeq \cdots \preccurlyeq \Gamma^\omega\bot \preccurlyeq \Gamma^{\omega+1}\bot \preccurlyeq \cdots \preccurlyeq \Gamma^\alpha\bot \preccurlyeq \cdots \quad \text{and}$$

$$\top \succcurlyeq \Gamma\top \succcurlyeq \Gamma^2\top \succcurlyeq \cdots \succcurlyeq \Gamma^\omega\top \succcurlyeq \Gamma^{\omega+1}\top \succcurlyeq \cdots \succcurlyeq \Gamma^\alpha\top \succcurlyeq \cdots ,$$

where $\Gamma^{\alpha+1}\bot = \Gamma(\Gamma^\alpha\bot)$ and $\Gamma^{\alpha+1}\top = \Gamma(\Gamma^\alpha\top)$ for a successor ordinal $\alpha+1$, $\Gamma^\alpha\bot = \sup\{\Gamma^\beta\bot : \beta < \alpha\}$ and $\Gamma^\alpha\top = \inf\{\Gamma^\beta\top : \beta < \alpha\}$ for a limit ordinal α.

Theorem 2.6 (Cousot–Cousot [15]). *Assume the setting of Definition 2.5. The bottom-up Cousot–Cousot sequence stabilizes, i.e., there is an ordinal α_0 such that $\Gamma^{\alpha_0}\bot = \Gamma^{\alpha_0+1}\bot = \cdots$. Its limit $\Gamma^{\alpha_0}\bot$ is the least fixed point (lfp) $\mu\Gamma$ of Γ.*

Dually, the top-down Cousot–Cousot sequence stabilizes: $\Gamma^{\alpha'_0}\top = \Gamma^{\alpha'_0+1}\top = \cdots$ with some α'_0. Its limit $\Gamma^{\alpha'_0}\top$ is the greatest fixed point (gfp) $\nu\Gamma$ of Γ.

Theorem 2.7 ((special case of) Kleene [6]). *Let $(L, \preccurlyeq)$ be a complete lattice and $\Gamma : L \to L$ be an ω-continuous function (i.e., $\Gamma(\sup L') = \sup\{\Gamma f : f \in L'\}$ for any increasing ω-chain $L' \subseteq L$). Then, the bottom-up Kleene sequence $\bot \preccurlyeq \Gamma\bot \preccurlyeq \Gamma^2\bot \preccurlyeq \cdots$ stabilizes at ω (i.e., $\Gamma^\omega\bot = \Gamma^{\omega+1}\bot = \cdots$). Its limit $\Gamma^\omega\bot$ is the lfp $\mu\Gamma$ of Γ.*

Dually, let Γ be an ω^{op}-cocontinuous function (i.e., $\Gamma(\inf L') = \inf\{\Gamma f : f \in L'\}$ for any decreasing ω-chain $L' \subseteq L$). Then, the top-down Kleene sequence $\top \succcurlyeq \Gamma\top \succcurlyeq \Gamma^2\top \succcurlyeq \cdots$ stabilizes at ω, with $\Gamma^\omega\top = \nu\Gamma$ giving the gfp.

The bottom-up sequence is the essence behind the *value iteration* technique in probabilistic model checking (§1). Thus, in this work, we generally refer to the iterative construction of such a sequence as *value iteration*. Note that the bottom-up and top-down sequences are the *under-* and *over-approximation sequences* of $\mu\Gamma$, respectively (i.e., $\Gamma^\alpha\bot \preccurlyeq \mu\Gamma \preccurlyeq \nu\Gamma \preccurlyeq \Gamma^{\alpha'}\top$ for any ordinals α and α').

2.3 Bounded Value Iteration

The problem we would like to solve is as follows.

Problem 2.8 (value function approximation problem). Given an SG $\mathcal{G}$ and a precision $\varepsilon > 0$, the *value function approximation problem* is to output a value that is ε-close to $V(s_{\mathrm{init}})$ (i.e., the difference from $V(s_{\mathrm{init}})$ is at most ε).

Problem 2.8 can be practically solved by approximating the lfp of the *(reachability) Bellman operator*. We first introduce the notion of the *state-action expectation* and then define the (reachability) Bellman operator based on this notion.

Definition 2.9 (state-action expectation $\phi_{f(s,a)}$). Let $\mathcal{G}$ be an SG as in Definition 2.2. The *state-action expectation* of a function $f \in [0,1]^S$ for a state-action pair $(s,a) \in S \times A$ is $\phi_f(s,a) := \sum_{s' \in S} \delta(s,a,s') \cdot f(s')$.

Definition 2.10 ((reachability) Bellman operator Φ). Let $\mathcal{G}$ be an SG as in Definition 2.2. The *(reachability) Bellman operator* is the function $\Phi : [0,1]^S \to [0,1]^S$ where, for $f \in [0,1]^S$,

$$(\Phi f)(s) := \begin{cases} 1 & \text{if } s \in T, \\ \max_{a \in \mathrm{Av}(s)} \phi_f(s,a) & \text{if } s \in S_\triangle \setminus T, \text{ and} \\ \min_{a \in \mathrm{Av}(s)} \phi_f(s,a) & \text{if } s \in S_\triangledown \setminus T. \end{cases}$$

Here is a well-known theorem on SG reachability probability (see, e.g., [11]).

Theorem 2.11. *Let V and Φ be as in Definitions 2.3 and 2.10. We have $\mu \Phi = V$.*

The (reachability) Bellman operator Φ is known to be ω-continuous and thus its lfp can be (under-)approximated using Kleene's theorem (Theorem 2.7): $\bot \preccurlyeq \Phi \bot \preccurlyeq \Phi^2 \bot \preccurlyeq \cdots$ converges to $\mu \Phi = V$. Nonetheless, one cannot know how close the approximation $(\Phi^i \bot)(s_{\mathrm{init}})$ is to $V(s_{\mathrm{init}})$ [18]. In particular, even when $(\Phi^i \bot)(s_{\mathrm{init}}) - (\Phi^{i-1} \bot)(s_{\mathrm{init}}) \leq 2\varepsilon$—a common stopping criterion for (non-bounded) VI—the approximation $(\Phi^i \bot)(s_{\mathrm{init}})$ may not be ε-close to $V(s_{\mathrm{init}})$ [18]. To overcome this, over-approximations of $\mu \Phi$ are brought into consideration.

Bounded value iteration (BVI) (also known as *interval iteration*) computes, in addition to the under-approximation sequence, the over-approximation sequence $\top \succcurlyeq \Phi \top \succcurlyeq \Phi^2 \top \succcurlyeq \cdots$ which converges to $\nu \Phi \succcurlyeq V$. If one finds $i \in \mathbb{N}$ such that $(\Phi^i \top)(s_{\mathrm{init}}) - (\Phi^i \bot)(s_{\mathrm{init}}) \leq 2\varepsilon$, then the value $\frac{1}{2}((\Phi^i \bot)(s_{\mathrm{init}}) + (\Phi^i \top)(s_{\mathrm{init}}))$ is guaranteed to be ε-close to $V(s_{\mathrm{init}})$. The issue with BVI is that $\nu \Phi$ is not necessarily equal to $\mu \Phi = V$. This means the over-approximation sequence may not converge to V and one may not be able to find $i \in \mathbb{N}$ that satisfies the condition. Several studies have been conducted to modify the over-approximation sequence in order to obtain convergence, e.g., by player reduction and end-component analysis. We refer to [23,25,33] for details; see also the related works in §6.

Example 2.12. Consider the SG in Fig. 1 (left). By representing $f \in [0,1]^S$ as $(f(s_0), \ldots, f(s_5))$, the under-approximation sequence is $\bot = (0,0,0,0,0,0) \preccurlyeq (0,0,1,0,0,0) \preccurlyeq (1/3, 0, 1, 0, 0, 0) \preccurlyeq (4/9, 1/4, 1, 0, 0, 0) \preccurlyeq (61/108, 1/3, 1, 0, 0, 0) \preccurlyeq \cdots$ converging to $V = (4/5, 3/5, 1, 0, 0, 0)$. On the other hand, the over-approximation sequence is $\top = (1,1,1,1,1,1) \succcurlyeq (1,1,1,1,1,1) \succcurlyeq \cdots$ stabilizing at $\nu \Phi = \top$.

3 The Maximality Inheritance Principle

To introduce our second key ingredient, we revisit [5, Thm. 10.19], a classical result well-known in the probabilistic model checking community.

Notation 3.1. The notations used in §3 are limited to this section (where we only consider Markov chains). For example, Φ denotes the one in §3 in this section, while it denotes the one in Definition 2.10 (for SGs) in other sections.

Let $\mathcal{M} = (S, s_{\text{init}}, \delta, T)$ be a Markov chain (MC), with a finite state space S, an initial state s_{init}, a transition kernel $\delta \colon S \to \text{DIST}(S)$, and a set $T \subseteq S$ of target states. Let $\Phi \colon [0,1]^S \to [0,1]^S$ be the Bellman operator for reachability probability, that is, for $f \in [0,1]^S$,

$$\Phi(f)(s) := \begin{cases} 1 & \text{if } s \in T, \text{ and} \\ \sum_{s' \in S} \delta(s, s') \cdot f(s') & \text{otherwise.} \end{cases}$$

It is standard that the *value function* $V \colon S \to [0,1]$, which assigns to each $s \in S$ the reachability probability to T, is the lfp of Φ (i.e., $V = \mu \Phi$).

Much like our discussion in §2.2–2.3, it is desired that the fixed point of Φ is unique (i.e., $\mu \Phi = \nu \Phi$), which would give us BVI with convergence. This is not the case in general; a counterexample can be given essentially like in Ex. 2.12.

Nonetheless, achieving fixed-point uniqueness for MC reachability is not difficult. Let $S_{=0} \subseteq S$ be the set of states that reach T with probability 0. We define the *modified Bellman operator*[1] $\Phi' \colon [0,1]^S \to [0,1]^S$ where, for $f \in [0,1]^S$,

$$\Phi'(f)(s) := \begin{cases} 1 & \text{if } s \in T, \\ 0 & \text{if } s \in S_{=0}, \text{ and} \\ \sum_{s' \in S} \delta(s, s') \cdot f(s') & \text{otherwise.} \end{cases} \quad (1)$$

We claim that Φ' has a unique fixed point. First, we state the following.

Lemma 3.2. (max. vs. average). *Let S be a finite set, $f \colon S \to [0,1]$ be a function, and $\delta \in \text{DIST}(S)$ be a distribution over S. Assume that $s^\star$ is an f-maximizer (meaning $f(s^\star) \geq f(s)$ for each $s \in S$).*

(i) $f(s^\star) \geq \sum_{s \in S} \delta(s) \cdot f(s)$ holds ("the maximum is above the average").
(ii) Assume further that we have an equality $f(s^\star) = \sum_{s \in S} \delta(s) \cdot f(s)$ ("the maximum coincides with the average"). Then, for each $s \in S$, $\delta(s) > 0$ implies $f(s^\star) = f(s)$.

We provide a uniqueness proof as follows.

Proposition 3.3 (unique solution [5, Thm. 10.19]). *Assume the setting of MC in §3. Then, the modified Bellman operator Φ' has a unique fixed point. Moreover, V is its fixed point; therefore we have $V = \mu \Phi' = \nu \Phi'$.*

Proof. We first show that $V = \mu \Phi'$. This follows the fact that the Kleene sequence $\bot \preccurlyeq \Phi'(\bot) \preccurlyeq (\Phi')^2(\bot) \preccurlyeq \cdots$ for the modified Bellman operator Φ' coincides with that for Φ. We show this by contradiction. Pick the smallest k

---

[1] In [5], the set $S_{=1} \subseteq S$ of states that reach T with probability 1 is also defined. However, $S_{=1}$ is not necessary for the uniqueness proof.

such that $(\Phi)^k(\bot) \neq (\Phi')^k(\bot)$. Since the only difference is in the second case of (1), there must be some $s \in S_{=0}$ such that $(\Phi)^k(\bot)(s) > 0$. But then we have $V(s) \geq (\Phi)^k(\bot)(s) > 0$, contradicting with $s \in S_{=0}$.

It follows that $V \preccurlyeq \nu\Phi'$. We show that this inequality is an equality. We argue by contradiction; assume $V \prec \nu\Phi'$. Then, there is $s \in S$ such that $V(s) < \nu\Phi'(s)$. Let $s^\star$ be a *gap maximizer*, i.e., a state that maximizes this gap: $(\nu\Phi' - V)(s^\star) \geq (\nu\Phi' - V)(s)$ for each $s \in S$. Note that we can pick such $s^\star$ since S is finite.

By this choice of $s^\star$, we have $(\nu\Phi' - V)(s^\star) > 0$. It follows that

$$s^\star \notin T \quad \text{and} \quad s^\star \notin S_{=0}. \qquad (2)$$

Indeed, if we assume otherwise, we have

$$(\nu\Phi' - V)(s^\star)$$
$$= \bigl(\Phi'(\nu\Phi') - \Phi'(V)\bigr)(s^\star) \quad \text{since } \nu\Phi' \text{ and } V = \mu\Phi' \text{ are fixed points of } \Phi'$$
$$= \bigl(\Phi'(\nu\Phi')\bigr)(s^\star) - \bigl(\Phi'(V)\bigr)(s^\star)$$
$$= 1 - 1 \quad (\text{if } s^\star \in T) \quad \text{or} \quad 0 - 0 \quad (\text{if } s^\star \in S_{=0}) \qquad \text{by (1)}$$
$$= 0, \quad \text{and this contradicts with } (\nu\Phi' - V)(s^\star) > 0.$$

Now, we reason as follows.

$$(\nu\Phi' - V)(s^\star) = \bigl(\Phi'(\nu\Phi') - \Phi'(V)\bigr)(s^\star)$$
$$= \bigl(\Phi'(\nu\Phi')\bigr)(s^\star) - \bigl(\Phi'(V)\bigr)(s^\star)$$
$$= \sum_{s' \in S} \delta(s^\star, s') \cdot (\nu\Phi')(s') - \sum_{s' \in S} \delta(s^\star, s') \cdot (V)(s') \quad \text{by (1) and (2)}$$
$$= \sum_{s' \in S} \delta(s^\star, s') \cdot (\nu\Phi' - V)(s').$$

We have proved that the average of $\nu\Phi' - V$ on the distribution $\delta(s^\star)$ coincides with its maximum taken at $s^\star$. Therefore, by Lemma 3.2, we have $(\nu\Phi' - V)(s^\star) = (\nu\Phi' - V)(s')$ for each successor s' of $s^\star$, where being a successor means $\delta(s^\star, s') > 0$. Hence, we have shown that being a gap maximizer is *inherited* to successors.

The above reasoning is valid for any gap maximizer $s^\star$. Thus, all offsprings of $s^\star$ (i.e., those reachable from $s^\star$) are gap maximizers. However, in (1) we showed that no gap maximizer is in T or in $S_{=0}$. Therefore, T is unreachable from $s^\star$. This implies $V(s^\star) = 0$ and thus $s^\star \in S_{=0}$, which is a contradiction with (2). □

We would like to signify a characteristic argument in the proof, calling it as the *maximality inheritance principle*. It has the following features.

- The goal is to show that two fixed points on $[0,1]^S$—the lfp for one operator Φ_1 (here Φ) and the gfp for another operator Φ_2 (here Φ')—coincide.
- One argues by contradiction. Assuming S is finite (this is necessary—see Rem. 5.7), we pick a *gap maximizer* $s^\star$.
- Then, one uses Lemma 3.2 (especially Item (ii)) to show that *maximality* (i.e., being a gap maximizer) *is inherited*. This proof method seems to work in many probabilistic settings beyond MCs; indeed we use it for SGs in §5.1.

– Finally, one derives a contradiction from this maximality inheritance. This is typically done by exploiting some "lfp structure" of $\mu\Phi_1$ or $\nu\Phi_2$. In Proposition 3.3, we used the former. Our proof in §5.1 will use the latter: while the fixed point $\nu\Phi_2$ itself is the gfp, the operator Φ_2 (Ω in §5.1) is defined with suitable lfps.

4 Widest Path Games

The maximality inheritance principle (§3) will be central to the correctness proof of our 2WP-BVI algorithm (§5). Here we introduce the other key ingredient, the *(2-player) widest path games*, which are used for formalizing the algorithm.

We define a non-stochastic (2-player) widest path game (WPG) from an SG $\mathcal{G}$ and a function $u \in [0,1]^S$. The game has a structure that mirrors that of $\mathcal{G}$: it has the same sets of states for Maximizer and Minimizer; these two players compete against each other under what we call the *widest path objective*.

4.1 Widest Path Objective

Given an SG $\mathcal{G}$ as in Definition 2.2, and a function $u \in [0,1]^S$, we associate each state-action pair $(s,a) \in S \times A$ with a *width* $\phi_u(s,a)$, where ϕ_u is the state-action expectation of u (Definition 2.9). Given an infinite path ρ, its *path width* with respect to u is the bottleneck width of the path. It is defined recursively as follows.

Definition 4.1 (path width $w_{u(\rho)}$, widest path width $\mathcal{W}_{u,s}^{(\sigma_\Delta,\sigma_\nabla)}$). Let $\mathcal{G}$ be an SG as in Definition 2.2, $\rho = s_0 a_0 s_1 a_1 \ldots \in (S \times A)^\omega$ be an infinite path (cf. §2.1), and $u \in [0,1]^S$. The *path width* $w_u(\rho)$ of ρ with respect to u is defined by

$$w_u(\rho) := \begin{cases} 1 & \text{if } s_0 \in T, \\ 0 & \text{if } s_i \notin T \text{ for all } i \in \mathbb{N}, \text{ and} \\ \min\bigl(\phi_u(s_0,a_0), w_u(s_1 a_1 s_2 a_2 \ldots)\bigr) & \text{otherwise.} \end{cases}$$

Note that only paths that reach T can have non-zero path width.

We extend the above to finite paths $\rho' = s_0 a_0 s_1 a_1 \ldots s_k \in ((S \setminus T) \times A)^* \times T$ with $s_k \in T$. In explicit terms, we have $w_u(\rho') = \min_{0 \le i < k} \phi_u(s_i, a_i)$. In fact, we can easily see that $w_u(\rho') = w_u(\rho'\rho'')$ for any infinite path ρ'' from s_k.

Given a pair of strategies $(\sigma_\Delta, \sigma_\nabla)$ and a state $s \in S$, we define $\text{PATH}_s^{(\sigma_\Delta,\sigma_\nabla)} := \{s_0 a_0 s_1 a_1 \ldots\}$ to be the set of all infinite paths such that $s_0 = s$, $a_i = \sigma_\Delta(s_i)$ if $s_i \in S_\Delta$, and $a_i = \sigma_\nabla(s_i)$ if $s_i \in S_\nabla$, for each $i \in \mathbb{N}$. Now we define

$$\mathcal{W}_{u,s}^{(\sigma_\Delta,\sigma_\nabla)} := \max\{w_u(\rho) : \rho \in \text{PATH}_s^{(\sigma_\Delta,\sigma_\nabla)}\}; \tag{3}$$

this is the *widest path width* from s following $(\sigma_\Delta, \sigma_\nabla)$ with respect to u.

The maximum in (3) is well-defined: although $\mathrm{PATH}_s^{(\sigma_\triangle,\sigma_\triangledown)}$ can be an infinite set, the maximum is asking for the widest path width from s to T in a suitably defined *finite* graph. It is well-known that this widest path width is well-defined, and efficient algorithms such as Dijkstra's algorithm [16] exploit this fact.

Now we define the *widest path objective*. Given a function $u \in [0,1]^S$, we are interested in the widest path width $W_{u,s}^{(\sigma_\triangle,\sigma_\triangledown)}$ when both players play optimally under the widest path objective. This is given by the *widest path value function* defined below.

Definition 4.2 (widest path value function W_u). Assume the setting of Definition 4.1. The *widest path value function* with respect to $u \in [0,1]^S$ is the function $W_u \colon S \to [0,1]$ defined by $W_u(s) := \min_{\sigma_\triangledown} \max_{\sigma_\triangle} W_{u,s}^{(\sigma_\triangle,\sigma_\triangledown)}$.

Note that a pair of strategies $(\sigma_\triangle, \sigma_\triangledown)$ does not determine a successor state $s_{i+1} \in \mathrm{POST}(s_i, a_i)$. Nevertheless, the widest path width $W_{u,s}^{(\sigma_\triangle,\sigma_\triangledown)}$ in (3) is defined as the maximum path width over all possible paths. Consequently, the widest path game can be interpreted as a non-stochastic game in which, at each state s, either Maximizer or Minimizer chooses an action $a \in \mathrm{Av}(s)$, and Maximizer subsequently chooses a successor state from $\mathrm{POST}(s,a)$.

Informally, by having Maximizer choose successor states in the widest path game, if u is an over-approximation of the optimal reachability probability, then so is W_u. This observation forms the main idea behind our 2WP-BVI algorithm presented in §5.

Example 4.3. Consider the non-stochastic (2-player) widest path game constructed from SG in Fig. 1 (left) and $u : s_i \mapsto i/5$ for $0 \le i \le 5$. The width $\phi_u(s,a)$ of each state-action pair is shown in Fig. 1 (right). Its widest path value function is $W_u = (1/5, 3/20, 1, 0, 0, 0)$ under a pair of optimal strategies $(\sigma_\triangle, \sigma_\triangledown)$ where $\sigma_\triangle(\cdot) = \alpha$ and $\sigma_\triangledown(\cdot) = \beta$. Notice that the widest paths require the successors of s_0 and s_1 under the mentioned pair of optimal strategies to be s_2 and s_0, respectively. These choices can be interpreted as being made by Maximizer.

4.2 Widest Path Value Function as a Fixed Point

The widest path value function can be computed by backward iteration from the target set using a suitable "Bellman operator". This is the intuition of Bellman–Ford's algorithm [7,17]. We formalize this with lattice-theoretic fixed points.

Definition 4.4 (widest path Bellman operator Ψ_u). Assume the setting of Definition 4.1. The *widest path Bellman operator* with respect to $u \in [0,1]^S$ is the function $\Psi_u \colon [0,1]^S \to [0,1]^S$ defined as follows. For $f \in [0,1]^S$ and $s \in S$,

$$(\Psi_u f)(s) := \begin{cases} 1 & \text{if } s \in T, \\ \max_{a \in \mathrm{Av}(s)} \min\left(\phi_u(s,a), \max_{s' \in \mathrm{POST}(s,a)} f(s')\right) & \text{if } s \in S_\triangle \setminus T, \text{ and} \\ \min_{a \in \mathrm{Av}(s)} \min\left(\phi_u(s,a), \max_{s' \in \mathrm{POST}(s,a)} f(s')\right) & \text{if } s \in S_\triangledown \setminus T. \end{cases}$$

Notice that Ψ_u incorporates $\phi_u(s,a)$ (Definition 2.9) in a way similar to the reachability Bellman operator Φ (Definition 2.10). Therefore, roughly speaking, an application of Ψ_u subsumes an application of Φ. This intuition will be useful later.

Lemma 4.5. *(i) Ψ_u is monotone, and (ii) $\mu\Psi_u = W_u$ (Definition 4.2).*

Lemma 4.5 suggests that one can compute $W_u = \mu\Psi_u$ using value iteration, that is, by computing $\bot \preccurlyeq \Psi_u\bot \preccurlyeq \cdots$ (§2.2). This is analogous to how Bellman–Ford's algorithm solves the shortest path problem in a weighted graph [7,17]. However, for shortest paths with non-negative weights, it is well-known that Bellman–Ford's algorithm can be improved to Dijkstra's algorithm [16].

We present a similar improvement for our current problem over widest path games. Note that our setting differs from classic Dijkstra's in two aspects: (i) the choice of weight semirings (i.e., shortest path vs. widest path, though this difference is not essential), and (ii) the presence of both Maximizer and Minimizer in our setting. The latter difference is nontrivial, and we address it by discarding Minimizer's suboptimal choices (Line 8).

Definition 4.6 (DIJKSTRAWIDESTPATHGAME($\mathcal{G}, u$)). Our Dijkstra-type algorithm for computing the widest path value function W_u (Definition 4.2) is in Algorithm 1.

Algorithm 1: our Dijkstra-type algorithm for computing W_u (Def. 4.2).

---
1 DIJKSTRAWIDESTPATHGAME($\mathcal{G}, u$)
2      $\mathbb{W}(s) \leftarrow 1$ for all $s \in T$; $\mathbb{W}(s) \leftarrow 0$ for all $s \in S \setminus T$
3   **while true do**
4   Find a state-action pair $(s,a) \in S \times A$ such that (i) $\mathbb{W}(s) = 0$,
            (ii) $a \in \mathrm{Av}(s)$, and (iii) $\min(\phi_u(s,a), \max_{s' \in \mathrm{POST}(s,a)} \mathbb{W}(s'))$ is
            the largest among those pairs which satisfy (i)–(ii)
5   **if** no such pair exist **then break**
6          $x \leftarrow \min(\phi_u(s,a), \max_{s' \in \mathrm{POST}(s,a)} \mathbb{W}(s'))$
7   **if** $x = 0$ **then break**
8   **if** $s \in S_\nabla$ **and** $|\mathrm{Av}(s)| > 1$ **then** $\mathrm{Av}(s) \leftarrow \mathrm{Av}(s) \setminus \{a\}$
9   **else** $\mathbb{W}(s) \leftarrow x$
10   **return** $\mathbb{W}$

Example 4.7. Consider an execution of Algorithm 1 with WPG constructed from SG in Fig. 1 (left) and $u : s_i \mapsto i/5$ for $0 \leq i \leq 5$. The width $\phi_u(s,a)$ of each state-action pair is shown in Fig. 1 (right). The algorithm begins with $\mathbb{W}(s_2) \leftarrow 1$ and $\mathbb{W}(s_i) \leftarrow 0$ for $i \neq 2$. In the while loop, the first pair selected is (s_5, α) with $x = 3/5$. As $s_5 \in S_\nabla$ and $|\mathrm{Av}(s_5)| > 1$, the action α is considered suboptimal and is removed from s_5. The next pairs are (s_1, γ) and (s_1, α). Both are removed for the same reason. Then, (s_0, α) with $x = 1/5$ is selected. Since $s_0 \in S_\Delta$, the algorithm assigns $\mathbb{W}(s_0) \leftarrow 1/5$. The loop continues with (s_1, β) selected. As now $\mathrm{Av}(s_1) = \{\beta\}$, the algorithm performs $\mathbb{W}(s_1) \leftarrow 3/20$. The next pair is (s_3, α) with $x = 0$. Therefore, the loop ends and the algorithm returns $\mathbb{W} = (1/5, 3/20, 1, 0, 0, 0)$.

Theorem 4.8. DIJKSTRAWIDESTPATHGAME$(\mathcal{G}, u)$ *always terminates and returns W_u for all inputs $(\mathcal{G}, u)$.*

Proof. Algorithm 1 always terminates since each pair (s, a) is considered at most once, and there are only finitely many such pairs. For its correctness, we show that, for each $s \in S$, when a positive value is assigned to $\mathbb{W}(s)$, that value is $W_u(s)$. The algorithm begins with $\mathbb{W}(s) \leftarrow 1$ for each $s \in T$, which is correct as $W_u(s) = 1$. We then argue that Line 9 assigns the correct value for each $s \in S \setminus T$.

First, we show that when a pair (s, a) is selected in Line 4, the value $x = \min(\phi_u(s, a), \max_{s' \in \text{POST}(s, a)} \mathbb{W}(s'))$ is the maximum widest path width that can be achieved at s. For contradiction, suppose x is not the maximum. Then, there must be a finite path $\rho = s_0 a_0 s_1 a_1 \ldots s_k$ where $s_0 = s$, $s_k \in T$, and $w_u(\rho) > x$. Along this path, there must be some s_i such that $\mathbb{W}(s_i) = 0$ and $\mathbb{W}(s_{i+1}) \neq 0$. As $\mathbb{W}(s_{i+1}) \neq 0$, its value must have been assigned and, by our invariant, equals $W_u(s_{i+1})$. Since $w_u(\rho) > x$, it follows that $\phi_u(s_i, a_i) > x$ and $\mathbb{W}(s_{i+1}) > x$. Hence, $\min(\phi_u(s_i, a_i), \max_{s' \in \text{POST}(s_i, a_i)} \mathbb{W}(s')) > x$, contradicting the assumption that the selected pair (s, a) in Line 4 has the largest such value.

Now, we consider two cases. If $s \in S_\triangle$, we set $\mathbb{W}(s) \leftarrow x$ in Line 9, and by the above argument, this equals $W_u(s)$. If $s \in S_\triangledown$, we remove a from $\text{Av}(s)$ (unless a is the last one), which is fine since doing so eliminates a suboptimal action for Minimizer. If the loop terminates with $x = 0$ at Line 7, then the maximum widest path width is zero for all remaining states. Thus, $\mathbb{W}(s) = 0 = W_u(s)$. □

5 Our 2WP-BVI Algorithm

We introduce a new operator built upon the widest path value function (Definition 4.2).

Definition 5.1 (widest path operator Ω). Let $\mathcal{G}$ be an SG as in Definition 2.2. Its *widest path operator* is $\Omega : [0, 1]^S \to [0, 1]^S$ where $\Omega u := W_u$ for $u \in [0, 1]^S$.

A similar name appears for 1WP-BVI in [33], but it refers to a different construction. The widest path operator Ω for our 2WP-BVI algorithm solves a *(2-player)* widest path game w.r.t. a function u. As discussed earlier, the structure of (2-player) widest path games closely mirrors that of SGs. In contrast, the operator for 1WP-BVI performs *(1-player, Maximizer-only)* widest path computation on a certain weighted directed graph. See §5.2 for a formal description of 1WP-BVI and a detailed comparison between the two approaches.

Definition 5.2 (2WP-BVI($\mathcal{G}, \varepsilon$)). Our 2WP-BVI algorithm for SG optimal reachability probabilities is in Algorithm 2.

Algorithm 2: our 2WP-BVI algorithm, using widest path games for over-approximation. The input $\varepsilon > 0$ is a desired precision.

1   2WP-BVI($\mathcal{G}, \varepsilon$)
2   $\ell(s) \leftarrow 0$ for all $s \in S$; $u(s) \leftarrow 1$ for all $s \in S$
3   **while** $u(s_{\text{init}}) - \ell(s_{\text{init}}) > 2\varepsilon$ **do**
4     $\ell \leftarrow \Phi \ell$ // Def. 2.10
5     $u \leftarrow \Omega u$ // Def. 5.1
6   **return** $\frac{1}{2}(\ell(s_{\text{init}}) + u(s_{\text{init}}))$

Example 5.3. We apply 2WP-BVI to Fig. 1 (left). The under-approximation sequence ℓ is the same as in Ex. 2.12. The over-approximation sequence u, however, differs from Ex. 2.12 as we apply Ω instead of Φ. Explicitly, our u is $\top = (1,1,1,1,1,1) \succcurlyeq (1,1,1,0,0,0) \succcurlyeq (1, 3/4, 1, 0, 0, 0) \succcurlyeq (11/12, 3/4, 1, 0, 0, 0) \succcurlyeq (8/9, 11/16, 1, 0, 0, 0) \succcurlyeq \cdots$ converging to $\nu\Omega = V = (4/5, 3/5, 1, 0, 0, 0)$ (by Theorem 5.5).

5.1 Correctness and Convergence

For our 2WP-BVI algorithm (Algorithm 2), we prove its correctness (that ℓ and u are under- and over-approximations, respectively) and convergence (of ℓ and u to V). The latter also implies termination.

Lemma 5.4. *(i) Ω is monotone and ω^{op}-cocontinuous (see Theorem 2.7), and (ii) $V = \Omega V = W_V$.*

Proof (of (ii)). We first show $W_V \preccurlyeq V$ by contradiction. Assume there is $s \in S$ such that $W_V(s) > V(s) \geq 0$. It is not possible that $s \in T$ as $W_V(s) = V(s) = 1$, thus $s \in S \setminus T$. By $W_V(s) > 0$, there is a finite path $\rho' = s_0 a_0 s_1 a_1 \ldots s_k$ where $s_0 = s$, $s_k \in T$, and $W_V(s) = w_V(\rho')$. By Definition 4.1, $w_V(\rho') = \min_{0 \leq i < k} \phi_V(s_i, a_i)$ and we have $w_V(\rho') \leq \phi_V(s, a_0)$ in particular. In case of $s \in S_\triangle \setminus T$, this leads to a contradiction $\phi_V(s, a_0) \geq W_V(s) > V(s) = \max_{a \in \text{Av}(s)} \phi_V(s, a)$, where the last equality is from Definition 2.10. In case of $s \in S_\triangledown \setminus T$, we know that ρ' gives the minimum widest path width at s. However, $\phi_V(s, a_0) \geq W_V(s) > V(s) = \min_{a \in \text{Av}(s)} \phi_V(s, a)$. Therefore, taking an action $\arg\min_{a \in \text{Av}(s)} \phi_V(s, a)$ would lead to a path with a smaller widest path width (its bottleneck is at most $\min_{a \in \text{Av}(s)} \phi_V(s, a)$), contradicting the optimality of ρ'.

We prove $V = \mu\Phi \preccurlyeq \mu\Psi_V = W_V$ (cf. Lemma 4.5) via induction that $\Phi^i \bot \preccurlyeq (\Psi_V)^i \bot$ for $i \in \mathbb{N}$. It is trivial for $i = 0$. For the induction $i + 1$, we show $\Phi(\Phi^i \bot) \preccurlyeq \Psi_V((\Psi_V)^i \bot)$ by cases. It holds when $s \in T$. When $s \in S \setminus T$, we have $\Phi^i \bot \preccurlyeq V$, implying $\phi_{\Phi^i \bot}(s, a) \leq \phi_V(s, a)$ for $a \in \text{Av}(s)$. Also, $\phi_{\Phi^i \bot}(s, a) \leq \max_{s' \in \text{Post}(s,a)}(\Phi^i \bot)(s') \leq \max_{s' \in \text{Post}(s,a)}((\Psi_V)^i \bot)(s')$ by our hypothesis. So, $\phi_{\Phi^i \bot}(s, a) \leq \min(\phi_V(s, a), \max_{s' \in \text{Post}(s,a)}((\Psi_V)^i \bot)(s'))$. As LHS is $(\Phi(\Phi^i))\bot$ and RHS is $(\Psi_V(\Psi_V)^i)\bot$ (Defs 2.10 and 4.4), the proof concludes. □

The following is our key theorem regarding a unique fixed point of the widest path operator Ω. It exploits the maximality inheritance principle (§3); observe its similarity to the proof of Proposition 3.3, especially towards its end.

Theorem 5.5 (key theorem: unique fixed point of Ω). *In the setting of Definition 5.1, we have $V = \mu\Omega = \nu\Omega$. In particular, Ω has a unique fixed point.*

Proof. We first show that $V = \mu\Omega$. Because $V = \Omega V$ (Lemma 5.4), it suffices to prove that $f = \Omega f$ implies $f \succcurlyeq V$. Suppose $f = \Omega f$, which yields $f = \Omega f = W_f = \mu\Psi_f$, and thus $f = \Psi_f f$. It is also easy to see from Lemma 3.2 that $\phi_f(s,a) \leq \max_{s' \in \text{POST}(s,a)} f(s')$ for all $s \in S \setminus T$ and $a \in \text{Av}(s)$. Thus, the term $\min(\phi_f(s,a), \max_{s' \in \text{POST}(s,a)} f(s'))$ in Definition 4.4 for $\Psi_f f$ becomes $\phi_f(s,a)$, matching exactly with Definition 2.10 for Φf. This implies $\Psi_f f = \Phi f$, and so $f = \Phi f$. Because $V = \mu\Phi$ and f is a fixed point of Φ, we get $f \succcurlyeq V$.

It follows that $V \preccurlyeq \nu\Omega$. We shall show that $V = \nu\Omega$. We argue by contradiction; assume $V \prec \nu\Omega$. Then, there is $s \in S$ with $V(s) < \nu\Omega(s)$. Let $s^\star$ be a *gap maximizer*, i.e., $(\nu\Omega - V)(s^\star) \geq (\nu\Omega - V)(s)$ for each $s \in S$. Note that we can pick such $s^\star$ as S is finite. By our choice of $s^\star$, we get $(\nu\Omega - V)(s^\star) > 0$. It follows that $s^\star \notin T$ (otherwise $V(s^\star) = 1$ and the gap is ≤ 0).

We now distinguish cases on whether $s^\star \in S_\triangle$ or $s^\star \in S_\triangledown$, and show that, in both cases, maximality is inherited under suitable actions.

Assume $s^\star \in S_\triangle$. Since $\nu\Omega = \Omega(\nu\Omega) = W_{\nu\Omega} = \mu\Psi_{\nu\Omega}$, we get $\nu\Omega = \Psi_{\nu\Omega}(\nu\Omega)$ and there must be an action $a_\Psi \in \text{Av}(s^\star)$ such that a_Ψ is optimal for the widest path objective (i.e., $\nu\Omega(s^\star) = \min(\phi_{\nu\Omega}(s^\star, a_\Psi), \max_{s' \in \text{POST}(s^\star, a_\Psi)} \nu\Omega(s')))$. By Lemma 3.2, $\nu\Omega(s^\star) = \phi_{\nu\Omega}(s^\star, a_\Psi)$. This action a_Ψ, however, can be suboptimal for the reachability objective, giving $V(s^\star) \geq \phi_V(s^\star, a_\Psi)$. Thus, $(\nu\Omega - V)(s^\star) \leq \phi_{\nu\Omega}(s^\star, a_\Psi) - \phi_V(s^\star, a_\Psi) = \phi_{(\nu\Omega - V)}(s^\star, a_\Psi) \leq \max_{s' \in \text{POST}(s^\star, a_\Psi)}(\nu\Omega - V)(s') \leq (\nu\Omega - V)(s^\star)$. Hence, by Lemma 3.2, $(\nu\Omega - V)(s^\star) = (\nu\Omega - V)(s')$ for all $s' \in \text{POST}(s^\star, a_\Psi)$. Therefore, being a gap maximizer is inherited under a_Ψ.

Now assume $s^\star \in S_\triangledown$. Since $V = \mu\Phi$, we get $V = \Phi V$ and there must be an action $a_\Phi \in \text{Av}(s^\star)$ such that a_Φ is optimal for the reachability objective (i.e., $V(s^\star) = \phi_V(s^\star, a_\Phi)$). This action, however, can be suboptimal for the widest path objective, giving $\nu\Omega(s^\star) \leq \min(\phi_{\nu\Omega}(s^\star, a_\Phi), \max_{s' \in \text{POST}(s^\star, a_\Phi)} \nu\Omega(s')) = \phi_{\nu\Omega}(s^\star, a_\Phi)$, where the equality is by Lemma 3.2(i). So, $(\nu\Omega - V)(s^\star) \leq \phi_{\nu\Omega}(s^\star, a_\Phi) - \phi_V(s^\star, a_\Phi) \leq (\nu\Omega - V)(s^\star)$. Thus, by Lemma 3.2(ii), $(\nu\Omega - V)(s^\star) = (\nu\Omega - V)(s')$ for all $s' \in \text{POST}(s^\star, a_\Phi)$. Hence, being a gap maximizer is inherited under a_Φ.

We now look at the stochastic game in which Maximizer always chooses $\sigma_\triangle(\cdot) = a_\Psi$ and Minimizer always chooses $\sigma_\triangledown(\cdot) = a_\Phi$. The above reasoning is valid for any gap maximizer $s^\star$. So we conclude that all states s reachable from $s^\star$ under $(\sigma_\triangle, \sigma_\triangledown)$ are gap maximizers (w.r.t. $\nu\Omega - V$). Since $\nu\Omega(s) = V(s) = 1$ for $s \in T$, it follows that T is unreachable from $s^\star$ under $(\sigma_\triangle, \sigma_\triangledown)$.

Now note that, under the widest path objective and $(\sigma_\triangle, \sigma_\triangledown)$, Maximizer plays optimally while Minimizer may not. Thus, the widest path width at a state s is at least $\nu\Omega(s)$. This is true for $s^\star$. Since $(\nu\Omega - V)(s^\star) > 0$, it implies $\nu\Omega(s^\star) > 0$. Therefore, under $(\sigma_\triangle, \sigma_\triangledown)$ and by the definition of the widest path width, there is a path from $s^\star$ to T of width at least $\nu\Omega(s^\star) > 0$. This contradicts the above that T is unreachable from $s^\star$ under $(\sigma_\triangle, \sigma_\triangledown)$. □

Theorem 5.6. *Our proposed algorithm $2\text{WP-BVI}(\mathcal{G}, \varepsilon)$ surely terminates and returns a value that is ε-close to $V(s_{\text{init}})$ for all inputs $(\mathcal{G}, \varepsilon)$.*

Proof. We get $\bot \preccurlyeq \Phi\bot \preccurlyeq \cdots \preccurlyeq \mu\Phi = V = \nu\Omega \preccurlyeq \cdots \preccurlyeq \Omega\top \preccurlyeq \top$ from the properties of Φ and Ω (Thms 2.11 and 5.5). Moreover, both under- and over-approximation sequences converge after ω steps, because the continuity of Φ (well-known) and Ω (Lemma 5.4). Thus, $(\Omega^i\top)(s_{\text{init}}) - (\Phi^i\bot)(s_{\text{init}}) \leq 2\varepsilon$ holds for some $i \in \mathbb{N}$ and $\frac{1}{2}((\Phi^i\bot)(s_{\text{init}}) + (\Omega^i\top)(s_{\text{init}}))$ is ε-close to $V(s_{\text{init}})$. □

Remark 5.7. The maximality inheritance principle (cf. §3) requires the state space to be finite. Consider Fig. 2 (left) as an example. For $i > 0$, the chance to go from s_i to s_{i+1} is $\frac{2-(1/2)^{i-1}}{2-(1/2)^i}$ while to s_0 is $\frac{1}{2^{i+1}-1}$. This results in $\mu\Phi = \mu\Omega = V$, where $V(s_i) = 1 - \frac{2-(1/2)^{i-1}}{2} = \frac{1}{2^i}$ for $i \in \mathbb{N}$, whereas $V \prec \nu\Phi = \nu\Omega = \top$.

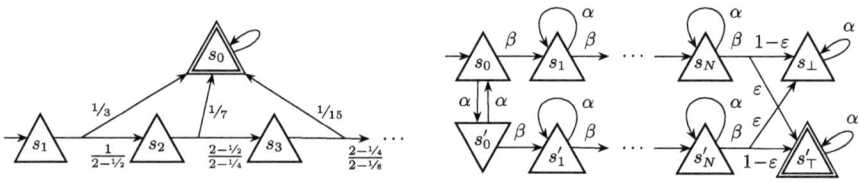

Fig. 2. Left: an infinite-state SG giving $\mu\Phi \prec \nu\Phi$ and $\mu\Omega \prec \nu\Omega$. Right: the benchmark *ECchain* (N is the model parameter). The labels 1 for $\delta(s,a,s') = 1$ are omitted.

5.2 1WP-BVI and Its Comparison with 2WP-BVI

Algorithm 3: 1WP-BVI algorithm of [33].
---
1   1WP-BVI($\mathcal{G}, \varepsilon$)
2     $\ell(s) \leftarrow 0$ for all $s \in S$; $u(s) \leftarrow 1$ for all $s \in S$
3   **while** $u(s_{\text{init}}) - \ell(s_{\text{init}}) > 2\varepsilon$ **do**
4       $\ell \leftarrow \Phi\ell$
5       $\mathcal{G}' \leftarrow \text{PLYRRDCT}(\mathcal{G}, \ell); u \leftarrow \Omega_{\mathcal{G}'} u$
6   **return** $\frac{1}{2}(\ell(s_{\text{init}}) + u(s_{\text{init}}))$

Recall that our 2WP-BVI improves upon *1WP-BVI* of [33]. Here, we formally describe 1WP-BVI and provide a comparison between 1WP-BVI and 2WP-BVI.

1WP-BVI is shown as Algorithm 3 and works as follows: the under-approximation sequence is computed using the Bellman operator Φ (Definition 2.10). For the over-approximation sequence, it starts with *player reduction* $\mathcal{G}' \leftarrow \text{PLYRRDCT}(\mathcal{G}, \ell)$, which removes Minimizer's suboptimal actions w.r.t. ℓ and converts all Minimizer's states into Maximizer's. Formally, this yields an MDP $\mathcal{G}'$ where (i) for $s \in S_\nabla$, $\text{Av}'(s) = \arg\min_{a \in \text{Av}(s)} \phi_\ell(s,a)$, and (ii) $S'_\triangle = S$, $S'_\nabla = \emptyset$.

Then, 1WP-BVI computes a (1-player, Maximizer-only) widest path width on a certain graph derived from the resulting MDP. In Algorithm 3, this is $u \leftarrow \Omega_{\mathcal{G}'} u$. In this work's notation, it corresponds to $u \leftarrow$

DijkstraWidestPathGame($\mathcal{G}', u$) (Algorithm 1). Since $S'_\forall = \emptyset$, Line 8 of Algorithm 1 is skipped. So, 1WP-BVI can outperform 2WP-BVI, as removing Minimizer's suboptimal actions in 2WP-BVI is costly.

However, 1WP-BVI has two drawbacks. Firstly, player reduction complicates the convergence proof for 1WP-BVI. Since the MDP $\mathcal{G}'$ can vary in each iteration, [33, Thm. 4.11] provides a non-constructive proof via the infinitary pigeonhole principle. In contrast, the fixed-point uniqueness proof for 2WP-BVI (Theorem 5.5) is cleaner and more structured, potentially enabling further extensions.

Secondly, player reduction in 1WP-BVI imposes a dependency between the under- and over-approximations. For example, slow convergence of the under-approximations delays that of the over-approximations.

As an instance, this is seen in the SGs of the *ECchain* benchmarks (Fig. 2, right). In these SGs, the top path has reachability ε and the bottom path $1-\varepsilon$. In the execution of 1WP-BVI (Algorithm 3), it takes roughly N iterations for $\ell(s'_\top) = 1$ to propagate to s'_1. Thus, player reduction is ineffective: no actions of s'_0 are removed, and $u(s_0)$ remains $1-\varepsilon$ for about N iterations, until $\ell(s'_1) \neq 0$. In contrast, 2WP-BVI detects the suboptimal action β for s'_0 in the first iteration, and can assign $u(s_0) = \varepsilon$. Since $\ell(s_0) = 0$, 2WP-BVI immediately terminates.

6 Related Work

Besides the works discussed elsewhere, we review the following closely related works. To our best knowledge, these are the only available VI-based tools for SG reachability that provide precision guarantees. They are compared with 1WP-BVI and our 2WP-BVI via experiments in §7.

End Component-Based BVI (EC-BVI) [23]. This is the first work on BVI for SG reachability. In each iteration, it first performs *player reduction* to obtain an MDP. Then, end-component analysis [8,18]—called *deflating*—is applied to the MDP to produce a tighter over-approximation. This work was later extended to other quantitative objectives such as total reward and mean payoff [25].

PET2[2] [31]. It extends PET [29] and is based on EC-BVI. It incorporates partial exploration techniques and various performance optimizations.

Optimistic Value Iteration (OVI) [3]. It extends OVI for MDPs [35] to SGs. Given $\ell \preccurlyeq \mu\Phi$, it checks if $\mu\Phi \preccurlyeq u := \ell + 2\varepsilon$. If so, $\ell + \varepsilon$ is ε-close to $\mu\Phi$. This can be done via Knaster–Tarski's theorem [24,37] or Park's induction [32]: $\Phi u \preccurlyeq u$ implies $\mu\Phi \preccurlyeq u$. End-component analysis is needed to ensure termination.

---

[2] On the Name PET [2] vs. PET2 [31]: in [2], the tool from the PET2 team is called PET ("PET has recently been extended to support reachability objectives for SGs."). Meanwhile, [31] says "PET2 is an extension of PET1 [29] (only applicable to MDPs)." Given these, we assume that the discussions on PET in [2] pertain to PET2 from [31]. This aligns with our understanding of PET2 based on [31] and its source code.

Sound Value Iteration (SVI) [4]. It extends SVI for MDPs [20] to SGs. Using the set $S_{=0}$ (cf. §3), the reachability from s to T is over-approximated by that of reaching T from s in k steps, plus that of remaining in $S \setminus (T \cup S_{=0})$ for k steps. It employs end-component analysis and other iterative mechanisms. According to [4], SVI can take fewer iterations to terminate compared to EC-BVI.

7 Experiments

We implemented our proposed 2WP-BVI (Algorithm 2) as an extension of PRISM-games [27]. Our artifact is available at [34]. The procedure $u \leftarrow \Omega u$ in Algorithm 2 is concretely implemented as $u \leftarrow$ DIJKSTRAWIDESTPATHGAME$(\mathcal{G}, u)$ (Algorithm 1).

Experiments were performed on MacBook Pro® with 2.3 GHz Intel® Core™ i9 and 32 GB of RAM. Each tool was executed inside a Docker container with OpenJDK JRE-17. The time-out (T/O) is 10 min. The precision is $\varepsilon = 10^{-6}$.

The experimental results are in Table 1. Most benchmarks are from existing works [9,12,13,21,26–28,33]; several are real-world case studies. The last four are artificial: *BigMec*, *ManyMecs*, *manyECs* feature large or numerous end components, while *ECchain* (Fig. 2, right) are newly designed to make the under-approximation sequence converge slowly.

The results demonstrate notable performance advantages of WP-based BVIs (2WP-BVI and 1WP-BVI) in benchmarks with many end components—chiefly, *manyECs* and *ECchain*, where either 2WP-BVI or 1WP-BVI performs best. Note that *ECchain* contains many self-loop end components (see Fig. 2, right).

The difference between 2WP-BVI and 1WP-BVI is signified in *ECchain*, where 2WP-BVI is constantly faster than 1WP-BVI. This is because, in 1WP-BVI, the over-approximation depends on the under-approximation. In *ECchain*, the latter converges slowly, which drags the convergence of the former. Conversely, 2WP-BVI is free from this performance burden (see §5.2 for details).

Regarding OVI's performance, it is comparable to 2WP-BVI and 1WP-BVI, except on SGs with many end components (*ManyMecs*, *manyECs*). EC-BVI and SVI are generally slower than the others across many benchmarks. That said, they perform quite well on certain cases (e.g., *investors* for EC-BVI, *cloud* for SVI). Thus, EC-BVI or SVI may be preferable depending on the benchmark.

We find that PET2 is the fastest on many benchmarks—this is consistent with the results from the QComp 2023 Competition [2]. Still, we find that (i) even in those cases, the performance gap with 2WP-BVI is rarely substantial (an exception is *hallway human*), and (ii) there are some benchmarks where 2WP-BVI clearly outperforms PET2 (namely, *cloud*, *manyECs*, and *ECchain*).

Moreover, a discussion in [2] attributes a large part of PET2's performance advantage to engineering efforts such as partial exploration, loop unrolling, and time-memory trade-offs [31]. This discussion, together with Table 1, points to the performance potential of 2WP-BVI. It would be interesting to observe its performance after similar engineering efforts have been applied.

Table 1. Experimental results. Following each benchmark name is a model parameter (the bigger the more complex). The execution times are in seconds; T/O (time-out) is 600 s. The fastest algorithms for each benchmark are shown in bold.

Benchmarks	Sources	EC-BVI	PET2	OVI	SVI	1WP-BVI	2WP-BVI (ours)
avoid (10×10, exit)	[12]	21.4	**7.6**	24.7	T/O	8.5	8.5
avoid (10×10, find)		13.4	**5.0**	17.6	13.8	15.5	17.2
avoid (15×15, exit)		185.4	28.0	191.6	T/O	**26.8**	32.2
avoid (15×15, find)		208.4	**19.1**	127.3	117.4	63.2	67.0
avoid (20×20, exit)		T/O	104.7	T/O	T/O	**90.3**	110.4
avoid (20×20, find)		551.1	**68.6**	T/O	564.3	178.5	188.0
cloud (5)	[9]	293.8	T/O	2.8	2.8	**1.9**	**1.9**
cloud (6)		T/O	T/O	5.8	5.4	**3.2**	3.7
cloud (7)		T/O	T/O	19.2	20.2	**6.9**	8.1
dice (25)	[27]	2.9	**2.7**	2.9	3.7	2.8	3.0
dice (50)		7.6	**4.3**	8.2	8.8	6.9	8.8
dice (100)		45.3	**11.3**	49.9	51.5	20.2	24.5
hallway human (5×5)	[12]	2.5	2.7	**2.4**	2.5	15.8	13.4
hallway human (10×10)		11.7	**10.2**	11.7	11.9	T/O	T/O
hallway human (15×15)		78.0	**48.7**	59.3	59.3	T/O	T/O
investor (50)	[28]	21.8	**11.5**	27.1	38.5	25.2	26.3
investor (100)		155.2	**78.0**	189.6	228.1	138.9	141.9
investors (2, 10)	[13]	8.4	**6.0**	12.5	12.3	8.4	8.1
investors (2, 20)		31.9	**20.1**	39.5	82.6	46.8	50.3
investors (2, 40)		166.6	**86.4**	200.2	346.5	252.8	271.3
mdsm (3)	[21]	4.8	**4.2**	5.0	8.8	5.1	5.2
mdsm (4)		20.2	**12.1**	19.1	31.2	14.1	17.5
mdsm (5)		90.5	54.1	82.8	139.3	**52.9**	61.0
BigMec (5000)	[26]	T/O	**6.9**	9.9	T/O	8.4	9.2
BigMec (7500)		T/O	**8.7**	19.7	T/O	17.2	19.8
BigMec (10000)		T/O	**18.7**	33.0	T/O	28.6	35.3
BigMec (25000)		T/O	**90.2**	252.5	T/O	196.7	267.1
ManyMecs (5000)	[26]	T/O	**24.6**	T/O	T/O	56.6	42.3
ManyMecs (7500)		T/O	**55.0**	T/O	T/O	127.2	102.5
ManyMecs (10000)		T/O	**112.9**	T/O	T/O	233.6	201.6
ManyMecs (25000)		T/O	T/O	T/O	T/O	T/O	T/O
manyECs (5000)	[33]	T/O	27.2	T/O	T/O	**7.3**	7.7
manyECs (7500)		57.6	T/O	T/O	T/O	17.4	**16.8**
manyECs (10000)		T/O	108.6	T/O	T/O	**30.5**	30.6
manyECs (25000)		T/O	T/O	T/O	T/O	221.8	**220.7**
ECchain (5000)	ours	T/O	T/O	15.3	76.8	12.4	**5.5**
ECchain (7500)		T/O	T/O	36.9	202.5	28.4	**12.6**
ECchain (10000)		T/O	T/O	64.7	393.3	48.5	**22.7**
ECchain (25000)		T/O	T/O	539.8	T/O	374.2	**183.9**

Overall, the results demonstrate 2WP-BVI's potential for broad applicability: there are benchmarks for which ours is the best performer; for most of the other benchmarks, ours is at most several times slower than the best performer. We note that the current implementation of 2WP-BVI is a prototype and leaves room for optimization, as discussed above.

8 Conclusions and Future Work

We presented 2WP-BVI, a novel BVI algorithm for SG reachability that is based on widest path computations—thereby avoiding the need for end-component analysis—and improves upon 1WP-BVI [33] in terms of theoretical clarity. 2WP-BVI is built on a construct called widest path games, and we introduced a proof principle referred to as the maximality inheritance principle. Our experimental evaluation demonstrated the algorithm's practical relevance.

We plan to optimize our prototype in various ways, such as incorporating partial exploration and applying low-level performance enhancements. Additionally, we aim to further investigate the theoretical foundations of our constructions through the lens of lattice theory.

Acknowledgments. The authors would like to thank the reviewers for their comments on improving the manuscript and acknowledge the implementations of Azeem et al. [4], Kelmendi et al. [23], Meggendorfer [30], Meggendorfer–Weininger [31], and Phalakarn et al. [33], which we use as basis for our implementation and experiments. This work is supported by ERATO HASUO Metamathematics for Systems Design Project (No. JPMJER1603) and the ASPIRE grant No. JPMJAP2301, JST.

Appendix: Omitted Proofs

Lemma 3.2 (max. vs. average). *Let S be a finite set, $f\colon S \to [0,1]$ be a function, and $\delta \in \mathrm{DIST}(S)$ be a distribution over S. Assume that $s^\star$ is an f-maximizer (meaning $f(s^\star) \geq f(s)$ for each $s \in S$).*

(i) $f(s^\star) \geq \sum_{s \in S} \delta(s) \cdot f(s)$ holds ("the maximum is above the average").
(ii) Assume further that we have an equality $f(s^\star) = \sum_{s \in S} \delta(s) \cdot f(s)$ ("the maximum coincides with the average"). Then, for each $s \in S$, $\delta(s) > 0$ implies $f(s^\star) = f(s)$.

Proof. For (i), it is clear that $\sum_{s \in S} \delta(s) \cdot f(s) \leq \sum_{s \in S} \delta(s) \cdot f(s^\star) = f(s^\star)$, as $f(s) \leq f(s^\star)$ for all $s \in S$. For (ii), we prove by contraposition. Let there be $s' \in S$ with $\delta(s') > 0$ and $f(s^\star) > f(s')$. Then, $\sum_{s \in S} \delta(s) \cdot f(s) = \sum_{s \in S \setminus \{s'\}} \delta(s) \cdot f(s) + \delta(s') \cdot f(s') \leq \sum_{s \in S \setminus \{s'\}} \delta(s) \cdot f(s^\star) + \delta(s') \cdot f(s') < f(s^\star)$. □

Lemma 4.4. *(i) Ψ_u is monotone, and (ii) $\mu\Psi_u = W_u$ (Definition 4.2).*

Proof (of (ii)). For $k \in \mathbb{N}$ and $s \in S_\triangle$, the value $((\Psi_u)^{k+1}\bot)(s)$ is the maximum widest path width that can be achieved at s over all strategies when looking at all finite paths of length at most k (i.e., $s_0 a_0 s_1 a_1 \ldots s_k$) that start at s. For $s \in S_\triangledown$, the same applies with $((\Psi_u)^{k+1}\bot)(s)$ being the minimum widest path width. Due to the fact that, if $W_u(s) > 0$ then there is a path of width $W_u(s)$ from s to T of length at most $|S|-1$ (i.e. with no loops), we know that $W_u = (\Psi_u)^{|S|}\bot = (\Psi_u)^{|S|+1}\bot$. By Lemma 4.5 and Theorem 2.6, we obtain the under-approximation sequence $\bot \preccurlyeq \Psi_u \bot \preccurlyeq \cdots \preccurlyeq (\Psi_u)^{|S|}\bot = (\Psi_u)^{|S|+1}\bot = \mu\Psi_u = W_u$. □

Lemma 5.4. *(i) Ω is monotone and ω^{op}-cocontinuous (see Theorem 2.7), and (ii) $V = \Omega V = W_V$.*

Proof (of (i)). Monotonicity is straightforward. For ω^{op}-cocontinuity (that is, $\Omega(\inf_{n<\omega} u_n) = \inf_{n<\omega} \Omega(u_n)$ for a decreasing chain $u_0 \succcurlyeq u_1 \succcurlyeq \cdots$), we notice the following: for any positive ε, there is $N \in \mathbb{N}$ that is large enough, such that (i) $u_N(s) < (\inf_{n<\omega} u_n)(s) + \varepsilon$ for each $s \in S$, and thus (ii) $\phi_{u_N}(s,a) < \phi_{\inf_{n<\omega} u_n}(s,a) + \varepsilon$ for each $s \in S$ and $a \in \mathrm{Av}(s)$. This holds because there are only finitely many s's and a's.

Moreover, when ε is small enough—say, it is smaller than the smallest difference of widths under $\inf_{n<\omega} u_n$—we can show that $\Omega(u_N) = W_{u_N}$ is given by the same strategies ($\sigma_\triangle, \sigma_\triangledown$) (cf. Definition 4.2) and moreover by the same path ρ (cf. (3)). In this case, by Definition 4.1, we have $\Omega(u_N) \preccurlyeq \Omega(\inf_{n<\omega} u_n) + \varepsilon$. We can take such N for any positive ε that is small enough; this establishes $\Omega(\inf_{n<\omega} u_n) = \inf_{n<\omega} \Omega(u_n)$. □

References

1. Andersson, D., Miltersen, P.B.: The complexity of solving stochastic games on graphs. In: Dong, Y., Du, D., Ibarra, O.H. (eds.) ISAAC 2009. vol. 5878, pp. 112–121. Springer (2009). https://doi.org/10.1007/978-3-642-10631-6_13
2. Andriushchenko, R., et al.: Tools at the frontiers of quantitative verification. In: Beyer, D., Hartmanns, A., Kordon, F. (eds.) TOOLympics Challenge 2023, pp. 90–146. Springer (2025)
3. Azeem, M., Evangelidis, A., Křetínský, J., Slivinskiy, A., Weininger, M.: Optimistic and topological value iteration for simple stochastic games. In: Bouajjani, A., Holík, L., Wu, Z. (eds.) ATVA 2022, vol. 13505, pp. 285–302. Springer (2022). https://doi.org/10.1007/978-3-031-19992-9_18
4. Azeem, M., Křetínský, J., Weininger, M.: Sound value iteration for simple stochastic games. CoRR abs/2411.11549 (2024). https://doi.org/10.48550/arXiv.2411.11549
5. Baier, C., Katoen, J.: Principles of Model Checking. MIT Press (2008)
6. Baranga, A.: The contraction principle as a particular case of Kleene's fixed point theorem. Discret. Math. **98**(1), 75–79 (1991)
7. Bellman, R.: On a routing problem. Q. Appl. Math. **16**(1), 87–90 (1958)
8. Brázdil, T., et al.: Verification of Markov decision processes using learning algorithms. In: Cassez, F., Raskin, J. (eds.) ATVA 2014, vol. 8837, pp. 98–114. Springer (2014). https://doi.org/10.1007/978-3-319-11936-6_8

9. Calinescu, R., Kikuchi, S., Johnson, K.: Compositional reverification of probabilistic safety properties for large-scale complex IT systems. In: Calinescu, R., Garlan, D. (eds.) Monterey Workshop 2012, vol. 7539, pp. 303–329. Springer (2012). https://doi.org/10.1007/978-3-642-34059-8_16
10. Chatterjee, K., Fijalkow, N.: A reduction from parity games to simple stochastic games. In: D'Agostino, G., Torre, S.L. (eds.) GandALF 2011. EPTCS, vol. 54, pp. 74–86 (2011). https://doi.org/10.4204/EPTCS.54.6
11. Chatterjee, K., Henzinger, T.A.: Value iteration. In: Grumberg, O., Veith, H. (eds.) 25 Years of Model Checking - History, Achievements, Perspectives. Lecture Notes in Computer Science, vol. 5000, pp. 107–138. Springer (2008). https://doi.org/10.1007/978-3-540-69850-0_7
12. Chatterjee, K., Katoen, J., Weininger, M., Winkler, T.: Stochastic games with lexicographic reachability-safety objectives. In: Lahiri, S.K., Wang, C. (eds.) CAV 2020, vol. 12225, pp. 398–420. Springer (2020). https://doi.org/10.1007/978-3-030-53291-8_21
13. Chen, T., Forejt, V., Kwiatkowska, M.Z., Parker, D., Simaitis, A.: Automatic verification of competitive stochastic systems. Formal Meth. Syst. Des. **43**(1), 61–92 (2013). https://doi.org/10.1007/S10703-013-0183-7
14. Condon, A.: The complexity of stochastic games. Inf. Comput. **96**(2), 203–224 (1992). https://doi.org/10.1016/0890-5401(92)90048-K
15. Cousot, P., Cousot, R.: Abstract interpretation: a unified lattice model for static analysis of programs by construction or approximation of fixpoints. In: Graham, R.M., Harrison, M.A., Sethi, R. (eds.) POPL 1977, pp. 238–252. ACM (1977). https://doi.org/10.1145/512950.512973
16. Dijkstra, E.W.: A note on two problems in connexion with graphs. Numer. Math. **1**, 269–271 (1959). https://doi.org/10.1007/BF01386390
17. Ford, L.R.: Network Flow Theory. Rand Corporation Paper, Santa Monica (1956)
18. Haddad, S., Monmege, B.: Interval iteration algorithm for MDPs and IMDPs. Theor. Comput. Sci. **735**, 111–131 (2018). https://doi.org/10.1016/J.TCS.2016.12.003
19. Hartmanns, A., Junges, S., Quatmann, T., Weininger, M.: A practitioner's guide to MDP model checking algorithms. In: Sankaranarayanan, S., Sharygina, N. (eds.) TACAS 2023. vol. 13993, pp. 469–488. Springer (2023). https://doi.org/10.1007/978-3-031-30823-9_24
20. Hartmanns, A., Kaminski, B.L.: Optimistic value iteration. In: Lahiri, S.K., Wang, C. (eds.) CAV 2020. vol. 12225, pp. 488–511. Springer (2020). https://doi.org/10.1007/978-3-030-53291-8_26
21. Hildmann, H., Saffre, F.: Influence of variable supply and load flexibility on demand-side management. In: EEM 2011, pp. 63–68 (2011). https://doi.org/10.1109/EEM.2011.5952980
22. Hoffman, A.J., Karp, R.M.: On nonterminating stochastic games. Manage. Sci. **12**(5), 359–370 (1966)
23. Kelmendi, E., Krämer, J., Kretínský, J., Weininger, M.: Value iteration for simple stochastic games: Stopping criterion and learning algorithm. In: Chockler, H., Weissenbacher, G. (eds.) CAV 2018, vol. 10981, pp. 623–642. Springer (2018). https://doi.org/10.1007/978-3-319-96145-3_36
24. Knaster, B.: Un theoreme sur les functions d'ensembles. Ann. Soc. Polon. Math. **6**, 133–134 (1928). https://cir.nii.ac.jp/crid/1571135651325476992
25. Kretínský, J., Meggendorfer, T., Weininger, M.: Stopping criteria for value iteration on stochastic games with quantitative objectives. In: LICS 2023, pp. 1–14. IEEE (2023). https://doi.org/10.1109/LICS56636.2023.10175771

26. Kretínský, J., Ramneantu, E., Slivinskiy, A., Weininger, M.: Comparison of algorithms for simple stochastic games. Inf. Comput. **289**(Part), 104885 (2022). https://doi.org/10.1016/J.IC.2022.104885
27. Kwiatkowska, M., Norman, G., Parker, D., Santos, G.: PRISM-games 3.0: stochastic game verification with concurrency, equilibria and time. In: Lahiri, S.K., Wang, C. (eds.) CAV 2020, vol. 12225, pp. 475–487. Springer (2020). https://doi.org/10.1007/978-3-030-53291-8_25
28. McIver, A., Morgan, C.: Results on the quantitative μ-calculus qMμ. ACM Trans. Comput. Log. **8**(1), 3 (2007). https://doi.org/10.1145/1182613.1182616
29. Meggendorfer, T.: PET - A partial exploration tool for probabilistic verification. In: Bouajjani, A., Holík, L., Wu, Z. (eds.) ATVA 2022, vol. 13505, pp. 320–326. Springer (2022). https://doi.org/10.1007/978-3-031-19992-9_20
30. Meggendorfer, T.: QComp 2023: Stochastic games - evaluation (2023). https://doi.org/10.5281/zenodo.7831409
31. Meggendorfer, T., Weininger, M.: Playing games with your PET: extending the partial exploration tool to stochastic games. In: Gurfinkel, A., Ganesh, V. (eds.) CAV 2024, vol. 14683, pp. 359–372. Springer (2024). https://doi.org/10.1007/978-3-031-65633-0_16
32. Park, D.: Fixpoint induction and proofs of program properties. Mach. Intell. **5** (1969). https://cir.nii.ac.jp/crid/1573950399497019904
33. Phalakarn, K., Takisaka, T., Haas, T., Hasuo, I.: Widest paths and global propagation in bounded value iteration for stochastic games. In: Lahiri, S.K., Wang, C. (eds.) CAV 2020, vol. 12225, pp. 349–371. Springer (2020). https://doi.org/10.1007/978-3-030-53291-8_19
34. Phalakarn, K., Tsai, Y.C., Hasuo, I.: ATVA 2025 artifact: widest path games and maximality inheritance in bounded value iteration for stochastic games (2025). https://doi.org/10.5281/zenodo.15845366
35. Quatmann, T., Katoen, J.: Sound value iteration. In: Chockler, H., Weissenbacher, G. (eds.) CAV 2018, vol. 10981, pp. 643–661. Springer (2018). https://doi.org/10.1007/978-3-319-96145-3_37
36. Svorenová, M., Kwiatkowska, M.: Quantitative verification and strategy synthesis for stochastic games. Eur. J. Control. **30**, 15–30 (2016). https://doi.org/10.1016/J.EJCON.2016.04.009
37. Tarski, A.: A lattice-theoretical fixpoint theorem and its applications. Pac. J. Math. **5**(2), 285–309 (1955)

Monitoring and Runtime Verification

Prompt Runtime Enforcement

Ayush Anand[1], Loïc Germerie Guizouarn[2], Thierry Jéron[2], Sayan Mukherjee[2], Srinivas Pinisetty[1(✉)], and Ocan Sankur[2]

[1] Indian Institute of Technology Bhubaneswar, Bhubaneswar, India
{a23cs09003,spinisetty}@iitbbs.ac.in
[2] Univ Rennes, Inria, CNRS, IRISA, Rennes, France
{loic.germerie-guizouarn,sayan.mukherjee}@irisa.fr,
Thierry.Jeron@inria.fr, ocan.sankur@cnrs.fr

Abstract. This paper deals with the problem of runtime enforcement (RE) in the context of reactive systems, which consists in modifying the outputs of a system minimally to ensure its correctness. In contrast to enforcers that can postpone events via buffering, enforcers for reactive systems must operate within the same reactive cycle, always yielding a (possibly modified) output. For safety properties, an enforcer makes sure to satisfy the property at each step. However, for general regular properties, one can only expect to satisfy the property eventually. There is then a risk that even under enforcement the satisfaction is indefinitely delayed, and the property is never actually satisfied. Forcing the satisfaction of regular or ω-regular properties has been considered using bounded fairness and prompt eventuality. In this paper, we propose a new runtime enforcement framework for regular properties with prompt eventualities. Given an automaton specifying a property φ and a bound k, the enforcer should never falsify φ more than k consecutive steps. We formally define this RE problem, characterize k-enforceability of automata, and exhibit the construction of the enforcer. Rather than fixing k, we also study whether k can be computed to ensure k-enforceability or some maximal coverage of φ. We implement the k-prompt enforcement framework, and demonstrate its behaviour with varying k.

1 Introduction

Runtime Enforcement (RE) techniques complement approaches such as model checking, with the goal to monitor the system and enforce a small set of crucial properties of the system at runtime. Such runtime techniques are essential as some properties may be difficult to prove due to scalability issues, and in cases when all the properties are proved statically, the system may still malfunction due to environmental changes or due to security concerns (attacks at runtime). Formal RE techniques focus on construction of enforcers automatically from

---

Research conducted within the context of the Inria and IIT Bhubaneswar SINCRET Associate Team supported by Inria and DST.
O. Sankur—The author is currently with Mitsubishi Electric R&D Centre Europe, France.

formal specification of the properties to be enforced. The constructed enforcer attached to the system monitors input/output of the system and corrects erroneous input/output values instantaneously. In addition to ensuring correctness, an enforcer should also guarantee that correct behaviour is unmodified.

Runtime enforcement has been an active area of research since its inception by F.B. Schneider in 2000 [16] in the context of security policies. Different actions like *suppress, store, delay, and reorder* [6,9,10,12,15] may be used to modify the system behaviour. Enforcement in the domain of cyber-physical systems (CPSs) is considerably different. CPSs, in general, are reactive systems which incessantly interact with their environments. This prohibits us to use actions like suppress or delay that interrupt the continuous execution of the system. Thus, approaches suitable for reactive systems such as [14] are proposed where the runtime enforcer continuously monitors the system, and instantaneously edits only those events which will lead to the violation of the property being enforced. The approach in [14] is restricted to enforcing safety (prefix closed) properties and in [13] it is extended to regular discrete-timed properties for reactive systems.

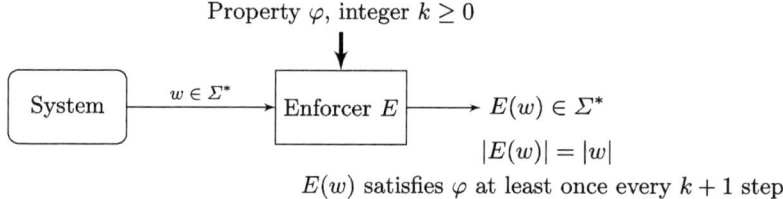

Fig. 1. General scheme of prompt enforcement.

In all the enforcement frameworks such as [13] which considers enforcement of regular properties for reactive systems, the notion of soundness that is defined ensures that whatever is released as output by the enforcer can be further extended so as to satisfy the property. That is, the enforcer ensures that it is always possible to extend the current execution to satisfy the property, but at the same time, it does not guarantee that the property will actually be satisfied eventually. Thus for some properties and observations, the output of the enforcer may continuously be a prefix of an accepting word without ever actually satisfying the property.

However, in some contexts it is important to bound the time before an eventuality is satisfied. To illustrate this, consider an autonomous driving application, where we want to enforce that the vehicle is moving within the speed limit. Let us consider that there are 3 ranges of speed (1) less than 80 (safe range), (2) between 80 to 90 (unsafe but not a violation), and (3) above 90 (violation). Here, we want the vehicle to never go beyond 90 but also never to remain between 80 and 90 indefinitely. Indeed, a good enforcer must eventually bring the vehicle to the safe range, rather than always leaving the possibility to do so without actually enforcing it.

This problem of indefinitely delaying the satisfaction of eventualities has already been considered in the literature. This has led to the study of prompt semantics of logics or Büchi automata, where these undesired infinite behaviours are withdrawn (see *e.g.*, [1,5]). In this paper, inspired by these works on prompt semantics, we consider the problem of satisfying eventualities in the context of enforcement. When enforcing a regular property, the expected behaviour of the runtime enforcer is still to produce prefixes of accepting words, but also to guarantee that the property is accepted eventually with regular intervals.

Contributions: We introduce the *prompt runtime enforcement* problem for regular properties, defined as follows and illustrated in Fig. 1. Given a regular property defined by a finite automaton, and an integer k, we build a k-prompt enforcer for φ, where a k-prompt enforcer transforms an input stream of actions of the system $w \in \Sigma^*$, (where Σ denotes the alphabet of actions) into an output stream of actions $E(w) \in \Sigma^*$ such that the $E(w)$ is a prefix of a word satisfying φ, and the property is satisfied at least once every $k+1$ steps. Moreover, the enforcer should be instantaneous (exactly one output action is produced for every input action), and should alter the actual input only when necessary.

After formalizing the problem, we characterize k-enforceability (existence of a k-prompt enforcer) in terms of a property of the automaton representing φ, and give polynomial-time algorithms to compute k-prompt enforcers. By fixing k, we fix an upper bound on the number of steps within which the property must be satisfied at least once, for every word generated by the enforcer. However, we may sometimes desire that this bound varies for different words generated by the enforcer. We show how *prompt enforcers* solve this problem, by modelling the problem as two-player game with Büchi objective. We show how prompt enforcers can be assumed to be k-prompt enforcer by choosing k to be the size of the state space of the game. We further show how to compute automatically the minimum k such that a given regular property φ is k-enforceable, thus ensuring that any input stream can satisfy φ at least once every $k+1$ steps. There is however a compromise to make between the promptness, that is, the value of k, and the permissiveness of the enforcer: while a small k ensures that the property is satisfied more often, an enforcer with a larger value of k can be less restrictive and changes the input less often. Unfortunately, for a given property, there is in general no upper bound (permissiveness can always be increased in the presence of loops with no accepting state). Nevertheless, when no such loops exist an upper bound can be computed, and we provide a procedure for computing this maximal k in this case. We implemented the k-prompt enforcer using Python. We test our enforcer with a number of policies and show how the promptness and permissiveness change with varying k.

2 Preliminaries

Let Σ be a finite alphabet of actions. A *finite word* on Σ is an element $w = \sigma_1 \cdot \sigma_2 \cdot \ldots \cdot \sigma_n$ of Σ^* whose length is $|w| = n$, where "$\cdot$" is the usual concatenation of words. An *infinite word* is an element $w = \sigma_1 \cdot \sigma_2 \cdot \ldots$ of Σ^ω; by convention $|w| = +\infty$. The empty word is denoted ε. A language of finite (respectively infinite) words is a subset of Σ^* (resp. Σ^ω). We write $w \preceq w'$ when w is a prefix of w', i.e., there exists w'' such that $w \cdot w'' = w'$. Let $w_{\leq i}$ denote the prefix of w of size i if $|w| \geq i$. We denote by $\mathsf{pref}(w)$ the language of prefixes of w, and for a language $\mathcal{L}$ of finite or infinite words, $\mathsf{pref}(\mathcal{L})$ is the language of finite prefixes of words in $\mathcal{L}$. In the remainder, we consider enforcement of finite words, but it will be convenient to reason about infinite words to talk about their unknown and unbounded continuations.

Definition 1. *A deterministic automaton is a tuple $\mathcal{A} = (Q, q_{\mathsf{init}}, \Sigma, \delta, Q_F)$, where Q is a set of states, $q_{\mathsf{init}} \in Q$ the initial state, $Q_F \subseteq Q$ a set of accepting states, Σ is an alphabet of actions, and $\delta : Q \times \Sigma \to Q$ a transition function.*

A *run* of an automaton $\mathcal{A}$ on a given word $w = \sigma_1 \cdot \sigma_2 \cdot \ldots \cdot \sigma_{n-1}$ is a sequence $q_1 q_2 \ldots q_n$ of states such that $q_1 = q_{\mathsf{init}}$, and for all $1 \leq i \leq n-1$, $q_{i+1} = \delta(q_i, \sigma_i)$. The run is accepting if $q_n \in Q_F$; rejecting otherwise. A word is accepted if one of its runs is accepting. Let $\mathcal{L}(\mathcal{A})$ denote the set of finite words accepted by $\mathcal{A}$ and $\mathcal{L}_\omega(\mathcal{A})$ the set of infinite words accepted by $\mathcal{A}$ by the Büchi acceptance condition (i.e., the set of infinite words w such that $\mathsf{Inf}(w) \cap Q_F \neq \emptyset$, where $\mathsf{Inf}(w)$ is the set of states appearing infinitely often in the run of $\mathcal{A}$ on w).

We will implicitly consider *complete automata*, i.e., for any state q and any action σ, if transition $\delta(q, a)$ is missing, it is directed to a non accepting trap state. This does not change its language.

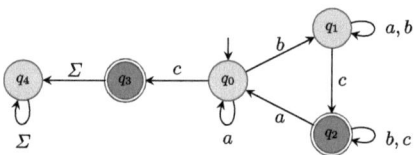

Fig. 2. An automaton $\mathcal{A}$.

Example 1. Fig. 2 represents an automaton $\mathcal{A}$. The nodes are the states, and the edges represent transitions from states, labelled with actions. The set of states is $Q = \{q_0, q_1, q_2, q_3, q_4\}$, $q_{\mathsf{init}} = q_0$ is the initial state, $Q_F = \{q_2, q_3\}$ is the set of accepting states, and $\Sigma = \{a, b, c\}$ is the alphabet. $\rho = q_0 q_1 q_2 q_2 q_0 q_3$ is the accepting run of $\mathcal{A}$ on the word $w = bccac$.

Given a state $q \in Q$, we define $\mathsf{Post}_\mathcal{A}(q) = \{q' \in Q \mid \exists \sigma \in \Sigma, q' = \delta(q, \sigma)\}$; and $\mathsf{Pre}_\mathcal{A}(q) = \{q' \in Q \mid \exists \sigma \in \Sigma, q = \delta(q', \sigma)\}$ respectively the successors and predecessors of q in one step. We extend Pre and Post to sets of states. Moreover, for $X \subseteq Q$ and $0 \leq k \leq l$, we write $\mathsf{Pre}_\mathcal{A}^{[k,l]}(X)$ for $\bigcup_{i \in [k,l]} \mathsf{Pre}_\mathcal{A}^i(X)$, i.e. the set of states from which a state in X is reachable in a number of steps comprised between k and l (where $\mathsf{Pre}_\mathcal{A}^i(X)$ is the composition of i-many $\mathsf{Pre}_\mathcal{A}$ on X, with the convention that $\mathsf{Pre}_\mathcal{A}^0(X) = X$).

We define the *surplus* of a finite word w w.r.t. $\mathcal{A}$, written $\mathsf{surplus}_\mathcal{A}(w)$, as the size of its minimal suffix w'' such that when writing $w = w' \cdot w''$, $w' \in \mathcal{L}(\mathcal{A})$; and we define $\mathsf{surplus}_\mathcal{A}(w) = |w| + 1$ when no such suffix exists. Intuitively, the surplus of a word is the number of actions after the last accepting prefix if there is one, and $|w| + 1$ otherwise. In other words, it is the number of non-accepting states traversed since the last accepting one (initially including q_{init} if q_{init} is not accepting). We have $\mathsf{surplus}_\mathcal{A}(w) = 0$ if and only if $w \in \mathcal{L}(\mathcal{A})$. In particular, $\mathsf{surplus}_\mathcal{A}(\varepsilon) = 0$ if $\varepsilon \in \mathcal{L}(\mathcal{A})$, and 1 otherwise.

We then come to the central notion of promptness. The *promptness* of a finite or infinite word w w.r.t an automaton $\mathcal{A}$ specifying φ, is the maximal surplus of its prefixes: $\mathsf{promptness}_\mathcal{A}(w) = \sup_{w' \in \mathsf{pref}(w)} \mathsf{surplus}_\mathcal{A}(w')$. This means, w falsifies φ at no more than $\mathsf{promptness}_\mathcal{A}(w)$-many consecutive steps. Note that, $\mathsf{promptness}_\mathcal{A}(w)$ is non-decreasing when w is extended with a suffix. The promptness of a language $\mathcal{L} \subseteq \Sigma^\omega$ w.r.t $\mathcal{A}$ is the supremum of the promptness of its words: $\mathsf{promptness}_\mathcal{A}(\mathcal{L}) = \sup\{\mathsf{promptness}_\mathcal{A}(w) \mid w \in \mathcal{L}\}$. We will not use the subscript $\mathcal{A}$ from the notations, when it is clear from the context.

By extension, the promptness of a (finite or infinite) run is the minimal number k such that accepting states are seen at least every $k+1$ steps in this run. Formally, for a run $\rho = q_1 q_2 \ldots q_n$ of $\mathcal{A}$ for all $1 \leq i \leq n-k$, $\{q_i, \ldots, q_{i+k}\} \cap Q_F \neq \emptyset$. The promptness of a word is then the promptness of its run in $\mathcal{A}$.

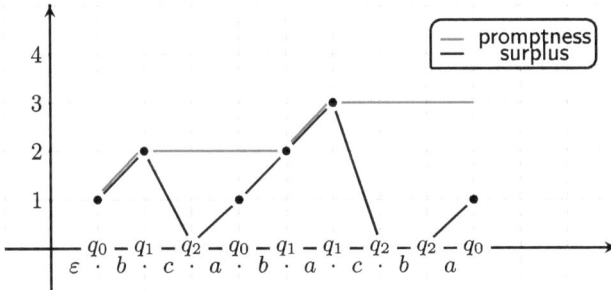

Fig. 3. surplus and promptness of the prefixes of the word $bcabacba$ with respect to the automaton $\mathcal{A}$ of Fig. 2.

Example 2. Figure 3 illustrates graphically these concepts for the word $bcabacba$ using automaton $\mathcal{A}$ of Fig. 2. The x-axis represents the consecutive actions and current state of the automaton, and the y-axis depicts the evolution of surplus and promptness. Note that $\mathsf{surplus}(\varepsilon) = 1$ since q_0 is not accepting, it then increases upon b, i.e. $\mathsf{surplus}(b) = 2$; then $\mathsf{surplus}(bc) = 0$ since bc is accepting. Later upon the next 3 actions aba it again increments by 1 upon each action, $\mathsf{surplus}(bcaba) = 3$, and it again becomes 0 upon the next action c as $bcabac$ is accepting $\mathsf{surplus}(bcabac) = 0$. Initially $\mathsf{promptness}(w)$ is 1, increments to 2 upon the first action b, then remains 2 for the next three actions and later increases to 3 upon the next action (when the word is $bcaba$, since $\mathsf{surplus}(bcaba) = 3$)

and then stays equal to 3. Note that, there are words (*e.g.* a^*) for which both surplus and promptness are unbounded here.

We define the *k-prompt sub-languages* $\mathcal{L}(\mathcal{A})$ and $\mathcal{L}_\omega(\mathcal{A})$, respectively, over finite and infinite words, as follows:

$$\mathcal{L}^k(\mathcal{A}) = \{w \in \mathcal{L}(\mathcal{A}) \mid \mathsf{promptness}_\mathcal{A}(w) \leq k\},$$
$$\mathcal{L}^k_\omega(\mathcal{A}) = \{w \in \mathcal{L}_\omega(\mathcal{A}) \mid \mathsf{promptness}_\mathcal{A}(w) \leq k\},$$

and let $\mathcal{L}^{<\infty}(\mathcal{A}) = \cup_{k \geq 0} \mathcal{L}^k(\mathcal{A})$ and $\mathcal{L}^{<\infty}_\omega(\mathcal{A}) = \cup_{k \geq 0} \mathcal{L}^k_\omega(\mathcal{A})$ denote the *unbounded prompt languages* respectively.

Here using non-strict inequality means that surpluses of prefixes are of size bounded by k, thus an accepting prefix will be seen at least once every subword of length $k + 1$. In other terms, for any run of a word in these languages, an accepting state is seen at least once every $k + 1$ steps.

Notice that, $\mathcal{L}^k(\mathcal{A})$ is not necessarily included in $\mathsf{pref}(\mathcal{L}^k_\omega(\mathcal{A}))$. Indeed a word in $\mathcal{L}^k_\omega(\mathcal{A})$ requires infinite repetition of both accepting states and promptness constraint; being in $\mathsf{pref}(\mathcal{L}^k_\omega(\mathcal{A}))$ means that a continuation in $\mathcal{L}^k_\omega(\mathcal{A})$ exists; while a word in $\mathcal{L}^k(\mathcal{A})$ may have no infinite continuation with promptness bounded by k, and even no infinite continuation at all. Notice that $\mathcal{L}^k_\omega(\mathcal{A})$ is the subset of infinite words in $\mathcal{L}_\omega(\mathcal{A})$ whose set of prefixes in $\mathcal{L}^k(\mathcal{A})$ is infinite.

Example 3. To illustrate this, consider the language of the automaton $\mathcal{A}$ described by Fig. 2 and let $k = 2$. The empty word ε is not accepted, thus has surplus and promptness 1. Then the word c is accepted, has surplus 0 and promptness 1, thus we have $c \in \mathcal{L}^1(\mathcal{A}) \subseteq \mathcal{L}^2(\mathcal{A})$. However, no extension of c is accepted, thus $c \notin \mathsf{pref}(\mathcal{L}^2_\omega(\mathcal{A}))$. On the other hand, bc has surplus 0, promptness 2 and is both in $\mathcal{L}^2(\mathcal{A})$ and $\mathsf{pref}(\mathcal{L}^2_\omega(\mathcal{A}))$ since $(bca)^\omega \in \mathcal{L}^2_\omega(\mathcal{A})$.

Promptness of Safety Properties. Safety properties (*i.e.*, prefix-closed languages) have promptness equal to 0: indeed prefixes of safe words have surplus 0 (otherwise said, safe runs visit accepting states at every 1 step). This entails that for any safety deterministic automaton $\mathcal{A}$, both $\mathcal{L}^0(\mathcal{A}) = \mathcal{L}(\mathcal{A})$ and $\mathcal{L}^0_\omega(\mathcal{A}) = \mathcal{L}_\omega(\mathcal{A})$.

3 Motivation

Enforcement of properties in a system for general regular properties is based on the idea that absolute violation of the property must be averted. When considering the existing enforcement frameworks such as [13], enforcers do not allow the system to deviate from the possibility of satisfying the property that is being enforced. In other words, they allow the system to exist in a state from which property satisfaction can be reached. The enforcers assure property satisfiability, but are incapable of exactly determining when the said property will be satisfied.

Consider an autonomous vehicle system that has an output channel, and let $\Sigma = \{a\_sn, d\_sn, a\_sb, d\_sb, a\_sv, d\_sv\}$ be the alphabet of actions. Action prefix 'a' in $\{a\_sn, a\_sb, a\_sv\}$ denote that the vehicle is accelerating, while

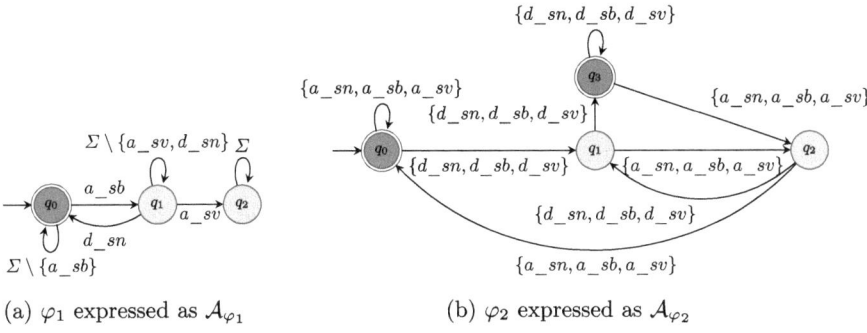

Fig. 4. Properties of autonomous vehicle system.

prefix 'd' denotes that the vehicle is decelerating. The suffix of the actions denotes whether the current speed of the vehicle is in *normal range (sn)*, *buffer range (sb)*, or *violation range (sv)*.

Let x be some speed-limit on a motorway, and v be the speed of the vehicle. The system outputs: a_sn or d_sn when $v \leq x$, a_sb or d_sb when $x < v \leq x + \Delta$ and a_sv or d_sv when $v > x + \Delta$, where Δ is some marginal buffer speed. Let φ_1 denote the property *"the vehicle should not accelerate to speed violation, and it should often remain within the speed-limit"*. Property φ_1 can be specified as an automaton $\mathcal{A}_{\varphi_1}$ shown in Fig. 4a. However a typical enforcer for regular properties obtained using frameworks such as [13], would still allow the system to forever remain in non-accepting state q_1, because there exists a path from q_1 to an accepting state q_0, thereby providing uncertainty over returning to or below the speed limit ($\leq x$).

In this work, we thus propose a prompt runtime enforcement framework for synthesis of a *k-prompt enforcer*, which for a given value k, will guarantee that state q_0 is reached at least once every $k + 1$ steps, thereby guaranteeing that the system will return to or is below the speed limit.

Consider another property φ_2 expressed as $\mathcal{A}_{\varphi_2}$ illustrated in Fig. 4b. Property φ_2 differentiates the 'non-jerk' $\{q_0, q_3\}$ states of the system from 'jerk' $\{q_1, q_2\}$ state. A 'jerk' state is identified by the sequence $(a\_..) \cdot (d\_..) \cdot (a\_..)$ or $(d\_..) \cdot (a\_..) \cdot (d\_..)$[1]. Using the parameter k in *k-prompt enforcer*, we can decide how many consecutive 'jerks' are allowed in the system. For example $k = 3$ will not allow more than 3 consecutive jerks, and for $k = 1$ the enforcer will not allow two or more consecutive jerks. Thus, the *k-prompt enforcer* allows to control the permissible number of consecutive jerks in the system.

---

[1] $a\_...$ denotes any action where the vehicle is accelerating, *i.e.*, $a\_.. = a\_sn/a\_sb/a\_sv$. Similarly, $d\_..$ denotes any action where the vehicle is decelerating, $d\_.. = d\_sn, d\_sb, d\_sv$.

4 Problem Definition

We want to define an enforcer that can change actions, but cannot remove them, and which ensures that a word belonging to the language $\mathcal{L}(\mathcal{A})$ will be produced regularly. We will consider two variants of this problem: either the designer chooses a parameter k and we look for an enforcer that ensures that the produced word satisfies $\mathcal{L}(\mathcal{A})$ every $k+1$ steps, or it is required that for each infinite word produced by the enforcer (assuming it is run over an infinite duration) there exists some k such that a prefix belonging to $\mathcal{L}(\mathcal{A})$ is seen every $k+1$ steps. Note the subtlety here: in the latter case, for each infinite word, a different bound k may apply (similar to the prompt-Büchi acceptance condition in [1]).

We call *word transducer* a function $E : \Sigma^* \to \Sigma^*$ that is monotonic for the prefix relation, that is, $w \preceq w' \Rightarrow E(w) \preceq E(w')$. A word transducer lifted to infinite words, is defined as: for $w \in \Sigma^\omega$, $E(w) = \lim_{i \geq 1} E(w_{\leq i})$. This limit is well defined due to the monotonicity of E. We say that a word transducer is *synchronous* when $\forall w \in \Sigma^*$, $|E(w)| = |w|$. All together, it entails that a synchronous enforcer is *instantaneous*: at each step, a given action σ is transformed into exactly one action σ'.

Definition 2. *Given an automaton $\mathcal{A}$ and an integer bound k, a k-prompt enforcer E for $\mathcal{A}$ is a synchronous word transducer $E : \Sigma^* \to \Sigma^*$ satisfying the following properties:*

Soundness: $\forall w \in \Sigma^\omega$, $E(w) \in \mathcal{L}_\omega^k(\mathcal{A})$.
Minimal Intervention: $\forall w \in \Sigma^*$, $\forall \sigma \in \Sigma$, $E(w) \cdot \sigma \in \mathsf{pref}(\mathcal{L}_\omega^k(\mathcal{A}))$ implies $E(w \cdot \sigma) = E(w) \cdot \sigma$.

We say that a language represented by $\mathcal{A}$ is k-*enforceable* if there exists a k-prompt enforcer for $\mathcal{A}$.

Soundness is defined for infinite words, even though the enforcer works on finite words. Intuitively, soundness means that the enforcer should always keep the possibility of an infinite continuation with promptness bounded by k, and can equivalently be defined as $\forall w \in \Sigma^*, E(w) \in \mathsf{pref}(\mathcal{L}_\omega^k(\mathcal{A}))$. Minimal intervention means that if some infinite extension of $E(w) \cdot \sigma$ with promptness k exists, σ should not be modified by the enforcer.

In [13], the minimal intervention property is called *transparency*. The *monotonicity* criterion of [13] is given here by the fact that E is a word transducer; and *instantaneity* of [13] follows from synchronicity of the word transducer.

Notice that by definition of a k-prompt enforcer for $\mathcal{A}$, the finite language it produces is exactly $\mathsf{pref}(\mathcal{L}_\omega^k(\mathcal{A}))$. Indeed by soundness any enforced word is in $\mathsf{pref}(\mathcal{L}_\omega^k(\mathcal{A}))$. Conversely, by minimal intervention, any input word in $\mathsf{pref}(\mathcal{L}_\omega^k(\mathcal{A}))$ is unmodified, thus can be produced. Therefore, in the limit, a k-prompt enforcer produces exactly $\mathcal{L}_\omega^k(\mathcal{A})$.

The second type of enforcers we are interested in are enforcers that guarantee promptness without a fixed bound k:

Definition 3. *Given an automaton $\mathcal{A}$, a prompt enforcer E for $\mathcal{A}$ is a synchronous word transducer $E : \Sigma^* \to \Sigma^*$ satisfying*

Soundness: $\forall w \in \Sigma^\omega$, $E(w) \in \mathcal{L}_\omega^{<\infty}(\mathcal{A})$.

In this case, we do not require any minimal intervention property. In fact, because the promptness of each infinite word can be different, and cannot be deduced from a finite prefix, one cannot impose a minimal intervention property as in Definition 2.

We are interested in determining when such k-prompt enforcers or prompt enforcers exist, and how to build them. In the next section, we will study algorithms for this problem.

5 Algorithms for Prompt Runtime Enforcement

5.1 k-Prompt Enforcers

By Sect. 4, the language of a k-prompt enforcer is exactly $\mathcal{L}_\omega^k(\mathcal{A})$. In this section, we show that enforceability requires the non-emptiness of $\mathcal{L}_\omega^k(\mathcal{A})$; interestingly, it turns out that this condition is also sufficient. Moreover, we also characterised enforceability by a property on automata and the proof is constructive: it shows how to build a k-prompt enforcer.

Before going into this result, we first define a few notations that will be used to formulate and prove this. Let $\mathcal{A} = (Q, q_{\mathrm{init}}, \Sigma, \delta, Q_F)$ be a deterministic automaton, we use Z^k to denote the greatest fixpoint: $Z^k = \nu X.\ Q_F \cap \mathrm{Pre}_\mathcal{A}^{[1,k+1]}(X)$. Intuitively, Z^k is the largest set consisting of all the states in Q_F from which another state in Z^k is reachable in at most $k+1$ steps. We now define a distance function $d_{Z^k} : Q \mapsto \mathbb{N}$ as $d_X(q) = \min\{\{+\infty\} \cup \{i \in \mathbb{N} \mid q \in \mathrm{Pre}_\mathcal{A}^i(X)\}\}$. In words, $d_{Z^k}(q)$ denotes the shortest distance of q from Z^k, when Z^k is non-empty and is reachable from q, and the distance is $+\infty$ otherwise. Note that, $d_{Z^k}(q) = 0, \forall q \in Z^k$.

Example 4. We illustrate these notions on the automaton $\mathcal{A}$ depicted in Fig. 2. Suppose $k = 2$, the fixpoint computation of Z^2 starts with $X^{(0)} = Q_F = \{q_2, q_3\}$; then since $\mathrm{Pre}_\mathcal{A}^{[1,2]}(\{q_2, q_3\}) = \{q_2\}$, we get $X^{(1)} = \{q_2\}$ and the fixpoint is reached, thus $Z^2 = \{q_2\}$. Note that, even though q_3 is accepting, it does not belong to Z^k for any k, since from q_3 no other accepting state (hence no states in Z^k) is reachable. On the other hand, the distances of the states from Z^2 are: $d_{Z^2}(q_0) = 2$, $d_{Z^2}(q_1) = 1$, $d_{Z^2}(q_2) = 0$, and $d_{Z^2}(q_3) = d_{Z^2}(q_4) = +\infty$. Note also that $Z^k = \{q_2\}$ for $k \geq 0$.

For a finite word w, we define $sum_{Z^k}(w) = \mathsf{surplus}(w) + d_{Z^k}(q_w)$ where $q_w = \delta(q_{\mathrm{init}}, w)$. In words, $sum_{Z^k}(w)$ is the sum of the surplus of w and the shortest distance to the set Z^k after reading w. The intention is to define a k-prompt enforcer E for $\mathcal{A}$ that will maintain the following invariant:

$$\forall w \in \Sigma^*,\ sum_{Z^k}(E(w)) \leq k+1 \qquad (1)$$

We then define, for $w \in \Sigma^*$, $\mathsf{filter}(w) = \{\sigma \in \Sigma \mid sum_{Z^k}(w \cdot \sigma) \leq k+1\}$, i.e., the set of all actions σ, that when concatenated with w still satisfy the invariant (1).

We now characterize k-enforceability by the following theorem:

Theorem 1. *Given a deterministic automaton $\mathcal{A} = (Q, q_{\mathsf{init}}, \Sigma, \delta, Q_F)$, and a bound $k \geq 0$, the following statements are equivalent: (1) $\mathcal{A}$ is k-enforceable, (2) $\mathcal{L}_\omega^k(\mathcal{A})$ is non-empty, and (3) $d_{Z^k}(q_{\mathsf{init}}) \leq k$.*

Proof. $\boxed{1 \implies 2}$ We assume $\mathcal{A}$ is k-enforceable. Then there exists a k-prompt enforcer E for $\mathcal{A}$. For any infinite word $w \in \Sigma^\omega$, by soundness of E we get that $E(w) \in \mathcal{L}_\omega^k(\mathcal{A})$, thus $\mathcal{L}_\omega^k(\mathcal{A}) \neq \emptyset$.

$\boxed{2 \implies 3}$ Let $w \in \mathcal{L}_\omega^k(\mathcal{A})$ by non-vacuity of this set. The run of $\mathcal{A}$ on w has promptness bounded by k, thus it visits Q_F at least once every $k+1$ steps. Since Q_F is finite, this run must visit some states in Q_F more than once. Let $q_f \in Q_F$ be the first state appearing twice in the run, this means that there exists a loop in $\mathcal{A}$ from q_f to q_f, moreover, this loop crosses Q_F at least once every $k+1$ steps (due to promptness). By definition of Z^k, those states belonging to Q_F in the loop belong to Z^k. Again, due to the promptness being bounded by k, the portion of the run from q_{init} to the first occurrence of q_f visits Q_F at least once every $k+1$ steps. This implies that all the accepting states in this part of the run are also in Z^k, and therefore $d_{Z^k}(q_{\mathsf{init}}) \leq k$.

$\boxed{3 \implies 1}$ We assume that $d_{Z^k}(q_{\mathsf{init}}) \leq k$. We define below a k-prompt enforcer of $\mathcal{A}$ as a word transducer $E : \Sigma^* \to \Sigma^*$ that will maintain the invariant (1). We construct E in an inductive manner. Initially, we define $E(\varepsilon) = \varepsilon$. The invariant (1) holds initially for ε because either $q_{\mathsf{init}} \in Z^k = Pre^0(Z^k)$ and then $\mathsf{surplus}(\varepsilon) = 0$ and $d_{Z^k}(q_{\mathsf{init}}) = 0$, or $q_{\mathsf{init}} \notin Z^k$, and then $\mathsf{surplus}(\varepsilon) = 1$ and $d_{Z^k}(q_{\mathsf{init}}) \leq k$ by hypothesis. In both of these cases, $sum_{Z^k}(\varepsilon) \leq k+1$ and the invariant is maintained.

Now, consider a finite word w, and assume that $E(w)$ has already been defined, satisfying (1). We claim that $\mathsf{filter}(E(w)) \neq \emptyset$. Define $q_{E(w)} = \delta(q_{\mathsf{init}}, E(w))$. Then, since $E(w)$ satisfies (1), $d_{Z^k}(q_{E(w)}) \leq k+1$. One can then observe that there must exist an action σ such that $d_{Z^k}(\delta(q_{E(w)}, \sigma)) = d_{Z^k}(q_{E(w)}) - 1$ when $\delta(q_{E(w)}, \sigma) \notin Z^k$, and is 0 when $\delta(q_{E(w)}, \sigma) \in Z^k$. Therefore, $sum_{Z^k}(E(w).\sigma) \leq k+1$, since the sum is either $\mathsf{surplus}_{\mathcal{A}}(E(w)) + 1 + d_{Z^k}(q_{E(w)}) - 1$ or it is reset to 0 when $\delta(q_{E(w)}, \sigma) \in Z^k$. Hence, $\sigma \in \mathsf{filter}(E(w))$ and thus $\mathsf{filter}(E(w)) \neq \emptyset$.

When receiving the next action $\sigma \in \Sigma$, the enforcer acts as follows: if $\sigma \in \mathsf{filter}(E(w))$ then $E(w.\sigma) = E(w).\sigma$; and otherwise $E(w.\sigma) = E(w).\sigma'$ for some $\sigma' \in \mathsf{filter}(E(w))$. From the argument presented in the previous paragraph, note that, the invariant (1) is maintained by this construction.

Satisfying the invariant for every word w means the following: $E(w)$ can be extended with a word w' that would reach Z^k within $k+1-\mathsf{surplus}(E(w))$ many steps. The surplus of a prefix of $E(w).w'$ then never exceeds k (surplus is 0 in Z^k). Moreover, the word $E(w).w'$ can be continued infinitely, hitting Z^k at least once every $k+1$ steps. Thus $E(w) \in \mathsf{pref}(\mathcal{L}_\omega^k(\mathcal{A}))$, hence soundness follows.

Furthermore, the construction of the enforcer ensures instantaneity and minimal intervention. Therefore, E is indeed a k-prompt enforcer for $\mathcal{A}$. □

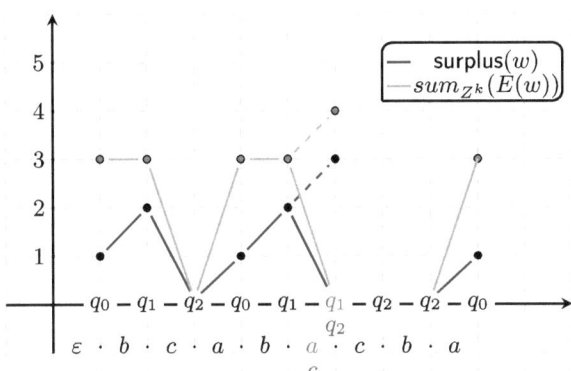

Fig. 5. Behaviour of a 2-enforcer for the automaton $\mathcal{A}$ of Fig. 2 on $bcabacba$. The dashed lines represent the values of the surplus and sum_{Z^k} if the enforcer would not have been in play in the last step. The modified action and the resulting states are written in red. (Color figure online)

Example 5. Let us consider the automaton $\mathcal{A}$ of Fig. 2 and suppose $k = 2$. Figure 5 represents the behaviour of the 2-enforcer on the input word $bcabacba$. Starting with ε at q_0, the surplus is 1 and distance d_{Z^k} is 2, thus their sum does not exceed $k + 1 = 3$. When reading b, q_1 is reached, the surplus increases by 1 while the distance decreases by 1, their sum is thus constant and the enforcer keeps b as output. Then reading c, q_2 is reached which is accepting; both surplus and distance are then set to 0. Then, receiving a, the surplus is 1 and the distance to q_2 is 2 and a is kept unmodified. Receiving b sets the surplus to 2 and distance to 1, then b is kept and we reach q_1. Now, receiving a would loop in q_1, leaving the distance unchanged but increasing the surplus to 3, the sum then is $4 > 3$, and the action a is changed to c which leads to q_2 with both surplus and distance reset to 0. The following actions c and b also lead to q_2 thus are kept as output, and finally a is kept, leading to q_0 again.

5.2 Prompt Enforcers

Rather than fixing a uniform bound k for all words generated under the enforcer, prompt enforcers (Definition 3) require from the enforcer that each generated infinite word must have bounded promptness for a possibly different bound k. In this section, we show that prompt enforcers can be assumed to be k-prompt enforcers for a well chosen k.

In order to study this case, we will model the prompt enforcement problem using two-player turn-based games [7]. Given $\mathcal{A} = (Q, q_{\text{init}}, \Sigma, \delta, Q_F)$, consider the two-player game $\mathcal{G}$ with a Büchi objective, defined as follows. The state space is $Q \cup (Q \times \Sigma)$ where Q is controlled by Player *Environment* and $(Q \times \Sigma)$ by Player *Enforcer*; at a state $q \in Q$, Environment selects $\sigma \in \Sigma$, and at any state $(q, \sigma) \in (Q \times \Sigma)$, Enforcer freely selects $\sigma' \in \Sigma$ and the game moves to state $q' = \delta(q, \sigma')$.

Let us put promptness aside for a moment and assume that the objective of Enforcer is to visit Q_F infinitely often, then this is a Büchi game. In any turn-based two-player game with a Büchi objective, if a player has a winning strategy, then he has a winning strategy under which all outcomes have promptness at most the size of the state space. This is because a winning player has a *positional*[2] winning strategy [7], which, against any adversary, ensures reaching an accepting state at least once every k steps, where k is the size of the state space.

Coming back to our game $\mathcal{G}$, if Enforcer has a winning strategy, then it has one that induces words with promptness at most $k = |Q| + |Q||\Sigma|$. Let $\gamma : Q \times \Sigma \to \Sigma$ denote such a positional winning strategy for Enforcer. Strategy γ corresponds to a prompt enforcer but not necessarily to a k-prompt enforcer since the minimal intervention property might not be satisfied. Nevertheless, a k-prompt enforcer can be derived as follows.

In the game $\mathcal{G}$, the set W of states from which a winning strategy exists can be partitioned into $W_0, W_1, \ldots, W_k$ where $W_0 \subseteq Q_F$, with the following properties:

- for all $1 \leq i \leq k$ and $q \in W_i, \forall \sigma \in \Sigma, \delta(q, \gamma(q, \sigma)) \in \cup_{0 \leq j \leq i-1} W_j$,
- for all $q \in W_0, \forall \sigma \in \Sigma, \delta(q, \gamma(q, \sigma)) \in W$.

Note that the sequence $(W_i)_i$ corresponds to the attractor computation when solving Büchi games; see [7]. In other terms, the strategy γ ensures that at each step, whatever the environment's action, we make progress towards accepting states, while from W_0, we remain within W.

In our case, given $q \in W$, we have $q \in W_i$ with $i \geq 1$ iff there is $w \in \Sigma^{\leq i}$ such that $\delta(q, w) \in W_0$.

Let us define a new strategy γ' as follows: For each $(q, \sigma) \in W_i$,

$$\gamma'(q) = \{\sigma' \in \Sigma \mid q \in W_0 \wedge \delta(q, \sigma') \in W$$
$$\vee \ \exists 1 \leq i \leq k, q \in W_i \wedge \delta(q, \sigma') \in \cup_{0 \leq j \leq i-1} W_j\}.$$

Thus, $\gamma'(q)$ denotes the set of all σ' which ensure making progress towards W_0. Note that for all $q \in W$, $\gamma(q, \sigma) \in \gamma'(q)$. Then any arbitrary strategy which, at all states (q, σ), selects some action from $\gamma'(q)$ is a winning strategy in $\mathcal{G}$ which induces words with promptness at most k. This is true regardless whether the strategy is positional or not.

Now, from γ' we can derive a k-prompt enforcer E, built recursively, as follows. Initially $E(\varepsilon) = \varepsilon$, and $q_{\text{init}} \in W$ (since we assumed that there exists a winning strategy). Consider any word w for which $E(w)$ is already defined and consider an input $\sigma \in \Sigma$. Let $q \in W$ be the state $\delta(q_{\text{init}}, E(w))$. Now if

---

[2] A positional strategy for Enforcer only depends on the current state.

$\sigma \in \gamma'(q)$, then $E(w.\sigma) = E(w).\sigma$; and otherwise $E(w.\sigma) = E(w).\sigma'$ for an arbitrary $\sigma' \in \gamma'(q)$. By the previous discussion, E is a winning strategy for Büchi with promptness at most k.

Moreover, E has the minimal intervention property. In fact, consider any word w and $\sigma \in \Sigma$, and let $q \in W_i$ denote the state $\delta(q_{\mathsf{init}}, E(w))$. Assume $E(w.\sigma) \in \mathsf{pref}(\mathcal{L}_\omega^k(\mathcal{A}))$. If $i > 0$, this means that there exists $w' \in \Sigma^{i-1}$ such that $\delta(q, \sigma \cdot w') \in W_0$, and so $E(w.\sigma) = E(w).\sigma$. If $i = 0$, then we necessarily have $\delta(q, \sigma) \in W$ since $E(w.\sigma) \in \mathsf{pref}(\mathcal{L}_\omega^k(\mathcal{A}))$ means that there is a winning strategy from $\delta(q, \sigma)$. In this case we also have $E(w.\sigma) = E(w).\sigma$.

Thus any prompt enforcer corresponds to a winning strategy for the Büchi objective in our game (it actually satisfies the prompt Büchi objective, which is stronger). Conversely, we just showed that a winning strategy for the Büchi objective can be assumed to be a k-prompt enforcer. We get the following theorem.

Theorem 2. *Consider an automaton $\mathcal{A} = (Q, q_{\mathsf{init}}, \Sigma, \delta, Q_F)$ and the Büchi game $\mathcal{G}$ described above. The following statements are equivalent:* (1) *Enforcer has a winning strategy in $\mathcal{G}$;* (2) *there exists a prompt enforcer for $\mathcal{A}$;* (3) *there exists a k-prompt enforcer for $\mathcal{A}$ with $k = |Q| + |Q||\Sigma|$.*

Theorem 2 can be used to decide the existence of prompt enforcers, and compute prompt enforcers using the bound $|Q| + |Q||\Sigma|$. However, this bound might in general be too large. We next discuss how to compute a minimal bound k.

5.3 Computing the Optimal k for Enforceability

Given an automaton $\mathcal{A}$, we will consider an abstraction in the form of a weighted graph $G_\mathcal{A}$ whose vertices are $Q_F \cup \{q_{\mathsf{init}}\}$ and there is an edge from $q \in Q_F \cup \{q_{\mathsf{init}}\}$ to $q' \in Q_F$ if there is a path in $\mathcal{A}$ from q to q' visiting no accepting states (other than q and q'), called a *non-accepting path*. $G_\mathcal{A}$ is parametrized by a function weight: we will define $\mathsf{weight}(q, q')$ labelling the edge $q \to q'$ if it exists in $G_\mathcal{A}$.

Minimal Promptness. If an automaton $\mathcal{A}$ is k-prompt enforceable, trivialy it is also k'-prompt enforceable for every $k' > k$. Thus, for a promptly enforceable property, we are interested in computing the minimal value $k_{\min}$ of k such that the property is k-prompt enforceable. Given $\mathcal{A}$, we can compute $k_{\min}$ in polynomial (in $|\mathcal{A}|$) time, as follows. We create a weighted graph $G_\mathcal{A}^{\min}$, where for every q, q', weight assigns to (q, q') the number of non-accepting states appearing in the shortest non-accepting path from q to q' in $\mathcal{A}$ (including q if it is q_{init} and is not in Q_F).

Let us write the set of all weights appearing in $G_\mathcal{A}^{\min}$, in ascending order, as $\zeta_1 \leq \zeta_2 \leq \cdots \leq \zeta_m$. Now, for each $1 \leq i \leq m$, we consider the graph $G_\mathcal{A}^{\leq i}$ obtained from $G_\mathcal{A}^{\min}$ by removing all edges having weight larger than ζ_i, and check the existence of a lasso that starts from q_{init}: such a lasso corresponds to an accepting lasso in $\mathcal{A}$. The procedure stops whenever such a lasso is found, or when we exhaust the search in all the graphs $G_{\mathcal{A}}^{\leq i}$. If we stop at step i, then $k_{\min} = \zeta_i$ is the minimal value for which there is a $k_{\min}$-prompt enforcer for $\mathcal{A}$. Indeed, the existence of a lasso means that $\mathcal{L}_\omega^{k_{\min}}(\mathcal{A})$ is non-empty, and by Theorem 1 this is equivalent to $\mathcal{A}$ being ζ_i-prompt enforceable. Conversely, note that, if there does not exist such a lasso in $G_{\mathcal{A}}^{\leq i}$ then $\mathcal{L}_\omega^{\zeta_i}(\mathcal{A})$ is empty and hence again from Theorem 1, there is no ζ_i-prompt enforcer for that ζ_i.

Theorem 3. *Given an automaton $\mathcal{A}$, one can compute in polynomial time if $\mathcal{A}$ is k-prompt enforceable for some $k \in \mathbb{N}$, and if it is, one can also compute the minimal k such that $\mathcal{A}$ is k-prompt enforceable.*

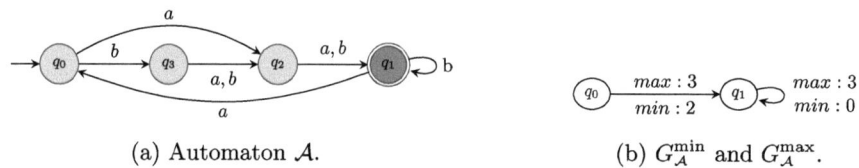

(a) Automaton $\mathcal{A}$.   (b) $G_{\mathcal{A}}^{\min}$ and $G_{\mathcal{A}}^{\max}$.

Fig. 6. An automaton and its $G_{\mathcal{A}}^{\min}$ and $G_{\mathcal{A}}^{\max}$ graph.

For example, consider the automaton $\mathcal{A}$ in Fig. 6. The graph $G_{\mathcal{A}}^{\min}$ is given by Fig. 6b using "min" weights attached to edges. Clearly $G_{\mathcal{A}}^{\leq 0}$ and $G_{\mathcal{A}}^{\leq 1}$ have no lasso while $G_{\mathcal{A}}^{\leq 2}$ does. We then get $k_{\min} = 2$.

Maximal Permissiveness. There is, in general, a trade-off between promptness of an enforcer and its *permissiveness*. In fact, while a small k is preferable because the produced words will satisfy $\mathcal{A}$ more often, it also means that the incoming words might be modified too often. An enforcer with a larger k is more permissive since it will let more words pass through and only modify them when necessary (according to the minimal intervention property). Here, we discuss whether there exists *most permissive enforcers* obtained by choosing some large enough k.

We already saw that if $\mathcal{A}$ is k-prompt enforceable it is k'-prompt enforceable for $k' \geq k$. However, in general, there is no maximal value $k_{\max}$ such that the prompt language is 'stable' after this value, that is, $\mathcal{L}_\omega^k(\mathcal{A}) = \mathcal{L}_\omega^{k_{\max}}(\mathcal{A})$, $\forall k \geq k_{\max}$. For instance, consider the automaton $\mathcal{A}$ in Fig. 2, we have already shown that this automaton is 2-prompt enforceable (see Fig. 5). Now, note that $bcaa^i bcb^\omega$ is in $\mathcal{L}_\omega^{2+i}(\mathcal{A})$ but not in $\mathcal{L}_\omega^{2+i-1}(\mathcal{A})$, for every integer $i \geq 1$. Therefore, in this example, $\mathcal{L}_\omega^k(\mathcal{A}) \subsetneq \mathcal{L}_\omega^{k'}(\mathcal{A})$, for every $k' > k \geq 2$. This happens essentially due to the presence of a loop that does not contain an accepting state (*e.g.* the self-loop at q_0) from which another loop (*e.g.* the loop $q_0 \to q_1 \to q_2 \to q_0$) that contains an accepting state is reachable.

Nevertheless, when no such loops exist, we argue that there indeed exists a maximal bound $k_{\max}$, computable in polynomial time. The algorithm starts by decomposing $\mathcal{A}$ into strongly connected components (SCC) in linear time using Tarjan's algorithm [17]. Let us call an SCC *winning* if it contains an accepting state, and *losing* otherwise. We construct the pruned automaton $\mathcal{A}' = (Q', q_{\text{init}}, \Sigma, \delta', Q'_F)$ from $\mathcal{A}$, by removing all the components from which no winning component is reachable. Note that, this procedure does not alter the language of $\mathcal{A}$, i.e. $\mathcal{L}_\omega(\mathcal{A}) = \mathcal{L}_\omega(\mathcal{A}')$. By hypothesis, $\mathcal{A}'$ contains no non-trivial losing component from which a winning component can be reached. If q_{init} was removed, then $\mathcal{A}$ is not enforceable. Otherwise we build a weighted graph $G_\mathcal{A}^{\max}$ from $\mathcal{A}'$ with the weight taken in $\mathcal{A}'$ as follows: for each pair of states $q \in Q'_F \cup \{q_{\text{init}}\}$, $q' \in Q'_F$, $\text{weight}(q, q')$ is the maximal number of non-accepting states in non-accepting paths from q to q'. We then define $k_{\max}$ as follows: $k_{\max} = \max_{q \in Q'_F \cup \{q_{\text{init}}\}, q' \in Q'_F} \text{weight}(q, q')$. Therefore, no prefix of an accepted word in $\mathcal{A}$ has promptness greater than $k_{\max}$. Otherwise said, in every accepting run of $\mathcal{A}'$ (hence, of $\mathcal{A}$ as well) an accepting state is seen every $k_{\max}+1$ steps. This immediately implies the following theorem.

Theorem 4. *Consider an automaton $\mathcal{A}$, and assume that from all reachable[3] and losing SCCs, no winning SCC is reachable. Then there exists $k_{\max} \geq 0$ such that $\forall k \geq k_{\max}, \mathcal{L}_\omega^k(\mathcal{A}) = \mathcal{L}_\omega^{k_{\max}}(\mathcal{A})$.*

Consider again $\mathcal{A}$ in Fig. 6. Since there is only one SCC in $\mathcal{A}$ which is accepting, we get $\mathcal{A}' = \mathcal{A}$ here. The graph $G_\mathcal{A}^{\max}$ is then the graph of Fig. 6b using "max" weights attached to edges. We then get $k_{\max} = 3$.

Algorithm 1. Pseudocode for implementation of k-enforcer E. The algorithm assumes that the property defined by $\mathcal{A}$ is k-enforceable, that $Z = \nu X. Q_F \cap \text{Pre}_{\mathcal{A}_\varphi}^{[1,k]}(X)$ is known, as well as the distance function $d_{Z^k} : Q \to \mathbb{N}$.

1: Input k, $\mathcal{A} = (Q, q_{init}, \Sigma, \delta, Q_F)$
2: cs ← 0 if $q_{init} \in Q_F$ else 1
3: $q \leftarrow q_{init}$
4: $w_E \leftarrow \varepsilon$
5: **while** true:
6:    $\sigma \leftarrow$ next_action()
7:    $\mathcal{F} \leftarrow \emptyset$
8:    **for all** $\sigma' \in \Sigma$:
9:       cs$_{\text{temp}}$ ← 0 if $\delta(q, \sigma') = q' \in Q_F$ else cs + 1
10:       **if** cs$_{\text{temp}}$ + $d_{Z^k}(q') \leq k+1$: $\mathcal{F} \leftarrow \mathcal{F} \cup \{\sigma'\}$
11:    $\sigma' \leftarrow \sigma$ **if** $\sigma \in \mathcal{F}$ **else** pick some σ' in $\mathcal{F}$
12:    $q \leftarrow \delta(q, \sigma')$
13:    cs ← 0 if $q \in Q_F$ else cs + 1
14:    $w_E \leftarrow w_E \cdot \sigma'$

---

[3] An SCC is *reachable* when its states are reachable from the initial state.

6 Implementation and Evaluation

Given a regular property specified as an automaton $\mathcal{A}$, in Algorithm 1, we present the implementation of constructing a k-prompt enforcer E (discussed in 5.1) as an online algorithm. We assume that $\mathcal{A}$ indeed has a k-prompt enforcer. We compare the results produced by our algorithm with that of [13].

Algorithm 1 takes as input an automaton $\mathcal{A}$ and a positive integer k. The actions emitted by the system are fed to the algorithm one at a time and the algorithm modifies this action whenever necessary. The word enforced so far is stored in the variable w_E, initially $w_E = \varepsilon$; the current surplus is maintained in the variable cs: initially 0 if $q_{init} \in Q_F$, otherwise 1. Further, the algorithm maintains the current state q of the property automaton, initially set to q_{init}. The online enforcement starts with the while loop in step 5. The enforcer receives the next action σ from the system (step 6). Steps 7 through 10 implement the filter function as defined in Page 9. We initialize the filter set $\mathcal{F}$ with $\emptyset$. Then, for each possible action σ', we update the value of the current surplus (in step 9) and compute the sum_{Z^k} (as defined also in Page 9) in step 10. Note here that we assume that Algorithm 1 is also provided with the distance function d_{Z^k}, we implement this function as a simple fixpoint computation. We add σ' to $\mathcal{F}$ if the computed value of sum_{Z^k} does not exceed $k+1$. Step 11 chooses the enforced letter $\sigma' \in \mathcal{F}$, respecting minimal intervention, *i.e.* keeping $\sigma' = \sigma$ if $\sigma \in \mathcal{F}$. The current word is then updated, and the while loop continues with the next action.

An execution of the algorithm on the automaton $\mathcal{A}$ in Example 1 is provided in the Appendix [2].

Algorithm 1 is implemented in Python. The implementation consists of a class called DFA that provides the required functionalities related to defining an automaton and its traversal on a word. We then encode Algorithm 1 as a function enforce_event(). This function is defined as a member function of the DFA class in the automata module. It takes the current state q, current action σ, and k as arguments, and updates the action and the word according to Algorithm 1 described above. Using a driver program in Python, we import the automata module, and create an object of the DFA class to specify the property as an automaton. We import the trace of the system dynamically, action by action, and call enforce_event() to enforce the specified property.

6.1 Results and Observations

We tested the *k-prompt* enforcer by enforcing 50 different properties. We used a random automata generator [19] to generate DFA specifications of 50 random properties. We enforced each property on 10 words of varying length (100 to 1000) using our *k-prompt* enforcer. For consistent results, all the words were such that no prefix of any word satisfied the property being enforced. We computed the number of times the property was satisfied, and the number of times the actions in the words were edited. We calculated three normalized frequencies:

- frequency of property satisfaction $\nu_{\text{sat}} = \dfrac{\text{number of accepting prefixes}}{\text{word length}}$,

- frequency of edited events (by the enforcer) $\nu_{\text{edited}} = \frac{\text{number of edited events}}{\text{word length}}$,
- and frequency of unedited events $\nu_{\text{unedited}} = 1 - \nu_{\text{edited}}$.

We first demonstrate the behaviours of the enforcer with varying k.

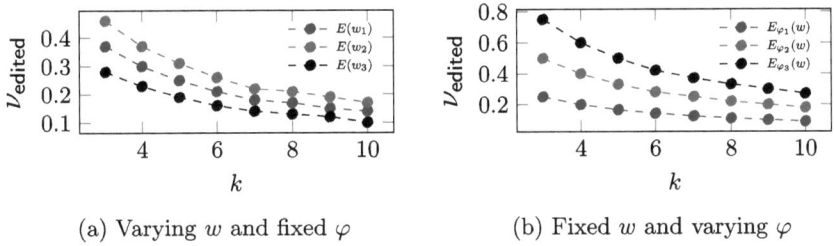

Fig. 7. Plot showing change in frequency of 'edited' actions with increasing k.

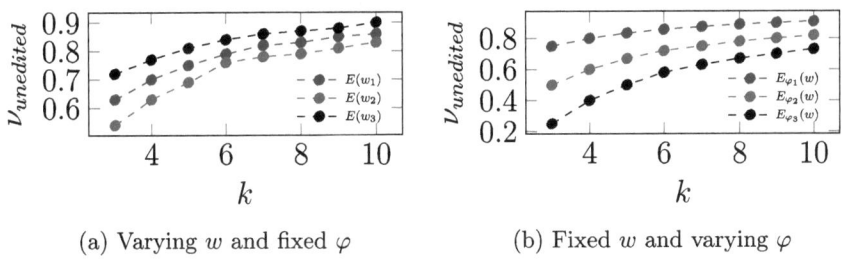

Fig. 8. Plot showing change in frequency of 'unedited' actions with increasing k.

Figure 7a shows that an enforcer designed for a particular property modifies different words differently. On the other hand, in Fig. 7b, we keep the input word w fixed, and use enforcers for three different properties. Here, w is chosen such that no prefixes of w satisfy any of φ_1, φ_2, or φ_3. We now make the following observations about ν_{edited} with respect to k from both of the figures: (i) frequency of edited actions (ν_{edited}) depends on both the input word as well as the enforced property; (ii) ν_{edited} monotonically decreases with increasing k, more precisely, $\nu_{\text{edited}} \propto \frac{1}{k}$; (iii) consequently, the frequency of unedited actions $\nu_{\text{unedited}} = 1 - \nu_{\text{edited}}$ monotonically increases with increasing k (see Fig. 8).

Higher ν_{unedited} implies lesser deviation from the original output of the system, while higher ν_{sat} implies more frequent property satisfaction. Through above experiments, we observed that ν_{edited} (thus ν_{unedited}) depends on the property being enforced, and the input word. However, for words with no prefix satisfying the property, $\nu_{\text{sat}} \propto \frac{1}{k}$. Therefore, choosing appropriate k is significant to maintain optimum trade-off between ν_{unedited} and ν_{sat} (see Fig. 9).

Comparison with [13]. We ported the implementation of [13] (available online) and compared the behaviours of our enforcer with this on the same machine.

For the words considered in the previous part, the chosen words had no prefix satisfying the property but always had an extension to property satisfaction. We observed that indeed the enforcer of [13] emitted the words unedited, thereby never satisfying the property (over the length of the word). However, our enforcer ensured the property is satisfied periodically. To illustrate the difference further, we compared the two enforcers (ours with $k = 3$) computed for a fixed property on 10 randomly generated words, the comparison (see Figs. 10, 11) showed that our enforcer ensures the property is satisfied more often by editing more letters.

7 Related Work

Runtime enforcement is a formal monitoring method that guarantees a system's behaviour consistently conforms to specified properties. An enforcement monitor acts as a guard on top of an executing system that observes its execution and transforms the events if necessary to avoid violation of the property being monitored. In order to correct/edit the execution of the system and avoid violation of the policy being monitored, different enforcement actions such as *halt, suppress, store, delay, and reorder* [6,9,10,12,15,16] are applied.

When we consider enforcement techniques for reactive systems which continuously interact with its environment, enforcement actions such as halting, delaying and suppression are not suitable.

In another approach for runtime enforcement in reactive systems [4], Bloem *et al.* propose synthesis of online safety enforcers called *shields*. Shields are capable

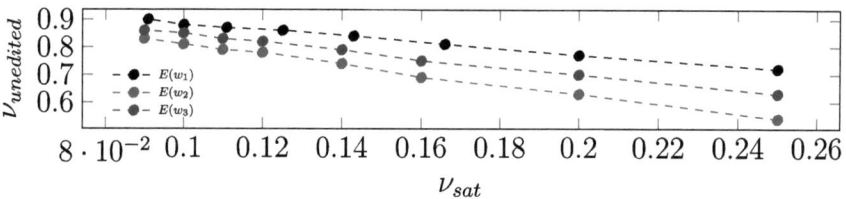

Fig. 9. Plot showing relationship between $\nu_{unedited}$ and ν_{sat}.

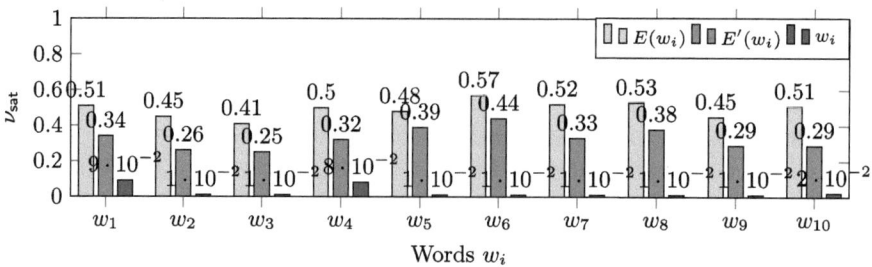

Fig. 10. Plot showing frequency of policy satisfaction ν_{sat} by output of 3-prompt enforcer $E(w)$, output of enforcer in [13] $E'(w)$, and original (unedited) input word w.

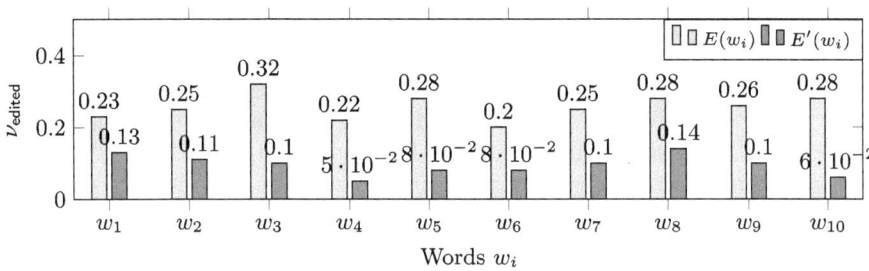

Fig. 11. Plot showing frequency of edited events ν_{edited} by output of 3-prompt enforcer $E(w)$, and output of enforcer in [13] $E'(w)$.

of efficiently enforcing a smaller number of safety critical properties, by allowing deviation from non-critical properties of the system. They have a notion of *k-stabilization* where minimum deviation from original output of the system (and consequently deviation from non-critical properties) is allowed for at most k consecutive steps after the initial violation of a safety critical property. However if a second violation (of a critical property) occurs within those k steps, the shield enters *fail-safe* mode where minimum deviation is permanently ignored in order to satisfy the critical safety property. In a similar work [18], Wu et al. propose an approach that provides instantaneous recovery from property violation, thereby allowing persistent minimum deviation from system's outputs. The notion of *k*-promptness in our work is different from that of k-stabilization in shields. The k-stabilization refers to the recovery phase (of k-steps) after a violation of the property has occurred, while *k*-promptness refers to property satisfaction at least once every $k + 1$ steps.

Könighofer et al. in [8] propose an *online shielding* approach for reinforcement learning (RL) systems. *Online shielding* ensures safe action in a decision state. Their framework is suitable for enforcing controllable learning agents where there is sufficient time gap between the decisions by the agent. The *shielding* is used in the learning phase as well as in the execution phase; however, our enforcement approach is instantaneous, and ensures property satisfaction at regular fixed intervals during the execution phase only.

In [3], the authors consider *shields* with mean payoff of 1/k, which means an accepting state is visited at least once every k steps *in the limit*. This allows execution to start with long prefixes where no accepting state is visited, and only then enter a cycle where an accepting state is seen every k steps. Our framework does not accept those. We require our k-prompt enforcers to have minimal intervention. The approach in [3] allows to quantify the interference score (how often actions are modified) as a mean payoff, only in the limit. Furthermore, their method computes a shield that optimizes a linear combination of the behavioral score (how frequently accepting states are visited) and the interference score. However, the approach only provides bounds on the combined score only in the limit, and does not offer separate guarantees on the individual scores.

There are other streams of work related to enforcement for reactive systems such as [14]. The framework in [14] focuses only on prefix-closed (safety) properties that instantaneously edits actions (only when necessary) to enforce the property being monitored. The approach is later extended to general regular properties in the discrete-time context [11,13] where properties to be enforced are modeled using an extension of finite state automata with discrete clocks.

Similar to approaches in [11,13,14] we focus on enforcement for reactive systems where the enforcer has to instantaneously correct the events. To simplify the presentation and formalization, in this work we do not explicitly take into account input-output pairs in formalizing events for bi-directional enforcement considered in approaches such as [11,13,14]. Our work can be easily adapted to the bi-directional setup. In [11,13,14] when enforcing a prefix-closed property (*i.e.*, a safety property), the synthesized enforcer ensures that the output emitted satisfies the property being monitored at every step. However in [11,13] when considering general regular properties it is not possible to ensure that the output after every step satisfies the property. For regular properties, the enforcer thus ensures that the output can always be extended to eventually to satisfy the property (the output emitted is a prefix of a word that satisfies the property). However, there is also a possibility that eventually it may never end up in a word that actually satisfies the property being monitored.

As far as we know, none of the existing enforcement frameworks of regular properties for reactive systems can ensure periodic satisfaction of the property by the output emitted by the enforcer. In this work, we thus propose a new enforcement framework for regular properties with prompt eventualities. Given any regular property defined as an automaton and a bound k, the synthesized enforcer ensures that the output emitted by it satisfies the property being monitored at least once every $k+1$ steps. The enforcer obtained using the proposed framework also fulfils other constraints such as monotonicity and transparency.

As already mentioned, bounding the number of steps before an event in temporal logics was considered in [5], and in other subsequent works. In particular, prompt Büchi acceptance is defined in [1] by existentially quantifying the bound k: a word is in the language if there exists k such that a k-prompt run can be built in $\mathcal{A}$. Our work is clearly based on these.

8 Conclusion and Future Work

We formalize for the first time the prompt runtime enforcement synthesis problem for reactive systems. We developed a new RE framework with prompt eventualities for regular properties. For any given property φ and a bound k, the enforcer synthesized using the framework ensures that φ is never violated for more that k consecutive steps. We formally define this RE problem, delineate the k-enforceability of automata, and provide algorithms for the design of the enforcer. We consider the prompt-enforcement problem where the bound k is not fixed, and show how the problem reduces to k-enforcement problem for sufficiently large k. We show the computation of minimal k for the property to be

k-enforceable. We also implement the k-prompt enforcer in Python and show how promptness and permissiveness of the enforcer change with varying k. In the near future, we will consider extending the prompt enforcement framework in multiple directions including tackling regular timed properties.

References

1. Almagor, S., Hirshfeld, Y., Kupferman, O.: Promptness in ω-regular automata. In: Automated Technology for Verification and Analysis: 8th International Symposium, ATVA 2010, Singapore, September 21-24, 2010. Proceedings 8, pp. 22–36. Springer (2010)
2. Anand, A., Guizouarn, L.G., Jéron, T., Mukherjee, S., Pinisetty, S., Sankur, O.: Prompt runtime enforcement. https://github.com/TimedProperties/PromptEnforcement/blob/main/Appendix/appendix.pdf (2025). technical Appendix. Accessed 16 July 2025
3. Avni, G., Bloem, R., Chatterjee, K., Henzinger, T.A., Könighofer, B., Pranger, S.: Run-time optimization for learned controllers through quantitative games. In: Dillig, I., Tasiran, S. (eds.) Computer Aided Verification, pp. 630–649. Springer International Publishing, Cham (2019)
4. Bloem, R., Könighofer, B., Könighofer, R., Wang, C.: Shield synthesis: runtime enforcement for reactive systems. In: International Conference on Tools and Algorithms for the Construction and Analysis of Systems (TACAS), pp. 533–548. Springer (2015)
5. Dershowitz, N., Jayasimha, D., Park, S.: Bounded fairness. Verification: Theory and Practice: Essays Dedicated to Zohar Manna on the Occasion of His 64th Birthday, pp. 304–317 (2003)
6. Falcone, Y., Mounier, L., Fernandez, J.C., Richier, J.L.: Runtime enforcement monitors: composition, synthesis, and enforcement abilities. Formal Methods Syst. Design **38**(3), 223–262 (2011)
7. Fijalkow, N., et al.: Games on graphs. arXiv preprint arXiv:2305.10546 (2023)
8. Könighofer, B., Rudolf, J., Palmisano, A., Tappler, M., Bloem, R.: Online shielding for reinforcement learning. Innovations Syst. Softw. Eng. **19**(4), 379–394 (2023)
9. Ligatti, J., Bauer, L., Walker, D.: Edit automata: Enforcement mechanisms for run-time security policies. Int. J. Inf. Secur. **4**, 2–16 (2005)
10. Ligatti, J., Bauer, L., Walker, D.: Run-time enforcement of nonsafety policies. ACM Trans. Inf. Syst. Secur. **12**(3) (2009)
11. Pearce, H.A., Pinisetty, S., Roop, P.S., Kuo, M.M.Y., Ukil, A.: Smart I/O modules for mitigating cyber-physical attacks on industrial control systems. IEEE Trans. Ind. Inf. **16**(7), 4659–4669 (2020)
12. Pinisetty, S., Falcone, Y., Jéron, T., Marchand, H., Rollet, A., Nguena Timo, O.: Runtime enforcement of timed properties revisited. Formal Methods Syst. Design **45**(3), 381–422 (2014). https://doi.org/10.1007/s10703-014-0215-y
13. Pinisetty, S., Roop, P.S., Smyth, S., Allen, N., Tripakis, S., von Hanxleden, R.: Runtime enforcement of cyber-physical systems. ACM Trans. Embed. Comput. Syst. **16**(5s), 178:1–178:25 (2017). https://doi.org/10.1145/3126500
14. Pinisetty, S., Roop, P.S., Smyth, S., Tripakis, S., von Hanxleden, R.: Runtime enforcement of reactive systems using synchronous enforcers. In: Erdogmus, H., Havelund, K. (eds.) Proceedings of the 24th ACM SIGSOFT International SPIN Symposium on Model Checking of Software, Santa Barbara, CA, USA, July 10-14, 2017, pp. 80–89. ACM (2017)

15. Pradhan, A., Akil, C.G.M., Pinisetty, S.: Runtime enforcement with event reordering. In: Anutariya, C., Bonsangue, M.M. (eds.) Theoretical Aspects of Computing - ICTAC 2024 - 21st International Colloquium, Bangkok, Thailand, November 25-29, 2024, Proceedings. Lecture Notes in Computer Science, vol. 15373, pp. 386–407. Springer (2024). https://doi.org/10.1007/978-3-031-77019-7_22
16. Schneider, F.B.: Enforceable security policies. ACM Trans. Inf. Syst. Secur. **3**(1), 30–50 (2000)
17. Tarjan, R.: Depth-first search and linear graph algorithms. SIAM J. Comput. **1**(2), 146–160 (1972)
18. Wu, M., Zeng, H., Wang, C.: Synthesizing runtime enforcer of safety properties under burst error. In: Rayadurgam, S., Tkachuk, O. (eds.) NFM 2016. LNCS, vol. 9690, pp. 65–81. Springer, Cham (2016). https://doi.org/10.1007/978-3-319-40648-0_6
19. Zuzak, I., Jankovic, V.: FSM simulator. https://ivanzuzak.info/noam/webapps/fsm_simulator/. Accessed 21 Apr 2025

Efficient Dynamic Shielding for Parametric Safety Specifications

Davide Corsi[1], Kaushik Mallik[2(✉)], Andoni Rodríguez[2,3], and César Sánchez[2]

[1] University of California, Irvine, USA
dcorsi@uci.edu
[2] IMDEA Software Institute, Madrid, Spain
{kaushik.mallik,andoni.rodriguez,cesar.sanchez}@imdea.org
[3] Universidad Politécnica de Madrid, Madrid, Spain

Abstract. Shielding has emerged as a promising approach for ensuring safety of AI-controlled autonomous systems. The algorithmic goal is to compute a shield, which is a runtime safety enforcement tool that needs to monitor and intervene the AI controller's actions if safety could be compromised otherwise. Traditional shields are designed statically for a specific safety requirement. Therefore, if the safety requirement changes at runtime due to changing operating conditions, the shield needs to be recomputed from scratch, causing delays that could be fatal. We introduce *dynamic shields* for *parametric* safety specifications, which are succinctly represented sets of all possible safety specifications that may be encountered at runtime. Our dynamic shields are statically designed for a given safety parameter set, and are able to dynamically adapt as the true safety specification (permissible by the parameters) is revealed at runtime. The main algorithmic novelty lies in the dynamic adaptation procedure, which is a simple and fast algorithm that utilizes known features of standard safety shields, like maximal permissiveness. We report experimental results for a robot navigation problem in unknown territories, where the safety specification evolves as new obstacles are discovered at runtime. In our experiments, the dynamic shields took a few minutes for their offline design, and took between a fraction of a second and a few seconds for online adaptation at each step, whereas the brute-force online recomputation approach was up to 5 times slower.

Keywords: Dynamic shields · parametric safety · symbolic control

1 Introduction

Most critical autonomous systems like self-driving cars are nowadays controlled by machine-learned (ML) controllers, and ensuring their safety is an important agenda in artificial intelligence and formal methods research. Despite the recent advancements in the formal verification of ML controllers [3,21,23], most methods either do not scale to the size and complexity of the ML components, or they do not support infinite-horizon safety properties [3]. Moreover, all these verification approaches assume knowledge of the ML components' parameters, which might not be true if the controller is designed by a third party and appears as a black-box. One promising solution is *shielding* [2,6,7,28], where we deploy a formally verified runtime enforcement tool, called the *shield*, that monitors—and, if necessary, overrides—the actions of an ML controller during deployment. Usually shield synthesis is cheaper than verifying the entire system, because the synthesis happens on a small system abstraction that concerns only the safety aspects. Furthermore, the synthesis process treats the ML controller as a black-box, thereby bypassing the aforementioned shortcomings of the traditional verification approaches. Shielding has been successfully applied in tandem with complex machine-learned controllers in a large variety of applications, including safe human-robot interactions [20] and safe autonomous driving [38].

State-of-the-art shield synthesis algorithms offer *statically* designed shields, crafted for a specific safety objective provided at the design time. In reality, safety specifications often vary over time, and there are no principled approaches to *dynamically* adapt a (statically designed) shield as new safety objectives are uncovered at runtime. This type of dynamic safety specifications appears naturally in designing navigation controllers for robots in previously unknown workspaces, which is the motivating use case of our work and is described as follows. We are given a robot in a workspace filled with static obstacles, and the robot must always avoid colliding with them. However, the visibility of the robot is limited by the range of its sensors, and therefore it can see the obstacles only when it gets close to them. If the entire map were visible to the shield, it could use the locations of the obstacles to define its static safety specification. However, due to its limited sensing power, the safety specification would only concern its immediate neighborhood, and would keep changing in real-time as it moves.

We present a novel framework of *dynamic shielding* with respect to evolving safety specifications. We assume that we are given a perturbed, discrete-time dynamical model of the system, and a parameterized (finite) set of all possible safety specifications that could be encountered at runtime. Specifically, as the specification, we are given a finite collection of safety objectives of the form $\{\Box\, G_i\}_i$, called the *parameter set*, where G_i is a set of safe states of the system, and $\Box\, G_i$ is a linear temporal logic (LTL) formula specifying that G_i must not be left at any time. Each formula $\Box\, G_i$ represents an *atomic* safety objective, and the actual safety specification encountered at runtime will be the conjunction of an arbitrary subset of atomic safety objectives. The aim is to statically design a shield for the statically provided parameter set $\{\Box\, G_i\}_i$, such that the shield can dynamically adapt itself for every dynamically generated safety specification.

Naturally, shielding against parametric safety would require coordination between the offline and online design phases, and the two extreme ends of the coordination spectrum are as follows. The pure offline approach would design one (static) shield for each subset of $\{\Box G_i\}_i$, so that the right shield could be instantly deployed at runtime. However, this would require solving an exponential number of offline shield synthesis problems which will not scale if the parameter set is large. In contrast, the pure online approach would perform no computation in the offline phase, and at runtime, whenever a new safety specification is revealed, it would compute the corresponding (static) shield at that moment. This would create delays in deploying the shield, and could be fatal in most cases.

We present an efficient dynamic shielding algorithm that creates a harmony between the offline and online design phases. In the offline design phase, one (static) *atomic* shield $\mathcal{S}_i$ is computed for each atomic safety specification $\Box G_i$, solving a linear number of shield synthesis problems as opposed to the exponential case of the pure offline algorithm. In the online deployment phase, as a new safety specification $\Phi = \Box G_j \wedge \Box G_k \wedge \ldots$ is encountered, the respective atomic shields $\mathcal{S}_j, \mathcal{S}_k, \ldots$ are *composed* to obtain the shield for the specification Φ. The composition operation utilizes simple known features like maximal permissiveness of safety shields, giving rise to a fast composition algorithm involving shield "intersections" followed by iterative deadlock removals. Similar style of composition operations are known in the literature in the context of the richer class of parity specifications [4], though their use in the specialized case of (dynamic) safety shielding is novel. In summary, our composition algorithm leads to a lightweight shield adaptation mechanism that is significantly cheaper than computing a new shield for Φ from scratch (the naïve pure online approach).

We propose abstraction-based synthesis algorithms for our dynamic shields, though other alternatives could also be pursued [45]. Concretely, we first create an abstract model of the system by following standard procedure [39], namely discretizing the system's state and input space using uniform grids, and then conservatively approximating the system dynamics over the discrete spaces. Afterwards, we adapt existing abstraction-based synthesis algorithms [39] for the offline design and online adaptation of our dynamic shields. These procedures are compatible with symbolic data structures, particularly binary decision diagrams (BDD), giving rise to efficient implementation of our dynamic shields.

We also provide practical strategies to address the following *safe handover* question that naturally arises: If the safety specification evolves at each step, it may not be the case that the current shield's actions would keep the system within the domain of the next shield. How to guarantee safety in such cases? We address this question for the specific problem of safe robot navigation in unknown territories, where the shield may encounter previously unknown (stationary) obstacles from time to time. We propose the most conservative solution to the safe handover problem, namely at each step, the shield needs to assume that the entire unobservable state space is unsafe, guaranteeing infinite-horizon safety that also keeps the system *inside* the current observable region. This shield is continued to be used until it is possible to find a new shield, based on the new surrounding, whose domain contains the current state of the robot. We prove that our safe handover mechanism will guarantee safety and non-blockingness, i.e., some safe actions will always be available.

We demonstrate the practical effectiveness and feasibility of the dynamic shields using a prototype implementation within the tool Mascot-SDS [30]. The safety rate of the shields were 100%, which is unsurprising since they are correct by construction. The offline design of our dynamic shields ended within minutes, and the online adaption per step on an average took between a fraction of a second upto a few seconds, which was upto 5 times faster compared to the pure online baseline. This demonstrates the practical feasibility of dynamic shields.

In short, our contributions are as follows:

(a) We propose the dynamic shielding framework for parametric safety specifications, orchestrating offline atomic shield synthesis with a lightweight online adaptation procedure.
(b) We show how our algorithms can be symbolically implemented using the abstraction-based control paradigm.
(c) We present a practical approach to address the safe handover question for dynamic shields in navigation tasks in unknown territories.
(d) We present the superior computational performance of our dynamic shields using a prototype implementation.

Related Works

Shielding has become one of the enabling technologies in guaranteeing safety of arbitrarily complex machine-learned controllers in autonomous systems [2,5,6, 13,26,28]. It has been studied in two operational settings, namely pre-shielding and post-shielding. In pre-shielding, shields are used to guarantee safety during the learning process, while in post-shielding, shields are used during deployment. While most classical works considered the qualitative safety specifications, recent works have developed shields for quantitative safety specifications [11,25,40,41, 47]. Our dynamic shields consider qualitative safety specifications, which makes them usable either as a pre-shield or as a post-shield [35].

Recent works have considered various different types of dynamic shielding frameworks. When the underlying model parameters like environment probability distributions are unknown or partially known, shields will need to dynamically adapt to account for newly discovered model parameters [9,12,15,36,46,48]. When shields' objectives are quantitative, e.g., requiring to keep some cost metric below a given threshold, they may need to adapt to changing requirements like changing cost thresholds under different conditions [22]. When an exhaustive computation of the shield for all possible state-action pairs is computationally infeasible, shields could be dynamically computed at runtime by only analyzing the relatively small set of forward reachable states upto a given horizon [10,27]. Surprisingly, none of the existing works considered our setting of changing qualitative safety specifications. While the shields based on forward reachable sets [10,27] could be used, their safety guarantee would be valid up to a fixed horizon only. This is an important gap in the shielding literature, since runtime controller adaptation due to changing safety goals is an important topic in AI and control theory [16,29,32,37].

Our synthesis algorithms are powered by abstraction-based control (ABC), which is a collection of model-based synthesis algorithms for formally verified controllers of nonlinear and hybrid dynamical systems [33,39,43]. Our work uses a particular ABC algorithm based on feedback refinement relations [39], which uses a uniform grid-based abstraction of the system and offers a fast controller refinement process that is crucial for the fast runtime deployment of our shields. In principle, our dynamic algorithm can be adapted to more advanced abstraction techniques, particularly the ones involving state space transformations in the pre-processing stage to achieve higher efficiency [8].

2 Preliminaries

Notation. Given an alphabet X, we will write X^* and X^ω to respectively denote the set of finite and infinite sequences over X, and will write X^∞ to denote $X^* \cup X^\omega$. Given a set $S \subseteq X^\infty$, we will write $Pref(S)$ to denote the set of every finite prefix of S, i.e., $Pref(S) := \{w \in X^* \mid \exists w' \in X^\infty \ . \ ww' \in S\}$.

Control Systems. We consider *continuous-state, discrete-time control systems*, described as tuples of the form $(\mathcal{X}, \mathcal{U}, \mathcal{W}, f)$, where $\mathcal{X} \subset \mathbb{R}^n$, $\mathcal{U} \subset \mathbb{R}^m$, and $\mathcal{W} \subset \mathbb{R}^p$ are all compact sets respectively called the *state space*, the *control input space*, and the *disturbance input space*, and the function $f \colon \mathcal{X} \times \mathcal{U} \times \mathcal{W} \to \mathcal{X}$ is called the *transition function*. The constants n, m, and p are all positive integers and are called the *dimensions* of the respective spaces.

The semantics of the control system $\Sigma = (\mathcal{X}, \mathcal{U}, \mathcal{W}, f)$ is described using its transitions and trajectories. For any given state $x \in \mathcal{X}$, control input $u \in \mathcal{U}$, and disturbance input $w \in \mathcal{W}$ of Σ at a given time step, the new state at the next time step is given by $x' = f(x, u, w)$, and we will express this as the transition $x \xrightarrow{u,w} x'$ The *trajectory* ξ of Σ starting at a given *initial* state $x_0 \in \mathcal{X}$ and caused by control and disturbance input sequences $u_0, u_1, \ldots$ and $w_0, w_1, \ldots$ is a sequence of transitions $x_0 \xrightarrow{u_0,w_0} x_1 \xrightarrow{u_1,w_1} x_2 \ldots$. The sequence of states $x_0, x_1, \ldots \in \mathcal{X}^\infty$ appearing in the trajectory ξ will be called the *path* of ξ. Trajectories and paths can be either finitely or infinitely long.

Controllers. Let $\Sigma = (\mathcal{X}, \mathcal{U}, \mathcal{W}, f)$ be a control system. A *controller* of Σ is a *partial* function of the form $\mathcal{X}^* \to 2^\mathcal{U}$, which determines the set of allowed control inputs given the history of past states at each point in time. Every controller $\mathcal{C}$ of Σ produces a set of paths from a given initial state $x_0 \in \mathcal{X}$, defined as

$$Paths(\Sigma, \mathcal{C}, x_0) := \Big\{ x_0 x_1 \ldots \in \mathcal{X}^\infty \Big| \exists w_0 w_1 \ldots \in \mathcal{W}^\infty \ . $$
$$x_0 \xrightarrow{u_0,w_0} x_1 \xrightarrow{u_1,w_1} x_2 \ldots \text{ is a trajectory of } \Sigma \text{ where } \forall i \geq 0 \ . \ u_i \in \mathcal{C}(x_0 \ldots x_i) \Big\}.$$

We will encounter the following three orthogonal subclasses of controllers, where each subclass can be combined with other subclasses.

- A *state-feedback (memoryless) controller* is a controller $\mathcal{C}$ that only considers the current state while selecting control inputs. Formally, $\mathcal{C}(y) = \mathcal{C}(y')$ for every y, y' whose last states are the same. We will represent state-feedback controllers as functions of the form $\mathcal{C} \colon \mathcal{X} \to 2^\mathcal{U}$, whose domain is defined as the set of every $x \in \mathcal{X}$ for which $\mathcal{C}(x)$ is defined, and written as $Dom(\mathcal{C})$.

- A *deterministic controller* is a controller $\mathcal{C}$ that selects a single control input at each step, i.e., has the form $\mathcal{X}^* \to \mathcal{U}$.
- A *nonblocking controller* is a controller $\mathcal{C}$ if its every generated finite path has an infinite extension, i.e., $Paths(\Sigma, \mathcal{C}, x_0) \cap \mathcal{X}^* \subseteq Pref(Paths(\Sigma, \mathcal{C}, x_0) \cap \mathcal{X}^\omega)$. In other words, every nonblocking controller $\mathcal{C}$ must disallow every control input u for every finite path $x_0 \ldots x_k$ if there exists a disturbance $w \in \mathcal{W}$ with $x_{k+1} = f(x_k, u, w)$ such that $\mathcal{C}(x_0 \ldots x_k x_{k+1})$ is undefined.

Safety Specifications. Let $\Sigma = (\mathcal{X}, \mathcal{U}, \mathcal{W}, f)$ be a control system, and let $G \subseteq \mathcal{X}$ be a set of states, designated as the set of *safe* states. The complement of the safe states will be called the *unsafe* states. The *safety specification* (with respect to Σ and G) is the set of every sequence of states of Σ that never leaves G, formally written as $Safety_\Sigma(G) := \{\rho = x_0 x_1 \ldots \in \mathcal{X}^\infty \mid \forall i \geq 0 \,.\, x_i \in G\}$. When the system is clear from the context, we will drop the suffix and write $Safety(G)$.

Safety Controllers. Let $\Sigma = (\mathcal{X}, \mathcal{U}, \mathcal{W}, f)$ be a control system and $Safety(G)$ be a safety specification. A state-feedback controller $\mathcal{C}$ of Σ is called a *safety controller* for $Safety(G)$, if, intuitively, $\mathcal{C}$ guarantees that all paths of the system stay forever inside G no matter what disturbance inputs are experienced; formally, $\mathcal{C}$ must fulfill $Paths(\Sigma, \mathcal{C}, x_0) \subseteq Safety(G)$ for every $x_0 \in Dom(\mathcal{C})$. It is known that for fulfilling safety specifications of the form $Safety(G)$, state-feedback controllers suffice [45]. It is also easy to see that $Dom(\mathcal{C}) \subseteq G$. From now on, we will denote a safety controller for $Safety(G)$ using $\mathcal{C}_G$.

We add one final subclass of controllers to the list of other subclasses presented earlier. For this, we say a controller $\mathcal{C}'$ is a *sub-controller* of $\mathcal{C}$, written $\mathcal{C}' \sqsubseteq \mathcal{C}$, if (a) $Dom(\mathcal{C}') \subseteq Dom(\mathcal{C})$ and (b) for every state $x \in Dom(\mathcal{C}')$, $\mathcal{C}'(x) \subseteq \mathcal{C}(x)$. Equivalently, we say $\mathcal{C}$ is the *super-controller* of $\mathcal{C}'$.

- For a given safety specification $Safety(G)$, a *maximally permissive safety controller* is a safety controller $\mathcal{C}_G^*$ such that every other safety controller $\mathcal{C}_G$ for $Safety(G)$ is a sub-controller of $\mathcal{C}_G^*$, i.e., $\mathcal{C}_G \sqsubseteq \mathcal{C}_G^*$.

It is known that if safety specifications admit controllers, then these controllers are *unique* nonblocking, maximally permissive (and state-feedback) controllers [45], written *n.m.p. controllers* in short. Specifications other than safety (like liveness) lack this feature, though workarounds exist in the literature [4].

3 Dynamic Shielding for Parametric Safety Specifications

3.1 Preliminaries: The Existing (Safety) Shielding Framework

We assume that the given control system needs to fulfill some functional tasks (like reaching a target in minimum time, etc.) while maintaining safety. The functional tasks are served by a *learned*[1] black-box controller, and the safety constraints are enforced by the shield, which monitors the learned controller's decisions and overrides them if safety would be at risk otherwise.

---
[1] The term "learned controller" is a placeholder. Any unverified controller can be used.

Definition 1 (Shields). *Suppose $\Sigma = (\mathcal{X}, \mathcal{U}, \mathcal{W}, f)$ is a control system and Safety(G) is a given safety specification. A shield is a partial function $\mathcal{S}_G \colon \mathcal{X} \times \mathcal{U} \to \mathcal{U}'$ with $\mathcal{U}' \subseteq \mathcal{U}$, such that for every $x \in \mathcal{X}$, $\mathcal{S}_G(x, u)$ is defined either for every $u \in \mathcal{U}$ or for none of $u \in \mathcal{U}$. The domain of the shield $\mathcal{S}_G$ is defined as: $\mathrm{Dom}(\mathcal{S}_G) \coloneqq \{x \in \mathcal{X} \mid \mathcal{S}_G(x, u) \text{ is defined for all } u \in \mathcal{U}\}$.*

Suppose the shield $\mathcal{S}_G$ is deployed with the learned controller $\overline{\mathcal{C}} \colon \mathcal{X}^* \to \mathcal{U}$. Let x be the current state at a given time point. First, $\overline{\mathcal{C}}$ proposes the control input $u = \overline{\mathcal{C}}(\ldots x)$, and then, the shield $\mathcal{S}_G$ takes into account the pair (x, u), and selects the control input $u' = \mathcal{S}_G(x, u)$ that is possibly different from u. The set of resulting paths starting at a given initial state $x_0 \in \mathcal{X}$ is given as:

$$\mathrm{Paths}(\Sigma, \overline{\mathcal{C}}, \mathcal{S}_G, x_0) \coloneqq \left\{ x_0 x_1 \ldots \in \mathcal{X}^\infty \,\middle|\, \exists w_0 w_1 \ldots \in \mathcal{W}^\infty \right. \\ \left. x_0 \xrightarrow{\mathcal{S}_G(x_0, \overline{\mathcal{C}}(x_0)), w_0} x_1 \xrightarrow{\mathcal{S}_G(x_1, \overline{\mathcal{C}}(x_0 x_1)), w_1} x_2 \ldots \text{ is a trajectory of } \Sigma \right\}.$$

The shield $\mathcal{S}_G$ guarantees safety under the learned controller $\overline{\mathcal{C}}$ from the initial state x_0 if $\mathrm{Paths}(\Sigma, \overline{\mathcal{C}}, \mathcal{S}_G, x_0) \subseteq \mathrm{Safety}(G)$.

Whenever the output u' of the shield $\mathcal{S}_G$ is different from the output of the controller $\overline{\mathcal{C}}$, we say that $\mathcal{S}_G$ has *intervened*, and we want minimal interventions while fulfilling safety. Formally, a shield is said to be *minimally intervening* if every intervention is a necessary intervention, i.e., without the intervention, disturbances could push the trajectory outside of the shield's domain, and therefore safety guarantees would be lost. Our definition of minimal intervention is adapted from the definition by Bloem et al. [7], which formalizes minimal intervention with respect to a generic intervention-penalizing cost metric.

Problem 1 (Minimally intervening shield synthesis).
Inputs: A control system Σ and a safety specification $\mathrm{Safety}(G)$.
Output: A shield $\mathcal{S}_G^*$ such that for every learned controller $\overline{\mathcal{C}}$ and for every $x_0 \in \mathrm{Dom}(\mathcal{S}_G^*)$, the following hold:

Safety: $\mathrm{Paths}(\Sigma, \overline{\mathcal{C}}, \mathcal{S}_G^*, x_0) \subseteq \mathrm{Safety}(G)$;
Minimal interventions: for every finite path $x_0 \ldots x_k \in \mathrm{Paths}(\Sigma, \overline{\mathcal{C}}, \mathcal{S}_G^*, x_0)$, if an intervention happens, i.e., if $\mathcal{S}_G^*(x_k, \overline{\mathcal{C}}(x_0 \ldots x_k)) \neq \overline{\mathcal{C}}(x_0 \ldots x_k)$, then there exists a $w \in \mathcal{W}$ such that $f(x, \overline{\mathcal{C}}(x_0 \ldots x_k), w) \notin \mathrm{Dom}(\mathcal{S}_G^*)$.

The output of Problem 1 will be called the minimally intervening shield for Σ and $\mathrm{Safety}(G)$, and can be obtained from n.m.p. safety controllers.

Theorem 1. *Let $\Sigma = (\mathcal{X}, \mathcal{U}, \mathcal{W}, f)$ be a control system, $\mathrm{Safety}(G)$ be a safety specification, and $\mathcal{C}_G^*$ be the (unique) nonblocking, maximally permissive (n.m.p.) controller of Σ for $\mathrm{Safety}(G)$. Then, every minimally intervening shield $\mathcal{S}_G^*$ for Σ and $\mathrm{Safety}(G)$ fulfills:*

$$\mathcal{S}_G^*(x, u) = \begin{cases} u & \text{if } u \in \mathcal{C}_G^*(x) \\ u' \in \mathcal{C}_G^*(x) & \text{otherwise.} \end{cases} \quad (1)$$

for every $(x, u) \in \mathcal{X} \times \mathcal{U}$.

Proof. By virtue of maximal permissiveness of $\mathcal{C}_G^*$, we can infer that every $u \notin \mathcal{C}_G^*(x)$ may potentially violate safety, since otherwise we could construct a safe super-controller of $\mathcal{C}_G^*$ that would allow u from x, and would otherwise mimic $\mathcal{C}_G^*$. This is not possible since it would contradict the maximal permissiveness assumption of $\mathcal{C}_G^*$. Since $\mathcal{S}_G^*$ needs to guarantee safety with its choice of control inputs, therefore it must select control inputs allowed by $\mathcal{C}_G^*$.

Now for the given x, u, if $u \in \mathcal{C}_G^*(x)$ but $\mathcal{S}_G^*(x, u) \neq u$, then the shield violates the minimal intervention requirement, since we know that selecting u instead would not lead to a violation of safety. □

Minimally intervening shields are not unique, since any $u' \in \mathcal{C}_G^*(x)$ can be selected when $u \notin \mathcal{C}_G^*(x)$ in Eq. (1). We will use the heuristics of selecting the u' that minimizes the Euclidean distance from the original input u. However, this does not provide any long-run optimality guarantees, and selecting the best intervening input is still an open problem in shield synthesis.

Remark 1. We consider the so-called post-shielding framework, where the shield operates alongside an already learned controller In contrast, in the pre-shielding framework, shields are used already during the training phase of the controller to prevent safety violations. It is known that safety shields—and by extension our dynamic safety shields—can be used in both pre and post settings [35], though we will only use the post-shielding view for simplicity.

3.2 Problem Statement

Traditional shield synthesis problems closely match the statement of Problem 1, implying that shields would need recomputation if safety specifications change. This is problematic when the precise safety specification is unknown apriori, and the shield needs to adapt as new safety requirements are discovered during runtime. To mitigate this, we propose a new dynamic variant of Problem 1.

We formalize parametric safety specifications. Suppose $\Sigma = (\mathcal{X}, \mathcal{U}, \mathcal{W}, f)$ is a control system, and R is a finite set of subsets of $\mathcal{X}$, i.e., $R = \{G_0, \ldots, G_l\} \subset 2^\mathcal{X}$. Each element of R is called an *atomic safe set*. The *parametric* safety specification P-*Safety*(R) on R is the family of all safety specifications generated by the safe sets that are conjunctions of subsets of R, i.e., P-*Safety*$(R) = \{Safety(G) \mid \exists S \subseteq R . G = \cap_{S' \in S} S'\}$. Clearly, the size of P-*Safety*(R) is $2^{|R|}$.

A *dynamic shield* for R is a function mapping every safety specification *Safety*$(G) \in$ P-*Safety*(R) to a regular, static shield for *Safety*(G). We assume that the set R is provided *statically* during the design of the dynamic shield, while the actual safety specification *Safety*$(G) \in$ P-*Safety*(R) is chosen *dynamically* during runtime.

Problem 2 (Dynamic shield synthesis).
Inputs: A control system $\Sigma = (\mathcal{X}, \mathcal{U}, \mathcal{W}, f)$ and a finite set $R \subset 2^\mathcal{X}$ of atomic safe sets.
Output: A dynamic shield $\mathcal{S}_R^*$ such that for every safety specification *Safety*$(G) \in$ P-*Safety*(R), $\mathcal{S}_R^*(G)$ is a minimally intervening (static) shield for Σ and *Safety*(G).

Using Theorem 1, Problem 2 reduces to the problem of synthesizing dynamic safety controllers, which are functions that map every safety specification $Safety(G) \in \text{P-}Safety(R)$ to an n.m.p. safety controller for $Safety(G)$.

Problem 3 (Dynamic safety controller synthesis).
Inputs: A control system $\Sigma = (\mathcal{X}, \mathcal{U}, \mathcal{W}, f)$ and a finite set $R \subset 2^{\mathcal{X}}$ of atomic safe sets.
Output: A dynamic safety controller $\mathcal{C}_R^*$ such that for every safety specification $Safety(G) \in \text{P-}Safety(R)$, $\mathcal{C}_R^*(G)$ is a nonblocking, maximally permissive (static) safety controller for Σ and $Safety(G)$.

Clearly, every solution to Problem 3 leads to a solution to Problem 2 via Eq. (1). Therefore, in what follows, we shift our focus to solving Problem 3.

3.3 Efficient Dynamic Safety Controller Synthesis

In theory, Problem 3 can be solved using two different types of brute-force approaches: The first one is a pure offline algorithm, where we iterate over the set of all safety specifications in P-$Safety(R)$, and for each of them, compute an n.m.p. (static) safety controller. The second one is a pure online algorithm, where we compute a new n.m.p. (static) safety controller after observing the current safety specification at each time point during runtime. While the pure offline algorithm would be prohibitively expensive, owing to the exponential size of P-$Safety(R)$, the pure online algorithm would be expensive enough to be deployed during runtime, especially when controller latency could have detrimental effects.

Our dynamic algorithm strikes a balance between offline design and online adaptation, and proves to be significantly more efficient compared to both on their own. Our new algorithm has an offline design phase and an online deployment phase. During the offline design phase, we compute the n.m.p. safety controller $\mathcal{C}_G^*$ for each atomic safety specification $Safety(G)$ for $G \in R$. These controllers may be called the *atomic* safety controllers. During the online deployment phase, at each step the true safe set $G = G' \cap G'' \cap \dots$ is revealed, where $G', G'', \dots \in R$, and the required safety controller for $Safety(G)$ is obtained by dynamically composing the corresponding atomic safety controllers $\mathcal{C}_{G'}^*, \mathcal{C}_{G''}^*, \dots$.

The process of composing atomic safety controllers at runtime involves two steps, namely a *product* operation, followed by enforcing *non-blockingness*, both described below. An illustration is provided in Fig. 1.

Definition 2 (Controller product). *Let $\mathcal{C}$ and $\mathcal{C}'$ be a pair of state-feedback controllers of a given control system $\Sigma = (\mathcal{X}, \mathcal{U}, \mathcal{W}, f)$. We define the product $\mathcal{C}$ and $\mathcal{C}'$ as the state-feedback controller $\mathcal{C} \otimes \mathcal{C}'$ such that for every $x \in Dom(\mathcal{C}) \cap Dom(\mathcal{C}')$, $\mathcal{C} \otimes \mathcal{C}'(x) = \mathcal{C}(x) \cap \mathcal{C}'(x)$, and for every $x \notin Dom(\mathcal{C}) \cap Dom(\mathcal{C}')$, $\mathcal{C} \otimes \mathcal{C}'(x)$ is undefined.*

Intuitively, the product controller $\mathcal{C} \otimes \mathcal{C}'$ outputs only those control inputs that are safe for both $\mathcal{C}$ and $\mathcal{C}'$, and suppresses those that are unsafe for at least one of them. This, however, does not guarantee the nonblockingness of $\mathcal{C} \otimes \mathcal{C}'$ itself, as is illustrated in Fig. 1b, where the product controller $\mathcal{C}_G^* \otimes \mathcal{C}_H^*$ blocks at the state e. Luckily, we will apply the product on the atomic safety controllers, which are n.m.p., and it follows that all nonblocking safety controllers for the overall safety specification will be sub-controllers of the product.

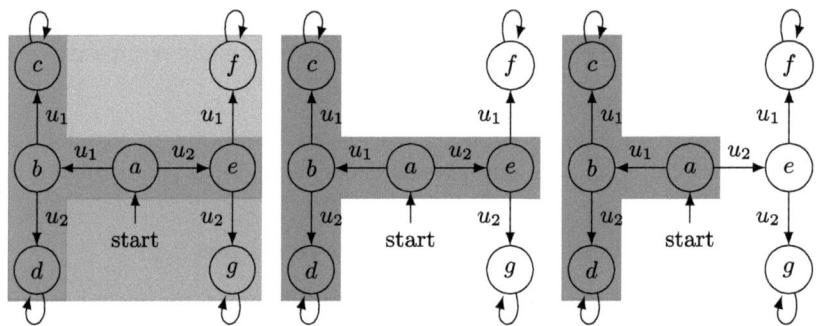

(a) $Dom(\mathcal{C}_G^*)$ is in red and $Dom(\mathcal{C}_H^*)$ is in blue.

(b) Product construction: $Dom(\mathcal{C}_G^* \otimes \mathcal{C}_H^*)$

(c) Ensuring nonblockingness: The domain of the largest nonblocking sub-controller of $\mathcal{C}_G^* \otimes \mathcal{C}_H^*$.

Fig. 1. Illustration of composition of atomic safety controllers. The transition system represents a finite-state control system with two control inputs u_1, u_2 and no disturbance inputs. The nodes are the states and the arrows represent the transition function. Suppose there are two safety specifications $Safety(\text{red})$ and $Safety(\text{blue})$, where red = $\{a, b, c, d, e, f\}$ and blue = $\{a, b, c, d, e, g\}$. The colored regions represent the domains of the respective controllers (purple is the intersection), and each controller's output at a given state is the set of control inputs for which the next state is in the domain. (Color figure online)

Theorem 2. Let $\Sigma = (\mathcal{X}, \mathcal{U}, \mathcal{W}, f)$ be a given control system, $Safety(G)$ and $Safety(H)$ be safety specifications, and $\mathcal{C}_G^*$ and $\mathcal{C}_H^*$ be the nonblocking, maximally permissive (n.m.p.) controllers for $Safety(G)$ and $Safety(H)$, respectively. A nonblocking controller is a safety controller for $Safety(G \cap H)$ if and only if it is a nonblocking sub-controller of $\mathcal{C}_G^* \otimes \mathcal{C}_H^*$.

Proof. First, observe that $Safety(G \cap H) = Safety(G) \cap Safety(H)$. This follows from the definition of safety specifications.

[If:] Suppose $\mathcal{C}$ is a nonblocking sub-controller of $\mathcal{C}_G^* \otimes \mathcal{C}_H^*$. Since this is a sub-controller of $\mathcal{C}_G^* \otimes \mathcal{C}_H^*$, which outputs control inputs that are allowed by both $\mathcal{C}_G^*$ and $\mathcal{C}_H^*$, it follows that $\mathcal{C}$ satisfies both $Safety(G)$ and $Safety(H)$, and therefore it satisfies $Safety(G \cap H)$. (Moreover, $\mathcal{C}$ is already assumed to be nonblocking.)

[Only if:] Suppose $\mathcal{C}$ is a nonblocking safety controller for $Safety(G \cap H)$. Therefore $\mathcal{C}$ is a nonblocking safety controller for both $Safety(G)$ and $Safety(H)$, separately. I.e., the control inputs selected by $\mathcal{C}$ fulfill both $Safety(G)$ and $Safety(H)$ simultaneously, and therefore they are also allowed by $\mathcal{C}_G^* \otimes \mathcal{C}_H^*$. Therefore, $\mathcal{C}$ is a (nonblocking, by assumption) sub-controller of $\mathcal{C}_G^* \otimes \mathcal{C}_H^*$. □

Theorem 2 dramatically narrows down the search space for the sought n.m.p. safety controller for $Safety(G \cap H)$, which is stated as follows.

Corollary 1. *The nonblocking, maximally permissive (n.m.p.) safety controller $\mathcal{C}_{G \cap H}^*$ for $Safety(G \cap H)$ fulfills:*

(a) $\mathcal{C}_{G \cap H}^*$ is nonblocking,
(b) $\mathcal{C}_{G \cap H}^* \sqsubseteq \mathcal{C}_G^* \otimes \mathcal{C}_H^*$, and
(c) for every nonblocking $\mathcal{C}$ with $\mathcal{C} \sqsubseteq \mathcal{C}_G^* \otimes \mathcal{C}_H^*$, $\mathcal{C} \sqsubseteq \mathcal{C}_{G \cap H}^*$.

The nonblocking sub-controller of $\mathcal{C}_G^* \otimes \mathcal{C}_H^*$ fulfilling (b) and (c) in Corollary 1 will be referred to as the *largest nonblocking sub-controller* of $\mathcal{C}_G^* \otimes \mathcal{C}_H^*$.

The computation of n.m.p. safety controllers and largest nonblocking sub-controllers may or may not be decidable, depending on the nature of the state space (finite or infinite) and the nature of the transition function (linear or non-linear) of the system [45]. We will present a sound but incomplete abstraction-based synthesis algorithm in the next section. For the moment, assuming largest nonblocking sub-controllers can be algorithmically computed, we summarize the overall dynamic safety controller synthesis algorithm in the following.

Inputs: Control system Σ and the set R of atomic safe sets
Output: Dynamic safety controller $\mathcal{C}_R^*$ for the parameterized safety specification P-$Safety(R)$
The algorithm:
(A) **The offline design phase:** Compute the set of atomic safety controllers $\{\mathcal{C}_{G_i}^*\}_{G_i \in R}$, where $\mathcal{C}_{G_i}^*$ is the n.m.p. safety controller for G_i.
(B) **The online deployment phase:** Let x be the current state and $G = G_1 \cap \ldots \cap G_k$ be the current obstacle, where $G_i \in R$ for all $i \in [1;k]$. We need to output $\mathcal{C}_R^*(G)(x)$, which is obtained by composing the atomic safety controllers $\mathcal{C}_{G_1}^*, \ldots, \mathcal{C}_{G_k}^*$ using the following two-step process:
1. Compute the product $\mathcal{C} := \mathcal{C}_{G_1}^* \otimes \ldots \otimes \mathcal{C}_{G_k}^*$.
2. Compute the largest nonblocking sub-controller $\mathcal{C}'$ of $\mathcal{C}$, and output $\mathcal{C}_R^*(G)(x) := \mathcal{C}'(x)$.

Fig. 2. The dynamic safety controller synthesis algorithm

4 Synthesis Algorithm Using Abstraction-Based Control

We now present a sound but incomplete procedure for implementing the algorithm in Fig. 2. Most of the results in this section are closely related to the existing works from the literature, but are adapted to our setting.

4.1 Preliminaries: Abstraction-Based Control (ABC)

Abstraction-based control (ABC) is a collection of controller synthesis algorithms, which use systematic grid-based abstractions of continuous control systems and performs synthesis over these abstractions using automata-based approaches. The strengths of ABC algorithms are in their expressive power, namely they support almost all widely used control system models alongside rich temporal logic specifications [31,39]. Besides, ABC algorithms are usually implementable using efficient symbolic data structures, such as BDDs, helping us to devise efficient push-button controller synthesis algorithms in practice.

The typical workflow of an ABC algorithm has three stages, namely *abstraction*, *synthesis*, and (controller) *refinement*. We describe each stage one by one in the following, where we assume that we are given a control system $\Sigma = (\mathcal{X}, \mathcal{U}, \mathcal{W}, f)$ and a generic specification $\Phi \subseteq \mathcal{X}^\infty$ as inputs, and the aim is to compute a controller $\mathcal{C}_\Phi \colon \mathcal{X} \to 2^\mathcal{U}$ whose domain is as large as possible such that $Paths(\Sigma, \mathcal{C}_\Phi, x_0) \subseteq \Phi$ for all $x_0 \in Dom(\mathcal{C}_\Phi)$.

Abstraction. In the abstraction stage, the given control system Σ is approximated by a finite grid-based *abstraction*. There are many alternative approaches to construct the abstraction, and we use the one based on *feedback refinement relations* (FRR) [39]. In FRR, the abstraction is modeled as a separate control system $\widehat{\Sigma} = \left(\widehat{\mathcal{X}}, \widehat{\mathcal{U}}, \widehat{f}\right)$ without disturbances, where $\widehat{\mathcal{X}}$ and $\widehat{\mathcal{U}}$ are finite sets, and $\widehat{f}$ is a nondeterministic transition function, i.e., has the form $\widehat{\mathcal{X}} \times \widehat{\mathcal{U}} \to 2^{\widehat{\mathcal{X}}}$. The set $\widehat{\mathcal{X}}$ is obtained as the collection of the finitely many grid cells created by partitioning the continuous state space $\mathcal{X}$; therefore, every element of $\widehat{\mathcal{X}}$ is a subset of $\mathcal{X}$. The set $\widehat{\mathcal{U}}$ is obtained as the collection of finitely many usually equidistant points selected from $\mathcal{U}$, i.e., $\widehat{\mathcal{U}}$ is a finite subset of $\mathcal{U}$.

Suppose $Q \colon x \mapsto \widehat{x}$ with $x \in \widehat{x}$ is a mapping that maps every continuous state of Σ to the (unique) cell of $\widehat{\mathcal{X}}$ it belongs to. We will extend Q to map sets of states and sets of state sequences of Σ to their counterparts for $\widehat{\Sigma}$ in the obvious manner. We say Q is an FRR from Σ to $\widehat{\Sigma}$, written $\Sigma \preccurlyeq_Q \widehat{\Sigma}$, if for every $x \in \mathcal{X}$, for every $\widehat{u} \in \widehat{\mathcal{U}}$, and for every $w \in \mathcal{W}$, there exists $\widehat{x}' \in \widehat{f}(Q(x), \widehat{u})$ such that $(f(x, \widehat{u}, w), \widehat{x}') \in Q$. We omit the details of how to construct $\widehat{f}$ such that $\Sigma \preccurlyeq_Q \widehat{\Sigma}$ holds, and refer the reader to the original paper [39].

When $\Sigma \preccurlyeq_Q \widehat{\Sigma}$, it is guaranteed that for every controller $\mathcal{C} \colon \mathcal{X} \to \widehat{\mathcal{U}}$ of the system Σ and for every initial state x_0, $Q(Paths(\Sigma, \mathcal{C}, x_0)) \subseteq Paths(\widehat{\Sigma}, \mathcal{C}, Q(x_0))$. In other words, the paths of the abstraction $\widehat{\Sigma}$ conservatively over-approximates (with respect to the mapping Q) the paths of the control system Σ under the same controller $\mathcal{C}$ and for every sequence of disturbance inputs.

Synthesis. In the synthesis stage, first, the given specification Φ is conservatively abstracted to the specification $\widehat{\Phi}$ for $\widehat{\Sigma}$ such that $\widehat{\Phi} \subseteq Q(\Phi)$. When Φ is a safety specification $Safety(G)$ for some $G \subseteq \mathcal{X}$, the abstract specification can be chosen as $\widehat{\Phi} = Safety_{\widehat{\Sigma}}(Q(G))$, i.e., the paths of $\widehat{\Sigma}$ which avoid $Q(G)$ at all time.

Next, we treat the abstraction $\widehat{\Sigma}$ as a two-player, turn-based adversarial game arena, where the controller player chooses a control input $\widehat{u}$ at each state $\widehat{x}$, while the environment player resolves the nondeterminism in $\widehat{f}(\widehat{x},\widehat{u})$. The objective of the controller player is to come up with an abstract controller $\widehat{\mathcal{C}}_{\widehat{\Phi}}\colon \widehat{\mathcal{X}} \to 2^{\widehat{\mathcal{U}}}$ such that no matter what the environment player does, the resulting sequence of states remains inside the set $\widehat{\Phi}$. In the next subsection, we will describe the algorithm for finding such abstract controllers for safety specifications.

Refinement. The (controller) refinement is the stage where the abstract controller $\widehat{\mathcal{C}}_{\widehat{\Phi}}$ of $\widehat{\Sigma}$ for $\widehat{\Phi}$ is mapped back to a concrete controller $\mathcal{C}_{\Phi}$ for the system Σ, which amounts to simply defining $\mathcal{C}_{\Phi}(x) := \widehat{\mathcal{C}}_{\widehat{\Phi}}(Q(x))$ for every $x \in Dom(\mathcal{C}) = \cup_{\widehat{x} \in Dom(\widehat{\mathcal{C}}_{\widehat{\Phi}})}\widehat{x}$. By virtue of the FRR Q between Σ and $\widehat{\Sigma}$, it is guaranteed that $Paths(\Sigma, \mathcal{C}_{\Phi}, x_0) \subseteq \Phi$ for all $x_0 \in Dom(\mathcal{C}_{\Phi})$; in other words, $\mathcal{C}_{\Phi}$ is a sound controller of Σ. It is worthwhile to mention that such a simple refinement stage is one unique strength of FRR, since the other alternatives [34,43] usually require a significantly more involved refinement mechanism.

Remark 2. Even though ABC produces sound controllers, it lacks completeness. This means that sometimes we will not find a controller even if there exists one, and even if we find a controller, its domain could be smaller than the one with the largest possible domain that exists in reality. This is unavoidable if we are uncompromising with soundness, since temporal logic control of nonlinear control systems is undecidable in general [19]. The side-effect of using ABC to solve Problem 3 is that the maximal permissiveness guarantee can no longer be achieved, though our safety controllers will be maximally permissive with respect to the abstraction. One way to improve the permissiveness would be to reduce the discretization granularity in the abstraction, though this will increase the computational complexity due to larger abstraction size.

4.2 ABC-Based Dynamic Safety Control

We now present ABC-based procedure to implement the algorithm in Fig. 2. For this, we fix the abstraction $\widehat{\Sigma}$ of the system Σ, assuming $\Sigma \preccurlyeq_Q \widehat{\Sigma}$ for a given FRR Q, and present our algorithms on $\widehat{\Sigma}$. Using the standard refinement process of ABC, we will obtain an dynamic safety controller for Σ.

Step A: Computing Atomic Safety Controllers. Suppose $G_i \subseteq \mathcal{X}$ be an atomic unsafe set of states of Σ. As described above, the abstract atomic safety specification $Safety_{\widehat{S}}(\widehat{G_i})$ is the set of paths of $\widehat{\Sigma}$ that remain safe with respect to $\widehat{G_i} = Q(G_i) = \{\widehat{x} \in \widehat{\mathcal{X}} \mid \widehat{x} \cap G \neq \emptyset\}$. The respective n.m.p. abstract controller $\widehat{\mathcal{C}}_{\widehat{G_i}}$ (n.m.p. with respect to $\widehat{\Sigma}$) can be computed using a standard iterative procedure from the literature [45] and presented using the function SafetyControl in Algorithm 1. SafetyControl uses the set S as an over-approximation of the set of states from which the safety specification can be fulfilled (aka, controlled invariant set). Initially S spans the entire state space $\widehat{\mathcal{X}}$ of $\widehat{\Sigma}$ (Line 1). Afterwards, the over-approximation S is iteratively refined (the do-while loop) as states from the current S are discarded owing to inability of fulfilling safety from them. This is implemented using the $CPre \colon 2^{\widehat{\mathcal{X}}} \to 2^{\widehat{\mathcal{X}}}$ operator defined as $CPre(S) := \left\{ \widehat{x} \in \widehat{\mathcal{X}} \mid \exists \widehat{u} \in \widehat{\mathcal{U}} \,.\, \widehat{f}(\widehat{x}, \widehat{u}) \subseteq S \right\}$. When no more refinement of S is possible, we stop the iteration and extract the safety controller $\widehat{\mathcal{C}_{G_i}}$ (Line 6) as the one that keeps the abstract system inside S. It is guaranteed that $\widehat{\mathcal{C}_{G_i}}$ is an n.m.p. safety controller of $\widehat{\Sigma}$ for $Safety_{\widehat{\Sigma}}(\widehat{G_i})$, and that its refinement is a nonblocking safety controller for $Safety_{\Sigma}(G_i)$. Unfortunately, the maximal permissiveness is not guaranteed with respect to Σ, as explained in Remark 2.

Algorithm 1. SafetyControl

Input: $\widehat{\Sigma} = (\widehat{\mathcal{X}}, \widehat{\mathcal{U}}, \widehat{f})$, $Safety_{\widehat{\Sigma}}(\widehat{G_i})$
Output: Safety controller $\widehat{\mathcal{C}_{G_i}}$ of $\widehat{\Sigma}$
1: $S \leftarrow \widehat{\mathcal{X}}$
2: do
3:     $S_{\text{old}} \leftarrow S$
4:     $S \leftarrow CPre(S) \cap \widehat{G_i}$
5: while $S \neq S_{\text{old}}$
6: $\forall \widehat{x} \in S \,.\, \widehat{\mathcal{C}_{G_i}}(\widehat{x}) \leftarrow \left\{ \widehat{u} \in \widehat{\mathcal{U}} \mid \widehat{f}(\widehat{x}, \widehat{u}) \subseteq S \right\}$
7: **return** $\widehat{\mathcal{C}_{G_i}}$

Algorithm 2. NBControl

Input: $\widehat{\Sigma} = (\widehat{\mathcal{X}}, \widehat{\mathcal{U}}, \widehat{f})$, $\widehat{\mathcal{C}} \colon \widehat{\mathcal{X}} \to 2^{\widehat{\mathcal{U}}}$
Output: Largest nonblocking sub-controller $\widehat{\mathcal{C}}'$ of $\widehat{\mathcal{C}}$
1: $\widehat{\mathcal{X}}' \leftarrow \widehat{\mathcal{X}} \cup \{\bot\}$
2: Define $\widehat{f}' \colon \widehat{\mathcal{X}}' \times \widehat{\mathcal{U}} \to 2^{\widehat{\mathcal{X}}'}$:
    $\forall \widehat{x} \in \widehat{\mathcal{X}} \,.\, \forall \widehat{u} \in \widehat{\mathcal{C}}(\widehat{x}) \,.\, \widehat{f}'(\widehat{x}, \widehat{u}) \leftarrow \widehat{f}(\widehat{x}, \widehat{u})$
    $\forall \widehat{x} \in \widehat{\mathcal{X}} \,.\, \forall \widehat{u} \notin \widehat{\mathcal{C}}(\widehat{x}) \,.\, \widehat{f}'(\widehat{x}, \widehat{u}) \leftarrow \{\bot\}$
    $\forall \widehat{u} \in \widehat{\mathcal{U}} \,.\, \widehat{f}'(\bot, \widehat{u}) \leftarrow \{\bot\}$
3: $\widehat{\Sigma}' \leftarrow (\widehat{\mathcal{X}}', \widehat{\mathcal{U}}, \widehat{f}')$
4: **return** SafetyControl($\widehat{\Sigma}'$, $\widehat{\mathcal{X}} = \widehat{\mathcal{X}}' \setminus \{\bot\}$)

Step B1: Computing the Product. Computing the product involves the straightforward application of Definition 2 on two abstract safety controllers.

Step B2: Computing Largest Nonblocking Sub-Controllers. The largest nonblocking sub-controller is computed using the function NBControl, presented in Algorithm 2. NBControl first modifies $\widehat{\Sigma}$ to a new system $\widehat{\Sigma}'$ by keeping those transitions that are allowed by $\widehat{\mathcal{C}}$, and redirecting the rest to a new sink state $\bot$ (Line 2). With this modification, any safety controller of $\widehat{\Sigma}'$ that is nonblocking and avoids the unsafe state $\bot$ is by construction a nonblocking sub-controller of $\widehat{\mathcal{C}}$. If the subcontroller is in addition maximally permissive with respect to the unsafe state $\bot$, then it follows that it is the largest nonblocking sub-controller of $\widehat{\mathcal{C}}$. Therefore, the largest nonblocking sub-controller of $\widehat{\mathcal{C}}$ is obtained by invoking the subroutine SafetyControl with arguments $\widehat{\Sigma}'$ and $Safety_{\widehat{\Sigma}'}(\widehat{\mathcal{X}})$.

In contrast, the naïve pure online shield synthesis algorithm would at each step run SafetyControl($\widehat{\Sigma}$, $Safety_{\Sigma}(\widehat{\mathcal{X}})$), which is significantly more expensive than the procedure outlined above. This is because in B2 (dominates B1), each invocation of $CPre(\cdot)$ in SafetyControl is significantly faster on $\widehat{\Sigma}'$ compared to invoking $CPre(\cdot)$ on $\widehat{\Sigma}$ (the pure online case), as the complexity of $CPre(\cdot)$ is linear in the number of transitions of the abstract system, and this number effectively becomes small for $\widehat{\Sigma}'$ since we can ignore all the transitions that lead to "$\bot$" (*surely* unsafe transitions). The smaller effective number of transitions also contributes to a smaller number of iterations of the while loop in SafetyControl, creating a compounding effect in reducing the overall complexity.

4.3 Symbolic Implementation

Our dynamic safety controller synthesis algorithm is implemented symbolically using BDDs, where the states and inputs and transitions of abstract control systems are modeled using boolean formulas represented by BDDs, and all the steps of Algorithm 1 and 2 and the product operation are implemented using logical operations over the BDDs and existential and universal quantifications. The implementation details follow standard procedures used by ABC algorithms from the literature [30,42]. In particular, our tool is built within the ABC tool Mascot-SDS [30], which supports efficient, parallelized BDD libraries like Sylvan [44]. These implementation details enabled us to create a prototype dynamic shielding tool that whose offline computation stage takes a few minutes, and, more importantly, the online computations finish within just a few seconds on an average at each step. More details on the experiments are included in Sect. 6.

5 Dynamic Shields for Robot Navigation in Unknown Territories

We consider a mobile robot placed in an unknown world filled with static obstacles (Fig. 3). The robot is controlled by an unknown AI controller with unknown motives. We want to design a shield whose safety objective is to avoid colliding with the obstacles at all time. We assume that the shield only has limited observation of the world, and it can only observe obstacles that are within a certain distance d along each dimension of the X-Y coordinate axes. This creates a *visible region* that is a square whose sides have the length $2d$ centered around the current location of the robot at each time step. This is a realistic scenario experienced by many mobile agents, including self-driving cars and exploratory robots.

The dynamic shield assumes that the robot's state space spans only the size of the visible region. At the design time, the shield assumes that obstacles can be arranged in all possible ways within this visible region at each step. At runtime, the shield observes the obstacles in the current snapshot of visible region, and does its online computations to quickly deploy the suitable shield. This shield is deployed just for the current time step. In the next step, the obstacle arrangements would have shifted,

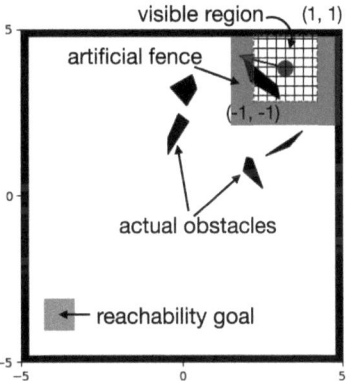

Fig. 3. Illustration of dynamic shielding of the robot (blue dot) in an unknown environment. Dynamic shields are computed using ABC, but not over the entire state space, rather over the tiny visible region of the robot. The corners "$(-1,-1)$" and "$(1,1)$" of the visible region are in the robot's own reference coordinates. (Color figure online)

because the robot and its visible region could have moved, and therefore the shield must dynamically adapt and recompute the safe control inputs. And the process repeats.

We need to ensure a *safe handover* of two dynamically adapted shields at consecutive steps, i.e., every action that a shield allows must guarantee that the new state is in the domain of the shield at the next step. The challenge comes from the lack of knowledge of obstacles that are currently outside of the visible region, but might suddenly appear in the next step and could seriously endanger safety. We take a conservative approach. We add *artificial fences* in the outer periphery of the visible region, to over-approximate the uncertainty that awaits in the unobservable parts. The safety specification for the shield at each step involves—other than avoiding the obstacles inside the visible region—avoiding the artificial fences all the time. We formalize this as a dynamic shield synthesis problem. The state space of the robot spans the visible region extended with the artificial fences of a given thickness $\epsilon > 0$, i.e., $\mathcal{X} = [-d-\epsilon, d+\epsilon] \times [-d-\epsilon, d+\epsilon]$ with respect to the robot's own reference coordinate frame, in which the robot's initial state is always the origin. We use the grid-based abstraction $\widehat{\mathcal{X}}$ of $\mathcal{X}$, and assume that each element of $\widehat{\mathcal{X}}$ is an atomic *unsafe* state set. This is because at runtime, no matter what obstacles are encountered within the visible region, they can be over-approximated as the union of the right subset of $\widehat{\mathcal{X}}$. In addition, the fence is included in each atomic unsafe set. Therefore, the set of atomic *safe* sets is $\left\{ \mathcal{X} \setminus (\{\widehat{x}\} \cup \textit{fence}) \mid \widehat{x} \in \widehat{\mathcal{X}} \right\}$ where $\textit{fence} = \mathcal{X} \setminus [-d, d] \times [-d, d]$.

Unfortunately, just adding artificial fences would not always lead to a safe handover. This is illustrated in Fig. 4, where for staying safe starting at the center of a given visible region, the shield needs to make a maneuver that requires all the states inside the visible region be safe (see configurations (a) and (f)). Starting at the configuration (a), the robot moves to its right—an action allowed by the shield. But now the visible region includes the obstacle, causing the shield to have an empty domain (as shown in (d)). Therefore, the new shield cannot be yet deployed and the handover would not be successful. Luckily, the shield designed for (a) would still be sound, because, by construction, the robot would still stay within its domain. This way, the shield designed at (a) remains in use until the new shield can be deployed, which happens in the configuration (f).

We formally present this procedure in Algorithm 3, where, as before, instead of shields, we consider the handover problem for the equivalent n.m.p. safety controllers. The subroutine Init takes as input the system dynamics in the visible region augmented with the fences, denoted as Σ, as well as the initial safety specification $Safety(G)$, and checks if a shield is feasible or not for this initial configuration of the unsafe states. Subsequently, as time progresses and the state changes, the subroutine Next is invoked, which takes as input the new safety specification $Safety(G')$ and the new state x within the previous configuration, and it performs the safe handover operation by updating the global variables config.-in-use, state-in-use, and cont.-in-use that store which configuration and safety controller is currently in use. The soundness is stated in Theorem 3.

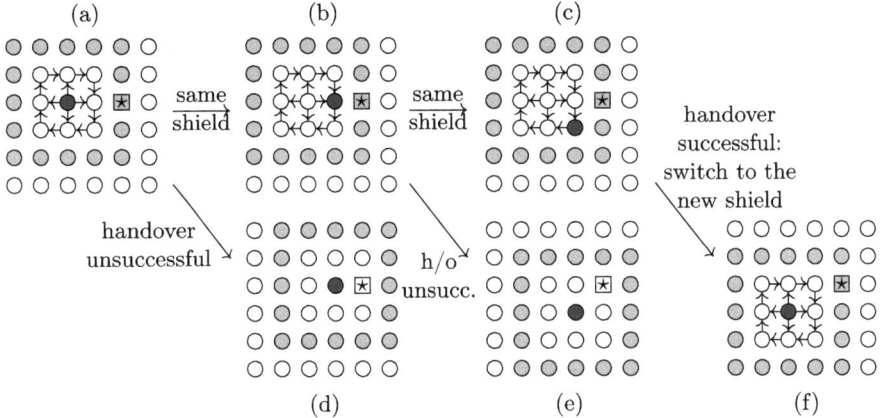

Fig. 4. Illustration of the safe handover framework on a simplified discrete state space: Above is a sequence of configurations during the handover mechanism, where each configuration captures the state of the robot (blue), and the current locations of the unsafe states, including the fence (pink). The single square shaped state marked with "⋆" represents the obstacle, and the arrows represent the only safe actions allowed by the shield at a given configuration. (Color figure online)

Theorem 3 (Soundness of SafeHandover). *Let $\Sigma = (\mathcal{X}, \mathcal{U}, \mathcal{W}, f)$ be the control system representing the dynamics of the underlying system within the visible region, and let all obstacles (including the ones outside the visible region) be stationary. Suppose at a given time $t > 0$, $x \in \mathcal{X}$ be the current state (in the visible region's reference frame), and $U \subseteq \mathcal{U}$ be the output of Next. Then for every $u \in U$ and for every $w \in \mathcal{W}$, the new state $x' = f(x, u, w)$ is safe and, moreover, no matter what the new safety specification $Safety(G')$ at time $t+1$ is, the output of $\text{Next}(Safety(G'), x')$ is non-empty.*

Proof. The safety of x' follows from the property of the n.m.p. controller in the given visible region, and from the assumption that the obstacles are stationary. At time $t+1$, there are two possibilities: (1) The handover is successful, i.e., the n.m.p. safety controller $\mathcal{C}^*_{G'}$ of Σ for $Safety(G')$ contains the origin $(0,0)$ in its domain, which coincides with x' from the reference frame of the visible region at time t. In this case, the output of $\mathcal{C}^*_{G'}((0,0))$ will by definition of "domain" be non-empty. (2) The handover is unsuccessful, i.e., $(0,0) \notin Dom(\mathcal{C}^*_{G'})$. In this case, Next would output $\mathcal{C}^*_G(x')$, where $\mathcal{C}^*_G$ is the n.m.p. safety controller that was used at the previous time step t. It follows from the non-blockingness property of $\mathcal{C}^*_G$ and from the stationarity assumption on the obstacles that $\mathcal{C}^*_G(x') \neq \emptyset$.

Algorithm 3. SafeHandover

1: **function** Init(Σ, Safety(G))	1: **function** Next(Safety(G'), x) ▷ x: new state in the current config.-in-use
2: $\Sigma \leftarrow \Sigma$ ▷ global variable	2: Compute the n.m.p. cont. $\mathcal{C}^*_{G'}$ of Σ for Safety(G')
3: Compute the n.m.p. cont. $\mathcal{C}^*_G$ of Σ for Safety(G)	3: **if** $(0,0) \in Dom(\mathcal{C}^*_{G'})$ **then** ▷ handover successful
4: **if** $(0,0) \in Dom(\mathcal{C}^*_G)$ **then**	4: config.-in-use $\leftarrow$ Safety(G')
5: config.-in-use $\leftarrow$ Safety(G)	5: state-in-use $\leftarrow (0,0)$
6: cont.-in-use $\leftarrow \mathcal{C}^*_G$	6: cont.-in-use $\leftarrow \mathcal{C}^*_{G'}$
7: **return** $\mathcal{C}^*_G((0,0))$	7: **else** ▷ keep using the old shield
8: **else** ▷ initially unsafe	8: state-in-use $\leftarrow x$
9: **return** failure	9: **end if**
10: **end if**	10: **return** cont.-in-use(state-in-use)
11: **end function**	11: **end function**

6 Experiments

We implemented our algorithm within the tool Mascot-SDS, which can be accessed in the following url: https://gitlab.com/kmallik/mascotsds.

The Experimental Setup. The dynamics of the mobile robot is modeled as a discrete-time Dubins vehicle. The system has three state variables x, y, and θ, where x and y represent the location in the X-Y coordinate, and θ represents the heading angle in radians (measured counter-clockwise from the positive X axis); two control input variables v and a, representing the forward velocity and the angular velocity of the steering; and three disturbance variables w^1, w^2, w^3, which affect the dynamics in the three individual states. The transitions are:

$$x' = x + (v\cos\theta)\tau + w^1, \qquad y' = y + (v\sin\theta)\tau + w^2, \qquad \theta' = \theta + a\tau + w^3,$$

where the primed variables on the left side represent the states at the next time step, and τ represents the sampling time. We use the following spaces for the states, control inputs, and disturbance inputs: $x \in [-1,1]$, $y \in [-1,1]$, $\theta \in [-\pi,\pi]$, $v \in \{-0.4, -0.2, \ldots, 0.2, 0.4\}$, $a \in \{-4, -3.5, \ldots, 3.5, 4\}$, $w^1 \in [-0.01, 0.01]$, $w^2 \in [-0.01, 0.01]$, and $w^3 \in [-0.02, 0.02]$. Furthermore, we fix $\tau = 0.1\,s$, and the thickness of the fence to $\epsilon = 0.3$.

The underlying AI controller is generated using reinforcement learning (RL) with reach-avoid objectives. In our experiments, the RL controller is made aware of the entire map, even though the shield's visibility range is limited to a tiny region ranging $[-1, 1] \times [-1, 1]$ in its own reference frame.

Performance Evaluations. We report the offline and online computation times of our dynamic shields for three different levels of abstraction coarseness used in the ABC algorithms. The abstraction coarseness is measured as the (uniform) grid size used for discretizing the state and input spaces, which are respectively 3 and 2-dimensional vectors representing the dimension-wise side lengths of the square-shaped grid elements. All synthesized shields are by-construction safe and minimally permissive, and therefore these aspects are not reported. The code was run on a personal computer powered by Intel Core Ultra 7 255U processor and 32 GB RAM.

We report the offline computation times for the three different abstractions in Table 1. As expected, as the abstraction gets finer (smaller grid sizes), the computation time increases. Nonetheless, all computation finished within reasonable amount of time. In comparison, the pure offline baseline would timeout even for the coarsest abstraction, because with its X-Y state variables' grid sizes $[0.10, 0.10]$, it would create $20 \times 20 = 400$ grid cells in the domain $[-1, 1] \times [-1, 1]$, and since we choose the number of atomic safety specifications to be equal to the number of grid cells, we would need to solve 2^{400} instances of safety controller synthesis problems! Although the pure online baseline takes zero time in the offline phase, it will take more time at the online phase as we discuss next.

For each of the three abstraction classes, we deployed the pure online and dynamic shields alongside a learned controller and tested them on 70 randomly generated reach-avoid control problem instances.

Table 1. Computation times of the offline phase (atomic shield synthesis) of dynamic shields.

Grid size		Computation time	
$\widehat{\mathcal{X}}$	$\widehat{\mathcal{U}}$	Abstraction	Synthesis
$[0.10, 0.10, 0.30]$	$[0.2, 0.5]$	2 m 12 s	1 m
$[0.08, 0.08, 0.25]$	$[0.2, 0.5]$	4 m 40 s	2 m 35 s
$[0.06, 0.06, 0.20]$	$[0.2, 0.5]$	9 m 35 s	9 m 25 s

In each instance and for each shield, we measured the computation time per step on an average, and report them in Fig. 5. We observe that the dynamic shields are almost always faster than the pure online shields, and as the abstraction gets finer, their difference becomes more prominent. With the finest abstraction, the dynamic shield was upto five times faster! Furthermore, any efficiency improvement of the pure online shield would benefit the dynamic shield too, because both rely on the SafetyControl algorithm for their online computation phase.

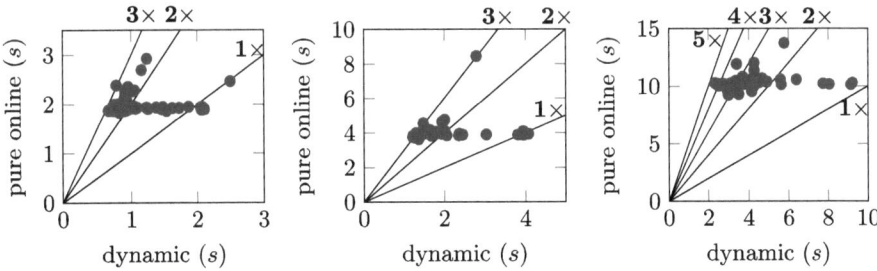

Fig. 5. Average online computation times of the pure online algorithm (the baseline) and our dynamic algorithm. Each point in the scatter plots represents one randomly generated problem instance for the navigation task. The three plots correspond to three different abstraction granularities used in the ABC procedure, with the leftmost plot representing the coarsest (Row 1, Table 1) and the rightmost plot representing the finest (Row 3, Table 1) abstraction sizes.

7 Discussions and Future Work

We propose dynamic shields that can adapt to changing safety specifications at runtime. While the problem can be solved using pure offline or pure online approaches using brute force, our dynamic approach is significantly more efficient and combines both offline and online computations. We presented concrete algorithms using the abstraction-based control framework, and demonstrated the effectiveness of dynamic shields on a robot motion planning problem.

Several future directions exist. Firstly, in our work, we use the atomic safe set as it is given, and we will investigate if this set can be first processed in a way that the online deployment phase of shield computation can be benefited (e.g., by simplifying the nonblockingness process). Secondly, in our simulations of the experiments, sometimes the system would get stuck and would not be able to make progress. This is a known issue in shielding and we will study how to eliminate this by taking inspiration from other works dealing with similar problems [27]. Thirdly, we proposed a conservative but simple approach to the safe handover problem, and more advanced procedures [32] will be incorporated in subsequent versions. Finally, we will extend our framework to richer classes of safety properties, expressible in LTL modulo theories [11,25,40,41,47], LTL over finite traces [14,17], and quantitative or discounted safety specifications [1,24], as well as to control systems with dynamic obstacles for world models [18].

Acknowledgments. This work was funded in part by the grant CEX2024-001471-M/funded by MICIU/AEI/10.13039/501100011033, and the DECO Project (PID2022-138072OB-I00) funded by MCIN/AEI/10.13039/501100011033 and by the ESF+.

References

1. Almagor, S., Boker, U., Kupferman, O.: Discounting in LTL. In: Ábrahám, E., Havelund, K. (eds.) TACAS 2014. LNCS, vol. 8413, pp. 424–439. Springer, Heidelberg (2014). https://doi.org/10.1007/978-3-642-54862-8_37
2. Alshiekh, M., Bloem, R., Ehlers, R., Könighofer, B., Niekum, S., Topcu, U.: Safe reinforcement learning via shielding. In: Proceedings of the AAAI Conference on Artificial Intelligence, vol. 32 (2018)
3. Amir, G., Schapira, M., Katz, G.: Towards scalable verification of deep reinforcement learning. In: Proceedings of 21st International Conference on Formal Methods in Computer-Aided Design (FMCAD), pp. 193–203 (2021)
4. Anand, A., Nayak, S.P., Schmuck, A.K.: Synthesizing permissive winning strategy templates for parity games. In: International Conference on Computer Aided Verification, pp. 436–458. Springer (2023)
5. Banerjee, A., Rahmani, K., Biswas, J., Dillig, I.: Dynamic model predictive shielding for provably safe reinforcement learning. Adv. Neural. Inf. Process. Syst. **37**, 100131–100159 (2024)
6. Bharadwaj, S., Bloem, R., Dimitrova, R., Konighofer, B., Topcu, U.: Synthesis of minimum-cost shields for multi-agent systems. In: 2019 American Control Conference (ACC), pp. 1048–1055. IEEE (2019)

7. Bloem, R., Könighofer, B., Könighofer, R., Wang, C.: Shield synthesis: runtime enforcement for reactive systems. In: Baier, C., Tinelli, C. (eds.) TACAS 2015. LNCS, vol. 9035, pp. 533–548. Springer, Heidelberg (2015). https://doi.org/10.1007/978-3-662-46681-0_51
8. Brorholt, A.H., Høeg-Petersen, A.H., Larsen, K.G., Schilling, C.: Efficient shield synthesis via state-space transformation. In: International Conference on Bridging the Gap between AI and Reality, pp. 206–224. Springer (2024)
9. Carr, S., Jansen, N., Junges, S., Topcu, U.: Safe reinforcement learning via shielding under partial observability. In: Thirty-Seventh AAAI Conference on Artificial Intelligence, AAAI 2023, Thirty-Fifth Conference on Innovative Applications of Artificial Intelligence, IAAI 2023, Thirteenth Symposium on Educational Advances in Artificial Intelligence, EAAI 2023, Washington, DC, USA, 7–14 February 2023, pp. 14748–14756. AAAI Press (2023). https://doi.org/10.1609/AAAI.V37I12.26723
10. Córdoba, F.C., Palmisano, A., Fränzle, M., Bloem, R., Könighofer, B.: Safety shielding under delayed observation. In: Proceedings of the Thirty-Third International Conference on Automated Planning and Scheduling (ICAPS 2023), pp. 80–85. AAAI Press (2023). https://doi.org/10.1609/ICAPS.V33I1.27181
11. Corsi, D., Amir, G., Rodríguez, A., Katz, G., Sánchez, C., Fox, R.: Verification-guided shielding for deep reinforcement learning. RLJ **4**, 1759–1780 (2024)
12. Debot, D., Venturato, G., Marra, G., Raedt, L.D.: Neurosymbolic reinforcement learning: playing minihack with probabilistic logic shields. In: AAAI-25, Sponsored by the Association for the Advancement of Artificial Intelligence, 25 February–4 March 2025, Philadelphia, PA, USA, pp. 29631–29633. AAAI Press (2025). https://doi.org/10.1609/AAAI.V39I28.35349
13. ElSayed-Aly, I., Bharadwaj, S., Amato, C., Ehlers, R., Topcu, U., Feng, L.: Safe multi-agent reinforcement learning via shielding. arXiv preprint arXiv:2101.11196 (2021)
14. Favorito, M.: Forward LTLF synthesis: DPLL at work. CoRR abs/2302.13825 (2023). https://doi.org/10.48550/arXiv.2302.13825
15. Feng, Y., Zhu, J., Platzer, A., Laurent, J.: Adaptive shielding via parametric safety proofs. Proc. ACM Program. Lang. **9**(OOPSLA1), 816–843 (2025)
16. Fridovich-Keil, D., Herbert, S.L., Fisac, J.F., Deglurkar, S., Tomlin, C.J.: Planning, fast and slow: a framework for adaptive real-time safe trajectory planning. In: 2018 IEEE International Conference on Robotics and Automation (ICRA), pp. 387–394. IEEE (2018)
17. Giacomo, G.D., Vardi, M.Y.: Linear temporal logic and linear dynamic logic on finite traces. In: Proceedings of the 23rd International Joint Conference on Artificial Intelligence (IJCAI 2013), pp. 854–860. IJCAI/AAAI (2013). http://www.aaai.org/ocs/index.php/IJCAI/IJCAI13/paper/view/6997
18. Ha, D., Schmidhuber, J.: World models. CoRR abs/1803.10122 (2018). http://arxiv.org/abs/1803.10122
19. Henzinger, T.A., Raskin, J.-F.: Robust undecidability of timed and hybrid systems. In: Lynch, N., Krogh, B.H. (eds.) HSCC 2000. LNCS, vol. 1790, pp. 145–159. Springer, Heidelberg (2000). https://doi.org/10.1007/3-540-46430-1_15
20. Hu, H., Nakamura, K., Fisac, J.F.: Sharp: shielding-aware robust planning for safe and efficient human-robot interaction. IEEE Robot. Autom. Lett. **7**(2), 5591–5598 (2022)
21. Ivanov, R., Weimer, J., Alur, R., Pappas, G.J., Lee, I.: Verisig: verifying safety properties of hybrid systems with neural network controllers. In: Proceedings of the 22nd ACM International Conference on Hybrid Systems: Computation and Control, pp. 169–178 (2019)

22. Jansen, N., Könighofer, B., Junges, S., Bloem, R.: Shielded decision-making in MDPs. arXiv preprint arXiv:1807.06096 (2018)
23. Katz, G., Barrett, C., Dill, D.L., Julian, K., Kochenderfer, M.J.: Reluplex: an efficient SMT solver for verifying deep neural networks. In: Majumdar, R., Kunčak, V. (eds.) CAV 2017. LNCS, vol. 10426, pp. 97–117. Springer, Cham (2017). https://doi.org/10.1007/978-3-319-63387-9_5
24. Khoury, R., Hallé, S.: Tally keeping-LTL: an LTL semantics for quantitative evaluation of LTL specifications. In: 2018 IEEE International Conference on Information Reuse and Integration, IRI 2018, pp. 495–502. IEEE (2018). https://doi.org/10.1109/IRI.2018.00079
25. Kim, K., et al.: Realizable continuous-space shields for safe reinforcement learning. In: Proceedings of the 7th Annual Learning for Dynamics & Control Conference (L4DC'25). PMLR (2025). https://proceedings.mlr.press/v242/zhou24a.html
26. Könighofer, B., et al.: Shield synthesis. Formal Methods Syst. Des. **51**(2), 332–361 (2017). https://doi.org/10.1007/s10703-017-0276-9
27. Könighofer, B., Rudolf, J., Palmisano, A., Tappler, M., Bloem, R.: Online shielding for reinforcement learning. Innovations Syst. Softw. Eng. **19**(4), 379–394 (2023)
28. Li, S., Bastani, O.: Robust model predictive shielding for safe reinforcement learning with stochastic dynamics. In: 2020 IEEE International Conference on Robotics and Automation (ICRA), pp. 7166–7172. IEEE (2020)
29. Majumdar, A., Tedrake, R.: Funnel libraries for real-time robust feedback motion planning. Int. J. Robot. Res. **36**(8), 947–982 (2017)
30. Majumdar, R., Mallik, K., Rychlicki, M., Schmuck, A.K., Soudjani, S.: A flexible toolchain for symbolic rabin games under fair and stochastic uncertainties. In: International Conference on Computer Aided Verification, pp. 3–15. Springer (2023)
31. Majumdar, R., Mallik, K., Schmuck, A.K., Soudjani, S.: Symbolic control for stochastic systems via finite parity games. Nonlinear Anal. Hybrid Syst **51**, 101430 (2024)
32. Nayak, S.P., Egidio, L.N., Della Rossa, M., Schmuck, A.K., Jungers, R.M.: Context-triggered abstraction-based control design. IEEE Open J. Control Syst. **2**, 277–296 (2023)
33. Nilsson, P., Ozay, N., Liu, J.: Augmented finite transition systems as abstractions for control synthesis. Discret. Event Dyn. Syst. **27**(2), 301–340 (2017). https://doi.org/10.1007/s10626-017-0243-z
34. Pola, G., Tabuada, P.: Symbolic models for nonlinear control systems: alternating approximate bisimulations. SIAM J. Control. Optim. **48**(2), 719–733 (2009)
35. Pranger, S., Könighofer, B., Posch, L., Bloem, R.: TEMPEST - synthesis tool for reactive systems and shields in probabilistic environments. In: Hou, Z., Ganesh, V. (eds.) ATVA 2021. LNCS, vol. 12971, pp. 222–228. Springer, Cham (2021). https://doi.org/10.1007/978-3-030-88885-5_15
36. Pranger, S., Könighofer, B., Tappler, M., Deixelberger, M., Jansen, N., Bloem, R.: Adaptive shielding under uncertainty. In: 2021 American Control Conference (ACC), pp. 3467–3474. IEEE (2021)
37. Quan, L., Zhang, Z., Zhong, X., Xu, C., Gao, F.: Eva-planner: environmental adaptive quadrotor planning. In: 2021 IEEE International Conference on Robotics and Automation (ICRA), pp. 398–404. IEEE (2021)
38. Raeesi, H., Khosravi, A., Sarhadi, P.: Safe reinforcement learning by shielding based reachable zonotopes for autonomous vehicles. Int. J. Eng. **38**(1), 21–34 (2025)
39. Reissig, G., Weber, A., Rungger, M.: Feedback refinement relations for the synthesis of symbolic controllers. IEEE Trans. Autom. Control **62**(4), 1781–1796 (2016)

40. Rodríguez, A., Amir, G., Corsi, D., Sánchez, C., Katz, G.: Shield synthesis for LTL modulo theories. In: Proceedings of the 39th AAAI Conference on Artificial Intelligence (AAAI 2025), pp. 15134–15142. AAAI Press (2025). https://doi.org/10.1609/AAAI.V39I14.33660
41. Rodríguez, A., Shaik, I., Corsi, D., Fox, R., Sanchez, C.: Explanations for unrealizability of infinite-state safety shields. In: Proceedings of the 22nd International Conference on Principles of Knowledge Representation and Reasoning (KR 2025) (2025)
42. Rungger, M., Zamani, M.: Scots: a tool for the synthesis of symbolic controllers. In: Proceedings of the 19th International Conference on Hybrid Systems: Computation and Control, pp. 99–104 (2016)
43. Tabuada, P.: An approximate simulation approach to symbolic control. IEEE Trans. Autom. Control **53**(6), 1406–1418 (2008)
44. Dijk, T., Pol, J.: Sylvan: multi-core decision diagrams. In: Baier, C., Tinelli, C. (eds.) TACAS 2015. LNCS, vol. 9035, pp. 677–691. Springer, Heidelberg (2015). https://doi.org/10.1007/978-3-662-46681-0_60
45. Vidal, R., Schaffert, S., Lygeros, J., Sastry, S.: Controlled invariance of discrete time systems. In: Lynch, N., Krogh, B.H. (eds.) HSCC 2000. LNCS, vol. 1790, pp. 437–451. Springer, Heidelberg (2000). https://doi.org/10.1007/3-540-46430-1_36
46. Waga, M., Castellano, E., Pruekprasert, S., Klikovits, S., Takisaka, T., Hasuo, I.: Dynamic shielding for reinforcement learning in black-box environments. In: International Symposium on Automated Technology for Verification and Analysis, pp. 25–41. Springer (2022)
47. Wu, M., Wang, J., Deshmukh, J., Wang, C.: Shield synthesis for real: enforcing safety in cyber-physical systems. In: Proceedings of 19th Formal Methods in Computer Aided Design, (FMCAD 2019), pp. 129–137. IEEE (2019). https://doi.org/10.23919/FMCAD.2019.8894264
48. Yang, W., Marra, G., Rens, G., Raedt, L.D.: Safe reinforcement learning via probabilistic logic shields. In: Proceedings of the 32nd International Joint Conference on Artificial Intelligence, (IJCAI 2023), pp. 5739–5749. ijcai.org (2023). https://doi.org/10.24963/IJCAI.2023/637

Learning Verified Monitors for Hidden Markov Models

Luko van der Maas(✉) and Sebastian Junges

Radboud University, Nijmegen, The Netherlands
{luko.vandermaas,sebastian.junges}@ru.nl

Abstract. Runtime monitors assess whether a system is in an unsafe state based on a stream of observations. We study the problem where the system is subject to probabilistic uncertainty and described by a hidden Markov model. A stream of observations is then unsafe if the probability of being in an unsafe state is above a threshold. A correct monitor recognizes the set of unsafe observations. The key contribution of this paper is the first correct-by-construction synthesis method for such monitors, represented as finite automata. The contribution combines four ingredients: First, we establish the coNP-hardness of checking whether an automaton is a correct monitor, i.e., a monitor without misclassifications. Second, we provide a reduction that reformulates the search for misclassifications into a standard probabilistic system synthesis problem. Third, we integrate the verification routine into an active automata learning routine to synthesize correct monitors. Fourth, we provide a prototypical implementation that shows the feasibility and limitations of the approach on a series of benchmarks.

1 Introduction

Runtime assurance is an essential ingredient in the deployment of safe autonomous systems [18,41]. Runtime monitors provide assurance by flagging potentially dangerous system behavior, based on a system execution. More precisely, a monitor receives a stream of observations about the system and outputs a verdict, e.g., it raises an alarm that the system has left some safety envelope. A monitor is correct if it correctly raises such alarms based on a formal specification. Various challenges in creating correct runtime monitors for (semi-)autonomous systems have been identified [41], such as: (1) the state of the system is only partially observable, i.e., the stream of observations comes from sensor readings and does not uniquely identify the state of a system, (2) the behavior of the system and/or the sensors may be subject to probabilistic uncertainty, (3) the monitor itself is subject to resource constraints (time, memory, etc.), and (4) the monitor is itself safety-critical and should therefore be subject to extensive validation. Challenges (1,2) can be addressed by modelling the system as a hidden Markov model (HMM), and Challenges (3,4) can be addressed

---

This work has been partially funded by the NWO grant FuRoRe (OCENW.M.22.282).

© The Author(s), under exclusive license to Springer Nature Switzerland AG 2026
M. D'Souza et al. (Eds.): ATVA 2025, LNCS 16145, pp. 180–203, 2026.
https://doi.org/10.1007/978-3-032-08707-2_9

by representing a monitor as, e.g., a (small) finite automaton. Concretely, this paper focuses on the following question: *Is a given finite automaton a correct monitor for a given and known HMM?* This paper studies the complexity of this problem, provides a practical verification approach, and embeds it into a framework to learn monitors.

What are HMMs? In this paper, we assume that the system including its sensors is adequately modeled as a discrete Hidden Markov Model (HMM) [39] and that we have full access to this HMM. Markov chains (MCs) describe system behavior subject to probabilistic uncertainty. Paths through an MC are sequences of states that describe system executions. HMMs extend MCs by labelling their states with *observations*. Intuitively, the observations can be used to model the information that the monitor receives in every state. In HMMs, every path can be lifted to a sequence of observations, which we call a *trace*. The trace associated to a system execution describes the information received by the monitor.

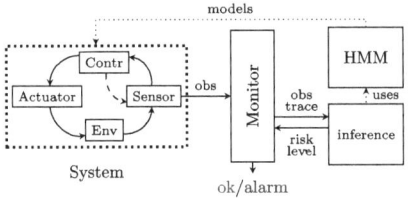

Fig. 1. White-box monitoring of systems

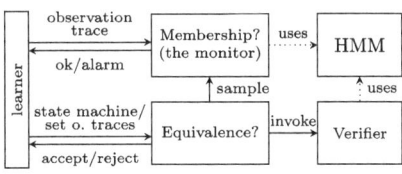

Fig. 2. Learning monitors.

Monitoring with HMMs. Monitoring with HMMs assumes that a monitor receives a trace from the system and performs inference on the HMM modelling the system (see Fig. 1). In the inference step, the key task is to estimate whether the current system state is dangerous, based on the available information in the form of a trace. Intuitively, the *risk of a trace* [34] quantifies how likely it is that the system state is dangerous. Formally, this can be defined as the probability of ending in a dangerous state, conditioned on the fact that the system execution matches the trace. For a given trace, we may compute this risk, e.g., either via model checking [16] or by a (forward) filtering that tracks a distribution over the current states [34,39]. We call a trace *unsafe* if its risk exceeds an acceptable threshold. Monitors should raise alarms only for unsafe traces.

What are Correct Monitors? Like in [1], we summarize the behavior of monitors by the set of traces (i.e., a formal language) on which they raise an alarm. A monitor is correct iff it raises an alarm on all unsafe traces. We highlight that a monitor can be correct without doing inference at run time [23]! The key verification problem in this paper asks whether a monitor, represented as a deterministic finite automaton, accepts (i.e., raises an alarm on) exactly the unsafe traces. In this paper, we only consider traces that are bounded by some fixed horizon.

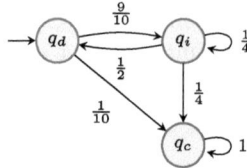 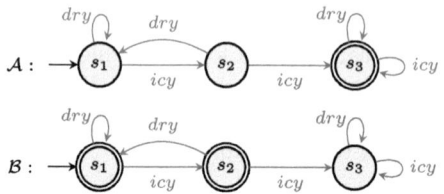

(a) HMM. States q_i, q_c have the observation icy, state q_d has dry. In state q_c the vehicle is off the road.

(b) A correct monitor $\mathcal{A}$ and an incorrect monitor $\mathcal{B}$ (for $\lambda = 0.25$ and $h = 3$).

Fig. 3. Running example: HMM (a) and two monitors (b).

Illustrative Toy Example. As a running example, we consider an oversimplified car driving scenario, loosely inspired by runtime monitors obtained from high-fidelity simulations [46]. A car can be in three states: It can be on a dry road, on an icy patch, or it has drifted off the road. The HMM in Fig. 3a describes how a car alternates between dry and icy road segments, and where being on an icy (dry) segment positively affects the probability that the next segment is icy (dry). When on an icy road, there is a higher probability to drift off the road. Our sensor can detect dry roads, but cannot distinguish between icy roads and off-road conditions. For a trace τ such as $dry \cdot icy \cdot icy$, we can define the trace risk as the probability to be off-road conditioned on τ, $13/22$ (for this trace, see Example 2). In Fig. 3a, monitor $\mathcal{A}$ is a finite automaton that describes the set of traces that end with two consecutive icy patches. The verification question in this paper is now: *Is this a correct monitor for threshold* 0.25? That is, is an alarm raised iff the trace risk is above 0.25?

Model-Based Approach. In this paper, we assume we are given a *useful* model of the system. While such white-box methods can be efficient and explainable, they require a model of the system, which is not always realistic. Alternatively, model-free approaches [20] require no such assumptions, but they have weaker guarantees. Black-box methods [13] fit in between, they learn a model of the system and then use a white-box algorithm to provide the monitor. While we focus on the white-box approach, the results thus contribute towards black-box settings.

Computational Complexity Results. Deciding whether a monitor is correct is coNP-complete (Theorem 4), assuming that the horizon is unary encoded. In particular, we study the dual problem that asks whether a monitor misclassifies at least one trace as safe/unsafe. A simpler variant of this problem asks whether there is a bounded trace in the HMM that is unsafe. This problem is already strongly NP-hard (Lemma 5) and the optimization problem that asks to compute (the risk of) most risky trace is APX-hard (Lemma 6), which indicates that it is intractable to even approximate this risk.

Our Verification Approach. While deciding whether a monitor is correct is in general not tractable, we suggest utilizing recent advances in the synthesis of probabilistic systems [9]. Our presentation focusses on proving the absence of *missed alarms*, i.e., we concentrate on showing that the monitor correctly identifies every unsafe trace, but we show that a similar reduction can be used to show that a monitor correctly identifies the safe traces. First, for a single trace, computing the risk can be reduced to computing a reachability probability in an MC that is some kind of product between a deterministic finite automata (DFA) that accepts exactly the trace and the HMM [34]. Thus, inspired by [14], we reduce our problem to the question: *Is there a DFA (accepting exactly one trace, accepted by our monitor) such that the probability in the product MC exceeds a threshold?* The answer is no iff the monitor has no missed alarms. We formalize the problem using colored MDPs and solve it using (exact) probabilistic model synthesis methods [8], as implemented in the tool PAYNT [9].

Our Learning Approach. Ultimately, we do not only want to verify monitors, but we want to *synthesize* correct monitors. We already mentioned that the monitors are formal languages. When considering bounded traces, these are regular, and can thus be captured using DFAs. Thus, we aim to synthesize DFAs. We do this using active automata learning (AAL, [11,47]), which is similar to other oracle-guided inductive synthesis loops [32]. Consider Fig. 2: To use AAL, we must provide a *membership oracle* that decides for a single trace whether the risk of the trace exceeds a threshold and an *equivalence oracle* that decides whether a given hypothesis monitor is indeed correct. The membership oracle can be implemented via inference for standard monitors on HMMs (see above), while the equivalence oracle can be implemented by verifying the correctness of the monitor, as popularized in *black-box checking* [37]. Practically, some minor modifications are necessary to embed our approach in an AAL framework: We have to handle the finite horizon, ignore traces that cannot occur, and combine our equivalence oracle with a conformance oracle to boost performance.

Contributions. In summary, this paper provides a first framework to learn runtime monitors—encoded as finite automata—that are verified to be correct with respect to a given HMM. The main contributions are: **(1)** We solve the verification problem by exhaustively searching for a counterexample using probabilistic system synthesis (Sect. 3). **(2)** We learn monitors by using the verifier above to answer equivalence queries in conjunction with active automata learning (Sect. 4). **(3)** We prove hardness of the verification problem (Sect. 5). **(4)** We demonstrate the feasibility and limitations of both the verifier and the learner on a series of benchmarks (Sect. 6). Our prototype finds monitors that are provably correct on 10^{22} traces by verifying HMMs with thousands of states, up to a hundred observations, and monitors with over 100 states.

The extended edition [35, App. A and B] contains proof (sketches) for all lemmas and theorems.

2 Formal Problem Statement

Let X be a finite set. A distribution μ over X is a mapping $\mu\colon X \to [0,1]$ such that $\sum_{x \in X} \mu(x) = 1$. The set of all distributions over X is written $\Delta(X)$.

DFAs. A *deterministic finite automaton* (DFA) is a tuple $\mathcal{A} := (Q, \Sigma, \delta, \iota, F)$. Q is a finite set of *states*, Σ is an *alphabet*, $\delta \colon Q \times \Sigma \rightharpoonup Q$ is a (partial) *transition function*, ι is the *initial state*, and $F \subseteq Q$ is a set of *accepting* states[1]. Let ε denote the empty word. We lift the transition relation to words, which is defined recursively as: $\delta^*(q, \varepsilon) := \varepsilon$ if $a \in \Sigma$ and $\delta^*(q, w \cdot a) := \delta(\delta^*(q, w), a)$. The *language* $\mathcal{L}(\mathcal{A})$ of a DFA $\mathcal{A}$ is the set of all words that end in a final state of $\mathcal{A}$, $\mathcal{L}(\mathcal{A}) := \{ w \in \Sigma^* \mid \delta^*(\iota, w) \in F \}$. We say that $\mathcal{A}$ accepts w if $w \in \mathcal{L}(\mathcal{A})$.

2.1 Models

We introduce MDPs and HMMs: The former are integral to our approach and the latter are crucial to the problem statement. Details can be found in [15].

Definition 1 (MDP). *A* Markov decision process *(MDP) is a tuple $(S, \iota, Act, \mathbf{P})$ with a countable nonempty set S of states, the initial state $\iota \in S$, and the partial transition function $\mathbf{P} \colon S \times Act \rightharpoonup \Delta(S)$.*

We use $Act(s) := \{ a \mid \mathbf{P}(s, a) \neq \bot \}$ as the set of *enabled actions*. We assume no deadlocks, i.e., for every $s \in S$, $Act(s) \neq \emptyset$. A path π is a (possibly infinite) sequence $s_0 \cdot a_0 \cdots \in S \times ((S \times Act)^* \cup (S \times Act)^\omega)$, such that $a_i \in Act(s_i)$ and $P(s_i, a_i)(s_{i+1}) > 0$ for every $i \geq 0$. The last state of a finite path is denoted by $\pi_\downarrow$. The set of paths in MDP $\mathcal{M}$ is denoted as $\Pi^\mathcal{M}$, the set of finite paths is $\Pi^\mathcal{M}_{fin}$, the set of paths of at most length h is $\Pi^\mathcal{M}_h$, and the set of paths of exactly length h are $\Pi^\mathcal{M}_{=h}$. We write $\mathbf{P}(s, a, s')$ for $\mathbf{P}(s, a)(s')$.

A *Markov chain* (MC) is an MDP where $|Act(s)| = 1$ for every state $s \in S$. We simplify notation and write MCs as a tuple $(S, \iota, \mathbf{P})$, $\mathbf{P}(s)$ to refer to the unique distribution $\mathbf{P}(s, a)$, and $\mathbf{P}(s, s')$ for $\mathbf{P}(s)(s')$. Paths in an MC are sequences of (only) states. As in [15], the probability measure $Pr^\mathcal{M}$ of an MC $\mathcal{M}$ is the unique probability measure following from the canonical σ-algebra associated with $\mathcal{M}$. A reachability property on target states T is the set of paths which contain a state $t \in T$. The reachability probability $Pr(\lozenge T)$ for $\lozenge T$ is defined using the standard cylinder set construction.

Definition 2 (HMMs). *A (risk-labelled) HMM is a tuple $(S, \iota, \mathbf{P}, Z, obs, r)$ such that $(S, \iota, \mathbf{P})$ is an MC, Z is a finite set of observations, $obs \colon S \to Z$ is the (deterministic) observation function[2], and $r \colon S \to \mathbb{R}_{\geq 0}$ is the risk function.*

Notions such as paths are lifted from MCs. Furthermore, a *trace* τ is a sequence of observations. We lift *obs* from states to paths. We define $Pr(\tau \mid \pi) := 1$ if $obs(\pi) = \tau$ and zero otherwise. The probability of a trace τ is $\sum_{\pi \in \Pi^\mathcal{M}} Pr(\pi) \cdot Pr(\tau \mid \pi)$. Finally, the conditional probability on a trace $\tau \in \mathcal{L}(\mathcal{M})$ is defined using Bayes' rule $Pr(\pi \mid \tau) := {Pr(\tau \mid \pi) \cdot Pr(\pi)}/{Pr(\tau)}$. We define $\mathcal{L}(\mathcal{M}) := \{ obs(\pi) \mid \pi \in \Pi^\mathcal{M} \}$.

---

[1] F is named after the synonymous final states to avoid confusion with actions.
[2] We use deterministic observation functions for concise definitions. Stochastic observation functions can be expressed via a blow-up of the HMM, see e.g., [34].

Example 1. We consider the HMM from Fig. 3a and $\tau = dry \cdot icy \cdot icy$. The conditional probability $Pr(q_d \cdot q_i \cdot q_i \mid \tau)$ is $Pr(\tau \mid q_d \cdot q_i \cdot q_i) \cdot Pr(q_d \cdot q_i \cdot q_i)/Pr(\tau)$. $Pr(\tau \mid q_d \cdot q_i \cdot q_i)$ is 1, and $Pr(q_d \cdot q_i \cdot q_i)$ is $9/40$. The sum of the probabilities of all paths which observe τ is $11/20$. Thus, $Pr(q_d \cdot q_i \cdot q_i \mid \tau)$ is $9/22$.

2.2 Formal Problem Statement

Definition 3 (Monitor). *A DFA $\mathcal{A}$ is a monitor for HMM $\mathcal{M}$ if the alphabet for $\mathcal{A}$ coincides with the observations in $\mathcal{M}$.*

Monitors should accept unsafe traces, which we define via their risk (level) [34]:

Definition 4 (Trace risk, safe/unsafe traces). *Given HMM $\mathcal{M}$, the risk of $\tau \in \mathcal{L}(\mathcal{M})$ is:*

$$R(\tau) := \sum_{\pi \in \Pi_{|\tau|}^{\mathcal{M}}} Pr(\pi \mid \tau) \cdot r(\pi_\downarrow).$$

Let $\lambda_s \leq \lambda_u \in \mathbb{R}_{\geq 0}$ be the safe threshold and the unsafe threshold, respectively. A trace $\tau \in \mathcal{L}(\mathcal{M})$ with $R(\tau) > \lambda_u$ is unsafe, while τ is safe if $R(\tau) < \lambda_s$.

We deliberately do not require $\lambda_s = \lambda_u$. By picking $\lambda_s < \lambda_u$, some traces are neither safe nor unsafe, also called inconclusive. We write $\mathbb{S}_{\mathcal{M},\lambda_s}^{\leq h}$ (and $\mathbb{U}_{\mathcal{M},\lambda_u}^{\leq h}$) for the set of safe (and unsafe) traces of length at most h.

Example 2. We consider the HMM from Fig. 3a, with the risk function assigning 1 to q_c and 0 to all other states. Taking the trace $dry \cdot icy \cdot icy$, there are three paths which could generate this trace. Two paths end in q_c, one ends in q_i. The paths ending in q_c have a conditional probability of $13/22$. Since only these paths have a non-zero risk, the risk of the trace is $13/22 \cdot r(q_c) = 13/22$.

Definition 5 (Missed/False alarms). *Given a monitor $\mathcal{A}$ for HMM $\mathcal{M}$, a horizon h, and thresholds $\lambda_s \leq \lambda_u \in \mathbb{R}_{\geq 0}$, the set of missed alarms is $\mathsf{mA}_{\mathcal{M},\lambda_u}^{\leq h}(\mathcal{A}) := \mathbb{U}_{\mathcal{M},\lambda_u}^{\leq h} \setminus \mathcal{L}(\mathcal{A})$. The set of false alarms is $\mathsf{fA}_{\mathcal{M},\lambda_s}^{\leq h}(\mathcal{A}) := \mathbb{S}_{\mathcal{M},\lambda_s}^{\leq h} \cap \mathcal{L}(\mathcal{A})$.*

Definition 6 (Correct monitor). *Given thresholds λ_s, λ_u and horizon h, a monitor $\mathcal{A}$ for HMM $\mathcal{M}$ is correct if $\mathsf{mA}_{\mathcal{M},\lambda_u}^{\leq h}(\mathcal{A}) = \emptyset = \mathsf{fA}_{\mathcal{M},\lambda_s}^{\leq h}(\mathcal{A})$.*

A correct monitor raises an alarm for all unsafe traces and for no safe trace, i.e., missed alarms are false negatives, while false alarms are false positives.

Corollary 1. *A monitor $\mathcal{A}$ is correct iff $\mathbb{U}_{\mathcal{M},\lambda_u}^{\leq h} \subseteq \mathcal{L}(\mathcal{A}) \subseteq \Sigma^* \setminus \mathbb{S}_{\mathcal{M},\lambda_s}^{\leq h}$.*

Problem statements. Given HMM $\mathcal{M}$, thresholds λ_s, λ_u and horizon h:
1. Given monitor $\mathcal{A}$ for $\mathcal{M}$, are there missed alarms, i.e., is $\mathsf{mA}_{\mathcal{M},\lambda_u}^{\leq h}(\mathcal{A}) = \emptyset$?
2. Given monitor $\mathcal{A}$ for $\mathcal{M}$, are there false alarms, i.e., is $\mathsf{fA}_{\mathcal{M},\lambda_s}^{\leq h}(\mathcal{A}) = \emptyset$?
3. Find a correct monitor $\mathcal{A}$ for $\mathcal{M}$ w.r.t. λ_s, λ_u and h.

Problems 1 and 2 together allow checking whether a monitor is correct. Furthermore, a correct monitor must exist, as $\mathbb{U}^{\leq h}$ is finite and thus regular.

Example 3. We discuss monitor correctness for the example from Fig. 3 using the correct monitor $\mathcal{A}$. Given the risk function assigning 1 to q_c and 0 to all other states, the traces $\tau_1 = dry \cdot icy \cdot icy$ and $\tau_2 = dry \cdot icy$ have risks $13/22$, $1/10$ respectively. If λ_s is $1/4$ and the horizon h is 3, τ_2 is the trace with maximum risk not accepted by the monitor. Given that its risk is below λ_s, the monitor does not have any missed alarms. Similarly, monitor $\mathcal{A}$ does not have any false alarms for $\lambda_u = 1/4$. Thus, $\mathcal{A}$ is a correct monitor for $\mathcal{M}$ with h, λ_s, and λ_u.

3 Monitor Verification

We present our approach to the monitor correctness problem, which reduces checking the existence of missed alarms to the well-studied policy synthesis problem on colored MDPs, defined below. We first formalize this policy synthesis problem and then present the step-wise transformation. Here, we focus on showing that there are no missed alarms of exactly the length of the horizon (an adaption of Problem 1). At the end of the section, we generalize our construction to traces of length *at most* the horizon (Problem 1) and to finding false alarms (Problem 2).

3.1 Relating Missed Alarms to Color-Consistent Policies

A (memoryless) *policy* for an MDP $\mathcal{M}$ is a function $\sigma \colon S \to Act$, which selects actions for every state. An MDP and a policy induce an MC by only keeping the state-action pairs in the transition function selected by the policy. We denote the probability measure on the MC induced by a policy σ of the MDP $\mathcal{M}$ as $Pr_\sigma^{\mathcal{M}}$. Policy synthesis for an MDP of a (reachability) property ϕ entails finding a policy for an MDP such that the induced MC entails ϕ. Colored (aka: labelled) MDPs [10] are an extension to MDPs that allow expressing dependencies between states that policies must adhere to. The following definition suffices for our needs:

Definition 7 (Colored MDP). *Given an MDP $\mathcal{M}$ with states S, a colored MDP is a tuple $\mathcal{M}^C := (\mathcal{M}, C, c)$, where C is a set of colors, and $c \colon S \to C$.*

Definition 8 (Color consistent). *A memoryless policy σ for a colored MDP $\mathcal{M}^C$ is color consistent[3] if for states s, s', $c(s) = c(s')$ implies $\sigma(s) = \sigma(s')$.*

The set of all color-consistent policies is denoted Σ_c. Policy synthesis for colored MDPs asks to find a color-consistent policy such that the reachability probability to a set of target states is above a certain threshold, or to report that no such policy exists. This problem is NP-hard [22], but efficient heuristics exist [9]. Policy synthesis for colored MDPs can prove the absence of missed alarms:

---

[3] Colored MDPs with color-consistent policies coincide with memoryless policies for partially observable MDPs. However, POMDPs often consider history-dependent (belief-based) policies. We use *colored MDPs* to avoid any confusion.

Theorem 1. *Given an HMM $\mathcal{M}$, monitor $\mathcal{A}$, unsafe threshold λ_u, and horizon h, there is a colored MDP $\mathcal{M}^C$ with target state T and threshold λ s.t.*

$$\exists \sigma \in \Sigma_c.\ Pr^{\mathcal{M}^C}_\sigma(\Diamond T) \geq \lambda \quad \text{iff} \quad \exists \tau \in \mathsf{mA}^{=h}_{\mathcal{M},\lambda_u}(\mathcal{A}).$$

Our proof, outlined in this section, is constructive and we show that we can use the construction to find a $\tau \in \mathsf{mA}(\mathcal{A})$, whenever such a τ exists.

Outline of the Proof. The proof is a direct consequence of Lemmas 1 to 3 below. We observe that on the left-hand side of Theorem 1, the monitor, horizon, observations, and risk do not occur, they must be encoded into the colored MDP. Furthermore, while missed alarms are defined using conditional probabilities, the policy synthesis problem is over reachability probabilities. We describe our transformation in several steps. In Sect. 3.2, we encode the monitor into the HMM and transform the HMM to include both the horizon and the risk. In Sect. 3.3, we resolve the conditioning and replace observations by nondeterminism.

Corollary 2. *There exists a map $t(\sigma) = \tau$, which, given a color-consistent policy σ, finds its associated trace τ.*

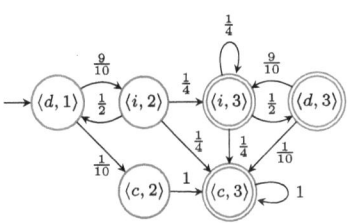

Fig. 4. The HMM for Example 4. States are named by the HMM state, $\{d, i, c\}$ and the monitor state, $\{1, 2, 3\}$. The alarm states are marked accepting.

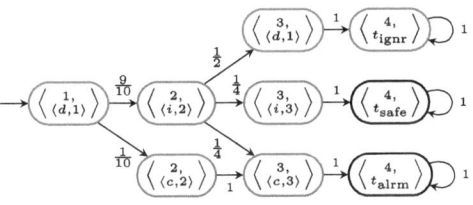

Fig. 5. The HMM for Example 5, brown and cyan are dry and icy observations. Black is the new z_{end} observation, and gray is the new z_{ignore} observation. All states are named with the step i, model state s and monitor state j as $\langle i, \langle s, j \rangle \rangle$.

3.2 The (Acyclic) Conditional Trace Risk Problem

First, we show how asking for a missed alarm can be rephrased into the conceptually simpler *conditional trace risk* (CTR) problem. We will further simplify the problem such that we are left with a problem on acyclic HMMs.

CTR Problem. We build (a mild variation of) a standard product construction [15] between HMM and the DFA. We define the *alarm states* T as those states which correspond to non-accepting states in the DFA. This is equivalent to taking a product with the complement of the monitor.

Example 4. Figure 4 shows the product of the HMM and monitor $\mathcal{B}$ from Fig. 3. Starting in the initial states d and 1, the HMM transitions to the i state with probability $9/10$. This is an *icy* state, and thus the monitor takes the *icy* transition to state 2. In the product, this is a transition from $\langle d, 1 \rangle$ to $\langle i, 2 \rangle$ with probability $9/10$. The alarm states are any product states of the form $\langle \_, 3 \rangle$.

Definition 9 (HMM product). *Given an HMM $\mathcal{M} = (S, \iota^{\mathcal{M}}, \mathbf{P}, Z, obs, r)$ and monitor $\mathcal{A} = (Q, \Sigma, \delta, \iota^{\mathcal{A}}, F)$, the product HMM $\langle \mathcal{M}_{\times \mathcal{A}}, T \rangle$ is the HMM $\mathcal{M}_{\times \mathcal{A}} := (S \times Q, \langle \iota^{\mathcal{M}}, \iota^{\mathcal{A}} \rangle, \mathbf{P}', Z, obs', r')$ with $obs'(\langle s, q \rangle) := obs(s)$, $r'(\langle s, q \rangle) := r(s)$, $\mathbf{P}'(\langle s, q \rangle, \langle s', \delta(q, obs(s')) \rangle) := \mathbf{P}(s, s')$ and $\mathbf{P}'(x, x') := 0$ otherwise, and finally the alarm states $T := S \times F$.*

In the product, we can find a trace τ whose conditional trace risk exceeds a threshold iff τ is a missed alarm. We state the decision problem that needs to be solved: It is key to our computational complexity analysis in Sect. 5.

Definition 10 (CTR Decision Problem). *Given HMM $\mathcal{M}$ with states S and risk r, horizon h, alarm states $T \subseteq S$, and threshold $\lambda_u \in \mathbb{R}_{\geq 0}$, decide if*

$$\exists \tau \in \mathcal{L}(\mathcal{M}). \sum_{\pi \in \Pi^{\mathcal{M}}_{=h} | \pi_{\downarrow} \in T} Pr^{\mathcal{M}}(\pi \mid \tau) \cdot r(\pi_{\downarrow}) > \lambda_u.$$

We denote the set of witnesses τ to a CTR decision problem as $\mathsf{CTR}(\mathcal{M}, h, T, \lambda_u)$. The following lemma states the correctness of the transformation. It follows directly from the definition of missing alarms and the product with the complement.

Lemma 1. *Using the notation from Theorem 1, Definition 9 and Definition 10:*

$$\exists \tau \in \mathsf{mA}^{=h}_{\mathcal{M}, \lambda_u}(\mathcal{A}) \quad \text{iff} \quad \exists \tau \in \mathsf{CTR}(\mathcal{M}_{\times \overline{\mathcal{A}}}, h, T, \lambda_u)$$

ACTR Problem. We further simplify the problem by unrolling the model along the horizon h and eliminating the risk function. For the first h steps, the unrolling is standard. At the horizon we transition to three dedicated states $\langle h+1, t_{\text{alrm}} \rangle$, $\langle h+1, t_{\text{safe}} \rangle$ and $\langle h+1, t_{\text{ignr}} \rangle$[4] according to the risk and alarm states T.

Example 5. Consider the HMM $\mathcal{M}$ depicted in Fig. 4, which was defined in Example 4. We unroll $\mathcal{M}$ with a horizon $h = 3$. This yields the HMM in Fig. 5. The states are tuples of the unrolled step and the CTR state from $\mathcal{M}$. The initial state becomes $\langle 1, \langle d, 1 \rangle \rangle$, which corresponds to a state at step 1 and $\langle d, 1 \rangle$ from the $\mathcal{M}$. This state transitions to $\langle 2, \langle i, 2 \rangle \rangle$ and $\langle 2, \langle c, 2 \rangle \rangle$. States with a step value equal to the horizon are treated differently. From states at the horizon, we transition to either of three states that help classify the trace. Consider $\langle 3, \langle i, 3 \rangle \rangle$, it is at the horizon $h = 3$, and it is in T. We want to classify such terminal states.

---

[4] We add the $\langle h+1, t_{\text{ignr}} \rangle$ state to easily modify the transformation for the no-false-alarms problem (See Sect. 3.4).

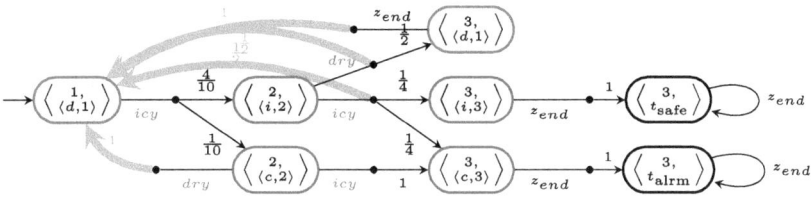

Fig. 6. The MDP from Example 6. Unreachable states are omitted, as are any actions which return to the initial state from every state at the same step.

As the (normalized) risk of $\langle 3, \langle i, 3 \rangle \rangle$ is 0, the state is safe and $\langle 3, \langle i, 3 \rangle \rangle$ transitions with probability 1 to $\langle 4, t_{\mathsf{safe}} \rangle$. Next, Consider $\langle 3, \langle d, 1 \rangle \rangle$, $\langle d, 1 \rangle$, it is not in T, but the state is at the horizon. This state can be ignored, and we transition to the ignore state, $\langle 4, t_{\mathsf{ignr}} \rangle$.

Definition 11 (Unrolling with risk). *The (risk-)unrolled HMM $\mathcal{M}_{\blacktriangleright h}$ of an HMM $\mathcal{M} = (S, \iota, \mathbf{P}, Z, obs, r)$ with alarm states T and horizon h is the HMM*

$$\mathcal{M}_{\blacktriangleright h} := (\{1, \ldots, h\} \times S \cup S_{\mathsf{end}}, \langle 1, \iota \rangle, \mathbf{P}', Z \cup \{z_{end}, z_{ignore}\}, obs', r'),$$

with $S_{\mathsf{end}} := \{\langle h+1, t_{\mathsf{alrm}} \rangle, \langle h+1, t_{\mathsf{safe}} \rangle, \langle h+1, t_{\mathsf{ignr}} \rangle\}$, $r'(\cdot) = 0$, obs' given by (1) $obs'(\langle i, s \rangle) := obs(s)$, (2) $obs'(\langle h+1, t_{\mathsf{ignr}} \rangle) := z_{ignore}$, and (3) $obs'(\langle h+1, t_{\mathsf{alrm}} \rangle) = obs'(\langle h+1, t_{\mathsf{safe}} \rangle) := z_{end}$, and $\mathbf{P}'$ given by:

$$\forall_{i \in \{1, \ldots, h-1\}} \quad \mathbf{P}'(\langle i, s \rangle, \langle i+1, s' \rangle) := \mathbf{P}(s, s'),$$

$$\mathbf{P}'(\langle h, s \rangle, \langle h+1, t \rangle) := \begin{cases} \frac{r(s)}{\max_{s \in S} r(s)} & \text{if } s \in F \text{ and } t = t_{\mathsf{alrm}}, \\ 1 - \frac{r(s)}{\max_{s \in S} r(s)} & \text{if } s \in F \text{ and } t = t_{\mathsf{safe}}, \\ 1 & \text{if } s \notin F \text{ and } t = t_{\mathsf{ignr}}, \\ 0 & \text{otherwise}, \end{cases}$$

$$\mathbf{P}'(\langle h+1, t \rangle, \langle h+1, t \rangle) := 1.$$

Lemma 2. *toactp Given an HMM $\mathcal{M}$, horizon h, alarm states T, and threshold λ_u, there exists a $\lambda \in (0, 1]$ such that, using z_{end} and t_{alrm} from Definition 11:*

$$\exists \tau \in \mathsf{CTR}(\mathcal{M}, h, t, \lambda_u) \quad \text{iff} \quad \exists \tau \in \mathcal{L}(\mathcal{M}_{\blacktriangleright h}). \sum_{\pi \in \Pi^{\mathcal{M}}} Pr^{\mathcal{M}}(\pi \cdot t_{\mathsf{alrm}} \mid \tau \cdot z_{end}) \geq \lambda.$$

3.3 Reduction to Consistent Policy Synthesis

For Lemma 2, we must find a trace such that a conditional reachability probability exceeds a threshold. We reformulate this into a policy synthesis problem (Sect. 3.1). The transformation combines two ideas: First, in every state, the policy can select the next observation, loosely inspired by [14]. Second, we reformulate conditional reachability probabilities into reachability probabilities, as in [16,34].

Example 6. We transform the HMM from Fig. 5 to the colored MDP in Fig. 6. Consider $\langle 2, \langle i, 2 \rangle \rangle$ in the HMM. The next observation is either dry or icy, which corresponds to the two actions from $\langle 2, \langle i, 2 \rangle \rangle$ in the colored MDP. The dry action transitions to the ensuing states with the dry observation. The remaining probability of $1/2$ for the dry action is directed to the initial state. This is similarly applied to the icy action. State $\langle 2, \langle c, 2 \rangle \rangle$ does not reach any dry states, we still add a dry action redirecting to the initial state, as *all* states with the same step value must have the same actions. State $\langle 3, \langle d, 1 \rangle \rangle$ in the HMM only has a transition to an z_{ignore} state. We fully remove the z_{ignore} state and the z_{ignore} observation in the MDP. Finally, we make sure all states with step 3 have the same actions, which explains the z_{end} action from state $\langle 3, \langle d, 1 \rangle \rangle$.

Definition 12. *Given the HMM from Definition 11*

$$\mathcal{M}_{\blacktriangleright h} := (S' := \{1, \ldots, h\} \times S \cup S_{\mathsf{end}}, \langle 1, \iota \rangle, \mathbf{P}, Z' := Z \cup \{z_{end}, z_{ignore}\}, obs, r),$$

we define the colored MDP $\mathcal{M}_{\gtrdot h} := ((S' \setminus \{\langle h+1, t_{ignr} \rangle\}, \iota, Act, \mathbf{P}'), C, c)$ *with* $Act := Z' \setminus \{z_{ignore}\}$, $C := \{1, \ldots, h\}$, *coloring* c *s.t.* $c(\langle i, s \rangle) := i$, *and*

$$\mathbf{P}'(\langle i, s \rangle, z, \langle j, q \rangle) := \begin{cases} \mathbf{P}(\langle i, s \rangle, \langle j, q \rangle) & \text{if } obs(\langle j, q \rangle) = z, \\ \sum_{(\langle k, q' \rangle) \in S \mid obs(\langle k, q' \rangle) \neq z} \mathbf{P}(\langle i, s \rangle, \langle k, q' \rangle) & \text{if } (\langle j, q \rangle) = \iota, \\ 0 & \text{otherwise} \end{cases}$$

Thus, we transition normally to a state if the action and observation of the target state are equal, otherwise we set the transition probability to zero. All the remaining probability mass is redirected towards the initial state[5].

The above construction allows for conditioning on a trace τ by constructing a policy σ that selects the ith observation of τ in the state with step i.

Definition 13 (Trace consistent policy). *Given a colored MDP* $\mathcal{M}_{\gtrdot h}$ *as in Definition 12 and a trace* $\tau \in (Z')^*$, *a trace consistent policy satisfies* $\sigma_\tau(\langle i, s \rangle) := \tau^{(i)}$, *where* $\tau^{(i)}$ *is the* ith *observation in* τ, *for* $i \leq |\tau|$ *and* $\sigma_\tau(\langle i, s \rangle) := z_{end}$ *otherwise.*

Using the coloring as described in Definition 12, the trace consistent policies coincide with color-consistent policies (Definition 8). Finding a missed-alarm trace now reduces to solving the color-consistent policy synthesis problem for targets $\{\langle h+1, t_{\mathsf{alrm}} \rangle\}$.

Lemma 3. *Given an HMM* $\mathcal{M}$, *horizon* h *alarm states* T, *and threshold* λ, *it holds that*

$$\exists \tau \in \mathcal{L}(\mathcal{M}_{\blacktriangleright h}). \sum_{\pi \in \Pi^{\mathcal{M}_{\blacktriangleright h}}} Pr^{\mathcal{M}_{\blacktriangleright h}}(\pi \cdot \langle h+1, t_{alrm} \rangle \mid \tau \cdot z_{end}) \geq \lambda$$
$$\Updownarrow$$
$$\exists \sigma \in \Sigma_c. Pr^{\mathcal{M}_{\gtrdot h}}_\sigma(\Diamond \{\langle h+1, t_{alrm} \rangle\}) \geq \lambda$$

Where σ *is trace consistent for* τ.

---
[5] In the implementation, we can prune actions where, from every state with the same color, the action redirects to the initial state.

Note that the colored part of the colored MDPs is absolutely necessary in order to map a policy of the colored MDP to a trace.

Example 7. Consider the MDP from Fig. 6 while ignoring the coloring. A function mapping $\langle 2, \langle i, 2 \rangle \rangle$ to icy and $\langle 2, \langle c, 2 \rangle \rangle$ to dry is a valid policy for the MDP. However, there does not exist a trace which describes the actions taken in the model, i.e., the trace starts with icy but then sometime contains icy and sometimes dry.

Restricting our policies to color-consistent policies makes sure in every step of the model we only ever take one action, corresponding with one observation in the trace at that step.

3.4 Adapting to No-False-Alarms and Smaller Traces

Traces of length at most the horizon. The approach for Theorem 1 only works for traces of length exactly equal to the horizon. We generalize this approach to traces of length at most the horizon.

Theorem 2. *Given an HMM $\mathcal{M}$, a monitor $\mathcal{A}$, unsafe threshold λ_u, horizon h, and risk r, there is a colored MDP $\mathcal{M}^C$ with target states T, and threshold λ s.t.*

$$\exists \sigma \in \Sigma_c. \ Pr_\sigma^{\mathcal{M}^C}(\Diamond T) \geq \lambda \quad \text{iff} \quad \exists \tau \in \mathsf{mA}_{\mathcal{M},\lambda_u}^{\leq h}(\mathcal{A}).$$

The main insight for this theorem is shown in Fig. 7. We combine the colored MDPs given by Theorem 1 for horizons 1 to h into one colored MDP, such that a policy starts by choosing which length trace to use (Fig. 7a). We can also instead directly construct a bisimulation quotient $\mathcal{M}_{\geqslant h}$ of this combined MDP with a small addition (Fig. 7b). We detail this construction in [35, App. A].

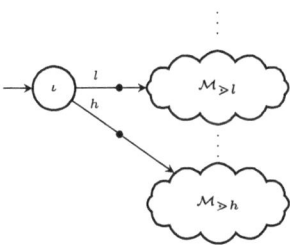
(a) A colored MDP combining the colored MDPs from Def. 12 for horizons up to h, $\{\mathcal{M}_{\geqslant l} \mid l \in \{1, \ldots, h\}\}$, into one MDP.

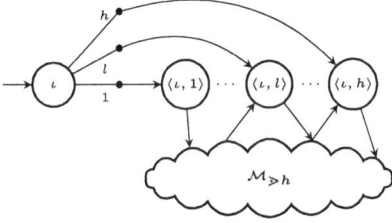
(b) A bisimilar colored MDP of Fig. 7a, containing only $\mathcal{M}_{\geqslant h}$. States $\langle \iota, 1 \rangle$ through $\langle \iota, h \rangle$ from $\mathcal{M}_{\geqslant h}$ are shown separate in order to show their relation to ι.

Fig. 7. Transformation steps needed for Theorem 2.

Finding False Alarms (Solving Problem 2). We modify the transformation from Theorem 2 such that it solves the no-false-alarms problem. This problem differs in two ways from the no-missed-alarms problem. We are finding a trace *accepted* by the monitor, and we find a trace whose risk is *below* the *safe* threshold.

Theorem 3. *Given an HMM $\mathcal{M}$, a monitor $\mathcal{A}$, safe threshold λ_s, horizon h, and risk r, there is a colored MDP $\mathcal{M}^C$ with target states T, and threshold λ s.t.*

$$\exists \sigma \in \Sigma_c.\ Pr_\sigma^{\mathcal{M}^C}(\lozenge T) \geq \lambda \quad \textit{iff} \quad \exists \tau \in \mathsf{fA}_{\mathcal{M},\lambda_s}^{\leq h}(\mathcal{A}).$$

We highlight the ideas here, for details see [35, App. A]. In order to find a trace accepted by the monitor, we no longer take the complement of the monitor while transforming to CTR. To find a safe trace we compute reachability on $\langle h+1, t_{\text{safe}} \rangle$ instead of $\langle h+1, t_{\text{alrm}} \rangle$ while taking as a threshold $1 - \lambda$. Thus, we find a trace whose probability of being safe is above a threshold[6].

4 Learning Correct Monitors

We present *learning* correct monitors (Problem 3), by combining automata learning using a *Minimally Adequate Teacher* (MAT, [11]) and monitor verification.

MAT Framework. We briefly recap the MAT framework, for details see [47]. A minimally adequate teacher answers two types of questions: A *membership query* (MQ), which in our setup means *should a trace be accepted by the monitor?*, and an *equivalence query* (EQ), *is this monitor correct?* Furthermore, if the answer to an equivalence query is negative, we must provide a counterexample that witnesses why the monitor is not correct. Various algorithms implementing the MAT framework for DFA learning exist. For the purpose of this paper, we use the L* algorithm [11] to learn a monitor. The learner asks MQs to the teacher until a *hypothesis monitor* can be constructed which is consistent with the MQs. Once such a hypothesis is constructed, its correctness is verified using an EQ.

Verification as a MAT. To learn a monitor $\mathcal{A}$, we provide the HMM $\mathcal{M}$, a risk function r, a horizon h, a learning threshold λ_l, and the safe and unsafe thresholds λ_s and λ_u. The additional learning threshold λ_l is used to define an MQ whenever $\lambda_s \neq \lambda_u$: In particular, for MQs, each trace must be unambiguously safe or unsafe: the MAT framework does not allow for flagging certain traces as *don't care*, while traces with a risk between λ_s and λ_u can be considered don't care in our setting. Likewise, the MQ must also be defined for traces $\tau \notin \mathcal{L}(\mathcal{M})$ or traces longer than the horizon. We thus adapt the notion of safe traces from Definition 4.

Definition 14. *Given any trace $\tau \in Z^\star$ and a horizon h, membership query MQ_{λ_l} is a function such that $\text{MQ}_{\lambda_l}(\tau)$ is unsafe iff $\tau \in \mathcal{L}(\mathcal{M})$[7] and $\tau \in \mathbb{U}_{\lambda_l}^{\leq h}$.*

---

[6] We cannot directly aim to compute a trace whose risk is below a threshold since minimizing reachability of $\langle h+1, t_{\text{alrm}} \rangle$ will result in a scheduler that always resets to the initial state if possible. Consider the colored MDP in Fig. 6, the color-consistent policy with the lowest probability of reaching the alarm state is as follows: take the dry action in step 2, and z_{end} in step 3. This policy has probability zero of reaching either $\langle h+1, t_{\text{alrm}} \rangle$ or $\langle h+1, t_{\text{safe}} \rangle$, and thus does not map to a valid trace.

[7] Defining traces $\tau \notin \mathcal{L}(\mathcal{M})$ as safe is an arbitrary design decision.

Such a function for MQ_{λ_l} can be defined by keeping track of the probability of being in each state after every observation from the trace *or* by model checking the induced Markov chain that reflects the trace-consistent policy in Sect. 3 [34, 39]. For EQs, we simply use the notion of correctness from Definition 6.

Definition 15. *Given an HMM $\mathcal{M}$, and a monitor $\mathcal{A}$, an $\text{EQ}_{\lambda_s,\lambda_u}$ is a function $\text{EQ}_{\lambda_s,\lambda_u}(\mathcal{A}) \in \{\top\} \cup Z^\star$, such that, $\text{EQ}^{\mathcal{M}}_{\lambda_s,\lambda_u}(\mathcal{A})$ holds if $\mathcal{A}$ is correct for $\mathcal{M}$ with λ_s and λ_u (in the sense of Definition 6), and $\text{EQ}^{\mathcal{M}}_{\lambda_s,\lambda_u}(\mathcal{A})$ returns a missed alarm or false alarm trace for an incorrect $\mathcal{A}$.*

The EQ requires checking both for no-missing-alarms, and for no-false-alarms. We perform these checks using our novel verification algorithm described in Sect. 3.

Lemma 4. *Given a MAT with a $\text{EQ}_{\lambda_s,\lambda_u}$ and a MQ_{λ_l}, a monitor learned with $L^\star$ is correct as long as $\lambda_s \leq \lambda_l \leq \lambda_u$.*

When $\lambda_s < \lambda_u$, the EQ has an inconclusive area given by the interval (λ_s, λ_u). This means that our EQ does not check for equivalence, but simply accepts any correct monitor [37]. We investigate the effect of this inconclusive area in Sect. 6.

Conformance Queries. An alternative to the EQ in Definition 15 is a conformance query [26]. It tests a monitor by sampling traces from the HMM and checking if the MQ and the monitor agree. If the monitor and the MQ don't agree on a trace, it is given as a counterexample. In our approach we use a hybrid of conformance and verification EQs. Monitors produced early in the learning process often contain many missed alarms and false alarms. Verification can find them, however, applying the transformation from Sect. 3 has a constant cost. Conformance queries can often find a counterexample faster if they have a high probability of occurring. We thus first try to find easy counterexamples using conformance, when this does not produce any we perform our verification routine.

5 Computational Complexity

This section discusses the hardness of monitor verification (Theorem 4) and the inapproximability of a related optimization problem (Lemma 6).

Theorem 4. *Is a monitor correct? (w. unary coded horizon) is coNP-complete.*

In fact, we study the dual to this problem, i.e., checking the existence of a counterexample. We call this problem *monitor co-verification*. For monitor co-verification, *membership* in NP follows from false alarms or missed alarms (of length up to horizon) being the witnesses. Verifying whether a trace is a false or missed alarm can be done in polynomial time, by checking whether the automaton accepts it and computing the trace risk (see Sect. 4).

To establish NP-hardness, we consider the CTR problem from Definition 10. As a solution to the monitor co-verification problem solves the CTR problem (using a trivial monitor), this implies NP-hardness of the former problem.

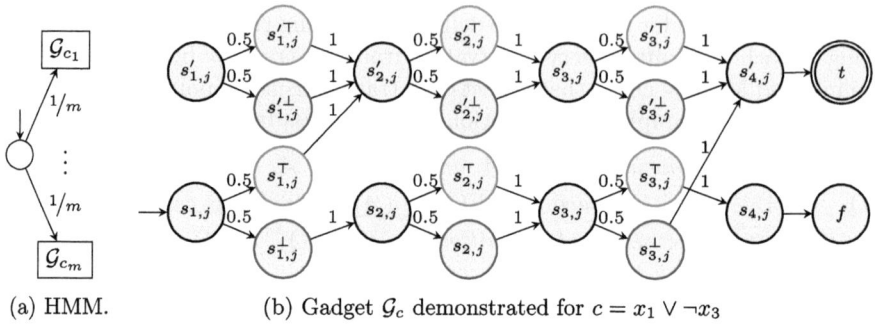

Fig. 8. Illustrations for Lemma 5, with m clauses and variables x_1, x_2, x_3.

Lemma 5. *The CTR Decision Problem is (strongly) NP-hard.*

The proof features a reduction from CNF-SAT, the problem of satisfiability of a propositional formula. We illustrate the reduction, details are in [35, App. B].

We construct HMM $\mathcal{M}_\varphi$ from CNF φ over variables X such that there is a trace with risk 1 iff there is a satisfying assignment to φ. In particular, that trace exists iff there is a trace τ s.t. all corresponding paths π with $obs(\pi) = \tau$ reach state t. The traces are of the form $\#\# \cdot \{\bot, \top\} \cdot \# \cdot \{\bot, \top\} \cdots \#$: Trace $\#\# \cdot \alpha(x_0) \cdot \# \cdot \alpha(x_1) \cdots \#$ represents an assignment $\alpha \colon X \to \{\bot, \top\}$. We construct $\mathcal{M}_\varphi$ such that any trace that ensures reaching t with probability one encodes a satisfying assignment for φ. We create gadgets for every clause. The gadgets are connected as in Fig. 8a: That is, to ensure reaching t along every path, we must reach t in every gadget. The gadget $\mathcal{G}_j$ intuitively 'evaluates' c_j with respect to an assignment, as exemplified in Fig. 8b. A path (or its trace) through $\mathcal{G}_j$ 'reads' variable x_i in state $s_{i,j}$ and transitions to $s_{i,j}^\top$ or to $s_{i,j}^\bot$. The states are labelled $\#, \top, \bot$, respectively. However, for a trace where $\alpha(x_i) = \top$, only the former path corresponds to the trace (and symmetrically for $\alpha(x_i) = \bot$). That path reaches state t iff the assignment satisfies at least one literal in the clause.

We now show that the construction above suffices to show that it is hard to approximate the maximal risk that a monitor admits.

Definition 16 (CTR Optimization Problem). *Given an HMM $\mathcal{M}$ with states in S, a unary encoded horizon h, a set of alarm states $T \subseteq S$:*

$$\max_{\tau \in \mathcal{L}(\mathcal{M})} \sum_{\pi \in \Pi_{=h}^{\mathcal{M}} | \pi_\downarrow \in T} Pr^{\mathcal{M}}(\pi \mid \tau) \cdot r(\pi_\downarrow).$$

Lemma 6. *The CTR Optimization Problem is APX-hard.*

This follows from a strict reduction from MAX-3SAT, which is an inapproximable and APX-hard problem [28]. The construction coincides with the reduction in Lemma 5 by observing that the conditional probability to reach a t state is given by $1/m$ times the number of satisfied clauses, i.e., we can compute the maximal number of satisfied clauses in φ using the HMM $\mathcal{M}_\varphi$.

6 Experiments

We empirically evaluate the monitor verification (Sect. 3) and monitor learning (Sect. 4) algorithms using our prototype implementation called ToVer. Code, benchmarks, and logs will be publicly available via the artifact evaluation.

Setup. The ToVer tool is implemented in Python and C++ on top of the model checker STORM [30] for data structures and for the MQs in Sect. 4 [34]. We use PAYNT [9] to verify colored MDPs (Definition 7), using exact arithmetic to avoid numerical problems on these types of benchmarks [27]. The learner uses the AAlpy framework [36]. All experiments are run on a single thread of an AMD Ryzen TRP 5965WX, with a memory limit of 15 GiB, and a time-out of 12 h.

Benchmarks. We take the benchmarks AIRPORT, REFUEL, EVADE, and HIDDEN-INCENTIVE from [34], adapted to HMMs. We add ICY-DRIVING, a scaled-up version of the running example and SNL based on the game "Snakes and Ladders". While the benchmarks from the literature contain many observations, i.e., few states share an observation, the new benchmarks only have a few different observations. All benchmarks are scalable. The risk function is defined by a temporal property, e.g., the probability of reaching a bad state within a few steps.

Efficiency of Monitor Verification. We first investigate scalability along different dimensions and identify the bottlenecks of our verification method.

Setup. We verify the HMMs with respect to three monitors obtained during the learning experiments (below, with $\lambda_s = \lambda_u = 0.3$). Every version of the benchmark is run on the first (incorrect) monitor that passed a limited conformance check, an (incorrect) monitor obtained halfway through the learning process, and the final correct monitor. We verify correctness w.r.t. the same λ_s, λ_u.

Results. We present our results in Table 1, which is a subset of the 516 benchmarks shown in [35, App. C.2]. Generally, we observe that we verify the correctness of monitors on at least billions of traces, which shows that enumerating the traces is not a feasible alternative. Our verification handles monitors and HMMs with both hundreds of states and up to hundred thousands of transitions, see benchmarks E-40, E-42, H-10. Benchmarks A-180, A-182 reflect verification w.r.t. almost trivial monitors, for which it is typically easy to find a counterexample, A-184, A-186, S-76, S-78 reflect a semi-correct monitor, and A-188, A-190, S-80, S-82 reflect verification of the same HMM with respect to a larger correct monitor. Increasing the horizon significantly increases the runtime, even for small models, e.g., I-34 compared to I-10 and I-22. In all benchmarks, the runtime consists almost exclusively of creating the input to PAYNT (taking the product and creating the MDP) and in running PAYNT. The former runs in polynomial time in the size of the input (see [35, App. C.1]), whereas the latter uses various heuristics to avoid the exponential computation time. In the current implementation, except for the (comparably) large EVADE benchmarks, the vast majority of time is spent on PAYNT. The transformation is never the bottleneck (see [35, App. C.2]).

Table 1. Subset of verification results found in [35, App. C.2]. The columns give the family name, an ID, horizon, and whether we check for missed alarms or false alarms. We give the size of the HMM (states, transitions), the number of observations, the size of the DFA (states, transitions), and the size of the language after pruning unreachable states. Furthermore, we list the run time for the complete verification procedure as well as the time spent on transforming the problem into a policy synthesis problem and the policy synthesis in PAYNT. Lastly, we list the size of the colored MDP produced by the transformation and the risk of the found counterexample. If no trace was found with a risk above (or below, for FA) the indicated threshold, the monitor is correct (✓).

				Benchmark					ToVer				
		h	MA/FA	$|S^{\mathcal{M}}|$	$|\mathbf{P}^{\mathcal{M}}|$	$|Z|$	$|S^{\mathcal{A}}|$	$|\mathbf{P}^{\mathcal{A}}|$	$|\mathcal{L}^{\leq h}|$	Time (s)	Trans (s)	PAYNT (s)	$|\mathcal{M}_{\geq h}|$	λ^{found}
AirportB-7	A-180	9	MA	470	2550	50	66	3300	10^{12}	5	1	4	2275	0.69
AirportB-7	A-182	9	FA	470	2550	50	66	3300	10^{12}	3	$\leq 1s$	3	2275	0.10
AirportB-7	A-184	9	MA	470	2550	50	319	15950	10^{12}	23	1	22	3503	0.41
AirportB-7	A-186	9	FA	470	2550	50	319	15950	10^{12}	17	1	15	3503	0.24
AirportB-7	A-188	9	MA	470	2550	50	569	28450	10^{12}	367	2	365	5111	✓
AirportB-7	A-190	9	FA	470	2550	50	569	28450	10^{12}	340	3	338	5111	✓
Evade	E-40	9	MA	385	1473	325	197	64025	10^{14}	34	26	4	680	1.00
Evade	E-42	9	FA	385	1473	325	197	64025	10^{14}	25	23	2	680	✓
Hidden-Incen.	H-2	10	FA	397	1649	100	106	10600	10^{18}	10	3	6	1261	0.30
Hidden-Incen.	H-10	10	FA	397	1649	100	298	29800	10^{18}	2972	4	2968	1411	✓
Icy-Driving	I-34	3	FA	3	6	2	8	16	10^{0}	$\leq 1s$	$\leq 1s$	$\leq 1s$	8	✓
Icy-Driving	I-10	10	FA	3	6	2	2	4	10^{4}	$\leq 1s$	$\leq 1s$	$\leq 1s$	29	✓
Icy-Driving	I-22	25	FA	3	6	2	2	4	10^{11}	1126	$\leq 1s$	1126	74	✓
RefuelB	R-20	10	MA	263	7127	72	31	2232	10^{22}	3	1	2	1812	✓
RefuelB	R-22	10	FA	263	7127	72	31	2232	10^{21}	5	2	3	1812	✓
SnL	S-76	16	MA	101	502	4	427	1708	10^{11}	393	$\leq 1s$	392	13547	0.54
SnL	S-78	16	FA	101	502	4	427	1708	10^{10}	1418	$\leq 1s$	1417	13547	0.00
SnL	S-80	16	MA	101	502	4	588	2352	10^{11}	4601	2	4600	14381	✓
SnL	S-82	16	FA	101	502	4	588	2352	10^{10}	2414	1	2413	14381	✓

Efficiency of Monitor Learning. A key contribution of this paper is the ability to use verification for the EQs in monitor learning. We consider the necessity of these EQs, the size of the learned monitors, and the efficiency of learning them, both for $\lambda_s = \lambda_u$ and $\lambda_s \neq \lambda_u$.

Setup. We use the MAT framework from Sect. 4. Before every EQ, we run conformance checking (max. 100 samples using as threshold λ_s and 100 samples with λ_u, see Sect. 4). As hyper-parameters, we investigate (1) $\lambda_s = 0.1, \lambda_l = 0.3, \lambda_u = 0.35$, with inconclusive trace, and (2) $\lambda_s = \lambda_l = \lambda_u = 0.3$, without inconclusive traces[8]. We compare against a baseline that does not use EQs, i.e., the baseline uses the MAT framework with only conformance checking (max. 100000 samples, different numbers of samples are tested in [35, App. D]).

Are the Monitors Correct? Using verification in the EQ, we always learn correct monitors. We validate this experimentally *and* show that the baseline does not

---

[8] We study correctness of monitors learned by the baseline w.r.t. different λ_l in [35, App. D].

always yield correct monitors. For every monitor we determine the unsafe trace with the lowest risk (*actual alarm threshold*, $\lambda_u^{\min}$) and the safe trace with the highest risk (*actual no-alarm threshold*, $\lambda_s^{\max}$). In a correct monitor, we have $\lambda_u^{\min} \geq \lambda_u$ and $\lambda_s^{\max} \leq \lambda_s$. Figures 9a to 9c show $\lambda_u^{\min}$ and $\lambda_s^{\max}$ for ToVer and for the baseline. Visually, a monitor is correct if its red bar never touches the green area and the green bar never touches the red area. In 14 out of 87 benchmarks the baseline learns a monitor that misses alarms. One baseline learned monitor has false alarms.

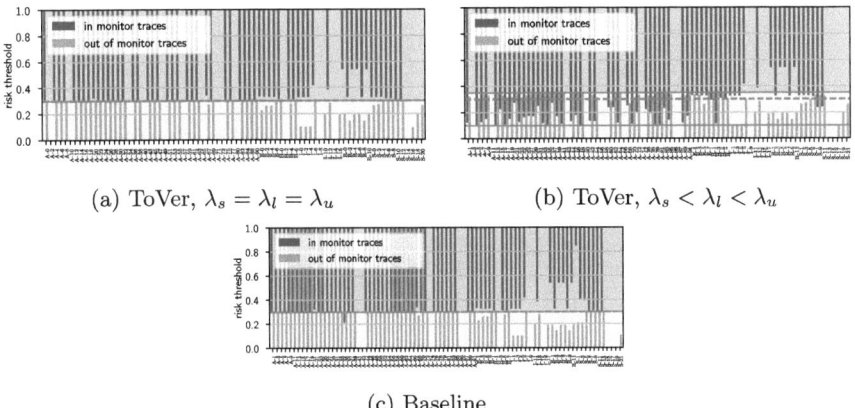

Fig. 9. Actual alarm and actual no-alarm thresholds from monitors learned with ToVer and baseline. The line between the green/gray is λ_u, the line between red/gray area is λ_s. The dotted line is λ_l. Missing bars reflect either time-outs or out-of-memory. (Color figure online)

How Big are the Monitors? ToVer learns monitors with hundreds of states and tens of thousands transitions, see Figs. 10a and 10b (log-scale!) and [35, App. E.2]. For the literature on AAL, these are large automata [2,44,49]. Comparing the sizes of the monitors learned using ToVer and the baseline, monitors are smaller (up to 8 times, mostly at least 1.5 times smaller)[9].

How Fast do we Learn the Monitors? We compare the runtime of ToVer and baseline in the Figs. 10c and 10d (log-scale!). We remark that only ToVer is guaranteed to be correct. Neither of the two learning algorithms is clearly faster than the other, but ToVer has the potential to significantly accelerate the learning process, despite the high complexity. One reason could be that ToVer needs half or fewer EQs to learn a monitor as can be seen in [35, App. E.2]. In Fig. 11, we detail where the time is spent. For most benchmarks, the EQ (in particular, PAYNT) is the bottleneck. However, for several EVADE benchmarks, most time

---

[9] For $\lambda_s = \lambda_u$, the language of correct monitors learned with ToVer and baseline are equivalent up to the horizon, but the monitors respond differently on longer traces.

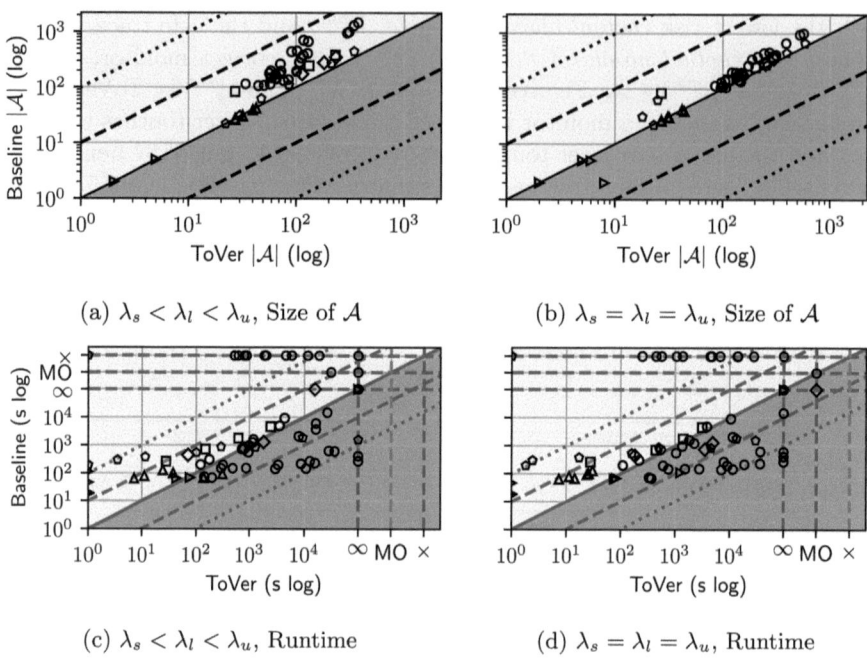

Fig. 10. States in learned monitors and runtimes: ToVer vs. baseline. The runtime includes labels for time-outs (∞), out-of-memory (MO), and incorrect ($\times$).

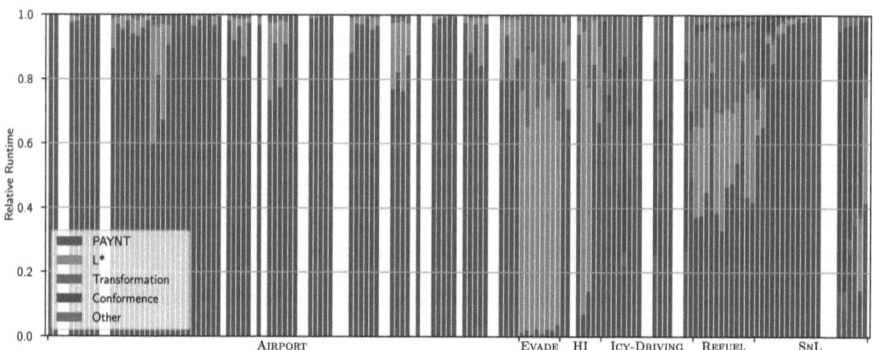

Fig. 11. Division of runtime for ToVer learning for different models. *PAYNT* is the time spent by PAYNT verifying colored MDPs. $L^\star$ is the time spent by the $L^\star$ algorithm creating a hypothesis including doing MQs. *Transformation* is the time spent transforming HMMs and monitors into colored MDPs for PAYNT. *Conformance* is the time spent on conformance testing during the EQs. Lastly, *Other* denotes any time not spent in the aforementioned processes. Empty bars denote HMMs for which learning did not finish.

is spent within L* code. We conjecture this happens as finding counterexamples is simple in these models.

The Role of an Inconclusive Area. We compare between $\lambda_s < \lambda_l < \lambda_u$ and $\lambda_s = \lambda_l = \lambda_u$, i.e., with and without an inconclusive area. The baseline does not actively support such an inconclusive area. With an inconclusive area, more monitors are correct (i.e., strictly speaking, we do not test equivalence but acceptance). The learner indeed finds monitors that are two to five times smaller (also compare Figs. 10a and 10b). For benchmarks ICY-DRIVING, EVADE, and AIRPORT, this also translates to faster runtimes than using conformance checking, sometimes by orders of magnitudes.

7 Related Work

This work studies *monitoring based on stochastic systems* and combines *active learning* with *probabilistic verification*. We consider related work in those directions.

Model-Based Monitoring for Stochastic Systems. Runtime verification is a wide field, see [24,29,41] for surveys. We review work on *model-based* runtime monitoring for stochastic systems. In particular, using state estimation on HMMs to decide whether to raise an alarm given a particular trace has been investigated in [42,45,48], extended to hybrid models [43], models with nondeterminism [34] and randomly timed models [14]. We use these techniques to answer membership queries. The HMMs for runtime monitoring can be learned from a set of traces, see, e.g., [12,13] and more recently [23], where they find the state risks at design time using model checking and use state estimation for runtime verification. Related to runtime monitoring is runtime enforcement, in particular shielding [19,25,31,40]. Shielding is successful in fully observable models but less studied in partial observable settings, in [21], shields are computed for qualitative properties. Finally, in [1], a more general notion of correct monitors via linear time μ-calculus is investigated, while in [17] a notion of correct *predictors* is introduced. Both can be seen as generalizations of our definitions.

Learning Monitors. Learning monitors has been advocated in, e.g., [20,38,46,50]. Closest to our setting is recent work in [33], which also uses state estimation for membership queries, but combines this with conformance queries and learns decision trees rather than automata. Crucially, by using conformance queries, the guarantees are significantly weaker, see also our experiments.

Probabilistic Verification. The verification of our monitors applies model checking of conditional probabilities [5,16] to runtime verification, similar to [14,34]. Most related is recent work in [14], where the models are CTMCs and the observation trace is uncertain itself. They also encounter a notion of trace-consistent policies, but instead of using synthesis, they overapproximate the verification by considering all policies. In contrast, our method is *complete*. Verification with partial observability as in our HMMs also occurs in the verification of partially observable MDPs [6], which can also be tackled using synthesis approaches [7]. Finally, considering MDPs as *distribution transformers* yields related but semantically different computationally hard problems that have been solved using (different) inductive synthesis approaches [3,4].

8 Conclusion and Future Work

This paper presented a first approach to verification of monitors with respect to hidden Markov models. It embeds this verification procedure in an automata learning framework. The empirical evaluation is encouraging but also shows the limitations of the off-the-shelf frameworks. We see three avenues for future work: (1) Dedicated synthesis methods for conditional probabilities and the specific structure of our colored MDPs. (2) Automata learning for acyclic models and don't-care results. (3) Faster verification for longer (or even unbounded) traces.

References

1. Aceto, L., et al.: On probabilistic monitorability. In: Principles of Systems Design. Lecture Notes in Computer Science, vol. 13660, pp. 325–342. Springer (2022)
2. Aichernig, B.K., Tappler, M., Wallner, F.: Benchmarking combinations of learning and testing algorithms for automata learning. Formal Aspects Comput. **36**(1), 3:1–3:37 (2024)
3. Akshay, S., Chatterjee, K., Meggendorfer, T., Zikelic, D.: MDPs as distribution transformers: affine invariant synthesis for safety objectives. In: CAV (3). Lecture Notes in Computer Science, vol. 13966, pp. 86–112. Springer (2023)
4. Akshay, S., Chatterjee, K., Meggendorfer, T., Zikelic, D.: Certified policy verification and synthesis for MDPs under distributional reach-avoidance properties. In: IJCAI, pp. 3–12. ijcai.org (2024)
5. Andrés, M.E., Rossum, P.: Conditional probabilities over probabilistic and nondeterministic systems. In: Ramakrishnan, C.R., Rehof, J. (eds.) TACAS 2008. LNCS, vol. 4963, pp. 157–172. Springer, Heidelberg (2008). https://doi.org/10.1007/978-3-540-78800-3_12
6. Andriushchenko, R., et al.: Tools at the frontiers of quantitative verification. CoRR abs/2405.13583 (2024)
7. Andriushchenko, R., Bork, A., Ceska, M., Junges, S., Katoen, J., Macák, F.: Search and explore: symbiotic policy synthesis in pomdps. In: CAV (3). Lecture Notes in Computer Science, vol. 13966, pp. 113–135. Springer (2023)
8. Andriushchenko, R., Ceska, M., Junges, S., Katoen, J.: Inductive synthesis of finite-state controllers for pomdps. In: UAI. Proceedings of Machine Learning Research, vol. 180, pp. 85–95. PMLR (2022)
9. Andriushchenko, R., Češka, M., Junges, S., Katoen, J.-P., Stupinský, Š: PAYNT: a tool for inductive synthesis of probabilistic programs. In: Silva, A., Leino, K.R.M. (eds.) CAV 2021. LNCS, vol. 12759, pp. 856–869. Springer, Cham (2021). https://doi.org/10.1007/978-3-030-81685-8_40
10. Andriushchenko, R., Ceska, M., Macák, F., Junges, S., Katoen, J.: An oracle-guided approach to constrained policy synthesis under uncertainty. J. Artif. Intell. Res. **82**, 433–469 (2025)
11. Angluin, D.: Learning regular sets from queries and counterexamples. Inf. Comput. **75**(2), 87–106 (1987)

12. Babaee, R., Ganesh, V., Sedwards, S.: Accelerated learning of predictive runtime monitors for rare failure. In: Finkbeiner, B., Mariani, L. (eds.) RV 2019. LNCS, vol. 11757, pp. 111–128. Springer, Cham (2019). https://doi.org/10.1007/978-3-030-32079-9_7
13. Babaee, R., Gurfinkel, A., Fischmeister, S.: Prevent: a predictive run-time verification framework using statistical learning. In: SEFM. Lecture Notes in Computer Science, vol. 10886, pp. 205–220. Springer (2018)
14. Badings, T.S., Volk, M., Junges, S., Stoelinga, M., Jansen, N.: Ctmcs with imprecisely timed observations. In: TACAS (2). Lecture Notes in Computer Science, vol. 14571, pp. 258–278. Springer (2024)
15. Baier, C., Katoen, J.: Principles of Model Checking. MIT Press (2008)
16. Baier, C., Klein, J., Klüppelholz, S., Märcker, S.: Computing conditional probabilities in Markovian models efficiently. In: Ábrahám, E., Havelund, K. (eds.) TACAS 2014. LNCS, vol. 8413, pp. 515–530. Springer, Heidelberg (2014). https://doi.org/10.1007/978-3-642-54862-8_43
17. Baier, C., Klüppelholz, S., Piribauer, J., Ziemek, R.: Formal quality measures for predictors in Markov decision processes. CoRR abs/2412.11754 (2024)
18. Bartocci, E., Falcone, Y. (eds.): Lectures on Runtime Verification - Introductory and Advanced Topics, Lecture Notes in Computer Science, vol. 10457. Springer (2018)
19. Bloem, R., Könighofer, B., Könighofer, R., Wang, C.: Shield synthesis: runtime enforcement for reactive systems. In: Baier, C., Tinelli, C. (eds.) TACAS 2015. LNCS, vol. 9035, pp. 533–548. Springer, Heidelberg (2015). https://doi.org/10.1007/978-3-662-46681-0_51
20. Cairoli, F., Bortolussi, L., Paoletti, N.: Neural predictive monitoring under partial observability. In: Feng, L., Fisman, D. (eds.) RV 2021. LNCS, vol. 12974, pp. 121–141. Springer, Cham (2021). https://doi.org/10.1007/978-3-030-88494-9_7
21. Carr, S., Jansen, N., Junges, S., Topcu, U.: Safe reinforcement learning via shielding under partial observability. In: AAAI, pp. 14748–14756. AAAI Press (2023)
22. Chatterjee, K., Chmelik, M., Davies, J.: A symbolic sat-based algorithm for almost-sure reachability with small strategies in pomdps. In: AAAI, pp. 3225–3232. AAAI Press (2016)
23. Cleaveland, M., Sokolsky, O., Lee, I., Ruchkin, I.: Conservative safety monitors of stochastic dynamical systems. In: NFM. Lecture Notes in Computer Science, vol. 13903, pp. 140–156. Springer (2023)
24. Falcone, Y., Fernandez, J., Mounier, L.: What can you verify and enforce at runtime? Int. J. Softw. Tools Technol. Transfer **14**(3), 349–382 (2012)
25. Fulton, N., Platzer, A.: Safe reinforcement learning via formal methods: toward safe control through proof and learning. In: AAAI. AAAI Press (2018)
26. Groce, A., Peled, D.A., Yannakakis, M.: Adaptive model checking. Log. J. IGPL **14**(5), 729–744 (2006)
27. Hartmanns, A., Junges, S., Quatmann, T., Weininger, M.: A practitioner's guide to MDP model checking algorithms. In: TACAS (1). Lecture Notes in Computer Science, vol. 13993, pp. 469–488. Springer (2023)
28. Håstad, J.: Some optimal inapproximability results. J. ACM **48**(4), 798–859 (2001)
29. Havelund, K., Reger, G., Roşu, G.: Runtime verification past experiences and future projections. In: Steffen, B., Woeginger, G. (eds.) Computing and Software Science. LNCS, vol. 10000, pp. 532–562. Springer, Cham (2019). https://doi.org/10.1007/978-3-319-91908-9_25
30. Hensel, C., Junges, S., Katoen, J., Quatmann, T., Volk, M.: The probabilistic model checker storm. Int. J. Softw. Tools Technol. Transf. **24**(4), 589–610 (2022)

31. Jansen, N., Könighofer, B., Junges, S., Serban, A., Bloem, R.: Safe reinforcement learning using probabilistic shields (invited paper). In: International Conference on Concurrency Theory (CONCUR). LIPIcs, vol. 171, pp. 3:1–3:16. Schloss Dagstuhl - Leibniz-Zentrum für Informatik (2020)
32. Jha, S., Seshia, S.A.: A theory of formal synthesis via inductive learning. Acta Informatica **54**(7), 693–726 (2017). https://doi.org/10.1007/s00236-017-0294-5
33. Junges, S., Seshia, S.A., Torfah, H.: Active learning of runtime monitors under uncertainty. In: IFM. Lecture Notes in Computer Science, vol. 15234, pp. 297–306. Springer (2024)
34. Junges, S., Torfah, H., Seshia, S.A.: Runtime monitors for Markov decision processes. In: Silva, A., Leino, K.R.M. (eds.) CAV 2021. LNCS, vol. 12760, pp. 553–576. Springer, Cham (2021). https://doi.org/10.1007/978-3-030-81688-9_26
35. van der Maas, L., Junges, S.: Learning verified monitors for hidden Markov models (2025). https://arxiv.org/abs/2504.05963. Technical report of this paper
36. Muskardin, E., Aichernig, B.K., Pill, I., Pferscher, A., Tappler, M.: Aalpy: an active automata learning library. Innov. Syst. Softw. Eng. **18**(3), 417–426 (2022)
37. Peled, D.A., Vardi, M.Y., Yannakakis, M.: Black box checking. J. Autom. Lang. Comb. **7**(2), 225–246 (2002)
38. Phan, D.T., Grosu, R., Jansen, N., Paoletti, N., Smolka, S.A., Stoller, S.D.: Neural simplex architecture. In: Lee, R., Jha, S., Mavridou, A., Giannakopoulou, D. (eds.) NFM 2020. LNCS, vol. 12229, pp. 97–114. Springer, Cham (2020). https://doi.org/10.1007/978-3-030-55754-6_6
39. Rabiner, L.R.: A tutorial on hidden Markov models and selected applications in speech recognition. Proc. IEEE **77**(2), 257–286 (1989)
40. Ramadge, P.J., Wonham, W.M.: Supervisory control of a class of discrete event processes. SIAM J. Control. Optim. **25**(1), 206–230 (1987). https://doi.org/10.1137/0325013
41. Sánchez, C., et al.: A survey of challenges for runtime verification from advanced application domains (beyond software). Formal Methods Syst. Des. **54**(3), 279–335 (2019)
42. Sistla, A.P., Srinivas, A.R.: Monitoring temporal properties of stochastic systems. In: Logozzo, F., Peled, D.A., Zuck, L.D. (eds.) VMCAI 2008. LNCS, vol. 4905, pp. 294–308. Springer, Heidelberg (2008). https://doi.org/10.1007/978-3-540-78163-9_25
43. Sistla, A.P., Žefran, M., Feng, Y.: Runtime monitoring of stochastic cyber-physical systems with hybrid state. In: Khurshid, S., Sen, K. (eds.) RV 2011. LNCS, vol. 7186, pp. 276–293. Springer, Heidelberg (2012). https://doi.org/10.1007/978-3-642-29860-8_21
44. Smeenk, W., Moerman, J., Vaandrager, F., Jansen, D.N.: Applying automata learning to embedded control software. In: Butler, M., Conchon, S., Zaïdi, F. (eds.) ICFEM 2015. LNCS, vol. 9407, pp. 67–83. Springer, Cham (2015). https://doi.org/10.1007/978-3-319-25423-4_5
45. Stoller, S.D., et al.: Runtime verification with state estimation. In: Khurshid, S., Sen, K. (eds.) RV 2011. LNCS, vol. 7186, pp. 193–207. Springer, Heidelberg (2012). https://doi.org/10.1007/978-3-642-29860-8_15
46. Torfah, H., Xie, C., Junges, S., Vazquez-Chanlatte, M., Seshia, S.A.: Learning monitorable operational design domains for assured autonomy. In: ATVA. Lecture Notes in Computer Science, vol. 13505, pp. 3–22. Springer (2022)
47. Vaandrager, F.W.: Model learning. Commun. ACM **60**(2), 86–95 (2017)

48. Wilcox, C.M., Williams, B.C.: Runtime verification of stochastic, faulty systems. In: Barringer, H., et al. (eds.) RV 2010. LNCS, vol. 6418, pp. 452–459. Springer, Heidelberg (2010). https://doi.org/10.1007/978-3-642-16612-9_34
49. Yang, N., et al.: Improving model inference in industry by combining active and passive learning. In: SANER, pp. 253–263. IEEE (2019)
50. Zolfagharian, A., Abdellatif, M., Briand, L.C., S., R.: SMARLA: a safety monitoring approach for deep reinforcement learning agents. CoRR abs/2308.02594 (2023)

Probabilistic Verification and Quantum Computing

Generalized Parameter Lifting: Finer Abstractions for Parametric Markov Chains

Linus Heck[1](✉), Tim Quatmann[2], Jip Spel[2], Joost-Pieter Katoen[2], and Sebastian Junges[1]

[1] Radboud University, Nijmegen, The Netherlands
{linus.heck,sebastian.junges}@ru.nl
[2] RWTH Aachen University, Aachen, Germany
{tim.quatmann,jip.spel,katoen}@cs.rwth-aachen.de

Abstract. Parametric Markov chains (pMCs) are Markov chains (MCs) with symbolic probabilities. A pMC encodes a family of MCs, where each member is obtained by replacing parameters with constants. The parameters allow encoding dependencies between transitions, which sets pMCs apart from interval MCs. The verification problem for pMCs asks whether each MC in the corresponding family satisfies a given temporal specification. The state-of-the-art approach for this problem is parameter lifting (PL)—an abstraction-refinement loop that abstracts the pMC to a non-parametric model analyzed with standard probabilistic model checking techniques. This paper presents two key improvements to tackle the main limitations of PL. First, we introduce generalized parameter lifting (GPL) to lift various restrictive assumptions made by PL. Second, we present a big-step transformation algorithm that reduces parameter dependencies in pMCs and, therefore, results in tighter approximations. Experiments show that GPL is widely applicable and that the big-step transformation accelerates pMC verification by up to orders of magnitude.

1 Introduction

Markov chains (MCs) describe system behavior under probabilistic uncertainty: They are used to model hardware circuits with faults, network communication over unreliable channels, and randomized protocols for distributed systems. Given an MC, probabilistic model checking tools like Storm [32] or Prism [38] can determine, e.g., the probability of a system failure or the expected time

---

This work has been partially funded by the NWO Veni Grant ProMiSe (222.147), DFG RTG 2236/2 (UnRAVeL), the KI-Starter Project 'Verifying AI Systems under Partial Observability' of the Ministry of Culture and Science of the German State of North Rhine-Westphalia and the European Union's Horizon 2020 research and innovation programme under the Marie Skłodowska-Curie grant agreement No. 101008233 (MISSION).

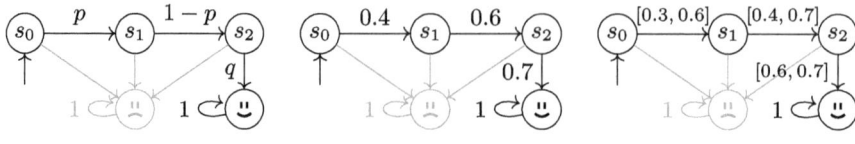

Fig. 1. Different types of (uncertain) MCs

until a successful packet transmission. However, verification results are only valid for fixed transition probabilities—which may not be known exactly—and it is unclear how sensitive results are to perturbations of these probabilities.

Parametric MCs. A variety of *uncertain MCs* allow representing uncertainty about the probabilities as a first-class citizen [4]. Prominent examples are *interval MCs* (iMCs) [27,34], where transition probabilities are given by intervals, and *parametric MCs* (pMCs) [20,39]. This paper improves the ability to verify the latter. In pMCs, we consider a finite set of symbols, called *parameters*. Contrary to (parameter-free) MCs, transition probabilities are polynomial functions over these parameters. By replacing the parameters with fixed values, we obtain MCs. A pMC is a generator for a set of MCs, given by all possible parameter instantiations. The main advantage of pMCs over iMCs is their ability to model *dependencies* between different states: by using the same parameter, we can encode that, e.g., the probability of successful network transmission is dependent on the value of a counter on the receiver. Dependencies are crucial for encoding finite memory policies in partially observable MDPs (POMDPs) as pMCs [36].

Example 1. Consider the pMC $\mathcal{D}$ in Fig. 1a over parameters p and q. Replacing them in $\mathcal{D}$ using a parameter instantiation $u \colon p \mapsto 0.4, q \mapsto 0.7$ yields the MC in Fig. 1b. We can also replace the parameters with intervals given by a parameter region $R = [0.3, 0.6] \times [0.6, 0.7]$, which yields the iMC in Fig. 1c.

Decision Problems for pMCs. Parameter instantiations are mappings from parameters to their domain. A pMC $\mathcal{D}$ and an instantiation u together define an instantiated MC $\mathcal{D}[u]$. Regions describe sets of parameter instantiations with a geometric interpretation as rectangular sets of points in Euclidean space. Given a pMC $\mathcal{D}$, a region R, and a temporal specification φ, two classical problems on pMCs are *feasibility*: Is there a parameter instantiation $u \in R$ such that $\mathcal{D}[u]$ satisfies φ? and its dual problem, *verification*: Does $\mathcal{D}[u]$ satisfy φ for every instantiation $u \in R$? The verification problem is particularly relevant to demonstrate that a system is robust against perturbations of the parameter assignments and it is a subroutine to parameter space partitioning [35, Section 9]. The feasibility problem is $\exists\mathbb{R}$-complete [37], i.e., it is as hard as answering whether a multivariate polynomial has a real-valued root [49], while the verification problem is co-$\exists\mathbb{R}$-complete. In contrast, verifying iMCs is possible in polynomial time [44].

Example 2. Consider $\mathcal{D}$ and R from Example 1. Two verification problem instances are: *Is the probability to reach ☺ in $\mathcal{D}$ below 20% for all instantiations in R?* and *Is the probability also below 15%?* The former holds, as the global maximum probability in R is 17.5% at $u\colon p \mapsto 0.5, q \mapsto 0.7$. For the latter problem, u is a counterexample. On the other hand, the iMC in Fig. 1c violates both specifications as its maximum probability is 29.4%. In the pMC, the instantiated transition probabilities at states s_0 and s_1 are dependent as both refer to the same parameter p. Such global dependencies are no longer present in the iMC.

Practically Solving pMCs. Practically solving feasibility positively only requires making a good guess, for which various incomplete approaches handling thousands of parameter exist [19,31]. For the verification problem, the literature considers two approaches: either an encoding as a nonlinear equation system solved by a constraint solver or *parameter lifting (PL)*—an abstraction-refinement algorithm. For anything but toy examples, the latter is the only viable approach [35]. Given a pMC $\mathcal{D}$ and a region R, PL replaces possible parameter instantiations with nondeterministic choices by constructing a (non-parametric) Markov decision process (MDP). The resulting MDP $\mathcal{M}_{\text{abstr}}$ yields an abstraction of the instantiated MCs of $\mathcal{D}$ in R: If $\mathcal{M}_{\text{abstr}}$ satisfies the specification φ, then φ also holds for every instantiation $\mathcal{D}[u]$, $u \in R$. If φ does not hold in $\mathcal{M}_{\text{abstr}}$, the abstraction is refined by partitioning R into smaller subregions $R = R_1 \cup \cdots \cup R_m$ that are verified individually. The key enabler of PL in practice is that the abstraction can be efficiently analyzed. However, the applicability of PL is often limited:

(i) PL is only applicable to pMC $\mathcal{D}$ and its region R, if transitions of $\mathcal{D}$ are monotonic functions, and R is well defined and graph preserving, i.e., the instantiated model $\mathcal{D}[u]$ for any $u \in R$ is guaranteed to be a valid MC and the topology of the underlying graphs is invariant under all instantiations.
(ii) The MDP abstraction in PL discards any parameter dependencies between states, often leading to an immense number of required refinement steps.

We improve the original PL approach and present solutions to both shortcomings. Both improvements build on the same conceptual basis: using iMCs instead of MDPs as the abstraction layer in the abstraction-refinement loop.

Fewer Restrictions with Generalized Parameter Lifting. As a first step, we reformulate the PL abstraction in terms of iMCs (Sect. 4). We call this conservative generalization of the original (standard) PL approach *generalized parameter lifting* (GPL). GPL is the first approach that can verify every induced Markov chain of a given pMC: By using iMCs, we support arbitrary (potentially non-monotonic) parametric transition functions in the input pMC. Furthermore, the iMC formalism supports verifying regions for which some instantiations do not yield an MC (Sect. 5.2). Finally, a novel and tailored variation of end component elimination for iMCs (Sect. 4.2) yields support for regions that are not graph preserving. GPL thus relaxes these restrictions for PL. This has significant practical implications as outlined in Sect. 3. In particular, the support for regions that are not graph preserving and/or not well defined enables mixing families of MCs—such as software product lines [14,17]—with continuous parameters (Sect. 5.3).

The Big-Step Transformation Yields Finer Abstractions. The abstraction of pMCs into either MDPs (for standard PL) or iMCs (for GPL) discards dependencies between transition probabilities at different states, often leading to coarse abstractions (see Example 2). We remedy this by a novel *big-step transformation* step, which is a pMC-to-pMC transformation that merges transitions over some fixed parameter (Sect. 6). This transformation, inspired by flip-hoisting techniques on probabilistic programs [16], reduces the number of dependencies while preserving specification satisfaction. The subsequently executed GPL algorithm provides much tighter approximations and thus requires far fewer refinement steps. GPL with this transformation enabled can provide speedups up to multiple orders of magnitude. As the big-step transformation results in pMCs with arbitrary transition functions, it is enabled by GPL's capability to verify such pMCs.

Contributions. This paper introduces *generalized* parameter lifting (GPL) and the *big-step* transformation for pMCs: In contrast to standard PL, GPL can prove specifications for *every* induced Markov chain of *any* given pMC, including pMCs with nonlinear transitions, e.g., from [54]. Additionally, GPL is the first scalable approach for the verification of families of pMCs. The experiments show that GPL retains the scalability of standard PL. The big-step transformation is introduced as part of a novel framework of *pMC-to-pMC transformations*, which also captures state elimination [20]. It yields finer abstractions in GPL and thereby significantly reduces the number of refinement steps. This allows verifying pMCs with many parameters, including a benchmark from [45] that was out of reach and is solved in seconds with the big-step transformation.

2 Problem Statement

We fix an ordered finite set $V = \{p_1, \ldots, p_n\}$ of *parameters* with subset of discrete parameters $V_D \subseteq V$ and *domain* $\mathbb{D}_p = \mathbb{Z}$ if $p \in V_D$ and $\mathbb{D}_p = \mathbb{R}$ otherwise. A *parameter instantiation* is a mapping $u \colon V \to \mathbb{R}$—or equivalently a vector $u \in \mathbb{R}^n$—with $u(p) \in \mathbb{D}_p$. $\mathbb{D}^V = \mathbb{D}_{p_1} \times \cdots \times \mathbb{D}_{p_n} \subseteq \mathbb{R}^n$ is the set of all parameter instantiations. $\mathbb{Q}[V]$ is the set of (multivariate) polynomials over V with rational coefficients. $f[u] \in \mathbb{R}$ denotes the evaluation of polynomial $f \in \mathbb{Q}[V]$ at $u \in \mathbb{D}^V$. The set of closed intervals with rational boundaries is given by $\mathrm{Int}(\mathbb{Q}) = \{[a,b] \mid a, b \in \mathbb{Q}, a \leq b\}$. An n-dimensional *region* $R = (I_1 \times \cdots \times I_n) \cap \mathbb{D}^V$ is a product of intervals $I_1, \ldots, I_n \in \mathrm{Int}(\mathbb{Q})$ restricted to parameter instantiations.

Definition 1 (Parametric Markov chain). *A parametric Markov chain (pMC) is a tuple $\mathcal{D} = (S, V, s_I, \mathcal{P})$ with finite set S of states and parameters V, initial state $s_I \in S$, and transition function $\mathcal{P}\colon S \times S \to \mathbb{Q}[V] \cup [0,1]$. $\mathcal{D}$ is a Markov Chain (MC) if $\mathcal{P}(s, s') \in [0, 1]$ and $\sum_{s'' \in S} \mathcal{P}(s, s'') = 1$ for all $s, s' \in S$.*

We may drop the variable set V for MCs and write them as $\mathcal{M} = (S, s_I, \mathcal{P})$. An instantiation $u \in \mathbb{D}^V$ is *well defined* for a pMC $\mathcal{D} = (S, V, s_I, \mathcal{P})$, if the *instantiated pMC* $\mathcal{D}[u] = (S, V, s_I, \mathcal{P}_u)$ with $\mathcal{P}_u(s, s') = \mathcal{P}(s, s')[u]$ is an MC. A region R induces a potentially infinite family of instantiated pMCs. We write $wd_{\mathcal{D}}(R) = \{u \in R \mid \mathcal{D}[u] \text{ is an MC}\}$ for the well-defined instantiations in R and drop the subscript $\mathcal{D}$ if it is clear. Region R is *well defined* if $wd_{\mathcal{D}}(R) = R$ and *graph preserving* if for all $u, u' \in R$, $s, s' \in S$: $\mathcal{P}(s, s')[u] = 0$ iff $\mathcal{P}(s, s')[u'] = 0$.

The transition function of an MC $\mathcal{M} = (S, s_I, \mathcal{P})$ defines a probability distribution $\mathcal{P}(s, \cdot)$ for the direct successor of each state $s \in S$. We lift the distributions to a probability measure $\Pr^{\mathcal{M}}$ (or simply $\Pr$ if $\mathcal{M}$ is clear) on measurable sets of infinite paths in the usual way, see [6]. $\Pr(s \leadsto \underline{u})$ is the probability to eventually reach a given set of target states $\underline{u} \subseteq S$ starting from $s \in S$. We denote by $\underline{\overset{..}{u}} \subseteq S$ the set of all states s where $\Pr(s \leadsto \underline{u}) = 0$. A *BSCC* is a strongly connected set of states where no outside state is reachable. A *(reachability probability) specification* is given by $\varphi = \mathbb{P}_{\sim \lambda}(\Diamond \underline{u})$, where $\sim \in \{<, \leq, \geq, >\}$. An MC $\mathcal{M}$ satisfies the specification φ, written $\mathcal{M} \models \varphi$, if $\Pr^{\mathcal{M}}(s_I \leadsto \underline{u}) \sim \lambda$. Our goal is to verify φ for *all* induced MCs in a region.

> Given a pMC $\mathcal{D}$, a region R, and a specification $\varphi = \mathbb{P}_{\sim \lambda}(\Diamond \underline{u})$, does $\mathcal{D}[u] \models \varphi$ hold for all Markov chains $\mathcal{D}[u]$ with $u \in wd_{\mathcal{D}}(R)$?

Note that R does not have to be well defined. Our results generalize to expected rewards in a straightforward way. All proofs can be found in [30, Appendix A].

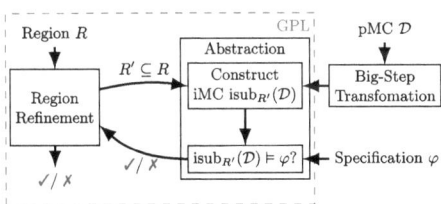

Fig. 2. Generalized Parameter Lifting Abstraction-Refinement Loop

Table 1. Comparison of Standard PL and Generalized PL

	Standard PL	GPL
Abstraction	MDPs	iMCs
pMCs	monotonic	arbitrary
Parameters	must be continuous	discrete or continuous
Regions	must be well defined and graph preserving	arbitrary hyperintervals

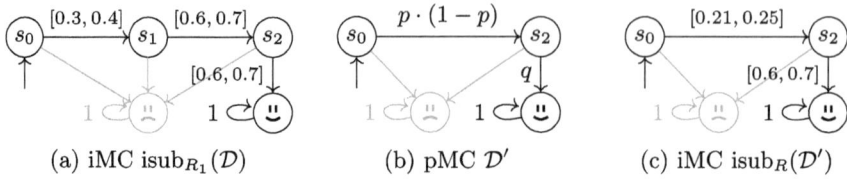

Fig. 3. More Markov models

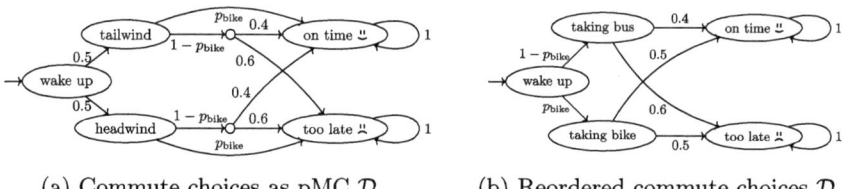

Fig. 4. Reordering commute choices

3 Our Approach in a Nutshell

We present generalized parameter lifting (GPL) and the big-step transformation. We first outline the steps of GPL and then compare to the approach in [45].

3.1 Overview

Figure 2 illustrates the approach, which is an instantiation of an abstraction-refinement loop that reduces solving the co-$\exists \mathbb{R}$-hard verification problem for pMCs by iteratively solving a set of iMCs. We also give a pseudocode description in [30, Appendix B]. As a running example, we use the pMC $\mathcal{D}$ from Fig. 1a, region $R = [0.3, 0.6] \times [0.6, 0.7]$ and specification $\varphi = \mathbb{P}_{<0.2}(\Diamond \smiley)$ as in Examples 1 and 2. Our goal is to verify that $\mathcal{D}[u] \models \varphi$ holds for all MCs $\mathcal{D}[u]$ with $u \in wd_\mathcal{D}(R)$—simply written as $\mathcal{D}, R \models \varphi$.

pMC Abstraction via iMCs. To show that $\mathcal{D}, R \models \mathbb{P}_{<0.2}(\Diamond \smiley)$, GPL computes an upper bound on the reachability probability by evaluating the iMC, written $isub_R(\mathcal{D})$, that substitutes the functions in $\mathcal{D}$'s transitions with their intervals in the region R. Figure 1c shows $isub_R(\mathcal{D})$ for our running example. This iMC is a proper abstraction: For any well-defined instantiation $u \in wd_\mathcal{D}(R)$, the instantiated MC $\mathcal{D}[u]$ can also be generated by the iMC $isub_R(\mathcal{D})$. However, the iMC also captures MCs that do not correspond to any instantiated MC $\mathcal{D}[u]$ of pMC $\mathcal{D}$. Recall from Example 2 that $\mathcal{D}, R \models \mathbb{P}_{<0.2}(\Diamond \smiley)$. The specification does not hold for the iMC abstraction since the maximal probability to reach $\smiley$ in the iMC is 0.294—achieved by picking the upper interval boundary for all transitions along the single path to $\smiley$. This a is a counterexample to the specification, but it is *spurious* since it is impossible to instantiate the pMC in the same way.

Region Refinement. GPL employs a divide-and-conquer refinement. Whenever a region R can not be verified through abstraction, it is *split* into smaller subregions $R = R_1 \cup \cdots \cup R_m$. We have $\mathcal{D}, R \models \varphi$ iff $\mathcal{D}, R_i \models \varphi$ for all $1 \leq i \leq m$. The initial verification problem thus reduces to verify φ for a series of subregions. Smaller regions $R_i \subsetneq R$ intuitively yield a refined abstraction, because the interval transitions for iMC $\mathrm{isub}_{R_i}(\mathcal{D})$ are tighter. Such a split can be done repeatedly until the subregions are sufficiently small to conclude that $\mathcal{D}, R \models \varphi$ or we find some $u \in wd_\mathcal{D}(R_i)$, e.g., by sampling, s.t. $\mathcal{D}[u] \not\models \varphi$. See [35] for further details on the refinement procedure, including splitting and sampling strategies. For our example, we (choose to) split R along the value for p into $R_1 = [0.3, 0.4] \times [0.6, 0.7]$ and $R_2 = R \setminus R_1$. Recursively, GPL verifies the iMCs $\mathrm{isub}_{R_1}(\mathcal{D})$ (Fig. 3a) and $\mathrm{isub}_{R_2}(\mathcal{D})$. Checking R_1 yields a maximal probability to reach ☺ of $0.196 < 0.2$, implying $\mathcal{D}, R_1 \models \mathbb{P}_{<0.2}(\Diamond ☺)$. For R_2, we get a value of $0.252 \not< 0.2$, resulting in further splitting of R_2. Depending on how the split is performed, at least three more subregions have to be considered to infer that the specification holds in R_2. GPL proves R to be satisfied by checking at least six iMCs in total.

Big-Step Transformation to Require Fewer Splits. The number of iterations, i.e., the number of iMCs that GPL verifies, can be prohibitively large, especially if there are many parameters. Indeed, while [45] evenly splits regions along every parameter, more refined splitting mechanisms were investigated later [35]. However, the coarse abstraction mechanism is the *root cause* for the required number of iterations. Here, the novel idea to reduce the number of iterations is to transform the pMC prior to abstraction. We give two examples to show the effectiveness of this transformation.

Example 3. Consider the pMCs $\mathcal{D}$ in Fig. 1a and $\mathcal{D}'$ in Fig. 3b. We obtain $\mathcal{D}'$ by applying state elimination [20], a transformation that preserves the reachability probability for every parameter value. Verifying only the iMC $\mathrm{isub}_R(\mathcal{D}')$ in Fig. 3c suffices to verify that the reachability probability in $\mathcal{D}$ in R is below 0.2.

Example 4. Consider the pMC $\mathcal{D}_c$ in Fig. 4a modeling a randomized decision to commute by bus or bike. Depending on the wind direction, taking the bike leads to arriving on time, while the bus is randomly late 60% of the time. Analyzing $\mathrm{isub}_R(\mathcal{D}_c)$ for $R = [0,1]$ yields a minimal reachability probability of 0.2. We can "reorder" $\mathcal{D}_c$ into pMC $\mathcal{D}_r$ (Fig. 4b) without affecting reachability probabilities. Analyzing $\mathrm{isub}_R(\mathcal{D}_r)$ for $R = [0,1]$ yields a tight lower bound of 0.4.

Intuitively, the big-step transformation takes advantage of the fact that pMCs have sub-pMCs in which the same parameter occurs multiple times, and these sub-pMCs can be merged efficiently into one transition. Such a sub-pMC can represent initiating communication between two stations or navigating through a particular room. Shortcuts eliminate sequential occurrences of a parameter within a sub-pMC, while grouping eliminates parallel occurrences within a sub-pMC. We refer to Sect. 6.4 for further details.

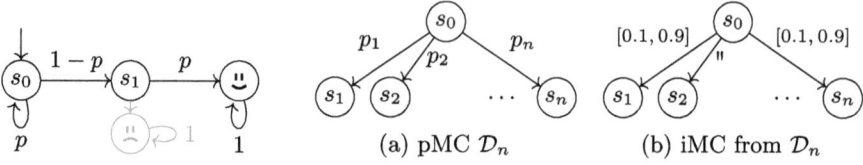

Fig. 5. pMC $\mathcal{D}$ **Fig. 6.** pMC and corresponding iMC

3.2 Comparing GPL and Standard Parameter Lifting

The standard parameter lifting (PL) approach [45] considers an abstraction-refinement loop similar to GPL. In fact, region refinement is performed in an identical way. The key difference between standard PL and GPL is the abstraction. While standard PL abstracts possible pMC instantiations using (non-parametric) MDPs, GPL is based on iMCs. The semantics of iMCs yield various advantages that allow us to lift restrictions (see Table 1).

Support for Regions that are Not Well Defined. Consider the pMC $\mathcal{D}_n$ in Fig. 6a and $R = [0.1, 0.9]^n$. Some points in this region do not induce MCs, e.g., for $n = 5$ and the point $u(p_i) = 0.9$, the probabilities of the distribution from s_0 add up to 4.5. We call R not well defined. Such regions naturally occur, e.g., for controllers that randomly execute some action a with probability p_a. Standard PL does not handle not-well-defined regions, while GPL supports them due to iMC semantics. *For any region R, GPL will analyze $wd(R)$, i.e., the Markov chains in R* (Sect. 5.2).

Support for Arbitrary Polynomials as Transition Probabilities. The MDP abstraction of standard PL requires transition functions to be monotonic. *GPL supports arbitrary polynomials by computing their intervals within each region* to get the iMC (Sect. 4, [30, Appendix F]). For example, the pMC $\mathcal{D}'$ from Fig. 3b is supported by GPL but not by standard PL. The more general support also enables more elaborate transformations of the pMC. In particular, the proposed big-step transformation algorithm (Sect. 6.4) yields pMCs with non-monotonic transition functions and is thus not applicable for standard PL.

Support for Regions that are Not Graph Preserving. Verifying sets of MCs, where different MCs have different topologies, is at the heart of probabilistic software product line verification [17,53]. These sets can be represented using pMCs with regions that are not graph preserving and the additional constraint that a parameter is either 0 or 1. In contrast to standard PL, *GPL supports not-graph-preserving regions via end component analysis* (Sect. 4.2). In particular, GPL supports the verification of sets of pMCs, i.e., it allows mixing discrete, graph-changing parameters and continuous parameters (see Sect. 5.3), which is not possible with existing abstraction-refinement techniques for software product line verification [3,14]. Region $R = [0,1]$ on the pMC $\mathcal{D}$ in Fig. 5 is not graph preserving and yields discontinuous reachability probabilities, as seen when comparing $p = 1$ and $p = 1 - \varepsilon$. Indeed, the verification results for $R' = [\varepsilon, 1-\varepsilon]$ and R are significantly different for almost every threshold $\varepsilon > 0$!

4 Verifying Interval Markov Chains

GPL uses interval Markov chains (iMCs). This section reviews iMC verification and describes a tailored version of end component elimination on iMCs.

4.1 Interval Markov Chains

Interval Markov chains (iMCs) can be seen as simplistic pMCs, where each transition has a unique real-valued parameter, combined with a region that assigns an interval to each such parameter.

Definition 2 (Interval Markov chain). *An interval Markov chain (iMC) is a tuple $\mathcal{I} = (S, s_I, \mathcal{P})$ with S and s_I as in Definition 1 and transition function $\mathcal{P} \colon S \times S \to \mathrm{Int}(\mathbb{Q})$. The set of MCs induced by iMC $\mathcal{I}$ is given by $\mathrm{MC}(\mathcal{I}) := \{\mathcal{M} = (S, s_I, \mathcal{P}_\mathcal{M}) \mid \mathcal{M}$ is an MC s.t. $\mathcal{P}_\mathcal{M}(s, s') \in \mathcal{P}(s, s')$ for all $s, s'\}$.*

We define the *reachability interval* of iMC $\mathcal{I}$ as

$$\langle\!\langle \mathcal{I} \rangle\!\rangle := \left[\, \min\nolimits_{\mathcal{M} \in \mathrm{MC}(\mathcal{I})} \Pr\nolimits^\mathcal{M}(s_I \rightsquigarrow \smile),\ \max\nolimits_{\mathcal{M} \in \mathrm{MC}(\mathcal{I})} \Pr\nolimits^\mathcal{M}(s_I \rightsquigarrow \smile) \,\right].$$

The reachability interval $\langle\!\langle \mathcal{I} \rangle\!\rangle$ can be described by a system of Bellman equations.

Definition 3 (iMC system of equations). *Let $\mathcal{I} = (S, s_I, \mathcal{P})$ be an iMC and $\mathrm{opt} \in \{\min, \max\}$. The system of equations for variables $x_s = \Pr^{\mathrm{opt}}(s \rightsquigarrow \smile)$ is given by $x_s = 1$ for all $s \in \smile$, $x_s = 0$ for all $s \in \frown$, and otherwise*

$$x_s = \mathrm{opt}\left\{ \sum\nolimits_{t \in S} a_{s,t} \cdot x_t \,\Big|\, a_{s,t} \in \mathcal{P}(s,t) \text{ for } s,t \in S \text{ such that } \sum\nolimits_{t \in S} a_{s,t} = 1 \right\}.$$

The solution of this system of equations is unique if all intervals of the iMC preserve its graph structure [28]. The solution can be computed via a linear program encoding [7,44] or a value iteration procedure [42,50].

4.2 Verifying iMCs with Not-Graph-Preserving Intervals

Most methods for pMCs assume that regions are graph preserving [33]. Any not-graph-preserving region can be decomposed into exponentially many graph-preserving hyperintervals, which may be open, and are thus not regions suitable for PL [35]. We drop the assumption that regions must be graph preserving. The challenge is that the iMC system of equations may not have a unique solution.

Example 5. Consider the pMC in Fig. 5. The probability to reach $\smile$ is p if $p < 1$ and zero if $p = 1$. Replacing all parametric transitions with the interval $[0, 1]$ yields an iMC $\mathcal{I}$. Its minimizing system of equations has a distinct (thus non-unique) solution for each $r \in [0, 1]$ given by $x_{s_0} = r$, $x_\smile = 1$, and $x_{s_1} = x_\frown = 0$.

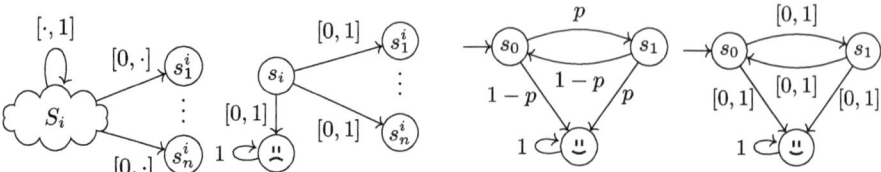

Fig. 7. Illustration of EC elimination

Fig. 8. Substituting $R = [0, 1]$

By eliminating the end components of the iMC, we can construct an iMC with a unique fixed point [10, 28, 40]. Eliminating end components on iMCs is all we will need to verify pMCs on not-graph-preserving regions in the next section.

Definition 4 (iMC end component). *Let* $\mathcal{I} = (S, s_I, \mathcal{P})$ *be an iMC. A set* S' *of states is an* end component (EC) *if* $S' \subseteq S$ *is a BSCC for some* $\mathcal{M} \in \mathrm{MC}(\mathcal{I})$.

The union of two overlapping ECs is again an EC [28]. Thus, a state belongs to at most one *maximal EC (MEC)*. The states in ☺ and ☹ each form an MEC.

Lemma 1 ([28, Prop. 3]). *The iMC* $\mathcal{I}$*'s system of equations has a unique solution if the only MECs in* $\mathcal{I}$ *consist of the states in* ☺ ∪ ☹.

Proof. This follows from [28, Prop. 3]. Use the fact that such a pMC's min-reduction is the pMC itself.

We identify MECs as in [28, Alg. 3] and eliminate them while preserving optimal reachability probabilities. Our transformation is a variant of the ones in [28], the difference being that we give a single transformation instead of two. Each MEC S_i is collapsed into a single state s_i as sketched in Fig. 7. To reflect the possibility to never exit the MEC, an additional transition to ☹ is added.

Definition 5 (EC elimination). *Let iMC* $\mathcal{I} = (S, s_I, \mathcal{P})$ *and* $E_{\mathcal{I}} = \{S_1, \ldots, S_n\}$ *the set of MECs with* $S_i \cap (☺ \cup ☹) = \emptyset$ *for all* $1 \leq i \leq n$. *For* $s \in S$, *define* $\langle s \rangle = S_i$ *if* $s \in S_i$ *for some* $S_i \in E_{\mathcal{I}}$ *and* $\langle s \rangle = s$ *otherwise. The EC elimination of* $\mathcal{I}$ *is the iMC* $\mathrm{elim}(\mathcal{I}) = (\{\langle s \rangle \mid s \in S\}, \langle s_I \rangle, \hat{\mathcal{P}})$, *where for* $s, s' \in S$

$$\hat{\mathcal{P}}(\langle s \rangle, \langle s' \rangle) = \begin{cases} [0, 1] & \text{if } \langle s \rangle \in E_{\mathcal{I}},\ \langle s \rangle \neq \langle s' \rangle,\ \text{and } \mathcal{P}(\langle s \rangle, \langle s' \rangle) \neq [0, 0], \\ [0, 1] & \text{if } \langle s \rangle \in E_{\mathcal{I}} \text{ and } \langle s' \rangle \cap ☹ \neq \emptyset, \\ \mathcal{P}(s, \langle s' \rangle) & \text{if } \langle s \rangle \notin E_{\mathcal{I}}, \\ [0, 0] & \text{otherwise.} \end{cases}$$

Theorem 1. *For any iMC* $\mathcal{I}$, *(a)* $\mathrm{elim}(\mathcal{I})$*'s system of equations has a unique solution and (b)* $\langle\!\langle \mathcal{I} \rangle\!\rangle = \langle\!\langle \mathrm{elim}(\mathcal{I}) \rangle\!\rangle$, *i.e., the reachability intervals coincide.*

5 Generalized Parameter Lifting

We have seen how one can verify iMCs with arbitrary intervals. This section introduces GPL. We first introduce Parameter Lifting on iMCs and then show how GPL verifies not-well-defined regions and handles discrete parameters.

5.1 Computing Region Estimates and Splitting Regions

PL is based on computing *region estimates*, i.e., upper and lower bounds to the reachability probability within a region.

Definition 6 (Region estimate). *A region estimate for pMC $\mathcal{D}$ in region R is an interval $[a, b] \in \text{Int}(\mathbb{Q})$ such that $a \leq \Pr^{\mathcal{D}[u]}(s_I \leadsto \underline{\smile}) \leq b$ for all $u \in wd(R)$.*

To obtain region estimates for pMCs, we replace the transition functions by intervals that cover all instantiations within the region, yielding an iMC. We say an iMC $\mathcal{I}$ substitutes a pMC $\mathcal{D}$ in region R if for all $u \in wd(R)$: $\mathcal{D}[u] \in \text{MC}(\mathcal{I})$.

Theorem 2. *Given a pMC $\mathcal{D}$, a region R, and an iMC $\mathcal{I}$ that substitutes $\mathcal{D}$ in R, the reachability interval $\langle\!\langle \mathcal{I} \rangle\!\rangle$ is a region estimate for $\mathcal{D}$ in R.*

Proof. For all $u \in wd(R)$: $\mathcal{D}[u] \in \text{MC}(\mathcal{I})$. Thus, $\min_{\mathcal{M} \in \text{MC}(\mathcal{I})} \Pr^{\mathcal{M}}(s_I \leadsto \underline{\smile}) \leq \min_{u \in wd(R)} \Pr^{\mathcal{D}[u]}(s_I \leadsto \underline{\smile})$. There is a symmetric argument for the maximum.

An iMC $\mathcal{I}$ *refines* another iMC $\mathcal{I}'$ if both share states S and for all $s, s' \in S$: $\mathcal{P}^{\mathcal{I}}(s, s') \subseteq \mathcal{P}^{\mathcal{I}'}(s, s')$ [34]. Let the *interval substitution* iMC $\text{isub}_R(\mathcal{D})$ be defined as the maximally refined iMC that substitutes $\mathcal{D}$ in R. It is obtained by substituting $\mathcal{D}$'s parametric transition probabilities with their intervals within R:

Proposition 1. *For pMC $\mathcal{D} = (S, s_I, \mathcal{P}, V)$, region R, $\text{isub}_R(\mathcal{D}) = (S, s_I, \mathcal{P}_{sub})$: $\mathcal{P}_{sub}(s, s') = [\, \min_{u \in wd(R)} \mathcal{P}(s, s')[u], \ \max_{u \in wd(R)} \mathcal{P}(s, s')[u] \,]$ for all s, s'.*

Proof. The iMC $\text{isub}_R(\mathcal{D})$ is the maximally refined iMC s.t. for all $u \in wd(R)$: $\mathcal{D}[u] \in \text{MC}(\mathcal{I})$. Thus, its transition probability intervals encompass exactly the transition probabilities of all $\mathcal{D}[u]$ with $u \in wd(R)$.

GPL's abstraction is the interval substitution $\text{isub}_R(\mathcal{D})$. Transition intervals in $\text{isub}_R(\mathcal{D})$ may include 0 as we allow not-graph-preserving regions—unlike standard PL [45]. Consequently, an EC $S' \subseteq S$ of $\text{isub}_R(\mathcal{D})$ might not be a BSCC in any of the instantiations of $\mathcal{D}[u]$. Handling such ECs as in Sect. 4.2 is the key to providing region estimates for not-graph-preserving regions.

Example 6. The interval substitution $\text{isub}_R(\mathcal{D})$ for pMC $\mathcal{D}$ and region $R = [0, 1]$ in Fig. 8 has an EC $\{s_0, s_1\}$ which is no BSCC of any instantiation $\mathcal{D}[u]$, $u \in R$.

The iMC $\text{isub}_R(\mathcal{D})$ might induce MCs that do not correspond to any instantiation of the pMC $\mathcal{D}$ due to two reasons. First, for transition functions over discrete parameters, the (continuous) intervals of $\text{isub}_R(\mathcal{D})$ potentially contain values not realizable by a discrete parameter assignment. Second, iMC transition intervals can be instantiated at each state independently, while pMC transition functions with common parameters are coupled. If region estimates obtained through interval substitution are not adequate to prove the specification, we may *split* the region into smaller regions which yields *refined* estimates.

Definition 7 (Region split [35]). *Let R be a region and $R_1, \ldots, R_m$ be regions with $R = \bigcup_{j=1}^m R_j$. Then we say that R splits into $R_1, \ldots, R_m$.*

Proposition 2. *If R splits into $R_1, \ldots, R_m$ and $\mathcal{I}_1, \ldots, \mathcal{I}_m$ are iMCs s.t. $\mathcal{I}_j$ substitutes $\mathcal{D}$ in R_j, then $\bigcup_{j=1}^m \langle\!\langle \mathcal{I}_j(\mathcal{D}) \rangle\!\rangle$ is a region estimate for pMC $\mathcal{D}$ in R.*

Proof. For each $u \in R$, there exists a $k \in \{1, \ldots, m\}$ such that $u \in R_k$ and $\Pr^{\mathcal{D}[u]}(s_0 \rightsquigarrow \smile) \in \langle\!\langle \mathcal{I}_k \rangle\!\rangle \subseteq \bigcup_{j=1}^m \langle\!\langle \mathcal{I}_j \rangle\!\rangle$.

Example 7. For $\mathcal{D}$ and $\text{isub}_R(\mathcal{D})$ as in Fig. 8, we have $\Pr^{\mathcal{D}[u]}(s_0 \rightsquigarrow \smile) = 1$ for all $u \in R$, but $\langle\!\langle \text{isub}_R(\mathcal{D}) \rangle\!\rangle = [0, 1]$. Splitting R into $R_1 = [0, 0.5]$ and $R_2 = [0.5, 1]$ yields $\langle\!\langle \text{isub}_{R_1}(\mathcal{D}) \rangle\!\rangle = \langle\!\langle \text{isub}_{R_2}(\mathcal{D}) \rangle\!\rangle = [1, 1]$ which results in estimate $[1, 1]$ for R.

Intuitively, splitting a region R into increasingly smaller subregions R_j yields tighter intervals in the iMCs $\text{isub}_{R_j}(\mathcal{D})$ and therefore tighter reachability intervals $\langle\!\langle \text{isub}_{R_j}(\mathcal{D}) \rangle\!\rangle$. This enables obtaining arbitrarily precise region estimates for R.

For a specification $\varphi = \mathbb{P}_{\geq \lambda}(\Diamond \smile)$, a region estimate $[a, b]$ for pMC $\mathcal{D}$ in region R yields three cases: If $a \geq \lambda$ or $b < \lambda$, *all* well-defined instantiations in R *satisfy* or *violate* φ, immediately answering our main problem statement. If $a < \lambda \leq b$, we successively apply region splitting to find an answer by either showing that φ holds in all subregions or finding a subregion where φ is violated. This terminates unless the optimum and the threshold coincide. We refer to [35] for further details.

5.2 Verifying Not-Well-Defined Regions

GPL supports the verification of not-well-defined regions, i.e., regions in which some points do not induce a Markov chain as the transition probabilities do not sum up to one. Such pMCs naturally occur when studying POMDPs [36]. For example, the region $R_n = [0.1, 0.9]^n$ is not well defined on pMC $\mathcal{D}_n$ in Fig. 6a. Reasoning about such regions involves ignoring not-well-defined instantiations. GPL achieves this by exploiting iMC semantics. Correctness follows from Theorem 2 and the fact that $\text{isub}_R(\mathcal{D})$ substitutes $\mathcal{D}$ in R:

Corollary 1. *Let $\mathcal{D}$ be a pMC and R a not-well-defined region. Then for all well-defined instantiations $u \in R$: $\Pr^{\mathcal{D}[u]}(s_I \rightsquigarrow \smile) \in \langle\!\langle \text{isub}_R(\mathcal{D}) \rangle\!\rangle$.*

A pMC is *simple* if all transitions are constant or of the form p or $1-p$ for $p \in V$. In simple pMCs, all regions $R \subseteq [0,1]^{|V|}$ are well defined. The pMC $\mathcal{D}_n$ in Fig. 6a is not simple. A transformation in [36] yields the simple pMC $\mathcal{D}'_n$ in Fig. 9 over new

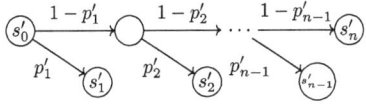

Fig. 9. Simple pMC $\mathcal{D}'_n$ from $\mathcal{D}_n$

parameters, with a bijection between valuations of $\mathcal{D}_n$ and $\mathcal{D}'_n$. $\mathcal{D}'_n$ can be checked with standard PL over the new parameters. However, this transformation does not enable us to check R_n: R_n in $\mathcal{D}_n$ has no equivalent hyperinterval region R'_n in $\mathcal{D}'_n$ with $R'_n = wd(R'_n)$. Thus, the region "go from s_0 to s_i with probabilities between 0.1 and 0.9" cannot be verified with standard PL. This query only becomes possible with GPL.

5.3 Reasoning About Families of pMCs Using Discrete Parameters

Suppose $\mathfrak{M}$ is a finite family (i.e., a finite set) of Markov chains. Each such $\mathfrak{M}$ can be described by a single pMC with additional discrete parameters $V_D = \{p_1, \ldots, p_n\}$ that take values $p_i \in \{0,1\}$ [13]. For example, consider the pMC in Fig. 4 with $p_{\text{bike}} \in \{0,1\}$. This pMC encodes two MCs and models buying either a bus subscription ($p_{\text{bike}} = 0$) or a bike ($p_{\text{bike}} = 1$). This encoding is used for the analysis of software product lines in, e.g., [13,47]. Previously, these pMCs could not be analyzed with parameter lifting as such regions are not graph preserving.

A similar procedure can be applied to finite families of pMCs $\mathfrak{D}$ over parameters V_C, resulting in a single pMC over $V_D \cup V_C$ that describes all pMCs in $\mathfrak{D}$. With GPL, and given a region R_C over the parameters V_C, all pMCs can be simultaneously checked by checking the joint pMC over the region $\{0,1\}^n \times R_C$. If necessary, GPL splits a parameter over $\{0,1\}$ into $\{0\}$ and $\{1\}$. To the best of our knowledge, GPL is the first verification method that explicitly supports a mix of discrete and continuous parameters, and thus finite families of pMCs.

6 Tightening Region Estimates by Transforming pMCs

As shown in Examples 3 and 4 on page 7, transforming the pMC before applying interval substitution can improve its region estimates. In this section, we introduce the requirements for such transformations, present two approaches based on shortcuts and transition grouping, and describe an algorithm combining both ideas.

6.1 Tightening Transformations

Definition 8 (Tightening transformation). *An iMC $\mathcal{I}$ tightens iMC $\mathcal{I}'$ if $\langle\!\langle \mathcal{I} \rangle\!\rangle \subseteq \langle\!\langle \mathcal{I}' \rangle\!\rangle$. Let $\mathfrak{D}_V$ be the set of pMCs with parameters V. A function $\mathtt{t} \colon \mathfrak{D}_V \to \mathfrak{D}_V$ is a tightening transformation if for all pMCs $\mathcal{D}$, the pMC $\mathtt{t}(\mathcal{D})$ satisfies for all regions R: $wd_{\mathtt{t}(\mathcal{D})}(R) = wd_\mathcal{D}(R)$ and $\mathrm{isub}_R(\mathtt{t}(\mathcal{D}))$ tightens $\mathrm{isub}_R(\mathcal{D})$.*

A tightening transformation preserves reachability probabilities induced by well-defined pMC instantiations. Let $\mathcal{D} \equiv \mathcal{D}'$ denote that two pMCs $\mathcal{D}, \mathcal{D}' \in \mathfrak{D}_V$ have the same reachability probabilities, i.e., their well-defined instantiations coincide and $\Pr^{\mathcal{D}[u]}(s_0 \leadsto \underline{\smile}) = \Pr^{\mathcal{D}'[u]}(s_0 \leadsto \underline{\smile})$ for all well-defined $u \in \mathbb{D}^V$.

Lemma 2. *For tightening transformation* $\mathfrak{t}$, *we have* $\mathcal{D} \equiv \mathfrak{t}(\mathcal{D})$ *for all pMCs* $\mathcal{D}$.

Proof. A tightening transformation $\mathfrak{t}$, pMC $\mathcal{D}$, and well-defined $u \in \mathbb{R}^V$ yield $\{\Pr_{\mathcal{D}[u]}(s_0 \leadsto \underline{\smile})\} = \langle\!\langle \mathrm{isub}_{\{u\}}(\mathcal{D})\rangle\!\rangle \subseteq \langle\!\langle \mathrm{isub}_{\{u\}}(\mathfrak{t}(\mathcal{D}))\rangle\!\rangle = \{\Pr_{\mathfrak{t}(\mathcal{D})[u]}(s_0 \leadsto \underline{\smile})\}$.

Intuitively, the region estimates obtained after applying a tightening transformation shall be at least as tight as the estimates obtained using the original pMC. The identity $\mathfrak{t}_{\mathrm{id}}$ with $\mathfrak{t}_{\mathrm{id}}(\mathcal{D}) = \mathcal{D}$ is a (trivial) tightening transformation that does not improve any region estimates. Another example is the function $\mathfrak{t}_{\mathrm{exact}}$ that transforms a pMC $\mathcal{D}$ into a pMC $\mathcal{D}'$ over fractions of multivariate polynomials with three states $\{s_0, \underline{\smile}, \underline{\frown}\}$ and the single rational transition function that encodes the reachability probabilities in $\mathcal{D}$ as in [20]. $\mathfrak{t}_{\mathrm{exact}}$ is a tightening transformation, since for any region R, $\langle\!\langle \mathrm{isub}_R(\mathfrak{t}_{\mathrm{exact}}(\mathcal{D}))\rangle\!\rangle$ is the tightest possible estimate and thus a subset of $\langle\!\langle \mathrm{isub}_R(D)\rangle\!\rangle$ by Theorem 2. The result $\mathfrak{t}_{\mathrm{exact}}(\mathcal{D})$ has exponentially large fractions of polynomials as transition probabilities [5].

From a practical perspective, neither $\mathfrak{t}_{\mathrm{id}}$ nor $\mathfrak{t}_{\mathrm{exact}}$ are useful: The transformation $\mathfrak{t}_{\mathrm{exact}}$ yields the tightest region estimates, but is hard to compute and evaluate, the identity $\mathfrak{t}_{\mathrm{id}}$ is easy to compute, but effectless. Our aim is to find a tightening transformation that (1) strictly tightens many region estimates and (2) is effectively computable, with a fast evaluation of region estimates.

6.2 Shortcuts in pMCs

Our transformation algorithm is based on two main ideas: *Creating shortcuts* in single-parameter sub-pMCs as in Example 3 and *grouping parametric choices* as in Example 4. It works on single-parameter *sub-pMCs* rooted in a state $\hat{s}$.

Definition 9 (Sub-pMC rooted in $\hat{s}$ over p). *A sub-pMC of $\mathcal{D}$ rooted in $\hat{s} \in S$ over $p \in V$ is a pMC $\mathcal{D}_{\hat{s},p} = (\hat{S}, \hat{s}, \hat{\mathcal{P}}, \{p\})$ such that $\hat{s} \in \hat{S} \subseteq S$ and*

- *the underlying graph $\mathcal{G}_{\hat{s},p} = (\hat{S}, \{(s,t) \in \hat{S} \times \hat{S} \mid \hat{\mathcal{P}}(s,t) \neq 0\})$ is acyclic, i.e., all maximal paths end in $\hat{S}_{\mathrm{exit}} = \{s \in \hat{S} \mid \hat{\mathcal{P}}(s,t) = 0 \text{ for all } t \in \hat{S}\}$,*
- *every $s \in \hat{S}$ is reachable from $\hat{s}$ in $\mathcal{G}_{\hat{s},p}$, and*
- *$s \notin \hat{S}_{\mathrm{exit}}$ implies $\hat{\mathcal{P}}(s,t) = \mathcal{P}(s,t) \in \mathbb{Q}[\{p\}]$ for all $t \in S$.*

Note that cyclic sub-pMCs can be made acyclic by removing transitions. A sub-pMC of the pMC in Fig. 10a rooted in s_0 over p is indicated in orange. We have $\hat{S}_{\mathrm{exit}} = \{s_3, s_4, \underline{\frown}\}$. Our approach is to take *shortcuts* from s_0 directly to $\hat{S}_{\mathrm{exit}}$—skipping over the intermediate states s_1 and s_2. To this end, the outgoing transitions of s_0 are replaced in Fig. 10b. We now fix $\mathcal{D}_{\hat{s},p}$ and $\hat{S}_{\mathrm{exit}}$ as in Definition 9.

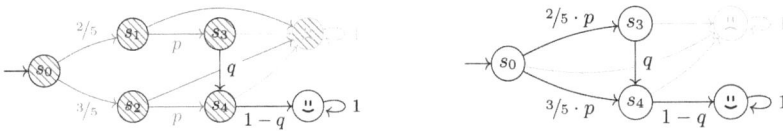

(a) Identify sub-pMC for (s_0, p) (step 1) (b) Create shortcuts in sub-pMC (step 2)

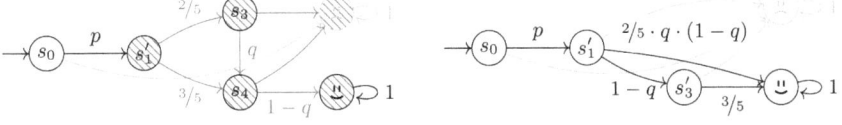

(c) Group p (step 3), id. sub-pMC for (s_1', q) (d) After an iteration on (s_1', q)

Fig. 10. Big-step transformation algorithm on an example pMC

Definition 10 (Shortcut pMC). *The shortcut pMC of $\mathcal{D}$ and its sub-pMC $\mathcal{D}_{\hat{s},p}$ is the pMC $\mathsf{t}_{\text{shortcut}}(\mathcal{D}, \mathcal{D}_{\hat{s},p}) = (S, s_I, \mathcal{P}_{\text{shortcut}}, V)$, with $\mathcal{P}_{\text{shortcut}}(s,t) = \mathcal{P}(s,t)$ for $s, t \in S$, $s \neq \hat{s}$, $\mathcal{P}_{\text{shortcut}}(\hat{s},t) = 0$ for $t \notin \hat{S}_{\text{exit}}$, and*

$$\mathcal{P}_{\text{shortcut}}(\hat{s}, t) = \Pr^{\mathcal{D}_{\hat{s},p}}(\hat{s} \rightsquigarrow t) = \sum_{s_0 \ldots s_n \in \text{Paths}(\hat{s},t)} \prod_{i=1}^n \mathcal{P}(s_{i-1}, s_i)$$

for $t \in \hat{S}_{\text{exit}}$, where $\text{Paths}(\hat{s}, t)$ denotes the set of paths from $\hat{s}$ to t.

The set $\text{Paths}(\hat{s}, t)$ for $t \in \hat{S}$ is finite as Definition 9 requires $\mathcal{D}_{\hat{s},p}$ to be acyclic. It follows that $\mathcal{P}_{\text{shortcut}}(\hat{s},t) = \Pr^{\mathcal{D}_{\hat{s},p}}(\hat{s} \rightsquigarrow t)$ is a univariate polynomial over parameter p. The polynomials $\Pr^{\mathcal{D}_{\hat{s},p}}(\hat{s} \rightsquigarrow t)$ for all $t \in \hat{S}$ can effectively be computed in a dynamic programming fashion by traversing the states of $\mathcal{D}_{\hat{s},p}$ in a topological order. Our implementation uses a factorized representation, cf. [30, Appendix D].

Lemma 3. $\text{isub}_R(\mathsf{t}_{\text{shortcut}}(\mathcal{D}, \mathcal{D}_{\hat{s},p}))$ *tightens* $\text{isub}_R(\mathcal{D})$ *for any region R.*

Proof. The two iMCs only differ at state $\hat{s}$. For $t \in S_{\text{exit}}$, we have $\mathcal{P}_{\text{shortcut}}(\hat{s}, t) = \{\Pr^{\mathcal{D}}(\hat{s} \rightsquigarrow t)[u] \mid u \in wd_{\mathcal{D}}(R)\}$. The claim follows as $\text{isub}_R(\mathcal{D})$ substitutes $\mathcal{D}$.

6.3 Grouping Transitions

Our approach is to iteratively apply transformations using shortcuts. The following example suggests interleaving shortcuts with a grouping of transitions.

Example 8. After adding an intermediate state s_1' as in Fig. 10c, we obtain a sub-pMC rooted in s_1' over q. This is a larger sub-pMC than the candidates in Fig. 10b. Figure 10d shows the corresponding shortcut pMC.

Definition 11 (Grouped pMC). *Suppose we have $\hat{s} \in S$, $S' = \{s_1, \ldots, s_k\} \subseteq S$ s.t. $\mathcal{P}(\hat{s}, s_i) = g_i + c_i \cdot f$ for some polynomials $f, g_i \in \mathbb{Q}[V]$ and factors $c_i \in \mathbb{Q}$ with $c = \sum_{j=1}^k c_j$. Then for the grouped pMC $\mathsf{t}_{\text{group}}(\mathcal{D}, \hat{s}, f) = (S \uplus \{s'\}, s_I, \mathcal{P}_{\text{group}}, V)$ we have $\mathcal{P}_{\text{group}}(\hat{s}, s') = c \cdot f$, $\mathcal{P}_{\text{group}}(\hat{s}, s_i) = g_i$, $\mathcal{P}_{\text{group}}(s', s_i) = c_i/c$, $\mathcal{P}_{\text{group}}(s', t') = 0$ for all $t' \notin S'$, and $\mathcal{P}_{\text{group}}(t, t') = \mathcal{P}(t, t')$ in all other cases.*

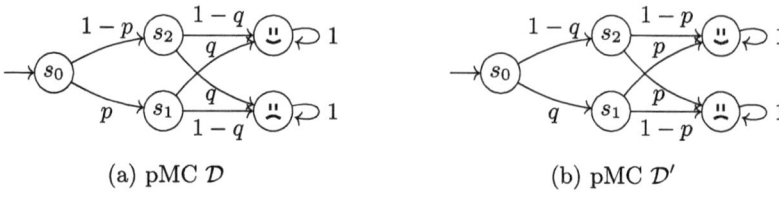

Fig. 11. Two pMCs over parameters $V = \{p, q\}$ with different orderings

Lemma 4. $\mathrm{isub}_R(\mathbf{t}_{\mathrm{group}}(\mathcal{D}, \hat{s}, f))$ *tightens* $\mathrm{isub}_R(\mathcal{D})$ *for any region* R, $f \in \mathbb{Q}[V]$.

Proof. Let $\mathcal{I}_1 = \mathrm{isub}_R(\mathcal{D})$ and $\mathcal{I}_2 = \mathrm{isub}_R(\mathbf{t}_{\mathrm{group}}(\mathcal{D}, \hat{s}, f))$. We have to prove that $\langle\!\langle \mathcal{I}_2 \rangle\!\rangle \subseteq \langle\!\langle \mathcal{I}_1 \rangle\!\rangle$, i.e., $\{\mathrm{Pr}^{\mathcal{M}}(s_I \leadsto \smiley) \mid \mathcal{M} \in \mathrm{MC}(\mathcal{I}_2)\} \subseteq \{\mathrm{Pr}^{\mathcal{M}}(s_I \leadsto \smiley) \mid \mathcal{M} \in \mathrm{MC}(\mathcal{I}_1)\}$. We consider an MC induced by $\mathcal{I}_2$ and show that we can (re)construct another MC induced by $\mathcal{I}_1$ with the same reachability probability. Let $c, c_1, \ldots, c_k$ and $y_1, \ldots, y_k$ be defined as in Definition 11. For $\mathcal{M} \in \mathrm{MC}(\mathcal{I}_2)$, let $x = \mathcal{P}^{\mathcal{M}}(\hat{s}, s')$ and $y_i = \mathcal{P}^{\mathcal{M}}(\hat{s}, s_i)$, then (re)construct $\mathcal{M}' \in \mathrm{MC}(\mathcal{I}_1)$ s.t. $\mathcal{P}(\hat{s}, s_i) = y_i + c_i \cdot x/c$. Then, $\mathrm{Pr}^{\mathcal{M}}(s_I \leadsto \smiley) = \mathrm{Pr}^{\mathcal{M}'}(s_I \leadsto \smiley)$. □

Example 9. Creating shortcuts and grouping together *reorders* parametric transitions to come before constant transitions. Consider the pMCs $\mathcal{D}_a$ in Fig. 10c and $\mathcal{D}_c$ in Fig. 10c. $\mathcal{D}_c$ takes the p-transition before taking the constant transitions.

Our algorithm never changes the order in which parameters occur along a path, because reordering parameters tends to lead to non-tightening transitions.

Example 10. Consider $\mathcal{D}$ and $\mathcal{D}'$ with $\mathcal{D} \equiv \mathcal{D}'$ in Fig. 11. Regions $R = [0.1, 0.5] \times [0.6, 0.7]$, $R' = [0.6, 0.7] \times [0.1, 0.5]$ yield $\langle\!\langle \mathrm{isub}_R(\mathcal{D}) \rangle\!\rangle = \langle\!\langle \mathrm{isub}_{R'}(\mathcal{D}') \rangle\!\rangle = [0.22, 0.66]$ and $\langle\!\langle \mathrm{isub}_R(\mathcal{D}') \rangle\!\rangle = \langle\!\langle \mathrm{isub}_{R'}(\mathcal{D}) \rangle\!\rangle = [0.33, 0.55]$. Consequently, any transformation $\mathbf{t}$ with either $\mathbf{t}(\mathcal{D}) = \mathcal{D}'$ or $\mathbf{t}(\mathcal{D}') = \mathcal{D}$ is *not* tightening. A similar observation appears in flip-hoisting [16]. Note that one could intersect these region estimates and always tighten estimates with the result. We leave this as future work.

6.4 Big-Step Transformation Algorithm for pMCs

We combine shortcuts and grouping into the big-step algorithm. Its steps are:

Step 1: Find a suitable sub-pMC rooted in some $\hat{s} \in S$ over $p \in V$ (or terminate).
Step 2: Construct the shortcut pMC $\mathbf{t}_{\mathrm{shortcut}}(\mathcal{D}, \mathcal{D}_{\hat{s},p})$.
Step 3: If possible, construct grouping pMCs $\mathbf{t}_{\mathrm{group}}(\mathcal{D}', \hat{s}, \cdot)$. Go to step 1.

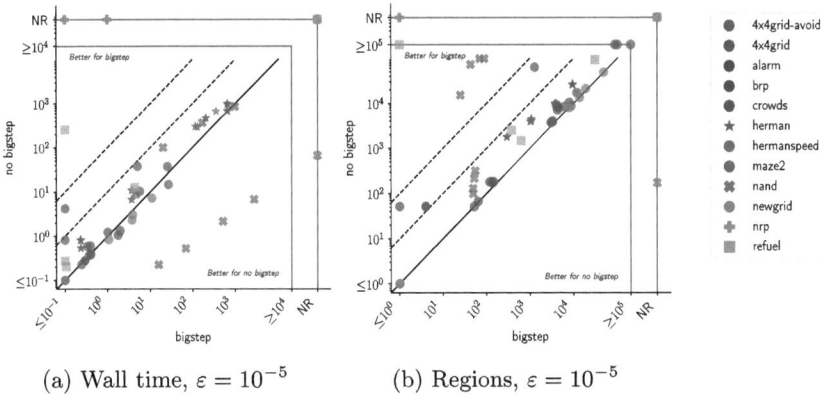

Fig. 12. Effectiveness of the big-step transformation (Q1)

Step 1: Picking transformations over $(\hat{s}, p)$. States $\hat{s} \in S$ are selected through a stack, which is initially a topological ordering from the initial state, and all parameters $p \in V$ are selected such that each $(\hat{s}, p)$ is visited once. Applying transformations only makes sense if $\mathcal{D}_{\hat{s},p}$ has more than one occurrence of p. To check this efficiently, we define a map $\gamma \colon S \times V \to 2^S$, such that for all $s \in \gamma(\hat{s}, p)$, s is reachable from $\hat{s}$ by constant transitions and s has a p-transition. The mapping γ is computable by a standard graph search. We pick $(\hat{s}, p)$ if

$$|\gamma(\hat{s},p)| \geq 2 \quad \text{or} \quad \Big(\gamma(\hat{s},p) = \{s\} \text{ and } \exists s' \in S : \mathcal{P}(s,s') \neq 0 \wedge \gamma(s',p) \neq \emptyset\Big).$$

The above condition implies the existence of a suitable sub-pMC $\mathcal{D}_{\hat{s},p}$ with more than one occurrence of p. Additionally, checking that we will make at least one state from $\mathcal{D}$ unreachable in an iteration on $(\hat{s}, p)$ makes the algorithm terminate.

Step 2: Applying $\mathsf{t}_{\text{shortcut}}$. We compute $\mathcal{D}_{\hat{s},p}$ using a DFS, where we add reachable states s if they conform to Definition 9 and if $|\gamma(s,p)| \neq \emptyset$. We then compute $\mathsf{t}_{\text{shortcut}}(\mathcal{D}, \mathcal{D}_{\hat{s},p})$ as discussed in [30, Appendix D].

Step 3: Applying $\mathsf{t}_{\text{group}}$. With $\mathcal{D}'$ starting as the shortcut pMC, we compute $\mathcal{D}' \leftarrow \mathsf{t}_{\text{group}}(\mathcal{D}', \hat{s}, f)$ if we find at least two shortcuts with a common factor f. This is done repeatedly until no more common factors are found. Assuming a factorized representation of polynomials, their common factors can be identified by a syntactical comparison. The new states s' are pushed to the top of the stack. Grouping changes the map γ, which has to be recomputed locally.

Theorem 3. *The big-step transformation is tightening in the sense of Definition 8.*

Theorem 3 follows from Lemmas 3 and 4. The big-step transformation may result in iMCs with large polynomial transitions. We use a Newton method to compute an iMC that substitutes $\mathcal{D}$ in R, cf. [30, Appendix F].

7 Experiments

Research Questions and Methodology. We evaluate the performance of GPL and the big-step transformation (Q1&2) and the wider applicability of GPL (Q3&4):

- (Q1) What is the effect of the big-step transformation (Sect. 6.4)?
- (Q2) How does GPL's performance compare against standard PL [45]? Can GPL compete with standard PL on benchmarks supported by both?
- (Q3) Is GPL efficient on regions that standard PL cannot handle?
- (Q4) Can GPL efficiently analyze a family of pMCs using discrete parameters?

We implemented GPL and the big-step transformation in Storm [32], improving upon its implementation of robust value iteration (VI) on iMCs [42]. The implementation is released as an open-source component of Storm. The experiments ran on a single core of an AMD Ryzen TRP 5965WX with 60 min timeout and 32 GB available memory. We use VI with default precision of 10^{-6}. For region refinement (Sect. 5), we split on four parameters. Preliminary experiments indicated that the results are not sensitive to this hyperparameter. Our benchmarks consist of a model $\mathcal{D}$, a region R, and a specification φ.

Q1: What is the effect of the big-step transformation? We compare number of regions and runtime for GPL with and without big-step transformation.

Setup. We consider simple pMCs (`4x4grid`, `evade`, `maze2`, `nrp`, `refuel`) synthesized from POMDPs [1,36], pMCs from [45,54] (`brp`, `crowds`, `nand`, `herman`, `hermanspeed`), and a pMC generated from a Bayesian network (`alarm`) from [48]. Of those pMCs, we choose multiple instances that (a) require at least one refinement step and (b) are solvable in 60 minutes in at least one case. We verify five different regions on each benchmark: $[0.2, 1]^{|V|}$, $[0, 0.8]^{|V|}$, and $[\delta, 1 - \delta]^{|V|}$ for $\delta \in \{0, 10^{-6}, 0.1\}$. Note that most of these regions are not graph preserving. We obtain challenging probability thresholds for the specifications using gradient descent (GD) [31] by running GD for at least ten converging iterations and using the best value that it has found. We add an $\varepsilon \in \{10^{-1}, 10^{-2}, 10^{-4}, 10^{-5}\}$ away from the optimum and ask GPL to verify it. The task thus is to prove the ε-optimality of the bound found by GD. We do not run experiments on trivial probability thresholds like $\lambda = 1.01$. Instances where the specification does not hold are excluded from our evaluation, as they can be efficiently solved by GD. Here, we enabled the standard splitting heuristic in PL. In [30, Appendix H], we confirm that our observations also hold when regions are split by round-robin.

Results. Figures 12a and 12b compare the performance of GPL with and without the big-step transformation for $\varepsilon = 10^{-5}$. The (log-scale!) plots show the wall time of the entire Storm execution and the number of regions needed to prove the specification φ. A point (x, y) indicates that GPL needed x seconds (regions) to prove φ with the big-step transformation and y seconds (regions) without. Points above the diagonal mean that the big-step transformation is beneficial, the two dashed lines indicate an improvement of factor 10 and 100 respectively. Detailed results, also for other values of ε, are in [30, Appendix G]. Smaller ε constitute

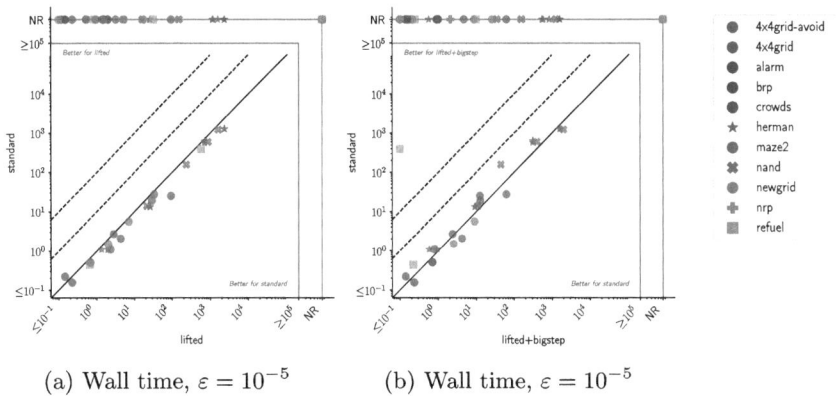

(a) Wall time, $\varepsilon = 10^{-5}$ (b) Wall time, $\varepsilon = 10^{-5}$

Fig. 13. Comparison of generalized and standard PL (Q2). Many no-result points for standard PL indicate that the benchmark is not supported as the region is not graph preserving

more difficult benchmarks that require more region refinements, as they imply the statement for all larger ε. In [30, Appendix I], we compare against standard PL.

Discussion. The big-step transformation reduces the number of regions on almost all models. GPL with big-step solves nrp within one region and two seconds, even on an instance with 100 parameters, while GPL without big-step already times out on the instance with five parameters. We illustrate what happens on nrp in [30, Appendix E]. Big-step also helps tremendously in other cases, such as refuel (34 parameters) and some nand (2 parameters). While nrp has many parameters that big-step reorders, nand has many parameters from which big-step creates shortcuts. While proving the bound on some regions on nand is much faster with the big-step algorithm enabled, the algorithm without is faster on other regions, outcompeting the transformation time. The big-step overhead usually pays off, as it is rarely the case that the added transformation time outweighs the time saved while running GPL. Further experiments show that the transformation scales to many states, but handling large shortcuts, as in nand, is expensive in our implementation, which can be improved in the future.

Q2: How does GPL's performance compare against standard PL?

Setup. We now compare GPL without big-step transformation to standard PL. We use the benchmarks from Q1 with graph-preserving regions, as the others cannot be handled by standard PL. We drop the non-monotonic hermanspeed benchmark as it is not supported by standard PL. We measure wall-clock time on the benchmarks where the execution took more than one second.

Results. On average, GPL needs 1.46x the runtime of standard PL on these benchmarks, with a median of 1.37x. In Fig. 13a, we compare wall-time between generalized and standard PL on simple pMCs. In Fig. 13b, we show the same with the big-step transformation enabled on generalized PL. The runtimes of the algorithms scale equally on harder benchmarks. The `4x4grid-avoid` benchmark is comparatively much slower for generalized PL than for standard PL, we have not investigated why this is. It becomes faster than standard PL with big-step enabled. We present more detailed results in [30, Appendix I].

Discussion. The runtime overhead of GPL is mostly due to performing VI on iMCs which takes slightly more time per iteration compared to value iteration on MDPs, which is used by PL. A hybrid iMC/MDP approach could speed up GPL.

Q3: Is GPL efficient on regions that standard PL cannot handle?

Setup. We have already seen in Q1 that GPL can handle not-graph-preserving regions. We further evaluate performance on a handcrafted, parameterized pMCs $\mathcal{D}_n = (\{s_0, \ldots, s_n, ☺, ☹\}, \{p_1, \ldots, p_{n-1}\}, s_0, \mathcal{P})$, where $1 \leq n \leq 32$, $\mathcal{P}(s_0, s_i) = p_i$ $(1 \leq i < n)$, $\mathcal{P}(s_0, s_n) = 1 - \sum_{1 \leq i < n} p_i$, and $\mathcal{P}(s_i, ☺) = 1/i = 1 - \mathcal{P}(s_i, ☹)$ $(1 \leq i \leq n)$. $\mathcal{D}_n$ reflects a multi-parameter distribution coming out of the initial state s_0—a worst-case scenario for standard PL as the used MDP abstraction requires 2^{n-1} distinct actions. See [30, Appendix J]. We consider the specification $\varphi = \Pr(s_0 \leadsto ☺) \geq 0.01$ with regions $R_1 = [10^{-6}, 1/n]^{n-1}$, $R_2 = [0, 1/n]^{n-1}$, and $R_3 = [0, 2/n]^{n-1}$. Only R_1 is supported by standard PL. R_2 and R_3 are not graph preserving and R_3 is also not well defined.

Results. Standard PL takes 126.0 s to verify R_1 for $n = 23$ and has a mem-out (>32 GB) for $n \geq 24$ allocating 2^{n-1} MDP actions. R_2 and R_3 are not supported.

Our proposed GPL proves φ on R_1, R_2 and R_3 without region refinement for all $1 \leq n \leq 32$ in under 1 s. Detailed results are in [30, Appendix J].

Discussion. GPL can efficiently verify the scaling benchmark on not-well-defined and not-graph-preserving regions. Verifying properties on pMCs with many parameters in a single state's distribution, even on graph-preserving and well-defined regions like R_1, only becomes feasible with generalized PL. As we discuss in Sect. 5.2, there is no simple way around this limitation in standard PL.

Q4: Can GPL efficiently analyze a family of pMCs?

Setup. We run an experiment on a pMC generated from a family of pMCs as discussed in Sect. 5.3. We use a variant of *Dynamic Power Management* [8,13] with 16 discrete and two continuous parameters. We choose the region $\{0, 1\}^{16} \times [0.4, 0.6] \times [0.7, 0.9]$. The discrete parameters describe the topology of DPM's controller, while the continuous parameters describe probabilities to start and continue sending packets. The bound we use is the one found by gradient descent[1] minus $\varepsilon = 10^{-5}$. We compare against enumerating all 2^{16} possible discrete parameter valuations and verifying each resulting pMC using (standard) PL.

---

[1] Ignoring the discreteness of some parameters. The bound is correct as GPL proves it.

Results and Discussion. GPL proves the property with a refinement into 128 subregions within 0.62 s. For 90 regions, verifying a *single* iMC implies the specification for *multiple* family members. GPL thus reasons effectively about the pMC family. Enumerating and solving all family members with PL takes 698.51 s.

8 Related Work

Closest to our work are abstraction-refinement loops for verifying pMCs [45], discussed in Sect. 1, and for related models in [2,12,14,26]. Crucially, the abstraction in these approaches ignores parameter dependencies between different states. Global monotonicity of certain parameters [51] allows avoiding useless region splits [52]. An application of PL to distributed protocols [54] overcomes the necessity for monotonic transition functions by splitting the region a-priori.

We compute solution functions in our shortcut transformation. Their computation is heavily studied, originally in [20,29,35,39]. A polynomial-time algorithm for a fixed number of parameters is given in [5]. Improvements of state-elimination include exploiting similarities between multiple models [25] and achieving speed-ups with a graph-like function representations [24]. Similarly to our pMC transformation, solution function computation that first considers fragments is investigated in [23]. Other computational problems on pMCs have gained quite some attention: For feasibility, dual to verification, incomplete approaches are popular [15,19,31] and scale to thousands of parameters. Discrete and continuous parameters are mixed in [11] to find locally Pareto-optimal designs. More work considers verification of pMDPs [43,46], pCTMCs [9], and MDPs with latent parameters [18].

Our pMC transformations have parallels in probabilistic programming. Flip-hoisting [16] merges parallel equivalent flip statements, while we merge parallel parameter transitions on the same parameter. Big-step semantics [55, p. 24] join sequential statements, while we join sequential parametric transitions. Our use on Newton's method to compute iMCs from pMCs given regions is taken from [41, p. 105]. Specialized variations of Newton's method have been used to verify recursive MCs [22] and recursive stochastic games [21].

9 Conclusion and Outlook

This paper presents generalized parameter lifting (GPL), an abstraction-refinement loop for pMC verification. GPL enhances the state of the art by its ability to solve a wider class of practically motivated pMCs on a wider class of parameter regions. In particular, in contrast to standard PL, GPL can prove specifications for every induced Markov chain of any given pMC. GPL also allows for a novel big-step transformation of pMCs that yields finer abstractions. Future work includes exploring new application areas of pMCs enabled by GPL and investigating pMC transformations that reorder parameters.

References

1. Andriushchenko, R., et al.: Tools at the frontiers of quantitative verification: QComp 2023 competition report. In: International TOOLympics Challenge, pp. 90–146. Springer (2024)
2. Andriushchenko, R., Bork, A., Ceska, M., Junges, S., Katoen, J., Macák, F.: Search and explore: symbiotic policy synthesis in POMDPs. In: CAV (3). Lecture Notes in Computer Science, vol. 13966, pp. 113–135. Springer (2023)
3. Andriushchenko, R., Ceska, M., Junges, S., Katoen, J., Stupinský, S.: PAYNT: a tool for inductive synthesis of probabilistic programs. In: CAV (1). Lecture Notes in Computer Science, vol. 12759, pp. 856–869. Springer (2021)
4. Badings, T.S., Simão, T.D., Suilen, M., Jansen, N.: Decision-making under uncertainty: beyond probabilities. Int. J. Softw. Tools Technol. Transf. **25**(3), 375–391 (2023)
5. Baier, C., Hensel, C., Hutschenreiter, L., Junges, S., Katoen, J., Klein, J.: Parametric Markov chains: PCTL complexity and fraction-free Gaussian elimination. Inf. Comput. **272**, 104504 (2020)
6. Baier, C., Katoen, J.: Principles of Model Checking. MIT Press (2008)
7. Benedikt, M., Lenhardt, R., Worrell, J.: LTL model checking of interval Markov chains. In: TACAS. Lecture Notes in Computer Science, vol. 7795, pp. 32–46. Springer (2013)
8. Benini, L., Bogliolo, A., Paleologo, G.A., Micheli, G.D.: Policy optimization for dynamic power management. IEEE Trans. Comput. Aided Des. Integr. Circuits Syst. **18**(6), 813–833 (1999)
9. Bortolussi, L., Silvetti, S.: Bayesian statistical parameter synthesis for linear temporal properties of stochastic models. In: TACAS (2). Lecture Notes in Computer Science, vol. 10806, pp. 396–413. Springer (2018)
10. Brázdil, T., et al.: Verification of Markov decision processes using learning algorithms. In: ATVA. Lecture Notes in Computer Science, vol. 8837, pp. 98–114. Springer (2014)
11. Calinescu, R., Ceska, M., Gerasimou, S., Kwiatkowska, M., Paoletti, N.: Designing robust software systems through parametric Markov chain synthesis. In: ICSA, pp. 131–140. IEEE Computer Society (2017)
12. Ceska, M., Dannenberg, F., Paoletti, N., Kwiatkowska, M., Brim, L.: Precise parameter synthesis for stochastic biochemical systems. Acta Informatica **54**(6), 589–623 (2017)
13. Ceska, M., Hensel, C., Junges, S., Katoen, J.: Counterexample-driven synthesis for probabilistic program sketches. In: FM. Lecture Notes in Computer Science, vol. 11800, pp. 101–120. Springer (2019)
14. Ceska, M., Jansen, N., Junges, S., Katoen, J.: Shepherding hordes of Markov chains. In: TACAS (2). Lecture Notes in Computer Science, vol. 11428, pp. 172–190. Springer (2019)
15. Chen, T., Hahn, E.M., Han, T., Kwiatkowska, M.Z., Qu, H., Zhang, L.: Model repair for Markov decision processes. In: TASE, pp. 85–92. IEEE Computer Society (2013)
16. Cheng, Y.H., Millstein, T., Van den Broeck, G., Holtzen, S.: flip-hoisting: exploiting repeated parameters in discrete probabilistic programs. In: International Conference on Probabilistic Programming (PROBPROG) (2021)
17. Chrszon, P., Dubslaff, C., Klüppelholz, S., Baier, C.: Profeat: feature-oriented engineering for family-based probabilistic model checking. Formal Aspects Comput. **30**(1), 45–75 (2018)

18. Costen, C., Rigter, M., Lacerda, B., Hawes, N.: Planning with hidden parameter polynomial MDPs. In: AAAI, pp. 11963–11971. AAAI Press (2023)
19. Cubuktepe, M., Jansen, N., Junges, S., Katoen, J., Topcu, U.: Convex optimization for parameter synthesis in MDPs. IEEE Trans. Autom. Control **67**(12), 6333–6348 (2022)
20. Daws, C.: Symbolic and parametric model checking of discrete-time Markov chains. In: ICTAC. Lecture Notes in Computer Science, vol. 3407, pp. 280–294. Springer (2004)
21. Esparza, J., Gawlitza, T., Kiefer, S., Seidl, H.: Approximative methods for monotone systems of min-max-polynomial equations. In: ICALP (1). Lecture Notes in Computer Science, vol. 5125, pp. 698–710. Springer (2008)
22. Etessami, K., Yannakakis, M.: Recursive Markov chains, stochastic grammars, and monotone systems of nonlinear equations. J. ACM **56**(1), 1:1–1:66 (2009)
23. Fang, X., Calinescu, R., Gerasimou, S., Alhwikem, F.: Fast parametric model checking with applications to software performability analysis. IEEE Trans. Software Eng. **49**(10), 4707–4730 (2023)
24. Gainer, P., Hahn, E.M., Schewe, S.: Accelerated model checking of parametric Markov chains. In: ATVA. Lecture Notes in Computer Science, vol. 11138, pp. 300–316. Springer (2018)
25. Gainer, P., Hahn, E.M., Schewe, S.: Incremental verification of parametric and reconfigurable Markov chains. In: QEST. Lecture Notes in Computer Science, vol. 11024, pp. 140–156. Springer (2018)
26. Giro, S., Rabe, M.N.: Verification of partial-information probabilistic systems using counterexample-guided refinements. In: ATVA. Lecture Notes in Computer Science, vol. 7561, pp. 333–348. Springer (2012)
27. Givan, R., Dean, T.L., Greig, M.: Equivalence notions and model minimization in Markov decision processes. Artif. Intell. **147**(1–2), 163–223 (2003)
28. Haddad, S., Monmege, B.: Interval iteration algorithm for MDPs and IMDPs. Theor. Comput. Sci. **735**, 111–131 (2018)
29. Hahn, E.M., Hermanns, H., Zhang, L.: Probabilistic reachability for parametric Markov models. Int. J. Softw. Tools Technol. Transf. **13**(1), 3–19 (2011)
30. Heck, L., Quatmann, T., Spel, J., Katoen, J., Junges, S.: Generalized parameter lifting: finer abstractions for parametric Markov chains. CoRR abs/2504.05965 (2025)
31. Heck, L., Spel, J., Junges, S., Moerman, J., Katoen, J.: Gradient-descent for randomized controllers under partial observability. In: VMCAI. Lecture Notes in Computer Science, vol. 13182, pp. 127–150. Springer (2022)
32. Hensel, C., Junges, S., Katoen, J., Quatmann, T., Volk, M.: The probabilistic model checker storm. Int. J. Softw. Tools Technol. Transf. **24**(4), 589–610 (2022)
33. Jansen, N., Junges, S., Katoen, J.: Parameter synthesis in Markov models: a gentle survey. In: Principles of Systems Design. Lecture Notes in Computer Science, vol. 13660, pp. 407–437. Springer (2022)
34. Jonsson, B., Larsen, K.G.: Specification and refinement of probabilistic processes. In: LICS, pp. 266–277. IEEE Computer Society (1991)
35. Junges, S., et al.: Parameter synthesis for Markov models: covering the parameter space. Formal Methods Syst. Des. **62**(1), 181–259 (2024)
36. Junges, S., et al.: Finite-state controllers of POMDPs using parameter synthesis. In: UAI, pp. 519–529. AUAI Press (2018)
37. Junges, S., Katoen, J., Pérez, G.A., Winkler, T.: The complexity of reachability in parametric Markov decision processes. J. Comput. Syst. Sci. **119**, 183–210 (2021)

38. Kwiatkowska, M.Z., Norman, G., Parker, D.: PRISM 4.0: verification of probabilistic real-time systems. In: CAV. Lecture Notes in Computer Science, vol. 6806, pp. 585–591. Springer (2011)
39. Lanotte, R., Maggiolo-Schettini, A., Troina, A.: Parametric probabilistic transition systems for system design and analysis. Formal Aspects Comput. **19**(1), 93–109 (2007)
40. Meggendorfer, T., Weininger, M., Wienhöft, P.: Solving robust Markov decision processes: generic, reliable, efficient. In: AAAI, pp. 26631–26641. AAAI Press (2025)
41. Moore, R.E., Kearfott, R.B., Cloud, M.J.: Introduction to Interval Analysis. SIAM (2009)
42. Nilim, A., Ghaoui, L.E.: Robust control of Markov decision processes with uncertain transition matrices. Oper. Res. **53**(5), 780–798 (2005)
43. Polgreen, E., Wijesuriya, V.B., Haesaert, S., Abate, A.: Automated experiment design for data-efficient verification of parametric Markov decision processes. In: QEST. Lecture Notes in Computer Science, vol. 10503, pp. 259–274. Springer (2017)
44. Puggelli, A., Li, W., Sangiovanni-Vincentelli, A.L., Seshia, S.A.: Polynomial-time verification of PCTL properties of MDPs with convex uncertainties. In: CAV. Lecture Notes in Computer Science, vol. 8044, pp. 527–542. Springer (2013)
45. Quatmann, T., Dehnert, C., Jansen, N., Junges, S., Katoen, J.: Parameter synthesis for Markov models: faster than ever. In: ATVA. Lecture Notes in Computer Science, vol. 9938, pp. 50–67 (2016)
46. Rickard, L., Abate, A., Margellos, K.: Learning robust policies for uncertain parametric Markov decision processes. In: L4DC. Proceedings of Machine Learning Research, vol. 242, pp. 876–889. PMLR (2024)
47. Rodrigues, G.N., et al.: Modeling and verification for probabilistic properties in software product lines. In: HASE, pp. 173–180. IEEE Computer Society (2015)
48. Salmani, B., Katoen, J.: Automatically finding the right probabilities in Bayesian networks. J. Artif. Intell. Res. **77**, 1637–1696 (2023)
49. Schaefer, M., Cardinal, J., Miltzow, T.: The existential theory of the reals as a complexity class: a compendium. CoRR abs/2407.18006 (2024)
50. Sen, K., Viswanathan, M., Agha, G.: Model-checking Markov chains in the presence of uncertainties. In: TACAS. Lecture Notes in Computer Science, vol. 3920, pp. 394–410. Springer (2006)
51. Spel, J., Junges, S., Katoen, J.: Are parametric Markov chains monotonic? In: ATVA. Lecture Notes in Computer Science, vol. 11781, pp. 479–496. Springer (2019)
52. Spel, J., Junges, S., Katoen, J.: Finding provably optimal Markov chains. In: TACAS (1). Lecture Notes in Computer Science, vol. 12651, pp. 173–190. Springer (2021)
53. Vandin, A., ter Beek, M.H., Legay, A., Lluch-Lafuente, A.: Qflan: a tool for the quantitative analysis of highly reconfigurable systems. In: FM. Lecture Notes in Computer Science, vol. 10951, pp. 329–337. Springer (2018)
54. Volk, M., Bonakdarpour, B., Katoen, J., Aflaki, S.: Synthesizing optimal bias in randomized self-stabilization. Distributed Comput. **35**(1), 37–57 (2022)
55. Winskel, G.: The Formal Semantics of Programming Languages - An Introduction. Foundation of Computing Series. MIT Press (1993)

Towards Unified Probabilistic Verification and Validation of Vision-Based Autonomy

Jordan Peper[1](✉), Yan Miao[2], Sayan Mitra[2], and Ivan Ruchkin[1]

[1] University of Florida, Gainesville, FL 32611, USA
jpeper@ufl.edu
[2] University of Illinois at Urbana-Champaign, Champaign, IL 61820, USA

Abstract. Precise and comprehensive situational awareness is a critical capability of modern autonomous systems. Deep neural networks that perceive task-critical details from rich sensory signals have become ubiquitous; however, their black-box behavior and sensitivity to environmental uncertainty and distribution shifts make them challenging to verify formally. Abstraction-based verification techniques for vision-based autonomy produce safety guarantees contingent on rigid assumptions, such as bounded errors or known unique distributions. Such overly restrictive and inflexible assumptions limit the validity of the guarantees, especially in diverse and uncertain test-time environments. We propose a methodology that unifies the verification models of perception with their offline validation. Our methodology leverages interval MDPs and provides a flexible end-to-end guarantee that adapts directly to the out-of-distribution test-time conditions. We evaluate our methodology on a synthetic perception Markov chain with well-defined state estimation distributions and a mountain car benchmark. Our findings reveal that we can guarantee tight yet rigorous bounds on overall system safety.
Code: https://github.com/Trustworthy-Engineered-Autonomy-Lab/unified-perception-vnv.

Keywords: Neural perception · Safety verification · Probabilistic validation · Interval Markov decision process

---

The authors thank Alessandro Abate for a discussion of Bayesian validation of Markov models, and Thomas Waite and Radoslav Ivanov for sharing their implementation of the vision-based mountain car.

 This material is based on research sponsored by AFRL/RW under agreement number FA8651-24-1-0007 and the NSF CAREER award CNS-2440920. The U.S. Government is authorized to reproduce and distribute reprints for Governmental purposes notwithstanding any copyright notation thereon. The opinions, findings, views, or conclusions contained herein are those of the authors and should not be interpreted as representing the official policies or endorsements, either expressed or implied, of the DAF, AFRL, NSF, or the U.S. Government.

© The Author(s), under exclusive license to Springer Nature Switzerland AG 2026
M. D'Souza et al. (Eds.): ATVA 2025, LNCS 16145, pp. 231–259, 2026.
https://doi.org/10.1007/978-3-032-08707-2_11

1 Introduction

Deep vision models are used to process rich sensory signals in safety-critical closed-loop systems – from autonomous driving [11,77] and robotic surgery [86] to aircraft control [25,26]. Nevertheless, verifying neural-perception systems remains a formidable challenge [69] due to their fragile nature [52,88]. The foremost obstacles include accurate modeling of visual signals in a verifiable way [77] and devising logical specifications for the neural models [3,45].

Assume-Guarantee (A/G) reasoning is a standard method for modular verification of complex systems [10,84]. In the A/G framework, one specifies the assumptions on the system's components and then verifies each component's guarantees under these assumptions, and this chain of reasoning establishes the system-level properties. To apply A/G reasoning to vision-based autonomous systems, a typical decomposition would be into *observer* and *controller* components. The observer process would include the image formation (from the state) as well as state estimation (from one or more images).

A/G reasoning has indeed been applied to vision-based systems with such decompositions. First, as a precursor to modeling visual uncertainties, A/G specifications have been extended to probabilistic uncertainties [74]. Another A/G-style technique, called *perception contracts* [3,44], computes bounds on the accuracy of the observer such that these bounds are sufficient to verify the closed-loop system. Similarly, constructing stochastic assumptions on the observer has enabled the probabilistic verification of vision-based systems in [13,17,18,77]. However, vision-based observers are well-known to be fragile and vulnerable to distribution shifts [33,95], which can violate the assumptions when the system is deployed in a new environment. Thus, a fundamental gap remains between A/G verification and the validity of those assumptions in the deployed system.

This paper aims to extend the scope of verification guarantees for vision-based systems by measuring the validity of modeling assumptions. To this end, we introduce a *unified verification & validation methodology* to obtain a safety guarantee that is flexibly degraded when the assumptions – in the form of a probabilistic model – are likely to be invalid in a new environment. The key idea is that a probabilistic safety guarantee for the ground truth system M_E modeled in environment E is contingent on a statistical claim about the model's validity in a new environment E', in the style of the Probably Approximately Correct (PAC) bounds [37]. This will be represented with nested probabilistic assertions.

Our methodology consists of three steps: abstraction, verification, and validation. The abstraction step represents neural perception's uncertainty with confidence intervals, leading to an *interval Markov decision process (IMDP)* abstraction $\mathcal{M}_E$. This abstraction overapproximates the concrete system M_E with confidence α (i.e., with probability $1 - \alpha$, $\mathcal{M}_E$ will contain the behavior distribution of M_E). At a high level, $\mathcal{M}_E$ represents a set of possible closed-loop systems with uncertainties in observer and dynamics, that are consistent with the data obtained from M_E.

The verification step checks a system-level temporal property φ on the constructed IMDP $\mathcal{M}_E$ with a probabilistic model checker [40,54]. It produces an upper bound β on the chance that a trajectory falsifies property φ. A combination of the first and second steps gives rise to a frequentist-style guarantee of the form: with confidence α in the dataset from which $\mathcal{M}_E$ was built, the chance that the underlying system M_E produces a safe trajectory is at least $1-\beta$.

The third step is to validate our IMDP abstraction $\mathcal{M}_E$ in a new environment E'. Here, we aim to measure the probability that the new concrete model $M_{E'}$ is contained in $\mathcal{M}_E$ – and thus we pivot to the Bayesian perspective. Instead of formulating a frequentist hypothesis test (which would merely detect a significant difference between E and E'), we construct a belief on the *parameters* of $M_{E'}$ based on the new data. Then, "intersecting" it with the probability intervals in IMDP $\mathcal{M}_E$ gives us a quantitative posterior $1-\gamma$ chance of the new environment E' falling within the uncertainty of $\mathcal{M}_E$. Hence, with confidence $1-\gamma$, the system $M_{E'}$ satisfies the property φ with probability $1-\beta$. This nested guarantee elegantly combines the two approaches: frequentist and Bayesian.

We evaluate our methodology on two case studies: (1) a synthetic waypoint-following task and (2) a vision-based mountain car system. Results demonstrate that our methodology yields a flexible trade-off between safety within a model and validity of the model in the presence of perceptual uncertainty. Furthermore, our validation procedure reliably discriminates between systems operating within the training distribution and those operating in domain-shifted environments.

This paper makes three contributions:

1. A unified framework for verifying the safety of vision-based autonomous systems and validating them in a deployment environment.
2. A flexible nested probabilistic guarantee for both verification and validation.
3. An evaluation of our framework in two case studies.

The rest of this paper is organized as follows. Section 2 surveys related work. Section 3 formulates our problem of making rigorous yet flexible guarantees that unify verification and validation. In Sect. 4, we describe our approach to addressing each subproblem in order, Finally, we evaluate this methodology on two case studies in Sect. 5, and then conclude with Sect. 6.

2 Related Work

Contracts and Assume/Guarantee Reasoning. Methodologies for assuring safety-critical software and systems originate from a rich tradition of compositionality [7,57,80,83], contracts [38,46,62,82], and assume-guarantee reasoning [35,36,56,81]. An engineer annotates each component with assumptions on its inputs and guarantees on its outputs; then, the two can be composed if the first component's guarantees satisfy the second's assumptions. Recently, stochastic [60,73,74] and neural-network [27,71] contracts attempt to handle uncertainties in learning components. Unfortunately, they do not offer a complete or straightforward solution to specifying and verifying vision-based systems.

Probabilistic Modeling and Verification. Probabilistic model checking [49,55] is a well-developed technique to check properties of various system models that exhibit probabilistic and non-deterministic transitions [43,53]. The oft-cited scalability issue can be tackled with assume-guarantee reasoning [32,51,56] and model counting [41,91], as well as model reduction [9], sampling [30,59], and restructuring [22,79]. There is a vast literature about creating automata-based abstractions from detailed system descriptions [1,42,63,65,96]. The uncertainty from data can be accounted for by inferring confidence intervals over model parameters [2,4,21]. This leads us to a class of models with sets of transition probabilities, known under the diverse names of uncertain/imprecise/interval/set/robust Markov models [5,23,48,76,89,90,94,99]. Our approach leverages these insights to construct and verify an interval Markov model of a vision-based closed-loop system.

Probabilistic Model Validation. Whether a probabilistic model is valid can be quantified in several ways. If model validity is conceptualized as a stochastic binary event, it can be characterized by a probability estimate [20] or confidence interval [8,34,39]. Numerical notions of robustness [24,31,58] and risk [16,64] offer directional, smooth uncertainty quantification. At run time, model validity can be determined via confidence monitoring [78] or parameter sampling [14]. Our methodology adopts a distributional perspective [15,29]: model validity is the inclusion of the true distribution into the modeled set, operationalized via the Bayesian approach to safety validation [70].

Perception Abstractions and Contracts. To model vision-based perception, most formal approaches use simple error probabilities and noise parameters [6,18,28,93,96]. Other approaches build detailed models of specific vision systems, such as aircraft landing cameras [85] or racing car LiDARs [47]. Sadly, such approaches have limited expressiveness and do not generalize to real-world systems. To obtain guarantees, perception contracts [3,44,61,87] assume a bound on the accuracy of a vision-based state estimator such that these bounds are sufficient for formally verifying closed-loop invariants [44] or Lyapunov functions [61]. In a similar vein, recent works on model checking vision systems have constructed a verifiable probabilistic model [17–19,77]. None of these approaches have been investigated (let alone provide guarantees) when the visual distribution changes from the one for which the model was built.

3 Problem Formulation

In this paper, we address the *composite problem* of (i) building a sound abstraction of perception from sample executions of a vision-based autonomous system, (ii) providing rigorous safety guarantees, and (iii) validating these guarantees in an offline deployment setting. We first introduce our system notation, then transition into our *three primary subproblems*.

Consider the closed-loop discrete-time dynamical system M_E that is composed of black-box sensing and perception processes (hereafter, "state estimation") operating under the randomness of the latent environment distribution E, and subsequently a deterministic, known control loop:

$$M_E : \begin{cases} \text{Sensing:} & o_t = g(s_t, e_t \sim E) \\ \text{Perception:} & \hat{s}_t = h(o_t) \end{cases} \text{State estimation} \\ \begin{cases} \text{Control policy:} & u_t = \pi(\hat{s}_t) \\ \text{Dynamics:} & s_{t+1} = f(s_t, u_t) \end{cases} \text{Control loop} \quad (1)$$

The operational domain of the closed-loop system M_E is deployed in an environment E – an unknown probability distribution that characterizes the uncertain behavior of a domain. At any time t, a single realization $e_t \in \mathcal{E}$ is drawn from the probability distribution E. Further, $s_t \in S \subset \mathbb{R}^n$ is the system state (e.g., position, class label); $o_t \in O \subset \mathbb{R}^k$ is the observation of this state and environment (e.g., a camera image or a LiDAR scan); $\hat{s}_t \in \hat{S} \subset \mathbb{R}^n$ is an estimate of the system state; and $u_t \in U \subset \mathbb{R}^m$ is the control action. An observation of the latent environment at a given state is made with the sensor $g : S \times \mathcal{E} \to O$, and the state estimates are made with the estimator $h : O \to \hat{S}$. Once $\hat{s}_t$ is computed from the state estimation process, a control action is determined with the policy $\pi : \hat{S} \to U$, and the state is updated with the dynamics $f : S \times U \to S$.

Given system M_E in some environment E (e.g., an autonomous drone or self-driving car), its *execution* is a pair of true and estimated trajectories $\tau = (s, \hat{s}) \sim [\![M_E]\!]$, where operator $[\![.]\!]$ means the model semantics (in this case, the distribution over trajectories). Each trajectory is based on the trace of *environment realizations* e. In the case of a model M with a fixed environment E, $[\![M_E]\!]$ can be interpreted as the distribution over all possible τ executions of M_E.

Furthermore, we will construct an abstraction function ψ such that $\psi(\tau) = \tau^\psi$, where τ^ψ is a discrete-space execution of M_E. This induces an abstract model $\mathcal{M}_E$. Here, the semantics $[\![\mathcal{M}_E]\!]$ is a set of distributions over τ resulting from conservative over-approximation. We slightly abuse the notation $[\![\psi(M_E)]\!]$ to mean the distribution over abstract, discrete-space executions of M_E.

With this notation, we describe the three problems solved in this work:

Problem 1 (Data-driven abstraction). Suppose we have a real physical system M_E, with a known controller π and dynamics f, from which we collect a dataset of *executions* $\mathcal{D}^{train}$ drawn according to $[\![M_E]\!]$. Our goal is to use this dataset to derive an abstract model $\mathcal{M}_E$ that satisfies:

$$[\![\psi(M_E)]\!] \in [\![\mathcal{M}_E]\!], \quad (2)$$

Problem 2 (Safety verification). Suppose we are given $\mathcal{M}_E$, which is an abstract model of M_E, and a co-safe linear temporal logic (LTL) property φ. The problem is to compute the worst-case logical satisfaction probability of the LTL predicate φ on $\mathcal{M}_E$:

$$\Pr^{min}_{[\![\mathcal{M}_E]\!]}(\varphi) \geq 1 - \beta \quad (3)$$

Problem 3 (Design-time validation). Suppose we are given $\mathcal{M}_E$, which is an abstract model of M_E, a novel deployment environment E', a dataset $\mathcal{D}^{val}$ of *executions* τ, where $\tau \sim [\![M_{E'}]\!]$, and a prior belief $\mathbb{M}^{pr}$ about the model $M_{E'}$ which is a distribution over candidate models M. The problem is to obtain the posterior $\mathbb{M}^{po}$ by updating the belief $\mathbb{M}^{pr}$ with $\mathcal{D}^{val}$, and then compute the conformance confidence γ that $[\![M_{E'}]\!]$ is characterized by some distribution in $\mathcal{M}$. Formally:

$$\Pr\nolimits_{\mathbb{M}^{po}}([\![M]\!] \in [\![\mathcal{M}_E]\!] \mid M \sim \mathbb{M}^{po}) \geq 1 - \gamma \qquad (4)$$

4 Approach: Abstraction, Verification, and Validation

This section describes our three-step methodology illustrated in Fig. 1:

- Subsect. 4.1 expands on Problem 1 of forming a sound abstraction of a vision-based autonomous system and proposes leveraging an *interval Markov decision process* (IMDP) to model imprecise knowledge about the true distribution of state estimates.
- Subsect. 4.2 addresses Problem 2 of verifying the system abstraction by leveraging well-explored probabilistic model checking techniques.
- Subsect. 4.3 reiterates Problem 3 of probabilistically validating the abstraction under a novel deployment environment and proposes a technique for modeling a posterior distribution over model parameters to measure their similarity to the abstraction parameters.

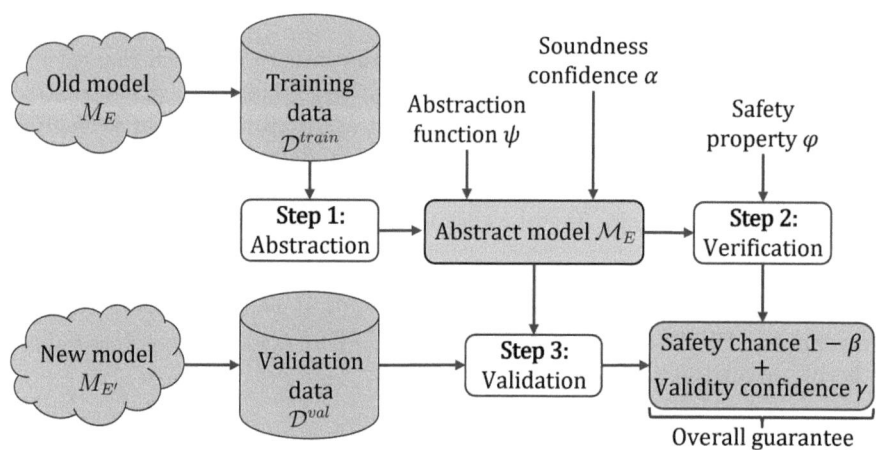

Fig. 1. Our verification & validation methodology in three steps.

Running Example. We utilize the OpenAI Gym [12] MountainCar-v0 benchmark (a widely adopted testbed for reinforcement learning) as a running example to clarify the algorithms throughout this section. This environment models a two-dimensional control problem with state variables $s = (x, v) \in [-1.2, 0.6] \times$

$[-0.07, 0.07]$, where x is the horizontal position of the vehicle and v is its velocity. At each timestep, the agent selects from actions $u \in \{0, 1, 2\}$, corresponding respectively to the application of a negative force (throttle leftward), no force, or a positive force (throttle rightward).

The objective of the Mountain Car is to reach the top of a steep incline by gaining momentum between the hills. The system is equipped with a pre-trained vision module that predicts the x-position of the car from third-person scene images. These predictions, alongside the ground-truth velocity v, are fed into a pre-trained Deep Q-Network (DQN) control policy π to obtain control action u.

4.1 Constructing Abstraction from Data

Recall the real-world closed-loop, discrete-time dynamical system M_E introduced in Eq. 1, which consists of a stochastic perception pipeline $h \circ g$ for state estimation—where g represents the observation process and h denotes the perception or inference model—governed by the randomness induced by a latent environment distribution E. This is followed by a known, deterministic control policy and dynamics composition $f \circ \pi$, where π is the policy mapping state estimates to control actions, and f propagates the system state forward in time.

An execution τ of M_E is drawn by sampling e from the operational environment E, making an observation of this environment $g : S \times \mathcal{E} \rightarrow O$, estimating the manifest state variables $h : O \rightarrow \hat{S}$, computing a control action $\pi : \hat{S} \rightarrow U$, and propagating the state $f : S \times U \rightarrow S$. Fundamentally, τ is a random variable which follows the unknown distribution of trajectories $[\![M_E]\!]$ induced by E. This formulation enables the precise definition of a sound abstraction in Definition 1.

Definition 1 (Sound abstraction). *Given the system M_E composed of deterministic components g, h, π, and f, subject to stochasticity from the latent environment distribution E, and an abstraction function $\psi : \mathbb{R}^n \rightarrow \mathbb{Z}^n$, a sound abstraction $\mathcal{M}_E$ is an abstract model that satisfies the inclusion:*

$$[\![\psi(M_E)]\!] \in [\![\mathcal{M}_E]\!]$$

We aim to construct a *sound abstraction* of M_E that over-approximates its behavior, leading to conservative safety estimates in the next subsection. The abstraction problem is intentionally formulated in a distribution-agnostic manner, i.e., the parameters of $[\![M_E]\!]$ are unknown, so we must construct $\mathcal{M}_E$ from a dataset $\mathcal{D}^{train}$ of N trajectories τ. The *data-driven abstraction problem* becomes constructing a *statistically sound abstraction* per Definition 2 since $\mathcal{D}^{train}$ is a finite set of executions.

Definition 2 (Statistically sound abstraction). *Given the system M_E composed of deterministic components g, h, π, and f, subject to stochasticity from the latent environment distribution E, and an abstraction function $\psi : \mathbb{R}^n \rightarrow \mathbb{Z}^n$, a dataset $\mathcal{D}^{train}$ of trajectories τ sampled i.i.d from $[\![M_E]\!]$, and a confidence level α, a statistically sound abstraction $\mathcal{M}_E$ is an abstract model that satisfies:*

$$[\![\psi(M_E)]\!] \in [\![\mathcal{M}_E]\!]$$

We first demonstrate how the real system M_E can be soundly transformed into a probabilistic automaton, then reiterate that its unknown transition probabilities must be statistically inferred from data.

Our approach considers state estimation and state propagation within M_E to be separable, yet sequentially-composed processes. In the concrete spaces S and $\hat{S}$, $g \circ h : S \times \mathcal{E} \times \hat{S} \to [0,1]$ is a probabilistic mapping, and $f \circ \pi : \hat{S} \to S$ is an injective mapping. This behavior can be represented as a simple Markov chain, as in Definition 3 below, where the state space $X = S \times \hat{S}$ consists of pairs of states and estimates, and $T : (S \times \hat{S}) \times (S \times \hat{S}) \to [0,1]$ is induced by the latent environment distribution E:

Definition 3 (Markov Chain). *A* Markov chain *is a triple (X, x_0, T), where X is the state space, $x_0 \in X$ is the initial state, and $T : X \times X \to [0,1]$ is the probabilistic transition function.*

However, model checking continuous-state Markov processes is challenging with current tools. One common workaround is to discretize the state space of the Markov chain, yielding a countable set of states and transitions. Let $\psi : \mathbb{R}^n \to \mathbb{N}^n$ be an abstraction function that maps the otherwise continuous space S into a countably infinite space S^ψ (and $\hat{S} \to \hat{S}^\psi$) of n-dimensional hypercubes.

In the abstract spaces S^ψ and $\hat{S}^\psi$, $g \circ h : S^\psi \times \mathcal{E} \times \hat{S}^\psi \to [0,1]$ is still a probabilistic mapping, but $f \circ \pi : \hat{S} \twoheadrightarrow S$ becomes a surjective mapping to over-approximate the model behavior. From this, we construct a discrete state Markov decision process, seen in Definition 4 below, where $X = S^\psi \times \hat{S}^\psi$.

Definition 4 (Markov Decision Process). *A* Markov decision process *is a tuple $(X, x_0, \omega, \delta, T)$, where X is the state space, $x_0 \in X$ is the initial state, ω is an alphabet of action labels, $\delta : X \to \omega$ is an adversary that resolves non-determinism, and $T : X \times \omega \times X \to [0,1]$ is the probabilistic transition function.*

Recall that we do not actually know the exact probabilistic transition function T. However, the information about it is present in our dataset $\mathcal{D}^{train}$. To perform a statistically rigorous approximation of this ground-truth MDP, which is a conservative discrete-state abstraction of the ground-truth MC, we use confidence intervals (CI) in place of single transition probabilities, resulting in an interval Markov decision process outlined in Definition 5, still with $X = S^\psi \times \hat{S}^\psi$

Definition 5 (Interval Markov Decision Process). *An* interval Markov decision process *is a tuple $(X, x_0, \omega, \delta, \Delta)$, where X is the state space, $x_0 \in X$ is the initial state, ω is an alphabet of action labels, $\delta : X \to \omega$ is an adversary that resolves non-determinism, and $\Delta : X \times \delta \times X \to \{[a,b] \mid 0 \le a \le b \le 1\}$ is the interval probability transition function.*

The interval probability function Δ is computed with Algorithm 1 such that with $1 - \alpha$ confidence, the intervals in Δ bracket the true transition probabilities in T, thereby capturing our uncertain knowledge about the true distribution induced by E. In practice, we chose to use the Clopper-Pearson interval, which is the maximally conservative confidence interval for binomial processes. It is referred to as the "exact" interval since it offers precise $1 - \alpha$ coverage of the binomial density, unlike other CIs that rely on asymptotic assumptions like the central limit theorem [72].

The discovered interval probability function $\Delta = \texttt{ConfInt}\left(\mathcal{D}^{train}, \psi, \alpha\right)$ determines the parameters of the desired abstraction. In practice, the interval probabilities correspond to a particular abstract estimate $\hat{s}^\psi$ at an abstract state s^ψ. However, we still require an underlying structure that organizes the allowed transitions from one state to another, modeling sequential state estimation $h \circ g$ and conservatively modeling state propagation $f \circ \pi$. We utilize Algorithm 2 to abstract $\mathcal{M}_E$ into a codified automaton parameterized by Δ.

Algorithm 1. ConfInt: compute confidence intervals for IMDP $\mathcal{M}_E$

Require: Dataset $\mathcal{D}^{train}$, abstraction function ψ, confidence level α
Ensure: confidence intervals Δ indexed by abstract state s^ψ and abstract estimate $\hat{s}^\psi$
1: Initialize $\Delta \leftarrow \{\}$
2: Let $N \leftarrow |\hat{S}^\psi|$
3: $\boldsymbol{s}^\psi \leftarrow [\psi(\boldsymbol{s}_i) \mid (\boldsymbol{s}_i, \hat{\boldsymbol{s}}_i) \in \mathcal{D}^{train}]$ ▷ Bin the state data
4: $\hat{\boldsymbol{s}}^\psi \leftarrow [\psi(\hat{\boldsymbol{s}}_i) \mid (\boldsymbol{s}_i, \hat{\boldsymbol{s}}_i) \in \mathcal{D}^{train}]$
5: **for all** unique $s^\psi \in \boldsymbol{s}^\psi$ **do**
6:     Let $I \leftarrow \{i \mid \boldsymbol{s}^\psi[i] = s^\psi\}$ ▷ Vector indices where s^ψ exists
7:     Let $\hat{S}_{s^\psi} \leftarrow \{\hat{\boldsymbol{s}}^\psi[i] \mid i \in I_{s^\psi}\}$ ▷ Subset of $\hat{S}^\psi$ indexed by I
8:     **for all** unique $\hat{s}^\psi \in \hat{S}^\psi_{s^\psi}$ **do**
9:         $n \leftarrow \#\{\hat{s}^\psi \text{ in } \hat{S}^\psi_{s^\psi}\}$
10:        $CI \leftarrow [\text{Beta}^{-1}(\alpha/2N, n, |\hat{S}^\psi_{s^\psi}| - n + 1), \text{Beta}^{-1}(1 - \alpha/2N, n+1, |\hat{S}^\psi_{s^\psi}| - n)]$
11:        $\Delta[s^\psi, \hat{s}^\psi] \leftarrow CI$
12:     **end for**
13: **end for**
14: **return** Δ

Algorithm 2. DynStruct: build the transition structure of IMDP $\mathcal{M}_E$

Require: Control loop $f \circ \pi$, bounded state and estimate spaces $\mathcal{S}$ and $\hat{\mathcal{S}}$, abstraction function ψ
Ensure: IMDP mapping abstract states to possible successor abstract states
1: Initialize IMDP ← {}
2: Define $\mathcal{S}^\psi \leftarrow \psi(\mathcal{S})$
3: Define $\hat{\mathcal{S}}^\psi \leftarrow \psi(\hat{\mathcal{S}})$
4: **for all** $(s^\psi, \hat{s}^\psi) \in \mathcal{S}^\psi \times \hat{\mathcal{S}}^\psi$ **do**
5: $\quad s_{\text{lb}} \leftarrow \min[\psi^{-1}(s^\psi)], \; s_{\text{ub}} \leftarrow \max[\psi^{-1}(s^\psi)]$
6: $\quad \hat{s}_{\text{lb}} \leftarrow \min[\psi^{-1}(\hat{s}^\psi)], \; \hat{s}_{\text{ub}} \leftarrow \max[\psi^{-1}(\hat{s}^\psi)]$
7: $\quad \Delta s_{\min} \leftarrow \infty, \; \Delta s_{\max} \leftarrow -\infty$
8: $\quad$ **for all** $s \in \{s_{\text{lb}}, s_{\text{ub}}\}, \hat{s} \in \{\hat{s}_{\text{lb}}, \hat{s}_{\text{ub}}\}$ **do**
9: $\quad\quad \delta s \leftarrow s - f(s, \pi(\hat{s}))$
10: $\quad\quad$ Update $\Delta s_{\min}$ and $\Delta s_{\max}$ elementwise
11: $\quad$ **end for**
12: $\quad s_{\text{next, min}} \leftarrow s_{\text{lb}} + \Delta s_{\min}$
13: $\quad s_{\text{next, max}} \leftarrow s_{\text{ub}} + \Delta s_{\max}$
14: $\quad s^\psi_{\text{next}} \leftarrow \{\psi(s_i) \mid s_i \in [s_{\text{next, min}}, s_{\text{next, max}}]\}$
15: $\quad$ current_state ← $(s^\psi, \hat{s}^\psi)$
16: $\quad$ possible_states ← ∅
17: $\quad$ **for all** $s^\psi \in s^\psi_{\text{next}}$ **do**
18: $\quad\quad$ Add s^ψ to possible_states
19: $\quad$ **end for**
20: $\quad$ IMDP[current_state] ← possible_states
21: **end for**
22: **return** IMDP

Running Example. Recall the mountain car state space $s = (x, v) \in [-1.2, 0.6] \times [-0.07, 0.07]$. We select an abstraction function ψ partitioning the x-space by intervals of width 0.05 and the v-space by intervals of width 0.005, yielding $\mathcal{S}^\psi = \{-24, \ldots, 12\} \times \{-14, \ldots, 14\}$. Similarly, we abstract estimation errors $x - \hat{x} \in [-0.5, 0.5]$ into intervals of width 0.1, obtaining $\hat{\mathcal{S}}^\psi = \{-5, \ldots, 5\}$. For instance, a concrete state $s_k = (-0.3, 0.06)$ abstracts to $\psi(s_k) = (-6, 12)$ and concretizes to the subspace $\psi^{-1}(\psi(s_k)) = [-0.30, -0.25] \times [0.06, 0.065]$. The estimation abstraction follows similarly.

Algorithm 1 computes intervals Δ indexed by abstract state-estimate pairs $(s^\psi, \hat{s}^\psi)$ by abstracting samples in $\mathcal{D}^{train}$ (Lines 3–4), counting occurrences per abstract state (Lines 5–7), then applying Beta quantiles to estimate confidence intervals (Lines 8–11). For example, given samples $(0, 0, -1), (0, 0, 0), (0, 0, 0)$, $(0, 0, 1)$ at $s^\psi = (0, 0)$, relative frequencies are computed by simply dividing their relative occurrence n_i by $N = |\hat{S}^\psi| = 11$ (0.09, 0.18, and 0.09, respectively) and bracketed by confidence intervals discovered with the Beta quantile function.

Algorithm 2 constructs an IMDP by concretizing abstract states and estimates (Lines 2–6), iterating over every abstract state-estimate pair in $\mathcal{S}^\psi \times \hat{\mathcal{S}}^\psi$, such as $(-6, 12, 0)$, to define concrete subspaces (e.g., $[-0.30, -0.25] \times [0.060, 0.065] \times [0.0, 0.1]$). The algorithm loops through the corners of these subspaces, computes control actions from estimates using policy π, and propagates the concrete states through the dynamics f (Lines 7–11). For instance, the corner $(-0.3, 0.065, 0.0)$ yields a concrete future state by evaluating $u = \pi(0.0)$ and $(x, v) = (-0.3, 0.065)$ through f. The reachable subspace in one step is then abstracted into discrete successor states (Line 14), updating the IMDP structure accordingly.

4.2 Verifying the Safety of Abstraction

We now address the problem of formally verifying the safety of a vision-based autonomous system. We seek to verify that the model $\mathcal{M}_E$, which is an α-sound abstraction of M_E per Definition 2, satisfies a given co-safe linear temporal logic (LTL) property (a finite-time-horizon liveness property) φ with at least $1 - \beta$ probability. Formally, we aim to compute the logical satisfaction probability of the LTL predicate φ on $\mathcal{M}_E$. The property φ is a Boolean predicate that represents a real-world constraint on the temporal behavior of the closed-loop system M_E. The predicate is written in LTL, translated from a natural language safety requirement such as "the car must make an emergency stop within 5 s whenever it observes a pedestrian in the road" to $G(\text{pedestrian} \implies F_{[0,5]} [\text{speed} = 0])$.

Since the abstraction $\mathcal{M}_E$ of the real system M_E is stochastic due to the latent environment distribution E, we are interested in verifying that it is *probabilistically safe* with at least $1 - \beta$ probability per Definition 6:

Definition 6 (Probabilistic safety). *An abstract model $\mathcal{M}_E$ satisfies an LTL safety property φ, denoted $\mathcal{M}_E \models \varphi$, with at least $1 - \beta$ probability iff:*

$$\Pr\nolimits_{\tau \sim [\![\mathcal{M}_E]\!]} (\tau \models \varphi) \geq 1 - \beta,$$

where τ is a random trajectory sampled from $[\![\mathcal{M}_E]\!]$.

We approach this problem by leveraging an existing probabilistic model checker on the output of Algorithm 2. Since our derived abstraction $\mathcal{M}_E$ is an interval Markov decision process, tools like PRISM [54] and STORM [40] are capable of verifying PCTL properties on IMDPs. These model checkers can evaluate the minimum probability that any execution of the IMDP τ is satisfied on the property LTL φ. For standard MDP verification, the model checker resolves the nondeterminism by identifying the worst-case scheduler δ; however, for IMDPs, the procedure further requires determining the worst-case probability distributions encoded in the probability interval function Δ.

Since $\mathcal{M}_E$ is a statistically sound abstraction of M_E with at least $1 - \alpha$ confidence, and $\mathcal{M}_E$ is probabilistically safe on the property φ with at least $1 - \beta$ chance, we assert a nested guarantee that "the trajectories are likely safe assuming that the abstraction is sound" for the real system M_E in Theorem 1 below (see the online appendix [75] for the proof):

Theorem 1 (In-distribution soundness and safety). *Let M_E be a concrete system with the state/estimation spaces S and $\hat{S}$, composed of deterministic components g, h, π, and f, subject to stochasticity from the latent environment distribution E, from which originates training data $\mathcal{D}^{train}$ consisting of random trajectories τ drawn i.i.d. from $[\![M_E]\!]$; let ψ be an abstraction function; let $\mathcal{M}_E$ be an* IMDP $=$ DynStruct$(\pi, f, S, \hat{S}, \psi)$ *parameterized by $\Delta =$ ConfInt$\left(\mathcal{D}^{train}, \psi, \alpha\right)$, where α is a soundness confidence level. If it holds that:*

- $\mathcal{M}_E$ *is a statistically α-sound abstraction of M_E per Definition 2.*
- $\mathcal{M}_E$ *is safe for LTL safety property φ with probability $1-\beta$ per Definition 6.*

Then:
$$\Pr\nolimits_{\mathcal{D}^{train}}\left[\Pr\nolimits_{\tau \sim [\![M_E]\!]}(\tau \vDash \varphi) \geq 1-\beta\right] \geq 1-\alpha$$

4.3 Validating Abstraction on New Data

Although verification yields rigorous guarantees about the system M_E, what if the system is deployed to an environment E' that may differ from the original environment E? Since the original safety guarantees were derived using the IMDP abstraction $\mathcal{M}_E$, which is parameterized by the set of probability intervals $\Delta =$ ConfInt$\left(\mathcal{D}^{train}, \psi, \alpha\right)$, these guarantees no longer hold meaningful value without reconciling the new domain E' with the old domain E. Verifying that the abstract model $\mathcal{M}_E$ still describes the behaviors of the real system M under this novel environment E' is critical to asserting a meaningful end-to-end guarantee free of run-time domain assumptions.

This section tackles an *offline validation setting* where we collect a novel dataset $\mathcal{D}^{val}$, consisting of L trajectories drawn independently from the new environment's trajectory distribution $[\![M_{E'}]\!]$. The objective is to infer the posterior distribution $\mathbb{M}^{po}$ of the parameters of $M_{E'}$ by updating a prior distribution $\mathbb{M}^{pr}$ with data, and then compute the confidence that $M_{E'}$ is characterized by some distribution in $[\![\mathcal{M}]\!]$. Formally, we aim to check whether $\mathcal{M}_E$ is a *statistically valid abstraction* of $M_{E'}$:

Definition 7 (Statistically valid abstraction). *Given an abstract model $\mathcal{M}_E$, a validation dataset $\mathcal{D}^{val}$ sampled i.i.d. from $M_{E'}$, and a prior belief $\mathbb{M}^{pr}$ about the parameters of $M_{E'}$, $\mathcal{M}_E$ is a statistically valid abstraction of $M_{E'}$ with γ confidence if:*

$$\Pr\nolimits_{\mathbb{M}^{po}}\left([\![M]\!] \in [\![\mathcal{M}_E]\!] \mid M \sim \mathbb{M}^{po}\right) \geq 1-\gamma$$

where $\mathbb{M}^{po}$ is a posterior belief about the parameters of $M_{E'}$.

Bayesian Validation. The objective of model validation is to measure the *extent* to which the behaviors of $M_{E'}$ are characterized by the abstract model $\mathcal{M}_E$ through statistical inference. We begin by formulating our null hypothesis:

$$H_0 := [\![M_E]\!] \in [\![\mathcal{M}_E]\!], \tag{5}$$

asserting that the distribution of trajectories within the true system is contained within the abstract model's set of trajectory distributions. We then acquire a validation dataset $\mathcal{D}^{val}$.

Two fundamental paradigms exist for testing H_0: frequentist and Bayesian. In the frequentist paradigm, $\mathcal{D}^{val}$ is viewed as random data generated under a fixed hypothesis (either true or false). Hypothesis testing involves computing the probability $\Pr(\mathcal{D}^{val} \mid H_0)$ of observing the validation dataset under the assumption H_0 is true. This probability is then used to derive a p-value, resulting in a *binary* outcome (reject or fail to reject) based on its comparison to a pre-specified significance threshold, which controls the Type I error rate.

In contrast, the Bayesian paradigm treats H_0 as a binary random variable with $\mathcal{D}^{val}$ viewed as fixed evidence. Observing $\mathcal{D}^{val}$ updates prior beliefs about H_0 into a posterior distribution via Bayes' theorem:

$$\Pr(H_0 \mid \mathcal{D}^{val}) \propto \Pr(\mathcal{D}^{val} \mid H_0) \Pr(H_0) \qquad (6)$$

We quantify the statistical likelihood of H_0 by integrating $\Pr(H_0 \mid \mathcal{D}^{val})$ over relevant intervals of the IMDP parameters. Thus, Bayesian validation yields a continuous measure of system-wide conformance rather than a binary one.

Let $\mathbb{M}^{pr}$ denote the prior distribution over the parameters of M_E. Since estimating discrete future states probabilistically is a multinomial process, we select $\mathbb{M}^{pr}$ as the Dirichlet distribution, the conjugate prior of the multinomial distribution. Observed evidence from the validation dataset $\mathcal{D}^{val}$ is incorporated by directly updating the parameters of our Dirichlet prior, resulting in a posterior distribution $\mathbb{M}^{po}$ over the parameters of $M_{E'}$. For each state, this Dirichlet distribution is parameterized by concentration parameters $\boldsymbol{\alpha} = [\alpha_1, \alpha_2, \ldots, \alpha_n]$, where each α_i represents the prior pseudo-count (or relative occurrence) associated with the corresponding discrete state estimate $\hat{s}_i^\psi$. These concentration parameters are initialized to $\boldsymbol{\alpha} = \mathbf{1}$ (the uniform prior).

We update our Dirichlet prior $\text{Dir}(\boldsymbol{\alpha}_0)$ with the observed estimate counts from the validation set $\mathcal{D}^{val}$ for each discrete state s^ψ. To this end, we first define the count of estimates witnessed for each state:

$$n_i = \left| \{ j : \hat{s}_j^\psi = i,\ s_j^\psi = s^\psi \} \right| \quad \text{for } i = 1, \ldots, K.$$

The posterior Dirichlet parameters for each s^ψ are computed based on the counts n_i and the prior parameters $\boldsymbol{\alpha}_0 = (\alpha_{0,1}, \ldots, \alpha_{0,K})$ as $\alpha_i = \alpha_{0,i} + n_i$ for all $i \in \{1, \ldots, K\}$, or simply $\boldsymbol{\alpha} = \boldsymbol{\alpha}_0 + \boldsymbol{n}$.

Validity Confidence. The next step is to quantify the conformance between this posterior distribution of the $M_{E'}$ parameters and the previously derived abstraction IMDP $\mathcal{M}_E$. We do this on a state-wise basis: a per-state conformance confidence from posterior $\text{Dir}(\boldsymbol{\alpha})$ is defined as:

$$1 - \gamma_{s^\psi} = \int_{\Delta[\cdot, s^\psi]} \text{Dir}(\mathbf{p};\, \boldsymbol{\alpha})\, d\mathbf{p}, \qquad (7)$$

where $\mathbf{p} \sim \text{Dir}(\boldsymbol{\alpha})$, and $\Delta[\cdot, s^\psi]$ are the intervals over possible state estimates $\hat{s}^\psi$.

In practice, due to the absence of an analytical solution to the above integral, we approximate $1-\gamma$ by drawing N independent samples $\{\mathbf{p}^{(i)}\}_{i=1}^N$ from $\text{Dir}(\boldsymbol{\alpha})$ and compute it as follows for each abstract state s^ψ:

$$1 - \gamma_{s^\psi} = \frac{1}{N} \sum_{i=1}^N \mathbf{1}\left(\mathbf{p}^{(i)} \in \Delta[\cdot, s^\psi]\right) \tag{8}$$

We put these ideas of state-wise conformance checking together into a validation pipeline seen in Algorithm 3, which outputs a set of confidence values $\Gamma = \text{Validate}(\Delta, \psi, \mathcal{D}^{val})$ over all discrete states.

Algorithm 3. Validate: compute the conformance of a system to an abstraction
---
Require: Abstraction parameters Δ, abstraction function ψ, validation data $\mathcal{D}^{val}$, Dirichlet prior $\boldsymbol{\alpha}_0$
1: Initialize $\Gamma \leftarrow \{\}$ ▷ Confidence levels over states
2: $\mathbf{s}^\psi \leftarrow [\psi(s_i) \mid (s_i, \hat{s}_i) \in \mathcal{D}^{train}]$ ▷ Bin the state data
3: $\hat{\mathbf{s}}^\psi \leftarrow [\psi(\hat{s}_i) \mid (s_i, \hat{s}_i) \in \mathcal{D}^{train}]$
4: **for all** unique $s^\psi \in \mathbf{s}^\psi$ **do**
5:     Let $I \leftarrow \{i \mid \mathbf{s}^\psi[i] = s^\psi\}$ ▷ Vector indices where s^ψ exists
6:     Let $\hat{\mathbf{s}}^\psi_{s^\psi} \leftarrow [\hat{\mathbf{s}}^\psi[i] \mid i \in I_{s^\psi}]$ ▷ Subset of $\hat{\mathbf{s}}^\psi$ indexed by I
7:     Let $\mathbf{n} \leftarrow \left[\left|\{i \mid \hat{\mathbf{s}}^\psi_{s^\psi}[i] = s\}\right| \mid s \in \text{unique}(\hat{\mathbf{s}}^\psi_{s^\psi})\right]$
8:     Update $\boldsymbol{\alpha} \leftarrow \boldsymbol{\alpha}_0 + \mathbf{n}$
9:     **Monte Carlo integration:**
10:     Draw $\{\mathbf{p}^{(i)}\}_{i=1}^N \overset{iid}{\sim} \text{Dir}(\boldsymbol{\alpha})$
11:     $\gamma_{s^\psi} \leftarrow 1 - (1/N) \sum_{i=1}^N \mathbf{1}(\mathbf{p}^{(i)} \in \Delta[\cdot, s^\psi])$
12:     $\Gamma \leftarrow \Gamma \cup 1 - \gamma_{s^\psi}$
13: **end for**

There are several ways of aggregating the state-wise confidences Γ into the system-level confidence γ. One conservative system-level metric of conformance is the worst-case confidence $\min_{s^\psi \in S^\psi} \Gamma$. However, in practice, some bins s^ψ may have only a few data points from $\mathcal{D}^{val}$, yielding low counts n_i and thus an excessively low posterior confidence, even if most of the state space is well-covered by $\mathcal{D}^{val}$. This overly low confidence has high uncertainty, can lead to numeric instability, and generally does not lead to a high validation precision due to the sensitivity to data availability, making it a poor indicator of system-wide conformance. To overcome the above limitation, we propose aggregating state-wise confidences using the *median* among all states, which is robust to outliers ($\gamma = \text{median}(\Gamma)$). Furthermore, the median reflects the confidence of at least half of the states. As we show in Sect. 5, our selection of the median metric allows for easy discrimination between the validity of $\mathcal{M}_E$ on the old (M_E) and new ($M_{E'}$) systems.

Finally, this section wraps up with a theorem that states a theoretical guarantee for our most conservative method. It asserts the lower confidence bound on the validity of a probabilistic safety claim under a novel environment E':

Theorem 2 (Out-of-distribution validity and safety). *Let $M_{E'}$ be a concrete system subject to stochasticity from the latent environment distribution E', from which originates training data $\mathcal{D}^{val}$ consisting of random trajectories τ drawn i.i.d. from $[\![M_{E'}]\!]$; let ψ be an abstraction function; let $\mathcal{M}_E$ be an IMDP abstraction of the same system under E.*

If the following is true:

- $\mathcal{M}_E$ *is a statistically γ-valid abstraction of $M_{E'}$ with confidence γ per Definition 7.*
- $\mathcal{M}_E$ *is safe for LTL safety property φ with probability $1-\beta$ per Definition 6.*

Then:
$$\Pr\nolimits_{\mathcal{D}^{val}}\left[\Pr\nolimits_{\tau \sim [\![M_E]\!]}(\tau \vDash \varphi) \geq 1 - \beta\right] \geq 1 - \gamma$$

The proof can be found in the online appendix [75].

Running Example. Consider the mountain car system introduced earlier, with state $s = (x, v) \in [-1.2, 0.6] \times [-0.07, 0.07]$. Suppose we have an abstraction $\mathcal{M}_E$, and aim to measure the extent to which it describes the behavior of the novel system $M_{E'}$.

We begin by gathering a new dataset $\mathcal{D}^{val}$ of trajectories from $M_{E'}$. Using the same abstraction function ψ as before, each state is abstracted to discrete state tiles (e.g., a concrete state $s_k = (-0.3, 0.06)$ maps to $\psi(s_k) = (-6, 12)$), and estimation differences $x - \hat{x}$ map to discrete intervals $-5, \ldots, 5$.

Algorithm 3 proceeds by binning validation data into abstract states (Lines 2–3), then iterating through each state tile, counting the occurrences of each abstract state seen at the current tile (Lines 5–7), and updating the prior parameters $\boldsymbol{\alpha_0}$ (Line 8). For example, suppose at $s^{\psi} = (-6, 12)$, we observe the following state estimate relative occurrences: $\boldsymbol{n} = \{0, 3, 7, 11, 7, 0, \ldots, 0\}$. Since $\boldsymbol{\alpha_0}$ is uniformly initialized, the posterior parameters become $\boldsymbol{\alpha} = \{1, 4, 8, 12, 8, 1, \ldots, 1\}$.

We then approximate the integral for conformance confidence via Monte Carlo sampling (Lines 10–12). Drawing samples from the posterior Dirichlet distribution, we check whether each sampled probability vector falls within the previously computed confidence intervals $\Delta[\,\cdot\,, (-6, 12)]$. The fraction of samples within these intervals estimates our confidence $1 - \gamma_{(-6,12)}$.

Repeating this process for each abstract state, we obtain confidence values Γ across the entire discrete state space. Finally, we aggregate these confidences using the median to yield a robust system-level conformance metric γ, effectively validating the IMDP abstraction under environment E'.

5 Experimental Evaluation

Our experimental evaluation has three goals: (1) to demonstrate formal verification of safety for a vision-based autonomous system through an IMDP abstraction, (2) to check whether the validation framework effectively discriminates between systems deployed to in-distribution (ID) and out-of-distribution (OOD) scenarios, and (3) to characterize the tradeoffs among the confidence parameters involved in statistical abstraction and system-wide safety guarantees (namely, abstraction confidence α, safety chance $1 - \beta$, and conformance confidence γ). All experimental computation was performed on a modern laptop equipped with a 14th Gen Intel Core i9-14900HX 24-core processor, 64 GB DDR5 RAM, and an RTX 4090 GPU with 16 GB VRAM.

5.1 Synthetic Goal-Reaching System

Environment Description. We consider a synthetic autonomous system M_E where an agent must reach a waypoint located at coordinates $(10, 10)$, starting from $(0.0, 0.0)$, within a two-dimensional state space $S = [0, 12] \times [0, 12]$. The agent uses a proportional controller with gain 0.5, producing steps toward the waypoint with a maximum allowable magnitude of 0.7. An execution is considered successful if the agent reaches within a radius of 2.0 units of the waypoint in fewer than 100 discrete time steps, without colliding with the barricades at $x = 12$ and $y = 12$. A collision or timeout constitutes an unsuccessful execution.

The agent has perfect localization; however, the waypoint's position is subject to uncertain estimation modeled by additive, unbiased Gaussian sensor noise with variance bounded within the interval $[\sigma_{\min}^2, \sigma_{\max}^2]$, which varies across the experiments. The magnitude of this noise decays as the agent approaches the waypoint, with the variance given by:

$$\sigma^2(d) = \frac{(d - d_{\min})(\sigma_{\max}^2 - \sigma_{\min}^2)}{d_{\max} - d_{\min}} + \sigma_{\min}^2,$$

where d is the agent's Euclidean distance from the waypoint, bounded by $d_{\min} = 2.0$ and $d_{\max} = 14.14$ (the distance to the waypoint from the initial position).

Abstraction. To construct an α-sound abstraction of this goal-reaching system, we define an abstraction function ψ using uniform discretization with bins of size 0.5 units, partitioning the continuous 2-dimensional state space $[0, 12] \times [0, 12]$ into 576 discrete tiles. We instantiate a training environment E with fixed noise variance parameters $\sigma_{\min}^2 = 0.5$ and $\sigma_{\max}^2 = 0.5$, placing the agent at each discrete state tile and collecting 200 state estimates per tile to form the dataset $\mathcal{D}^{\text{train}}$. Using this dataset, we compute the IMDP parameters via $\Delta = $ ConfInt$(\mathcal{D}^{\text{train}}, \psi, \alpha)$, and subsequently construct the IMDP through IMDP $=$ DynStruct$(\pi, f, S, \hat{S}, \psi)$, where the functions π, f are inferred from closed-loop executions of M_E. Finally, we programmatically translate the IMDP into PRISM model syntax, resulting in approximately 16,000 transitions. For this chosen level of state-space granularity, the model construction procedure requires roughly 120 seconds of computation time on our laptop.

To confirm that the data-driven abstractions are a sound and over-approximate representation of the underlying system, we examined both the percentage of real trajectories covered by the abstraction, as well as the Jaccard similarity between the set of real and abstract transitions exiting a node, obtaining 100% coverage and ≈ 0.2 similarity (depending on the value of α).

Verification. We probabilistically model check the following PCTL property:

$$\Pr_{\geq?}^{\min}\left[(x < 12 \wedge y < 12) \cup_{[0,100]} \sqrt{(x-10)^2 + (y-10)^2} \leq 2\right]$$

which ensures that the agent never collides with a barricade and reaches within 2.0 of the waypoint within 100 time steps. The model was successfully verified at 10 notable positions, and the verification results are summarized in Table 1.

Table 1. Verified safety for the goal-reaching system from initial positions w/$\alpha = 0.05$

x_0	y_0	$1 - \beta$
0.0	0.0	0.6909
0.0	2.5	0.7201
2.5	0.0	0.7202
2.5	2.5	0.7466
0.0	5.0	0.7465
5.0	0.0	0.7465
5.0	5.0	0.7934
0.0	7.5	0.7689
7.5	0.0	0.7855
7.5	7.5	0.8430

Verification and Validation Tradeoff. We analyze the tradeoff between statistical abstraction confidence $1 - \alpha$ and the resulting safety guarantees by varying the binomial confidence parameter α used in the construction of Δ. We plot these safety probabilities against α in Fig. 2.

In addition to the model checking results, we also leverage the abstraction parameters Δ to measure how well the abstraction conforms to the in-distribution system through Algorithm 3. We instantiate another in-distribution environment with the same parameters as the training system ($\sigma^2 \in [0.5, 4.0]$), then collect 1000 independent trajectories of state/estimate pairs, which yields the dataset $\mathcal{D}^{val}$. From the output, we obtain a representative confidence level $1 - \gamma = \text{median}\left[\text{Validate}(\Delta, \psi, \mathcal{D}^{val})\right]$, and plot this against α in Fig. 2.

Discriminating ID and OOD Systems. To demonstrate the discriminative ability of our validation, we instantiate the agent in multiple domain-shifted environments, collect 1000 independent trajectories from each, and compute conformance confidences used as classification scores for the ID vs. OOD decision.

A domain shift is induced by biasing the distribution of state estimate noise with a scalar offset. To label which environments are truly outside of our IMDP, we compare their data-driven 99%-confidence interval with the model-checked interval from the IMDP. If these intervals do not overlap, the environment is

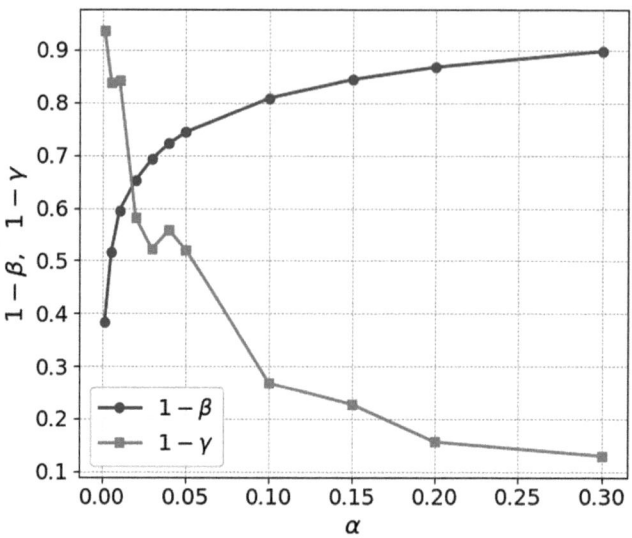

Fig. 2. Safety chance and conformance confidence are tradeoffs as functions of α for the goal-reaching system. A smaller α corresponds to higher binomial confidence, leading to looser IMDP intervals, thus providing the model checker with greater flexibility to select worst-case distributions, resulting in lower safety chances.

deemed to be OOD for the IMDP. We also collect four datasets from the non-shifted environment, which are considered ID for the IMDP.

Our validation results are shown in Table 2. Clearly, many reasonable thresholds (e.g., 0.5) on the γ values would lead to a perfect discrimination between the ID and OOD cases. Note that the environments with smaller shifts (between 0 and 2.45) could not be conclusively labeled ID or OOD, so they were excluded.

Effects of Discretization Granularity. We performed a small-scale ablation to assess how discretization granularity (tile size) affects verification and validation outcomes, holding the abstraction confidence at $\alpha = 0.05$, and checking the above property. As the state space was partitioned into finer tiles, the safety chance increased while the conformance confidence decreased. For example, with 1.0×1.0 tiles, the safety chance was 0.036 (model checking time: 7.8 s) and conformance confidence was 0.464. Refining to 0.8×0.8 tiles, safety chance increased to 0.067 (13.8 s) and conformance confidence was 0.450. At 0.75×0.75, safety chance rose to 0.695 (15.4) with conformance confidence 0.314. Using 0.5×0.5 tiles, safety chance increased to 0.9998 (15.4 s), while conformance confidence was 0.406.

5.2 Vision-Based Mountain Car

Environment Description. We evaluate our methodology using the Mountain Car benchmark used as a running example in Sect. 4. Here we briefly augment the description of this system with details relevant to the experiment.

Table 2. Validation confidences and empirical safety for four in-distribution and ten out-of-distribution environments. The ID safety chance from PRISM is $[0.5837, 1.0000]$.

Case	Distance	Success rate	99% success CI	$1 - \gamma$
ID	0.00	1.000	[0.9947, 1.0000]	0.7782
ID	0.00	1.000	[0.9947, 1.0000]	0.7593
ID	0.00	1.000	[0.9947, 1.0000]	0.7093
ID	0.00	1.000	[0.9947, 1.0000]	0.6530
OOD	2.45	0.505	[0.4638, 0.5461]	0.0000
OOD	2.47	0.454	[0.4132, 0.4952]	0.0000
OOD	2.50	0.405	[0.3651, 0.4459]	0.0000
OOD	2.52	0.391	[0.3514, 0.4317]	0.0000
OOD	2.55	0.289	[0.2527, 0.3274]	0.0000
OOD	2.60	0.263	[0.2278, 0.3004]	0.0000
OOD	2.70	0.176	[0.1461, 0.2091]	0.0000
OOD	2.80	0.092	[0.0700, 0.1180]	0.0000
OOD	2.90	0.061	[0.0431, 0.0832]	0.0000
OOD	3.00	0.025	[0.0141, 0.0407]	0.0000

For our experiments, we trained a lightweight Deep Q-Network (DQN) policy over 5000 episodes with $\epsilon_0 = 1.0$ and a decay rate of 0.9983. During closed-loop execution with non-linear dynamics, the policy is guided by intermediate position estimates generated by a pre-trained vision-based estimator [92], which predicts the car's position directly from a noisy image.

To induce noise in vision-based state estimation, the images are perturbed with Gaussian noise before being input to the vision model. We modeled the "in-distribution" environment by applying unbiased Gaussian noise with $\sigma = 0.1$ to the grayscale MountainCar images. Figure 3 shows example images perturbed with noise with parameters $\sigma \in \{0.00, 0.10, 0.25, 0.50\}$.

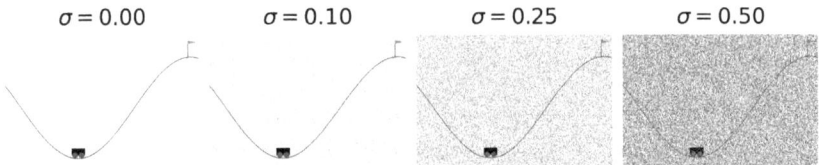

Fig. 3. Examples of noisy visual inputs from the MountainCar environment. The true car position is fixed at -0.46. The position estimation errors are 0.01, 0.25, 0.46, and 0.58 from left to right.

Abstraction. To construct an α-sound abstraction of the MountainCar, we define an abstraction function ψ using uniform discretization with bins of size 0.05

for x and 0.005 for v, partitioning the continuous 2-dimensional state space $[-1.2, 0.6] \times [-0.07, 0.07]$ into 1008 discrete tiles. We instantiate a training environment E with fixed noise standard deviation $\sigma = 0.1$. To collect the dataset $\mathcal{D}^{\text{train}}$, we place the mountain car at each of the discrete state tiles and collect 100 observations and subsequent position estimates. Using this dataset, we compute the IMDP parameters via $\Delta = \texttt{ConfInt}\left(\mathcal{D}^{\text{train}}, \psi, \alpha\right)$, and subsequently construct the IMDP through $\texttt{IMDP} = \texttt{DynStruct}(\pi, f, S, \hat{S}, \psi)$. In this experiment, π is a DQN policy, and the mountain car dynamics f are inferred by propagating the gym environment over one time step for particular state/action pairs. Finally, we programmatically translate the IMDP into PRISM model syntax, resulting in approximately 23,000 transitions. For this chosen level of state-space granularity, the model construction procedure requires roughly 300 seconds of computation time on a modern laptop. Similarly to the first case study, this abstraction is conservative: it has 100% coverage of concrete behaviors and ≈0.2 Jaccard similarity between the set of real and abstract transitions exiting a node.

Verification. We probabilistically model check the following PCTL property:

$$\Pr_{\geq ?}^{\min} \left[F_{[0, 200]} \left(x \geq 0.45 \right) \right]$$

which ensures that the car reaches the goal within 200 discrete time steps. The model was successfully verified at states such as $(0.2, 0.07)$, which yields a $1 - \beta$ safety chance of 0.9991, and $(0.3, 0.06)$, which yields the same safety chance.

Verification and Validation Tradeoff. We again analyze the tradeoff between the lower bound on safety of the IMDP, the conformance of a novel system to this IMDP, and the confidence level used to construct the binomial CIs for the IMDP from real data. We analyze the tradeoff between statistical abstraction confidence $1 - \alpha$ and the resulting safety guarantees by varying the binomial confidence parameter α exponentially between 0.001 and 0.3 to construct Δ.

We then collect another dataset $\mathcal{D}^{val}$ of state/estimate trajectories over 50 episodes in the environment with $\sigma = 0.1$. Then, for each α, we tabulate the lower bound of safety of the abstraction $1 - \beta$ and the median representative conformance confidence of the abstraction to the data $\mathcal{D}^{val}$ computed as $1 - \gamma = \text{median}\left[\texttt{Validate}(\Delta, \psi, \mathcal{D}^{val})\right]$, producing the results seen in Fig. 4. They confirm the observation that model soundness attenuates the safety-validity tradeoff.

Limitations. The most obvious limitation of our approach is its scalability: our abstraction method produces sizable PRISM models that consume time and computational resources when model checking. This makes it challenging to verify systems with non-linear dynamics and controls (such as the MountainCar) because they require carefully balancing non-determinism between overly conservative and overly large abstractions. Nonetheless, our theoretical approach is not inherently limited to low dimensions. This issue can be mitigated with more sophisticated abstraction in the future, like adaptive tiling. Secondly, measuring the conformance of the IMDP parameters at each discrete state is sample-inefficient. We anticipate that continuous statespace-wide distribution models, such as Gaussian processes, will be able to overcome this limitation.

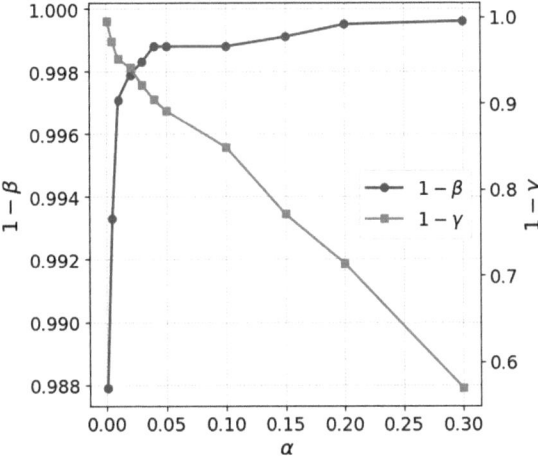

Fig. 4. Safety chance and conformance confidence are tradeoffs as functions of α for the mountain car, analogous to Fig. 2.

6 Conclusion

This paper contributes a unified verification & validation methodology for assuring vision-based autonomous systems. The methodology contains three steps: (1) statistical **soundness** of the vision-based system abstraction, (2) probabilistic **verification** of the safety of the vision-based system, and (3) statistical **validation** of the abstraction in a new operational environment. Our experiments have shown that our abstractions are sound: the IMDP trajectories robustly over-approximate those of the true system. In both case studies, we achieved 100% coverage of the real system trajectories with the IMDP, and a Jaccard similarity of approximately 0.2 (no. of transitions shared between the real and abstract systems divided by the total no. of transitions). For verification, we indeed produce genuine safety chance lower bounds in PRISM model checking. For validation, system-wide conformance checking via Bayesian inference effectively discriminates between in-distribution and shifted environments. Finally, end-to-end guarantees are established via Theorems 1 and 2 and their proofs.

This paper opens several fruitful directions for future research. First, our validation procedure can be targeted towards the states that carry the most probability mass in the verification. Second, one can apply more sophisticated uncertainty models to create abstractions, such as Gaussian processes. Third, there are promising models of photorealistic neural scene representation, such as Neural Radiance Fields (NeRF) [68] and Gaussian splats [50], which enables photorealistic simulation of vision-based robotics applications like zero-shot sim-to-real transfer for aerial navigation [66,67], self-driving [97], and manipulation tasks [98]; however, the soundness of those neural representation abstraction remains an open question. Lastly, state abstraction can be improved with more sophisticated procedures, such as adaptive tiling or polynomial representations. Furthermore, we plan to apply our approach to realistic physical systems, such as drone racing [67] and vision-based fixed-wing landing [66].

References

1. Aichernig, B.K., Tappler, M.: Probabilistic black-box reachability checking (extended version). Form. Methods Syst. Des. **54**(3), 416–448 (2019)
2. Alasmari, N., Calinescu, R., Paterson, C., Mirandola, R.: Quantitative verification with adaptive uncertainty reduction. J. Syst. Softw. **188**, 111275 (2022). https://doi.org/10.1016/j.jss.2022.111275, https://www.sciencedirect.com/science/article/pii/S016412122200036X
3. Astorga, A., Hsieh, C., Madhusudan, P., Mitra, S.: Perception contracts for safety of ML-enabled systems. Proc. ACM Program. Lang. **7**(OOPSLA2), 2196–2223 (2023)
4. Badings, T., Cubuktepe, M., Jansen, N., Junges, S., Katoen, J.P., Topcu, U.: Scenario-based verification of uncertain parametric MDPs. Int. J. Softw. Tools Technol. Transf. **24**(5), 803–819 (2022)
5. Badings, T., Junges, S., Marandi, A., Topcu, U., Jansen, N.: Efficient sensitivity analysis for parametric robust Markov chains. In: 35th International Conference on Computer Aided Verification (2023)
6. Badithela, A., Wongpiromsarn, T., Murray, R.M.: Evaluation Metrics for Object Detection for Autonomous Systems (2022). https://doi.org/10.48550/arXiv.2210.10298, http://arxiv.org/abs/2210.10298, arXiv:2210.10298 [cs, eess]
7. Bakirtzis, G., Subrahmanian, E., Fleming, C.H.: Compositional thinking in cyber-physical systems theory. Computer **54**(12), 50–59 (2021)
8. Bensalem, S., Cheng, C.H., Huang, W., Huang, X., Wu, C., Zhao, X.: What, indeed, is an achievable provable guarantee for learning-enabled safety-critical systems. In: Steffen, B. (eds.) Bridging the Gap Between AI and Reality. AISoLA 2023. LNCS, vol. 14380, pp. 55–76. Springer, Cham (2024). https://doi.org/10.1007/978-3-031-46002-9_4
9. Bharadwaj, S., Roux, S.L., Perez, G., Topcu, U.: Reduction Techniques for Model Checking and Learning in MDPs, pp. 4273–4279 (2017). https://www.ijcai.org/proceedings/2017/597
10. Blundell, C., Giannakopoulou, D., Păsăreanu, C.S.: Assume-guarantee testing. SIGSOFT Softw. Eng. Notes **31**(2), 1–es (2005). https://doi.org/10.1145/1118537.1123060, https://dl.acm.org/doi/10.1145/1118537.1123060
11. Bojarski, M., et al.: End to End Learning for Self-Driving Cars (2016). https://doi.org/10.48550/arXiv.1604.07316, http://arxiv.org/abs/1604.07316, arXiv:1604.07316 [cs]
12. Brockman, G., et al.: OpenAI Gym (2016). https://doi.org/10.48550/arXiv.1606.01540, http://arxiv.org/abs/1606.01540, arXiv:1606.01540 [cs]

13. Calinescu, R., et al.: Controller Synthesis for Autonomous Systems With Deep-Learning Perception Components. IEEE Transactions on Software Engineering (2024). https://www.computer.org/csdl/journal/ts/2024/06/10496502/1W28Vqz3hQc
14. Carpenter, T.J., Ivanov, R., Lee, I., Weimer, J.: ModelGuard: runtime validation of Lipschitz-continuous models. In: 7th IFAC Conference on Analysis and Design of Hybrid Systems (ADHS'21) (2021). arXiv: 2104.15006
15. Cauchois, M., Gupta, S., Ali, A., Duchi, J.C.: Robust validation: confident predictions even when distributions Shift. J. Am. Stat. Assoc. 1–66 (2024). https://doi.org/10.1080/01621459.2023.2298037
16. Chapman, M.P.: Risk-Sensitive Safety Analysis and Control for Trustworthy Autonomy. Ph.D., University of California, Berkeley, United States – California (2020). https://www.proquest.com/docview/2460739262/abstract/18015E97A18F4C45PQ/1, iSBN: 9798678171221
17. Cleaveland, M., Lu, P., Sokolsky, O., Lee, I., Ruchkin, I.: Conservative Perception Models for Probabilistic Verification (2025). https://doi.org/10.48550/arXiv.2503.18077, http://arxiv.org/abs/2503.18077, arXiv:2503.18077 [cs] version: 2
18. Cleaveland, M., Ruchkin, I., Sokolsky, O., Lee, I.: Monotonic safety for scalable and data-efficient probabilistic safety analysis. In: ACM/IEEE 13th International Conference on Cyber-Physical Systems (ICCPS), pp. 92–103 (2022). https://doi.org/10.1109/ICCPS54341.2022.00015
19. Cleaveland, M., Sokolsky, O., Lee, I., Ruchkin, I.: Conservative safety monitors of stochastic dynamical systems. In: Proceedings of the NASA Formal Methods Conference (May 2023)
20. Corso, A., Moss, R., Koren, M., Lee, R., Kochenderfer, M.: A survey of algorithms for black-box safety validation of cyber-physical systems. J. Artif. Intell. Rese. **72**, 377–428 (2022). https://doi.org/10.1613/jair.1.12716, https://dl.acm.org/doi/10.1613/jair.1.12716
21. Cubuktepe, M., Jansen, N., Junges, S., Katoen, J.P., Topcu, U.: Scenario-based verification of uncertain MDPs. In: In: Biere, A., Parker, D. (eds.) Tools and Algorithms for the Construction and Analysis of Systems. TACAS 2020, LNCS, pp. 287–305. Springer, Cham (2020). https://doi.org/10.1007/978-3-030-45190-5_16
22. Cámara, J.: HaiQ: synthesis of software design spaces with structural and probabilistic guarantees. In: Proceedings of the 8th International Conference on Formal Methods in Software Engineering, pp. 22–33. FormaliSE '20, Association for Computing Machinery, New York, NY, USA (2020). https://doi.org/10.1145/3372020.3391562
23. D'Innocenzo, A., Abate, A., Katoen, J.P.: Robust PCTL model checking. In: Proceedings of the 15th ACM international conference on Hybrid Systems: Computation and Control, pp. 275–286. HSCC '12, Association for Computing Machinery, New York, NY, USA (2012). https://doi.org/10.1145/2185632.2185673
24. Dong, Y., et al.: Reliability assessment and safety arguments for machine learning components in system assurance. ACM Trans. Embed. Comput. Syst. **22**(3), 48:1–48:48 (2023).https://doi.org/10.1145/3570918, https://dl.acm.org/doi/10.1145/3570918
25. Dong, Y., Huang, J., Ai, J.: Visual perception-based target aircraft movement prediction for autonomous air combat. J. Aircraft **52**(2), 538–552 (2015). https://doi.org/10.2514/1.C032764, https://arc.aiaa.org/doi/10.2514/1.C032764, publisher: American Institute of Aeronautics and Astronautics

26. Dong, Y., Tao, J., Zhang, Y., Lin, W., Ai, J.: Deep learning in aircraft design, dynamics, and control: review and prospects. IEEE Trans. Aerosp. Electron. Syst. **57**(4), 2346–2368 (2021)
27. Dreossi, T., Donzé, A., Seshia, S.A.: Compositional falsification of cyber-physical systems with machine learning components. J. Autom. Reason. **63**(4), 1031–1053 (2019)
28. Dreossi, T., et al.: VERIFAI: A Toolkit for the Design and Analysis of Artificial Intelligence-Based Systems. arXiv:1902.04245 [cs] (2019). http://arxiv.org/abs/1902.04245, arXiv: 1902.04245
29. Dutta, S., et al.: Distributionally Robust Statistical Verification with Imprecise Neural Networks. In: Proceedings of the HSCC 2025. Springer (2025). https://doi.org/10.48550/arXiv.2308.14815
30. D'Argenio, P., Legay, A., Sedwards, S., Traonouez, L.M.: Smart sampling for lightweight verification of markov decision processes. Int. J. Softw. Tools Technol. Transf. **17**(4), 469–484 (2015)
31. Fainekos, G.E., Pappas, G.J.: Robustness of temporal logic specifications for continuous-time signals. Theor. Comput. Sci. **410**(42), 4262–4291 (2009)
32. Feng, L., Han, T., Kwiatkowska, M., Parker, D.: Learning-based compositional verification for synchronous probabilistic systems. In: Bultan, T., Hsiung, P.-A. (eds.) ATVA 2011. LNCS, vol. 6996, pp. 511–521. Springer, Heidelberg (2011). https://doi.org/10.1007/978-3-642-24372-1_40
33. Filos, A., Tigkas, P., Mcallister, R., Rhinehart, N., Levine, S., Gal, Y.: Can autonomous vehicles identify, recover from, and adapt to distribution shifts? In: Proceedings of the 37th International Conference on Machine Learning, pp. 3145–3153. PMLR (2020). https://proceedings.mlr.press/v119/filos20a.html, iSSN: 2640-3498
34. Fleiss, J.L., Levin, B., Paik, M.C.: Statistical Methods for Rates & Proportions, 3rd edn. Wiley-Interscience, Hoboken, N.J. (2003)
35. Frehse, G., Han, Z., Krogh, B.: Assume-guarantee reasoning for hybrid I/O-automata by over-approximation of continuous interaction. In: Proceedings of the 43rd IEEE Conference on Decision and Control (CDC) (IEEE Cat. No. 04CH37601), vol. 1, pp. 479–484 (2004). https://doi.org/10.1109/CDC.2004.1428676
36. Frenkel, H., Grumberg, O., Păsăreanu, C.S., Sheinvald, S.: Assume, guarantee or repair: a regular framework for non regular properties. Int. J. Softw. Tools Technol. Transf. **24**(5), 667–689 (2022)
37. Fu, J., Topcu, U.: Probably Approximately Correct MDP Learning and Control With Temporal Logic Constraints. Robotics: Science and Systems X (2014). https://doi.org/10.15607/RSS.2014.X.039, http://www.roboticsproceedings.org/rss10/p39.pdf, conference Name: Robotics: Science and Systems 2014 ISBN: 9780992374709 Publisher: Robotics: Science and Systems Foundation
38. Graf, S., Passerone, R., Quinton, S.: Contract-based reasoning for component systems with rich interactions. In: Sangiovanni-Vincentelli, A., Zeng, H., Di Natale, M., Marwedel, P. (eds.) Embedded Systems Development. Embedded Systems, LNCS, vol. 20, pp. 139–154. Springer, New York (2014). https://doi.org/10.1007/978-1-4614-3879-3_8
39. Gupta, C., Podkopaev, A., Ramdas, A.: Distribution-free binary classification: prediction sets, confidence intervals and calibration. arXiv:2006.10564 [cs, math, stat] (2022). http://arxiv.org/abs/2006.10564, arXiv:2006.10564

40. Hensel, C., Junges, S., Katoen, J.P., Quatmann, T., Volk, M.: The Probabilistic Model Checker Storm (2020). https://doi.org/10.48550/arXiv.2002.07080, http://arxiv.org/abs/2002.07080, arXiv:2002.07080 [cs]
41. Holtzen, S., Junges, S., Vazquez-Chanlatte, M., Millstein, T., Seshia, S.A., Van den Broeck, G.: Model checking finite-horizon Markov chains with probabilistic inference. In: Silva, A., Leino, K.R.M. (eds.) Computer Aided Verification. CAV 2021. LNCS, vol. 12760, pp. 577–601. Springer, Cham (2021). https://doi.org/10.1007/978-3-030-81688-9_27
42. Holtzen, S., Millstein, T., Broeck, G.V.D.: Probabilistic Program Abstractions. arXiv:1705.09970 [cs] (2017),.http://arxiv.org/abs/1705.09970, arXiv: 1705.09970
43. Howard, R.A.: Dynamic Probabilistic Systems, Volume II: Semi-Markov and Decision Processes, 1 edn. Dover Publications, New York (June 2007)
44. Hsieh, C., Li, Y., Sun, D., Joshi, K., Misailovic, S., Mitra, S.: Verifying controllers with vision-based perception using safe approximate abstractions. IEEE Trans. Comput. Aided Des. Integr. Circuits Syst. **41**(11), 4205–4216 (2022). https://doi.org/10.1109/TCAD.2022.3197508
45. Huang, X., Kwiatkowska, M., Wang, S., Wu, M.: Safety verification of deep neural networks. In: Majumdar, R., Kunčak, V. (eds.) Computer Aided Verification. CAV 2017. LNCS, vol. 10426, pp. 3–29. Springer, Cham (2017). https://doi.org/10.1007/978-3-319-63387-9_1
46. Incer, I., Benveniste, A., Sangiovanni-Vincentelli, A., Seshia, S.A.: Hypercontracts. In: NASA Formal Methods: 14th International Symposium, NFM 2022, Pasadena, CA, USA, 24–27 May 2022, Proceedings, pp. 674–692. Springer, Berlin, Heidelberg (2022). https://doi.org/10.1007/978-3-031-06773-0_36
47. Ivanov, R., Carpenter, T.J., Weimer, J., Alur, R., Pappas, G.J., Lee, I.: Case study: verifying the safety of an autonomous racing car with a neural network controller. In: Proceedings of the 23rd International Conference on Hybrid Systems: Computation and Control, pp. 1–7. HSCC '20, Association for Computing Machinery, New York, NY, USA (2020). https://doi.org/10.1145/3365365.3382216, https://dl.acm.org/doi/10.1145/3365365.3382216
48. Jackson, J., Laurenti, L., Frew, E., Lahijanian, M.: Formal Verification of Unknown Dynamical Systems via Gaussian Process Regression (2021). https://www.semanticscholar.org/paper/Formal-Verification-of-Unknown-Dynamical-Systems-Jackson-Laurenti/8093250cc2b5876880717afc806ee7f2a35fd1ba
49. Katoen, J.P.: The probabilistic model checking landscape. In: Proceedings of the 31st Annual ACM/IEEE Symposium on Logic in Computer Science, pp. 31–45. LICS '16, Association for Computing Machinery, New York, NY, USA (2016). https://doi.org/10.1145/2933575.2934574
50. Kerbl, B., Kopanas, G., Leimkühler, T., Drettakis, G.: 3D gaussian splatting for real-time radiance field rendering. ACM Trans. Graph. **42**(4) (2023). https://repo-sam.inria.fr/fungraph/3d-gaussian-splatting/
51. Komuravelli, A., Pasareanu, C.S., Clarke, E.M.: Assume-Guarantee Abstraction Refinement for Probabilistic Systems. arXiv:1207.5086 [cs] **7358**, 310–326 (2012). https://doi.org/10.1007/978-3-642-31424-7_25, http://arxiv.org/abs/1207.5086, arXiv: 1207.5086
52. Kurakin, A., Goodfellow, I.J., Bengio, S.: Adversarial examples in the physical world. In: Proceedings of the ICLR 2016 (2017). https://openreview.net/forum?id=HJGU3Rodl
53. Kwiatkowska, M., Norman, G., Parker, D.: Stochastic model checking. In: Bernardo, M., Hillston, J. (eds.) Formal Methods for Performance Evaluation. SFM

2007. LNCS, vol. 4486, pp. 220–270. Springer, Berlin, Heidelberg (2007). https://doi.org/10.1007/978-3-540-72522-0_6
54. Kwiatkowska, M., Norman, G., Parker, D.: PRISM 4.0: verification of probabilistic real-time systems. In: Gopalakrishnan, G., Qadeer, S. (eds.) CAV 2011. LNCS, vol. 6806, pp. 585–591. Springer, Heidelberg (2011). https://doi.org/10.1007/978-3-642-22110-1_47
55. Kwiatkowska, M., Norman, G., Parker, D.: Probabilistic model checking and autonomy. Annu. Rev. Control Robot. Auton. Syst. **5**(1), 385–410 (2022). https://doi.org/10.1146/annurev-control-042820-010947, https://doi.org/10.1146/annurev-control-042820-010947, _eprint
56. Kwiatkowska, M., Norman, G., Parker, D., Qu, H.: Assume-guarantee verification for probabilistic systems. In: Esparza, J., Majumdar, R. (eds.) Tools and Algorithms for the Construction and Analysis of Systems. TACAS 2010. LNCS, vol. 6015, pp. 23–37. Springer, Berlin, Heidelberg (2010). https://doi.org/10.1007/978-3-642-12002-2_3
57. Kwiatkowska, M., Norman, G., Parker, D., Qu, H.: Compositional probabilistic verification through multi-objective model checking. Inf. Comput. **232**, 38–65 (2013)
58. Kwiatkowska, M., Zhang, X.: When to trust AI: advances and challenges for certification of neural networks. Ann. Comput. Sci. Inf. Syst. **35**, 25–37 (2023). https://annals-csis.org/Volume_35/drp/2324.html, iSSN: 2300-5963
59. Legay, A., Sedwards, S., Traonouez, L.M.: Scalable verification of markov decision processes. In: Canal, C., Idani, A. (eds.) Software Engineering and Formal Methods. SEFM 2014. LNCS, vol. 8938, pp. 350–362. Springer, Cham (2015). https://doi.org/10.1007/978-3-319-15201-1_23
60. Li, J., Nuzzo, P., Sangiovanni-Vincentelli, A., Xi, Y., Li, D.: Stochastic contracts for cyber-physical system design under probabilistic requirements. In: Proceedings of the 15th ACM-IEEE International Conference on Formal Methods and Models for System Design, pp. 5–14. MEMOCODE '17, Association for Computing Machinery, New York, NY, USA (2017). https://doi.org/10.1145/3127041.3127045
61. Li, Y., Ji, C., Anchalia, J., Mitra, S.: Lyapunov perception contracts. In: In Proceedings of Learning for Decision and Control (L4DC) (2025)
62. Liebenwein, L., et al.: Compositional and contract-based verification for autonomous driving on road networks. In: Amato, N., Hager, G., Thomas, S., Torres-Torriti, M. (eds.) Robotics Research. Springer Proceedings in Advanced Robotics, vol. 10, pp. 163–181. Springer, Cham (2020). https://doi.org/10.1007/978-3-030-28619-4_18
63. Lomuscio, A., Pirovano, E.: A Counter abstraction technique for the verification of probabilistic swarm systems. In: Proceedings of the 18th International Conference on Autonomous Agents and MultiAgent Systems, pp. 161–169. AAMAS '19, International Foundation for Autonomous Agents and Multiagent Systems, Richland, SC (May 2019)
64. Majumdar, A., Pavone, M.: How should a robot assess risk? Towards an axiomatic theory of risk in robotics. In: Amato, N., Hager, G., Thomas, S., Torres-Torriti, M. (eds.) Robotics Research. Springer Proceedings in Advanced Robotics, LNCS, vol. 10, pp. 75–84. Springer, Cham (2020). https://doi.org/10.1007/978-3-030-28619-4_10
65. Mallik, K., Schmuck, A.K., Soudjani, S., Majumdar, R.: Compositional synthesis of finite-state abstractions. IEEE Trans. Autom. Control **64**(6), 2629–2636 (2018). publisher: IEEE
66. Miao, Y., Shen, W., Cui, H., Mitra, S.: Falconwing: an open-source platform for ultra-light fixed-wing aircraft research (2025). https://arxiv.org/abs/2505.01383

67. Miao, Y., Shen, W., Mitra, S.: Zero-shot sim-to-real visual quadrotor control with hard constraints. In: IEEE/RSJ International Conference on Intelligent Robots and Systems. Hangzhou, China (October 2025)
68. Mildenhall, B., Srinivasan, P.P., Tancik, M., Barron, J.T., Ramamoorthi, R., Ng, R.: Nerf: representing scenes as neural radiance fields for view synthesis. Commun. ACM **65**(1), 99–106 (2021)
69. Mitra, S., et al.: Formal verification techniques for vision-based autonomous systems – a survey. In: Jansen, N., et al. (eds.) Principles of Verification: Cycling the Probabilistic Landscape. LNCS, vol. 15262, pp. 89–108. Springer, Cham (2025). https://doi.org/10.1007/978-3-031-75778-5_5
70. Moss, R.J., Kochenderfer, M.J., Gariel, M., Dubois, A.: Bayesian safety validation for black-box systems. In: Conference proceedings of the 2023 AIAA AVIATION Forum (May 2023). https://doi.org/10.48550/arXiv.2305.02449, http://arxiv.org/abs/2305.02449, arXiv:2305.02449 [cs, stat]
71. Naik, N., Nuzzo, P.: Robustness contracts for scalable verification of neural network-enabled cyber-physical systems. In: 2020 18th ACM-IEEE International Conference on Formal Methods and Models for System Design (MEMOCODE), pp. 1–12 (2020). https://doi.org/10.1109/MEMOCODE51338.2020.9315118
72. Newcombe, R.G.: Two-sided confidence intervals for the single proportion: comparison of seven methods. Stat. Med. **17**(8), 857–872 (1998)
73. Nuzzo, P.: From electronic design automation to cyber-physical system design automation: a tale of platforms and contracts. In: Proceedings of the 2019 International Symposium on Physical Design, pp. 117–121. ISPD '19, Association for Computing Machinery, San Francisco, CA, USA (2019). https://doi.org/10.1145/3299902.3311070
74. Nuzzo, P., Li, J., Sangiovanni-Vincentelli, A.L., Xi, Y., Li, D.: Stochastic assume-guarantee contracts for cyber-physical system design. ACM Trans. Embed. Comput. Syst. **18**(1), 2:1–2:26 (2019). https://doi.org/10.1145/3243216
75. Peper, J., Miao, Y., Mitra, S., Ruchkin, I.: Towards Unified Probabilistic Verification and Validation of Vision-Based Autonomy (2025). https://doi.org/10.48550/arXiv.2508.14181, http://arxiv.org/abs/2508.14181, arXiv:2508.14181 [eess]
76. Puggelli, A., Li, W., Sangiovanni-Vincentelli, A.L., Seshia, S.A.: Polynomial-time verification of PCTL properties of MDPs with convex uncertainties. In: Sharygina, N., Veith, H. (eds.) CAV 2013. LNCS, vol. 8044, pp. 527–542. Springer, Heidelberg (2013). https://doi.org/10.1007/978-3-642-39799-8_35
77. Păsăreanu, C.S., et al.: Closed-loop analysis of vision-based autonomous systems: a case study. In: Enea, C., Lal, A. (eds.) Computer Aided Verification. CAV 2023. LNCS, vol. 13964, pp. 289–303. Springer, Cham (2023). https://doi.org/10.1007/978-3-031-37706-8_15
78. Ruchkin, I., Sokolsky, O., Weimer, J., Hedaoo, T., Lee, I.: Compositional probabilistic analysis of temporal properties over stochastic detectors. IEEE Trans. Comput.-Aided Des. Integr. Circuits Syst. **39**(11), 3288–3299 (2020). https://doi.org/10.1109/TCAD.2020.3012643
79. Ruchkin, I.: Integration of Modeling Methods for Cyber-Physical Systems. PhD Thesis, Carnegie Mellon University (2019). https://doi.org/10.1184/R1/7970222.v1
80. Ruchkin, I., et al.: Confidence composition for monitors of verification assumptions. In: ACM/IEEE 13th International Conference on Cyber-Physical Systems (ICCPS), pp. 1–12 (2022). https://doi.org/10.1109/ICCPS54341.2022.00007

81. Ruchkin, I., de Niz, D., Chaki, S., Garlan, D.: ACTIVE: a tool for integrating analysis contracts. In: 5th Analytic Virtual Integration of Cyber-Physical Systems Workshop. Rome, Italy (2014)
82. Ruchkin, I., de Niz, D., Chaki, S., Garlan, D.: Contract-based integration of cyber-physical analyses. In: Proceedings of the International Conference on Embedded Software (EMSOFT). ACM, New York, NY, USA (2014). https://doi.org/10.1145/2656045.2656052
83. Rushby, J.: Composing safe systems. In: Arbab, F., Ölveczky, P.C. (eds.) Formal Aspects of Component Software. FACS 2011. LNCS, vol. 7253, pp. 3–11. Springer, Berlin, Heidelberg (2012). https://doi.org/10.1007/978-3-642-35743-5_2
84. Sangiovanni-Vincentelli, A., Damm, W., Passerone, R.: Taming Dr. Frankenstein: contract-based design for cyber-physical systems. Eur. J. Control **18**(3), 217–238 (2012). https://doi.org/10.3166/ejc.18.217-238
85. Santa Cruz, U., Shoukry, Y.: NNLander-VeriF: a neural network formal verification framework for vision-based autonomous aircraft landing. In: Deshmukh, J.V., Havelund, K., Perez, I. (eds.) NASA Formal Methods. NFM 2022. LNCS, vol. 13260, pp. 213–230. Springer, Cham (2022). https://doi.org/10.1007/978-3-031-06773-0_11
86. Shvets, A.A., Rakhlin, A., Kalinin, A.A., Iglovikov, V.I.: Automatic instrument segmentation in robot-assisted surgery using deep learning. In: 2018 17th IEEE International Conference on Machine Learning and Applications (ICMLA), pp. 624–628 (2018). https://doi.org/10.1109/ICMLA.2018.00100, https://ieeexplore.ieee.org/document/8614125
87. Sun, D., Yang, B.C., Mitra, S.: Learning-based inverse perception contracts and applications. In: 2024 IEEE International Conference on Robotics and Automation (ICRA), pp. 11612–11618 (2024). https://doi.org/10.1109/ICRA57147.2024.10610329
88. Szegedy, C., et al.: Intriguing properties of neural networks. In: International Conference on Learning Representations (2014)
89. Termine, A., Antonucci, A., Facchini, A., Primiero, G.: Robust model checking with imprecise markov reward models. In: Proceedings of the Twelveth International Symposium on Imprecise Probability: Theories and Applications, pp. 299–309. PMLR (2021). https://proceedings.mlr.press/v147/termine21a.html, iSSN: 2640-3498
90. Troffaes, M.C.M., Skulj, D.: Model checking for imprecise Markov chains. In: Proceedings of the Eighth International Symposium on Imprecise Probability: Theories and Applications, pp. 337–344. Society for Imprecise Probability: Theories and Applications (SIPTA), Compiegne, France (2013). http://www.sipta.org/isipta13/index.php?id=paper&paper=034.html, conference Name: ISIPTA'13: Proceedings of the Eighth International Symposium on Imprecise Probability: Theories and Applications Meeting Name: ISIPTA'13: Proceedings of the Eighth International Symposium on Imprecise Probability: Theories and Applications
91. Vazquez-Chanlatte, M., Rabe, M.N., Seshia, S.A.: A Model Counter's Guide to Probabilistic Systems. arXiv:1903.09354 [cs] (2019). http://arxiv.org/abs/1903.09354, arXiv: 1903.09354
92. Waite, T., Geng, Y., Turnquist, T., Ruchkin, I., Ivanov, R.: State-Dependent Conformal Perception Bounds for Neuro-Symbolic Verification of Autonomous Systems (2025). https://doi.org/10.48550/arXiv.2502.21308, http://arxiv.org/abs/2502.21308, arXiv:2502.21308 [eess]

93. Wang, Z., Huang, C., Wang, Y., Hobbs, C., Chakraborty, S., Zhu, Q.: Bounding perception neural network uncertainty for safe control of autonomous systems. In: 2021 Design, Automation & Test in Europe Conference & Exhibition (DATE), pp. 1745–1750 (2021). https://doi.org/10.23919/DATE51398.2021.9474204, iSSN: 1558-1101
94. Wolff, E.M., Topcu, U., Murray, R.M.: Robust control of uncertain Markov decision processes with temporal logic specifications. In: 2012 IEEE 51st IEEE Conference on Decision and Control (CDC), pp. 3372–3379 (2012). https://doi.org/10.1109/CDC.2012.6426174, iSSN: 0743-1546
95. Wu, H., et al.: Toward certified robustness against real-world distribution shifts. 2023 IEEE Conference on Secure and Trustworthy Machine Learning (SaTML), pp. 537–553 (2023). https://doi.org/10.1109/SaTML54575.2023.00042, https://ieeexplore.ieee.org/document/10136136/, conference Name: 2023 IEEE Conference on Secure and Trustworthy Machine Learning (SaTML) ISBN: 9781665462990 Place: Raleigh, NC, USA Publisher: IEEE
96. Xie, X., Song, J., Zhou, Z., Zhang, F., Ma, L.: Mosaic: Model-based Safety Analysis Framework for AI-enabled Cyber-Physical Systems (May 2023). http://arxiv.org/abs/2305.03882, arXiv:2305.03882 [cs]
97. Xie, Z., Liu, Z., Peng, Z., Wu, W., Zhou, B.: Vid2sim: realistic and interactive simulation from video for urban navigation. CVPR (2025)
98. Yang, S., et al.: Novel demonstration generation with gaussian splatting enables robust one-shot manipulation. arXiv preprint arXiv:2504.13175 (2025)
99. Zhao, X., Gerasimou, S., Calinescu, R., Imrie, C., Robu, V., Flynn, D.: Bayesian learning for the robust verification of autonomous robots. Commun. Eng. **3**(1), 1–14 (2024)

Q-Sylvan: A Parallel Decision Diagram Package for Quantum Computing

Sebastiaan Brand(✉)🆔 and Alfons Laarman🆔

Leiden Institute of Advanced Computer Science, Leiden University, Leiden, The Netherlands
{s.o.brand,a.w.laarman}@liacs.leidenuniv.nl

Abstract. As physical realizations of quantum computers move closer towards practical applications, the need for tools to analyze and verify quantum algorithms grows. Among the algorithms and data structures used to tackle such problems, decision diagrams (DDs) have shown much success. However, an obstacle with DDs is their efficient parallelization, and while parallel speedups have been obtained for DDs used in classical applications, attempts to parallelize operations for quantum-specific DDs have yielded only limited success. In this work, we present an efficient implementation of parallel edge-valued DDs, which makes use of fine-grained task parallelism and lock-free hash tables. Additionally, we use these DDs to implement two use cases: simulation and equivalence checking of quantum circuits. In our empirical evaluation we find that our tool, Q-Sylvan, shows a single-core performance that is competitive with the state-of-the-art quantum DD tool MQT DDSIM on large instances, and moreover achieves parallel speedups of up to ×18 on 64 cores.

Keywords: Quantum computing · Quantum circuit simulation · Equivalence checking · Decision diagrams · Parallelism

1 Introduction

Quantum computing is an emerging technology that aims to provide computational speedups on problems in areas such as cryptography [30], finance [26], and optimization [13], as well as on problems in quantum physics [16] and quantum chemistry [5]. As the number of available qubits on quantum chips grows, and the field moves closer towards practical applications, so grows the need for tools to analyze and verify quantum circuits.

In this paper, we focus on two tasks specifically: simulation and equivalence checking of quantum circuits. Although these are computationally hard problems [1,17,18,33], much like problems in classical verification, heuristic algorithms and data structures can significantly help with the scalability of these tasks. One particular data structure that has seen a lot of success in the classical evaluation of quantum circuits is decision diagrams (DDs). While different types

© The Author(s), under exclusive license to Springer Nature Switzerland AG 2026
M. D'Souza et al. (Eds.): ATVA 2025, LNCS 16145, pp. 260–273, 2026.
https://doi.org/10.1007/978-3-032-08707-2_12

of decision diagrams have been proposed in the context of quantum computing [24,28,31,35–37,39,40], edge-valued decision diagrams (EVDDs) [32] with complex edge values [24,40] have been shown to be very useful in practice.

However, a particular obstacle with decision diagrams is that computations on them are hard to efficiently parallelize [8]. And although the decision diagram library Sylvan [9] has shown good speedups for DDs without edge values, the storage and handling of floating-point values in EVDDs adds additional complications. This has thus far yielded limited scalability of EVDDs for quantum computing applications, with speedups of up to ×3 using 32 cores on the simulation of random circuits [14] and ×2–3 using 16 cores on Grover circuits [21].

In this paper, we present an efficient implementation of parallel EVDDs, building on the parallel decision diagram library Sylvan [9], which before now only supported decision diagrams without edge values, and we address several obstacles regarding floating-point values in DDs. We also provide implementations for two use cases: quantum circuit simulation and quantum circuit equivalence checking, both supporting the full set of standard quantum gates of Open QASM 2.0 [6]. We evaluate the performance of our resulting tool, Q-Sylvan,[1] against several other recent tools on a large set of benchmarks. We show that Q-Sylvan is capable of obtaining speedups of up to ×7 on 8 cores and up to ×18 on 64 cores, while also providing a single-core performance that is competitive with the state-of-the-art DD-based quantum circuit simulator MQT DDSIM [40] on large instances. The contributions of this paper are summarized as follows:

1. An efficient implementation of parallel EVDDs.
2. The implementation of two use cases using these EVDDs: simulation and equivalence checking of quantum circuits.
3. An evaluation against state-of-the-art tools on a large benchmark set.

2 Quantum Computing and EVDDs

For the convenience of the reader, we briefly explain the necessary basics of quantum computing and the role of decision diagrams in this context.

While there are many interesting intricacies in the mathematics of quantum computing, for the purposes of this paper, a high-level description of *quantum states* and *quantum gates* will be sufficient. The state of n quantum bits (qubits) can be described by a vector in $\mathbb{C}^{2^n}$, and can also be seen as a function $\psi : \{0,1\}^n \to \mathbb{C}$. Similarly, a quantum gate (i.e. a linear transformation that maps states to states) that acts on n qubits can be described by a matrix in $\mathbb{C}^{2^n \times 2^n}$ (or a function $U : \{0,1\}^{2n} \to \mathbb{C}$). The effect of a gate on a state can be computed through matrix-vector multiplication. A *quantum circuit* is a sequence of quantum gates, and can be classically simulated through repeated matrix-vector multiplication.

---

[1] Available online at https://github.com/System-Verification-Lab/q-sylvan under the Apache-2.0 license.

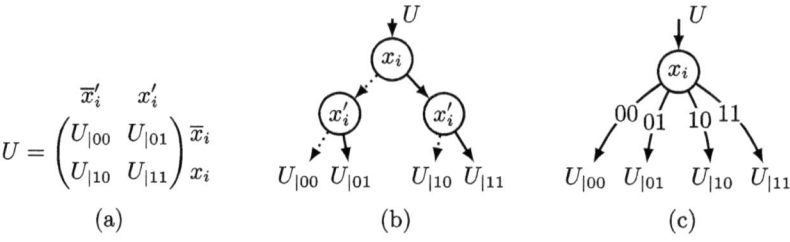

Fig. 1. A $2^n \times 2^n$ matrix (a) can be recursively encoded in a DD with two children per node (b), or four children per node (c), as in QMDD [24].

To store these exponentially large vectors and matrices compactly, people have turned to decision diagrams, a data structure for which it is well known how to compute matrix multiplications [12]. In this work we opt to use edge-valued DDs [24], which are also called quantum multi-valued DDs (QMDDs) [40].

An EVDD is a rooted, directed, acyclic graph whose edges have values associated with them. For our purposes these values are complex numbers. Each node v in an EVDD has a variable $\mathsf{var}v = x_i$, and two outgoing edges. For an EVDD that encodes an n-qubit state, we use the variables $\{x_0, \ldots, x_{n-1}\}$. EVDDs are always ordered, i.e. on every path the variables are encountered in the same order $x_0 \prec x_1 \prec \cdots \prec x_{n-1}$, although variables may be skipped. Every path through an EVDD corresponds to a single entry in the vector it encodes, with that value being equal to the product of the edge values on that path. As an example, the EVDD on the right encodes the vector $\psi = \begin{pmatrix} 1 & -2 & 1 & -2 & 1 & i & 3 & 3i \end{pmatrix}^\mathsf{T}$. The value $\psi(110)$, for example, can be read from the EVDD by following the 1 (solid) edges for x_0 and x_1, and the 0 (dashed) edge for x_2, obtaining $1 \cdot 3 \cdot 1 = 3$. Algorithms on DDs are typically defined recursively. Two examples are given in Algorithms 1 and 2.

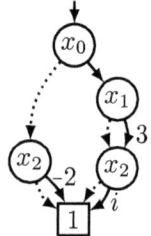

Figure 1 shows how DDs represent matrices. EVDDs do so by reinterpreting the matrix as a function $f(\boldsymbol{x}, \boldsymbol{x}')$, where $\boldsymbol{x}$ indexes rows and $\boldsymbol{x}'$ columns (Fig. 1b). The variables in $\boldsymbol{x}$ and $\boldsymbol{x}'$ are then interleaved to enable recursive descent on matrix quadrants (Fig. 1b). In contrast, a QMDD [24] is refined for matrices, as Fig. 1c shows. Because a QMDD can be translated into an EVDD in linear time and vice versa, they are effectively the same data structure [11].

Other types of DDs have also been used within quantum computing, such as multi-terminal binary DDs (MTBDDs) [28,36], context-free-language ordered BDDs (CFLOBDDs) [31], local invertible map DDs (LIMDDs) [37], and local invertible map tensor DDs (LimTDDs) [15]. EVDDs appear to strike a good balance between compression and practical efficiency: compared to MTBDDs, they benefit from better compression [40], while compared to LIMDDs and CFLOBDDs, they are practically more efficient on a wider array of circuits [31,38].

Algorithm 1: Vector addition with EVDDs. Here val(A) denotes the edge value of the root edge of A, and A[0] (A[1]) denotes the 0 (1) child of A.

1 **def** PLUS(EVDD A, EVDD B) ▷ assuming var(A) = var(B)
2   **if** A and B are terminals **then**
3   **return** val(A) + val(B)
4   **if** $R \leftarrow$ cache[PLUS,A,B] **then return** R ▷ Memoization to avoid
5     $R_0 \leftarrow$ PLUS(val(A) · $A[0]$, val(B) · $B[0]$) ▷ recomputing
6     $R_1 \leftarrow$ PLUS(val(A) · $A[1]$, val(B) · $B[1]$)
7     $R \leftarrow$ MAKENODE(var(A), R_0, R_1)
8   cache[PLUS,A,B] $\leftarrow R$
9   **return** R

Algorithm 2: Matrix-vector multiplication with EVDDs.

1 **def** MULTIPLY(EVDD M, EVDD V) ▷ assuming var(M) = var(V)
2   **if** M and V are terminals **then**
3   **return** val(M) · val(V)
4   **if** $R \leftarrow$ cache[MULTIPLY,M,V] **then return** R
5     $R_{00} \leftarrow$ MULTIPLY(val($M[0]$) · $M[00], V[0]$)
6     $R_{01} \leftarrow$ MULTIPLY(val($M[0]$) · $M[01], V[1]$)
7     $R_{10} \leftarrow$ MULTIPLY(val($M[1]$) · $M[10], V[0]$)
8     $R_{11} \leftarrow$ MULTIPLY(val($M[1]$) · $M[11], V[1]$)
9     $R_0 \leftarrow$ MAKENODE(var(v), R_{00}, R_{10})
10     $R_1 \leftarrow$ MAKENODE(var(v), R_{01}, R_{11})
11     $R \leftarrow$ PLUS(R_0, R_1) ▷ using Algorithm 1
12   cache[MULTIPLY,M,V] $\leftarrow R$
13   **return** R · val(M) · val(V)

3 EVDD Implementation

Since our goal is to provide an efficient implementation of parallel EVDDs, we choose to implement these on top of the parallel decision diagram library Sylvan [9]. Sylvan contains implementations of several different types of decision diagrams, among which are multi-terminal binary decision diagrams (MTBDDs), list decision diagrams (LDDs), and zero-suppressed decision diagrams (ZDDs). However, Sylvan does not yet support any decision diagrams with edge values.

Floating-Point Equality. A prominent hurdle in the implementation of DDs with real (or complex) edge values is handling floating-point values. Floating-point computations infamously do not always yield exact solutions, e.g. $0.1 + 0.2$ might give 0.30000000000000004, and so using exact floating-point equality would often prevent the merging of nodes, which in turn prevents the decision diagrams from

Algorithm 3: Find-or-put a complex value c in a hash table. δ is a configurable variable with a default value of 10^{-14}.

```
1  def FINDORPUT(c)
2      d.r ← ROUND(c.r, δ)                       ▷ Round real and imaginary components
3      d.i ← ROUND(c.i, δ)
4      index ← HASH(d)                           ▷ Compute hash based on rounded value
5      while not found or put do
6          if CAS(table[index], empty, c) then   ▷ Store unrounded value with
7              return index                      ▷ atomic compare-and-swap
8          else
9              v ← table[index]
10             if |c.r − v.r| < δ and |c.i − v.i| < δ then   ▷ If δ-close, return
11                 return index                               ▷ existing value
12             else
13                 index ← index + 1
```

staying compact. Therefore, we would like to consider edges with edge values that are very close to be equivalent. Specifically, we consider two floating-point values a, b equivalent if $|a − b| < \delta$, with $\delta = 10^{-14}$, and we consider two complex values equivalent if the same inequality holds for both their real and imaginary components. Although this can introduce numerical errors, setting $\delta = 0$ has been shown empirically to allow for almost no node-merging [25], and thus setting δ to a small but non-zero value appears to be a necessary evil of decision diagrams with floating-point edge values. Alternative representations of real or complex values, such as algebraic representations, have their own shortcomings. For example, the algebraic representation proposed in [25] only works for a limited gate set (specifically $\{H, T, CX\}$). And even though this gate set is technically universal for quantum computing, more general single-qubit rotation gates, which appear in ubiquitous quantum algorithms such as quantum approximate optimization algorithms (QAOA), variational quantum eigensolvers (VQE), and the quantum Fourier transform (QFT), can only be approximated by it. Specifically, an m-gate quantum circuit that contains general single-qubit rotation gates can be approximated up to an error of ε by a circuit with $O(m \log(m/\varepsilon))$ gates [7,19,29].

Storing Edge Values. In order to efficiently recognize equivalent edge values, we store them in a hash table. To facilitate efficient concurrent access we use a hash table with atomic compare-and-swap operations based on [20]. As mentioned above, due to the imperfection of floating-point arithmetic we cannot simply use floating-point equality to determine if two edge values are equivalent. Instead, when storing a complex edge value c we hash a rounded version of c to compute a bucket index, in which we store the (non-rounded) value of c. If the bucket is already occupied we compare the absolute values of the real and imaginary components to check if the stored value is equivalent to the value we want to store. A pseudocode description of this procedure is given in Algorithm 3.

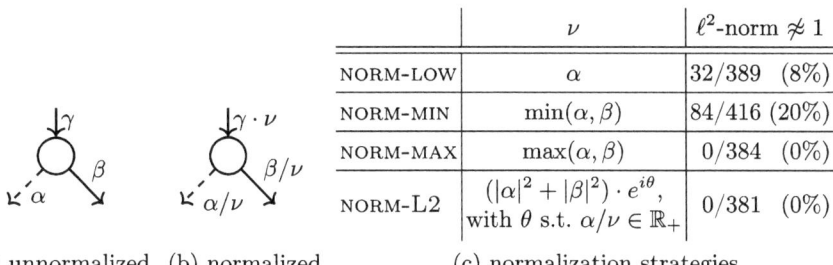

Fig. 2. An arbitrary tuple of edge values $\langle \alpha, \beta, \gamma \rangle$ is not generally in a canonical form, e.g. $\langle 2, 6, 1 \rangle \equiv \langle 1, 3, 2 \rangle$. Such a tuple can be normalized by dividing α and β, and multiplying γ, by some choice of ν. In the example, normalizing both tuples by $\nu = \alpha$ yields $\langle \frac{2}{2}, \frac{6}{2}, 1 \cdot 2 \rangle = \langle 1, 3, 2 \rangle$ and $\langle \frac{1}{1}, \frac{3}{1}, 2 \cdot 1 \rangle = \langle 1, 3, 2 \rangle$. The table in (c) shows different choices for ν, along with an empirical evaluation of the numerical errors when simulating circuits from MQT Bench [27] and checking the ℓ^2-norm of the output.

Normalizing Edge Values In order to recognize equivalent nodes, they must be stored in a canonical form. To bring an arbitrary EVDD node into a canonical form, the edge values need to be normalized (Figs. 2a and 2b). Four different methods, specified in Fig. 2c, have been implemented. Out of these the first three achieve canonicity by setting one of the edge values to 1, while the fourth is based on the way quantum states are normalized in quantum computing in general. These methods have been tested on the MQT Bench benchmark set [27] (discussed in Sect. 5) for circuits up to 30 qubits. For each run that terminated within the given timeout of 10 min we computed the ℓ^2-norm (the sum of absolute values squared) of the output and checked if this equals 1 ($\pm 10^{-3}$) as it should for quantum states. We find that while NORM-MAX and NORM-L2 did not have any issues, NORM-LOW and NORM-MIN suffered from a significant amount of numerical errors. This can be an indication that having larger values higher up in the decision diagram can increase issues with numerical instability, and it rules out NORM-LOW and NORM-MIN as viable methods. Between the remaining strategies we find that while NORM-L2 yields smaller decision diagrams on some instances, NORM-MAX is faster on most instances. This difference is likely due to the higher complexity of NORM-L2. We therefore choose to set NORM-MAX as the default, and have also used this for the evaluation in Sect. 5.

Parallelization. Sylvan makes use of the work-stealing framework Lace [10], which can be used for both intra- and inter-operational parallelism with its SPAWN (fork) and SYNC (join) commands. Since we aim to create efficient parallel quantum DD operations, we focus here on intra-operational parallelism, i.e. parallelism within a single (recursive) DD operation. As an example, consider the EVDD algorithm for vector addition, given in Algorithm 1. The algorithm contains two recursive calls (lines 5 and 6) that are typically executed sequentially. With Lace, these can be parallelized as follows:

```
5  SPAWN(PLUS(val(A) · A[1], val(B) · B[1]))     ▷ Spawn call as task (fork)
6  R₀ ← PLUS(val(A) · A[0], val(B) · B[0])       ▷ Call directly
7  R₁ ← SYNC                                     ▷ Obtain task result (join)
```

The spawned tasks are queued and can be executed by another thread, while the task on line 6 is executed by the current thread. After finishing its own task, the thread waits for the result of the spawned task.

Since all threads share the same hash table that stores unique nodes, a mechanism is required to protect against race conditions. Sylvan does this using a lock-free node table with atomic compare-and-swap operations, rather than locking (parts) of the table [8]. The same mechanism is also used for the table that stores the edge values (see Algorithm 3).

4 Use Cases

We now briefly describe the implementation of our two main use cases: simulation and equivalence checking of quantum circuits. Implementations of both are available as command line programs and take as input circuits in the standard quantum circuit format Open QASM 2.0 [6], with support for the full set of quantum gates defined by Open QASM's "qelib1.inc". Additionally, Q-Sylvan's C interface can also be used directly, supporting many functions for creating and manipulating vectors and matrices used in quantum computing.[2]

Simulating quantum circuits with DDs is straightforward: first a DD is constructed for the initial all-zero state (i.e. a vector $(1\ 0\ 0\ \cdots\ 0)^\mathsf{T}$), after which for every gate in the circuit the state is updated through matrix-vector multiplication (Algorithm 2). Q-Sylvan then allows for the final state to be either output directly, or to draw samples from it through simulated quantum measurements.

Our second use case is quantum circuit equivalence checking, which is defined as follows: given two n-qubit quantum circuits $U = \{U_1, \ldots, U_m\}$ and $V = \{V_1, \ldots, V_\ell\}$, where U_i and V_i are the individual gates composing the circuits, are U and V represented by the same matrices up to a global factor? I.e. does there exist some $c \in \mathbb{C}$ such that $U = cV$ (or equivalently we write $U \equiv V$)? There are a variety of ways to check quantum circuit equivalence. The naive method is to compute the full $2^n \times 2^n$ sized matrices U and V through multiplication of their individual gates. However, much like computing the composition of transition relations tends to be inefficient with DDs in classical model checking [22], the DDs resulting from multiplying quantum gates together tend to be much larger than those obtained from only updating states. However, as discussed below, one can be clever in choosing the order in which the gates are multiplied.

We implement two equivalence checking algorithms: "alternating" and "Pauli". The alternating algorithm was proposed in [4], and the idea is to first rewrite $U \equiv V$ as $UV^\dagger \equiv I$, where I is the identity matrix, $UV^\dagger = U_m \ldots U_2 U_1 V_1^\dagger V_2^\dagger \ldots V_\ell^\dagger$,

---

[2] See https://github.com/System-Verification-Lab/Q-Sylvan#Documentation.

and $V_i^\dagger = (V_i^*)^\mathsf{T}$ is the conjugate transpose of V_i. This product can then be computed from the inside out, e.g. if $m = \ell$ the computation order would be $(U_m \ldots (U_2(U_1 V_1^\dagger) V_2^\dagger) \ldots V_\ell^\dagger)$. If (w.l.o.g.) $m \geq \ell$ the algorithm takes $\frac{m}{\ell}$ gates from U for every gate from V. The motivation for this approach is that when U and V are identical, every step of the computation yields the identity matrix, and thus the computation remains easy. When U and V are equivalent but not identical, this approach can still heuristically yield matrices that have small DD encodings. The Pauli algorithm is based on [34, Thm.1], which notes that $U \equiv V \iff \forall j \in \{0, \ldots, n-1\}(U X_j U^\dagger = V X_j V^\dagger) \wedge (U Z_j U^\dagger = V Z_j V^\dagger)$, where X_j and Z_j special matrices (specifically tensor products of identity and Pauli matrices) that have an efficient classical description. Similar to the alternating algorithm, the terms can be computed from the inside out, e.g. compute $U X_j U^\dagger$ as $(U_m \ldots (U_2(U_1 X_j U_1^\dagger) U_2^\dagger) \ldots U_m^\dagger)$. The motivation here is that when U and V consist of a particular subset of quantum gates called Clifford gates this computation is provably efficient (i.e. polynomial time), and when they consist of more general gates there can still be heuristic benefits from the compression DDs provide. Ours is the first DD-based implementation of this algorithm.

5 Empirical Evaluation

We evaluate Q-Sylvan against several state-of-the-art tools.[3] The single and 8-core results were obtained on an AMD Ryzen 7 5800x CPU with 8 cores and 64 GB of memory. The 64-core results were obtained on a machine with two AMD EPYC 7601 CPUs with 32 physical cores each (64 in total) and 1 TB of memory.

5.1 Simulation

For testing simulation performance we use two sets of quantum circuits in the Open QASM 2.0 format. The first, MQT Bench [27], contains 22 types of quantum circuits for which the number of qubits can be arbitrarily scaled, as well as 6 types of non-scalable circuits with varying numbers of qubits. To obtain a greater variety of circuits, the second dataset we include is one generated by KetGPT [2], an instance of ChatGPT that was trained on the MQT Bench dataset, and consists of 1000 quantum circuits with varying numbers of qubits. The reported runtimes only include computing the final state vector. Simulating measurements given this state vector constitutes negligible overhead [40].

We first test Q-Sylvan's single-core performance against the well-established EVDD-based quantum circuit simulator MQT DDSIM [40], shown in Fig. 3. We find that while DDSIM outperforms Q-Sylvan on the smaller instances (presumably in part due to a more efficient initialization), on larger instances (where either tool takes $\geq 10\,\mathrm{s}$) Q-Sylvan outperforms DDSIM on 61% of the MQT Bench circuits, and 30% of KetGPT circuits. A comparison against Quasimodo [31] (see [3, App. A]) shows that, while CFLOBDDs can theoretically

---

[3] Reproducible benchmarks are available at https://github.com/sebastiaanbrand/q-sylvan-benchmarks.

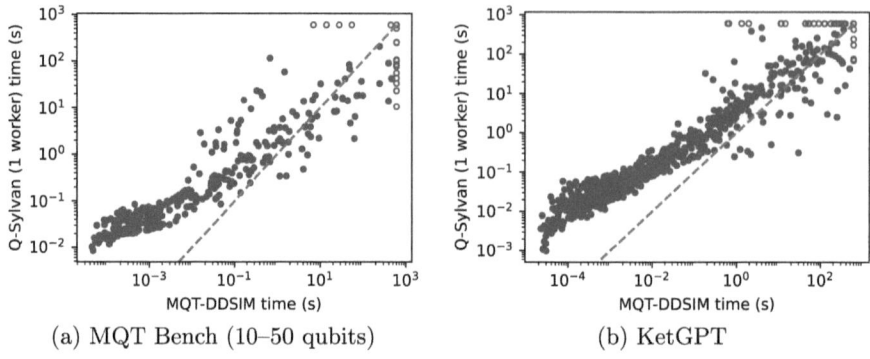

Fig. 3. Q-Sylvan vs DDSIM. Both order variables according to the qubit ordering in the QASM file. Open markers indicate timeouts. For both plots, we verified the full state vector output of both tools up to 20 qubits. While DDSIM is faster on the smaller circuits, on circuits where either tool takes $\geq$ 10 s Q-Sylvan beats DDSIM in 61% of MQT Bench circuits, and 30% of KetGPT circuits.

achieve much greater compactness than EVDDs, on this benchmark set they beat EVDDs only on the GHZ circuit. We omit SliQSim [35], as it does not support this benchmark set due to a lack of rotation-gate support.

Second, we evaluate Q-Sylvan's parallel performance. Since, when comparing single-core performance, Q-Sylvan performs well on a significant fraction of larger circuits, we evaluate Q-Sylvan's multi-core performance against its own single-core performance. As noted in [14], parallel speedups can greatly depend on the compactness of the decision diagrams. For example, it is easier to obtain speedups on a DD that is effectively a binary tree than it is to obtain speedups on a very compact DD. To evaluate this effect, we split the DDs resulting from the different benchmarks into three categories: *no sharing* (DDs which, for n qubits, have almost 2^n nodes), *high sharing* (DDs with less than $n \log n$ nodes), and *some sharing* (the DDs which fall in between these categories). Figures 4b and 4c show the distribution of decision diagram sizes for both benchmark sets. Obtaining speedups on the "no sharing" category would be the easiest, however these are instances where EVDDs offer little or no benefit. On the other hand, obtaining speedups on the "high sharing" category would be very difficult, since the DDs are so compact that little work remains that can be done in parallel. We are therefore mostly interested in speedups in the "some sharing" category.

The full parallel performance results are shown in Figs. 4d–4g, and a summary of the speedups at different percentiles is given in Fig. 4a. We find that, on the "some sharing" instances, Q-Sylvan is able to obtain speedups of up to ×7.2 and ×18 for 8 and 64 cores respectively. Unfortunately, we are unable to test directly against the two other parallel EVDD implementations [14,21], as one [14] does not have an implementation available anymore (neither public nor private), while the other [21] hard codes two circuits but does not allow for the parallel simulation of arbitrary circuits. However, for comparison, the first [14] reported

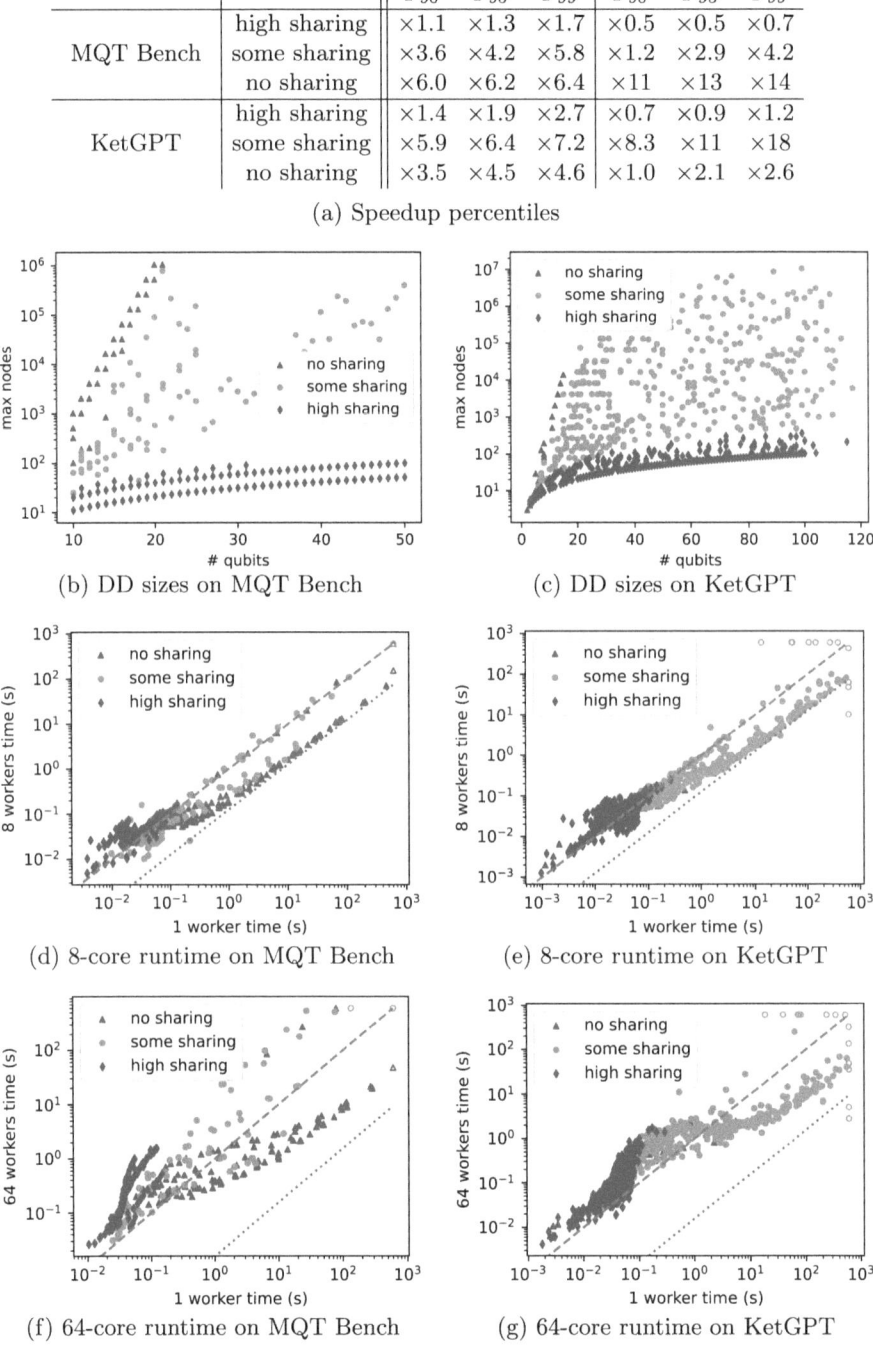

Fig. 4. Parallel performance. Open markers indicate timeouts, dashed lines indicate equal performance, and dotted lines indicate a $\times k$ speedup for k-cores.

speedups of up to ×3 using 32 cores on "no sharing" circuits, while the second [21] reported speedups of ×2–3 using 16 cores on "some sharing" circuits.

On the MQT Bench dataset we find that while the 8 core speedups are promising, the 64 core results are less strong. This could in part be caused by a higher communication overhead, since the 64 cores are split between two separate CPUs. Additionally, it might be that larger benchmarks (not just in numbers of qubits, but in number of DD nodes) are required to show greater speedups for 64 cores. The underperformance of Q-Sylvan on the "no sharing" subset of the KetGPT circuits can be explained by the fact that those types of circuits are almost not present in the KetGPT dataset.

5.2 Equivalence Checking

Next we compare our two equivalence checking implementations against two recent tools: MQT QCEC [4] and Quokka-Sharp [23]. We omit SliQEC [39] as it supports very few circuits due to a lack of rotation-gate support. MQT QCEC is a portfolio of different algorithms and makes use of both EVDDs as well a ZX-calculus, while Quokka-Sharp is based on weighted model counting. Both support multi-core computations. We use the benchmark set from [23], consisting of 78 pairs of equivalent circuits, and 146 non-equivalent pairs.

An overview of the number of completed benchmarks, as well as the speedups for 8-core computations, is given in Table 1. Detailed single-core results can be found in [3, App. A]. We find that Q-Sylvan shows a similar potential for speedups on the task of equivalence checking as it does on simulation. Using 8 cores it achieves a speedup of ×5.8 on both the equivalent and non-equivalent sets of circuits. Although Q-Sylvan is unable to match the single-core performance of QCEC, it still manages to solve some instances (19% of equivalent and 5% of non-equivalent circuits) faster than QCEC. QCEC, being a portfolio method, can parallelize computations naively, and greatly benefits from this on the equivalent instances. Its greater than ×8 parallel performance on these instances is likely a result of the way it prioritizes testing for non-equivalence over verifying equivalence when running on a single core. This might also explain

Table 1. Comparison of Q-Sylvan, Quokka-Sharp, and MQT QCEC, separated into equivalent and non-equivalent benchmarks. Timeout set to 5 min.

		Q-Sylvan alternating		Q-Sylvan Pauli		Quokka-Sharp		MQT QCEC	
	cores	1	8	1	8	1	8	1	8
equiv	% completed	59%	62%	49%	59%	39%	39%	64%	67%
	runtime reduction		×5.8		×2.1		×2.2		×15
non-equiv	% completed	56%	60%	47%	58%	50%	56%	82%	69%
	runtime reduction		×5.8		×2.2		×2.1		×1.3

its decrease in the number of solved non-equivalent instances when using more cores.

Overall we find that Q-Sylvan's equivalence checking algorithms show promising parallel performance, and would likely benefit from being embedded into a portfolio approach.

Acknowledgements. This work was supported by the NEASQC project, funded by the European Union's Horizon 2020, Grant Agreement No. 951821.

References

1. Aaronson, S.: BQP and the polynomial hierarchy. In: Proceedings of the Forty-Second ACM Symposium on Theory of Computing, pp. 141–150 (2010)
2. Apak, B., Bandic, M., Sarkar, A., Feld, S.: KetGPT–dataset augmentation of quantum circuits using transformers. In: International Conference on Computational Science, pp. 235–251. Springer (2024)
3. Brand, S., Laarman, A.: Q-sylvan: a parallel decision diagram package for quantum computing. arXiv preprint arXiv:2508.00514 (2025)
4. Burgholzer, L., Wille, R.: Advanced equivalence checking for quantum circuits. IEEE Trans. TCAD **40**(9), 1810–1824 (2020)
5. Cao, Y., et al.: Quantum chemistry in the age of quantum computing. Chem. Rev. **119**(19), 10856–10915 (2019)
6. Cross, A.W., Bishop, L.S., Smolin, J.A., Gambetta, J.M.: Open quantum assembly language. arXiv preprint arXiv:1707.03429 (2017)
7. Dawson, C.M., Nielsen, M.A.: The Solovay-Kitaev algorithm. arXiv preprint quant-ph/0505030 (2005)
8. van Dijk, T., Laarman, A., van de Pol, J.: Multi-core BDD operations for symbolic reachability. Electron. Not. Theoret. Comput. Sci. **296**, 127–143 (2013)
9. van Dijk, T., Van de Pol, J.: Sylvan: multi-core framework for decision diagrams. STTT **19**, 675–696 (2017)
10. van Dijk, T., van de Pol, J.C.: Lace: non-blocking split deque for work-stealing. In: Lopes, L., et al. (eds.) Euro-Par 2014. LNCS, vol. 8806, pp. 206–217. Springer, Cham (2014). https://doi.org/10.1007/978-3-319-14313-2_18
11. Fargier, H., Marquis, P., Niveau, A., Schmidt, N.: A knowledge compilation map for ordered real-valued decision diagrams. In: Proceedings of the AAAI Conference on Artificial Intelligence **28**(1) (2014)
12. Fujita, M., McGeer, P.C., Yang, J.Y.: Multi-terminal binary decision diagrams: an efficient data structure for matrix representation. Formal Methods Syst. Des. **10**, 149–169 (1997)
13. Harwood, S., Gambella, C., Trenev, D., Simonetto, A., Bernal, D., Greenberg, D.: Formulating and solving routing problems on quantum computers. IEEE Trans. Quantum Eng. **2**, 1–17 (2021)
14. Hillmich, S., Zulehner, A., Wille, R.: Concurrency in DD-based quantum circuit simulation. In: 2020 25th Asia and South Pacific Design Automation Conference (ASP-DAC), pp. 115–120. IEEE (2020)
15. Hong, X., Dai, A., Gao, D., Li, S., Ji, Z., Ying, M.: LimTDD: a compact decision diagram integrating tensor and local invertible map representations. arXiv preprint arXiv:2504.01168 (2025)

16. Huang, H.Y., Kueng, R., Torlai, G., Albert, V.V., Preskill, J.: Provably efficient machine learning for quantum many-body problems. Science **377**(6613) (2022)
17. Janzing, D., Wocjan, P., Beth, T.: "Non-identity-check" is QMA-complete. Int. J. Quant. Inf. **3**(03), 463–473 (2005)
18. Ji, Z., Wu, X.: Non-identity check remains QMA-complete for short circuits. arXiv preprint arXiv:0906.5416 (2009)
19. Kitaev, A.Y.: Quantum computations: algorithms and error correction. Russ. Math. Surv. **52**(6), 1191 (1997)
20. Laarman, A., van de Pol, J., Weber, M.: Boosting multi-core reachability performance with shared hash tables. In: Formal Methods in Computer Aided Design, pp. 247–255. IEEE (2010)
21. Li, S., Kimura, Y., Sato, H., Fujita, M.: Parallelizing quantum simulation with decision diagrams. IEEE Trans. Quant. Eng. (2024)
22. Matsunaga, Y., McGeer, P.C., Brayton, R.K.: On computing the transitive closure of a state transition relation. In: Proceedings of the 30th International Design Automation Conference, pp. 260–265 (1993)
23. Mei, J., Coopmans, T., Bonsangue, M., Laarman, A.: Equivalence checking of quantum circuits by model counting. In: International Joint Conference on Automated Reasoning, pp. 401–421. Springer (2024)
24. Miller, D.M., Thornton, M.A.: QMDD: a decision diagram structure for reversible and quantum circuits. In: 36th International Symposium on Multiple-Valued Logic (ISMVL'06), pp. 30–30. IEEE (2006)
25. Niemann, P., Zulehner, A., Drechsler, R., Wille, R.: Overcoming the tradeoff between accuracy and compactness in decision diagrams for quantum computation. IEEE TCAD **39**(12), 4657–4668 (2020)
26. Orús, R., Mugel, S., Lizaso, E.: Quantum computing for finance: overview and prospects. Rev. Phys. **4**, 100028 (2019)
27. Quetschlich, N., Burgholzer, L., Wille, R.: MQT Bench: Benchmarking software and design automation tools for quantum computing. Quantum (2023). MQT Bench is https://www.cda.cit.tum.de/mqtbench/
28. Samoladas, V.: Improved BDD algorithms for the simulation of quantum circuits. In: Halperin, D., Mehlhorn, K. (eds.) ESA 2008. LNCS, vol. 5193, pp. 720–731. Springer, Heidelberg (2008). https://doi.org/10.1007/978-3-540-87744-8_60
29. Selinger, P.: Efficient Clifford+T approximation of single-qubit operators. arXiv preprint arXiv:1212.6253 (2012)
30. Shor, P.W.: Algorithms for quantum computation: discrete logarithms and factoring. In: FOCS, pp. 124–134. IEEE (1994)
31. Sistla, M., Chaudhuri, S., Reps, T.: Symbolic quantum simulation with Quasimodo. In: CAV, pp. 213–225. Springer (2023)
32. Tafertshofer, P., Pedram, M.: Factored edge-valued binary decision diagrams. Formal Methods Syst. Des. **10**, 243–270 (1997)
33. Tanaka, Y.: Exact non-identity check is NQP-complete. Int. J. Quant. Inf. **8**(05), 807–819 (2010)
34. Thanos, D., Coopmans, T., Laarman, A.: Fast equivalence checking of quantum circuits of Clifford gates. In: International Symposium on Automated Technology for Verification and Analysis, pp. 199–216. Springer (2023)
35. Tsai, Y.H., Jiang, J.H.R., Jhang, C.S.: Bit-slicing the Hilbert space: Scaling up accurate quantum circuit simulation. In: 2021 58th ACM/IEEE Design Automation Conference (DAC). pp. 439–444. IEEE (2021)

36. Viamontes, G.F., Markov, I.L., Hayes, J.P.: High-performance QuIDD-based simulation of quantum circuits. In: Proceedings Design, Automation and Test in Europe Conference and Exhibition, vol. 2, pp. 1354–1355. IEEE (2004)
37. Vinkhuijzen, L., Coopmans, T., Elkouss, D., Dunjko, V., Laarman, A.: LIMDD: a decision diagram for simulation of quantum computing including stabilizer states. Quantum **7**, 1108 (2023)
38. Vinkhuijzen, L., Grurl, T., Hillmich, S., Brand, S., Wille, R., Laarman, A.: Efficient implementation of LIMDDs for quantum circuit simulation. In: International Symposium on Model Checking Software, pp. 3–21. Springer (2023)
39. Wei, C.Y., Tsai, Y.H., Jhang, C.S., Jiang, J.H.R.: Accurate BDD-based unitary operator manipulation for scalable and robust quantum circuit verification. In: Proceedings of the 59th Design Automation Conference, pp. 523–528 (2022)
40. Zulehner, A., Wille, R.: Advanced simulation of quantum computations. IEEE TCAD **38**(5), 848–859 (2018)

Learning

Inductive Generalization in Reinforcement Learning from Specifications

Vignesh Subramanian[1]($\boxtimes$), Rohit Kushwah[2], Subhajit Roy[2], and Suguman Bansal[1]

[1] School of Computer Science, Georgia Institute of Technology, Atlanta, USA
{vignesh,suguman}@gatech.edu
[2] Department of Computer Science and Engineering, Indian Institute of Technology Kanpur, Kanpur, India
{krohitk,subhajit}@cse.iitk.ac.in

Abstract. We present a novel *inductive generalization framework* for RL from logical specifications. Many interesting tasks in RL environments have a natural inductive structure. These *inductive tasks* have similar overarching goals but they differ inductively in low-level predicates and distributions. We present a generalization procedure that leverages this inductive relationship to learn a higher-order function, a *policy generator*, that generates appropriately *adapted* policies for instances of an inductive task in a zero-shot manner. An evaluation of the proposed approach on a set of challenging control benchmarks demonstrates the promise of our framework in generalizing to unseen policies for long-horizon tasks.

1 Introduction

Formal methods community has contributed strongly to *reinforcement learning (RL)*, especially from formal specifications [1,7,9,10,13,14,20,25,38,40]. These techniques may not provide strong guarantees. In fact, their inability to offer rigorous guarantees has been proven [2,39]. Nevertheless, these methods provide a principled approach for handling learning over long-horizon tasks.

Generalization remains one of the fundamental challenges in RL. While RL agents can achieve impressive performance on individual tasks, they often struggle to transfer learned behaviors to even slightly modified scenarios. Most RL approaches lack formal mechanisms to capture and exploit structural relationships between tasks, instead relying on implicit generalization through neural network function approximation. This often leads to superficial generalization that fails to capture deeper task similarities. Recent work has attempted to address these challenges through meta-learning and goal-conditioned learning, but developing RL algorithms that can generalize remains an open challenge.

While the challenge of overall generalization is too large to address, this work presents a novel notion of generalization, which we call *inductive generalization*. This is based on leveraging inductive similarities between tasks to generalize.

Inductive relationships are fundamental to computational tasks because they capture how complex behaviors can be built from simpler ones through systematic transformation. They appear naturally whenever tasks exhibit natural recursion or iteration. Our insight is that once we understand how to transform from step i to step $i + 1$, we can systematically generalize to handle arbitrarily many steps. This naturally arising pattern is particularly evident in robotics and control tasks, where physical constraints often impose regular structure. By formalizing these inductive relationships, we can move beyond treating each task instance as independent and instead leverage their inherent structural connections to enable systematic generalization.

To this end, we present a *logic-guided approach to inductive generalization* in RL. We use logical specifications to encode a class of *inductive tasks* which comprises of several similar tasks that can be enumerated from each other using an inductive relationship. We require that these tasks have identical logical structure but differ only in the low-level details of predicate values and/or environment parameters. Next, we leverage their similar structures to design a generalizable RL algorithm.

Formally, an inductive task is given by a tuple R = (R_0, update_pred, update_init) where R_0 is a *base task* given as a temporal logical specification over given predicates and update_pred and update_init define inductive updates to the predicates of the specification and environment parameters, respectively, to be applied to the base task repeatedly, so as to generate a family of tasks $R_1, R_2, \ldots$ and such. Intuitively, one can think of an inductive task to represent a complex task involving iterations as follows:

```
base_task = \task_0 // Encodes the base spec. and envt. conditions
current_task = base_task
repeat
    next_task = update_pred(current_task), update_init(current_task)
    current_task = next_task
```

For instance, in Fig. 1 the robot is required to transport the source pile of boxes to a target pile. This complex task can be decomposed into a series of inductively related tasks: for the i-th instance, pick the topmost box from a height of i in *Source* and place it at the top of the *Target* pile at height $(h - i)$ (where h is the total number of blocks). Here, the 0-th task instance forms the base task, and the update functions change the location of the topmost block in the source and target piles. Observe that all task instances in an inductive task have identical logical structure. They only differ in the instantiations of the low-level predicates and environment variables.

Our goal is to leverage this inductive relationship between tasks to design generalizable RL algorithms to learn policies for each task instance. Concretely, the question we ask is: if trained on a few task instances of an inductive task, can we obtain policies for the remaining tasks in a *zero-shot* manner?

Such generalization is difficult, in general. To solve this problem, we hypothesize that *inductively-related task instances may have inductively-related policies*. Based on this hypothesis, we attempt to learn an *inductive relationship*

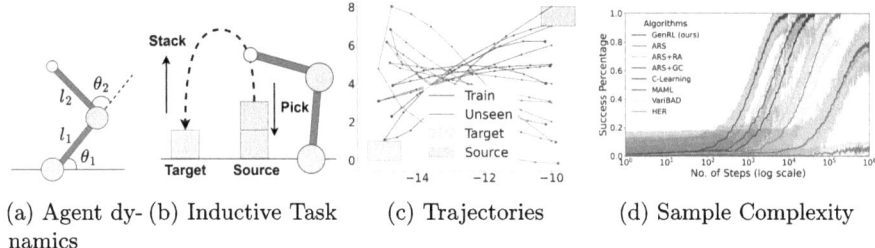

(a) Agent dynamics (b) Inductive Task (c) Trajectories (d) Sample Complexity

Fig. 1. Tower Destacking: The task is to pick boxes from *Source* and stack it on *Target*.(Color figure online)

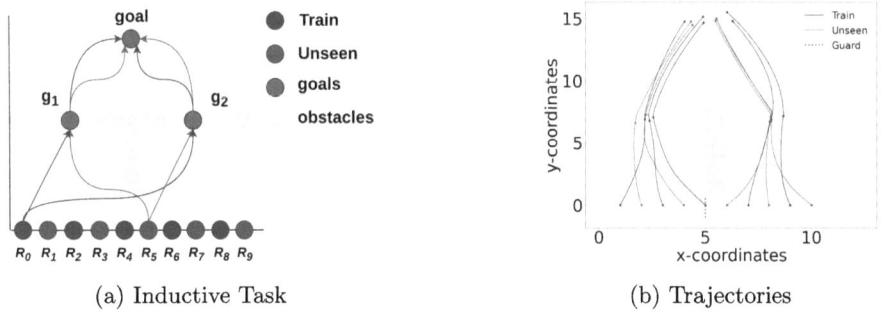

(a) Inductive Task (b) Trajectories

Fig. 2. Choice: visit either g_1 or g_2, then visit goal; task instances differ in initial state distribution. (Color figure online)

between the policies of simpler task instances to extract a *policy generator*: a higher-order function that returns an *adapted* policy for a given inductive task instance. Figure 1(c) shows the trajectories of the pickup head with $h = 8$ blocks: we trained a policy generator for the robot on picking and placing the first four blocks (shown in blue); The robot could complete the whole task, with adapted policies from the learned policy generator for the unseen task instances, i.e. pick-n-place of the bottom four blocks are shown in red. We see that the policy generator lends *significant adaptability* to the robot to control its θ_1 and θ_2, as the trajectories of the task instances are quite different.

However, our hypothesis may not always hold. It is possible that despite the task being inductive, the policies are not immediately inductive. The motivating example from Fig. 2 illustrates this complication. Figure 2 illustrates an *inductive task* in a 2D Cartesian plane: in a task instance, the agent is initially located in one of the blue or red regions marked R_k. The goal is to *visit the region* marked goal, *after visiting* one of the intermediate regions g_1 or g_2, while *always avoiding* the obstacles shown in light blue. The task is inductive on the initial position: the $(k+1)$-th task can be defined in terms of the k-th task, by shifting the initial location to the right by c units.

However, the policies are not inductive: there is a task R_k such that its policy needs to route through g_1 but the policy of task R_{k+1} must route through g_2 (e.g. R_4 and R_5). Yet, we may be able to *classify* the task instances into multiple groups, such that all tasks in each group is *inductive* (e.g. $\{\mathsf{R}_0, \ldots, \mathsf{R}_4\}$ and $\{\mathsf{R}_5, \ldots, \mathsf{R}_9\}$). Our policy generator learns such *branches* such that the task instances on the same decision of the branch have inductive policies.

The benchmark environments we utilize in this work are particularly well-suited for evaluating inductive generalization capabilities. Our tasks span a range from simple reachability in 2D environments to complex robotic manipulation scenarios, all unified by their inherent inductive structure. These environments feature continuous state and action spaces, long-horizon planning requirements, and varying degrees of physical constraints, which are challenging even for RL without generalization.

We summarize our contributions: (a). We introduce a framework to learn inductively generalizable policies for long-horizon tasks. This comprises formalizing the notion of inductively-related tasks based on their logical specification and describing the generalization problem as learning a higher-order policy generator (Sect. 3). (b). We describe a procedure to learn a neural policy generator by leveraging the inductive relationship between task instances (Sects. 4 and 5). (c). We perform an empirical evaluation of our inductive framework for generalization in learning unseen tasks in complex, long-horizon specifications in continuous environments, popular control environments, and robotic pick-n-place tasks. Our evaluation demonstrates the promise of our inductive approach (Sect. 6) as we are able to show that our approach outperforms mature policy-gradient state-of-the-art generalizable RL algorithms in their ability to generalize to unseen tasks and sample complexity.

2 Preliminaries

2.1 Markov Decision Process (MDP)

The environment in RL is given by a Markov Decision Process (MDP) $\mathcal{M} = (S, A, P, \eta)$ with continuous states $S \subseteq \mathbb{R}^n$, continuous actions $A \subseteq \mathbb{R}^m$, transitions $P(s, a, s') = p(s' \mid s, a) \in \mathbb{R}_{\geq 0}$ (i.e., probability density of transitioning from state s to state s' upon taking action a), and initial states $\eta : S \to \mathbb{R}_{\geq 0}$ (i.e., $\eta(s)$ is the probability of the initial state being s).

Let $\mathcal{Z}$ denote the set of all trajectories. A *trajectory* $\zeta \in \mathcal{Z}$ is either an infinite sequence $\zeta = s_0 \xrightarrow{a_0} s_1 \xrightarrow{a_1} \cdots$ or a finite sequence $\zeta = s_0 \xrightarrow{a_0} \cdots \xrightarrow{a_{t-1}} s_t$ where $s_i \in S$ and $a_i \in A$. A subtrajectory of ζ is a subsequence $\zeta_{\ell:k} = s_\ell \xrightarrow{a_\ell} \cdots \xrightarrow{a_{k-1}} s_k$. We let $\mathcal{Z}_f$ denote the set of finite trajectories. A (deterministic) *policy* $\pi : \mathcal{Z}_f \to A$ maps a finite trajectory to a fixed action.

Crucially, in RL we assume that the transition probabilities of the MDP are unknown. Hence, the MDP is accessed by sampling only. Concretely, given a policy π, we can sample a trajectory by sampling an initial state $s_0 \sim \eta(\cdot)$, and then iteratively taking the action $a_i = \pi(\zeta_{0:i})$ and sampling a next state $s_{i+1} \sim p(\cdot \mid s_i, a_i)$.

2.2 SPECTRL Specification Language and Their Abstract Graphs

We express RL tasks using the logical specification language SPECTRL [18]. Every SPECTRL specification can be expressed as an *abstract graph* which can be used to design scalable compositional algorithms for RL from logical specifications [19].

A SPECTRL specification is defined over a set of *atomic predicates* $\mathcal{P}_0$ that ground environment states, where every $p \in \mathcal{P}_0$ is associated with a function $[\![p]\!] : S \to \mathbb{B} = \{\texttt{true}, \texttt{false}\}$; we say a state s *satisfies* p (denoted $s \models p$) if and only if $[\![p]\!](s) = \texttt{true}$. For $b \in \mathcal{P}$, the syntax of SPECTRL is: $\phi ::= \texttt{achieve } b \mid \phi_1 \texttt{ ensuring } b \mid \phi_1; \phi_2 \mid \phi_1 \texttt{ or } \phi_2$. Each specification ϕ corresponds to a function $[\![\phi]\!] : \mathcal{Z} \to \mathbb{B}$, and we say $\zeta \in \mathcal{Z}$ satisfies ϕ (denoted $\zeta \models \phi$) if and only if $[\![\phi]\!](\zeta) = \texttt{true}$. Intuitively, 'achieve' and 'ensuring' are reachability and safety goals, respectively. ';' and 'or' refer to sequencing and disjunction, respectively. Letting ζ be a finite trajectory of length t, this function is defined by

$\zeta \models \texttt{achieve } b$ if $\exists\, i \le t,\ s_i \models b$

$\zeta \models \phi \texttt{ ensuring } b$ if $\zeta \models \phi$ and $\forall\, i \le t,\ s_i \models b$

$\zeta \models \phi_1; \phi_2$ if $\exists\, i < t,\ \zeta_{0:i} \models \phi_1$ and $\zeta_{i+1:t} \models \phi_2$

$\zeta \models \phi_1 \texttt{ or } \phi_2$ if $\zeta \models \phi_1$ or $\zeta \models \phi_2$.

Abstract Graph. An *abstract graph* of a SPECTRL specification is a DAG-like structure in which vertices represent sets of states (called subgoal regions) and edges represent sets of MDP trajectories that can be used to transition from the source to the target vertex without violating safety constraints.

Definition 1. *An abstract graph $\mathcal{G} = (U, E, u_0, F, \beta, \mathcal{Z}_{\text{safe}})$ is a directed acyclic graph (DAG) with vertices U, (directed) edges $E \subseteq U \times U$, initial vertex $u_0 \in U$, final vertices $F \subseteq U$, subgoal region map $\beta : U \to 2^S$ such that for each $u \in U$, $\beta(u)$ is a subgoal region, and safe trajectories $\mathcal{Z}_{\text{safe}} = \bigcup_{e \in E} \mathcal{Z}^e_{\text{safe}} \cup \bigcup_{f \in F} \mathcal{Z}^f_{\text{safe}}$, where $\mathcal{Z}^e_{\text{safe}} \subseteq \mathcal{Z}$ denotes the safe trajectories for edge $e \in E$ and $\mathcal{Z}^f_{\text{safe}} \subseteq \mathcal{Z}$ denotes the safe trajectories for final vertex $f \in F$.*

Intuitively, (U, E) is a DAG, and u_0 and F define a graph reachability problem for (U, E). Furthermore, β and $\mathcal{Z}_{\text{safe}}$ connect (U, E) back to the original MDP $\mathcal{M}$; in particular, for an edge $e = u \to u'$, $\mathcal{Z}^e_{\text{safe}}$ is the set of safe trajectories in $\mathcal{M}$ that can be used to transition from $\beta(u)$ to $\beta(u')$.

A trajectory $\zeta = s_0 \xrightarrow{a_0} s_1 \xrightarrow{a_1} \cdots \xrightarrow{a_{t-1}} s_t$ in $\mathcal{M}$ satisfies the abstract graph $\mathcal{G}$ (denoted $\zeta \models \mathcal{G}$) if there is a sequence of indices $0 = k_0 \le k_1 < \cdots < k_\ell \le t$ and a path $\rho = u_0 \to u_1 \to \cdots \to u_\ell$ in $\mathcal{G}$ such that (a). $u_\ell \in F$, (b). for all $z \in \{0, \ldots, \ell\}$, we have $s_{k_z} \in \beta(u_z)$, (c). for all $z < \ell$, letting $e_z = u_z \to u_{z+1}$, we have $\zeta_{k_z:k_{z+1}} \in \mathcal{Z}^{e_z}_{\text{safe}}$, and (d). $\zeta_{k_\ell:t} \in \mathcal{Z}^{u_\ell}_{\text{safe}}$. The first two conditions state that the trajectory should visit a sequence of subgoal regions corresponding to a path from the initial vertex to some final vertex, and the last two conditions state that the trajectory is composed of subtrajectories that are safe according to $\mathcal{Z}_{\text{safe}}$.

The *edge policy* π_e for an edge $e = u \to u'$ is one that safely transitions from a state in $\beta(u)$ to a state in $\beta(u')$. Given edge policies Π along with a path $\rho = u_0 \to u_1 \to \cdots \to u_k = u$ in $\mathcal{G}$, the *path policy* π_ρ navigates from $\beta(u_0)$ to $\beta(u)$. In particular, π_ρ executes $\pi_{u_j \to u_{j+1}}$ (starting from $j = 0$) until reaching $\beta(u_{j+1})$, after which it increments $j \leftarrow j+1$ (unless $j = k$). Learning an optimal policy for SPECTRL is reduced to learning an optimal path policy from the initial to final vertex. This gives rise to a natural compositional learning approach that first learns edge policies and then returns the path policy with the maximum probability of reaching a final vertex [19].

3 Inductive Tasks

We begin by describing *inductive tasks*. These appear naturally in several scenarios, as shown in Figs. 1 and 2.

Notation. An *RL task* is given by the tuple (ϕ, η) where ϕ is a SPECTRL specification and η is the initial state distribution in the MDP. We say a trajectory $\zeta = s_0 \ldots s_t$ satisfies an RL task (ϕ, η), denoted $\zeta \models (\phi, \eta)$, if $s_0 \sim \eta$ and $\zeta \models \phi$, I.e., ζ begins in a state sampled from η and ζ satisfies ϕ.

An *inductive task* is a family of *RL tasks* that demonstrate the same overarching structure but differ inductively in the low-level details. I.e., an *inductive task* is given by a set of enumerable RL tasks such that the $(i+1)$-th task builds on the i-th task by updating the predicates in the specification and/or the MDP initial distribution. Formally,

Definition 2. *Let $\mathcal{P}$ and $\mathcal{D}(S)$ denote the sets of predicates and state distributions in an MDP, respectively. Let $\phi(P)$ denote a* SPECTRL *specification defined over predicates $P \subseteq \mathcal{P}$. Then, an* inductive task *is given by* $\mathsf{R} = (\mathsf{R}_0,$ update_pred, update_init) *where RL task* $\mathsf{R}_0 = (\phi(\mathcal{P}_0), \eta_0)$ *is the base task,* update_pred $: \mathcal{P} \mapsto \mathcal{P}$ *is the predicate update function, and* update_init $: \mathcal{D}(S) \mapsto \mathcal{D}(S)$ *is the initial distribution update function. The enumerable task instances in* R *are given by* $\mathsf{R}_0 = (\phi(\mathcal{P}_0), \eta_0)$ *and* $\mathsf{R}_{i+1} = (\phi(\mathcal{P}_{i+1}), \eta_{i+1})$ *for $i > 0$ where* $\mathcal{P}_{i+1} = \{$update_pred$(p) \mid p \in \mathcal{P}_i\}$ *and* $\eta_{i+1}(s) = \eta_i($update_init$(s))$.

We denote the i-th task instance R_i by (ϕ_i, η_i) and refer to task instances R_i and R_{i+1} as *adjacent*.

Motivating Example #1. For Fig. 1, the inductive task is formalized as: For $j \in \{0, \ldots, h\}$, let the predicates source_j and target_j denote the location of the block at height j in the source and target tower, respectively; let η_source_j be a distribution around the block at height j in the source tower. The base task R_0 is given by

$$((\texttt{achieve (target\_0)}); (\texttt{achieve (source\_(h-1)))}, \eta\_\texttt{source\_h}).$$

The predicate update function updates predicates source_j and target_j to source_(j − 1) and target_(j + 1), resp. The initial distribution update function updates η_source_j to η_source_(j − 1). Then, the j-th task instance

R_j = ((achieve (target_j)); (achieve (source_(h − j − 1))), η_source_h − j).

Motivating Example #2. Choice tasks from Fig. 2 is an inductive task that updates the initial state distribution, by shifting to the right by constant units for adjacent task instances. They are stack of l levels, where each task R_k requires reaching a goal $goal_i$ while avoiding the obstacle obs, either through the (sub)goal g_{i1} or g_{i2},

$$(\text{achieve } (\text{reach } (g_{i1}) \text{ or reach } (g_{i2}));$$
$$\text{achieve } (\text{reach } (goal_i)))^l$$
$$\text{ensuring } (\text{avoid } (obs))$$

where, $1 \leq i \leq l$. We use the superscript l to indicate that the enclosed specification is repeated l times. Figure 2a illustrates a task with $l = 1$ and Fig. 9c illustrates a task with $l = 2$. The update functions for the initial distribution is defined as update_init($\eta(s)$) = $\eta(s + (c_1, 0))$, where $c_1 = 1$ unit. Intuitively, this corresponds to shifting the support of the distribution η to the left by c_1 units along the x-axis.

Lemma 1. *For an inductive task R, let $\mathcal{G}_i$ be the abstract graph of the specification of the i-th task instance R_i. Then, all the $\mathcal{G}_i$s share a common DAG structure with the same initial and final vertices.*

Proof. The proof follows from the construction of abstract graphs in [19].

This lemma asserts that all task instances within an inductive task have identical logical structures. They differ only in the low-level details of the abstract graph.

4 Generalizable RL for Inductive Tasks

We define the problem of learning generalizable policies for an inductive task by learning a *policy generator*. The *policy generator* for an inductive task R is a function $\mathbb{G} : R \to \Pi$, where Π is the set of all policies in the MDP. E.g., the policy generator for tower-destacking from Fig. 1 maps the j-th task instance to the policy that displaces the source's (h − j)-th block to the target's j-th block, then returns to the source's (h − j − 1)-th block by manipulating the motor controls θ_1, θ_2. Note these policies are different for each task instance R_j.

Definition 3 (Learning a Policy Generator). *Given an MDP with unknown transitions, an inductive task R and a set of a training task instances Train s.t. the base task $R_0 \in$ Train, the problem of generalizable RL is to learn a policy generator $\mathbb{G}^* : R \to \Pi$ such that*

$$\mathbb{G}^* \in \arg\max_{\mathbb{G}} \frac{1}{|\mathsf{Train}|} \cdot \sum_{\mathsf{R}_j \in \mathsf{Train}} \Pr_{s_0 \sim \eta_j, \zeta \sim \mathcal{D}_{\pi_j, s_0}} [\zeta \models \phi_j, \eta_j] \text{ where the policy } \pi_j = \mathbb{G}^*(\mathsf{R}_j)$$

Then, $\pi_j = \mathbb{G}^*(\mathsf{R}_j)$ for all $j \in \mathbb{N}$.

I.e., the policy generator optimizes the policies for all training task instances simultaneously, in an attempt to *generalize*, so as to also derive policies for all task instances not present in Train.

4.1 Learning Policy Generator

We present an overview of our approach to learning a policy generator. Learning a higher-order function such as the policy generator is difficult. To make learning a policy generator feasible, we (a) assume *inductive relations between policies* of task instances that are inductively related, (b) leverage similarity between the structure of inductive tasks (Lemma 1), and (c) leverage compositionality of SPECTRL specifications [19].

We leverage the inductive nature of the inductive tasks to learn the policy generator. We base our work on the following hypothesis: *As two adjacent task instances are related by an inductive relation, there may also exist an inductive relation over the corresponding policies of these tasks*. However, this may not hold for certain tasks (e.g. Fig. 2). We attempt to overcome this with *compositonality*: instead of learning an inductive policy for the whole task, we divide the task into *subtasks* via the abstract graph, where each edge in the abstract graph corresponds to a subtask.

[19] ensures that a policy for a task instance R_i is given by a path policy in its abstract graph $\mathcal{G}_i$. Lemma 1 informs that the DAG structure of all graphs $\mathcal{G}_i$ are identical, say $\mathcal{G}$. Hence, the policy generator can be viewed as a map from task instances to path policies from initial to final vertex in the same graph $\mathcal{G}$ (with appropriate instantiation for edge policies in each task instance). Hence, we learn an inductive relation between the corresponding edge policies of the abstract graphs. We formulate the problem to learn such inductive relations in Subsect. *Learning an Inductive Relation on Edges*.

Last but not least, the edge policies obtained from the inductive relation will result in multiple path policies for each task instance. We are interested in the policy generator to choose the optimal path policy for each task instance. We ensure this by incorporating *guards* along vertices in the common DAG $\mathcal{G}$ that route each task instance along the optimal path in the DAG (Subsect. *Learning the Policy Generator*).

Learning an Inductive Relation on Edges. This section defines an inductive relation between corresponding edges of the abstract graphs of an inductive task and formulates our approach to learn neural inductive relations.

Let $e = u \to v$ be an edge in the common DAG $\mathcal{G}$ of an inductive task. Let π_i denote the edge policy for the i-th task on the edge e in $\mathcal{G}_i$.

Then, an *inductive relation* between these policies is a function $\Omega : \Pi \to \Pi$ s.t. $\pi_{i+1} = \Omega(\pi_i)$. Thus, given the edge policy π_0 in the base task, the inductive relation Ω can be inductively "unrolled" to construct the edge policy for any instance R_i of an inductive task R. That is,

$$\pi_i = \Omega(\pi_{i-1}) = \Omega(\Omega(\pi_{i-2})) = \cdots = \Omega^i(\pi_0)$$

where Ω^i composes Ω with itself i times.

As learning the inductive relation Ω is difficult, we resort to *polynomial approximation*: we approximate the inductive relation Ω over the policies as an m-degree polynomial. Polynomial approximations are interesting as any function can be approximated as a polynomial up to an arbitrary precision using the Taylor expansion. This reduces learning Ω on edges to inferring the κ-coefficients $(\kappa_m, \cdots, \kappa_0)$ of an m-degree κ-polynomial. Details below:

Neural Policies. If the policy for the i-th task instance $\pi_i \in \Pi$ is implemented by a neural network with parameter vector $[\pi_i]$, then the m-degree polynomial inductive relation is given by

$$[\pi_{i+1}] = \kappa_m \odot [\pi_i]^m + \kappa_{m-1} \odot [\pi_i]^{m-1} + \cdots + \kappa_0 \qquad (1)$$

where, the polynomial coefficients, κ_i, are vectors with the same dimension as $[\pi_i]$; the $\odot$ operator is the Hadamard product (element-wise multiplication) of the coefficient vectors κ_i with the parameter vector (weights and biases) of the policy network π_i, and '+' is element-wise vector addition. Then as described earlier, with π_0 as the base policy with parameters $[\pi_0]$, the inductive relation Ω can be inductively "unrolled" to construct the policy network for π_i. Hence, in this case, we attempt to learn an inductive relation between the parameter vectors of the policy (neural) network of task instances.

Learning the Policy Generator. Next, we describe a policy generator on the common DAG $\mathcal{G}$ between all task instances in R. Given the inductive relation and base policy for every edge in $\mathcal{G}$, our goal is to describe a mapping for task instances in R to a path policy in $\mathcal{G}$, as per the edge policies inferred by Eq. 1.

Every path from the initial to the final vertex corresponds to a path policy for the i-th task. Elaborating further, for degree m, let $\kappa^e = (\kappa^e_m, \cdots, \kappa^e_0)$ denote the κ-coefficients on the edge $e \in \mathcal{G}$. Let $\rho = e_1 \cdots e_k$ be a path from the initial to a final vertex. Then, a policy for a task R_i is given by the path policy $\pi_i^{e_1} \cdots \pi_i^{e_k}$ where $[\pi_i^{e_j}] = \Omega^i[\pi_0^{e_j}]$. This requires *selection* of a path policy for each R_i.

We assign *guards* at vertices with multiple outgoing edges in $\mathcal{G}$ such that each vertex routes task instances to a unique outgoing edge, ensuring a unique path for every task instance from initial to a final vertex. Formally, a guard in a vertex maps task instances to the outgoing edges from the vertex.

Then, the policy generator for an abstract graph executes as follows: Given a task instance R_i, it uses the guard conditions to determine its unique path from the initial to a final vertex. It returns the path policy along this path as

Algorithm 1. GenRL(R, m, Train)
―――
1: $\mathcal{G} \leftarrow$ CommonDAG(R)
2: **while** vertex $u \in \mathcal{G}$ is chosen in topological order **do**
3:     Compute $P(u,i)$, bestIn(u,i) **for** all $i \in$ Train
4:     $\eta_i^u \leftarrow$ InduceDistrbution$(u,$ bestIn$(u,i))$ **for** all $i \in$ Train
5:     **for** edge $e = (u,v) \in$ OutEdges(u) **do**
6:         $\pi_0^e \leftarrow$ LearnBasePolicy(e, η_0^u)
7:         $\kappa^e \leftarrow$ LearnKappaCoefficients$(e, m+1, \pi_0^e, \eta^u,$ Train$)$
8: Guard $\leftarrow$ LearnGuardConditions$(\mathcal{G},$ bestIn$)$
9: **return** κ^e, π_0^e for all edge and Guard for all vertices
―――

described above. For example, Fig. 2a has two possible paths: via g_1 or g_2. We learn a guard, ($i \le 4$), that resolves this branching decision at the init node: a task like R$_2$ would select pass via g_1 while R$_6$ will via g_2.

Hence, learning a policy generator for a DAG entails learning the $(m+1)$ κ-coefficients of the m-degree κ-polynomial and a base policy for every edge, along with guard conditions for all vertices with multiple outgoing edges.

5 Algorithm

Algorithm 1 (GenRL) takes as input an inductive task R, the degree m of the κ-polynomial, and a finite set of training task instances Train (we assume $0 \in$ Train) and outputs a *policy generator* for R. As described above, this entails learning a base policy and the $(m+1)$ κ-coefficients for edges and guard conditions for vertices in the common DAG $\mathcal{G}$ (with initial vertex u_0) of the inductive task.

GenRL operates in two phases: (1) learn κ-coefficients and base policy for all edges, and (2) learn guard conditions at vertices with multiple outgoing edges.

In the first phase, GenRL traverses the vertices in $\mathcal{G}$ in topological order. While processing a vertex u, we record the *success probability* of the best probability path from the initial vertex u_0 to u for the i-th task instance in $P(u,i)$. We also record bestIn(u,i) to be the set of incoming vertices to u that are along a best probability path from u_0 to u for the task instance $i \in$ Train. Then,

$$P(u,i) = \begin{cases} 1 & \text{if } u = u_0 \\ \max\{P(w,i) \cdot p_i^{w \to u} \mid w \to u \in \text{InEdges}(u)\} & \text{if } u \ne u_0 \end{cases}$$

$$\text{bestIn}(u,i) = \begin{cases} \emptyset & \text{if } u = u_0 \\ \arg\max_w \{P(w,i) \cdot p_i^{w \to u} \mid w \to u \in \text{InEdges}(u)\} & \text{if } u \ne u_0 \end{cases}$$

where $p_i^{w \to u}$ is the estimated success probability of edge policy of i-th task instance on edge $w \to u$.

Next, we induce a state distribution η_i^u on vertex u for all task instances $i \in$ Train. $\eta_i^{u_0}$ is given by the initial distribution of the task instance R$_i$. For all other vertices $u \ne u_0$, the state distributions are induced along the *best*

Algorithm 2. LearnKappaCoefficients(e, m, π_e^0, Γ_u, Train)
Kappa Training using a modified Augmented Random Search

1: Initialize $\kappa(m)$
    where $m \leftarrow$ number of kappa in the polynomial template
2: **while** κ not converged **do**
3:     $\delta_{samples} \leftarrow \emptyset$
4:     **for** $s = 0$ to $n\_samples$ **do**
5:        $r_{plus} \leftarrow \emptyset, r_{minus} \leftarrow \emptyset$
6:        $\delta \leftarrow$ SampleDelta(κ)
7:        $\kappa_{plus} \leftarrow$ PerturbKappa($\kappa, \delta, \delta_{scale}$)
8:        $\kappa_{minus} \leftarrow$ PerturbKappa($\kappa, \delta, -\delta_{scale}$)
9:        **for** $k = 0$ to |Train| and task R_i where $i \in$ Train **do**
10:           $\pi_{plus} \leftarrow$ KappaPolicy($\kappa_{plus}, \pi_e^0, k, m$)
11:           $r_{plus}[k] \leftarrow$ Reward(π_{plus}, R_i)
12:           $\pi_{minus} \leftarrow$ KappaPolicy($\kappa_{minus}, \pi_e^0, k, m$)
13:           $r_{minus}[k] \leftarrow$ Reward(π_{minus}, R_i)
14:        $R_{plus} \leftarrow$ Score(r_{plus})
15:        $R_{minus} \leftarrow$ Score(r_{minus})
16:        $\delta_{samples}[s] \leftarrow (\delta, R_{plus}, R_{minus})$
17:     $\delta_\kappa \leftarrow$ DeltaUpdate($\delta_{samples}$)
18:     Update $\kappa \leftarrow$ PerturbKappa($\kappa, \delta_\kappa, 1$)
19: **return** κ

probability path from u_0 to u. To this end, η_i^u is induced from states in bestIn(u, i) using the leaned edge policies along these incoming edges.

Finally, for all outgoing edges $e = u \rightarrow v$, we learn the base policy and $(m + 1)$ κ-coefficients. The base policy π_0^e is learned as a neural-network policy using standard RL such that π_0^e maximizes the satisfaction of the edge e for the 0-th task instance. I.e., the rewards are designed to encourage π_0^e to safely transition from an MDP state in u to an MDP state in v for the 0-th task instance.

The κ-coefficients are learned using an adaptation of the ARS (Augmented Random Search) (see Algorithm 2). The κ-coefficients capture an inductive relation between the parameters of the policy networks of adjacent task instances; $[\pi_i^e]$ is the parameter vector for the policy network corresponding to the i-th task instance. Let π_i^e be obtained by unrolling the κ-polynomial on the base policy parameters for all $i \in$ Train. Taking rewards of π_i^e to be based on satisfaction of the edge for the i-th task instance (as done for the base policy), κ-polynomials are trained to optimize the softmin of the rewards over all training task instances.

The second phase learns the guard conditions (see Algorithm 3): In addition to ensuring the uniqueness of the path, we require that the guards choose an edge such that the resulting path policy has a high probability of satisfaction. To this end, for each edge e, we create a set S^e of task instances such that the e appears on a best probability path to a final vertex for those task instances, using backward DAG traversal and bestIn. Finally, the guard on a vertex u is learned as a multi-task classifier with (a) outgoing edges as the class labels, (b)

Algorithm 3. LearnGuardConditions($\mathcal{G}$, bestIn)

Training a Decision Tree Classifier at every edge where decision making is involved

1: \\ Creating Decision Sets
2: Initialize $O(v) \leftarrow$ OutVertices(v) for all $v \in \mathcal{G}$
3: Initialize $Q \leftarrow F$ \\ Q is a queue
4: **while** Q is not empty **do**
5:    vertex $u \leftarrow Q$.dequeue
6:    **for** vertex $v \in$ InVertices(u) **do**
7:      $O(v)$.remove(u)
8:      **for** $i \in$ Train **do**
9:        **if** $v \in$ (bestIn(u, i)) **then**
10:           $\mathcal{D}_e(e)$.append(i) where edge $e = (u \rightarrow v)$
11:      **if** $O(v)$ is empty **then**
12:        Q.enqueue(v)
13: \\ Learning Guard
14: dataset $D = \{(x, y) \mid x \in X, y \in Y\}$ where $X \leftarrow$ EnvInputValues(R), $Y \leftarrow$ edge e
15: Guard $\leftarrow$ TrainDecisionTree(D) where Guard $= (f : X \rightarrow Y)$
16: **return** Guard

---

task instance indices as features, and (c) the dataset consists of data points (i, e) s.t. $i \in S^e$ for all outgoing edges e from u.

6 Empirical Evaluation

We evaluate GenRL[1] across diverse environments, demonstrating superior generalization and sample efficiency compared to state-of-the-art approaches. Through experiments spanning navigation, long-horizon tasks, complex decision-making, and control benchmarks, we show that explicitly modeling inductive relationships between tasks provides a fundamentally more effective approach to generalization.

6.1 Experimental Setup

Evaluation Methodology. To rigorously evaluate generalization capabilities, each experiment involves training on a fixed set of task instances (Train) and testing on unseen task instances (Unseen) from the same inductive task family. We estimate the probability of success for each task based on 1000 rollouts. A policy π_i is considered successful on task instance $R_i : (\phi_i, \eta_i)$ if the rollouts ζ satisfy the specification with probability above δ, specifically $\Pr_{\zeta \sim \mathcal{D}_{\pi_i}}[\zeta \models \phi_i, \eta_i] > \delta$, where we set $\delta = 0.9$. All reported results represent the median of five independent runs with different random seeds. For fair comparison, all methods are evaluated on identical Train and Unseen sets.

---
[1] Complete codebase of GenRL and the experimental setup is available at https://anonymous.4open.science/r/GenRL_Zenith-7EEB/.

In all experiments, we train using a 1-degree κ-polynomial approximation of the inductive relationship. All experiments run on a cluster with Intel Xeon Gold 6226 CPUs (2.7 GHz, 24 cores per node) and 192 GB RAM per node.

6.2 Baselines and Comparisons

Baselines are state-of-the-art generalizable RL approaches and GenRL ablations:

- Generalizable RL algorithms across three categories:
  - *Inductive Generalization algorithms.* PSMP [16] leverages inductive structures between tasks but operates as a planning approach with known transition probabilities;
  - *Meta-Learning algorithms.* MAML-Reinforce [11] and VariBAD-A2C [42], which enable rapid adaptation through task-specific representations;
  - *Goal-Conditioned algorithms.* C-Learning [29] and HER-DDPG [4] enable generalization by incorporating goal-states directly into the policy input.
- Ablations of GenRL to analyze component contributions:
  - *Augmented Random Search (*ARS*)* [28]: This ablation uses the standard ARS algorithm, learning a single policy for all tasks in Train. Unlike GenRL, which trains an inductive policy generator that adapts to different tasks, ARS relies on a single reward signal rather than aggregating multiple task-specific rewards.
  - ARS + *Reward Aggregation (*ARS+RA*):* This ablation incorporates our reward aggregation mechanism (softmin function across tasks) but still learns a single policy instead of generating task-specific policies.
  - ARS + *Goal Conditioning (*ARS+GC*):* This ablation extends ARS+RA by providing the task index as additional input to the policy, enabling differentiation between tasks while maintaining a single policy.

6.3 Results and Analysis

Simple Reachability Tasks. We begin with simple reachability tasks in a 2D Cartesian plane. The inductive tasks (Figs. 3, 4 and 5) require navigating from initial positions (blue and red dots) to target positions (grey boxes) while avoiding obstacles when present. Task instances are generated by shifting either only the initial position (Figs. 4 and 5) or both initial and goal positions (Fig. 3).

The figures show representative trajectories for training tasks (blue) and unseen tasks (red). Despite the apparent simplicity, most baselines struggle with generalization. While PSMP performs adequately when task variations follow simple shifts (Fig. 3), it fails with more complex adaptations (Figs. 4 and 5). ARS+RA shows stronger performance in controlled variations but lacks consistent generalization across broader conditions.

In contrast, GenRL demonstrates substantially superior generalization by producing custom trajectories adapted to each specific task instance rather than applying nearly identical paths across all variations. For the simplest case (Fig. 3), GenRL successfully completes up to 99 unseen tasks after 400

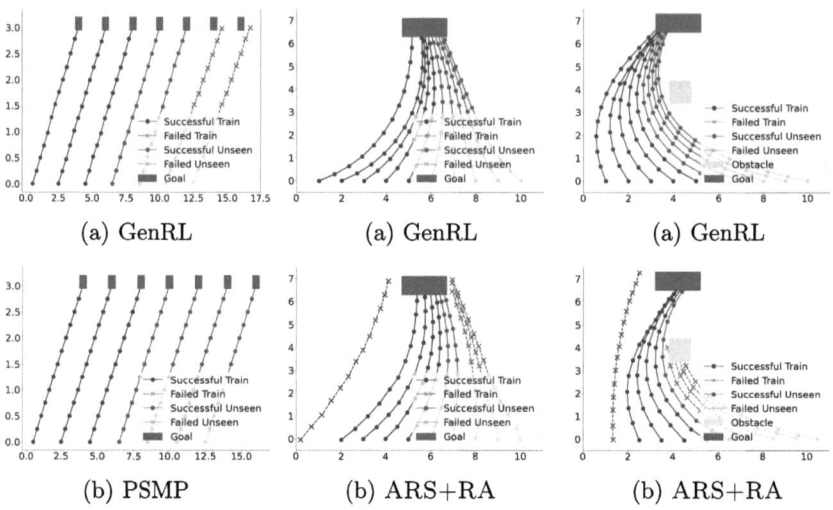

Fig. 3. Moving initial and goal distributions (Color figure online)

Fig. 4. Moving initial distribution, stationary goal (Color figure online)

Fig. 5. Moving initial distribution, stationary goal, with obstacle (Color figure online)

iterations—a remarkable 1650% generalization rate relative to the training set. Even with obstacles (Fig. 5), GenRL maintains impressive generalization with 22 successful unseen tasks (367% generalization rate). Successful trajectories (solid lines with •) vastly outnumber failures (dotted lines with ×) for GenRL even on unseen tasks, confirming its robust adaptation capabilities.

Long-Horizon Tasks. To evaluate scalability to longer horizons, we designed two classes of long-horizon tasks:

N-Reachability Tasks. These tasks (Fig. 6a and 6c) extend simple reachability by requiring the agent to visit N intermediate points sequentially. Both the initial distribution and goal positions shift inductively across task instances.

Figure 6b and 6d show generalization performance as N increases. GenRL maintains consistently high performance across all horizon lengths, successfully generalizing to 5 unseen tasks even in the most complex scenarios ($N = 5$)—an 83% generalization rate. While VariBAD achieves competitive results for $N = 1$, its performance deteriorates dramatically as horizon length increases, highlighting its difficulty with longer-horizon tasks. Other algorithms show poor generalization across the board, with performance declining rapidly as N increases.

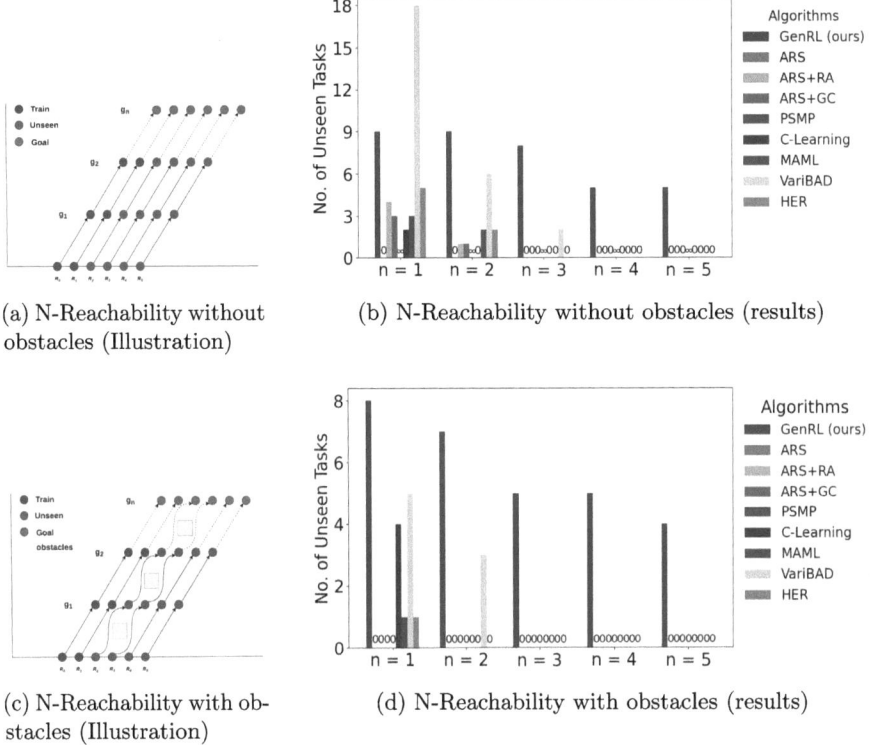

Fig. 6. *N*-Reachability Tasks: (a) and (c) illustrate the task environments without and with obstacles, respectively. (b) and (d) compare the number of successful unseen tasks for these environments.

Tower-Destacking. We evaluated several variations of a tower-destacking task using a robotic arm in the Reacher environment (Figs. 1 and 7). The source tower contains eight blocks, with algorithms trained on the top four blocks and tested on the remaining four.

Figure 8a shows that GenRL achieves generalization performance comparable to sophisticated methods like VariBAD and HER. However, the learning curves in Fig. 7 reveal a critical advantage: GenRL reaches optimal performance with an order of magnitude fewer samples than these alternatives. While GenRL converges after approximately 10^4 environment steps, VariBAD requires 10^5 steps, and HER-DDPG needs over 10^6 steps to achieve similar performance. This remarkable sample efficiency demonstrates the power of explicitly modeling inductive relationships rather than relying on implicit learning through neural networks.

Complex Decision-Making Tasks. Some of the most challenging scenarios involve optimal decision-making where the agent must choose between alter-

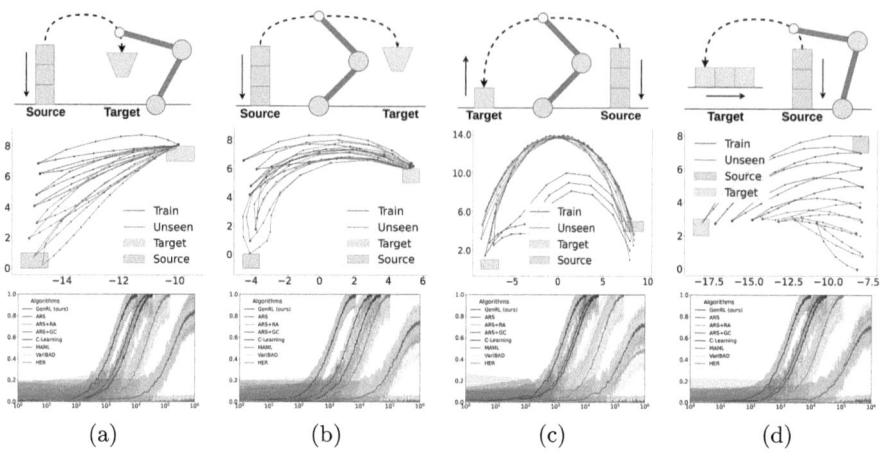

Fig. 7. Tower-destacking benchmarks on Reacher Environment: Task illustrations, trajectories, and learning curves: (a) Pick and Drop: Same side, (b) Pick and Drop: Opposite side, (c) Pick and Vertical Stack: Opposite side, (d) Pick and Horizontal Stack: Same side. Learning Curve: x-axis denotes the number of samples (steps) and y-axis denotes the average of the estimated probability of success of all tasks in **Train**. Results are averaged over 5 runs with the cloud indicating the minimum and maximum.

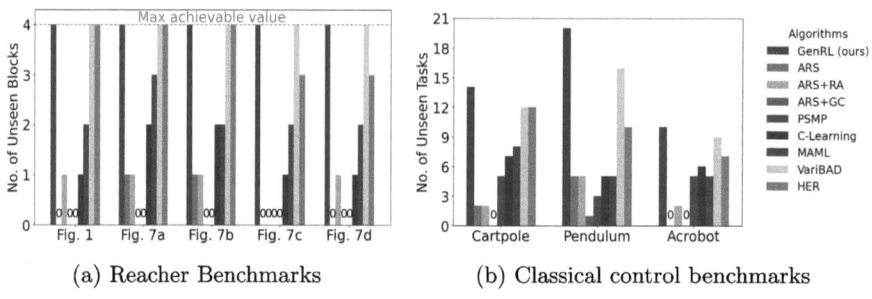

(a) Reacher Benchmarks

(b) Classical control benchmarks

Fig. 8. Comparison of the number of successful Unseen task instances. (a) Performance on Reacher benchmarks. (b) Performance on classical Control benchmarks.

Table 1. Choice benchmarks: No. of successful unseen tasks for the Car2D Choice benchmarks. **Successful Train** indicates if all training tasks were completed successfully ($|\text{Train}| = 6$), while **Successful Unseen** reports the number of successful instances on unseen tasks. **Learned Guard Predicate** represents the decision index where the agent must choose the optimal goal. For example, when $i \leq 4$, for task R_i where $i \leq 4$, goal g_1 is chosen; otherwise, goal g_2 is chosen. In more complex benchmarks (e.g., Fig. 9c with 2 levels), multiple predicates may emerge.

Benchmark	Successful Train	Successful Unseen	Learned Guard Predicate
Figure 2	All	7	$(i \leq 4)$
Figure 9a	All	5	$(i \leq 4)$
Figure 9c	All	5	$(i \leq 4), (i \leq 4)$

native paths based on task parameters. We evaluated GenRL on three "choice" tasks of increasing complexity: (a). Moving initial point with fixed goal (Fig. 2) (b). Moving initial point and moving goal (Fig. 9a) (c). Two-level choice with moving initial point and moving goal (Fig. 9c). These tasks require the agent to select between alternative subgoals (g_1 or g_2) based on the specific task instance. GenRL's unique ability to learn guard conditions enables optimal branching decisions. For example, in Fig. 2, GenRL learns the guard predicate: $i \leq 4$, directing tasks with index $i \leq 4$ through the first subgoal and tasks with $i > 4$ through the second subgoal.

Table 1 shows that GenRL successfully generalizes to 5-7 unseen tasks across these choice benchmarks, achieving up to 117% generalization on the most basic choice task (Fig. 2) and 84% generalization on more complex choice variants. Remarkably, no other algorithm demonstrates any meaningful generalization on these tasks, highlighting GenRL's distinctive capability to model complex decision boundaries.

Classical Control Benchmarks. To verify GenRL's applicability beyond navigation tasks, we evaluated it on classic OpenAI Gym control benchmarks: Pendulum, Acrobot, and Cartpole. These environments feature inductive variations in physical parameters (mass, length) rather than task specifications.

Figure 8b shows that GenRL achieves superior generalization across all three environments, with particularly impressive results in Pendulum (20 successful unseen tasks, 333% generalization) and Cartpole (14 successful unseen tasks, 233% generalization). Even in the challenging Acrobot environment, GenRL successfully generalizes to 10 unseen tasks (167% generalization) with sufficient training iterations, while competing methods plateau at much lower levels of generalization. This demonstrates that GenRL can effectively model inductive relationships in physical parameters and transfer knowledge between related control tasks.

6.4 Key Findings and Analysis

Superior Performance and Stability Across Complexity Scales. GenRL consistently outperforms all baselines across diverse specifications, particularly as task complexity increases. While baseline methods exhibit diminishing returns—evident in N-Reachability tasks where VariBAD's performance drops dramatically from N = 1 to N = 5, and in choice tasks where baselines fail to generalize at all—GenRL maintains stable performance even for longer horizons and complex branching tasks. This stability, coupled with remarkable sample efficiency (requiring only 10^4 environment steps compared to 10^5-10^6 for policy gradient methods), demonstrates that explicitly modeling inductive relationships is fundamentally more effective than implicit meta-learning or goal-conditioning approaches. GenRL achieves this despite using the simpler Augmented Random Search algorithm without gradients, yet matches or exceeds the performance of sophisticated methods like VariBAD and HER.

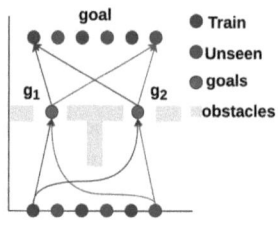
(a) Choice with moving goal - Illustration.

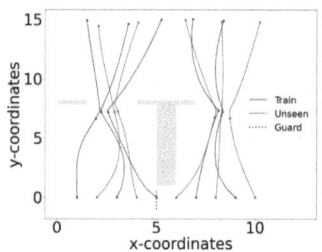
(b) Choice with moving goal - Trajectory.

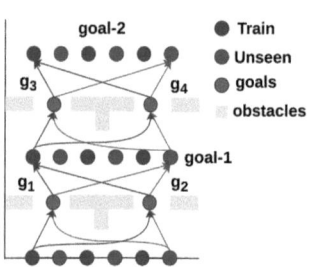
(c) Two levels of choice with moving goal - Illustration.

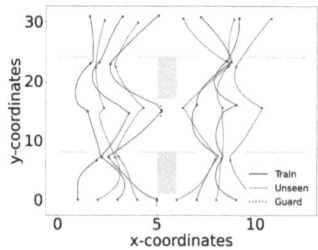
(d) Two levels of choice with moving goal - Trajectory.

Fig. 9. Choice benchmarks task illustration and corresponding trajectories: (a) and (b) illustrate the benchmark, while (c) and (d) show the agent's trajectory in the respective benchmarks.

This dramatic efficiency advantage demonstrates the power of leveraging logical specifications and inductive structure. For tasks with natural inductive relationships, explicitly modeling these relationships proves far more effective than attempting to learn them implicitly through meta-learning or policy gradients.

Policy Generator is key to GenRL's superior performance. Our ablation studies with ARS, ARS+RA, and ARS+GC consistently show these variants underperforming compared to the full GenRL framework. The base ARS algorithm has no mechanism to generalize over tasks, resulting in poor performance. Although incorporating Reward Aggregation (ARS+RA) and Goal Conditioning (ARS+GC) provides marginal improvements, these variants still fall far short of GenRL's capabilities.

When ARS leverages GenRL's inductive policy generator framework, it not only overcomes its high sample complexity but significantly enhances performance. This integration enables GenRL to outperform even sophisticated policy gradient methods, demonstrating the substantial advantages of our approach. GenRL's ability to efficiently generate adapted policies for diverse task instances—rather than learning or fine-tuning individual policies—underlies its exceptional sample efficiency and performance.

7 Related Work

Specification-Guided RL. Recent years have seen an emergence of RL from logical specifications [1,2,5,7,9,12–15,17,19,20,25,26,33,38,40]. Here, the task is expressed using high-level logical specifications rather than as low-level rewards. Logic specifications have received traction due to their ease in expressing complex long-horizon tasks and ability to efficiently scale learning. Prior works have focused primarily on scalability to long-horizon tasks and theoretical guarantees. Ours is the first work to leverage logical specifications specifically for generalization.

Zero-Shot Generalization. Zero-shot generalization relates to multi-task learning and skill transfer, distilling transferable skills from seen tasks to generalize to unseen ones [22,30–32]. With logical specifications, existing approaches learn policies for sub-specifications and generalize to their combinations [23,24, 27,35,37]. Our problem is orthogonal: in prior work, the predicate set remains constant while only specifications change. In our setting, both predicates and environment distributions vary between training and unseen tasks. [21] considers changing distributions but with fixed predicates. Reward-based generalizable RL has been explored in [34,43]. In meta-learning, algorithms like MAML [11] and VariBAD [42] enable rapid adaptation to new tasks by adjusting task-specific parameters and representations. Goal-conditioned algorithms like C-Learning [29] and HER [4] contribute by conditioning policies on desired outcomes, enhancing adaptation to new goals without additional training.

Inductive/Programmatic Approaches to Generalization. Closest to our work is PSMP [16], which learns inductive policies in the planning setting (known MDP) rather than RL (unknown MDP). Despite this advantage, PSMP cannot adapt to different task instances, as it learns a single policy for all instances. Our approach learns a higher-order policy generator that produces specialized policies for each task instance. Programmatic/logic-based policy representations generally demonstrate better generalizability than neural network policies [6,8,36,41]. Non-programmatic policy sketches have also been explored [3]. Our work differs by exploiting the natural inductiveness in task specifications to extract inductive relations for policies and learn a higher-order policy generator.

8 Concluding Remarks

While current advances in generalizable RL have focused primarily on making agents more adaptable through sophisticated architectures and training procedures, our work suggests an alternative path forward - one that leverages the inherent structure in specifications to enable systematic generalization. By making this structure explicit through formal specifications and inductive relationships, we not only achieve better generalization but also achieve better sample complexity by an order of magnitude. In doing so, we outperform several mature policy-gradient based state-of-the-art tools for generalization.

Currently, GenRL performs effectively in environments with lower-dimensional action and state spaces. However, its scalability to more complex environments with higher-dimensional spaces remains a challenge. Future work will focus on enhancing the algorithm's capability to handle these more complex scenarios. Additionally, while defining tasks via logical specifications is generally easier than specifying rewards, it still requires considerable effort to design these specifications accurately. To address these, future research will aim at developing more streamlined and user-friendly methods for task specification to make the specification process as lightweight as possible. This will help broaden the applicability of GenRL or any specification-guided learning to a wider range of tasks and environments. Even though the logic and formulation behind our research are principally motivated by a foundational hypothesis and empirically validated for its performance and results, we still not have investigated the possibilities of providing theoretical guarantees and this is also something our future work will focus on.

References

1. Aksaray, D., Jones, A., Kong, Z., Schwager, M., Belta, C.: Q-learning for robust satisfaction of signal temporal logic specifications. In: Conference on Decision and Control (CDC), pp. 6565–6570. IEEE (2016)
2. Alur, R., Bansal, S., Bastani, O., Jothimurugan, K.: A framework for transforming specifications in reinforcement learning. In: Principles of Systems Design: Essays Dedicated to Thomas A. Henzinger on the Occasion of His 60th Birthday, pp. 604–624. Springer (2022). https://doi.org/10.1007/978-3-031-22337-2_29
3. Andreas, J., Klein, D., Levine, S.: Modular multitask reinforcement learning with policy sketches. In: International Conference on Machine Learning, pp. 166–175. PMLR (2017)
4. Andrychowicz, M., et al.: Hindsight experience replay. In: Advances in Neural Information Processing Systems, vol. 30 (2017)
5. Bansal, S.: Specification-guided reinforcement learning. In: International Static Analysis Symposium, pp. 3–9. Springer (2022)
6. Bastani, O., Pu, Y., Solar-Lezama, A.: Verifiable reinforcement learning via policy extraction. In: Advances in Neural Information Processing Systems, vol. 31 (2018)
7. Brafman, R., De Giacomo, G., Patrizi, F.: LTLf/LDLf non-markovian rewards. In: Proceedings of the AAAI Conference on Artificial Intelligence, vol. 32 (2018)
8. Cao, Y., et al.: GALOIS: boosting deep reinforcement learning via generalizable logic synthesis. In: Advances in Neural Information Processing Systems, vol. 35, pp. 19930–19943 (2022)
9. De Giacomo, G., Iocchi, L., Favorito, M., Patrizi, F.: Foundations for restraining bolts: reinforcement learning with LTLf/LDLf restraining specifications. In: Proceedings of the International Conference on Automated Planning and Scheduling, vol. 29, pp. 128–136 (2019)
10. Dohmen, T., Perez, M., Somenzi, F., Trivedi, A.: Regular reinforcement learning. In: Gurfinkel, A., Ganesh, V. (eds.) Computer Aided Verification, pp. 184–208. Springer Nature Switzerland, Cham (2024)
11. Finn, C., Abbeel, P., Levine, S.: Model-agnostic meta-learning for fast adaptation of deep networks. In: International Conference on Machine Learning, pp. 1126–1135. PMLR (2017)

12. Hahn, E.M., Perez, M., Schewe, S., Somenzi, F., Trivedi, A., Wojtczak, D.: Omega-regular objectives in model-free reinforcement learning. In: Vojnar, T., Zhang, L. (eds.) TACAS 2019. LNCS, vol. 11427, pp. 395–412. Springer, Cham (2019). https://doi.org/10.1007/978-3-030-17462-0_27
13. Hasanbeig, M., Kantaros, Y., Abate, A., Kroening, D., Pappas, G.J., Lee, I.: Reinforcement learning for temporal logic control synthesis with probabilistic satisfaction guarantees. In: Conference on Decision and Control (CDC), pp. 5338–5343 (2019)
14. Hasanbeig, M., Abate, A., Kroening, D.: Logically-constrained reinforcement learning. arXiv preprint arXiv:1801.08099 (2018)
15. Icarte, R.T., Klassen, T., Valenzano, R., McIlraith, S.: Using reward machines for high-level task specification and decomposition in reinforcement learning. In: International Conference on Machine Learning, pp. 2107–2116. PMLR (2018)
16. Inala, J.P., Bastani, O., Tavares, Z., Solar-Lezama, A.: Synthesizing programmatic policies that inductively generalize. In: International Conference on Learning Representations (2020)
17. Jiang, Y., Bharadwaj, S., Wu, B., Shah, R., Topcu, U., Stone, P.: Temporal-logic-based reward shaping for continuing reinforcement learning tasks. In: Proceedings of the AAAI Conference on Artificial Intelligence, vol. 35, pp. 7995–8003 (2021)
18. Jothimurugan, K., Alur, R., Bastani, O.: A composable specification language for reinforcement learning tasks. In: Advances in Neural Information Processing Systems, vol. 32 (2019)
19. Jothimurugan, K., Bansal, S., Bastani, O., Alur, R.: Compositional reinforcement learning from logical specifications. In: Advances in Neural Information Processing Systems, vol. 34, pp. 10026–10039 (2021)
20. Jothimurugan, K., Bansal, S., Bastani, O., Alur, R.: Specification-guided learning of Nash equilibria with high social welfare. In: International Conference on Computer Aided Verification, pp. 343–363. Springer (2022)
21. Jothimurugan, K., Hsu, S., Bastani, O., Alur, R.: Robust subtask learning for compositional generalization. In: International Conference on Machine Learning (2023)
22. Kirk, R., Zhang, A., Grefenstette, E., Rocktäschel, T.: A survey of zero-shot generalisation in deep reinforcement learning. J. Artif. Intell. Res. **76**, 201–264 (2023)
23. Kuo, Y.L., Katz, B., Barbu, A.: Encoding formulas as deep networks: reinforcement learning for zero-shot execution of LTL formulas. In: 2020 IEEE/RSJ International Conference on Intelligent Robots and Systems (IROS), pp. 5604–5610. IEEE (2020)
24. León, B.G., Shanahan, M., Belardinelli, F.: Systematic generalisation through task temporal logic and deep reinforcement learning. arXiv preprint arXiv:2006.08767 (2020)
25. Li, X., Vasile, C.I., Belta, C.: Reinforcement learning with temporal logic rewards. In: IEEE/RSJ International Conference on Intelligent Robots and Systems (IROS), pp. 3834–3839. IEEE (2017)
26. Littman, M.L., Topcu, U., Fu, J., Isbell, C., Wen, M., MacGlashan, J.: Environment-independent task specifications via GLTL. arXiv preprint arXiv:1704.04341 (2017)
27. Liu, J., Shah, A., Rosen, E., Jia, M., Konidaris, G., Tellex, S.: Skill transfer for temporal task specification. In: CoRL 2023 Workshop on Learning Effective Abstractions for Planning (LEAP) (2023)
28. Mania, H., Guy, A., Recht, B.: Simple random search of static linear policies is competitive for reinforcement learning. In: Advances in Neural Information Processing Systems, pp. 1805–1814 (2018)

29. Naderian, P., et al.: C-learning: horizon-aware cumulative accessibility estimation. In: International Conference on Learning Representations (2021)
30. Oh, J., Singh, S., Lee, H., Kohli, P.: Zero-shot task generalization with multi-task deep reinforcement learning. In: International Conference on Machine Learning, pp. 2661–2670. PMLR (2017)
31. Sodhani, S., Zhang, A., Pineau, J.: Multi-task reinforcement learning with context-based representations. In: International Conference on Machine Learning, pp. 9767–9779. PMLR (2021)
32. Sohn, S., Oh, J., Lee, H.: Hierarchical reinforcement learning for zero-shot generalization with subtask dependencies. In: Advances in Neural Information Processing Systems, vol. 31 (2018)
33. Svoboda, J., Bansal, S., Chatterjee, K.: Reinforcement learning from reachability specifications: Pac guarantees with expected conditional distance. In: Forty-first International Conference on Machine Learning (2024)
34. Taiga, A.A., Agarwal, R., Farebrother, J., Courville, A., Bellemare, M.G.: Investigating multi-task pretraining and generalization in reinforcement learning. In: The Eleventh International Conference on Learning Representations (2023)
35. Vaezipoor, P., Li, A.C., Icarte, R.A.T., Mcilraith, S.A.: LTL2ACTION: generalizing LTL instructions for multi-task RL. In: International Conference on Machine Learning, pp. 10497–10508. PMLR (2021)
36. Verma, A., Murali, V., Singh, R., Kohli, P., Chaudhuri, S.: Programmatically interpretable reinforcement learning. In: International Conference on Machine Learning, pp. 5045–5054. PMLR (2018)
37. Xu, D., Fekri, F.: Generalizing LTL instructions via future dependent options. arXiv preprint arXiv:2212.04576 (2022)
38. Xu, Z., Topcu, U.: Transfer of temporal logic formulas in reinforcement learning. In: International Joint Conference on Artificial Intelligence, pp. 4010–4018 (2019)
39. Yang, C., Littman, M., Carbin, M.: On the (in) tractability of reinforcement learning for LTL objectives. arXiv preprint arXiv:2111.12679 (2021)
40. Yuan, L.Z., Hasanbeig, M., Abate, A., Kroening, D.: Modular deep reinforcement learning with temporal logic specifications. arXiv preprint arXiv:1909.11591 (2019)
41. Zhu, H., Xiong, Z., Magill, S., Jagannathan, S.: An inductive synthesis framework for verifiable reinforcement learning. In: Proceedings of the 40th ACM SIGPLAN Conference on Programming Language Design and Implementation, pp. 686–701 (2019)
42. Zintgraf, L., et al.: Varibad: variational bayes-adaptive deep RL via meta-learning. J. Mach. Learn. Res. **22**(289), 1–39 (2021)
43. Zisselman, E., Lavie, I., Soudry, D., Tamar, A.: Explore to generalize in zero-shot RL. In: Advances in Neural Information Processing Systems, vol. 36 (2024)

Solution-Aware Vs Global ReLU Selection: Partial MILP Strikes Back for DNN Verification

Yuke Liao[1]($\boxtimes$)[iD], Blaise Genest[2,3][iD], Kuldeep Meel[4][iD], and Shaan Aryaman[5][iD]

[1] CNRS@CREATE, Singapore, Singapore
yuke.liao@cnrsatcreate.sg
[2] CNRS@CREATE and IPAL, Singapore, Singapore
blaise.genest@cnrsatcreate.sg, blaise.genest@cnrs.fr
[3] CNRS, IPAL, Paris, France
[4] University of Toronto, Toronto, Canada
meel@cs.toronto.edu
[5] NYU Courant Institute of Mathematical Sciences, New York, USA

Abstract. Branch and Bound (BaB) is considered as the most efficient technique for DNN verification: it can propagate bounds over numerous branches, to accurately approximate values a given neuron can take even in large DNNs, enabling formal verification of properties such as local robustness. Nevertheless, the number of branches grows *exponentially* with important variables, and there are complex instances for which the number of branches is too large to handle even using BaB. In these cases, providing more time to BaB is not efficient, as the number of branches treated is *linear* with the time-out. Such cases arise with verification-agnostic DNNs, non-local properties (e.g. global robustness, computing Lipschitz bound), etc.

To handle complex instances, we revisit a divide-and-conquer approach to break down the complexity: instead of few complex BaB calls, we rely on many small *partial* MILP calls. The crucial step is to select very few but very important ReLUs to treat using (costly) binary variables. The previous attempts were suboptimal in that respect. To select these important ReLU variables, we propose a novel *solution-aware* ReLU scoring (SAS), as well as adapt the BaB-SR and BaB-FSB branching functions as *global* ReLU scoring (GS) functions. We compare them theoretically as well as experimentally, and SAS is more efficient at selecting a set of variables to open using binary variables. Compared with previous attempts, SAS reduces the number of binary variables by around 6 times, while maintaining the same level of accuracy. Implemented in *Hybrid MILP*, calling first α,β-CROWN with a short time-out to solve easier instances, and then partial MILP, produces a very accurate yet efficient verifier, reducing by up to 40% the number of undecided instances to low levels ($8-15\%$), while keeping a reasonable runtime ($46s-417s$ on average per instance), even for fairly large CNNs with 2 million parameters.

© The Author(s), under exclusive license to Springer Nature Switzerland AG 2026
M. D'Souza et al. (Eds.): ATVA 2025, LNCS 16145, pp. 299–320, 2026.
https://doi.org/10.1007/978-3-032-08707-2_14

1 Introduction

Deep neural networks (DNNs for short) have demonstrated remarkable capabilities, achieving human-like or even superior performance across a wide range of tasks. However, their robustness is often compromised by their susceptibility to input perturbations [23]. This vulnerability has catalyzed the verification community to develop various methodologies, each presenting a unique balance between completeness and computational efficiency [17,18,21]. This surge in innovation has also led to the inception of competitions such as VNNComp [6], which aim to systematically evaluate the performance of neural network verification tools. While the verification engines are generic, the benchmarks usually focus on local robustness, i.e. given a DNN, an image and a small neighbourhood around this image, is it the case that all the images in the neighbourhood are classified in the same way. For the past 5 years, VNNcomp has focused on rather easy instances, that can be solved within tens of seconds (the typical hard time-out is 300 s). For this reason, DNN verifiers in the past years have mainly focused on optimizing for such easy instances. Among them, NNenum [2], Marabou [18,27], and PyRAT [12], respectively 4th, 3rd and 2nd of the last VNNcomp'24 [5] and 5th, 2nd and 3rd of the VNNcomp'23 [4]; MnBAB [15], 2nd in VNNcomp'22 [20], built upon ERAN [21] and PRIMA [19]; and importantly, α, β-CROWN [25,29], the winner of the last 4 VNNcomp, benefiting from branch-and-bound based methodology [8,30]. We will thus compare mainly with α, β-CROWN experiments as gold standard in the following[1].

α, β-CROWN, as well as BaBSR [8] and MN-BaB [15], rely on Branch and Bound technique (BaB), which call BaB once per output neuron (few calls). In the worst case, this involves considering all possible ReLU configurations, though branch and bound typically circumvents most possibilities. For easy instances, BaB is highly efficient as all branches can be pruned early. However, BaB methods hit a complexity barrier when verifying more complex instances, due to an overwhelming number of branches (exponential in the height of branches that cannot be pruned as they need too many variables to branch over). This can be clearly witnessed on the verification-agnostic [9] DNNs of Table 1 (6 first DNNs), where vastly enlarging the time-out only enables to verify few more % of images, leaving a large proportion (20% − 50%) of images undecided despite the large runtime. As argued in [9], there are many situations (workflow, no access to the dataset...) where using specific trainers to learn easy to verify DNN is simply not possible, leading to *verification-agnostic* networks, and such cases should be treated as well as DNNs specifically trained to be easy to verify, e.g. using [28]. Verification-agnostic are the simplest instances to demonstrate the scaling behavior of BaB on complex instances using standard local robustness implementations. Other complex instances include solving non-local properties, e.g. global robustness computed through Lipschitz bound [26], etc. The bottom line is that one cannot expect to have only easy instances to verify. It is important

---

[1] GCP-CROWN [30] is slightly more accurate than α, β-CROWN on the DNNs we tested, but necessitates IBM CPLEX solver, which is not available to us.

Table 1. Accuracy of DNN (class predicted vs ground truth), upper bound on robustness (robustness attacks found on remaining images), and % of images verified by α, β-CROWN with different time-outs (TO) on 7 DNNs, and average runtime per image. The 6 first DNNs are complex instances. The last DNN (ResNet) is an easy instance (trained using Wong to be easy to verify, but with a very low accuracy level), provided for reference.

Network Perturbation	nbr activ.	Accur.	Upper Bound	α, β-CROWN TO=10s	α, β-CROWN TO=30s	α, β-CROWN TO=2000s
MNIST 5×100 $\epsilon = 0.026$	500 ReLU	99%	90%	33% 6.9s	35% 18.9s	40% 1026s
MNIST 5×200 $\epsilon = 0.015$	1000 ReLU	99%	96%	46% 6.5s	49% 16.6s	50% 930s
MNIST 8×100 $\epsilon = 0.026$	800 ReLU	97%	86%	23% 7.2s	28% 20.1s	28% 930s
MNIST 8×200 $\epsilon = 0.015$	1600 ReLU	97%	91%	35% 6.8s	36% 18.2s	37% 1083s
MNIST 6×500 $\epsilon = 0.035$	3000 ReLU	100%	94%	41% 6.4s	43% 16.4s	44% 1003s
CIFAR CNN-B-Adv $\epsilon = 2/255$	16634 ReLU	78%	62%	34% 4.3s	40% 8.7s	42% 373s
CIFAR ResNet $\epsilon = 8/255$	107496 ReLU	29%	25%	25% 2s	25% 2s	25% 2s

to notice that the number of activation functions of the DNN is a poor indicator of the hardness of the instance, e.g. 5 × 100 with 500 ReLUs is far more complex to certify (50% undecided images) than 100 times bigger ResNet (0% undecided images), see Table 1.

Table 2. Result of non-BaB methods on the hard 5 × 100 with TO = 10 000s. Only NNenum verifies more instances (9% out of 50% undecided images) than α, β-CROWN (40%), at the cost of a much larger runtime (4995s vs 1026s).

Network	Accuracy	Upper	Marabou 2.0	NNenum	Full MILP
MNIST 5×100 $\epsilon = 0.026$	99%	90%	28% 6200s	49% 4995s	40% 6100s

Other standard non-BaB methods such as Marabou, NNenum or a Full MILP encoding, show similar poor performance on such complex instances as well, even with a large 10 000s Time-out: Table 2 reveals that only NNenum succeeds to verify images not verified by α, β-CROWN, limited to 9% more images out of the 50% undecided images on 5 × 100, and with a very large runtime of almost 5000 s per image. It appeared pointless to test these verifiers on larger networks.

Our main contributions address the challenges to verify *complex* instances efficiently, as current methods are not appropriate to verify such instances:

1. We revisit the idea from [16] to consider small calls to a partial MILP (pMILP) solver, i.e. with few binary variables encoding few ReLU functions exactly (other being encoded with more efficient but less accurate linear variables), to compute bounds for each neuron inductively, hence many ($O(n)$, the number of neuron) small calls, with a complexity exponential only in the few binary variables (Sect. 4). Compared to the few (one per output neuron) complex call to BaB, each with a worst case complexity exponential in the number of neurons of the DNN (which is far from the actual complexity thanks to pruning branches in BaB - but which can be too large as we shown in the 6 first DNNs of Table 1). Two questions arise: how to select few very important ReLUs?, and is computing the bounds of intermediate neurons a good trade-off compared with the theoretical loss of accuracy due to selecting only some binary ReLUs? Answer to these questions were not looking very promising judging by previous attempt [16], which was using a simple selection heuristic of nodes in the previous layer only.
2. On the first question, we adapted from BaB-SR [8] and FSB [11], which choose branching nodes for BaB, *global scoring (GS)* functions to choose important ReLUs (Sect. 5). These revealed to be much more accurate than the simple heuristic in [16]. However, we also uncover that the *improvement function* that GS tries to approximate depends heavily upon the mode of the ReLU function, and as this mode is unavailable to GS, there are many cases in which GS is far from the improvement (with both under or over-approximation of the improvement function).
3. We thus designed a *novel solution-aware scoring (SAS)*, which uses the solution of a unique LP call, that provides the mode to consider (Sect. 6). Theoretically, we show that SAS is always an over-approximation of the improvement (Proposition 2), which implies that a small SAS value implies that the ReLU is unnecessary. Experimentally, we further show that SAS is very close to the actual improvement, closer than GS, and that overall, the accuracy from SAS is significantly better than GS. Compared with the heuristic in [16], SAS is much more efficient ($\approx$ 6 times less binary variables for same accuracy (Fig. 4)).
4. Compared with many calls using full MILP, where all the ReLUs are encoded as binary variables, SAS (and GS) encode only a subset of ReLUs as binary and others as linear variables. The model in full MILP is fully accurate, while SAS (and GS) are abstractions, and thus much faster to solve. While full MILP is thus *asymptotically* more accurate than SAS and GS, *experimentally*, every reasonable time-out leads to much better practical accuracy of SAS (and GS) (see Fig. 5).
5. For the second question, we propose a new verifier, called *Hybrid MILP*, invoking first α, β-CROWN with short time-out to settle the easy instances.

On those (*hard*) instances which are neither certified nor falsified, we call pMILP with few neurons encoded as binary variables. Experimental evaluation reveals that Hybrid MILP achieves a beneficial balance between accuracy and completeness compared to prevailing methods. It reduces the proportion of undecided inputs from $20-58\%$ (α, β-CROWN with 2000 s TO) to $8-15\%$, while taking a reasonable average time per instance (46 – 420s), Table 4. It scales to fairly large networks such as CIFAR-10 CNN-B-Adv [9], with more than 2 million parameters.

Limitation: We consider DNNs employing the standard ReLU activation function, though our findings can be extended to other activation functions, following similar extention by [16], with updated MILP models e.g. for maxpool.

1.1 Related Work

We compare Hybrid MILP with major verification tools for DNNs to clarify our methodology and its distinction from the existing state-of-the-art. It scales while preserving good accuracy, through targeting a limited number of binary variables, stricking a good balance between exact encoding of a DNN using MILP [24] (too slow) and LP relaxation (too inaccurate). MIPplanet [14] opts for a different selection of binary variables, and execute one large MILP encoding instead of Hybrid MILP's many small encodings, which significantly reduce the number of binary variables necessary for each encoding. In [16], small encodings are also considered, however with a straightforward choice of binary nodes based on the weight of outgoing edges, which need much more binary variables (thus runtime) to reach the same accuracy.

Compared with [1], which uses pMILP in an abstraction refinement loop, they iteratively call pMILP to obtain bounds for the same output neuron, opening more and more ReLUs. This scales only to limited size DNN (500 neurons), because of the fact that many ReLUs need to be open (and then Gurobi takes a lot of time) and the iterative nature which cannot be parallelized, unlike our method which scales up to 20.000 neurons.

The fact that pure BaB is not that efficient for e.g. verification-agnostic (even very small) DNNs has been witnessed before [22]. The workaround, e.g. in *refined* α, β-CROWN, was to precompute very accurate bounds for the first few neurons of the DNN using a complete full MILP encoding, and then rely on a BaB call from that refined bounds (more complex calls to full MILP and BaB). Non-surprisingly, this very slow technique does not scale but to small DNNs (max 2000 ReLU activation functions). Hybrid MILP on the other hand relies only on small calls: it is much more efficient on small DNNs, and it can scale to larger DNNs as well: we demonstrated strong performance with at least one order of magnitude larger networks (CNN-B-Adv).

Last, ERAN-DeepPoly [21] computes bounds on values very quickly, by abstracting the weight of every node using two functions: an upper function and a lower function. While the upper function is fixed, the lower function offers two choices. It relates to the LP encoding through Proposition 1 [10]: the LP relaxation precisely matches the intersection of these two choices. Consequently, LP is more accurate (but slower) than DeepPoly, and Hybrid MILP is considerably more precise. Regarding PRIMA [19], the approach involves explicitly maintaining dependencies between neurons.

Finally, methods such as Reluplex / Marabou [17,18] abstract the network: they diverge significantly from those abstracting values such as PRIMA, α,β-CROWN) [19,25], Hybrid MILP. These network-abstraction algorithms are designed to be *intrinsically complete* (rather than asymptotically complete as BaB), but this comes at the price of significant scalability challenges, and in practice they time-out on complex instances as shown in Table 2.

2 Notations and Preliminaries

In this paper, we will use lower case latin a for scalars, bold $\boldsymbol{z}$ for vectors, capitalized bold $\boldsymbol{W}$ for matrices, similar to notations in [25]. To simplify the notations, we restrict the presentation to feed-forward, fully connected ReLU Deep Neural Networks (DNN for short), where the ReLU function is ReLU : $\mathbb{R} \to \mathbb{R}$ with $\text{ReLU}(x) = x$ for $x \geq 0$ and $\text{ReLU}(x) = 0$ for $x \leq 0$, which we extend componentwise on vectors.

An ℓ-layer DNN is provided by ℓ weight matrices $\boldsymbol{W}^i \in \mathbb{R}^{d_i \times d_{i-1}}$ and ℓ bias vectors $\boldsymbol{b}^i \in \mathbb{R}^{d_i}$, for $i = 1, \ldots, \ell$. We call d_i the number of neurons of hidden layer $i \in \{1, \ldots, \ell-1\}$, d_0 the input dimension, and d_ℓ the output dimension.

Given an input vector $\boldsymbol{z}^0 \in \mathbb{R}^{d_0}$, denoting $\hat{\boldsymbol{z}}^0 = \boldsymbol{z}^0$, we define inductively the value vectors $\boldsymbol{z}^i, \hat{\boldsymbol{z}}^i$ at layer $1 \leq i \leq \ell$ with

$$\boldsymbol{z}^i = \boldsymbol{W}^i \cdot \hat{\boldsymbol{z}}^{i-1} + \boldsymbol{b}^i \qquad \hat{\boldsymbol{z}}^i = \text{ReLU}(\boldsymbol{z}^i). \qquad (1)$$

The vector $\hat{\boldsymbol{z}}$ is called post-activation values, $\boldsymbol{z}$ is called pre-activation values, and z^i_j is used to call the j-th neuron in the i-th layer. For $\boldsymbol{x} = \boldsymbol{z}^0$ the (vector of) input, we denote by $f(\boldsymbol{x}) = \boldsymbol{z}^\ell$ the output. Finally, pre- and post-activation neurons are called *nodes*, and when we refer to a specific node/neuron, we use a, b, c, d, n to denote them, and $W_{a,b} \in \mathbb{R}$ to denote the weight from neuron a to b. Similarly, for input $\boldsymbol{x}$, we denote by $\text{value}_{\boldsymbol{x}}(a)$ the value of neuron a when the input is $\boldsymbol{x}$.

Concerning the verification problem, we focus on the well studied local-robustness question. Local robustness asks to determine whether the output of a neural network will be affected under small perturbations to the input. Formally, for an input $\boldsymbol{x}$ perturbed by $\varepsilon > 0$ under distance d, then the DNN is locally ε-robust in $\boldsymbol{x}$ whenever:

$$\forall \boldsymbol{x}' \text{ s.t. } d(\boldsymbol{x}, \boldsymbol{x}') \leq \varepsilon, \text{ we have } argmax(f(\boldsymbol{x}')) = argmax(f(\boldsymbol{x})) \qquad (2)$$

3 Value Abstraction for DNN Verification

In this section, we describe different value (over-)abstractions on $\boldsymbol{z}$ that are used by efficient algorithms to certify robustness around an input $\boldsymbol{x}$. Over-abstractions

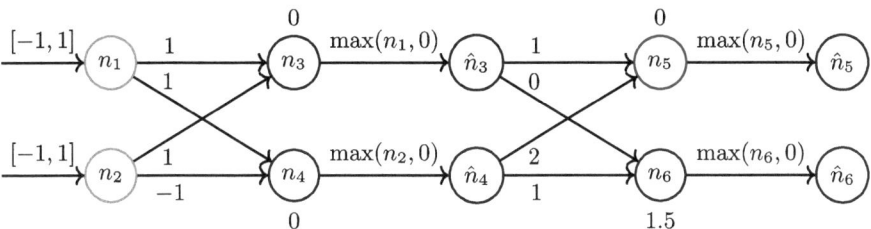

Fig. 1. A DNN. Every neuron is separated into 2 nodes, n pre- and $\hat{n}$ post-ReLU activation.

of values include all values for z in the neighbourhood of x, and thus a certificate for safety in the over-abstraction is a proof of safety for the original input x.

3.1 The Box Abstractions

The concept of value abstraction involves calculating upper and lower bounds for the values of certain neurons in a Deep Neural Network (DNN) when inputs fall within a specified range. This approach aims to assess the network's robustness without precisely computing the values for every input within that range.

Firstly, it's important to note that weighted sums represent a linear function, which can be explicitly expressed with relative ease. However, the ReLU (Rectified Linear Unit) function presents a challenge in terms of accurate representation. Although ReLU is a relatively straightforward piecewise linear function with two modes (one for $x < 0$ and another for $x \geq 0$), it is not linear. The complexity arises when considering the compounded effects of the ReLU function across the various layers of a ReLU DNN. It's worth noting that representing ReLU(x) precisely is feasible when x is "*stable*", meaning it's consistently positive or consistently negative, as there's only one linear mode involved in each scenario. Consequently, the primary challenge lies in addressing "*unstable*" neurons, where the linearity of the function does not hold consistently.

Consider the simpler abstraction, termed "Box abstraction", recalled e.g. in [21]: it inductively computes the bounds for each neuron in the subsequent layer independently. This is achieved by considering the weighted sum of the bounds from the previous layer, followed by clipping the lower bound at max(0, lower bound) to represent the ReLU function, and so forth. For all $i \geq 3$, define $x_i = \text{value}_x(n_i)$, where $x = (x_1, x_2)$. Taking the DNN example from Fig 1, assume $x_1, x_2 \in [-1, 1]$. This implies that $x_3, x_4 \in [-2, 2]$. After applying the ReLU function, $\hat{x}_3, \hat{x}_4$ are constrained to $[1.5, 3.5]$, leading to $x_5 \in [0, 6]$ and $x_6 \in [0, 2]$. The bounds for $n_1, \ldots, n_4$ are exact, meaning for every α within the range, an input y can be found such that $\text{value}_y(n_i) = \alpha$. However, this precision is lost from the next layer (beginning with n_5, n_6) due to potential dependencies among preceding neurons. For example, it is impossible for $x_5 = \text{value}_x(n_5)$ to reach 6, as it would necessitate both $x_3 = 2$ and $x_4 = 2$, which is not possible at the same time as $x_3 = 2$ implies $x_1 = x_2 = 1$ and $x_4 = 2$ implies $x_2 = -1$ (and $x_1 = 1$), a contradiction.

In [13,21] and others, the *triangular abstraction* was proposed:

$$\text{ReLU}(x) = \max(0, x) \leq \hat{x} \leq \text{UB} \frac{x - \text{LB}}{\text{UB} - \text{LB}} \quad (3)$$

It has two lower bounds (the 0 and identity functions), and one upper bound. DeepPoly [21] chooses one of the two lower bounds for each neuron x, giving rise to a greedy quadratic-time algorithm to compute very fast an abstraction of the value of $\hat{x}$ (but not that accurately).

3.2 MILP and LP Encodings for DNNs

At the other end of the spectrum, we find the Mixed Integer Linear Programming (MILP) value abstraction, which is a complete (but inefficient) method. Consider an unstable neuron n, whose value $x \in [\text{LB}, \text{UB}]$ with $\text{LB} < 0 < \text{UB}$. The value $\hat{x}$ of ReLU(x) can be encoded exactly in an MILP formula with one integer (actually even binary) variable a valued in $\{0, 1\}$, using constants UB, LB with 4 constraints [24]:

$$\hat{x} \geq x \quad \wedge \quad \hat{x} \geq 0 \quad \wedge \quad \hat{x} \leq \text{UB} \cdot a \quad \wedge \quad \hat{x} \leq x - \text{LB} \cdot (1 - a) \quad (4)$$

For all $x \in [\text{LB}, \text{UB}] \setminus 0$, there exists a unique solution $(a, \hat{x})$ that meets these constraints, with $\hat{x} = \text{ReLU}(x)$ [24]. The value of a is 0 if $x < 0$, and 1 if $x > 0$, and can be either if $x = 0$. This encoding approach can be applied to every (unstable) ReLU node, and optimizing its value can help getting more accurate bounds. However, for networks with hundreds of *unstable* nodes, the resulting MILP formulation will contain numerous binary variables and generally bounds obtained will not be accurate, even using powerful commercial solvers such as Gurobi.

MILP instances can be linearly relaxed into LP over-abstraction, where variables originally restricted to integers in $\{0, 1\}$ (binary) are relaxed to real numbers in the interval $[0, 1]$, while maintaining the same encoding. As solving LP instances is polynomial time, this optimization is significantly more efficient. However, this efficiency comes at the cost of precision, often resulting in less stringent bounds. This approach is termed the *LP abstraction*. We invoke a folklore result on the LP relaxation of (4), for which we provide a direct and explicit proof:

Proposition 1. *[10] The LP relaxation of (4) is equivalent with the triangular abstraction (3).*

Proof. Consider an unstable neuron n, that is $\text{LB} < 0 < \text{UB}$. The lower bound on $\hat{x}$ is simple, as $\hat{x} \geq 0 \wedge \hat{x} \geq x$ is immediately equivalent with $\hat{x} \geq \text{ReLU}(x)$.

We now show that the three constraints $\hat{x} \leq \text{UB} \cdot a \wedge \hat{x} \leq x - \text{LB} \cdot (1 - a) \wedge a \in [0, 1]$ translates into $\hat{x} \leq \text{UB} \frac{x - \text{LB}}{\text{UB} - \text{LB}}$. We have $\hat{x}$ is upper bounded

Algorithm 1: pMILP$_K$

Input: Bounds $[\text{LB}(m), \text{UB}(m)]$ for nodes m at layer 0
Output: Bounds $[\text{LB}, \text{UB}]$ for every node n

1 **for** *layer* $k = 1, \ldots, \ell$ **do**
2   **for** *neuron n in layer k* **do**
3   Compute X a set of K nodes most important for target neuron n.
4   Run pMILP$_X(n)$ to obtain $[\text{LB}(n), \text{UB}(n)]$ using MILP$_X$ and additional constraints $\bigvee_{m \text{ in layer } < k} \text{value}(m) \in [\text{LB}(m), \text{UB}(m)]$.

by $max_{a \in [0,1]}(min(\text{UB} \cdot a, x - \text{LB}(1 - a)))$, and this bound can be reached. Furthermore, using standard function analysis tools (derivative...), we can show that the function $a \mapsto min(\text{UB} \cdot a, x - \text{LB}(1 - a))$ attains its maximum when $\text{UB} \cdot a = x - \text{LB}(1 - a)$, leading to the equation $(\text{UB} - \text{LB})a = x - \text{LB}$ and consequently $a = \frac{x - \text{LB}}{\text{UB} - \text{LB}}$. This results in an upper bound $\hat{x} \leq \text{UB}\frac{x - \text{LB}}{\text{UB} - \text{LB}}$, which can be reached, hence the equivalence. □

4 Partial MILP

In this paper, we revisit the use of *partial MILP* (pMILP for short, see [16]), to get interesting trade-offs between accuracy and runtime. Let X be a subset of the set of unstable neurons, and n a neuron for which we want to compute upper and lower bounds on values: pMILP$_X(n)$ simply calls Gurobi to minimize/maximize the value of n with the MILP model encoding (Eq. (2) Sect. 3.2), where variable a is:

- binary for neurons in X (exact encoding of the ReLU),
- linear for neurons not in X (linear relaxation).

Formally, we denote by MILP$_X$ the MILP encoding where the variable a encoding ReLU(y) is binary for $y \in X$, and linear for $y \notin X$ (y being unstable or stable). We say that nodes in X are *opened*. That is, if X is a strict subset of the set of all unstable neurons, then MILP$_X$ is an abstraction of the constraints in the full MILP model. If X covers all unstable neurons, then MILP$_X$ is exact as there is only one linear mode for stable variables. The worst-case complexity to solve MILP$_X$ is NP-complete in $|X|$, ie the number of binary variables.

To reduce the runtime, we will limit the size of subset X. This a priori hurts accuracy. To recover some of this accuracy, we use an iterative approach similar to the box abstraction or DeepPoly [21], computing lower and upper bounds LB, UB for neurons n of each layer iteratively, that are used when computing values of the next layer. So we trade-off the NP-complexity in $|X|$ with a linear complexity in the number of neurons. Notice that all the neurons of a layer can be treated in parallel.

We provide the pseudo code for pMILP$_K$ in Algorithm 1. pMILP$_K$ has a worst case complexity bounded by $O(N \cdot \text{MILP}(N, K))$, where N is the number of nodes of the DNN, and MILP(N, K) is the complexity of solving a MILP program with K binary variables and N linear variables. We have MILP(N, K) $\leq$ 2^KLP(N) where LP(N) is the Polynomial time to solve a Linear Program with N variables, 2^K being an upper bound. Solvers like Gurobi are quite adept and usually do not need to evaluate all 2^K ReLU configurations to deduce the bounds. It is worth mentioning that the "for" loop iterating over neurons n in layer k (line 2) can be executed in parallel, because the computation only depends on bounds from preceding layers, not the current layer k. This worst-case complexity compares favorably when $K \ll N$ with the worst-case complexity of BaB which would be $O(out \times 2^N)$, where out is the number of output neurons. Of course, actual complexity is always much better than the worst case, thanks to different heuristics, such as pruning, which is what happens for easy instances, for which the linear cost N in pMILP (which cannot be avoided) is actually the limiting factor. Only experimental results can tell whether the accuracy lost using reduced variables in pMILP can be a good trade off vs efficiency, both depending on the number K chosen.

If K is sufficiently small, this approach is expected to be efficient. The crucial factor in such an approach is to *select* few opened ReLU nodes in X which are the most important for the accuracy. An extreme strategy was adopted in [16], where only ReLU nodes of the immediate previous layer can be opened, and the measure to choose ReLU a when computing the bounds for neuron b was to consider $|W_{ab}|(\text{UB}(a) - \text{LB}(a))$.

5 Global Scoring Functions

To select nodes X for pMILP$_X$, we first adapt from the BaB-SR [8] and FSB [11] functions, which originally iteratively select one node to branch on for BaB. Intuitively, we extract the scoring s_{SR} and s_{FSB} from both BaB-SR and FSB, as the BaB bounding step is not adapted for pMILP. We will call such functions *global scoring* (GS) functions.

They both work by backpropagating gradients vectors $\boldsymbol{\lambda}$ from the neurons under consideration in layer n, back to neurons to be potentially selected. To do so, they consider the rate of ReLU($\boldsymbol{u}_k$) to be $r(\boldsymbol{u}_k) = \frac{\max(0, \text{UB}(\boldsymbol{u}_k))}{\max(0, \text{UB}(\boldsymbol{u}_k)) - \min(0, \text{LB}(\boldsymbol{u}_k))} \in [0, 1]$, with $r(b) = 0$ iff UB(b) ≤ 0 and $r(b) = 1$ iff LB(b) ≥ 0.

$$\boldsymbol{\lambda}_{n-1} = -(\boldsymbol{W}^n)^T \mathbf{1}, \quad \boldsymbol{\lambda}_{k-1} = (\boldsymbol{W}^k)^T \big(r(\boldsymbol{u}_k) \odot \boldsymbol{\lambda}_k\big) \quad k \in [n-1, 2] \quad (5)$$

Then, the scoring functions s_{SR} and s_{FSB} for ReLUs in layer k are computed by approximating how each node would impact the neurons in layer n, using the computed $\boldsymbol{\lambda}$, differeing only in how they handle the bias $\boldsymbol{b}_k$:

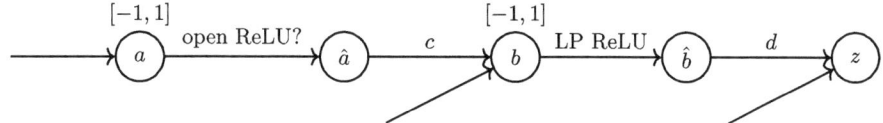

Fig. 2. A running example with parametric weights c (Color figure online) and d.

$$s_{SR}(k) = \left| r(\boldsymbol{u}_k) \odot \text{LB}(\boldsymbol{u}_k) \odot \max(\boldsymbol{\lambda}_k, 0) + \max\{0, \boldsymbol{\lambda}_k \odot \boldsymbol{b}_k\} - r(\boldsymbol{u}_k) \odot \boldsymbol{\lambda}_k \odot \boldsymbol{b}_k \right|$$

$$s_{FSB}(k) = \left| r(\boldsymbol{u}_k) \odot \text{LB}(\boldsymbol{u}_k) \odot \max(\boldsymbol{\lambda}_k, 0) + \min\{0, \boldsymbol{\lambda}_k \odot \boldsymbol{b}_k\} - r(\boldsymbol{u}_k) \odot \boldsymbol{\lambda}_k \odot \boldsymbol{b}_k \right|$$

Then, ReLU are ranked using these scores, to select the most important unstable ReLUs (with $\text{LB}(u_k) < 0 < \text{UB}(u_k)$).

Running Example: Consider Fig. 2. It has no bias, so $s_{SR} = s_{FSB}$. We have $\lambda(b) = d$, $\lambda(a) = \frac{cd}{2}$. The value of $s_{FSB}(a)$ depends on the signs of c, d.

We perform a novel comparison between $s_{FSB}(a)$ and $\Delta(z)$, the difference on the *maximal bound* computed by $\text{pMILP}_X(z)$ when opening the ReLU of node a ($X = \{a\}$), yielding $\text{value}(\hat{a}) = \text{ReLU}(\text{value}(a))$, versus having $X = \emptyset$, for which $\text{value}(\hat{a})$ can be any value in the triangle approximation (Prop. 1).

The most favorable cases are $c < 0 < d$ and $d < 0 < c$: as $cd < 0$, we have $s_{FSB}(a) = \max(0, \frac{cd}{4}) = 0$. Because $cd < 0$, both a and $\hat{a}$ need to be minimized by MILP_X in order to maximize the value of z. For $X = \emptyset$, the LP approximation ($=\text{MILP}_\emptyset$) will thus set $\text{value}(\hat{a}) = \text{ReLU}(\text{value}(a))$ as this is the minimum value in the triangle approximation. Notice that opening $X = \{a\}$ yields the same $\text{value}(\hat{a}) = \text{ReLU}(\text{value}(a))$. That is, opening node a is not improving the bound $\text{UB}(z)$, as correctly predicted by the score $s_{FSB}(a) = \Delta(a) = 0$.

Case $c > 0, d > 0$: we have $s_{FSB}(a) = \frac{cd}{4}$. The value of $a, \hat{a}, b, \hat{b}$ should be maximized to maximize the value of z, because $W_{bz} = d > 0$ and $W_{ab} = c > 0$. Now, let us call $val(a)$ the maximum value for a (same for $\text{MILP}_\emptyset$ and $\text{MILP}_{\{a\}}$). The maximum value for $\hat{a}$ under LP ($X = \emptyset$) is $\frac{1}{2} \cdot (\text{value}(a) - LB(a))$ following the triangle approximation. Now, if $X = \{a\}$, then the value of $\hat{a}$ is $\text{ReLU}(\text{value}(a))$: the difference $\Delta(\hat{a})$ is between 0 (for $\text{value}(a) \in \{LB, UB\}$) and $\frac{1}{2}$ (for $\text{value}(a) = 0$). The difference $\Delta(b)$ for the value of b is thus between 0 and $\frac{c}{2}$, which means $\Delta(\hat{b}) \in [0, \frac{c}{4}]$, using the upper function of the triangle approximation of rate $r(b) = \frac{1}{2}$, as the value of $\hat{b}$ should be maximized. This means a difference $\Delta(z) \in [0, \frac{cd}{4}]$ (depending on the maximal value $val(a)$), to compare with the fixed $s_{FSB}(a) = \frac{cd}{4}$.

The last case is the most problematic: Case $c < 0, d < 0$, implying that $s_{FSB}(a) = \frac{cd}{4}$, because $cd > 0$. Opening ReLU(a) will have the same impact on the value of $\hat{a}, b$ than in case $c > 0, d > 0$, with $\Delta(b) \in [0, \frac{c}{2}]$. However, as $d < 0$, value of $\hat{b}$ needs to be minimized to maximize the value of z. That is, the value of $\hat{b}$ will be the value of ReLU($sol(b)$), and the change $\Delta(\hat{b})$ will be either 0 in case value(b) < 0, or $\Delta(b) \in [0, \frac{c}{2}]$ for value(b) > 0. That is, z will be modified by either $\Delta(z) = 0$ or $\Delta(z) = d\Delta(b)$, to be compared with the fix value $s_{FSB}(a) = \frac{cd}{4}$, which is not always an overapproximation: we have $\Delta(z) = \frac{cd}{2} > s_{FSB}(a)$, if value($a$) = 0 and value($b$) > 0.

We call *global scoring* (GS) these functions s_{FSB}, s_{SR} because they score ReLUs as accurately as possible, considering that they do not have access to the values value(a), value(b) maximizing z. Following this analysis of s_{FSB}, s_{SR}, next Section presents a novel scoring function more accurate wrt $\Delta(z)$.

6 Solution-Aware Scoring

In this section, we propose *Solution-Aware Scoring* (SAS), to evaluate accurately how opening a ReLU impacts the accuracy. To do so, SAS considers explicitly a solution to a unique LP call, which is reasonably fast to obtain as there is no binary variables (polynomial time). Assume that we want to compute an upper bound for neuron z on layer ℓ_z. We write $n < z$ if neuron n is on a layer before ℓ_z, and $n \leq z$ if $n < z$ or $n = z$. We denote (Sol_ $\max_X^z(n))_{n \leq z}$ a solution of $\mathcal{M}_X$ maximizing z: Sol_ $\max_X^z(z)$ is the maximum of z under $\mathcal{M}_X$.

Consider $(sol(n))_{n \leq z} = $ (Sol_ $\max_\emptyset^z(n))_{n \leq z}$, a solution maximizing the value for z when all ReLU use the LP relaxation. Function Improve_ $\max^z(n) = sol(z) - $ Sol_ $\max_{\{n\}}^z(z)$, accurately represents how much opening neuron $n < z$ reduces the maximum computed for z compared with using only LP. We have Improve_ $\max^z(n) \geq 0$ as Sol_ $\max_{\{n\}}^z$ fulfills all the constraints of $\mathcal{M}_\emptyset$, so Sol_ $\max_{\{n\}}^z(z) \leq sol(z)$. Computing exactly Improve_ $\max^z(n)$ would need a MILP call on $\mathcal{M}_{\{n\}}$ for every neuron $n \leq z$, which would be very time consuming. Instead, the SAS function uses a (single) LP call to compute $(sol(n))_{n \leq z}$, with negligible runtime wrt the forthcoming MILP$_X$ call, and yet accurately approximates Improve_ $\max^z(n)$ (Fig. 4).

For a neuron b on the layer before layer ℓ_z, we define:

$$\text{SAS\_ max}^z(b) = W_{bz} \times (sol(\hat{b}) - \text{ReLU}(sol(b))) \tag{6}$$

Comparison: consider b with $W_{bz} < 0$: to maximize z, the value of $sol(\hat{b})$ is minimized by LP, ie $sol(\hat{b}) = $ ReLU($sol(b)$) thanks to Proposition 1. Thus, we have SAS_ $\max^z(b) = 0 = $ Improve$_{max}^z(b)$. Notice that the original scoring function $|W_{bz}|$(UB(b) − LB(b)) [16] would be possibly very large in this case. However, GS scoring functions from BaB-SR and FSB would also accurately compute $s_{FSB}(b) = s_{SR} = 0$. Notice that SAS does not need to consider bias explicitly, unlike s_{FSB}, s_{SR}, as they are already accounted for in the solution considered.

Consider a neuron a two layers before ℓ_z, b denoting neurons in the layer ℓ just before ℓ_z. Recall the rate $r(b) = \frac{\max(0, \text{UB}(b))}{\max(0, \text{UB}(b)) - \min(0, \text{LB}(b))} \in [0, 1]$. We define:

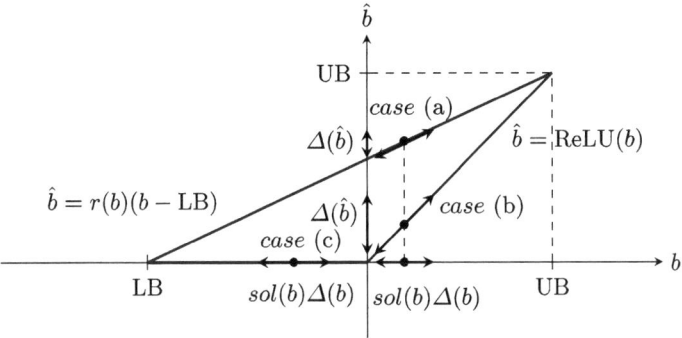

Fig. 3. Different cases for ReLU(b).

$$\Delta(\hat{a}) = \text{ReLU}(\text{sol}(a)) - \text{sol}(\hat{a}) \qquad (7)$$
$$\forall b \in \ell, \Delta(b) = W_{ab}\Delta(\hat{a}) \qquad (8)$$

$$\forall b \in \ell, \Delta(\hat{b}) = \begin{cases} r(b)\Delta(b), & \text{for } W_{bz} > 0 \quad (9a) \\ \max(\Delta(b), -\text{sol}(b)), & \text{for } W_{bz} < 0 \text{ and sol}(b) \geq 0 \quad (9b) \\ \max(0, \Delta(b) + \text{sol}(b)), & \text{for } W_{bz} < 0 \text{ and sol}(b) < 0 \quad (9c) \end{cases}$$

$$\text{SAS\_max}^z(a) = \Delta(z) = -\sum_{b \in \ell} W_{bz}\Delta(\hat{b}) \qquad (10)$$

Comparison: First, the original [16] does not propose a formula for node a two layers before z. So we will compare SAS with GS. Consider again the running example of Fig. 2.

In the case $c \cdot d < 0$, we have $\text{SAS\_max}^z(a) = \text{Improve}^z_{max}(b) = s_{FSB}(a) = s_{SR}(a) = 0$, as $\Delta(\hat{a}) = 0$.

In the case $c > 0, d > 0$, $\Delta(\hat{a}) = \text{ReLU}(\text{sol}(a)) - \text{sol}(\hat{a})$ is precise, whereas the corresponding $\Delta_{FSB}(\hat{a}) = \text{LB}(a)r(a)$ is only an upperbound.

The last case $c < 0, d < 0$ is the most extreme: $\Delta(\hat{b})$ adapts to the case (b),(c) in Fig. 3 leveraging the value sol(b), which yields very different values, whereas the corresponding $\Delta_{FSB}(\hat{b})$ is always $r(b)\Delta_{FSB}(b)$:

- For $\text{sol}(b) \ll 0$, we will have $\Delta(\hat{b}) = 0 < \Delta_{FSB}(\hat{b})$.
- For $\text{sol}(b) \gg 0$, we will have $\Delta(\hat{b}) = \Delta(b) > \frac{1}{2}\Delta_{FSB}(\hat{b})$ as $r(b) = \frac{1}{2}$.

Further, we can show that SAS is a safe overapproximation of Improve$\_\text{max}^z(a)$, which does not hold for s_{FSB}, s_{SR} (because of the case sol(b) $\gg 0$):

Proposition 2. $0 \leq \text{Improve\_max}^z(a) \leq \text{SAS\_max}^z(a)$.

In particular, for all nodes a with $\text{SAS\_max}^z(a) = 0$, we are sure that this node is not having any impact on $\text{Sol\_max}^z_{\{a\}}(z)$.

Proof. Consider $\text{sol}'(n)_{n \leq z}$ with $\text{sol}'(n) = \text{sol}(n)$ for all $n \notin \{z, \hat{a}\} \cup \{b, \hat{b} \mid b \in \ell\}$. In particular, $\text{sol}'(a) = \text{sol}(a)$. Now, define $\text{sol}'(\hat{a}) = \text{ReLU}(\text{sol}(a))$. That is, $\text{sol}'(\hat{a})$ is the correct value for $\hat{a}$, obtained if we open neuron a, compared to the LP abstraction for $\text{sol}(\hat{a})$. We define $\text{sol}'(b) = \text{sol}(b) + \Delta(b)$ and $\text{sol}'(\hat{b}) = \text{sol}(\hat{b}) + \Delta(\hat{b})$. Last, $\text{sol}'(z) = \text{sol}(z) + \sum_{b \in \ell} W_{bz} \Delta(\hat{b})$. We will show:

$$(\text{sol}'(n))_{n \leq z} \text{ satisfies the constraints in } \mathcal{M}_{\{a\}} \qquad (11)$$

This suffices to conclude: as $\text{sol}'(z)$ is a solution of $\mathcal{M}_{\{a\}}$, it is smaller or equal to the maximal solution: $\text{sol}'(z) \leq \text{Sol\_max}^z_{\{a\}}(z)$. That is, $\text{sol}(z) - \text{sol}'(z) \geq \text{sol}(z) - \text{Sol\_max}^z_{\{a\}}(z)$, i.e. $\text{SAS\_max}^z(a) \geq \text{Improve\_max}^z(a)$. In particular, we have that $\text{SAS\_max}^z(a) \geq 0$, which was not obvious from the definition.

Finally, we show (11). First, opening a changes the value of $\hat{a}$ from $\text{sol}(\hat{a})$ to $\text{ReLU}(\text{sol}(a)) = \text{sol}(\hat{a}) + \Delta(a)$, and from $\text{sol}(b)$ to $\text{sol}(b) + \Delta(b)$. The case of $\Delta(\hat{b})$ is the most interesting: If (a) $W_{bz} > 0$, to maximize z, the LP solver sets $\text{sol}(\hat{b})$ to the maximal possible value, which is $r(b)\text{sol}(b) + \text{Cst}$ according to Proposition 1. Changing b by $\Delta(b)$ thus results in changing $\text{sol}(\hat{b})$ by $r(b)\Delta(b)$. If $W_{bz} \leq 0$, then the LP solver sets $\text{sol}(\hat{b})$ to the lowest possible value to maximize z, which happens to be $\text{ReLU}(b)$ according to Proposition 1. If (b) $\text{sol}(b) > 0$, then $\text{sol}(\hat{b}) = \text{ReLU}(\text{sol}(b)) = \text{sol}(b)$, and the change to $\hat{b}$ will be the full $\Delta(b)$, unless $\Delta(b) < -\text{sol}(b) < 0$ in which case it is $-\text{sol}(b)$. If (c) $\text{sol}(b) < 0$, then we have $\text{sol}(\hat{b}) = \text{ReLU}(b) = 0$ and opening a moves away from 0 only if $\text{sol}(b) + \Delta(b) > 0$. □

7 Experimental Evaluation

We implemented Hybrid MILP in Python 3.8: it first calls α, β-CROWN with small time out (10 s for small and 30 s for larger DNNs), and then call pMILP on the undecided inputs. Gurobi 9.52 was used for solving LP and MILP problems. We conducted our evaluation on an AMD Threadripper 7970X (32 cores@4.0GHz) with 256 GB of main memory and 2 NVIDIA RTX 4090. The objectives of our evaluation was to answer the following questions:

1. How does the the choice of the set X impacts the accuracy of MILP_X?
2. How accurate is Hybrid MILP, and how efficient is it?

7.1 Comparison Between Different Scoring Functions (accuracy)

To measure the impact of the scoring function to select neurons to open, we considered the complex CNN-B-Adv, which has 16634 nodes. We tested over

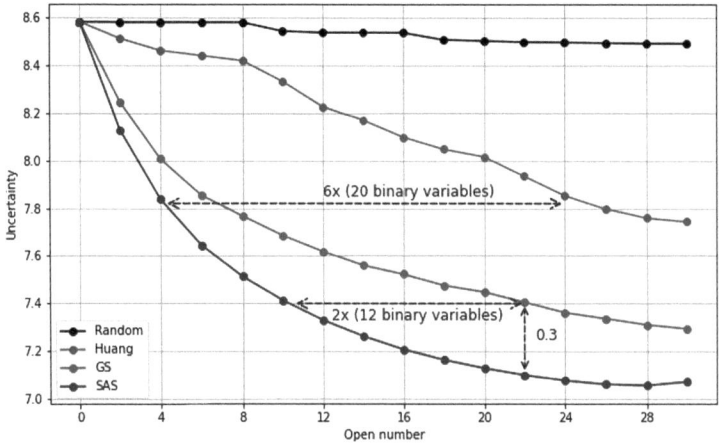

Fig. 4. Average uncertainty of pMILP for neurons of the fourth layer of CNN-B-Adv, when selecting between 0 and 30 ReLUs with different scoring functions.

the x = 85th image in the CIFAR-10 dataset. To measure the accuracy, we measure the uncertainty of all nodes in the 4th layer: the uncertainty of a node is the range between its computed lower and upper bound. We then average the uncertainty among all the nodes of the layer. Formally, the uncertainty of a node a with bounds [LB, UB] is uncert(a) = UB(a) − LB(a). The average uncertainty of layer ℓ is $\frac{\sum_{a \in l} \text{uncert}(a)}{size(\ell)}$.

We report in Fig. 4 the average uncertainty of MILP$_X$ following the choice of the K heaviest neurons of SAS, compared with a random choice, with Huang [16], based on strength(n) = (UB(n)−LB(n))·$|W_{nz}|$, and with GS (here, s_{FSB}).

Overall, SAS is more accurate than GS, more accurate than Huang, more accurate than random choice of variables. SAS significantly outperforms other solutions, with 2 times less binary variables for the same accuracy (10 vs 22) vs GS and 6 times vs Huang [16] (4 vs 24). Each node of the 4th layer displays a similar pattern, and the pattern is similar for different images.

Gurobi relies on a Branch and Bound procedure to compute bounds. We report in Table 3 experiments on changing the ordering on variables in Gurobi,

Table 3. Comparison of different orderings with selection of ReLUs by SAS.

Image 85 order	45 open ReLUs		50 open ReLUs		55 open ReLUs		60 open ReLUs	
	distance	time	distance	time	distance	time	distance	time
Gurobi	0.384	252 s	0.368	265 s	0.342	287 s	0.315	306 s
SAS (static)	0.384	448 s	0.368	759 s	0.365	971 s	0.355	971 s
GS (static)	0.384	**251 s**	0.368	**253 s**	0.342	**270 s**	0.315	**281 s**

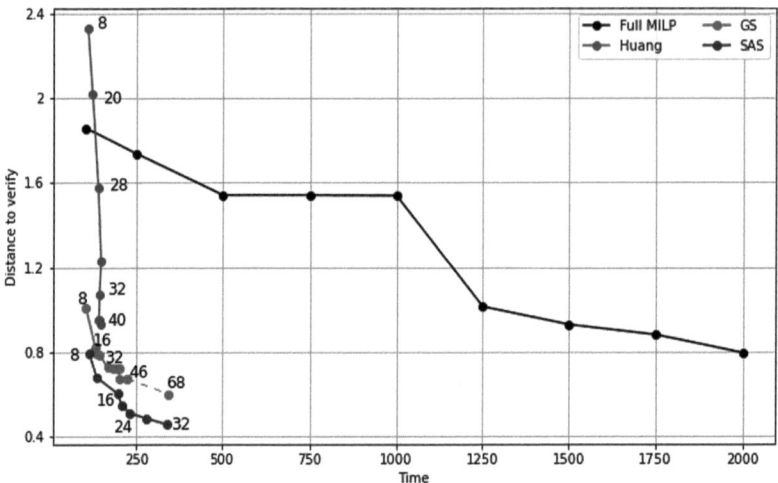

Fig. 5. Distance to verify vs runtime: comparison between SAS, GS, full MILP and Huang's method for different number of opened ReLUs/time-outs.

when the selection of ReLUs is fixed by SAS on CNN-B-Adv Image 85. We compared the standard Gurobi ordering of variables, which is adaptative in each branch, with the static order provided by SAS, as well as the static order provided by GS, wrt runtime at a fixed accuracy (we report the *distance* to verify the image).

SAS ordering is particularly counter-productive because it is accurate only for one branch (the most complicated one), whereas Gurobi can adapt the order to each branch. However, the GS *ordering* (with the SAS *selection*) is better as it is general and not local to a solution, with better runtime than Gurobi, despite its staticness whereas Gurobi order is adaptive.

7.2 Comparison with MILP (time and Accuracy)

Restricting the set X of open ReLU nodes potentially hurts accuracy. Another strategy could be to still compute inductively accurate bounds for each nodes, replacing pMILP (SAS, GS, etc.) with a full MILP model, and stopping it early after some fixed time-out (100 s, 250 s, ..., 2000 s).

We evaluate in Fig. 5 the full MILP and different pMILP models on the output layer of CNN-B-Adv. The bounds for hidden layers have been computed with the same SAS method. We compare the *distance to verify* the same Image 85, specifically the lower bound of an output neuron, the furthest away from verification. The curve is not as smooth as in Fig. 4, as a unique neuron is considered rather than an average over neurons.

SAS (even GS= s_{FSB}) is much more accurate than full MILP for every reasonable time-outs considered, with > 10 times fastest runtime at better accuracy. The reason is that even the advanced MILP solver Gurobi struggles to sort out all ReLUs. It is thus particulary important to have accurate scoring functions as SAS, in order to optimize both accuracy and runtime. Huang [16] is limited in ReLUs in the previous layer, reason why it is stuck at relatively poor accuracy. The accuracy/runtime curve from GS is closer to SAS than the number of nodes/accuracy curve of Fig. 4. This is because many ReLU nodes deemed important by GS are not relevant for accuracy, but they are also not penalizing runtime. Still, SAS is faster than GS at every accuracy. Importantly, SAS is more deterministic in its runtime given a number of ReLU nodes, with half the variance in runtime over different output neurons compared with GS for similar accuracy, which helps setting a number of ReLU nodes to open.

7.3 Ablation Study: on Usefulness of Computing Previous Layers Accurately

We explore the usefulness of computing accurately bounds for each neuron inductively on the layers, even on small networks. For that, we consider MNIST 5×100, computing bounds for nodes of layer 3, comparing when bounds for neurons of layer 2 have been computed inaccurately using LP rather than with the more accurate (partial) MILP (Fig. 6).

This experiment explains the rationale to use divide and conquer methodology, using many calls (one for each neuron) of pMILP with relatively small number $|X|$ of open ReLUs rather than few calls (one per output neuron) of pMILP with larger number $|X|$ of open nodes. The benefit is clear already from

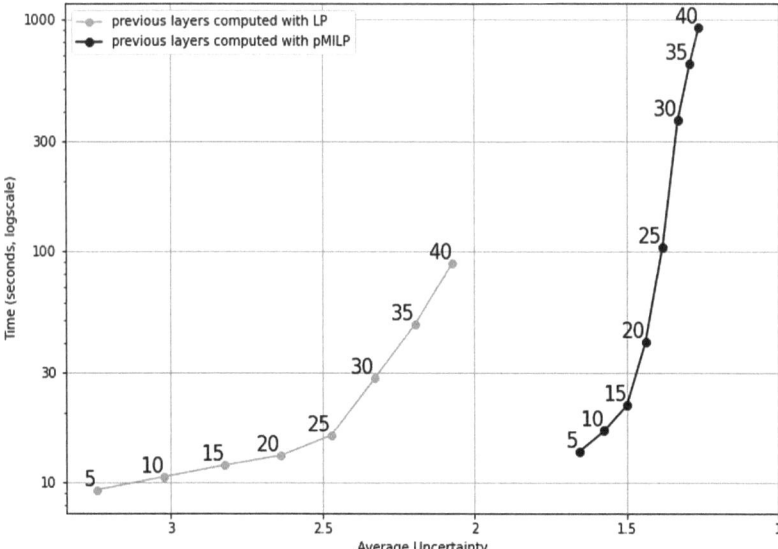

Fig. 6. Comparison of accuracy in layer 3 when bounds for neurons in layer 2 is computed inaccurately using LP vs when bounds of layer 2 are computed accurately using pMILP. Time is using logscale.

layer 3, obtaining much tighter bounds (lower uncertainty) when bounds for neurons in layer 2 have been computed accurately using pMILP.

7.4 Comparison with α, β-CROWN

To assess the verification efficiency and runtime vs α, β-CROWN, we conducted evaluations on neural networks tested in [25] which are mostly *complex* to verify (as easy instances are already appropriately taken care of). Namely, 6 ReLU-DNNs: 5 MNIST DNN that can be found in the ERAN GitHub (the 4th to the 8th DNNs provided) as well as 1 CIFAR CNN from [3], see also [9], which can be downloaded from the α, β-CROWN GitHub. We commit to the same ϵ settings as in [25], that are recalled in Table 1. For reference, we also report an easy but very large ResNet Network for CIFAR10, already tested with α, β CROWN. We report in Table 4 the % of undecided images, that is the % of images than can be neither falsified (by α, β-CROWN) nor verified by the tested verifier, among the 100 first images for each MNIST or CIFAR10 benchmark. The exact same DNNs, image set and ϵ are used in Tables 1 and 4.

Analysis: overall, Hybrid MILP is very accurate, only leaving 8%-15% of images undecided, with runtime taking less than $500s$ in average per image, and even 10 times less on smaller DNNs. It can scale up to quite large hard DNNs, such as CNN-B-Adv with 2M parameters.

Compared with α, β-CROWN: on easy instances, Hybrid MILP is virtually similar to α, β-CROWN (e.g. even on the very large ResNet), since Hybrid MILP calls first α, β-CROWN as it is very efficient for easy instances.

On hard instances (the 6 first DNNs tested), compared with α, β-CROWN with a time-out of TO=2000 s, Hybrid MILP is much more accurate, with a reduction of undecided images by $9\% - 43\%$. It is also from 20x faster on smaller networks to similar time on the largest DNN. Compared with α, β-CROWN with

Table 4. Undecided images (%, *lower is better*) as computed by α, β-CROWN, Refined β-CROWN and Hybrid MILP on 7 DNNs (average runtime per image). The 6 first DNNs are hard instances. The last DNN (ResNet) is an easy instance (trained using Wong to be easy to verify), provided for reference.

Network	α, β-CROWN TO=10 s	α, β-CROWN TO=30 s	α, β-CROWN TO=2000 s	Refined β-CROWN	Hybrid MILP
MNIST 5×100	57% (6.9 s)	55% (18.9 s)	50% (1026 s)	13% (92 s)	13% (**46 s**)
MNIST 5×200	50% (6.5 s)	47% (17 s)	46% (930 s)	9% (80 s)	**8%** (**71 s**)
MNIST 8×100	63% (7.2 s)	58% (20 s)	58% (1163 s)	21% (102 s)	15% (**61 s**)
MNIST 8×200	56% (6.8 s)	55% (18 s)	54% (1083 s)	16% (83 s)	**8%** (**78 s**)
MNIST 6×500	53% (6.4 s)	51% (16 s)	50% (1002 s)	–	**10%** (**402 s**)
CNN-B-Adv	28% (4.3 s)	22% (8.7 s)	20% (373 s)	–	**11%** (**417 s**)
ResNet	0% (2 s)	0% (2 s)	0% (2 s)	–	0% (2 s)

a time-out of TO=30 s, the accuracy gap is even larger (e.g. 11% for CNN-B-Adv, i.e. half the undecided images), although the average runtime is also obviously larger (solving hard instances takes longer than solving easy instances).

Last, compared with *Refined* β-CROWN, we can observe three patterns: on the shallowest DNNs (5×100, 5×200), Refined β-CROWN can run full MILP on almost all nodes, reaching almost the same accuracy than Hybrid MILP, but with longer runtime (up to 2 times on 5×100). As size of DNNs grows (8×100, 8×200), full MILP invoked by Refined β-CROWN can only be run on a fraction of the neurons, and the accuracy is not as good as Hybrid MILP, with 6% – 8% more undecided images (that is double on 8×200), while having longer runtime. Last but not least, Refined β-CROWN cannot scale to larger instances (6×500, CNN-B-Adv), while Hybrid MILP can.

7.5 Comparison with Other Verifiers

We voluntarily limited the comparison so far to α, β-CROWN because it is one of the most efficient verifier to date, which allowed us to consider a spectrum of parameters to understand α, β-CROWN scaling without too much clutter.

Interestingly, GCP-CROWN [30] is slightly more accurate than α, β-CROWN on the DNNs we tested, but necessitates IBM CPLEX solver, which is not available to us. We provide in Table 5 results from the Table 3 page 9 of [30], experimenting with different verifiers on the most interesting CIFAR CNN-B-Adv. Notice that results are not exactly comparable with ours because the testing images are not the same (ours has 62% upper bound while [30] has 65% upper bound, so the image set in [30] are slightly easier). There, GCP-CROWN is 2% more accurate (with higher runtime) than α, β-CROWN with 90 s TO, so we can deduce that Hybrid MILP, which is 9% more accurate than α, β-CROWN with 2000 s TO, is significantly more accurate than GCP-CROWN.

Results on other networks from other verifiers (PRIMA [19], SDP-FO [9], etc.) were already reported [25] on other tested DNNs, with unfavorable comparison vs α, β-CROWN. Further, we reported accuracy of NNenum [2], Marabou [18,27], respectively 4th, 3rd of the last VNNcomp'24 [5], as well as full MILP [24] in Table 2, showing that these verifiers are not competitive on complex (even small) instances. Concerning MnBAB [15], and it compares slightly unfavorably in time and accuracy towards α, β-CROWN on CNN-B-Adv and *complex* MNIST DNNs at several time-out settings. Last, Pyrat [12] (2nd in the latest VNNComp) is not open source, which made running it impossible.

Table 5. Images verified by different verifiers (%, higher is better) on CIFAR CNN-B-Adv. Results, from [30], are not fully comparable with Tables 1,4.

Upper Bound	SDP-FO	PRIMA	refined β-CROWN	β-CROWN	GCP-CROWN
65%	32.8%	38%	27%	46.5%	48.5%
$\epsilon = 2/255$	> 25h	344s	361s	32s	58s

8 Conclusion

In this paper, we developed a novel solution-aware scoring (SAS) function to select few ReLU nodes to consider with binary variables to compute accurately bounds in DNNs. The solution awareness allows SAS to compute an accurate score for each ReLU, which enables partial MILP to be very efficient, necessitating $\approx$ 6x less binary variables than previous proposals [16] for the same accuracy, and $\approx$ 2x less than GS scoring adapted from FSB [11]. As the worst-case complexity is exponential in the number of binary variables, this has large implication in terms of scalability to larger DNNs, making it possible to verify accurately quite large DNNs such as CNN-B-Adv with 2M parameters.

While α, β-CROWN is known to be extremely efficient to solve easier verification instances, we exhibit many cases (complex instances) where its worst-case exponential complexity in the number of ReLUs is tangible, with unfavorable scaling (Table 1). Resorting to Hybrid MILP, a divide-and-conquer approach [16], revisited thanks to the very efficient SAS, revealed to be a much better trade-off than augmenting α, β-CROWN time-outs, with 8% to 40% less undecided images at ISO runtime. Currently, for hard instances, there is no alternative to partial MILP, other methods being > 10 times slower.

This opens up interesting future research directions, to verify global [26], rather than local (robustness) properties, which need very accurate methodology and give rise to hard instances as the range of each neuron is no more local to a narrow neighborhood (most ReLUs are unstable, with both modes possible).

Acknowledgement. This research was conducted as part of the DesCartes program and was supported by the National Research Foundation, Prime Minister's Office, Singapore, under the Campus for Research Excellence and Technological Enterprise (CREATE) program, and partially supported by ANR-23-PEIA-0006 SAIF.

References

1. Afzal, M., Gupta, A., Akshay, S.: Using counterexamples to improve robustness verification in neural networks. In: Automated Technology for Verification and Analysis (ATVA'23), LNCS 14215, pp. 422–443 (2023)
2. Bak, S.: nnenum: verification of relu neural networks with optimized abstraction refinement. In: NASA Formal Methods Symposium, pp. 19–36. Springer (2021)
3. Balunović, M., Vechev, M.: Adversarial training and provable defenses: bridging the gap. In: International Conference on Learning Representations (ICLR'20) (2020)
4. Brix, C., Bak, S., Liu, C., Johnson, T.T.: The fourth international verification of neural networks competition (VNN-comp 2023): summary and results (2023)
5. Brix, C., Bak, S., Liu, C., Johnson, T.T., Shriver, D., Wu, H.: 5th International Verification of Neural Networks Competition (VNN-comp'24) (2024)
6. Brix, C., Müller, M.N., Bak, S., Johnson, T.T., Liu, C.: First three years of the international verification of neural networks competition (VNN-comp) (2023)
7. Bunel, R., Dvijotham, K., Kumar, M.P., De Palma, A., Stanforth, R.: Verified neural compressed sensing, Pawan Kumar (2024)

8. Bunel, R., Lu, J., Turkaslan, I., Torr, P.H., Kohli, P., Kumar, M.P.: Branch and bound for piecewise linear neural network verification. J. Mach. Learn. Res. **21**(42), 1–39 (2020)
9. Dathathri, S., et al.: Enabling certification of verification-agnostic networks via memory-efficient semidefinite programming. Adv. Neural Inf. Process. Syst. **33**, 5318–5331 (2020)
10. De Palma, A., Behl, H.S., Bunel, R., Torr, P., Kumar, M.P.: Scaling the convex barrier with active sets. In: International Conference on Learning Representations (ICLR'21). Open Review (2021)
11. De Palma, A., et al.: Improved branch and bound for neural network verification via lagrangian decomposition. arXiv preprint arXiv:2104.06718 (2021)
12. Durand, S., Lemesle, A., Chihani, Z., Urban, C., Terrier, F.: Reciph: relational coefficients for input partitioning heuristic. In: 1st Workshop on Formal Verification of Machine Learning (WFVML 2022) (2022)
13. Ehlers, R.: Formal Verification of Piece-Wise Linear Feed-Forward Neural Networks. In: D'Souza, D., Narayan Kumar, K. (eds.) ATVA 2017. LNCS, vol. 10482, pp. 269–286. Springer, Cham (2017). https://doi.org/10.1007/978-3-319-68167-2_19
14. Ehlers, R.: Formal Verification of Piece-Wise Linear Feed-Forward Neural Networks. In: D'Souza, D., Narayan Kumar, K. (eds.) ATVA 2017. LNCS, vol. 10482, pp. 269–286. Springer, Cham (2017). https://doi.org/10.1007/978-3-319-68167-2_19
15. Ferrari, C., Muller, M.N., Jovanovic, N., Vechev, M.: Complete verification via multi-neuron relaxation guided branch-and-bound. In: International Conference on Learning Representations (ICLR'22) (2022)
16. Huang, C., Fan, J., Chen, X., Li, W., Zhu, Q.: Divide and slide: layer-wise refinement for output range analysis of deep neural networks. IEEE Trans. Comput. Aided Des. Integr. Circuits Syst. **39**(11), 3323–3335 (2020)
17. Katz, G., Barrett, C., Dill, D.L., Julian, K., Kochenderfer, M.J.: Reluplex: an efficient SMT solver for verifying deep neural networks. In: Rupak Majumdar and Viktor Kunčak, editors, Computer Aided Verification, pp. 97–117, Cham (2017)
18. Katz, G., et al.: The marabou framework for verification and analysis of deep neural networks. In: Isil Dillig and Serdar Tasiran, editors, Computer Aided Verification, pp. 443–452. Springer International Publishing, Cham (2019)
19. Müller, M.N., Makarchuk, G., Singh, G., Püschel, M., Vechev, M.: Prima: general and precise neural network certification via scalable convex hull approximations. vol. 6, New York, NY, USA (2022). Association for Computing Machinery
20. Brix, C., Müller, M.N., Bak, S., Johnson, T.T., Liu, C.: The third international verification of neural networks competition (2022): summary and results (2022)
21. Singh, G., Gehr, T., Püschel, M., Vechev, M.: An abstract domain for certifying neural networks. Proc. ACM Program. Lang., 3(POPL) (2019)
22. Singh, G., Gehr, T., Püschel, M., Vechev, M.: Robustness certification with refinement. In: International Conference on Learning Representations (ICLR'19) (2019)
23. Szegedy, C., et al.: Intriguing properties of neural networks. In: International Conference on Learning Representations (ICLR'14) (2014)
24. Tjeng, V., Xiao, K., Tedrake, R.: Evaluating robustness of neural networks with mixed integer programming. In: International Conference on Learning Representations (ICLR'19) (2014)
25. Shiqi Wang, et al.: Beta-crown: efficient bound propagation with per-neuron split constraints for neural network robustness verification. In: Ranzato, M., Beygelz-

imer, A., Dauphin, Y., Liang, P.S., Wortman Vaughan, J., (eds), Advances in Neural Information Processing Systems, vol. 34, pp. 29909–29921. Curran Associates, Inc. (2021)
26. Wang, Z., Huang, C., Zhu, Q.: Efficient global robustness certification of neural networks via interleaving twin-network encoding. In: 2022 Design, Automation & Test in Europe Conference & Exhibition (DATE), pp. 1087–1092. IEEE (2022)
27. Wu, H., et al.: Marabou 2.0: a versatile formal analyzer of neural networks. In: Gurfinkel, A., Ganesh, V., (eds.), Proceedings of the 36th International Conferenceon Computer Aided Verification (CAV '24), vol. 14681 of Lecture Notes in Computer Science, pp. 249–264, Montreal, Canada. Springer (2024)
28. Xu, D., Mozumder, N.J., Duong, H., Dwyer, M.B.: Training for verification: Increasing neuron stability to scale DNN verification. In: Finkbeiner, B., Kovács, L., (eds.), Tools and Algorithms for the Construction and Analysis of Systems, pp. 24–44. Springer Nature Switzerland, Cham (2024)
29. Xu, K., et al.: Fast and complete: enabling complete neural network verification with rapid and massively parallel incomplete verifiers. In: International Conference on Learning Representations (ICLR'21). OpenReview.net (2021)
30. Zhang, H., et al.: General cutting planes for bound-propagation-based neural network verification. In: Advances in Neural Information Processing Systems 35: Annual Conference on Neural Information Processing Systems 2022, NeurIPS 2022, New Orleans, LA, USA, November 28 - December 9, 2022 (2022)

Locally Pareto-Optimal Interpretations for Black-Box Machine Learning Models

Aniruddha Joshi[1](✉), Supratik Chakraborty[2], S. Akshay[2], Shetal Shah[2], Hazem Torfah[3], and Sanjit Seshia[1]

[1] University of California at Berkeley, Berkeley, USA
{aniruddhajoshi,sseshia}@berkeley.edu
[2] Indian Institute of Technology Bombay, Mumbai, India
{supratik,akshayss,shetals}@cse.iitb.ac.in
[3] Chalmers University of Technology and University of Gothenburg, Gothenburg, Sweden
hazemto@chalmers.se

Abstract. Creating meaningful interpretations for black-box machine learning models involves balancing two often conflicting objectives: accuracy and explainability. Exploring the trade-off between these objectives is essential for developing trustworthy interpretations. While many techniques for multi-objective interpretation synthesis have been developed, they typically lack formal guarantees on the Pareto-optimality of the results. Methods that do provide such guarantees, on the other hand, often face severe scalability limitations when exploring the Pareto-optimal space. To address this, we develop a framework based on local optimality guarantees that enables more scalable synthesis of interpretations. Specifically, we consider the problem of synthesizing a set of Pareto-optimal interpretations with local optimality guarantees, within the immediate neighborhood of each solution. Our approach begins with a multi-objective learning or search technique, such as Multi-Objective Monte Carlo Tree Search, to generate a best-effort set of Pareto-optimal candidates with respect to accuracy and explainability. We then verify local optimality for each candidate as a Boolean satisfiability problem, which we solve using a SAT solver. We demonstrate the efficacy of our approach on a set of benchmarks, comparing it against previous methods for exploring the Pareto-optimal front of interpretations. In particular, we show that our approach yields interpretations that closely match those synthesized by methods offering global guarantees.

S. Chakraborty—Partly supported by a Qualcomm Faculty Award.
S. Akshay—Partly supported by the SBI Foundation Hub for Data Science and Analytics, IIT Bombay.
UC Berkeley authors were partly supported by the DARPA Provably Correct Design of Adaptive Hybrid Neuro-Symbolic Cyber Physical Systems (ANSR) program award number FA8750-23-C-0080, and by Nissan and Toyota under the iCyPhy Center.
H. Torfah—Partly supported by the Wallenberg AI, and Autonomous Systems and Software Program (WASP), funded by the Knut and Alice Wallenberg Foundation.

© The Author(s), under exclusive license to Springer Nature Switzerland AG 2026
M. D'Souza et al. (Eds.): ATVA 2025, LNCS 16145, pp. 321–341, 2026.
https://doi.org/10.1007/978-3-032-08707-2_15

1 Introduction

The use of machine learning (ML) components is rapidly increasing across various applications and domains. However, the complexity of ML models often makes it difficult to understand how these components function. As a result, their behavior is frequently treated as a black box. To build trust in ML models, especially in domains where accountability and safety are critical, it is essential to provide interpretations that accurately reflect the underlying functionality of the ML model, while being also understandable by humans.

Over the past decade, a vast body of research has focused on explaining the behavior of ML models (e.g., see [11] for a survey). A prominent approach in this area has been the development of post-hoc interpretation methods, i.e., techniques used to explain the behavior of an ML model after it has been trained. These methods often involve generating surrogate models (e.g., decision trees, decision lists, etc.) that serve as simplified approximations of the original complex model [11]. A key challenge in creating such models lies in finding the right balance between accuracy and explainability. In many cases, these two objectives are in direct conflict: a simple, human-understandable explanation may diverge significantly from the predictions of the original model, while a more accurate surrogate may be too complex for meaningful human interpretation. This raises a central question: how much accuracy are users willing to sacrifice for the sake of explainability, and vice versa?

While there are no easy answers to the above problem, a promising way to address it is by exploring the Pareto-optimal space of interpretations [27]. Rather than generating a single interpretation optimized for one objective (or even for a weighted combination of objectives), the Pareto-optimal interpretation problem involves examining the trade-off across multiple objectives, such as the balance between accuracy and explainability. This approach can be very beneficial for users aiming to understand these trade-offs; however, it also introduces significant challenges, particularly in efficiently navigating the space of possible interpretations. Previous work has demonstrated that it is possible to explore this space with formal statistical guarantees on the explored Pareto-optimal curve [27]. However, these approaches often struggle to scale due to their full reliance on computationally intensive symbolic techniques like constraint solvers. In this paper, we address the question of whether lighter and faster methods can be used to generate candidate Pareto-optimal interpretations, which can then be refined using more powerful tools such as Boolean satisfiability solvers.

Specifically, we propose the use of Multi-Objective Monte Carlo Tree Search (MO-MCTS) [28], a well-established technique from the field of reinforcement learning known for its strong empirical performance, to quickly approximate the Pareto-optimal curve. We integrate MO-MCTS with Boolean satisfiability solving, enabling us to obtain local guarantees on the Pareto-optimality of interpretations. This replaces earlier global Pareto-optimality guarantees with theoretically weaker local Pareto-optimality. However, since MO-MCTS is capable of recovering global guarantees over time, running our approach for a sufficient number of iterations yields interpretations whose local guarantees converge toward global ones. In our experiments, we show empirical evidence that the local guarantees obtained using MO-MCTS within a reasonable timeout are indeed close to the global guarantees. The notion of locally Pareto-optimal interpretations, that we introduce, also offers additional benefits. Theoretically, they support anytime guarantees, meaning that useful solutions can be extracted at any point during execution (unlike earlier MaxSAT-based approaches). Additionally, they capture locally imperturbable interpretations, where small changes in the interpretation do not alter the optimality within a local neighborhood.

In summary our contributions are the following:

1. We formalize the problem of locally Pareto-optimal interpretation synthesis for black-box ML models, where explainability is traded off for accuracy under user control.
2. We develop a new technique to solve the above problem by a two phase hybrid algorithm that integrates Multi-objective Monte-Carlo Tree search with Boolean satisfiability solving.
3. We show that our approach converges monotonically to the global optimal, with local optimality guarantees for early stopping.
4. Our experimental results show that in practice, our approach obtains results close to the global optimal in several benchmarks. For larger benchmarks, we obtain results (with local optimality guarantees), where earlier approaches fail to produce *any* globally Pareto-optimal solution.

Related Work. The literature contains a significant body of work focused on methods for interpreting black-box ML models. In certain applications, the goal is to explain the output of a black-box model in the vicinity of a specific input. To achieve this, specialized techniques have been developed that provide local and robust explanations [10,18,21,22]. Other applications use techniques like generation of surrogate models and model distillation (in the form of decision trees [7,13,15,16,29]). For further information on these techniques, we refer the reader to the surveys in [1,11].

The problem of synthesizing multi-objective interpretations of black-box ML models was introduced and formalized in [27]. In that work, a MaxSAT-based engine was used to synthesize a set of Pareto-optimal interpretations. This approach provides statistical global guarantees on the accuracy of the synthesized interpretations. Similar ideas were explored in [29], where the authors encoded the problem of finding an interpretation as optimal decision sets, and in [30], where sparse optimal decision trees were constructed using an objective function combining misclassification rate and the number of leaves. In comparison to the approach in [27], the solutions presented in [29] and [30] provide a single point in the Pareto-optimal space, yielding a single value for correctness and explainability measures. Our approach aligns with the goals of [27] in providing Pareto-optimal interpretations with guarantees on correctness. However, in contrast to [27], our method offers a much more scalable solution for exploring the Pareto-optimal front. In [5], the authors use multi objective optimization to find locally optimal Pareto solutions to the joint problem of generating a machine learning model and its surrogate. Our work is agnostic to the machine learning model, which is assumed to be a black box.

Monte-Carlo Tree Search (MCTS) is a highly effective procedure for heuristically searching through a complex space of actions and rewards. Browne et al. [4] provide an excellent review on MCTS techniques and heuristics, and Swiechowski et al. [25] give a review of recent modifications and advances on domain specific adaptations required for MCTS. Other papers [6,28] consider the multi-objective variant of MCTS that is relevant to our work.

2 Preliminaries and Problem Formulation

We borrow some terminology from [27] in presenting the problem formulation below. Let $\mathcal{I}$ be an input domain, $\mathcal{O}$ be an output domain, and $\Delta(\mathcal{I} \times \mathcal{O})$ be a distribution over the input-output space induced by a black-box ML model. Let $\mathcal{G}$ denote the class of interpretations mapping $\mathcal{I}$ to $\mathcal{O}$. For each interpretation $g \in \mathcal{G}$, we abuse notation and define the semantic function $g : \mathcal{I} \to \mathcal{O}$ that outputs $g(i) \in \mathcal{O}$ for every input $i \in \mathcal{I}$. We also assume that each interpretation $g \in \mathcal{G}$ is associated with a non-negative real-valued *correctness measure* $\mathcal{C}(g) \in \mathbb{R}_{\geq 0}$, and a non-negative real-valued *explainability measure* $\mathcal{E}(g) \in \mathbb{R}_{\geq 0}$. Intuitively, $\mathcal{C}(g)$ measures the accuracy of the interpretation g w.r.t. the input-output distribution $\Delta(\mathcal{I} \times \mathcal{O})$, and $\mathcal{E}(g)$ is a user-specified measure of the human understandability of the interpretation. In general we want to synthesize interpretations with high values of correctness and explainability measures.

For an interpretation $g \in \mathcal{G}$, we define $(\mathcal{C}(g), \mathcal{E}(g))$ to be the *goodness tuple* of g. The partial order $\preceq$ on goodness tuples is defined as follows: $(c, e) \preceq (c', e')$ iff $c \leq c'$ and $e \leq e'$. The strict partial-order $\prec$ on such tuples is defined as: $(c, e) \prec (c', e')$ iff $(c, e) \preceq (c', e')$ and at least one of $c < c'$ or $e < e'$ holds. Given a set $\mathcal{S}$ of goodness measures (c, e), we define $\max^{\preceq} \mathcal{S}$ to be the set of all $\preceq$-maximal tuples in $\mathcal{S}$.

Definition 1. (Pareto-Domination and Optimality *[17, 27]*)**.** *Given a class $\mathcal{G}$ of interpretations mapping $\mathcal{I}$ to $\mathcal{O}$, we say an interpretation g Pareto-dominates another interpretation g' if $(\mathcal{C}(g'), \mathcal{E}(g')) \prec (\mathcal{C}(g), \mathcal{E}(g))$. An interpretation g is said to be **Pareto-optimal** (or PO) in $\mathcal{G}$ if $g \in \mathcal{G}$, and there is no other interpretation $g' \in \mathcal{G}$ that Pareto-dominates g. In other words, $(\mathcal{C}(g), \mathcal{E}(g))$ is $\preceq$-maximal in the set of goodness tuples of all interpretations in $\mathcal{G}$.*

In general, there may be multiple PO interpretations in $\mathcal{G}$, with one or more interpretations corresponding to each $\preceq$-maximal tuple (c, e). In [27], Torfah et al. presented a technique to synthesize a set of PO interpretations, one for every $\preceq$-maximal tuple (c, e). This effectively gives the user a set of interpretations, none of which can be "improved" on both the accuracy and explainability measures together. Unfortunately, computing such PO interpretations is computationally expensive, and the technique of [27] does not scale large to problem instances. This motivates us to define locally Pareto-optimal interpretations.

Definition 2. (Locally Pareto-optimal Interpretation). *Let $\mathcal{G}$ be a class of interpretations mapping $\mathcal{I}$ to $\mathcal{O}$, with correctness measure $\mathcal{C}(\cdot)$ and explainability measure $\mathcal{E}(\cdot)$, as before. Let $\delta_c \in \mathbb{R}_{\geq 0}$ be the correctness slack, and $\delta_e \in \mathbb{R}_{\geq 0}$ be the explainabiility slack, where $\mathbb{R}_{\geq 0}$ denotes the set of all non-negative reals. We say that an interpretation $g \in \mathcal{G}$ is locally Pareto-optimal (LPO) w.r.t δ_c and δ_e if $\nexists g' \in \mathcal{G}$ such that $(\mathcal{C}(g), \mathcal{E}(g)) \prec (\mathcal{C}(g'), \mathcal{E}(g')) \preceq (\mathcal{C}(g) + \delta_c, \mathcal{E}(g) + \delta_e)$.*

Informally, if interpretation g is LPO w.r.t. δ_c and δ_e, then there is no other interpretation g' that Pareto-dominates g, while having its correctness (respectively, explainability) measure within a window of δ_c (respectively, δ_e) of the corresponding measure for g. Note that an LPO interpretation g may not be a PO interpretation. However, there cannot be a "nearby" (in the correctness-explainability measure space) interpretation g' that improves the correctness (respectively, explainability) measure of g by an amount bounded by δ_c (respectively, δ_e) without adversely affecting explainability (respectively, correctness). Clearly, every PO intepretation is also LPO w.r.t δ_c and δ_e, for every $\delta_c, \delta_e \in \mathbb{R}_{\geq 0}$. We can now define the problem of synthesizing LPO interpretations as follows.

Problem 1 (Locally Pareto-Optimal Interpretation Synthesis). Let $\mathcal{G}, \mathcal{C}(\cdot)$, $\mathcal{E}(\cdot), \delta_c$ and δ_e be as in Definition 2. The locally Pareto-optimal (or LPO) interpretation synthesis problem requires us to synthesize a set $\mathcal{S}$ of interpretations in $\mathcal{G}$ such that every $g \in \mathcal{S}$ is LPO w.r.t δ_c and δ_e, and every distinct $g, g' \in \mathcal{S}$ are incomparable, i.e. neither of them Pareto-dominates the other.

A few points about Problem 1 are worth noting. First, the requirement that interpretations in the solution must not Pareto-dominate each other ensures that we don't report LPO interpretations, one of which dominates the other. This can indeed happen for LPO interpretations g and g' if, for example, $\mathcal{C}(g) > \mathcal{C}(g') + \delta_c$ and $\mathcal{E}(g) > \mathcal{E}(g') + \delta_e$. In such cases, g is a "better" interpretation than g', and it is not meaningful to report both g and g'. Second, every set of PO interpretations serves as a solution to Problem 1, for every non-negative value of δ_c and δ_e. However, not every LPO interpretation may be a PO interpretation in general. Hence, the ask of Problem 1 is weaker than that of finding PO interpretations (as addressed in [27]). Third, if we set δ_c and δ_e to M and N respectively, where $M > \max_{g \in \mathcal{G}} \mathcal{C}(g)$ and $N > \max_{g \in \mathcal{G}} \mathcal{E}(g)$, then every solution to Problem 1 also gives a set of PO interpretations. Hence, Problem 1 can be technically used to obtain PO interpretations, if we know $\max_{g \in \mathcal{G}} \mathcal{C}(g)$ and $\max_{g \in \mathcal{G}} \mathcal{E}(g)$. Finally, note that Problem 1 does not require us to synthesize a maximal (by subset ordering) set of incomparable LPO interpretations. This makes it possible to synthesize increasingly larger (set cardinality-wise) solutions incrementally.

3 Our Approach and the Problem Instantiation

In order to solve Problem 1, at a high level, we use a hybrid approach that has two phases. In the first phase, we use techniques developed from the multi-objective learning/search literature. We assume a time budget for the first phase, and restrict ourselves to those techniques that maintain a best-effort solution at all times. Once the time budget is exhausted, we stop the first phase, retrieve the best-effort interpretations from the first phase, and then pass these interpretations to the second phase. We assume no guarantees about finding (locally) Pareto-optimal solutions from the first phase, since most multi-objective learning/search based techniques do not give strong anytime theoretical guarantees.

In the second phase, we take as inputs the set of interpretations obtained from the first phase, and also the correctness and explainability slacks δ_c and δ_e. We then verify that the interpretations obtained from the first phase are incomparable and also locally Pareto-optimal w.r.t. the given slacks. We do this in two steps. In the first step, we verify that the interpretations are incomparable. If they are not, we discard dominated interpretations. Then in the second step, we verify that the remaining interpretations are locally Pareto-optimal. If any of the interpretations are not locally Pareto-optimal, then we improve upon those interpretations. Thus, at the end we are able to output those interpretations that are incomparable and also locally Pareto-optimal. Figure 1 diagrammatically shows the two phases in our approach.

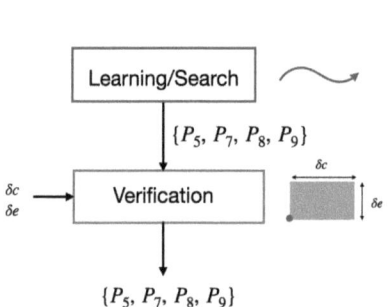
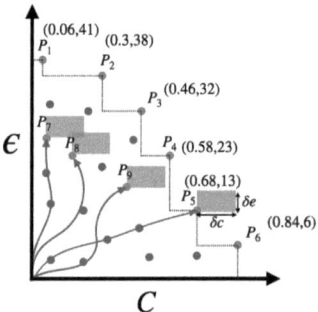

(a) The red curvy arrow represents a multi-objective search procedure with a time budget. If this outputs interpretations $\{P_5, P_7, P_8, P_9\}$, we then verify absence of a dominating solution within slack δ_c and δ_e, as represented by the blue rectangle.

(b) Illustrating our navigation of the search space. The x-axis (resp. y-axis) represents the correctness (resp. explainability) measure. The red curvy arrows indicate the search based phase, and the blue rectangles indicate the verification phase. $P_1, \ldots P_6$ are PO interpretations. Our approach finds the LPO interpretations P_5, P_7, P_8, P_9

Fig. 1. Our approach.

3.1 Instantiating the Interpretations and Measures

In order to solve Problem 1, we must first choose the class $\mathcal{G}$ of interpretations, and the explainability and correctness measures $\mathcal{C}(\cdot)$ and $\mathcal{E}(\cdot)$. We start by choosing decision trees as the class of interpretations, since these are the most widely used in the explainable AI literature. Note that the work of [27] considers decision diagrams for interpretations. Decision trees are essentially decision diagrams with the additional restriction that every node has at most one incoming edge. Hence, we can use the same correctness and explainability measures as used in [27] , making it easier to compare our results with those of [27].

Class of Interpretations: Decision Trees. Let $\mathcal{I}$ and $\mathcal{O}$ denote the input and output domains, respectively. We restrict the output domain $\mathcal{O}$ to a finite set $L := \{l_1, l_2, \ldots l_{|L|}\}$ of labels. Let $F := \{f_1, f_2, \ldots, f_{|F|} \mid f_i : \mathcal{I} \to \{1, 2, \ldots b_i\}\}$ be a set of functions f_i that map the input domain $\mathcal{I}$ to a finite set of branches $\{1, 2, \ldots b_i\}$. We use L and F to label the nodes of decision trees. Specifically, each internal node of a tree has an incoming edge and outgoing edges, and is labeled by a function f_i. Each branch $j \in \{1, 2, \ldots b_i\}$ in the range of f_i corresponds to an outgoing edge of the internal node. The leaf nodes in a decision tree are labeled by L. Figure 2a gives an example of a decision tree.

In order to represent (possibly partially constructed) decision trees at intermediate steps of our multi-objective search procedure, we consider a context-free grammar [12] $\mathfrak{G}$ that allows us to generate decision trees in a principled manner. Grammar $\mathfrak{G}$ uses the symbol N as the starting (non-terminal) symbol, and $\Sigma := \{\,[\,,\,]\,,\,,\,,\,f_1, f_2, \ldots f_{|F|}, l_1, l_2, \ldots l_{|L|}\}$ as the set of terminal symbols. It has the following production rules:

$$N := f_1\underbrace{[N, N, \ldots N]}_{b_1 \text{ times}} \mid f_2\underbrace{[N, N, \ldots N]}_{b_2 \text{ times}} \mid \ldots \mid f_{|F|}\underbrace{[N, N, \ldots N]}_{b_{|F|} \text{ times}} \mid l_1 \mid l_2 \mid \ldots \mid l_{|L|}$$

We can imagine the start symbol as representing a (partially constructed) decision tree with a single node that is not yet labeled by a function from F or by a label from L. Every application of a production rule assigns a function f_i or a label l_j to an unlabeled node N. If a function f_i is assigned to an unlabeled node, then b_i outgoing edges are created, and b_i new unlabeled nodes are created, one for each new outgoing edge. We represent each function f_i in the grammar rules as $f_i\underbrace{[N, N, \ldots N]}_{b_i \text{ times}}$ to indicate that b_i new unlabeled nodes are created, one for each branch in the range of the function f_i. If a label l_j is assigned to an unlabeled node, no new nodes are created. We call decision trees containing unlabeled nodes as partial decision trees, and those not containing unlabeled nodes as complete decision trees. Figure 2b gives an example of a partial decision tree. Unless specified otherwise, by decision trees we will henceforth mean complete decision trees.

We now give the semantics of a decision tree: given an input $x \in \mathcal{I}$, a decision tree D outputs a label $l \in \mathcal{O}$, which we denote by $D(x)$, as per the following rules:

- if D is of the form $f_i[D_1, D_2, \ldots D_{b_i}]$ then $D(x) := D_{f_i(x)}(x)$
- if D is a leaf labeled l_j, then $D(x) := l_j$

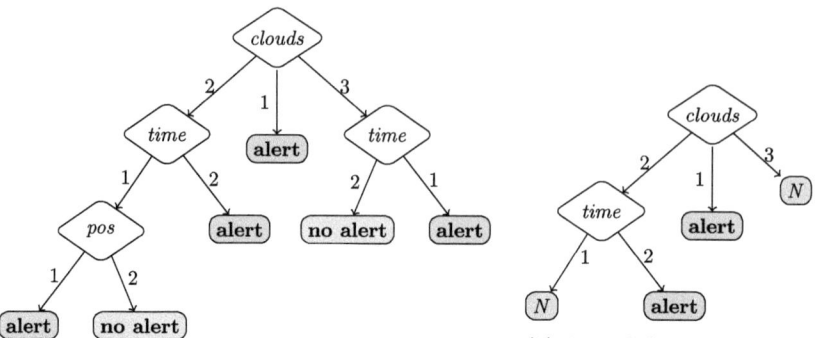

(a) Decision Tree with functions {*clouds, time, pos*} and labels {*alert, no alert*}. The functions *time* and *pos* have two outgoing branches, and *clouds* has tree.

(b) Partial decision tree with two unassigned nodes labeled N be default.

Fig. 2. (a) Complete and (b) Partial Decision Tree.

Note that $D_{f_i(x)}(x)$ is well defined since the range of f_i is $\{1, 2, \ldots b_i\}$.

As in [27], we assume that we have a node budget $B \in \mathbb{Z}_{>0}$—a positive integer—that bounds the number of internal nodes in our decision trees. Thus, the class of interpretations $\mathcal{G}$ is restricted to decision trees generated by the grammar $\mathfrak{G}$ with at most B internal nodes. We denote the grammar with this restriction by $\mathfrak{G}_B$ and the corresponding class of interpretations by $\mathcal{G}_B$. Note, however, that the above is not a real restriction, since the number of semantically different decision trees for a finite set of features/predicates (represented by $f_i \in F$) and labels (represented by $l_j \in L$) is finite. To see this, observe that along any directed path $f_{i_1} \xrightarrow{b_{i_1}} f_{i_2} \xrightarrow{b_{i_1}} \ldots f_{i_j} \xrightarrow{b_{i_j}} \ldots f_{i_{k-1}} \xrightarrow{b_{i_{k-1}}} f_{i_k}$ in a decision tree, if there are two nodes with the same function $f_{i_j} = f_{i_k}$, then the second occurrence of f_{i_k} can be removed from the tree, by simply attaching the sub-tree rooted at the $b_{i_j}^{th}$ branch of f_{i_j} to the $b_{i_{k-1}}^{th}$ branch of $f_{i_{k-1}}$. It is easy to see that this doesn't change the semantics since any input $x \in \mathcal{I}$ evaluated along the path already evaluates to $f_{i_j}(x) = f_{i_k}(x) = b_{i_j}$. Therefore, there are only finitely many semantically different decision trees for a given set of functions and labels, and setting B to the maximum number of internal nodes in this set of semantically different trees allows us to include all semantically different decision trees in the class $\mathcal{G}_B$.

Explainability and Accuracy Measures. We now define the explainability measure $\mathcal{E}$ and the correctness measure $\mathcal{C}$ on decision trees. Our correctness measure $\mathcal{C} : \mathcal{G}_B \rightarrow [0, 1]$ is a map from the set of decision trees to a number between 0 and 1. This gives the accuracy of the decision tree in predicting the output from an input, for samples drawn from the underlying distribution $\Delta(\mathcal{I} \times \mathcal{O})$. That is, given a decision tree $D \in \mathcal{G}_B$, its correctness measure $\mathcal{C}(D) :=$

$\mathcal{P}_{(i,o) \sim \Delta(\mathcal{I} \times \mathcal{O})}[D(i) = o]$ is the probability of correctly classifying an input-output sample (i, o) from the distribution $\Delta(\mathcal{I} \times \mathcal{O})$. We estimate this measure using the Probably Approximately Correct (PAC) [23] framework, as done in [27]. Specifically, for a given tolerance ε and confidence $1 - \delta$, where $0 < \varepsilon, \delta < 1$, we first compute the sample complexity, say $\mu(\mathcal{G}, \varepsilon, \delta)$, of the finite class $\mathcal{G}_B$ of decision trees using standard techniques [23]. Then, we draw $\mu(\mathcal{G}, \varepsilon, \delta)$ i.i.d. samples of (input, output) values from the distribution $\Delta(\mathcal{I} \times \mathcal{O})$, and compute the fraction of times the output is correctly predicted by the decision tree D under consideration for these samples. PAC theory then guarantees that with probability at least $1 - \delta$, the computed estimate of the fraction lies within an additive tolerance of ε of the expected value of the fraction, when i.i.d. samples are drawn from the distribution $\Delta(\mathcal{I} \times \mathcal{O})$.

Our explainability measure $\mathcal{E} : \mathcal{G}_B \to \mathbb{R}_{>0}$ is a map from the set of decision trees to the set of positive real numbers. Below, we describe a specific explainability measure that assigns higher scores to small decision trees (typically, more explainable than large trees), and also to decision trees that use predicate/features that are more desirable to be included in an interpretation. Our overall approach is however not restricted to this specific explainability metric, and applies to any metric that can be encoded symbolically (see Sect. 4.2).

We assume that each function f_i has an associated (user-provided) weight $w_i \in \mathbb{Z}_+$, that gives us a measure of the desirability of including f_i in an interpretation. Higher weights represent functions that are more desirable to be included. Let $W := \max_{1 \le i \le |F|} w_i$ be the highest such weight. Given a decision tree D with m internal nodes containing i_1 nodes corresponding to the function f_1, i_2 nodes corresponding to f_2, ..., $i_{|F|}$ nodes corresponding to $f_{|F|}$, the explainability measure is given by $\mathcal{E}(D) := (B - m)|W + 1| + \sum_{j=1}^{j=|F|} i_j * w_j$. That is, we first prioritize the unused nodes by giving them the highest weights. So, lower values of m correspond to more explainable the decision trees. This aligns with human intuition, that is, the smaller the decision tree, the easier it is to explain that decision tree. Then for a given size m, we prioritize the functions that are the most desirable to be included in an interpretation. This also aligns with human intuition as some functions may be difficult to explain than others.

4 A Two-Phase Algorithm: Search and Verification

Recall from our earlier discussion that our approach works in two phases. In the first phase, we use multi-objective Monte-Carlo Tree Search (MCTS) to solve a multi-objective optimization problem. Then, in the second phase we use SAT solvers to get local guarantees. In Sect. 4.1 we construct a Multi-Objective Markov Decision Process (MO-MDP). This MO-MDP has (partial or complete) decision trees as states, and uses actions that allow us to grow these decision trees. Then, we use Multi-Objective Monte-Carlo Tree Search [28] to search through the MO-MDP to synthesize best-effort Pareto-optimal decision trees.

Finally, we give local guarantees on the decision trees synthesized by the MO-MCTS using a Boolean satisfiability solver.

4.1 Multi-objective MDP and MCTS

In this section, we model the generation of decision trees by the grammar $\mathfrak{G}_B$ as a deterministic MO-MDP, where each state corresponds to a (partial or complete) decision tree, and the production rules of $\mathfrak{G}_B$ determine the actions. Specifically, the transitions only have a probability of 0 or 1 depending on the current and next state. The probability is 1 for transitions that correspond to the production rule of the chosen action, and 0 otherwise. We then assign a multi-objective reward to the states, and apply MO-MCTS [28] to synthesize a best-effort approximation to the Pareto-optimal front.

Definition 3. (Multi-objective MDP). *A MO-MDP $M := (S, A, T, s_0, R)$ is a tuple, where S is a set of states, A is the set of actions, $T : S \times A \times S \to [0,1]$ is the transition probability, s_0 is the initial state, and $R : S \times A \times S \to \mathbb{R}^2_{\geq 0}$ is a **two-dimensional vector-valued reward**.*

We assume that we are given a set $F := \{f_1, f_2, \ldots f_{|F|}\}$ of functions, a set $L := \{l_1, l_2, \ldots l_{|L|}\}$ of labels, a budget B bounding the number of internal nodes, and the grammar $\mathfrak{G}_B$ as defined in Sect. 2. We define the following deterministic MO-MDP $M_{\mathfrak{G}_B}$, where:

- Set of states $S := \{\alpha \mid N \stackrel{*}{\Rightarrow}_{\mathfrak{G}_B} \alpha\}$ is the set of all (partial or complete) decision trees generated by the application of zero or more rules from the grammar $\mathfrak{G}_B$ on the initial symbol N.
- The initial state s_0: $s_0 = N$ is the initial string N, which represents a partial decision tree with just one node corresponding to the non-terminal N.
- Set of actions A: $A := \{(i,j) \mid 1 \leq i \leq N_{max} \text{ and } 1 \leq j \leq |F| + |L|\}$ is the set of all actions. Here N_{max} is the maximum number of non-terminals of a decision tree in the set $\mathcal{G}_B$. Each action is a tuple (i,j) that represents the application of jth production rule of $\mathfrak{G}_B$ on the ith non-terminal node to generate the next (partial or complete) decision tree. If the number of non-terminals in the current decision tree is less than i, then the transition on this action loops to the same decision tree.
- Since we consider a deterministic MO-MDP, the transition on an action $a = (i,j)$ is just the application of jth production rule of $\mathfrak{G}_B$ on the ith non-terminal if it exists, otherwise the transition corresponding to the action just loops back. The transition probabilities are given by the following:

$$T((s, a = (i,j), s')) := \begin{cases} 1, & \text{if the number of non-terminals in } s \text{ is more than } i, \text{ and applying the } j^{th} \text{ production rule on } i^{th} \text{ non-terminal results in } s' \\ 1, & \text{if } s = s' \text{ and there are less than } i \text{ non-terminals in } s \\ 0, & \text{otherwise} \end{cases}$$

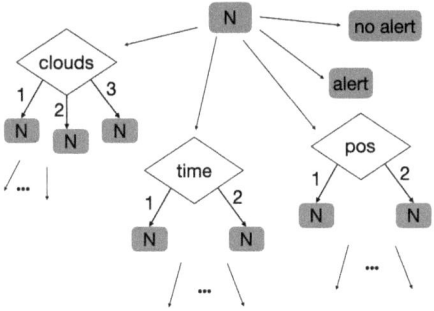

Fig. 3. Deterministic transitions in the MO-MDP.

– A two-dimensional reward is given by the correctness measure in one dimension and the explainability measure in the other. For every transition (s, a, s') where s' is not a complete decision tree the reward is defined as $R((s,a,s')) := [0,0]$. Otherwise, if s' is a complete decision tree, the reward is defined as $R((s,a,s')) := [\mathcal{C}(s'), \mathcal{E}(s')]$. i.e. the correctness and explainability measure of the (complete) decision tree s'. It is easy to see that we have a sparse setting for the reward.

Figure 3 shows some deterministic transitions from the initial node in an MO-MDP modeling one of our benchmarks (TaxiNet), where *clouds, time, pos* are elements of F, and *alert, noalert* are labels in L. The MO-MCTS algorithm developed in [28] works for deterministic MO-MDPs, and is therefore suitable use in our approach. The MO-MCTS procedure of [28] generates a search tree and maintains a set of best-effort approximations of Pareto-optimal interpretations over the search tree. This procedure has three phases. In the first phase, the procedure iteratively chooses an action until it arrives at a (search tree) node that has all unexplored actions, or until a Progressive Widening heuristic is triggered on a node with unexplored actions. This heuristic initially restricts the number of child nodes allowed for exploration. For each node, it only allows a limited number of child nodes for exploration at the start, and gradually increases this number as the visits to the parent node increase. This helps in managing the exploration initially by focusing on a smaller subset of actions. During the first phase, the actions chosen are those that maximize a quantity dependent on the hypervolume indicator [31] of the upper confidence bound, subtracted with an L_2-norm of the perspective projection of the upper confidence bound. Then it chooses an unexplored action using another heuristic that builds on the Rapid Action Value Estimation (RAVE) heuristic [9] by maximizing over all unexplored actions the L_2-norm of the difference between the perspective projection of the RAVE heuristic with itself. The second phase starts once an unexplored action is chosen. In this phase, the MO-MCTS procedure randomly selects actions until a terminal state is reached. Then in the third and final phase, the multi-dimensional rewards are collected and the quantities required for the heuristics are updated by backtracking.

The MO-MCTS procedure maintains a set of best-effort approximations of Pareto-optimal interpretations that it keeps on improving in each iteration. Lemma 1 below quantifies this formally.

Lemma 1. *Let PO_i be an incomparable set of best-effort Pareto optimal points in the MO-MCTS procedure at iteration i. Then for every iteration $j > i$ and for every point $p \in PO_i$ there is a point $p' \in PO_j$ such that $p \preceq p'$.*

4.2 SAT Encoding

In this section, we describe the verification procedure for the interpretations obtained from the MO-MCTS procedure. We assume that the MO-MCTS procedure outputs a set $S := \{(D, \mathcal{C}(D), \mathcal{E}(E))\}$ of decision trees along with their correctness and explainability measures. Let δ_c and δ_e be the user-provided correctness and explainability slacks respectively. For each interpretation $(D, \mathcal{C}(D), \mathcal{D}(D))$ in S, this phase searches for an interpretation $D' \in \mathcal{G}_B$ s.t. $(\mathcal{C}(D)+\delta_c, \mathcal{E}(D)+\delta_e) \succeq (\mathcal{C}(D'), \mathcal{E}(D')) \succ (\mathcal{C}(D), \mathcal{E}(D))$ by encoding the problem as one of Boolean satisfiability, and by using a Boolean satisfiability solver. If it finds such a D', then it replaces D with D' in the set S, and repeats the above search using the satisfiability solver. Otherwise, it declares D as locally PO w.r.t δ_c and δ_e and moves it from S to a set S'. This phase also filters out the decision trees in S' that are already Pareto-dominated by other locally PO trees in S'. Thus, if allowed to run till completion, this phase computes a set S' of locally Pareto-optimal (w.r.t. δ_c and δ_e) decision trees that are Pareto-incomparable, such that each tree in S is either present in S' or is Pareto-dominated by a tree in S'.

To search for an interpretation D' satisfying $(\mathcal{C}(D) + \delta_c, \mathcal{E}(D) + \delta_e) \succeq (\mathcal{C}(D'), \mathcal{E}(D')) \succ (\mathcal{C}(D), \mathcal{E}(D))$, we use the encoding ideas in [27]. Specifically, we construct a Boolean formula $\Phi(X, Y, Z, W)$, where X, Y, Z, W are binary encodings of integers, that is satisfiable if and only if there is a decision tree $D' \in \mathcal{G}_B$ such that $(X, Y) \prec (\mathcal{C}(D'), \mathcal{E}(D')) \preceq (Z, W)$. Moreover, the formula is constructed such that the interpretation D' can be obtained directly from the satisfying assignment of Φ. Once Φ is obtained, we invoke a Boolean satisfiability solver on $\Phi(\mathcal{C}(D), \mathcal{E}(D), \mathcal{C}(D) + \delta_c, \mathcal{E}(D) + \delta_e)$ to find the desired D'. If the formula is unsatisfiable, then we know that D is LPO w.r.t δ_c and δ_e.

Motivated by the encoding ideas in [27], we obtain the formula $\Phi(X, Y, Z, W)$ is as a conjunction of four sub-formulas

$$\Phi(X,Y,Z,W) := \Phi_{syntax} \wedge \Phi_{corr}(X,Z) \wedge \Phi_{exp}(Y,W) \wedge \Phi(X,Y).$$

Here, Φ_{syntax} encodes a syntactic restriction that allows only those decision trees generated by the grammar $\mathfrak{G}_B$. Similarly, $\Phi_{corr}(X, Z)$ encodes a correctness restriction that is satisfiable if there is a decision tree D' such that $X \leq \mathcal{C}(D') \leq Z$. The formula $\Phi_{exp}(Y, W)$ is s.t. it is satisfiable iff there is a decision tree D such that $Y \leq \mathcal{E}(D) \leq W$. Finally, the fourth component $\Phi(X, Y)$ is satisfiable iff there is a decision tree D such that the correctness and explainability measures dominate (X, Y), i.e., $(X, Y) \prec (\mathcal{C}(D'), \mathcal{E}(D'))$. The correctness of the encoding is formalized below.

Lemma 2. *There is a Boolean formula $\Phi(c, e, c + \delta_c, e + \delta_e)$ that is satisfiable if and only if there is a decision tree $D' \in \mathcal{G}_B$ such that $(c, e) \prec (\mathcal{C}(D'), \mathcal{E}(D')) \preceq (c + \delta_c, e + \delta_e)$.*

4.3 Overall Procedure

We now integrate the ideas in the previous two sections to come up with an anytime two-phase algorithm. Algorithm 1 takes as input the timeout $T_{\text{MO-MCTS}}$ of the first phase involving MO-MCTS, the overall timeout T_{overall}, and the slacks δ_c and δ_e. The algorithm runs in two phases. In the first phase, it executes the MO-MCTS procedure with a timeout $T_{\text{MO-MCTS}}$. Since MO-MCTS always maintains a set of best-effort Pareto-optimal points internally, we collect all these best-effort solutions in a set S once the time budget $T_{\text{MO-MCTS}}$ is exhausted. Specifically, we assume that at the end of the first phase, each element in set S is a decision tree $D \in \mathcal{G}_B$ along with the tuple $(\mathcal{C}(D), \mathcal{E}(D))$.

Algorithm 1: Anytime LPO Interpretation Synthesis

Input: Timeouts $T_{\text{MO-MCTS}}$ and T_{overall} of MO-MCTS and overall algorithm
  Slack δc of correctness measure $\mathcal{C}$
  Slack δe of explainability measure $\mathcal{E}$
Output: Set S' of incomparable interpretations that are LPO w.r.t. δc and δe
  Set S of best-effort interpretations

/* Execute the first phase of MO-MCTS   */
$S \leftarrow$ execute_with_timeout(MO-MCTS, $T_{\text{MO-MCTS}}$)

/* Execute the second phase of verification   */
$S' \leftarrow \{\}$
while $S \neq \emptyset$ *or* T_{overall} *not exceeded* **do**

  $(D, (c, e)) \leftarrow S.\text{pop}()$ // fetch and remove an element $D, (c, e)$ from S

  (status, assignment) = Check_SAT($\Phi(c, e, c + \delta_c, e + \delta_e)$, T_{overall})
  if *status is unsatisfiable* **then**
    $S' \leftarrow S' \cup \{(D, (c, e))\}$
    Remove Pareto-dominated interpretations from S'
  else if *status is satisfiable* **then**
    /* the satisfying assignment encodes a decision tree D' with measures (c', e')
       s.t. $(c, e) \prec (c', e') \preceq (c + \delta_c, e + \delta_e)$ */
    $(D', (c', e')) \leftarrow$ extract_decision_tree(assignment)
    $S \leftarrow S \cup \{(D', (c', e'))\}$
    Remove Pareto-dominated interpretations from S
  else
    /* T_{overall} exceeded during Check_SAT call   */
    $S \leftarrow S \cup \{(D, (c, e))\}$

return S' and S

In the second phase, Algorithm 1 maintains a set S' of confirmed locally Pareto-optimal interpretations, and initializes S' to the empty set. It then iterates through each tree D in S, and invokes the Check_SAT function on the Boolean formula $\Phi(\mathcal{C}(D), \mathcal{E}(D), \mathcal{C}(D) + \delta_c, \mathcal{E}(D) + \delta_e)$. Function Check_SAT checks if the formula fed to it as input is satisfiable. If so, it returns a decision tree D', along with $(\mathcal{C}(D'), \mathcal{E}(D'))$ such that $(\mathcal{C}(D), \mathcal{E}(D)) \prec (\mathcal{C}(D'), \mathcal{E}(D')) \preceq (\mathcal{C}(D) + \delta_c, \mathcal{E}(D) + \delta_e)$. Since D' Pareto-dominates D, we replace the entry $(D, (\mathcal{C}(D), \mathcal{E}(D)))$ in S by $(D', (\mathcal{C}'(D), \mathcal{E}(D')))$. If, on the other hand, Check_SAT reports that $\Phi(\mathcal{C}(D), \mathcal{E}(D), \mathcal{C}(D) + \delta_c, \mathcal{E}(D) + \delta_e)$ is unsatisfiable, we know that D is LPO w.r.t. δ_c and δ_e, and add $(C, (\mathcal{C}(D), \mathcal{E}(D)))$ to the set S', while ensuring that no two interpretations in S' Pareto-dominate each other. If the overall timeout T_{overall} is exceeded while Check_SAT is in execution, we assume that Check_SAT is forcibly terminated and the status returned indicates timeout. In such cases, we retain $(D, (\mathcal{C}(D), \mathcal{E}(D)))$ in the set S.

The second phase of Algorithm 1 iterates until the overall timeout T_{overall} is reached or the set S becomes empty. In either case, the algorithm returns the sets S' and S, with the guarantee that S' contains incomparable LPO interpretations w.r.t. δ_c and δ_e. The interpretations in S, however, are simply best-effort interpretations that may not be LPO w.r.t. δ_c and δ_e.

Theorem 1. *Suppose Algorithm 1 outputs sets S' and S of decision trees along with their associated measures on termination. Then, every decision tree D in S' is LPO w.r.t. δ_c and δ_e. Furthermore, for every decision tree D in S, there exists at least one tree D' output by MO-MCTS s.t. $(\mathcal{C}(D'), \mathcal{E}(D')) \preceq (\mathcal{C}(D), \mathcal{E}(D))$.*

Note that Theorem 1 holds regardless of whether Algorithm 1 terminates due to S becoming empty or T_{overall} being exceeded. It is also easy to verify that Algorithm 1 is guaranteed to output at least one decision tree (in either S or S') if the first phase of MO-MCTS does not return an empty set. This suggests the following corollary.

Corollary 1. *With sufficiently large overall timeout $T_{overall}$ and with sufficiently large values of δ_c and δ_e, Algorithm 1 is guaranteed to find at least one PO interpretation.*

5 Experiments

We have implemented the MO-MCTS procedure of [28] adapted to our setting, and the verification algorithm described above in a prototype tool called ALPO available at https://github.com/anirjoshi/ALPO. All our experiments were run on an Apple Mac M2 Pro with 32 GB memory. In the experiments, we set the timeout $T_{\text{MO-MCTS}}$ for MO-MCTS to be exactly half of the overall timeout T_{overall}. We experimented with two different values of the overall timeout T_{overall}, viz. 5 mins and 20 mins. We used the Kissat SAT solver [2] to solve the Boolean satisfiability queries in the verification phase of Algorithm 1. In the first phase involving MO-MCTS, we restricted the actions of MO-MDP to only allow those actions that involve the first non-terminal. Without this restriction, we empirically observed that the action set becomes very large. We also note that the restriction does not reduce the expressivity, as the actions may be applied in any order. For example, in Fig. 2b, actions for any of the two non-terminals can be taken first. This restriction just enforces an ordering on the actions by always selecting an action corresponding to the first non-terminal.

For each state, we also skipped explore the self-looping actions, since they do not contribute towards exploration. Finally, from the initial state of the MO-MDP we do not allow actions involving labels in the set L, since allowing such actions would give rise to single-node decision trees that classify every input to the same label. We compare our work with the tool Synplicate developed as part of [27], which is guaranteed to synthesize the full Pareto-optimal curve of interpretations, when it does terminate (which as we show is not always the case). Since Synplicate considers interpretations as decision diagrams, we modified it slightly to restrict the interpretations to decision trees. We used the same timeout T_{overall} for Synplicate as used by ALPO.

Benchmarks. For our benchmarks, we considered a set of 10 benchmarks from the UCI repository [19], 3 custom-made benchmarks, and 5 randomly generated benchmarks. In this section, we present the four most relevant benchmarks namely AutoTaxi, Balance Scale [24], Car Evaluation [3] and Yeast [20]. The remaining are detailed in the extended version [14].

All of our benchmarks have categorical outputs. The AutoTaxi benchmark, adapted from [8,26], is a decision module that predicts whether a perception module of an airplane behaves correctly under certain environment conditions. It uses the following features: time of day, types of clouds, and initial position of the airplane on the runway. The implementation of this module is a decision tree based on data collected from 200 simulations, using the XPlane (https://www.x-plane.com) simulator.

The other benchmarks Balance Scale, Car Evaluation, and Yeast are all collected from the UCI Machine Learning Repository [19]. These benchmarks are available as datasets. We first train these datasets on a fully connected neural network with four hidden layers containing seven neurons in each layer, and a ReLU activation function for each neuron. This neural network then serves as our black-box model. For the synthesis procedure, we restrict the space of decision trees to only those with size less than six internal nodes. The names of functions for the decision tree are the same as the names of features in the dataset. For every categorical feature, we assign a number to each category, and the feature function in the decision tree just outputs the number according to the category. For every numerical feature $\mathbf{f}$, we have a function f that has three output buckets. This function simply divides the range of the feature into three equal regions. Let $\mathbf{f}_{max}$ and $\mathbf{f}_{min}$ be the maximum and minimum values of $\mathbf{f}$ in the dataset. Then $f \colon \mathbb{R} \to \{0, 1, 2\}$ is defined as:

Table 1. List of feature names, weights and output branches in all benchmarks

Benchmark Name	Features	Weights	Output Branches
AutoTaxi	clouds, day time, init pos	1, 4, 3	6, 3, 4
Balance Scale	left distance, left weight	3, 3	3, 3
	right distance, right weight	3, 3	3, 3
Car Evaluation	buying, doors, lug boot	3, 3, 3	4, 4, 3
	maint, persons, safety	3, 3, 3	4, 3, 3
Yeast	alm, erl, gvh, mcg, mit	3, 3, 3, 3	3, 3, 3, 3
	nuc, pox, vac	3, 3, 3	3, 3, 3

$$f(i) := \begin{cases} 0, & \text{if } i < \mathbf{f}_{min} + \frac{\mathbf{f}_{max} - \mathbf{f}_{min}}{3} \\ 1, & \text{else if } i < \mathbf{f}_{min} + 2 * \frac{\mathbf{f}_{max} - \mathbf{f}_{min}}{3} \\ 2, & \text{otherwise} \end{cases}$$

In Table 1, we list the features used in these four benchmarks. We plot the results of executing ALPO and Synplicate on these benchmarks in Fig. 6. We first discuss the results with an overall timeout of 20 minutes. (10 mins for MO-MCTS, and 10 mins for the second phase in ALPO). The (δ_c, δ_e) windows for AutoTaxi, Car Evaluation, Balance Scale, and Yeast are $(0.023, 5)$, $(0.018, 5)$, $(0.021, 5)$ and $(0.017, 5)$, respectively. The δ_c values are obtained as $\frac{10}{K}$, where K is the total number of samples used for a benchmark. We use $\epsilon = 0.25$ and $\delta = 0.1$ for the PAC guarantees, without making any realizability assumption.

The Research Questions. We address the following three research questions.

- RQ1: Are locally Pareto-optimal solutions given by our approach close to the actual (global) Pareto-optimal solutions?
- RQ2: Does the MO-MCTS procedure output a good approximation of the Pareto-optimal curve?
- RQ3: Does our procedure scale empirically in comparison with Synplicate?

5.1 Our Results

RQ1: From Local Pareto-optimality to Global Pareto-optimality. Our experiments reveal that the search for locally Pareto-optimal solutions around the solutions of the MO-MCTS procedure often gives us globally Pareto-optimal solutions. We use the AutoTaxi and the Balance Scale benchmarks to demonstrate this. Indeed, these are the only benchmarks (among the four being discussed here) where the Synplicate tool terminates within 20 mins, and hence gives the Pareto-optimal curve, allowing us to perform this comparison.

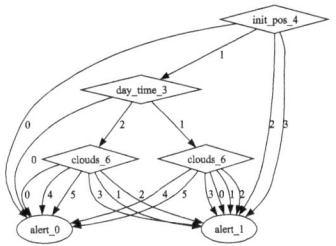
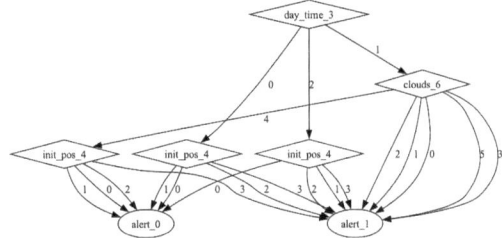

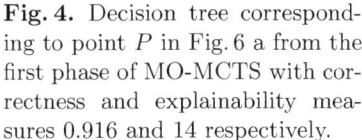

Fig. 4. Decision tree corresponding to point P in Fig. 6 a from the first phase of MO-MCTS with correctness and explainability measures 0.916 and 14 respectively.

Fig. 5. Decision tree corresponding to point Q from the second phase of verification procedure with correctness and explainability 0.918 and 14 resp.

In the AutoTaxi benchmark, we observe from the Pareto-optimal curve in Fig. 6a that all decision trees except one $[P=(0.916,14)]$ from the MO-MCTS procedure are Pareto-optimal. Also, we are able to discover a Pareto-optimal decision tree Q close to $P = (0.916, 14)$ in the second phase. We show the corresponding decision trees in Figs. 4 and 5 representing points P and Q respectively.

RQ2: MO-MCTS is a Good Approximation of the Pareto-Optimal Curve. The plots in Fig. 6a and Fig. 6b corresponding to the AutoTaxi and Balance Scale benchmarks, respectively, provide evidence that the MO-MCTS procedure gives a good approximation of the (actual) Pareto-optimal curve, as given by Synplicate. The MO-MCTS procedure outputs eight of the combined twelve Pareto-optimal points. We cannot use the other two benchmarks to answer this question, because the Synplicate tool times out before outputting even one Pareto-optimal point.

RQ3: Performance of ALPO vs Synplicate. Finally, we address whether our procedure performs better than Synplicate on a wider set of benchmarks. We answer this affirmatively by looking into the two benchmarks: Car Evaluation and Yeast. More evidence is presented in the extended version [14] via other benchmarks. As can be observed from the results of the Car Evaluation benchmark in Fig. 6c and the Yeast benchmark in Fig. 6d, the Synplicate tool cannot output even a single Pareto-optimal point for these benchmarks. Since the number of feature nodes in these benchmarks is more than those of the other two, this increases the size of the search space significantly. We believe this eventually causes Synplicate to choke. However, ALPO outputs at least four decision trees for each benchmark. Figure 7 shows the decision tree correponding to highest accuracy decision tree synthesized by this approach. Moreover, for each of the two benchmarks, we are able to verify that two decision trees are locally Pareto-optimal. Therefore, using our procedure, we are able to synthesize locally Pareto-optimal decision trees even in the cases where synthesizing a Pareto-optimal set is practically computationally intensive.

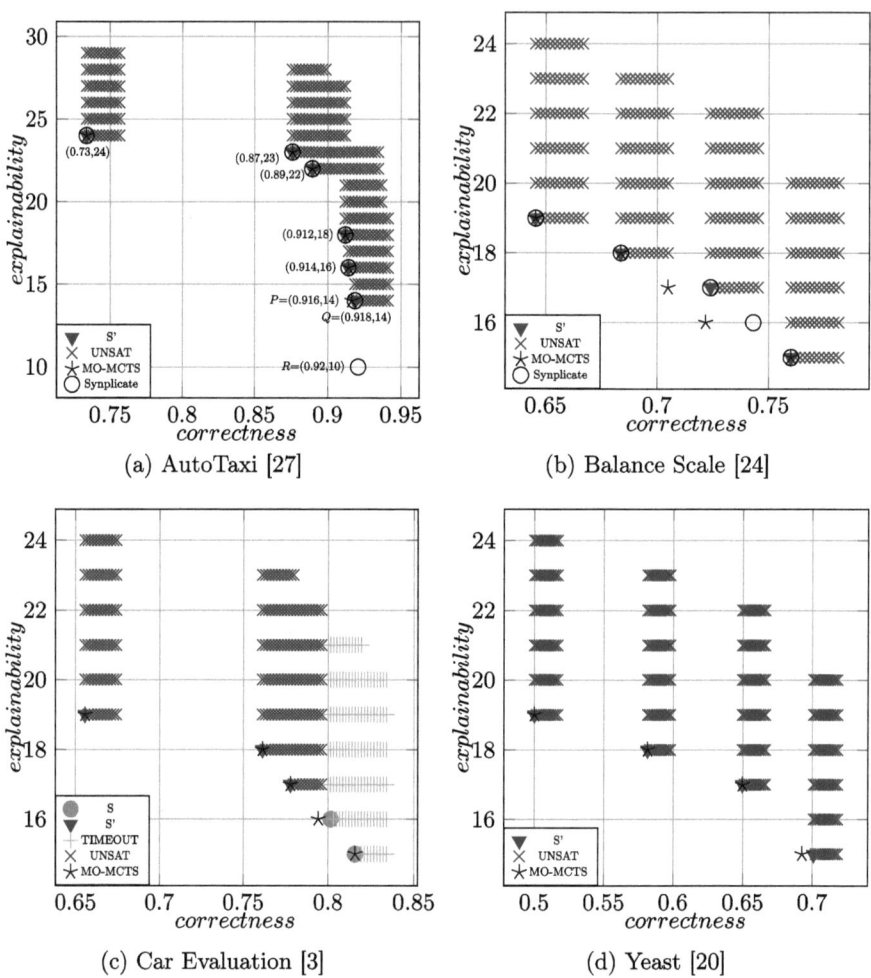

Fig. 6. Visualization of results: For each benchmark, correctness measure is plotted on X-axis and explainability measure on Y-axis. Blue stars indicate MO-MCTS results. Red inverted triangle indicate LPO interpretations found by ALPO. Red crosses indicate absence of interpretations with corresponding explainability-accuracy measures. Green solid circles indicate points that dominate an interpretation obtained from MO-MCTS, but not verified to be LPO. Yellow pluses indicate that ALPO timed out when checking for LPO here. Synplicate results are shown with hollow circles. (Color figure online)

In summary, our results answer RQ1-3 comprehensively and show the effectiveness of ALPO. We also conducted experiments on several other benchmarks (see the extended version [14]), and repeated the experiments on the four benchmarks presented above with a 5 mins timeout (see the extended version [14]).

Our results consistently support the conclusions w.r.t. RQ1-3 made above. In particular, when running with timeout of 5 mins, ALPO gives fewer (but non-empty) LPO interpretations than with 20 mins timeout, and hence degrades gracefully. This shows the value of ALPO as an anytime LPO interpretation synthesis algorithm.

6 Conclusion

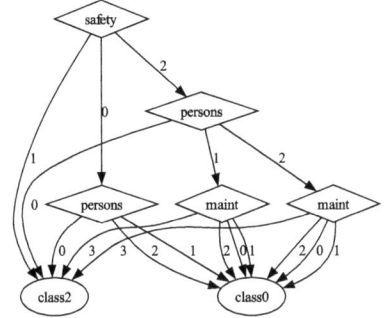

Fig. 7. Decision tree corresponding to the most accurate best-effort Pareto-point from the MO-MCTS for Car Evaluation benchmark.

In this paper, we have considered an integrated multi-objective MCTS-based search algorithm with SAT-based verification to synthesize Pareto-optimal interpretations with locally optimality guarantees. Our experimental results show that the interpretations we generate are close to globally Pareto-optimal illustrating the practical significance of the approach. As future work, it would be interesting to use the solutions from the SAT solver to improve search, leading to even better integration between these approaches. Future advancements in methods for MCTS-based search will directly transfer to our approach.

References

1. Adadi, A., Berrada, M.: Peeking inside the black-box: a survey on explainable artificial intelligence (XAI). IEEE Access **6**, 52138–52160 (2018). https://doi.org/10.1109/ACCESS.2018.2870052
2. Biere, A., Faller, T., Fazekas, K., Fleury, M., Froleyks, N., Pollitt, F.: CaDiCaL, Gimsatul, IsaSAT and Kissat entering the SAT Competition 2024. In: Heule, M., Iser, M., Järvisalo, M., Suda, M. (eds.) Proc. of SAT Competition 2024 – Solver, Benchmark and Proof Checker Descriptions. Department of Computer Science Report Series B, vol. B-2024-1, pp. 8–10. University of Helsinki (2024)
3. Bohanec, M.: Car Evaluation. UCI Machine Learning Repository (1988). https://doi.org/10.24432/C5JP48
4. Browne, C., et al.: A survey of monte carlo tree search methods. IEEE Trans. Comput. Intell. AI Games **4**(1), 1–43 (2012)
5. Charalampakos, F., Tsouparopoulos, T., Koutsopoulos, I.: Joint explainability-performance optimization with surrogate models for AI-driven edge services (2025). https://arxiv.org/abs/2503.07784
6. Chen, W., Liu, L.: Pareto monte carlo tree search for multi-objective informative planning. CoRR **abs/2111.01825** (2021)
7. Craven, M.W., Shavlik, J.W.: Extracting tree-structured representations of trained networks. In: Touretzky, D.S., Mozer, M., Hasselmo, M.E. (eds.) Advances in Neural Information Processing Systems 8, NIPS, Denver, CO, USA, November 27-30, 1995, pp. 24–30. MIT Press (1995). http://papers.nips.cc/paper/1152-extracting-tree-structured-representations-of-trained-networks

8. Fremont, D.J., Chiu, J., Margineantu, D.D., Osipychev, D., Seshia, S.A.: Formal Analysis and Redesign of a Neural Network-Based Aircraft Taxiing System with VERIFAI. In: Lahiri, S.K., Wang, C. (eds.) CAV 2020. LNCS, vol. 12224, pp. 122–134. Springer, Cham (2020). https://doi.org/10.1007/978-3-030-53288-8_6
9. Gelly, S., Silver, D.: Combining online and offline knowledge in UCT. In: ICML. ACM International Conference Proceeding Series, vol. 227, pp. 273–280. ACM (2007)
10. Guidotti, R., Monreale, A., Ruggieri, S., Pedreschi, D., Turini, F., Giannotti, F.: Local rule-based explanations of black box decision systems. CoRR **abs/1805.10820** (2018). http://arxiv.org/abs/1805.10820
11. Guidotti, R., Monreale, A., Ruggieri, S., Turini, F., Giannotti, F., Pedreschi, D.: A survey of methods for explaining black box models. ACM Comput. Surv. **51**(5), 93:1–93:42 (2019). https://doi.org/10.1145/3236009
12. Hopcroft, J.E., Ullman, J.D.: Introduction to Automata Theory. Addison-Wesley, Languages and Computation (1979)
13. Johansson, U., König, R., Löfström, T., Boström, H.: Evolved decision trees as conformal predictors. In: Proceedings of the IEEE Congress on Evolutionary Computation, CEC 2013, Cancun, Mexico, June 20-23, 2013, pp. 1794–1801. IEEE (2013). https://doi.org/10.1109/CEC.2013.6557778
14. Joshi, A., Chakraborty, S., Akshay, S., Shah, S., Torfah, H., Seshia, S.: Locally pareto-optimal interpretations for black-box machine learning models (2025). https://arxiv.org/abs/2508.15220
15. Krishnan, R., Sivakumar, G., Bhattacharya, P.: Extracting decision trees from trained neural networks. Patt. Recognit. **32**(12), 1999–2009 (1999). https://doi.org/10.1016/S0031-3203(98)00181-2
16. Krishnan, S., Wu, E.: PALM: machine learning explanations for iterative debugging. In: Binnig, C., Hellerstein, J.M., Parameswaran, A.G. (eds.) Proceedings of the 2nd Workshop on Human-In-the-Loop Data Analytics, HILDA@SIGMOD 2017, Chicago, IL, USA, May 14, 2017, pp. 4:1–4:6. ACM (2017). https://doi.org/10.1145/3077257.3077271
17. Luc, D.T.: Pareto Optimality, pp. 481–515. Springer New York, New York, NY (2008)
18. Lundberg, S.M., Lee, S.: A unified approach to interpreting model predictions. In: Guyon, I., et al., (eds.) Advances in Neural Information Processing Systems 30: Annual Conference on Neural Information Processing Systems 2017, December 4-9, 2017, Long Beach, CA, USA, pp. 4765–4774 (2017). https://proceedings.neurips.cc/paper/2017/hash/8a20a8621978632d76c43dfd28b67767-Abstract.html
19. Kelly, M., Rachel Longjohn, K.N.: The UCI Machine Learning Repository. https://archive.ics.uci.edu
20. Nakai, K.: Yeast. UCI Machine Learning Repository (1991). https://doi.org/10.24432/C5KG68
21. Ribeiro, M.T., Singh, S., Guestrin, C.: "why should I trust you?": Explaining the predictions of any classifier. In: Proceedings of the Demonstrations Session, NAACL HLT 2016, The 2016 Conference of the North American Chapter of the Association for Computational Linguistics: Human Language Technologies, San Diego California, USA, June 12-17, 2016, pp. 97–101. The Association for Computational Linguistics (2016). https://doi.org/10.18653/V1/N16-3020
22. Ribeiro, M.T., Singh, S., Guestrin, C.: Anchors: high-precision model-agnostic explanations. In: McIlraith, S.A., Weinberger, K.Q. (eds.) Proceedings of the Thirty-Second AAAI Conference on Artificial Intelligence, (AAAI-18), the 30th

innovative Applications of Artificial Intelligence (IAAI-18), and the 8th AAAI Symposium on Educational Advances in Artificial Intelligence (EAAI-18), New Orleans, Louisiana, USA, February 2-7, 2018, pp. 1527–1535. AAAI Press (2018). https://doi.org/10.1609/AAAI.V32I1.11491
23. Shalev-Shwartz, S., Ben-David, S.: Understanding Machine Learning - From Theory to Algorithms. Cambridge University Press (2014)
24. Siegler, R.: Balance Scale. UCI Machine Learning Repository (1976). https://doi.org/10.24432/C5488X
25. Swiechowski, M., Godlewski, K., Sawicki, B., Mandziuk, J.: Monte carlo tree search: a review of recent modifications and applications. Artif. Intell. Rev. **56**(3), 2497–2562 (2023)
26. Torfah, H., Junges, S., Fremont, D.J., Seshia, S.A.: Formal analysis of AI-based autonomy: from modeling to runtime assurance. In: Feng, L., Fisman, D. (eds.) Runtime Verification - 21st International Conference, RV 2021, Virtual Event, October 11-14, 2021, Proceedings. Lecture Notes in Computer Science, vol. 12974, pp. 311–330. Springer (2021). https://doi.org/10.1007/978-3-030-88494-9_19
27. Torfah, H., Shah, S., Chakraborty, S., Akshay, S., Seshia, S.A.: Synthesizing pareto-optimal interpretations for black-box models. In: FMCAD, pp. 153–162. IEEE (2021)
28. Wang, W., Sebag, M.: Multi-objective monte-carlo tree search. In: ACML. JMLR Proceedings, vol. 25, pp. 507–522. JMLR.org (2012)
29. Yu, J., Ignatiev, A., Stuckey, P.J., Bodic, P.L.: Computing optimal decision sets with SAT. In: Simonis, H. (ed.) Principles and Practice of Constraint Programming - 26th International Conference, CP 2020, Louvain-la-Neuve, Belgium, September 7-11, 2020, Proceedings. Lecture Notes in Computer Science, vol. 12333, pp. 952–970. Springer (2020). https://doi.org/10.1007/978-3-030-58475-7_55
30. Zhang, R., Xin, R., Seltzer, M.I., Rudin, C.: Optimal sparse regression trees. In: Williams, B., Chen, Y., Neville, J. (eds.) Thirty-Seventh AAAI Conference on Artificial Intelligence, AAAI 2023, Thirty-Fifth Conference on Innovative Applications of Artificial Intelligence, IAAI 2023, Thirteenth Symposium on Educational Advances in Artificial Intelligence, EAAI 2023, Washington, DC, USA, February 7-14, 2023, pp. 11270–11279. AAAI Press (2023). https://doi.org/10.1609/AAAI.V37I9.26334
31. Zitzler, E., Thiele, L.: Multiobjective optimization using evolutionary algorithms - a comparative case study. In: PPSN. Lecture Notes in Computer Science, vol. 1498, pp. 292–304. Springer (1998)

Hybrid and Dynamical Systems

Evaluation, Reduction, and Approximation of Dynamical Systems and Networks with ERODE

Luca Cardelli[1], Giuseppe Squillace[2(✉)], Mirco Tribastone[2], Max Tschaikowski[3], and Andrea Vandin[4]

[1] University of Oxford, Oxford, UK
[2] IMT Lucca, Lucca, Italy
giuseppe.squillace@imtlucca.it
[3] Aalborg University, Aalborg, Denmark
[4] Sant'Anna School for Advanced Studies Pisa, Pisa, Italy

Abstract. We present ERODE, a tool introduced in 2016 to analyze and reduce differential equations and chemical reaction networks. Over the years, it has been extended with further analysis and reduction techniques, as well as formalisms including differential algebraic equations, Boolean networks, networks, and Markov chains. ERODE can import-export towards several tools, including Matlab, BioNetGen, Modelica, PRISM, STORM, Stochkit, GINsim, SBML, and CoLoMoTo. It also has Python APIs.

1 Introduction

We present ERODE, a software tool originally introduced in [32] for the analysis and reduction of ordinary differential equations and chemical reaction networks (CRNs) [93]. Since its initial release, ERODE has seen substantial advancements, with expanded support for modeling formalisms and the addition of new analysis and reduction techniques.

This paper offers the first comprehensive overview of the current version of ERODE, emphasizing its major enhancements compared to the original release. Over the years, ERODE has been extended to support a broader class of dynamical models, including differential algebraic equations (DAEs), Boolean networks (BNs) [56], and general network structures [65]. In addition to exact reduction methods for ODEs presented in [32], the tool now offers exact reductions for DAEs and Boolean networks, as well as approximate reduction techniques for large-scale ODE systems.

Another key advancement is a newly introduced Python APIs that facilitate the interaction with data science libraries like NetworkX [50] and Pandas [63]. In this direction, the Python APIs provide new techniques for the computation of network embeddings, enabling their use in machine learning tasks and data-driven modeling. Interoperability has also been significantly improved, with import/export support for tools and formats such as Matlab [5], Modelica [46], SBML [52], PRISM [57], STORM [42], BioNetGen [15], StochKit [73], and the CoLoMoTo environment [64]. We summarize in Table 1 the main differences between the features provided by the previous ERODE version [32] with respect to the current version.

Table 1. Differences between the features provided by the old and the current version of ERODE.

Features	ERODE [32]	ERODE state-of-the-art
Exact ODE reduction	✓	✓
SMT-based exact reduction	✓	✓
CRNs reduction	✓	✓
Approximate ODE reduction	✗	✓
Exact DAE reduction	✗	✓
Networks reduction	✗	✓
Boolean networks reduction	✗	✓
Python extension	✗	✓
Network embedding	✗	✓

2 Overview

ERODE is a modern IDE offering several functionalities, including syntax highlighting, in-line error annotation, fix suggestions, and auto-completion. As depicted in Fig. 1, the tool presents a flexible and configurable GUI composed by several tabs with ERODE models in some of the supported formalisms. Independently from the used format, an ERODE model contains: *(i)* a model specification section comprising parameters, variables with optional initial values, model dynamics, etc.; *(ii)* a list of commands to analyze, reduce, and export the model.

The output of analyses is information on dynamics given in interactive plots and CSV files. Reductions generate new ERODE models with fewer variables while preserving the dynamics of interest, exactly or approximately, depending on the used technique. Import and export are available through appropriate commands or GUI's wizards. ERODE can also be accessed programmatically from Python.

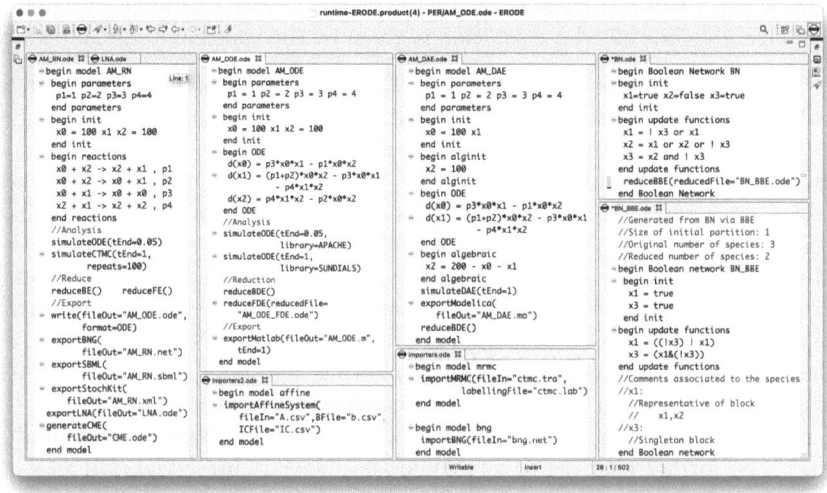

Fig. 1. ERODE: overview of input/output formats, and analysis/reduction commands

3 Input and Output Languages and Formalisms

Ordinary Differential Equations (ODEs).
Tab AM_ODE of Fig. 1 provides an ODE system with 3 variables, x0, x1, and x2, initialized to 100, 0, and 100, respectively. These variables change value continuously according to their derivatives (block begin/end ODE). This is a model of a cell cycle switch, needed to avoid genetic instability during replication [25]. Interestingly, it also describes a distributed algorithm for computing approximately majority among two outcomes (yes/no) [25]. Figure 2 depicts the model dynamics through an ERODE plot view. Here, x0 approaches 200, while x1 and x2 approach 0. Indeed, x0 and x2 denote the two different outcomes, while x1 is an intermediate status.

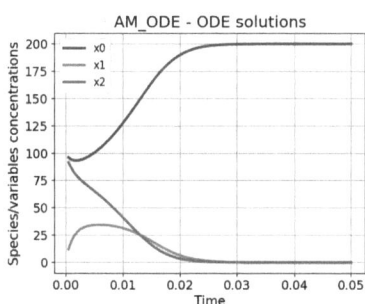

Fig. 2. Majority vote model dynamics

Differential Algebraic Equations (DAEs). DAEs [83] extend ODEs with algebraic constraints. DAEs are often used to describe quantities, following conservation laws like Kirchhoff's laws in electric circuits. The ODEs in tab AM_ODE of Fig. 1 model a closed system, meaning that x0+x1+x2 remains constant to 200. Once the values of two variables are known, that of the third one can be derived. Tab

AM_DAE of Fig. 1 shows a DAE system with two differential variables, x0 and x1, and an algebraic one x2 whose solution is given by the constraint x2=200-x0-x1.

Chemical Reaction Networks (CRNs). CRNs [93] are a popular model for biological processes supporting both a deterministic and a stochastic interpretation based on ODEs and continuous-time Markov chains (CTMCs), respectively [24,48]. Tab AM_RN of Fig. 1 shows a CRN encoding of AM. It has 3 variables, or *species*, x0, x1, and x2 that interact through 4 reactions (block begin-end reactions). A reaction contains multisets of species on the left-hand side, the *reagents*, that interact and produce the multiset of species on the right-hand side, the *products*. A reaction executes (or *fires*) with a rate proportional to the kinetic constant, given in ERODE after the products, and to the current amount of its reagents (following the *law of mass-action* [93]). Alternatively, a reaction can have an arbitrary rate (keyword arbitrary). The first reaction in the figure states that whenever an instance of x0 and x2 interact, the former changes to x1, while the latter is preserved. CRNs where all reactions have singleton reagents and products can be seen as CTMCs or weighted graphs, formalisms for which ERODE provides specific analysis techniques (see, e.g., [13,22,27,28,82]). CTMCs in explicit format supported by PRISM [57] and STORM [42] (.tra and .lab files) can be imported using the command importMRMC shown in tab importers of Fig. 1. Given the relationship between CRN and ODE systems [48], ERODE provides the write command, which enables conversion between an ODE system, its corresponding CRN, and vice versa. In Fig. 1 tab AM_RN, the command is invoked as write(fileOut=''AM_ODE.ode'',format=ODE), specifying both the output file name and the desired format. This generates the ODE system associated with the original CRN model.

Networks. Networks are mathematical structures used to model entities and their relationships [65]. The entities are given as a set of nodes $N = \{1,...,n\}$, while the relationships by a symmetric adjacency matrix $A = (a_{i,j}) \in \mathbb{R}^{n \times n}$, where $a_{i,j} = 1$ if there is an edge between node i and j, and $a_{i,j} = 0$ otherwise. In other words, we consider undirected unweighted networks [65]. Networks can be imported into ERODE, considering the associated linear dynamical system $\dot{x} = Ax$, with one equation and variable per node in the network. As discussed later, we have established a formal relation among the backward reductions in ERODE, and notions of network science like role equivalence [62], equitable partitions [49], and centralities [65].

Networks in the de facto standard of format known as *edgelist* can be imported in ERODE via Python APIs. The edgelist format, widely adopted by major network libraries, e.g., the widely-used Python library NetworkX [50], represents a network as a list of lines, each containing a pair of node identifiers

``IDnode1 IDnode2'', corresponding to a single edge. In the case of undirected unweighted networks, like ours, weights are implicitly assumed to be 1, and the edges ``i j'' and ``j i'' are identical. We show in Sect. 5.1 how ERODE has been integrated with NetworkX to import popular network repositories, process and visualize them.

Boolean Networks (BNs). BNs [56,79] are established models to qualitatively describe biological systems (e.g., [6,16]). In its simplest form, a BN can be seen as a discrete-time qualitative abstraction of an ODE system: it consists of a set of Boolean variables, each having a Boolean update function associated. Starting from an initial assignment for each variable, discrete-time dynamics is obtained by setting the new state of each variable as the evaluation of its associated function. Tab BN of Fig. 1 shows a BN with variables x1, x2, and x3.

4 Underlying Techniques

4.1 Analysis

Numerical Solution of Differential Equations. ERODE is integrated with state-of-the-art numerical solvers for ODEs and DAEs, namely Apache Commons Math library [8] and the SUNDIALS[1] library [51]. Given initial conditions for all variables, we can invoke these solvers to study the evolution of the variables' values over time for a given time horizon. Figure 1 shows the commands used for the different formats: simulateODE for CRNs and ODEs, for which we can specify the library to use, and simulateDAE for DAEs, where SUNDIALS is used by default. Alternatively, one can use the exporting commands exportMatlab, exportModelica, and exportBNG to use the state-of-the-art solvers offered by Matlab [5], OpenModelica [46] and BioNetGen [15].

Stochastic Analysis and Simulation. CRNs can also be analyzed stochastically by simulating their underlying CTMC, the *master equation* [48], whose states are integer vectors specifying the current *population* of each species. We interface with the FERN library [44] featuring Gillespie's Direct Method, Gibson and Bruck's Next Reaction, and tau-leaping (cf. [47]). Figure 1 shows the corresponding command, simulateCTMC. One can also export to the state-of-the-art simulator StochKit [73], or use generateCME to build the whole master equation.

Approximate Analysis for CRNs. ERODE supports the linear noise approximation (LNA) of CRNs [17,20] (exportLNA, tab AM_RN of Fig. 1). LNA analyzes CRNs using a Gaussian process approximating its first and second-order moments (Fig. 3).

---

[1] Due to upgrade issues, the SUNDIALS library is not currently supported in Ubuntu.

LNA extends the ODEs (the first order moments) of a CRN of N species with N^2 variables for the covariances of each pair of species (the second order moments). Tab LNA of Fig. 4 shows the LNA of AM. Another supported analysis is the novel finite state expansion (FSE) [94], which improves the approximation error when the CRN is analyzed by ODEs instead of the ground-truth master equation. FSE extends the ODEs of a CRN with

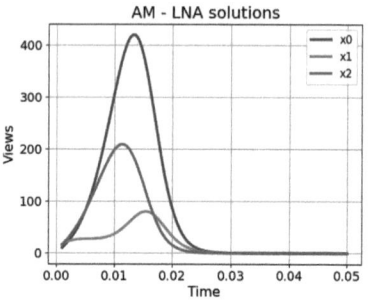

Fig. 3. Majority vote model LNA

a user-defined part of the master equation dynamics. It can be understood as an instance of a framework of Markov chain truncation where the truncated state space moves dynamically [71]. FSE can be applied to AM using fse(fileOut=AM_fse.ode,limits=[x0:1]), obtaining the model in tab AM_FSE of Fig. 4. For each species, one has to specify a limit below which the stochastic dynamics should be exactly preserved. Beyond such a limit, the species dynamics is given by the original ODE variable. In the figure, we gave limit 1 to x1 and 0 to the others, leading to species Dec0 (population 1 for x0 and 0 for the others) and Dec1 (only 0-populations).

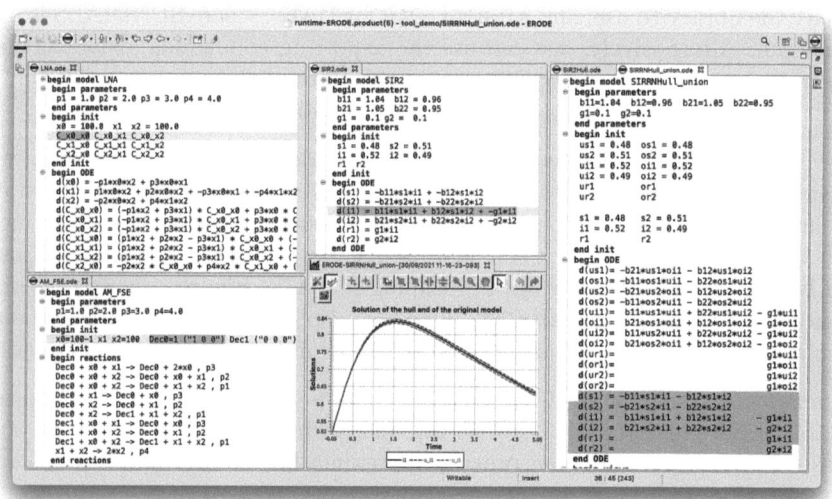

Fig. 4. Linear noise approximation (top-left) and finite state expansion (bottom-left) of AM. Differential hull approximation of a 2-class SIR [87] (centre and right).

4.2 Reduction

Exact Reduction of ODEs with Polynomial Derivatives. These models can be reduced by forward or backward equivalence (FE and BE, respectively) [22,31, 33]. The former (reduceFE, tab AM_RN of Fig. 1) reduces models such that each macro-variable represents the sum of variables in a block. The latter (reduceBE) ensures that all variables in a block have the same value at all time points.

SMT-Based Exact Reduction of ODEs with Richer Non-linearities. For ODEs with non-linearities beyond polynomials (e.g., min/max, absolute values, and in general Tarski's decidable theory of reals [78]), we can use forward and backward differential equivalence [23,37], conservative generalizations of FE and BE, respectively (commands reduceFDE and reduceBDE, resp. see tab AM_ODE of Fig. 1).

Exact Reduction of Stochastic CRNs via CRN-to-CRN Transformation. If interested in interpreting a CRN stochastically, one can reduce it by means of species equivalence (SE) [29,34]. SE, command reduceSE, identifies a partition of the CRN species and produces a reduced CRN where the marginal probability distribution of each macro-species corresponds to the probability distribution of the sum of the original species in the corresponding block from the original CRN.

Approximate Reduction of ODEs with Polynomial Derivatives. If interested in more aggressive reductions that do not preserve exactly the model dynamics, one can use ε-differential equivalences [30,35] (commands approxFDE and approxBDE) or differential hull [75,87] (command computeDifferentialHull). These are relaxations of differential equivalences where the macro-variables approximately represent the sum of the original variables within some computable bound. Intuitively, the main idea is to perturb the model parameters as little as possible to obtain a new model amenable to exact reduction. The error arising through the parameter change is formally estimated via linearization [35] or differential inequalities [87]. The centre and right of Fig. 4 exemplifies the differential hull for an epidemiologic model from [87] describing a 2-class SIR model. The model has six variables: si, ii, ri, for $i \in \{1,2\}$ describing the susceptible, infected, and recovered individuals in the two classes. The original ODEs are given in tab SIR2 of Fig. 4. Tab SIRRNHull_union of Fig. 4 contains the hull to which, to ease presentation, we added the original model (highlighted). The error estimation for i1 is depicted with dashed lines in the plot in the center of Fig. 4, while the original solution is provided in solid line.

Similarly, we consider a recurrent model in biochemistry from [30], where we analyze the dynamics of complexes such as receptors and scaffold proteins, which have multiple binding domains [18,40]. In our prototypical model, a molecule A possesses two independent binding sites, each capable of reversibly binding to a molecule B. We denote by A_{10}, A_{01}, and A_{11} the molecular species resulting from the binding of B to the first site, the second site, or both sites of A, respectively. In this model, species with the same number of occupied binding sites are assumed to exhibit identical dynamics, provided they share the same kinetic parameters. While this assumption simplifies the analysis, it is rather restrictive and often unrealistic in real-world scenarios.

We model the system with ERODE using CRNs, and demonstrate that it is possible to recover underlying symmetries even when the parameters are affected by noise through approximate BDE. In Fig. 5 we show a plot computed by ERODE, where A_{01} and A_{10}, exhibit nearly identical behaviors. This demonstrates the effectiveness of approximate differential equivalence to uncover symmetries and reduce the dimensionality of complex systems under uncertainty.

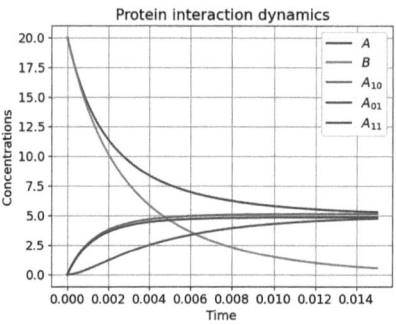

Fig. 5. Protein interaction plot.

Exact Reduction of DAEs with Linear Derivatives. Backward Invariance [81,83] is a generalization of backward equivalence that can be used for linear DAEs, i.e., linear differential equations complemented by algebraic constraints. As shown in tab AM_DAE of Fig. 1, this is performed in ERODE using command reduceBDE. We note that the considered model is polynomial. Indeed, part of the theory from [83] can be trivially extended to this case.

Network Reduction and Embedding. Networks with adjacency matrix A can be reduced exactly and approximately by ERODE through differential equivalences considering the associated dynamical system $\dot{x} = Ax$. This is because in previous works, we established formal relations among our reduction techniques and notions from network science. In particular, in [82] we showed how our exact reductions preserve centrality measures such as Page Rank, eigenvector, and Katz centrality [65]. Furthermore, we demonstrated how our backward equivalence corresponds to the notion of exact role assignment [62]. This notion, widely applied in the social sciences (see, e.g., [97]), assigns *roles* to each node and states that two nodes with the same role have the same number of neighbors of each role. Furthermore, these partitions are in line with the definition of equitable partitions [49] employed to compute the embedding of a network [76]. A network embedding consists of a matrix $E \in \mathbb{R}^{n \times d}$, with $d < n$, which encodes nodes in a lower-dimensional space while preserving key properties of the original network. The ERODE Python APIs provide exact and approximate versions of BE tailored for networks (methods reduceNetworkEpsBE) and the algorithm to compute the embedding (method computeEmbedding).

Exact Reduction of BNs. Boolean BE [10,12] is a recasting of BE to BNs. It finds species that maintain the same activation status if initialized equally (reduceBBE in tab BN of Fig. 1). BNs can be reduced by forward notions thanks to the generalized forward bisimulation (GFB) [9]. It is a reduction for general dynamical systems over commutative monoids, extending and unifying forward equivalences.

GFB can handle various monoids, e.g., on the reals $\mathbb{R}$ or Booleans $\mathbb{B}$, and is applicable to both discrete- and continuous-time dynamical systems. E.g., using monoid $(\mathbb{R}, +)$ we recover forward equivalence for ODEs; using $(\mathbb{B}, \vee)$ we obtain forward reductions of BNs with macro-variables representing the disjunction of the variables in a block. For monoids $(\mathbb{R}, \cdot)$ and $(\mathbb{B}, \wedge)$ we obtain non-linear reductions of non-linear systems. The command supporting it is reduceFME.

5 Integration with Python

Recently, ERODE has also been offered as an API to be invoked from Python, as exemplified in Fig. 6a. All features are made available through the ErodeHandler class. First, it is necessary to start and connect to a JVM (lines 1–2). ERODE models can be loaded as shown in line 4, while further formalisms can be imported with corresponding import methods. Line 4 loads KAIC [41], a biological system with 4 species: OO, PP, OP, and PO. The model is reduced using BE in line 5, obtaining the partition {OO,PP} and {OP,PO}.

Line 7 simulates KAIC specifying the time horizon (1), the number of steps (100), and the output file which can be processed using famous Python libraries such as Pandas and Matplotlib (not shown in the figure). Line 9 generates the plot in Fig. 6b. We can see pairwise equal lines in accordance with the BE reduction. Finally, in line 11, we stop the JVM. Additional features (approximations, initial partitions, etc.) are specified in the GitHub page [2], where we provide a Colab Notebook to use the tool online without any installation [1].

```
1  erodeHandler = ErodeHandler()
2  erode=erodeHandler.start_JVM()
3
4  erode.loadModel("kaic.ode")
5  obtained = erode.computeBE();
6
7  erode.simulateODE(1.0,100,"kaic")
8  df_csv=pd.read_csv("kaic.cdat")
9  df_csv.plot()
10
11 erodeHandler._stop_server()
```

(a) ERODE-Python snippet

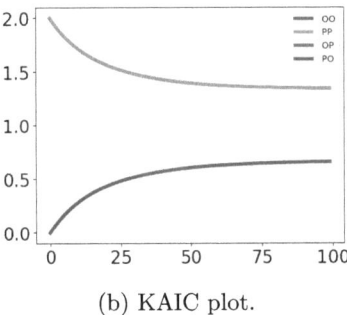

(b) KAIC plot.

Fig. 6. Example of loading, reduction, and plotting of a model with ERODE via Python and the resulting plot.

5.1 Extension for Network Embedding

We extended the functionalities of ERODE to compute network embeddings via Python, integrating with the popular NetworkX library. In this section, we present a guided toy example to illustrate how network embeddings are computed, demonstrate the interoperability between Python and ERODE, and clarify the connection between ODE model reduction and the field of network embedding. The example reported in this section and further experiments are available on the Colab Notebook in [1].

ERODE analyzed networks by modeling them as linear dynamical systems of the form $\dot{x} = Ax$. Each node corresponds to a variable and an associated differential equation. The backward reductions can be used on this dynamical system to find nodes with similar equations. Notably, these reductions are in line with several well-established concepts in network science, such as equitable partitions and exact role assignment, which are based on the idea that nodes sharing similar roles have the same number of neighbors of each role. In [76] we exploit this idea, proposing ε-BE, an approximate version of backward equivalence tailored for networks where the tolerance ε relaxes the original exact definition.

In Fig. 7, we report two partitions computed with ε-BE setting ε equal to 0 and 1, computed on the running example reported in [76]. Here, nodes belonging to the same block present the same color (i.e., role) and the same number of neighbors for each color, fostering the connections with exact role assignment and equitable partitions. Notably, the exact reduction fails to group structurally similar nodes into the same block, separating nodes 2 and 3 from node 1. This occurs because node 1 has a different degree compared to nodes 2 and 3, despite occupying a similar structural position within the network. In contrast, in the approximate setting, a tolerance of $\varepsilon = 1$ is sufficient to overcome this limitation. The reduction successfully groups these nodes together, effectively identifying their shared role and capturing their intuitive structural similarity.

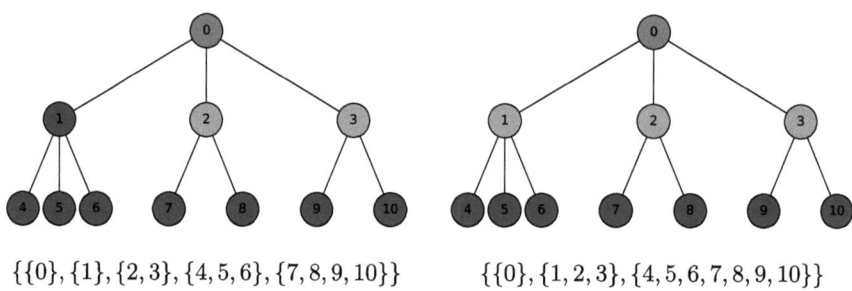

$\{\{0\}, \{1\}, \{2, 3\}, \{4, 5, 6\}, \{7, 8, 9, 10\}\}$ $\qquad$ $\{\{0\}, \{1, 2, 3\}, \{4, 5, 6, 7, 8, 9, 10\}\}$

Fig. 7. Resulting partitions with ε-BE equal to 0 (left) and 1 (right). Nodes in the same block have the same color.

In Fig. 8, we report a snippet of code illustrating how to compute the 1-BE partition and its corresponding embedding with the ERODE Python APIs. In line 1, we compute the partition (method `reduceNetworkEpsBE`) specifying the path to the edgelist file (``'example.edgelist''`), the number of nodes (11), and the ε value (1.0). In line 2, the resulting partition is converted into a Python list. Lines 4–8 show how to integrate with NetworkX to visualize the partition on

```
1  P = erode.reduceNetworkEpsBE("example.edgelist",11,1.0)
2  P_py=erodeHandler.j_to_py_list(P,int)
3
4  plt.figure(figsize=(6,2.8))
5  colors = ["brown","c","orange"]
6  nx.draw(G,pos, node_color=[colors[i-1] for i in P_py], font_color = 'k',
7          edgecolors = "k", node_size=node, with_labels=True )
8  plt.show()
9
10 matrix= np.array(nx.adjacency_matrix(G).todense())
11 E = erodeHandler.computeEmbedding(matrix,P_py)
```

Fig. 8. Snippet of code showing how to use the ERODE Python API and its integration with NetworkX.

networks. Finally, in line 10, the adjacency matrix is extracted using NetworkX, and in line 11 we compute the embedding (method computeEmbedding) using the adjacency matrix and the partition.

The resulting embedding $E \in \mathbb{R}^{n \times d}$ encodes each node in a smaller dimensional space $\mathbb{R}^d$ where nodes with the same role present similar vectors. The number of columns d in the embedding corresponds to the number of blocks in the partition, resulting in a significant reduction in matrix size.

Increasing the tolerance parameter ε leads to a more compact network embedding, but it may compromise the accuracy of node aggregation. To address this issue, we introduced in [76] an iterative ε-BE technique (method reduceIterativeNetworkEpsBE). This method accepts an initial tolerance ε_0, a maximum tolerance Δ, and a step size δ as inputs. It begins by computing the partition with ε_0 and incrementally increases the tolerance by δ. At each iteration, the partition is refined by collecting the blocks identified at different tolerance levels until reaching the maximum tolerance Δ. This approach avoids greedy node aggregation and allows the obtaining of useful aggregations of large-scale benchmark networks [76]. The ERODE integration with Python allows to carry further analysis on such embeddings using well-known machine-learning libraries like scikit-learn [68] and SciPy [92].

6 Tool Availability, Targets, Interoperability, Case Studies

The tool is freely available at [4] with a manual, and models. Its source code is available at [3]. ERODE is multi-platform and has a rich modern GUI. Tool papers [11,32], and tutorial-like presentations [85,90] have been provided. So far, the tool targeted both teaching and academics. As regards teaching, it is used in courses in the authors' institutions and has been presented in PhD schools [90]. As regards academics, it has been used in many publications, also by external researchers (e.g., [19,39,74]), or to compare with further techniques (e.g., [60,67]).

The import/export to several formalisms and the interoperability with languages like Python [2,80] and Matlab [21,36] made ERODE applicable in a wide variety of domains, including reachability analysis [35,75,77], model reduction with formal bounds [30], network reduction and role assignment [61,82,84], machine learning [76], control theory [14,28,43,55,58], biological systems [54,59,69,95] and others [26,53,86,88,91,96]. In some of these domains, ERODE was evaluated against state-of-the-art tools, providing competitive results in terms of effectiveness and efficiency. For example, in [35,75] we tested ERODE against state-of-the-art tools in reachability analysis such as CORA [7], FLOW* [38], and C2E2 [45]. In the machine learning field [76], we compare the quality of our embedding against struc2vec [72], SEGK [66], DRNE [89], and others.

Overall, ERODE has been applied for the reduction and analysis of many models, including the about 600 CRNs and ODEs from the BioModelsDB [69,70], several BioNetGen models (CRNs) [22], the rouhgly 100 BNs from GinSim [10], and several electrical networks [35]. A selection of these models and all the ones presented here is available at www.erode.eu/examples.html.

This paper summarizes the significant extensions made to ERODE through years of ongoing research and development. The tool is actively maintained and evolving, with new features targeting emerging application areas. Recent advancements, such as network embedding techniques and Python integration, demonstrate its growing versatility. In future work, we plan to continue the theoretical and technical development of ERODE, while also extending its applicability to new domains where formal analysis and reduction techniques can be effectively applied.

Acknowledgments. Several co-authors contributed to ERODE. We thank Georgios Argyres, Giorgio and Giovanni Bacci, Josu Doncel, Nicolas Gast, Alberto Lluch Lafuente, Isabel Perez-Verona, Stefano Tognazzi, Tabea Waizmann. This work was partially supported by the Poul Due Jensen Foundation (883901), the project SERICS (PE00000014), the project Tuscany Health Ecosystem (THE), CUP: B83C22003920001, SMaRT COnSTRUCT (CUP J53C24001460006), within FAIR (CUP I53C22001380006); the last two under the MUR National Recovery and Resilience Plan funded by the EU - NextGenerationEU.

References

1. Erode-python online notebook. https://colab.research.google.com/github/andrea-vandin/erode-python/blob/main/erodePython.ipynb
2. Erode-python website. https://github.com/andrea-vandin/erode-python/wiki
3. Erode source code. https://github.com/IMTAltiStudiLucca/ERODE4.18
4. Erode website. www.erode.eu
5. Matlab. https://www.mathworks.com/products/matlab.html
6. Abou-Jaoudé, W., et al.: Logical modeling and dynamical analysis of cellular networks. Front. Gen. **7**, 94–94 (05 2016). https://doi.org/10.3389/fgene.2016.00094

7. Althoff, M.: An introduction to Cora 2015. In: Proceeding of the Workshop on Applied Verification for Continuous and Hybrid Systems, pp. 120–151 (2015)
8. Apache commons mathematics library. http://commons.apache.org/proper/commons-math/
9. Argyris, G., Lluch-Lafuente, A., Leguizamon-Robayo, A., Tribastone, M., Tschaikowski, M., Vandin, A.: Minimization of dynamical systems over monoids. In: LICS, pp. 1–14 (2023). https://doi.org/10.1109/LICS56636.2023.10175697
10. Argyris, G., Lluch-Lafuente, A., Tribastone, M., Tschaikowski, M., Vandin, A.: Reducing Boolean networks with backward Boolean equivalence. In: 19th International Conference on Computational Methods in Systems Biology CMSB 2021, pp. 1–18 (2021). https://doi.org/10.1007/978-3-030-85633-5_1
11. Argyris, G., Lluch-Lafuente, A., Tribastone, M., Tschaikowski, M., Vandin, A.: An extension of ERODE to reduce Boolean networks by backward Boolean equivalence. In: Petre, I., Paun, A. (eds.) Computational Methods in Systems Biology - 20th International Conference, CMSB 2022, Bucharest, Romania, September 14-16, 2022, Proceedings. Lecture Notes in Computer Science, vol. 13447, pp. 294–301. Springer (2022). https://doi.org/10.1007/978-3-031-15034-0_16
12. Argyris, G., Lluch-Lafuente, A., Tribastone, M., Tschaikowski, M., Vandin, A.: Reducing Boolean networks with backward equivalence. BMC Bioinform. **24**(1), 212 (2023). https://doi.org/10.1186/S12859-023-05326-9
13. Bacci, G., Bacci, G., Larsen, K.G., Tribastone, M., Tschaikowski, M., Vandin, A.: Efficient local computation of differential bisimulations via coupling and up-to methods. In: 36th Annual ACM/IEEE Symposium on Logic in Computer Science, LICS 2021, pp. 1–14 (2021). https://doi.org/10.1109/LICS52264.2021.9470555
14. Bacci, G., Bacci, G., Larsen, K.G., Squillace, G., Tribastone, M., Tschaikowski, M., Vandin, A.: Dissimilarity for linear dynamical systems. In: Hillston, J., Soudjani, S., Waga, M. (eds.) Quantitative Evaluation of Systems and Formal Modeling and Analysis of Timed Systems - First International Joint Conference, QEST+FORMATS 2024, Calgary, AB, Canada, September 9-13, 2024, Proceedings. Lecture Notes in Computer Science, vol. 14996, pp. 125–142. Springer (2024). https://doi.org/10.1007/978-3-031-68416-6_8
15. Blinov, M.L., Faeder, J.R., Goldstein, B., Hlavacek, W.S.: BioNetGen: software for rule-based modeling of signal transduction based on the interactions of molecular domains. Bioinformatics **20**(17), 3289–3291 (2004)
16. Bloomingdale, P., Nguyen, V.A., Niu, J., Mager, D.E.: Boolean network modeling in systems pharmacology. J. Pharmacokinet Pharmacodyn. **45**(1), 159–180 (2018). https://doi.org/10.1007/s10928-017-9567-4
17. Bortolussi, L., Cardelli, L., Kwiatkowska, M., Laurenti, L.: Approximation of probabilistic reachability for chemical reaction networks using the linear noise approximation. In: Agha, G., Houdt, B.V. (eds.) QEST. vol. 9826, pp. 72–88. Springer (2016). https://doi.org/10.1007/978-3-319-43425-4_5
18. Camporesi, F., Feret, J., Koeppl, H., Petrov, T.: Combining model reductions. Electr. Notes Theor. Comput. Sci. **265**, 73–96 (2010)
19. Camporesi, F., Feret, J., Lý, K.Q.: Kade: a tool to compile kappa rules into (reduced) ODE models. In: Feret, J., Koeppl, H. (eds.) 15th International Conference on Computational Methods in Systems Biology CMSB 2017. Lecture Notes in Computer Science, vol. 10545, pp. 291–299. Springer (2017). https://doi.org/10.1007/978-3-319-67471-1_18
20. Cardelli, L., Csikász-Nagy, A., Dalchau, N., Tribastone, M., Tschaikowski, M.: Noise reduction in complex biological switches. Sci. Rep. **6**, 20214–20226 (2016)

21. Cardelli, L., Tribastone, M., Tschaikowski, M., Vandin, A.: Comparing chemical reaction networks: a categorical and algorithmic perspective. In: LICS, pp. 485–494 (2016)
22. Cardelli, L., Tribastone, M., Tschaikowski, M., Vandin, A.: Efficient syntax-driven lumping of differential equations. In: TACAS, pp. 93–111 (2016)
23. Cardelli, L., Tribastone, M., Tschaikowski, M., Vandin, A.: Symbolic computation of differential equivalences. In: POPL, pp. 137–150 (2016). https://doi.org/10.1145/2837614.2837649
24. Cardelli, L.: On process rate semantics. Theoret. Comput. Sci. **391**(3), 190–215 (2008)
25. Cardelli, L., Csikász-Nagy, A.: The cell cycle switch computes approximate majority. Sci. Rep. **2**, 656 EP – (2012)
26. Cardelli, L., Csikász-Nagy, A., Dalchau, N., Tribastone, M., Tschaikowski, M.: Noise reduction in complex biological switches. Sci. Rep. **6**(1), 20214 (2016)
27. Cardelli, L., Grosu, R., Larsen, K.G., Tribastone, M., Tschaikowski, M., Vandin, A.: Lumpability for uncertain continuous-time markov chains. In: Quantitative Evaluation of Systems - 18th International Conference, QEST 2021, pp. 391–409 (2021). https://doi.org/10.1007/978-3-030-85172-9_21
28. Cardelli, L., Grosu, R., Larsen, K.G., Tribastone, M., Tschaikowski, M., Vandin, A.: Algorithmic minimization of uncertain continuous-time Markov chains. IEEE Trans. Autom. Control **68**(11), 6557–6572 (2023). https://doi.org/10.1109/TAC.2023.3244093
29. Cardelli, L., Pérez-Verona, I.C., Tribastone, M., Tschaikowski, M., Vandin, A., Waizmann, T.: Exact maximal reduction of stochastic reaction networks by species lumping. Bioinform. **37**(15), 2175–2182 (2021). https://doi.org/10.1093/bioinformatics/btab081
30. Cardelli, L., Squillace, G., Tribastone, M., Tschaikowski, M., Vandin, A.: Formal lumping of polynomial differential equations through approximate equivalences. J. Log. Algebraic Methods Program. **134**, 100876 (2023). https://doi.org/10.1016/J.JLAMP.2023.100876
31. Cardelli, L., Tribastone, M., Tschaikowski, M., Vandin, A.: Forward and backward bisimulations for chemical reaction networks. In: 26th International Conference on Concurrency Theory, CONCUR, pp. 226–239 (2015). https://doi.org/10.4230/LIPIcs.CONCUR.2015.226
32. Cardelli, L., Tribastone, M., Tschaikowski, M., Vandin, A.: ERODE: a tool for the evaluation and reduction of ordinary differential equations. In: International Conference on Tools and Algorithms for the Construction and Analysis of Systems (TACAS), pp. 310–328 (2017)
33. Cardelli, L., Tribastone, M., Tschaikowski, M., Vandin, A.: Maximal aggregation of polynomial dynamical systems. Proc. Natl. Acad. Sci. **114**(38), 10029–10034 (2017)
34. Cardelli, L., Tribastone, M., Tschaikowski, M., Vandin, A.: Syntactic Markovian bisimulation for chemical reaction networks. In: Models, Algorithms, Logics and Tools, pp. 466–483 (2017). https://doi.org/10.1007/978-3-319-63121-9_23
35. Cardelli, L., Tribastone, M., Tschaikowski, M., Vandin, A.: Guaranteed error bounds on approximate model abstractions through reachability analysis. In: Quantitative Evaluation of Systems - 15th International Conference, QEST 2018, pp. 104–121 (2018). https://doi.org/10.1007/978-3-319-99154-2_7
36. Cardelli, L., Tribastone, M., Tschaikowski, M., Vandin, A.: Comparing chemical reaction networks: a categorical and algorithmic perspective. Theor. Comput. Sci. **765**, 47–66 (2019). https://doi.org/10.1016/j.tcs.2017.12.018

37. Cardelli, L., Tribastone, M., Tschaikowski, M., Vandin, A.: Symbolic computation of differential equivalences. Theoret. Comput. Sci. (2019). https://doi.org/10.1016/j.tcs.2019.03.018
38. Chen, X., Ábrahám, E., Sankaranarayanan, S.: Flow*: an analyzer for non-linear hybrid systems. In: Proceedings of the 25th International Conference on Computer Aided Verification (CAV), pp. 258–263. Springer (2013)
39. Chodak, J., Heiner, M.: Spike - reproducible simulation experiments with configuration file branching. In: 17th International Conference on Computational Methods in Systems Biology CMSB 2019. Lecture Notes in Computer Science, vol. 11773, pp. 315–321. Springer (2019). https://doi.org/10.1007/978-3-030-31304-3_19
40. Conzelmann, H., Fey, D., Gilles, E.: Exact model reduction of combinatorial reaction networks. BMC Syst. Biol. **2**(1), 78 (2008)
41. Dalchau, N., et al.: Computing with biological switches and clocks. Nat. Comput. **17**(4), 761–779 (2018). https://doi.org/10.1007/s11047-018-9686-x
42. Dehnert, C., Junges, S., Katoen, J., Volk, M.: A storm is coming: a modern probabilistic model checker. In: Majumdar, R., Kuncak, V. (eds.) Computer Aided Verification - 29th International Conference, CAV 2017. Lecture Notes in Computer Science, vol. 10427, pp. 592–600. Springer (2017). https://doi.org/10.1007/978-3-319-63390-9_31
43. Doncel, J., Gast, N., Tribastone, M., Tschaikowski, M., Vandin, A.: Utopic: underapproximation through optimal control. In: International Conference on Quantitative Evaluation of Systems, pp. 277–291. Springer (2019)
44. Erhard, F., Friedel, C.C., Zimmer, R.: FERN - a Java framework for stochastic simulation and evaluation of reaction networks. BMC Bioinform. **9**(1), 356 (2008). https://doi.org/10.1186/1471-2105-9-356
45. Fan, C., Qi, B., Mitra, S., Viswanathan, M., Duggirala, P.S.: Automatic reachability analysis for nonlinear hybrid models with C2E2. In: CAV, pp. 531–538 (2016)
46. Fritzson, P.: Principles of Object-Oriented Modeling and Simulation with Modelica 3.3. Wiley-IEEE Press, 2 edn. (2014)
47. Gillespie, D.T.: Stochastic simulation of chemical kinetics. Ann. Rev. Phys. Chem. **58**(1), pp. 35–55 (2007)
48. Gillespie, D.T.: Exact stochastic simulation of coupled chemical reactions. J. Phys. Chem. **81**(25), 2340–2361 (1977)
49. Godsil, C.D.: Compact graphs and equitable partitions. Linear Algebra Appl. **255**(1–3), 259–266 (1997)
50. Hagberg, A., Swart, P.J., Schult, D.A.: Exploring network structure, dynamics, and function using networkx. Tech. rep, Los Alamos National Laboratory (LANL), Los Alamos, NM (United States) (2008)
51. Hindmarsh, A.C., et al.: SUNDIALS: suite of nonlinear and differential/algebraic equation solvers. ACM Trans. Math. Softw. (TOMS) **31**(3), 363–396 (2005)
52. Hucka, M., et al.: Systems biology markup language (SBML) level 2 version 5: structures and facilities for model definitions. J. Integrative Bioinformat. **12**(2), 271–271 (2015). https://doi.org/10.2390/biecoll-jib-2015-271
53. Iacobelli, G., Tribastone, M., Vandin, A.: Differential bisimulation for a Markovian process algebra. In: Italiano, G.F., Pighizzini, G., Sannella, D.T. (eds.) Mathematical Foundations of Computer Science 2015, pp. 293–306. Springer, Berlin Heidelberg, Berlin, Heidelberg (2015)
54. Ilieva, M., Tschaikowski, M., Vandin, A., Uchida, S.: The current status of gene expression profilings in Covid-19 patients. Clin. Transl. Discovery **2**(3), e104 (2022)

55. Jiménez-Pastor, A., Leguizamon-Robayo, A., Tschaikowski, M., Vandin, A.: Approximate reductions of rational dynamical systems in clue. In: International Conference on Computational Methods in Systems Biology, pp. 108–116. Springer (2024)
56. Kauffman, S.: Homeostasis and differentiation in random genetic control networks. Nature **224**(5215), 177–178 (1969). https://doi.org/10.1038/224177a0
57. Kwiatkowska, M.Z., Norman, G., Parker, D.: PRISM 4.0: verification of probabilistic real-time systems. In: Gopalakrishnan, G., Qadeer, S. (eds.) 23rd International Conference on Computer Aided Verification (CAV'11). Lecture Notes in Computer Science, vol. 6806, pp. 585–591. Springer (2011). https://doi.org/10.1007/978-3-642-22110-1_47
58. Larsen, K.G., Toller, D., Tribastone, M., Tschaikowski, M., Vandin, A.: Optimality-preserving reduction of chemical reaction networks. In: International Symposium on Leveraging Applications of Formal Methods, pp. 13–32. Springer (2024)
59. Leguizamon-Robayo, A., Jiménez-Pastor, A., Tribastone, M., Tschaikowski, M., Vandin, A.: Approximate constrained lumping of chemical reaction networks. Proc. Royal Soc. A **481**(2317), 20240754 (2025)
60. Leguizamon-Robayo, A., Jiménez-Pastor, A., Tribastone, M., Tschaikowski, M., Vandin, A.: approximate constrained lumping of polynomial differential equations. In: Pang, J., Niehren, J. (eds.) Computational Methods in Systems Biology - 21st International Conference, CMSB 2023, Luxembourg City, Luxembourg, September 13-15, 2023, Proceedings. Lecture Notes in Computer Science, vol. 14137, pp. 106–123. Springer (2023). https://doi.org/10.1007/978-3-031-42697-1_8
61. Leguizamon-Robayo, A., Tschaikowski, M.: Efficient estimation of agent networks. In: International Symposium on Leveraging Applications of Formal Methods, pp. 199–214. Springer (2022)
62. Lerner, J.: Role assignments. In: Network analysis: methodological foundations, pp. 216–252. Springer (2005)
63. McKinney, W., et al.: pandas: a foundational python library for data analysis and statistics. Python High Perform. Sci. Comput. **14**(9), 1–9 (2011)
64. Naldi, A., et al.: The colomoto interactive notebook: accessible and reproducible computational analyses for qualitative biological networks. Front. Physiol. **9**, 680 (2018). https://doi.org/10.3389/fphys.2018.00680
65. Newman, M.: Networks. Oxford University Press (2018)
66. Nikolentzos, G., Vazirgiannis, M.: Learning structural node representations using graph kernels. IEEE TKDE **33**(5), 2045–2056 (2019)
67. Ovchinnikov, A., Pérez-Verona, I.C., Pogudin, G., Tribastone, M.: CLUE: exact maximal reduction of kinetic models by constrained lumping of differential equations. Bioinform. **37**(12), 1732–1738 (2021). https://doi.org/10.1093/BIOINFORMATICS/BTAB010
68. Pedregosa, F., et al.: Scikit-learn: machine learning in python. J. Mach. Learn. Res. **12**, 2825–2830 (2011)
69. Pérez-Verona, I.C., Tribastone, M., Vandin, A.: A large-scale assessment of exact model reduction in the biomodels repository. In: 17th International Conference on Computational Methods in Systems Biology CMSB 2019, pp. 248–265 (2019). https://doi.org/10.1007/978-3-030-31304-3_13
70. Pérez-Verona, I.C., Tribastone, M., Vandin, A.: A large-scale assessment of exact model reduction in the biomodels repository. Theoret. Comput. Sci. (2021). https://doi.org/10.1016/j.tcs.2021.06.026

71. Randone, F., Bortolussi, L., Tribastone, M.: Refining mean-field approximations by dynamic state truncation. Proc. ACM Meas. Anal. Comput. Syst. **5**(2), 25:1–25:30 (2021). https://doi.org/10.1145/3460092, SIGMETRICS 2021
72. Ribeiro, L.F., Saverese, P.H., Figueiredo, D.R.: struc2vec: learning node representations from structural identity. In: Proceedings of 23rd ACM SIGKDD KDD, pp. 385–394 (2017)
73. Sanft, K.R., Wu, S., Roh, M.K., Fu, J., Lim, R.K., Petzold, L.R.: Stochkit2: software for discrete stochastic simulation of biochemical systems with events. Bioinform. **27**(17), 2457–2458 (2011). https://doi.org/10.1093/bioinformatics/btr401
74. Spaccasassi, C., Yordanov, B., Phillips, A., Dalchau, N.: Fast enumeration of non-isomorphic chemical reaction networks. In: 17th International Conference on Computational Methods in Systems Biology CMSB 2019. Lecture Notes in Computer Science, vol. 11773, pp. 224–247. Springer (2019). https://doi.org/10.1007/978-3-030-31304-3_12
75. Squillace, G., Tribastone, M., Tschaikowski, M., Vandin, A.: An algorithm for the formal reduction of differential equations as over-approximations. In: Ábrahám, E., Paolieri, M. (eds.) Quantitative Evaluation of Systems - 19th International Conference, QEST 2022, Warsaw, Poland, September 12-16, 2022, Proceedings. Lecture Notes in Computer Science, vol. 13479, pp. 173–191. Springer (2022). https://doi.org/10.1007/978-3-031-16336-4_9
76. Squillace, G., Tribastone, M., Tschaikowski, M., Vandin, A.: Efficient network embedding by approximate equitable partitions. In: 2024 IEEE International Conference on Data Mining (ICDM), pp. 440–449 (2024). https://doi.org/10.1109/ICDM59182.2024.00051
77. Squillace, G., Tribastone, M., Tschaikowski, M., Vandin, A.: Approximate regular equivalence by partition refinement. Appl. Netw. Sci. **10**(1), 39 (2025). issn = 2364–8228. https://doi.org/10.1007/s41109-025-00726-7.
78. Tarski, A.: A decision method for elementary algebra and geometry. In: Caviness, B.F., Johnson, J.R. (eds.) Quantifier Elimination and Cylindrical Algebraic Decomposition, pp. 24–84. Springer Vienna, Vienna (1998)
79. Thomas, R.: Boolean formalization of genetic control circuits. J. Theor. Biol. **42**(3), 563–585 (1973)
80. Tognazzi, S., Tribastone, M., Tschaikowski, M., Vandin, A.: EGAC: a genetic algorithm to compare chemical reaction networks. In: The Genetic and Evolutionary Computation Conference (GECCO) (2017)
81. Tognazzi, S., Tribastone, M., Tschaikowski, M., Vandin, A.: backward invariance for linear differential algebraic equations. In: 57th IEEE Conference on Decision and Control, CDC 2018, pp. 3771–3776 (2018). https://doi.org/10.1109/CDC.2018.8619710
82. Tognazzi, S., Tribastone, M., Tschaikowski, M., Vandin, A.: Differential equivalence yields network centrality. In: 8th International Symposium on Leveraging Applications of Formal Methods, Verification and Validation. Distributed Systems ISoLA 2018, pp. 186–201 (2018). https://doi.org/10.1007/978-3-030-03424-5_13
83. Tognazzi, S., Tribastone, M., Tschaikowski, M., Vandin, A.: Differential equivalence for linear differential algebraic equations. IEEE Trans. Autom. Control **67**(7), 3484–3493 (2022). https://doi.org/10.1109/TAC.2021.3108530
84. Toller, D., Tribastone, M., Tschaikowski, M., Vandin, A.: Coarse-graining complex networks for control equivalence. IEEE Trans. Autom. Control (2024)
85. Tribastone, M., Vandin, A.: Speeding up stochastic and deterministic simulation by aggregation: an advanced tutorial. In: 2018 Winter Simulation Conference, WSC 2018, pp. 336–350 (2018). https://doi.org/10.1109/WSC.2018.8632364

86. Tschaikowski, M., Tribastone, M.: Exact fluid Lumpability in Markovian process algebra. Theor. Comput. Sci. **538**, 140–166 (2014). Quantitative Aspects of Programming Languages and Systems (2011-12)
87. Tschaikowski, M., Tribastone, M.: Approximate reduction of heterogenous nonlinear models with differential hulls. IEEE Trans. Autom. Control **61**(4), 1099–1104 (2016). https://doi.org/10.1109/TAC.2015.2457172
88. Tschaikowski, M., Tribastone, M.: Spatial fluid limits for stochastic mobile networks. Perform. Evaluation **109**, 52–76 (2017)
89. Tu, K., Cui, P., Wang, X., Yu, P.S., Zhu, W.: Deep recursive network embedding with regular equivalence. In: Proceedings of 24th ACM SIGKDD KDD, pp. 2357–2366 (2018)
90. Vandin, A., Tribastone, M.: Quantitative abstractions for collective adaptive systems. In: SFM 2016, Bertinoro Summer School, pp. 202–232 (2016). https://doi.org/10.1007/978-3-319-34096-8_7
91. Vandin, A., Tribastone, M.: Quantitative abstractions for collective adaptive systems, pp. 202–232. Springer International Publishing, Cham (2016)
92. Virtanen, P., et al.: Scipy 1.0: fundamental algorithms for scientific computing in python. Nat. Methods **17**(3), 261–272 (2020)
93. Voit, E.O., Martens, H.A., Omholt, S.W.: 150 years of the mass action law. PLOS Comput. Biol. **11**(1), 1–7 (2015). https://doi.org/10.1371/journal.pcbi.1004012
94. Waizmann, T., Bortolussi, L., Vandin, A., Tribastone, M.: Improved estimations of stochastic chemical kinetics by finite-state expansion. Proceedings of the Royal Society A: Mathematical, Physical and Engineering Sciences 477(2251), 20200964 (2021). https://doi.org/10.1098/rspa.2020.0964
95. Waizmann, T., Bortolussi, L., Vandin, A., Tribastone, M.: Improved estimations of stochastic chemical kinetics by finite-state expansion. Proc. Royal Soc. A **477**(2251), 20200964 (2021)
96. Waizmann, T., Tribastone, M.: Difflqn: differential equation analysis of layered queuing networks. In: Companion Publication for ACM/SPEC on International Conference on Performance Engineering, pp. 63–68. ICPE '16 Companion, Association for Computing Machinery, New York, NY, USA (2016)
97. Wasserman, S., Faust, K.: Social network analysis: Methods and applications (1994)

Deriving Liveness Properties of Hybrid Systems from Reachable Sets and Lyapunov-Like Certificates

Ludovico Battista[✉] and Stefano Tonetta

Fondazione Bruno Kessler, 38123 Trento, Italy
lbattista@fbk.eu

Abstract. In this paper we tackle the problem of proving generic LTL properties of hybrid systems with a particular focus on liveness properties such as recurrence of regions, response to stimuli, or region stability. Although many advances have been made in the analysis of reachability and safety properties of dynamic and hybrid systems, there is a lack of tool support for the automated verification of liveness properties. We propose a fully automated approach that combines Lyapunov synthesis, reachability analysis, and SMT-based quantifier elimination to build a discrete abstraction and then applies standard model checking algorithms. A key step of the algorithm is the derivation of LTL constraints from reachable sets computations and Lyapunov-like certificates. We implemented the approach on top of the CORA and nuXmv tools and show how it can scale in the size of the discrete structure and how it can prove properties over linear and non-linear complex dynamics.

Keywords: Hybrid Systems · Linear Temporal Logic · Discrete Abstraction · Lyapunov Functions · Certificate Functions · Reachable Sets Overapproximation

1 Introduction

The verification of temporal properties in hybrid systems [Hen96, ACH+95, GST12] poses significant challenges due the interaction between continuous dynamics and discrete transitions. This problem is further exacerbated when considering properties of reactive systems that need to hold on infinite executions, and in particular liveness properties such as recurrence of regions, response to stimuli, and region stability.

These properties can be expressed in LTL [Pnu77], but while model-checking techniques have been successful in verifying LTL on discrete-time transition systems, most approaches to the verification of hybrid systems focus on safety and reachability properties (cfr., e.g., [SÁW+24] for a recent overview of the state-of-the-art technology). Although a number of works also proposed techniques

---

L. Battista, S. Tonetta—The authors acknowledge the support of the MUR PNRR project FAIR - Future AI Research (PE00000013), under the NRRP MUR program funded by the NextGenerationEU.

© The Author(s), under exclusive license to Springer Nature Switzerland AG 2026
M. D'Souza et al. (Eds.): ATVA 2025, LNCS 16145, pp. 363–386, 2026.
https://doi.org/10.1007/978-3-032-08707-2_17

Table 1. Table that summarizes the form of LTL properties generated from each analysis technique. R_i are regions expressed as Boolean combination of polynomial constraints and q represents a location of the hybrid automaton.

Object	Property	Type
Lyapunov Function	$G(F(G(\neg R) \vee (\neg q)))$	Liveness
Descent Function	$G(F(G(\neg R) \vee (\neg q)))$	Liveness
Barrier Function	$G(R_1 \rightarrow (G(\neg R_2)W(\neg q)))$	Safety
Reachable Set Overapproximation	$R_1 \wedge (R_1 U(R_2 \wedge R_2 U(R_3 \wedge R_3 U \ldots)))$	Liveness

for LTL (e.g., [PKV13,CGMT14,HS20]), they are typically limited either in the expressiveness of the dynamics and the properties or in the automation and scalability of the verification.

In the direction of closing such gap, we propose a new algorithm, called LTLConstraints4HS, to prove that a hybrid system H satisfies an LTL formula ϕ based on the following steps steps: 1) generate a set of regions from the property to prove, sublevel sets of Lyapunov functions, and post-images through discrete jumps, 2) derive a set Γ of LTL properties that are satisfied by H from certificate functions and from Reachability Set Overapproximation (RSO) applied to the regions, 3) build a discrete-time coarse overappoximation D_H of the hybrid system based on the regions, 4) call a model checker to prove $D_H \models (\bigwedge_{\gamma \in \Gamma} \gamma) \rightarrow \phi$. The core of the method is the second step, which exploits existing analysis techniques such as Lyapunov-like functions, barrier certificates and reachability analysis to generate LTL properties that are satisfied by H. Such generation is focused on liveness properties as summarized in the Table 1.

We implemented the approach on top of the CORA [Alt15] and nuXmv [CCD+14] tools and show the effectiveness of the method both in handling systems with large discrete structures, and in proving properties over linear and non-linear complex dynamics. The method is fully automated but not complete (the problem is in general undecidable).

The precision of the abstraction depends on the set of regions and we allow to specify additional regions in input to the algorithm. Nevertheless, we are able to automatically prove many interesting properties on complex models without any additional regions. No other tool is currently able to automatically tackle such a task. The experimental results show that LTLConstraints4HS can generate and handle up to ~ 150 regions and ~ 1000 LTL constraints. Code and complete results are available at [BTa].

Our contributions may be summarized as follows:

- a new general method that integrates standard techniques for hybrid dynamical systems with LTL discrete-time model checking;
- a method to synthesize regions for the discrete abstraction that is empirically proven to be effective in several benchmarks;
- derivation of LTL properties from certificate functions and RSO;

– an implementation of the method that automates the four steps of synthesizing certificate functions and regions, generating the LTL properties, abstracting, and model checking the result;
 – an experimental evaluation that shows the effectiveness of the approach on new or existing benchmarks [FI04, BKRS24].

Related Work. Various abstraction techniques have been proposed for hybrid systems [AGRS25], typically with some assumptions on the dynamics. For linear hybrid systems, predicate abstraction and CEGAR have been proved to be effective for verifying safety properties [ADI06]; liveness-related properties have been proved under some conditions on equilibrium points [CN12]; complete discrete abstractions have been found if the continuous or discrete evolution are restricted to specific types [AHLP00]; SMT-based model checking has been applied to rectangular hybrid automata [CGMT14]. Our approach builds a rather simple abstraction, but potentially tackles arbitrary polynomial systems.

Other works focus on the use of certificate functions, but usually for safety and reachability analysis. Lyapunov-like functions have been considered to build sublevel sets to create an abstract timed automaton [WS11] or generalized to recover ideas similar to k-induction [Bak18, AMTZ21]. Contrary to these works, here we use Lyapunov-like functions in combination with other methods to derive general liveness properties for the systems.

Reachability analysis [Alt10, AFG21] is a powerful way to study properties of hybrid systems, and several tools are devoted to this task [dC16, CBGV12, BFF+19, Alt15]. They efficiently prove safety properties for bounded times and have been used to approach unbounded time safety properties for specific systems [PA18]. Although we make use of several tools and approaches that were already available (*e.g.* numerical solvers to compute Lyapunov-like functions, CORA to compute RSO, SMT-solvers to build the discrete abstraction and to check the validity of the generated certificate functions, nuXmv for the model checking), we are able to provide a framework that integrates all of them to successfully prove LTL properties on hybrid systems.

Some works have approached the verification of liveness properties, using Lyapunov-like functions as certificates for the validity of temporal properties [HS20, NEDR+23], and, in the context of non-linear systems, to invalidate substrings to prove general LTL properties implied by safety properties [WTL14]. KeYmaera X [FMQ+15] provides an excellent framework for proving temporal properties also using certificate functions. Compared to these, we provide an automated method that combines regions and certificates synthesis, RSO, and discrete-time symbolic model checking in a unique novel way.

2 Background

2.1 Finite-State Transition Systems and LTL

Given a finite set V of Boolean variables, let V' denote a copy of the variables V, which are used to represent the values of V after a transition. A *Finite-state*

Transition System (FTS) S is a tuple $S = \langle V, Init, Inv, Trans \rangle$, where V is a set of (state) variables, $Init$ is a formula over V representing the initial condition, Inv is a formula over V representing the invariant condition, and $Trans$ is a formula over $V \cup V'$ representing the transition condition. A state $s \subseteq 2^V$ of S is a Boolean assignment to the variables V, represented as a subset of V.

A trace σ of S is an infinite sequence of states $\sigma = s_0, s_1, \cdots$ such that $s_0 \models Init$ and for all $i \geq 0$, $s_i \models Inv$, and $s_i \cup s'_{i+1} \models Trans$.

LTL. We define the set of LTL formulas over the variables V with the following grammar rule: $\phi := p \mid \phi \vee \phi \mid \neg \phi \mid \phi U \phi$ where $p \in V$. Note that we do not consider here the standard next (X) operator. We use the following standard abbreviations: $\top := p \vee \neg p$, $\bot := \neg \top$, $\phi \wedge \psi := \neg(\neg \phi \vee \neg \psi)$, $\phi \rightarrow \psi := (\neg \phi) \vee \psi$, $F\phi := \top U \phi$, $G\phi := \neg F \neg \phi$, $\psi W \phi := (\psi U \phi) \vee G(\psi)$. Traces over V are infinite sequences of assignments to V. Given a trace $\sigma = s_0, s_1, \ldots$, we denote with $\sigma[i]$ the $i+1$-th state s_i and with σ^i the suffix trace starting from $s[i]$. Given a trace σ and an LTL formula ϕ over V, we define $\sigma \models \phi$ in the usual way as follows: $\sigma \models p$ iff p evaluates to true given the assignment $\sigma[0]$; $\sigma \models \phi \vee \psi$ iff $\sigma \models \phi$ or $\sigma \models \psi$; $\sigma \models \neg \phi$ iff $\sigma \not\models \phi$; $\sigma \models \phi U \psi$ iff there exists $i \geq 0$ s.t. $\sigma^i \models \psi$ and for all j, $0 \leq j < i$, $\sigma^j \models \phi$. Given an FTS S and an LTL formula ϕ over V, $S \models \phi$ if for all traces σ of S, $\sigma \models \phi$.

2.2 Hybrid Systems

Several formal models fall under the name of hybrid systems. Here, we consider the classical definition of hybrid automaton [Hen96]:

Definition 1. *A Hybrid Automaton (HA) is a tuple* $H = (X, Q, q_{init}, E, init, flow, inv, guard, jump)$, *where:*

- *X is a finite set of real variables $x_1, \ldots, x_n$;*
- *Q is a finite set of discrete modes (also called locations);*
- *$q_{init} \in Q$ is the initial location;*
- *$E \subseteq Q \times Q$ is the set of possible discrete transitions;*
- *$init \subseteq \mathbb{R}^n$ specifies the set of initial continuous states;*
- *$inv \colon Q \to 2^{\mathbb{R}^n}$ assigns an invariant set $inv(q)$ to each location q, that specifies where the system is allowed to remain while in mode q;*
- *$flow \colon Q \times \mathbb{R}^n \to \mathbb{R}^n$ is a partial function that defines the continuous evolution of the system in each discrete mode $q \in Q$ via a set of differential equations;*
- *$guard \colon E \to 2^{\mathbb{R}^n}$ is a guard condition, specifying when the transition (q, q') is enabled based on the continuous state;*
- *$jump \colon E \to 2^{\mathbb{R}^n \times \mathbb{R}^n}$ assigns a relation to each edge that specifies the possible jumps of the continuous variables.*

A state of H is a pair $\langle q, s \rangle$, where $q \in Q$ and s is an assignment to the variables in X; s is also called a continuous state.

We consider a symbolic representation of the conditions $init$, $inv(q)$, $flow(q,s)$, $guard(e)$, and $jump(e)$, in the sense that they are defined by symbolic formulas over the variables X, taken from a set denoted by $Expr(X)$ (or $Expr(X, X')$ in the case of $jump$). In this work, we focus on *polynomial automata*, where $Expr(X)$ contains Boolean combinations of polynomial constraints over X. This is mainly due to limitations of theory solvers and simulators, but the proposed method can be generalized to more general forms. We also assume, for simplicity, that E does not contain elements of the form (q,q).

To describe the evolution of a hybrid system H we will use the notion of *hybrid trace* [dAM95,CRT09]. We briefly recall it. Given an interval $I \subseteq \mathbb{R}$, we denote by $l(I)$ its infimum and by $u(I)$ its supremum.

Definition 2. *A hybrid trace for H is an infinite sequence* $\sigma = \langle f_0, I_0, q_0 \rangle$, $\langle f_1, I_1, q_1 \rangle, \ldots$ *such that: I_i are adjacent intervals, i.e. $l(I_{i+1}) = u(I_i)$; q_i are locations, i.e. $q_i \in Q$; the intervals cover $\mathbb{R}^{\geq 0}$, i.e. $\bigcup_{i \in \mathbb{N}} I_i = \mathbb{R}^{\geq 0}$; $f_i \colon I_i \to \mathbb{R}^n$ is analytic. We sometimes denote q_i with $loc(\sigma_i)$.*

Definition 3. *A hybrid trace is a* trajectory *(also called a* run *or a* solution*) for H if:*

- *the image of f_i is contained in $inv(q_i)$.*
- *if $l(I_i) \neq u(I_i)$, then $\frac{df_i}{dt}(t) = flow(q_i)(f_i(t))$ for all $t \in I_i$;*
- *if $q_i = q_{i+1}$, then $f_i \cup f_{i+1}$ is well defined and analytic on $I_i \cup I_{i+1}$. In particular, either I_i is right-closed or I_{i+1} is left-closed;*
- *if $q_i \neq q_{i+1}$, then I_i is right-closed, I_{i+1} is left-closed, $e = (q_i, q_{i+1}) \in E$, $f_i(u(I_i)) \in guard(e)$, and $(f_i(u(I_i)), f_{i+1}(l(I_{i+1}))) \models jump(e)$.*

We say that a run *starts in* (R, q) if $f_0(0) \in R$ and $loc(\sigma_0) = q$. An *initial run* is a run that starts in $(init, q_{init})$. We notice that different traces may describe the same dynamics. Intuitively, a trace is a sampling refinement of another one if it has been obtained by splitting an interval into two parts [dAM95].

Definition 4 (Partitioning Function - Sampling Refinement [dAM95]). *A partitioning function μ is a sequence $\mu_0, \mu_1, \mu_2, \ldots$ of non-empty, adjacent and disjoint intervals of $\mathbb{N}$ partitioning $\mathbb{N}$. Formally, $\bigcup_{i \in \mathbb{N}} \mu_i = \mathbb{N}$ and $u(\mu_i) = l(\mu_{i+1}) - 1$.*

Given two hybrid traces $\sigma = \langle f_0, I_0, q_0 \rangle, \langle f_1, I_1, q_1 \rangle, \ldots$ and $\sigma' = \langle f'_0, I'_0, q'_0 \rangle$, $\langle f'_1, I'_1, q'_1 \rangle, \ldots$, we say that σ' is a sampling refinement of σ by the partitioning μ (denoted by $\sigma' \preceq_\mu \sigma$) iff, for all $i \in \mathbb{N}$, $I_i = \bigcup_{j \in \mu_i} I'_j$, and for all $j \in \mu_i$, $f'_j = f_i$ and $q'_j = q_i$.

2.3 LTL on Hybrid Traces (HLTL)

We extend LTL replacing propositions with predicates over a set Q of locations and a set X of real variables. To distinguish it from the propositional version defined in Sect. 2.1, we refer to this extension as HLTL, whose syntax is given by the following grammar rules: $\phi := q \mid R \mid \phi \vee \phi \mid \neg \phi \mid \phi U \phi$, where $q \in Q$ and R ranges over $Expr(X)$. We use the same abbreviations defined for LTL.

Given a hybrid trace $\sigma = \langle f_0, I_0, q_0 \rangle, \langle f_1, I_1, q_1 \rangle, \ldots$ and an HLTL formula ϕ over Q and X, we define $\sigma \models \phi$ as follows:

- $\sigma, i \models q$ iff $q_i = q$;
- $\sigma, i \models R$ iff for all $t \in I_i$, $f_i(t) \models R$;
- $\sigma, i \models \phi \vee \psi$ iff $\sigma, i \models \phi$ or $\sigma, i \models \psi$
- $\sigma, i \models \neg \phi$ iff $\sigma, i \not\models \phi$
- $\sigma, i \models \phi U \psi$ iff there exists $k \geq i$ s.t. $\sigma, k \models \psi$ and for all j, $i \leq j < k$, $\sigma, j \models \phi$

Finally, $\sigma \models \phi$ iff $\sigma, 0 \models \phi$. We say that a hybrid trace σ is ground for a a predicate R if its interpretation over intervals is constant, i.e., $\forall (t_1, t_2) \in I_i$, $(f_i(t_1) \models R \Leftrightarrow f_i(t_2) \models R)$. We say that σ is ground for an HLTL formula ϕ iff it is ground for every predicate in ϕ. Given a hybrid automaton H and an HLTL formula ϕ over Q and X, $H \models \phi$ iff, for all initial runs σ of H that are ground for ϕ, $\sigma \models \phi$. Notice that it is always possible to refine a run to make it ground for a HLTL formula [dAM95,CRT09].

Definition 5. *We sometimes identify a formula $R \in Expr(X)$ with the set of states that satisfy it, i.e., $\{s \in \mathbb{R}^n \mid s \models R\}$. We call both the formula and the associated set a* region *of H.*

We denote by $\overline{R}$ the formal closure of R, obtained by performing the following steps: 1) rewrite R into DNF; 2) remove negations in front of the polynomial constraints by interchanging $<$ with $\geq$, $>$ with $\leq$, $=$ with $\neq$; 3) apply the substitutions $a > b \Rightarrow a \geq b$, $a < b \Rightarrow a \leq b$, $a \neq b \Rightarrow \top$. Note that this is not the topological closure $clos(R)$ of R. In general, it holds that $\overline{R} \supseteq clos(R)$.

Definition 6. *Predicates of the form $R_Z \wedge (\bigvee_{q \in Q_Z} q)$ are often very natural and useful. These corresponds to the combination of a region $R_Z \in Expr(X)$ and a set of locations $Q_Z \subseteq Q$. We support them natively: a* local region Z *is a pair (R_Z, Q_Z). Notice that a region is logically equivalent to a particular case of local region, where $Q_Z = Q$. For this reason, we will only consider local regions in the main algorithm. A local region Z in a HLTL predicate is interpreted as $R_Z \wedge (\bigvee_{q \in Q_Z} q)$.*

2.4 Lyapunov-Like, Descent, Barrier Functions

Certificate functions are used to ensure the satisfaction of some properties such as Lyapunov-like functions to prove stability or Barrier functions to prove safety properties.

Lyapunov-Like Function. Even when a hybrid system does not converge to a single attracting point, it can admit functions that decrease along trajectories. To better exploit this property, we give the following definition of Lyapunov-like function [Kel14,Bra94] using class-κ functions [Kha02]:

Definition 7. *A couple $L = (L_f, L_Q)$ where L_Q is a subset of Q and L_f is a function $L_f \colon \mathbb{R}^n \times L_Q \to \mathbb{R}$; is a Lyapunov-like function for H if:*

- *for every $q \in L_Q$, and for every (x, q) such that $x \in inv(q)$, we have $L_f(x, q) \geq 0$, and the Lie derivative is non-positive: $\mathcal{L}_{flow(q)} L_f(x, q) \leq 0$;*
- *for every edge $(q, q') \in E$ such that $\{q, q'\} \subseteq L_Q$, $x \in guard(e)$ and $(x, x') \models jump(e)$, we have $L_f(x', q') \leq L_f(x, q)$;*
- *there exists a κ-function α such that for every $q \in L_Q$ and $x \in inv(q)$, we have $\mathcal{L}_{flow(q)} L_f(x, q) \leq -\alpha(L_f(x, q))$.*

Informally, L_f is the value of the Lyapunov-like function in the different locations and L_Q is the set of locations where the Lyapunov-like conditions hold. We will generalize results such as the Comparison Principle [Kel14, Section 5] to our setting in Sect. 3.3.

Descent Function. An analogue tool that proved to be useful is:

Definition 8. *A couple $D = (D_f, D_Q)$ where D_Q is a subset of Q and D_f is a function $D_f \colon \mathbb{R}^n \times Q \to \mathbb{R}$ is a Descent function for H if there is $\varepsilon > 0$ such that*

- *for every $q \in D_Q$, if $x \in inv(q)$, we have $\mathcal{L}_{flow(q)} D_f(x, q) < -\varepsilon$;*
- *for every edge $(q, q') \in E$ such that $\{q, q'\} \subseteq D_Q$, $x \in guard(e)$ and $(x, x') \models jump(e)$, we have $D_f(x', q') \leq D_f(x, q)$*

Informally, D_f is a function that decreases indefinitely over trajectories that stay in the locations D_Q.

Barrier Function Another important tool that we use is the following:

Definition 9. *A couple $B = (B_f, B_Q)$ where B_Q is a subset of Q and B_f is a function $B_f \colon \mathbb{R}^n \times Q \to \mathbb{R}$ is a Barrier function for H if:*

- *for every $q \in B_Q$, if $x \in inv(q)$ and $B_f(x, q) = 0$, $\mathcal{L}_{flow(q)} B_f(x, q) < 0$;*
- *for every edge $(q, q') \in E$ such that $\{q, q'\} \subseteq B_Q$, $x \in guard(e)$ and $(x, x') \models jump(e)$, we have $B_f(x, q) \leq 0 \to B_f(x', q') \leq 0$.*

Informally, B_f provides a certificate that a trajectory will not get from $B_f \leq 0$ to $B_f > 0$ while staying in locations B_Q.

Definition 10. *In the context of this paper, a certificate function is either a Lyapunov-like, or a descent, or a barrier function.*

Notation 1. *With abuse of notation, we sometimes denote with $L_f(q)$ the restriction of L_f to the set $\mathbb{R}^n \times \{q\}$. This also reflects the implementation, where $L_f(q)$ is represented by a polynomial expression. We do the same for descent and barrier functions.*

Methods for Synthesis of Certificate Functions. Many numerical methods exist to synthesize certificate functions for continuous systems [Par00,ZZCL20], and several variations had been proposed more recently to work with hybrid systems [BT24,Oeh11]. Several works are also devoted to the formal verification of the correctness of such functions [APA20]. We support the synthesis of candidate certificate functions through: 1) the use of Sum of Squares (SOS) programming, followed by a soundness check through an SMT solver; 2) directly using an SMT solver to synthesize a valid function (see *e.g.* [APA20]). We elaborate on this in Sect. 3.5.

Notice that these approaches are by no means exhaustive: synthesizing certificate functions (in particular for non-linear systems) is an active area of research. One important aspect of our framework is that it can be easily extended to support any method for the synthesis of certificate functions.

2.5 Reachable Set Overapproximation (RSO)

Tools that provide reachable sets [GG08] using RSO form a powerful way to obtain information on the behaviour of a hybrid system.

Definition 11. *Given a hybrid system H, a starting region R, and a starting location q, a Reachable Set Overapproximation (or RSO) with granularity τ up to time T $(= \tau N$ for some $N \in \mathbb{N})$ for (R, q) is a finite set $\mathcal{B} = \{(Y_i, J_i, p_i)\}$ where: Y_i is a region of H, $J_i = [l_i \tau, u_i \tau]$ is an interval, and $p_i \in Q$, such that for every run $\sigma = \langle f_j, I_j, q_j \rangle$ with $f_0(0) \in R$ and $q_0 = q$, for every $0 \le t \le T$ and every j such that $t \in \mathrm{Dom}\, f_j$, the point $f_j(t)$ is inside $\bigcup_{i \mid t \in J_i, p_i = q_j} Y_i$.*

Informally, a RSO gives information on where a solution that starts in the region R and location q can be at any time $0 \le t \le T$.

3 Discrete Abstraction with LTL Constraints

3.1 Overview

In this section, we detail the steps of Algorithm LTLConstraints4HS, that we use to verify the validity of an HLTL property for a hybrid system H, using a discrete abstraction and LTL constraints. The algorithm takes as input:

- a hybrid system H as defined in Definition 1;
- a set $\mathcal{Z}_\phi$ of local regions $Z = (R_Z, Q_Z)$ (as defined in Definition 6) that are used to define the HLTL property ϕ, and a (possibly empty) set $\mathcal{Z}_{add}$ of additional regions to be used in the abstraction. Let $\mathcal{Z}_{in} := \{(init, q_{init})\} \cup \mathcal{Z}_\phi \cup \mathcal{Z}_{add}$;
- an HLTL property ϕ defined over Q and $\mathcal{Z}_\phi$.

Algorithm LTLConstraints4HS consists of the following steps:

1. it synthesizes and validates Lyapunov-like and descent functions;

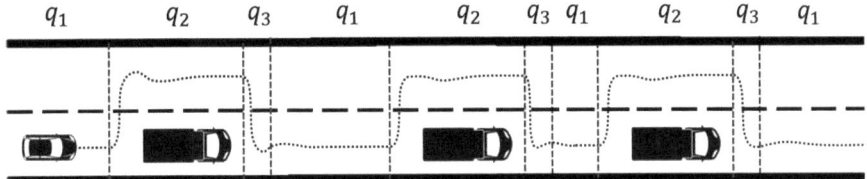

Fig. 1. Simple example of a car overtaking obstacles on the right lane of a highway.

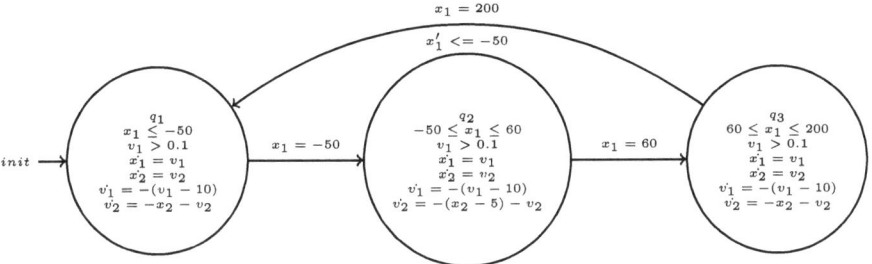

Fig. 2. Hybrid automaton for the car example.

2. it synthesizes local regions $\mathcal{Z}_{Lyap}$, defined as some sublevels sets of Lyapunov-like functions and possibly their images through admissible *jump* functions; let $\mathcal{Z} = \mathcal{Z}_{in} \cup \mathcal{Z}_{Lyap}$;
3. it computes the barrier functions corresponding to the local regions $\mathcal{Z}_{Lyap}$; let $\mathcal{F}$ be all the certificate functions found;
4. it computes an HLTL formula γ_f over $\mathcal{Z}$ and Q for each $f \in \mathcal{F}$;
5. it performs RSO for each local region $(R_Z, Q_Z) \in \mathcal{Z}$ and each $q \in Q_Z$ and computes the HLTL formula $\gamma_{Z,q}$ over $\mathcal{Z}$ and Q (the granularity τ and time T are fixed parameters of the algorithm).
6. it computes the discrete abstraction D_H, which has a variable v_Z for each local region $(R_Z, Q_Z) \in \mathcal{Z}$ and a variable v_q for each location $q \in Q$;
7. it transforms ϕ and each generated γ_i into LTL properties $\widehat{\phi}$ and $\widehat{\gamma}_i$ substituting Z with v_Z and q with v_q;
8. if $D_H \models (\bigwedge_{f \in \mathcal{F}} \widehat{\gamma_f} \wedge \bigwedge_{Z \in \mathcal{Z}, q \in Q_Z} \widehat{\gamma_{Z,q}}) \to \widehat{\phi}$, then it returns $True$;
9. else it returns $Unknown$.

We detail steps 4-5-6 in the next sections, postponing steps 1-2-3 to Sect. 3.5 (since it contains more standard arguments). We start by defining an example that will help us in the description of the algorithm.

3.2 Running Example

We present a simple hybrid system model to exemplify the method. The model represents a car running on a two-lane highway, overtaking obstacles on the road, like depicted in Fig. 1. For simplicity, the obstacles are always on the right lane and not moving. The movement of the car is divided in three phases that are repeated in sequence infinitely often: q_1 where the car approaches the obstacle, q_2 where it changes lane, q_3 where it returns to the original lane after overtaking the obstacle. After the overtake (q_3) the car returns to q_1 to approach another obstacle.

The hybrid automaton formalizing the example is shown in Fig. 2, where x_1, x_2, v_1, v_2 are the continuous variables representing the distance from the engaged obstacle x_1, the distance from the center of the right lane x_2, and the velocity (v_1, v_2) of the vehicle; the initial region is *init* defined as $x_1 \leq -100 \wedge -0.1 \leq x_2 \leq 0.1 \wedge 9.9 \leq v_1 \leq 10.1 \wedge -0.1 < v_2 < 0.1$, and every jump condition is abbreviated so that if a variable is not mentioned is implicitly not changed.

The local regions $\mathcal{Z}_\phi$ are those that we want to avoid: the part beyond the right lane $B_1 = (x_2 < -2, \{q_1, q_2, q_3\})$, the one beyond the left lane $B_2 = (x_2 > 7, \{q_1, q_2, q_3\})$, and the part surrounding the engaged obstacle $B_3 = (0 \leq x_1 \leq 50 \wedge -0.5 \leq x_2 \leq 0.5, \{q_2\})$. We add no other local regions, i.e. $\mathcal{Z}_{add} = \emptyset$.

We would like to prove that the car overtakes all obstacles, or in other words that whenever the car has an obstacle in front of it (q_1), it will eventually reach a position after the obstacle (q_3) while avoiding the bad states defined as $B := B_1 \vee B_2 \vee B_3$. This is formalized by the HLTL property

$$\phi := G(q_1 \to ((\neg(B))Uq_3)).$$

Lyapunov-Like and Descent Functions. Using SOS (see Sect. 2.4) we compute (and validate symbolically) the following Lyapunov-like functions:

$$L^1 = (L_f^1(x, q_1) = L_f^1(x, q_3) = \kappa_1 v_2^2 + (\kappa_2 v_2 + \kappa_3 x_2)^2 + \kappa_4 (v_1 - 10)^2, \{q_1; q_3\});$$
$$L^2 = (L_f^2(x, q_2) = \kappa_5 v_2^2 + (\kappa_6 v_2 + \kappa_7 (x_2 - 5))^2 + \kappa_8 (v_1 - 10)^2, \{q_2\});$$

where κ_i are positive constants. Using symbolic methods (see Sect. 2.4) we also compute the following descent functions:

$$D^1 = (D_f^1(x, q_1) = D_f^1(x, q_2) = -\kappa_{11} v_1 - \kappa_{12} x_1, \{q_1; q_2\});$$
$$D^2 = (D_f^2(x, q_3) = -\kappa_{11} v_1 - \kappa_{12} x_1, \{q_3\}).$$

Additional Local Regions and Barrier Functions. We automatically select 9 sub-level sets of each of the two Lyapunov-like function. We add them and the images through the jump functions of their non-empty intersections with guards to the local regions, for a total of $36 = |\mathcal{Z}_{Lyap}|$ regions. For clarity and space reasons, we now list only four of these local regions, that are shown in Fig. 3:

$$Z_1 := (L_f^1 \leq \kappa_9, \{q_1; q_3\}); \qquad Z_2 := (L_f^1 \leq \kappa_9 \wedge x_1 = -50, \{q_2\});$$
$$Z_3 := (L_f^2 \leq \kappa_{10}, \{q_2\}); \qquad Z_4 := (L_f^2 \leq \kappa_{10} \wedge x_1 = 60, \{q_3\});$$

For each sublevel set we add the associated barrier function. For example, for Z_1 we have: $B^1 = (B_f^1(x, q_1) = B_f^1(x, q_3) = L_f^1 - \kappa_9, \{q_1; q_3\})$.

In Sect. 3.5, we detail the process we follow for the above computation. However, we focus first on how we derive the LTL constraints and the discrete abstraction from these objects.

3.3 LTL Constraints

In this section we are going to define HLTL formulae that hold for the system H. We will then use that $H \models \gamma$ and that $D_H \models (\widehat{\gamma} \to \widehat{\psi})$ to conclude $H \models \psi$. The complete proofs are available at [BTb, Appendix B].

Certificate Functions. We start by listing HLTL properties that can be derived from the existence of certificate functions (recall Definition 10), together with the intuition behind their construction.

Lyapunov-Like Functions. Suppose that $L = (L_f, L_Q)$ is a valid Lyapunov-like function for H. If a solution will eventually be contained in the locations L_Q, the value of L_f along such solution will converge to 0. For this reason, if a local region $Z = (R_Z, Q_Z)$ is such that the infimum of $L_f(q)$ is strictly positive on R_Z for some $q \in Q_Z \cap L_Q$, we know that such a solution will eventually leave R or L_Q. We formalize this intuition in the following theorem:

Theorem 1. *Let $L = (L_f, L_Q)$ be a Lyapunov-like function for H. Let (R_Z, Q_Z), $q \in L_Q \cap Q_Z$ be such that for some $\varepsilon > 0$ the following formula is valid: $((R_Z \land inv(q))) \to L_f(q) > \varepsilon$. Then:*

$$H \models G\Big(G\Big(\bigvee_{p \in L_Q} p\Big) \to F(G(\neg(Z \land q)))\Big) \text{ , or, equivalently,}$$

$$H \models G\Big(F\Big(G(\neg(Z \land q)) \lor \neg\Big(\bigvee_{q \in L_Q} q\Big)\Big)\Big).$$

Given L, for every $q \in L_Q$ and every $Z \in \mathcal{Z}, q \in Q_Z$ we look for the existence of a valid ε for $R_Z \land inv(q)$ and $\neg R_Z \land inv(q)$. This is done by checking the validity of the formula in the proposition for $\varepsilon = 10^{-4}$. Finally, for every Lyapunov function L we compute γ_L as the conjunction of the HLTL propositions on the pairs (Z, q) for which we are able to prove the existence of such ε. Details can be found in [BTb, Appendix D].

Running Example: Since $L_f^1(q_1)$ has a positive minimum on $\neg R_{Z_1} \land inv(q_1)$, we have $H \models G(G(q_1 \lor q_3) \to F(G(\neg(\neg Z_1 \land q_1))))$, and similarly for other combinations.

Descent Functions. The case of descent functions is similar to the one of Lyapunov-like functions. Also in this case, these functions decrease along solutions that are contained in the locations D_Q, and we can deduce that such solution will leave local regions that have a finite infimum of D_f on them. This is formalized in the following theorem:

Theorem 2. Let $D = (D_f, D_Q)$ be a descent function for H. Let (R_Z, Q_Z), $q \in D_Q \cap Q_Z$ be such that for some $M \in \mathbb{R}$ the following formula is valid: $(R_Z \wedge inv(q)) \rightarrow D_f(q) > M$. Then: $H \models G\Big(G\big(\bigvee_{p \in D_Q} p\big) \rightarrow F(G((\neg(Z \wedge q))))\Big)$.

We compute γ_D in the same way we did for Lyapunov-like functions.

Running Example: Every pair (Z, q) satisfies the hypotheses of Theorem 2 for some D^i. As an example, for the pair (Z_1, q_1) the HLTL proposition is modeled by H: $H \models G(G(q_1 \vee q_2) \rightarrow F(G((\neg(Z_1 \wedge q_1)))))$.

Barrier Functions. Suppose that $B = (B_f, B_Q)$ is a valid barrier function for H. Let Z_1 and Z_2 be two local regions such that, for some locations $q_1, q_2 \in B_Q \cap Q_{Z_1} \cap Q_{Z_2}$, the value of $B(q_1)$ on R_{Z_1} is strictly positive and the value of $B(q_2)$ on R_{Z_2} is negative. Since the barrier function will not pass from negative to positive values along a solution that stays in the locations in B_Q, we know that if such solution gets to R_{Z_2} in location q_2, it will not get to R_{Z_1} in location q_1, unless it passes through locations outside B_Q. This is formalized in the following theorem:

Theorem 3. Let $B = (B_f, B_Q)$ be a barrier function for H. Let (R_{Z_1}, Q_{Z_1}), (R_{Z_2}, Q_{Z_2}), $q_1 \in B_Q \cap Q_{Z_1}$, $q_2 \in B_Q \cap Q_{Z_2}$, be such that
$((R_{Z_1} \wedge inv(q_1)) \rightarrow B_f(q_1) > 0) \wedge ((R_{Z_2} \wedge inv(q_2)) \rightarrow B_f(q_2) \leq 0)$, Then:
$H \models G\Big((Z_2 \wedge q_2) \rightarrow \big((\neg(Z_1 \wedge q_1))W\big(\neg \bigvee_{p \in B_Q} p\big)\big)\Big)$.

Given B, let $(Z_i, q_i)_{i \in I}$ be such that $((R_{Z_i} \wedge inv(q_i)) \rightarrow B_f(q_i) > 0)$ and $(Z_j, q_j)_{j \in J}$ such that $((R_{Z_j} \wedge inv(q_j)) \rightarrow B_f(q_j) \leq 0)$. We define γ_B as the following formula, whose validity is a straightforward consequence of Theorem 3:
$\gamma_B := G\Big(\big(\bigvee_{i \in I}(Z_i \wedge q_i)\big) \rightarrow \big(\big(\bigwedge_{j \in J}(\neg(Z_j \wedge q_j))\big)W\big(\neg \bigvee_{p \in B_Q} p\big)\big)\Big)$.

Running Example: Since $(R_{Z_1} \wedge inv(q_1)) \rightarrow B_f^1(q_1) \leq 0$ and $(\neg R_{Z_1} \wedge inv(q_1)) \rightarrow B_f^1(q_1) > 0$, it holds: $H \models G((Z_1 \wedge q_1) \rightarrow ((\neg((\neg Z_1) \wedge q_1))W(\neg(q_1 \vee q_3))))$, and similarly for other combinations.

Reachability Matrices from RSO. Here, we transform the information contained in a RSO $\mathcal{B} = \langle Y_i, J_i, p_i \rangle$ (Definition 11) in an HLTL property that is satisfied by the system H.

To do this, we start by creating a schematic object that can be easily manipulated, called *reachability matrices*:

Definition 12. *Given $\mathcal{B}$ for (R_Z, q) with $q \in Q_Z$, let $\mathcal{Z} = \{Z_1, \ldots, Z_k\}$, $Q = \{q_1, \ldots, q_h\}$, and $\tau = \frac{T}{N} \in \mathbb{R}^+$, we define:*

- *the associated* containment *matrices $C_{\mathcal{B}}^{\mathcal{Z}}$ and $C_{\mathcal{B}}^{Q}$ as the $(N+1) \times k$ and $(N+1) \times h$ matrices:*

$$C_{\mathcal{B}}^{\mathcal{Z}}(a,b) = \begin{cases} 1 & \text{if } \bigcup_{a\tau \in J_i} Y_i \subseteq R_{Z_b} \wedge \bigwedge_{a\tau \in J_i} p_i \in Q_{Z_b} \\ 0 & \text{otherwise} \end{cases} ; \quad C_{\mathcal{B}}^{Q}(a,b) = \begin{cases} 1 & \text{if } \forall i \mid a\tau \in J_i, q_b = p_i \\ 0 & \text{otherwise} \end{cases} ;$$

- *the associated* overapproximation *matrices $O_{\mathcal{B}}^{\mathcal{Z}}$ and $O_{\mathcal{B}}^{Q}$ as the $(N+1) \times k$ and $(N+1) \times h$ matrices:*

$$O_{\mathcal{B}}^{\mathcal{Z}}(a,b) = \begin{cases} 1 & \text{if } R_{Z_b} \cap \bigcup_{a\tau \in J_i \wedge p_i \in Q_{Z_b}} Y_i \neq \emptyset \\ 0 & \text{otherwise} \end{cases} ; \quad O_{\mathcal{B}}^{Q}(a,b) = \begin{cases} 1 & \text{if } \exists i \mid a\tau \in J_i, q_b = p_i \\ 0 & \text{otherwise} \end{cases} .$$

Informally, the a-rows of such matrices gives us information on where a solution that starts in (R_Z, q) can be at time $t = a\tau$ with respect to the local regions $\mathcal{Z}$: matrix C tracks containments and matrix O tracks intersections. We now transform this information in HLTL constraints that allow us to refine the behavior of the FTS.

Definition 13. *Given reachability matrices $C_{\mathcal{B}}^{\mathcal{Z}}, C_{\mathcal{B}}^{Q}, O_{\mathcal{B}}^{\mathcal{Z}}, O_{\mathcal{B}}^{Q}$, the associated a-constraint for $a = 0, \ldots, N$ is defined as:*
$$\gamma_a = \bigwedge_{b \mid C_{\mathcal{B}}^{\mathcal{Z}}(a,b)=1} Z_b \wedge \bigwedge_{b \mid C_{\mathcal{B}}^{Q}(a,b)=1} q_b \wedge \bigwedge_{b \mid O_{\mathcal{B}}^{\mathcal{Z}}(a,b)=0} \neg(Z)_b \wedge \bigwedge_{b \mid O_{\mathcal{B}}^{Q}(a,b)=0} \neg q_b.$$

Theorem 4. *Let $\mathcal{B}$ be a RSO for the system H for (R_Z, q), and let γ_a be the formulae built as in Definition 13 using the associated reachability matrices $C_{\mathcal{B}}^{\mathcal{Z}}, C_{\mathcal{B}}^{Q}, O_{\mathcal{B}}^{\mathcal{Z}}, O_{\mathcal{B}}^{Q}$. The system H satisfies the HLTL formula*

$$H \models G((Z \wedge q) \rightarrow (\gamma_0 \wedge (\gamma_0 U(\gamma_1 \wedge (\gamma_1 U(\gamma_2 \wedge \ldots \gamma_{N-2} U(\gamma_{N-1} \wedge (\gamma_{N-1} U \gamma_N))) \ldots)$$

Remark. It is often the case that several consecutive lines of $C_{\mathcal{B}}^{\mathcal{Z}}, C_{\mathcal{B}}^{Q}, O_{\mathcal{B}}^{\mathcal{Z}}$, and $O_{\mathcal{B}}^{Q}$ are equal. One can get rid of these multiple occurrences without losing expressive power of the formula presented in Theorem 4.

For each couple $Z \in \mathcal{Z}, q \in Q_Z$, we compute the RSO for $(R_Z, q)_{q \in Q_Z}$ and the associated reachability matrices. The constraint $\gamma_{Z,q}$ is the one that appears in Theorem 4.

Running Example. In Fig. 3 we show two out of the 18 successfully computed RSOs for the running example. From the picture, it is clear that every trajectory that starts in R_{Z_2} reaches R_{Z_3} without intersecting B. We refrain from writing the full formula obtained applying Theorem 4; however, from it one can deduce: $H \models (Z_2 \wedge q_2) \rightarrow ((\neg B)U(Z_3 \wedge q_2))$, and similarly for Z_4, q_3 and Z_1, q_3. Notice that RSO computation may fail for certain local region (*e.g.* unbounded ones); in these cases $\gamma_{Z,q}$ is set to $\top$.

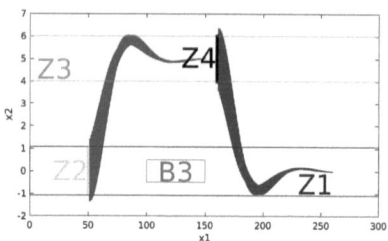

Fig. 3. Two RSO for the running example, starting from (Z_2, q_2) and (Z_4, q_3). In the plot, also projections on (x_1, x_2) for Z_1, Z_3 and part of B are depicted.

Remark 1. Certain classes of hybrid systems are stable iff there exist a piecewise quadratic Lyapunov function [DBPL00]. Since the verification of any LTL property can be reduced to the verification of a property of the form $F(G(p))$ on the hybrid system (in product with a discrete automaton), there is in principle no limitation on the form of the LTL properties that can be proven using this method. However, the problem is in general undecidable.

3.4 Discrete Abstraction

In this section, we define an FTS D_H that abstracts the behavior of the hybrid system H, given a set of local regions $\mathcal{Z}$. Informally, we approximate the predicate abstraction of H with respect to $\mathcal{Z}$, by computing the precise abstraction of the discrete structure of H and adding some simple constraints that capture the consistency and adjacency of the regions with respect to the locations of H. Additional constraints derived from the certificate functions and RSO (computed in Sect. 3.3) are added later on top of D_H.

Definition 14. *Given a HA* $H = (X, Q, q_{init}, E, init, flow, inv, guard, jump)$, *the discrete abstraction* D_H *of* H *w.r.t.* $\mathcal{Z}$ *is an FTS* $\langle V, Init, Inv, Trans \rangle$ *where:*

- *V is the set of Boolean variables* $\{v_Z\}_{Z=(R_Z, Q_Z) \in \mathcal{Z}} \cup \{v_q\}_{q \in Q}$;
- $Init(V) = v_{(init, \{q_{init}\})}$;
- *$Inv(V)$ is the conjunction of the following:* 0) $\bigwedge_{Z \in \mathcal{Z}} \left(v_Z \rightarrow \bigvee_{q \in Q_Z} v_q \right)$;
  1) $count(\{v_q\}_{q \in Q}) = 1$;
  2) $\bigwedge_{q \in Q} \left(v_q \rightarrow \left(\exists x. \bigwedge_{q \in Q_Z} (v_Z \leftrightarrow R_Z(x)) \wedge inv(q)(x) \right) \right)$;
- *$Trans(V, V')$ is the conjunction of the following:*
  3) $\bigwedge_{(q,q') \in E} ((v_q \wedge v'_{q'}) \rightarrow \exists x, x'. \, inv(q)(x) \wedge inv(q')(x') \wedge jump(e)(x, x') \wedge guard(e)(x) \wedge \bigwedge_{q \in Q_Z} (R_Z(x) \leftrightarrow v_Z) \wedge \bigwedge_{q' \in Q_Z} (R_Z(x') \leftrightarrow v'_Z))$;
  4) $\left(\bigwedge_{q \in Q} v_q = v'_q \right) \rightarrow \bigwedge_{q \in Q} \wedge \bigwedge_{q \in Q_{Z_1}, q \in Q_{Z_2}} ((v_q \wedge v_{Z_1} \wedge v'_{Z_2}) \rightarrow (\exists x. \, inv(q)(x) \wedge ((\overline{Z}_1(x) \wedge Z_2(x)) \vee (Z_1(x) \wedge \overline{Z}_2(x)))))$;

where:

- the formula 1) is the Boolean encoding of the constraints that force one and only one variable in $\{v_q\}_{q \in Q}$ to be true;
- the quantifiers in formulas 2), 3), and 4) are removed with standard ALLSMT procedure [LNO06], optimized using static learning [Seb07].

Given an HLTL formula γ, we denote by $\widehat{\gamma}$ the LTL formula obtained from γ by substituting each occurrence of q with v_q and each occurrence of Z with v_Z. This FTS is an abstraction of the hybrid automaton H in the following sense:

Theorem 5. Let ψ be a HLTL property over $\mathcal{Z} \cup Q$. It holds:
$D_H \models \widehat{\psi} \implies H \models \psi$.

Details of the proof can be found in [BTb]; here, we provide some implications of the constraints in Definition 14 to clarify the intuition, relating to Fig. 4:

- Constraint 0): if v_Z is true, a variable v_q with $q \in Q_Z$ must be true;
- Constraint 1): one location variable is true at each step;
- Constraint 2): empty combinations are not allowed, e.g. we cannot have $v_{loc_1} \wedge v_{Z_1} \wedge v_{Z_2}$;
- Constraint 3): the set of true variables before and after a transition where at least one location variable changes its value must be consistent with the jump and guard conditions, e.g. we do not admit $(v_{loc_1} \wedge v_{Z_2}) \wedge (v_{loc_2} \wedge v_{Z_2})'$, but we admit $(v_{loc_1} \wedge v_{Z_1}) \wedge (v_{loc_2} \wedge v_{Z_2})'$;
- Constraint 4): we do not admit a transition within a location among two regions that are not adjacent, e.g. we do not admit $(v_{loc_1} \wedge v_{Z_1}) \wedge (v_{loc_1} \wedge v_{Z_2})'$, but we admit $(v_{loc_1} \wedge v_{Z_1}) \wedge (v_{loc_1} \wedge v_{Z_3})'$;

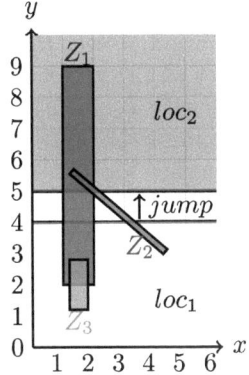

Fig. 4. A configuration of local regions in a hybrid system, used to explain the constraints in Definition 14. Invariant sets of locations are highlighted, and the jump condition is $x' = x \wedge y' = y + 1$.

The following is a consequence of Theorems 1 - ... - 5:

Corollary 1. If $D_H \models (\bigwedge_{f \in \mathcal{F}} \widehat{\gamma_f} \wedge \bigwedge_{Z \in \mathcal{Z}, q \in Q_Z} \widehat{\gamma_{Z,q}}) \to \widehat{\phi}$, then $H \models \phi$.

3.5 Computation of Certificate Functions and Regions

We now detail the first three steps of the algorithm presented in Sect. 3.1.

Lyapunov-Like and Descent Functions. We briefly describe the synthesis of a Lyapunov-like function for the system H, and refer to [BTb] (in particular to Algorithm 2) for further details.

Given a subset S of variables, we define $flow(q)|_S$ the coordinates of $flow(q)$ corresponding to the variables in S. Given a location q and a subset S of variables such that the formulae $flow(q)|_S$ contain only variables in S, we look for a classic Lyapunov function for $flow(q)$ restricted to the variables S.

Let z_e be an equilibrium point for $flow(q)|_S$. The candidate Lyapunov function $V(z)$ is constructed as a polynomial of a specified degree d by requiring: $V(z) > 0 \wedge \dot{V}(z) < 0 \quad$ for all $z_e \neq z \in inv(q)$, These conditions can be given to an LMI or an SOS solver. Once the function V is synthesized, we validate it through the use of an SMT solver. If either the synthesis or the validation fails, we try to synthesize a Lyapunov function by finding a solution to a symbolic equation. If also this one fails, we move on with a different subset of variables or a different location. Notice that the requirements on V imply that the extension of V to the set of all variables is a Lyapunov-like function as in Definition 7 for the system H with $L_Q = \{q\}$.

If the Lyapunov-like function is found and validated, we try to expand L_Q by picking another location q_{new} and checking if the dynamics restricted to S is still independent from the other variables, verifying whether conditions on V holds in q_{new}, and whether it does not increase on jumps from q to q_{new} (or vice versa). If this is the case, we can add q_{new} to L_Q and repeat the process for other locations, until we cannot add any other location.

The synthesis of a descent function is similar to the synthesis of a Lyapunov-like function, by modifying the requirements according to the definition.

Region Synthesis and Barrier Functions. Starting with the Lyapunov-like functions that we have found, we create a list of local regions to be considered in the discrete abstraction. We here outline the method, and refer to the complete Algorithm 3 in [BTb] for the details. For each valid Lyapunov-like function (L_f, L_Q) synthesized, we create a list of *critical values* $CV_{(L_f, L_Q)}$. These are obtained by computing maxima and minima of L_f on the local regions $\mathcal{Z}_{in}$ given in input that share a location with L_Q, and adding the mid-points of two consecutive critical values. The local regions to add to the abstraction are the sublevels of the Lyapunov-like function given by these values: $\{(L_f \leq a, L_Q) \mid a \in CV_{(L_f, L_Q)}\}$. For each such local region, we add the *associated barrier function* $(L_f - a, L_Q)$ that is a valid barrier certificate and a witness that once a sublevel is reached, the system will not leave it. As a final step, for each local region $(L_f \leq a, L_Q)$ and each $e = (q_1, q_2) \in E$ such that $q_1 \in L_Q$, we compute the image of $(L_f \leq a) \cap guard(e)$ through $jump(e)$, and add it to the list of local regions the ones that are non-empty.

Table 2. Characteristics of the six benchmarks. When $|\mathcal{Z}_{add}| = 0$, we did not need any additional handcrafted region to prove the properties.

Benchmark	dim	$|Q|$	flow	$|\mathcal{Z}_\phi|$	$|\mathcal{Z}_{add}|$
Linear Overtake	4	3	Linear	3	0
Multiple choice example	2	$2 + 2n$	Linear	1	0
Navigation Benchmark	4	25	Linear	1	14
Non-linear circular	2	1	Nonlinear	2	11
Multilayer control	3	n	Lin - Nonlin	2	0

4 Experimental Evaluation

4.1 Overview

In this section, we present six experiments designed to evaluate the effectiveness and robustness of the proposed algorithm in proving liveness properties of hybrid systems. We apply out method to: 1) Linear Overtake (the running example presented in Sect. 3.2); 2) Multiple choice: a scalable benchmark; 3) Navigation Benchmark: an instance of the benchmark from [FI04]; 4) Non-linear circular dynamics: a system with one location and non-linear dynamics converging to the unit circle; 5–6) Multilayer Control (linear and nonlinear): a hybrid system where the location decides the point to which the system converges and the dynamics can be linear or non-linear. Table 2 reports for each benchmark the number of continuous variables, the number of locations, the type of flow conditions, and the cardinality $|\mathcal{Z}_{add}|$. For each benchmark, we run the algorithm in four configurations: with or without adding images through $jump$ functions to $\mathcal{Z}_{Lyap}$ during Step 2, and using or not using stabilizing constraints [CS12] in the model checking. Adding images through $jump$ functions results in an increased time execution for the algorithm, but it is sometimes necessary to be able to prove the properties.

How to Read the Tables. The complete logs from the benchmarks are available at [BTa]. We report in the tables the most interesting entries. They are the time used for, respectively: T_{TOT}^{ic3-e}: total using IC3 without stabilizing constraints; T_{TOT}^{ic3}: total using with IC3 with stabilizing constraints; $T_{TOT}^{vb} := \min\{T_{TOT}^{ic3-e}; T_{TOT}^{ic3}\}$; T_{Lyap}: Lyapunov-like function; T_{ASJump}: AllSMT with discrete jumps - formula 3) in Definition 14; T_{ASReg}: AllSMT within a location - formula 2) in Definition 14; T_{AdReg}: adjacency constraints - formula 4) in Definition 14; T_{RSO}: the RSOs; T_{RSOMat}: the RSO matrices; T_{ic3} - T_{ic3-e}: to solve the model checking problem with k-liveness and IC3 using (resp. not using) stabilizing constraints [CS12]; $T_{vb} := \min\{T_{ic3}; T_{ic3-e}\}$. Furthermore, we provide the average of: md_{RSO}: temporal depth of LTL properties coming from the RSO; ms_{RSO}: size of LTL properties coming from the RSO; ms_{bar}: size of LTL properties coming from the barriers. We also show: N_{LTL}: the number of LTL constraints synthesized by the algorithm; $|\mathcal{Z}|$: the number of regions in the set $\mathcal{Z}$. Notice

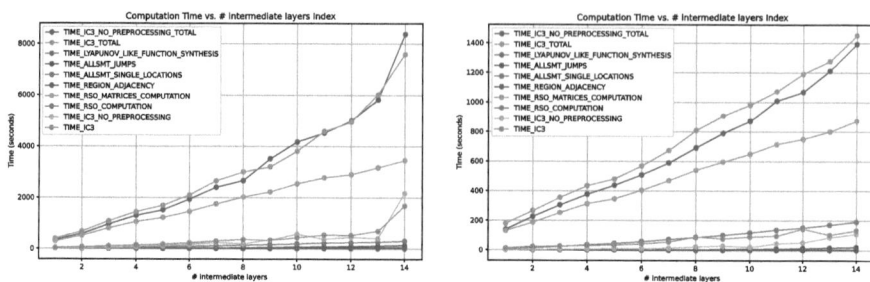

Fig. 5. Computation times for multiple choice benchmark, with (left) and without (right) images through jump functions.

that the value of the temporal depth and size that are not reported may vary only up to ±1 because of the way such LTL constraints are built.

Algorithm `LTLConstraints4HS` is implemented using an extension of pySMT [GM15] for VMT format [VMT11] called pyVMT [pyV22] for the model construction, z3 [dMB08] and cvc5 [BBB+22] to check the validity of the polynomial conditions, nuXmv [CCD+14] for model checking and CORA [Alt15] inside MATLAB [Inc22] for RSO with $T = 10$ and $\tau = 0.1$ or 0.01 depending on the complexity of the system, and for computation of reachability matrices. We ran experiments on a machine with 32 GB of RAM and a 12-core, 3.5 GHz processor. You can find additional information at [BTb] and [BTa].

4.2 Benchmarks

Linear Overtake. We already presented the benchmark in Sect. 3.2. We apply our algorithm to the properties: the car gets infinitely often to the initial location, i.e. $p_1 = G(F(q_1))$, then $p_2 = \phi$ as defined in Sect. 3.2, and that the bad states are never reached, i.e. $p_3 = G(\neg B)$. Results are shown in Table 3. We were not able to prove p_2 and p_3 without considering images through jumps, and using stabilizing constraints in the model checking resulted in a timeout.

Table 3. Data for linear overtake benchmark with images through jump functions.

T_{TOT}^{vb}	T_{Lyap}	T_{ASJump}	T_{ASReg}	T_{AdReg}	T_{RSOMat}	T_{RSO}	$T_{vb}p_1$	$T_{vb}p_2$	$T_{vb}p_3$	md_{RSO}	ms_{RSO}	ms_{bar}	N_{LTL}	$|\mathcal{Z}|$
359.88	0.45	4.11	1.37	32.85	93.63	4.07	68.94	49.70	6.72	15.50	532.17	68.33	153	40

Multiple Choice. This 2-dimensional linear hybrid system MC_n schematize a 2-dimensional system that moves with $\dot{x}_1 = 10$ and that can have a discrete jump after traveling a fixed distance in the x_1-coordinate: to move close to $x_2 = 5$ or close to $x_2 = 0$. The parameter n decides how many times this choice can be made before arriving in a final location with globally asymptotically stable dynamics. Precise definitions and complete results are given at [BTb], together with some figures to visualize the system. The initial local region is $Z_0 = ([-1,1] \times [-1,1], Loc_1)$. We want to prove that we eventually end up in the local region $Z_{target} = ([5(n+2) - 1, 5(n+2) + 1] \times [-1,1], Loc_{2n+2})$, therefore we define property $p_1 = F(G(Z_{target}))$. Results are shown in Fig. 5. For $n = 14$ with images through jumps, we have $N_{LTL} = 1223$ and $|\mathcal{Z}| = 169$.

Navigation Benchmark. This example is taken from [FI04, Section 2.1] and its simplification is used as a benchmark for the ARCH-competition [BKRS24]. Details can be found at [BTb], and we refer to the original paper for the full definition of the hybrid automaton and the *map* of a specific instance. It consists in a 4-dimensional hybrid system with linear intricate dynamics, where proving the existence of recurrent trajectories is not trivial. This demonstrates how our algorithm can verify complex properties when appropriate regions are carefully selected. We consider the system corresponding to the instance with the map: $[4, 5, 6, 6, 6; 4, 3, 2, 0, 6; 4, 3, 2, 0, 6; 4, 3, 2, 0, 6; 2, 2, 1, 0, 7]$. Some simulations of the system are presented in [BTb, App. C.3]. Based on these, we defined the local region $Z_0 = ([3.49; 3.55] \times [4.26; 4.32] \times [-0.35; -0.29] \times [0.65; 0.69], \{Loc_3\})$ as the initial local region, for which we want to prove the liveness property $p_1 := G(F(Z_0))$. In order to be able to do this, we needed the regions $\mathcal{Z}_{add}$ that can be found in [BTb, App. C.3]. Results are presented in Table 4. Considering images through jumps or stabilizing constraints resulted in timeout.

Table 4. Data for navigation benchmark, without images through jump functions.

T_{TOT}^{vb}	T_{Lyap}	T_{ASJump}	T_{ASReg}	T_{AdReg}	T_{RSOMat}	T_{RSO}	$T_{vb}p_1$	md_{RSO}	ms_{RSO}	ms_{bar}	N_{LTL}	$|\mathcal{Z}|$
15633.64	6.54	79.88	11.00	33.75	177.83	20.98	14090.35	35.67	2273.33	148.64	222	37

Non-linear Circular. The fourth experiment explores a non-linear system with only one location aiming to prove the existence of a loop that avoids a specified bad region. The dynamics is given by:
$\dot{x}_1 = -x_1 \left(x_1^2 + x_2^2 - 1\right) - x_2; \quad \dot{x}_2 = -x_2 \left(x_1^2 + x_2^2 - 1\right) + x_1$.

Notice that regions and local regions are equivalent when we have only one location. The starting region is $R_{0,\alpha} = [1 - \alpha; 1 + \alpha] \times [-\alpha; \alpha]$ for the values $\alpha = 0.05, 0.08, 0.11$. We also define a bad region $B = [0.3; 0.5] \times [-0.7; -0.5]$, that we want to prove that we avoid. The other regions in $\mathcal{Z}_{add}$ can be found in [BTb, App. C.4]. We prove the properties $p_1 := G(F(R_{0,\alpha}))$ and $p_2 := G(\neg B)$. Results are shown in Table 5. Notice that in this case we have no jumps, so there is no difference in considering images through them or not. Performances of $ic3$ and $ic3 - e$ are similar in this case.

Multilayer Control. The last benchmark consists in a hybrid systems on 3 variables (x, y, t) with $n \geq 4$ locations. Let $\{o_i\}_{i=1,\ldots,n}$ be the vertices of the

Table 5. Computation times for nonlinear circular benchmark.

α	T_{TOT}^{vb}	T_{Lyap}	T_{ASReg}	T_{AdReg}	T_{RSOMat}	T_{RSO}	$T_{vb}p_1$	$T_{vb}p_2$	md_{RSO}	ms_{RSO}	N_{LTL}	$|\mathcal{Z}|$
0.05	182.03	0.15	0.04	3.54	107.50		85.64	15.59	0.70	12.00	255.67	6	13
0.08	115.70	0.14	0.04	3.56	31.65		66.53	21.92	0.49	12.00	263.00	2	13
0.11	103.01	0.14	0.04	3.44	32.38		49.42	21.10	0.41	12.00	255.00	2	13

regular n-gon centered in the origin ordered counterclockwise with $o_1 = (1,0)$. The flow $flow(q_i)$ converges to o_i. We consider two configurations: one where the dynamics is linear ($\dot{x} = -x + x_{o_i}, \dot{y} = -y + y_{o_i}, \dot{t} = 1$) and one where the dynamics is non-linear ($\dot{x} = (-x + x_{o_i})^3, \dot{y} = (-y + y_{o_i})^3, \dot{t} = 1$). A switch may happen between any pair of locations when $t \geq 10$, and the reset function is $x' = x, y' = y, t' = 0$. The starting local region is $Z_0 = ([0.9, 1.1] \times [-0.1, 0.1] \times \mathbb{R}, q_1)$. Let $B = ([-0.1, 0.1] \times [-0.1, 0.1], Q)$. We check two properties: that the bad region is avoided if switches may only occur among consecutive locations, i.e. $p_1 := \left(G\left(\bigwedge_{i=1}^{n} \left(q_i \rightarrow \left(\left(\bigwedge_{j=1,\ldots,n;j\neq i-1,i,i+1} \neg q_j \right) W(q_{i-1} \vee q_{i+1}) \right) \right) \right) \right) \rightarrow G(\neg B)$, where $q_{-1} := q_n$ and $q_{n+1} := q_1$; and that if a solution eventually remains in q_1, it will get and remain in Z_0, i.e. $p_2 := G(G(q_1) \rightarrow F(G(Z_0)))$.

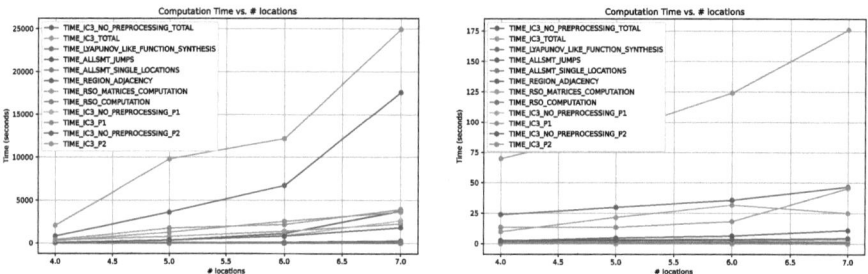

Fig. 6. Computation times for multilayer linear control benchmark, with (left) and without (right) images through jump functions.

As far as the linear control is concerned, we do not need images through jumps to prove p_2, while we are not able to prove p_1 without them. When considering the nonlinear control, we are not able to prove p_1 even with images through jumps. The difference between these two cases is given by the RSO, that is much more complex in the nonlinear case and struggles to prove that trajectories after the switch does not intersect B. Results are shown in Fig. 6 (linear case) and in [BTb, Appendix] (nonlinear case).

5 Conclusions and Future Works

In this paper, we addressed the problem of verifying liveness properties, expressed in LTL, on hybrid systems, with linear or non-linear dynamics. The method leverages Lyapunov-like functions and reachable set overapproximation to synthesize regions and LTL properties to be used for the discrete-time abstraction. We then use standard LTL model checking techniques to prove the property on the abstraction. We implemented the approach on top of the CORA and nuXmv tools, showing how it can scale in the size of the discrete structure and how it can prove properties over linear and non-linear complex dynamics. The work paves the way to different future directions. The automation for the set of regions, the set of functions, and the parameters for the reachable set overapproximation can be improved; it is an open challenge to fully automate and guide their generation for finding the inputs sufficient to prove the property. This would be very important specifically for barrier functions, whose computation without initial/unsafe region can be challenging. Several tools and ideas developed along these lines could be integrated into the workflow [APA20,BT24]. Complexity could be addressed in many points: semi-algebraic reasoning can be very expensive, and LTL-to-automata translation can be probably optimized, even though the symbolic approach of nuXmv is already very efficient. We will consider the generalization of the properties with metric operators as in MTL or STL, for example leveraging the exponential decay of Lyapunov functions.

References

[ACH+95] Alur, R., et al.: The algorithmic analysis of hybrid systems. Theor. Comput. Sci. **138**(1), 3–34 (1995)

[ADI06] Alur, R., Dang, T., Ivančić, F.: Counterexample-guided predicate abstraction of hybrid systems. Theor. Comput. Sci. **354**(2), 250–271 (2006)

[AFG21] Althoff, M., Frehse, G., Girard, A.: Set propagation techniques for reachability analysis. Ann. Rev. Control Rob. Auton. Syst. **4**(1), 369–395 (2021)

[AGRS25] Abate, A., Giacobbe, M., Roy, D., Schnitzer, Y.: Model checking and strategy synthesis with abstractions and certificates, pp. 360–391. Springer, Cham (2025). https://doi.org/10.1007/978-3-031-75775-4_16

[AHLP00] Alur, R., Henzinger, T.A., Lafferriere, G., Pappas, G.J.: Discrete abstractions of hybrid systems. Proc. IEEE **88**(7), 971–984 (2000)

[Alt10] Althoff, M.: Reachability Analysis and its Application to the Safety Assessment of Autonomous Cars. PhD thesis, Technische Universität München (2010)

[Alt15] Althoff, M.: An introduction to CORA 2015. In: Proceedings of the 1st and 2nd Workshop on Applied Verification for Continuous and Hybrid Systems, pp. 120–151. EasyChair (2015)

[AMTZ21] Anand, M., Murali, V., Trivedi, A., Zamani, M.: Safety verification of dynamical systems via k-inductive barrier certificates. In: 2021 60th IEEE Conference on Decision and Control (CDC), pp. 1314–1320 (2021)

[APA20] Ahmed, D., Peruffo, A., Abate, A.: Automated and Sound Synthesis of Lyapunov Functions with SMT Solvers (2020). https://doi.org/10.1007/978-3-030-45190-5_6

[Bak18] Bak, S.: t-barrier certificates: a continuous analogy to k-induction. IFAC-PapersOnLine **51**(16), 145–150 (2018)

[BBB+22] Barbosa, H., et al.: cvc5: a versatile and industrial-strength SMT solver. In: TACAS 2022. LNCS, vol. 13243, pp. 415–442. Springer, Cham (2022). https://doi.org/10.1007/978-3-030-99524-9_24

[BFF+19] Bogomolov, S., Forets, M., Frehse, G., Potomkin, K., Schilling, C.: Juliareach: a toolbox for set-based reachability. In: Proceedings of the 22nd ACM International Conference on Hybrid Systems: Computation and Control, HSCC '19, pp. 39–44. Association for Computing Machinery, New York (2019)

[BKRS24] Bu, L., Kundu, A., Ray, R., Shi, Y.: Arch-comp24 category report: hybrid systems with piecewise constant dynamics and bounded model checking. In: Frehse, G., Althoff, M. (eds.) Proceedings of the 11th Int. Workshop on Applied Verification for Continuous and Hybrid Systems, vol. 103 of EPiC Series in Computing, pp. 1–14. EasyChair (2024)

[Bra94] Branicky, M.S.: Stability of switched and hybrid systems. In: Proceedings of 1994 33rd IEEE Conference on Decision and Control, vol. 4, pp. 3498–3503 (1994)

[BTa] Battista, L., Tonetta, S.: Artifact evaluation link. https://zenodo.org/records/15846315

[BTb] Battista, L., Tonetta, S.: Extended version. https://es-static.fbk.eu/people/lbattista/pages/hybrid_ltl.html

[BT24] Battista, L., Tonetta, S.: Formal verification of stability for parametric affine switched systems. IFAC-PapersOnLine **58**(11), 37–42 (2024). https://doi.org/10.1016/j.ifacol.2024.07.422

[CBGV12] Collins, P., Bresolin, D., Geretti, L., Villa, T.: Computing the evolution of hybrid systems using rigorous function calculus*. IFAC Proc. Vol. **45**(9), 284–290 (2012)

[CCD+14] Cavada, R., et al.: The NUXMV symbolic model checker. In: Biere, A., Bloem, R. (eds.) CAV 2014. LNCS, vol. 8559, pp. 334–342. Springer, Cham (2014). https://doi.org/10.1007/978-3-319-08867-9_22

[CGMT14] Cimatti, A., Griggio, A., Mover, S., Tonetta, S.: Verifying LTL properties of hybrid systems with K-LIVENESS. In: Biere, A., Bloem, R. (eds.) CAV 2014. LNCS, vol. 8559, pp. 424–440. Springer, Cham (2014). https://doi.org/10.1007/978-3-319-08867-9_28

[CN12] Carter, R., Navarro-López, E.M.: Dynamically-driven timed automaton abstractions for proving liveness of continuous systems. In: Jurdziński, M., Ničković, D. (eds.) FORMATS 2012. LNCS, vol. 7595, pp. 59–74. Springer, Heidelberg (2012). https://doi.org/10.1007/978-3-642-33365-1_6

[CRT09] Cimatti, A., Roveri, M., Tonetta, S.: Requirements validation for hybrid systems. In: Bouajjani, A., Maler, O. (eds.) CAV 2009. LNCS, vol. 5643, pp. 188–203. Springer, Heidelberg (2009). https://doi.org/10.1007/978-3-642-02658-4_17

[CS12] Claessen, K., Sörensson, N.: A liveness checking algorithm that counts. In: FMCAD, pp. 52–59. IEEE (2012)

[dAM95] de Alfaro, L., Manna, Z.: Verification in continuous time by discrete reasoning. In: Alagar, V.S., Nivat, M. (eds.) AMAST 1995. LNCS, vol. 936, pp. 292–306. Springer, Heidelberg (1995). https://doi.org/10.1007/3-540-60043-4_60

[DBPL00] Decarlo, R.A., Branicky, M.S., Pettersson, S., Lennartson, B.: Perspectives and results on the stability and stabilizability of hybrid systems. Proc. IEEE **88**(7), 1069–1082 (2000)

[dC16] Sandretto, J.A.D., Chapoutot, A.: Validated explicit and implicit Runge-Kutta methods. Reliable Comput. **22**(1), 79–103 (2016)

[dMB08] Moura, L., Bjørner, N.: Z3: an efficient SMT solver. In: Ramakrishnan, C.R., Rehof, J. (eds.) TACAS 2008. LNCS, vol. 4963, pp. 337–340. Springer, Heidelberg (2008). https://doi.org/10.1007/978-3-540-78800-3_24

[FI04] Fehnker, A., Ivančić, F.: Benchmarks for hybrid systems verification. In: Alur, R., Pappas, G.J. (eds.) HSCC 2004. LNCS, vol. 2993, pp. 326–341. Springer, Heidelberg (2004). https://doi.org/10.1007/978-3-540-24743-2_22

[FMQ+15] Fulton, N., Mitsch, S., Quesel, J.-D., Völp, M., Platzer, A.: KeYmaera X: an axiomatic tactical theorem prover for hybrid systems. In: Felty, A.P., Middeldorp, A. (eds.) CADE 2015. LNCS (LNAI), vol. 9195, pp. 527–538. Springer, Cham (2015). https://doi.org/10.1007/978-3-319-21401-6_36

[GG08] Girard, A., Guernic, C.: Efficient reachability analysis for linear systems using support functions. IFAC Proc. Vol. **41**(2), 8966–8971 (2008)

[GM15] Gario, M., Micheli, A.: Pysmt: a solver-agnostic library for fast prototyping of smt-based algorithms. In: SMT Workshop 2015 (2015)

[GST12] Goebel, R., Sanfelice, R.G., Teel, A.R.: Hybrid Dynamical Systems: Modeling, Stability, and Robustness. Princeton University Press, New Jersey (2012)

[Hen96] Henzinger, T.A.: The theory of hybrid automata. In: Proceedings 11th Annual IEEE Symposium on Logic in Computer Science, pp. 278–292 (1996)

[HS20] Han, H., Sanfelice, R.G.: Linear temporal logic for hybrid dynamical systems: characterizations and sufficient conditions. Nonlinear Anal. Hybrid Syst **36**, 100865 (2020)

[Inc22] The MathWorks Inc. Matlab version: 9.13.0 (r2022b) (2022)

[Kel14] Kellett, C.M.: A compendium of comparison function results. Math. Control Signals Syst. **26**(3), 339–374 (2014). https://doi.org/10.1007/s00498-014-0128-8

[Kha02] Khalil, H.K.: Nonlinear Systems, 3rd edn. Prentice-Hall, Upper Saddle River (2002)

[LNO06] Lahiri, S.K., Nieuwenhuis, R., Oliveras, A.: SMT techniques for fast predicate abstraction. In: Ball, T., Jones, R.B. (eds.) CAV 2006. LNCS, vol. 4144, pp. 424–437. Springer, Heidelberg (2006). https://doi.org/10.1007/11817963_39

[NEDR+23] Nayak, S.P., Egidio, L.N., Rossa, M.D., Schmuck, A.-K., Jungers, R.M.: Context-triggered abstraction-based control design. IEEE Open J. Control Syst. **2**, 277–296 (2023)

[Oeh11] Oehlerking, J.: Decomposition of stability proofs for hybrid systems. PhD thesis, Universität Oldenburg (2011)

[PA18] Pek, C., Althoff, M.: Efficient computation of invariably safe states for motion planning of self-driving vehicles. In: 2018 IEEE/RSJ International Conference on Intelligent Robots and Systems (IROS), pp. 3523–3530 (2018)

[Par00] Parrilo, P.: Structured semidenite programs and semialgebraic geometry methods in robustness and optimization. PhD thesis (2000)

[PKV13] Plaku, E., Kavraki, L.E., Vardi, M.Y.: Falsification of LTL safety properties in hybrid systems. Int. J. Softw. Tools Technol. Transf. **15**(4), 305–320 (2013)

[Pnu77] Pnueli, A.: The temporal logic of programs. In: FOCS, pp. 46–57. IEEE Computer Society (1977)

[pyV22] PyVmt: a python library to interact with transition systems (2022). https://github.com/pyvmt/pyvmt. [Github repository]

[SÁW+24] Schupp, S., Erika Ábrahám, Md., Waez, T.B., Rambow, T., Qiu, Z.: On the applicability of hybrid systems safety verification tools from the automotive perspective. Int. J. Softw. Tools Technol. Transf. **26**(1), 49–78 (2024)

[Seb07] Sebastiani, R.: Lazy satisability modulo theories. J. Satisf. Boolean Model. Comput. **3**(3–4), 141–224 (2007)

[VMT11] VMT-LIB: Verification Modulo Theories (Language, Benchmarks and Tools) (2011). https://vmt-lib.fbk.eu/

[WS11] Wisniewski, R., Sloth, C.: Abstraction of dynamical systems by timed automata. Model. Identificat. Control (Online Ed.) **32**(2), 79–90 (2011)

[WTL14] Wongpiromsarn, T., Topcu, U., Lamperski, A.G.: Automata theory meets barrier certificates: temporal logic verification of nonlinear systems. IEEE Trans. Autom. Control **61**, 3344–3355 (2014)

[ZZCL20] Zhao, H., Zeng, X., Chen, T., Liu, Z.: Synthesizing barrier certificates using neural networks. In: Proceedings of the 23rd International Conference on Hybrid Systems: Computation and Control, HSCC '20. Association for Computing Machinery, New York (2020)

Control Closure Certificates

Vishnu Murali[✉], Mohammed Adib Oumer, and Majid Zamani

University of Colorado Boulder, Boulder, USA
vishnu.murali@colorado.edu

Abstract. This paper introduces the notion of control closure certificates (C^3) to synthesize controllers for discrete-time control systems against ω-regular specifications. Typical functional approaches to synthesize controllers against ω-regular specifications rely on combining inductive invariants (for example, via barrier certificates) with proofs of well-foundedness (for example, via ranking functions). Transition invariants, provide an alternative where instead of standard well-foundedness arguments one may instead search for disjunctive well-foundedness arguments that together ensure a well-foundedness argument. Closure certificates, functional analogs of transition invariants, provide an effective, automated approach to verify discrete-time dynamical systems against linear temporal logic and ω-regular specifications. We build on this notion to synthesize controllers to ensure the satisfaction of ω-regular specifications. To do so, we first illustrate how one may construct control closure certificates to visit a region infinitely often (or only finitely often) via disjunctive well-founded arguments. We then combine these arguments to provide an argument for parity specifications. Thus, finding an appropriate C^3 over the product of the system and a parity automaton specifying a desired ω-regular specification ensures that there exists a controller κ to enforce the ω-regular specification. We propose a sum-of-squares optimization approach to synthesize such certificates and demonstrate their efficacy in designing controllers over some case studies.

Keywords: discrete-time control systems · transition invariants · control synthesis · ω-regular properties · parity automata

1 Introduction

We introduce a notion of control closure certificates to synthesize controllers for discrete-time control systems against ω-regular specifications. Closure certificates [19], are a functional analog of transition invariants to verify discrete-time systems against ω-regular specifications. Unlike barrier certificates [24], which seek to overapproximate the reachable states of a system, closure certificates are real-valued functions that seek to overapproximate the reachable *transitions* of a system. When used for safety specifications, such certificates often allow

---

Majid Zamani—This work was supported by the NSF grants CNS-2111688 and CNS-2145184.

for much simpler templates [19, Section 3.1] to prove safety when compared to traditional barrier certificates. When combined with proofs of well-foundedness [8], such certificates may be leveraged to prove ω-regular specifications. Similar to barrier certificates, one may automate the search for closure certificates via optimization techniques such as sum-of-squares (SOS) [22], satisfiability modulo theory solvers (SMT) [9,11,17], and neural networks [1,21]. In the above cases, one fixes the certificate to be within a template class, $e.g.$, polynomials of a fixed degree or neural networks of a fixed size, and then proceeds to search for such a certificate within the template class. We build on this work to show how one may simultaneously search for both a certificate, as well as a controller to ensure the satisfaction of a desired ω-regular specification. To do so we first provide certificate conditions to ensure that a set is visited infinitely often, or that it is visited only finitely often. We then show how one may combine these proof techniques to design controllers for more general ω-regular specifications.

Functional Proofs for ω-regular Specifications. Functional approaches to synthesize controllers for ω-regular specifications rely on a combination of finding inductive invariants with well-foundedness arguments [2,7,10]. Such proofs of well-foundedness, similar to proofs of termination [8], can be reduced to finding an appropriate ranking function $\mathcal{V}$. To illustrate these approaches, let $\mathcal{X}$ denote the set of states of the system, and assume that one is able to determine the exact reachable set of a system (denoted Reach), and let $\mathcal{X}_{VF}$ be a set of states of a system that must be visited only finitely often. Consider a function $\mathcal{V} : \mathcal{X} \to \mathbb{R}$ from the states of the system to the reals such that:

$$\mathcal{V}(x') \leq \mathcal{V}(x) - \xi, \qquad \text{if } x \in \mathcal{X}_{VF} \cap \text{Reach and}$$
$$\mathcal{V}(x') \leq \mathcal{V}(x) \qquad \text{if } x \in \text{Reach} \setminus \mathcal{X}_{VF},$$

where x' is the one-step transition from state x and ξ is some positive value. Then the existence of a function $\mathcal{V}$ that is bounded from below and satisfies the above conditions provides a proof that the system visits the set $\mathcal{X}_{VF}$ only finitely often. As one typically does not know the set Reach, one instead tries to ensure that the above conditions hold over an inductive state invariant that overapproximates the set Reach. The promise of such functional proofs lie in their automatability. One may effectively search for them via optimization [22,24] or learning-based [1] techniques.

Transition Invariants. In the above discussion we considered the existence of a single function $\mathcal{V}$ to prove a set $\mathcal{X}_{VF}$ is visited only finitely often. Practically, one may want to instead consider partitions over relevant sets and try to find independent ranking function arguments to prove this. Unfortunately, such a strategy fails to be sound in general. This insight was observed in [23], which showed that one cannot prove a relation to be well-founded if it is a union of well-founded relations. However, it is possible to prove a relation is well-founded if its transitive closure (cf. Section 2) is disjunctively well-founded. To overapproximate the transitive closure, they introduced a notion of *transition invariants*, that overapproximate the reachable transitions of a system. Hence one is able to leverage transition invariants to find independent ranking functions to prove well-foundedness. While transition invariants provide an approach to prove a set is visited only finitely often, one often requires to show the dual, that a set be visited infinitely often, or both. This is the case when dealing with deterministic automata that describe ω-regular languages such as Rabin, Streett, or parity automata. Thus, we consider the question of how disjunctive well-founded proofs help in designing controllers for ω-regular specifications.

Our Contributions.

1. We introduce a notion of control closure certificates to synthesize controllers for discrete-time control systems against ω-regular specifications.
2. We show how proofs of disjunctive well-foundedness are useful not just for showing a set is visited only finitely often but also in proofs of showing a set is visited infinitely often, thus making them amenable to provide conditions for synthesis against ω-regular properties.
3. We rely on an optimization-based approach to automate the search for these control closure certificates and demonstrate their use in some case studies.

Related Works. The results in [24] introduced a notion of barrier certificates to act as functional inductive invariants for hybrid systems. These results illustrated how one may effectively automate the search for such certificates via optimization techniques such as sum-of-squares programming [22]. Building on this idea, the results in [10] considered a notion of parity certificates to synthesize controllers for objectives specified by parity automata and then demonstrated how one may use such certificates in verifying alternating-time temporal logic properties [4]. These certificates relied on a combination of invariant arguments (characterized as barrier certificates) with ranking functions (described as Lyapunov functions) to design controllers. Similar to these results, the results in [2] proposed a notion of Streett supermartingales to synthesize controllers for stochastic systems against Streett objectives. The results in [7] introduced a notion of Büchi ranking functions to provide a sound and semi-complete proof rule for real-valued programs via Putinar's Positivestellensatz [25]. More recent works consider extensions for stochastic systems [3,13,16]. The results in [19] proposed a notion of closure certificates to describe functional transition invariants analogous to barrier certificates and considered techniques to automate the search for these certificates via sum-of-squares (SOS) programming and satisfiability modulo theory (SMT) [9] solvers. Building on this, the results in [31] considered their use for recurrence (showing a set is visited infinitely often). Our work builds on the notion of closure certificates to find transition invariants and proofs of disjunctive well-foundedness to synthesize controllers for specifications characterized by parity automata. We show that while one may directly adapt conditions for recurrence as in [31], one faces challenges when trying to prove disjunctive well-foundedness (cf. Section 3.2). We thus propose alternative conditions to show a set is visited infinitely often by relying on proofs of disjunctive well-foundedness. These disjunctive well-foundedness proofs may be used as acceleration lemmas [12], similar to the ones used for ranking functions and state invariants. An extended version with more detailed proofs and coefficients for our computed certificates can be found in [18].

2 Preliminaries

We denote the set of natural numbers and reals by $\mathbb{N}$ and $\mathbb{R}$ respectively. Given a number $a \in \mathbb{R}$, we use $\mathbb{R}_{\geq a}$ and $\mathbb{R}_{>a}$ to denote the intervals $[a, \infty[$ and $]a, \infty[$ respectively, and similarly, for any natural number $n \in \mathbb{N}$, we use $\mathbb{N}_{\geq n}$ to denote the set of natural numbers greater than or equal to n. Let $R \subseteq A \times B$ be a relation, and $a \in A$, we use $R(a)$ to denote the set $\{b \mid (a, b) \in R\}$. Given two sets A, B, we use $A \setminus B$ to denote the set containing those elements that are present in A but not in B, and as usual use $A \cup B$ and $A \cap B$ to represent their union and intersection. Given a set $R \subseteq A \times A$ and any $i \in \mathbb{N}_{\geq 1}$, we define R^i recursively as $R^1 = \{(a_1, a_2) \mid (a_1, a_2) \in R\}$ if $i = 1$, and $R^i = \{(a_1, a_2) \mid (a_1, a_3) \in R^{i-1}, \text{ and } (a_3, a_2) \in R\}$. That is R^i is the i-fold self-composition of the relation with itself. Given a relation $R \subseteq A \times A$, its transitive closure is defined as the set $R^+ := \bigcup_{i \in \mathbb{N}_{\geq 1}} R^i$. Finally, we use logical operators $\wedge$, and $\implies$ as shorthands for conjunction, and implication, respectively. Given a pair $(a, b) \in A \times B$, we use $\pi_1(a, b) = a$, and $\pi_2(a, b) = b$ to denote projections of these pairs. We say that a function $f : A \to \mathbb{R}$ is bounded from below (resp. bounded from above) if there exists some $l \in \mathbb{R}$, such that $l \leq f(a)$ for all $a \in A$ (resp. if there exists some $u \in \mathbb{R}$ such that $f(a) \leq u$ for all $a \in A$). A function is bounded if it is bounded from below and above. Similarly, we say a function $f : A \times B \to \mathbb{R}$ is bounded from below (resp. above) in A if, for all $b \in B$ there exist $l \in \mathbb{R}$ (resp. $u \in \mathbb{R}$) such that $l \leq f(a, b)$ ($f(a, b) \leq u$) for all $a \in A$. Given a set A, denote the set of finite and countably infinite sequences of elements in A by sets A^* and A^ω respectively. We use the notation $\boldsymbol{a} = \langle a_1, a_2, \ldots, a_n \rangle \in A^*$ for finite length sequences and $\boldsymbol{s} = \langle a_0, a_1, \ldots \rangle \in A^\omega$ for infinite-sequences. Given a sequence $\boldsymbol{s} = \langle a_0, a_1, \ldots \rangle$ we say that the sequence $\langle b_0, b_1, \ldots \rangle$ is a subsequence of $\boldsymbol{s}$ iff $b_i = a_{j_i}$ where $j_0 \leq j_1 \leq \ldots$ for all $i \in \mathbb{N}$, Let $\mathsf{Inf}(\boldsymbol{s})$ be the set of infinitely often occurring elements in the sequence $\boldsymbol{s} = \langle a_0, a_1, \ldots \rangle$. Given a possibly infinite sequence $\boldsymbol{s} = \langle a_0, a_1, \ldots \rangle$, and two natural numbers $i, j \in \mathbb{N}$ where $i \leq j$, we use $\boldsymbol{s}[i, j]$ to indicate the finite sequence $\langle a_i, a_{i+1}, \ldots, a_j \rangle$, and $\boldsymbol{s}[i, \infty[$ to indicate the infinite sequence $\langle a_i, a_{i+1}, \ldots \rangle$. Finally, we use $\boldsymbol{s}[i]$ to denote the ith element in the sequence $\boldsymbol{s}$ for any $i \in \mathbb{N}$. With a slight abuse of notation, following [23], we say that a relation $R \subseteq A \times A$ is well-founded if there exists no infinite sequence $\langle a_0, a_1, \ldots \rangle$ such that $(a_i, a_{i+1}) \in R$ for all $i \in \mathbb{N}$. In this work, we consider a relation $R \subseteq A \times A$ to be well-founded with respect to a set $B \subseteq A$, if for every infinite sequence $\langle a_0, \ldots \rangle \in A^\omega$, where $(a_i, a_{i+1}) \in R$, there does not exist a subsequence $\langle b_0, b_1, \ldots \rangle \in B^\omega$. A relation $R \subseteq A \times A$ is said to be disjunctively well-founded if it is the finite union of well-founded relations, i.e., $R = \bigcup_{i=1}^{m} R_i$ for some $m \in \mathbb{N}$, where the relations R_i are well-founded.

2.1 Discrete-Time Control Systems

A discrete-time control system (simply, a control system) $\mathfrak{S}$ is a tuple $(\mathcal{X}, \mathcal{X}_0, U, f)$, where $\mathcal{X} \subseteq \mathbb{R}^n$ denotes the state set, $\mathcal{X}_0 \subseteq \mathcal{X}$ denotes a set of initial states, $U \subseteq \mathbb{R}^m$ denotes the set of control inputs, and $f : \mathcal{X} \times U \to \mathcal{X}$ the state transition function. We assume that state set of the systems under consideration are compact. Given a control sequence $\boldsymbol{u} = \langle u_0, u_1, \ldots \rangle \in U^\omega$, and an initial state $x_0 \in \mathcal{X}_0$, the corresponding *state sequence* is the infinite sequence $\boldsymbol{x_u} = \langle x_0, x_1, \ldots \rangle \in \mathcal{X}^\omega$ where and $x_{i+1} = f(x_i, u_i)$, for all $i \in \mathbb{N}$. In this paper, we consider the systems to be controlled with state feedback controllers, i.e., controllers of the form $\kappa : \mathcal{X} \to 2^U$, where for all states $x \in \mathcal{X}$ one may select a choice of input[1] $u \in \kappa(x)$ or controllers with a finite memory, where $\kappa : \mathcal{X} \times \{0, \ldots mem\} \to 2^U$ (cf. Definitions 7 and 2, where we use a counter j as memory). Thus, given an initial state $x_0 \in \mathcal{X}_0$, a state trajectory of the system under controller κ is the infinite sequence $\langle x_0, x_1, \ldots \rangle$ such that $x_{i+1} = f(x_i, u_i)$, where $u_i \in \kappa(x_i)$ for all $i \in \mathbb{N}$. For a finite alphabet set Σ, we associate a labeling function $\mathcal{L} : \mathcal{X} \to \Sigma$ which maps each state of the system to a letter in Σ. This naturally generalizes to mapping a state sequence of the system $\langle x_0, x_1, \ldots \rangle \in \mathcal{X}^\omega$ to a trace or word $w = \langle \mathcal{L}(x_0), \mathcal{L}(x_1), \ldots \rangle \in \Sigma^\omega$. Finally, let $\mathsf{Tr}_{(\mathfrak{S}, \mathcal{L}, \kappa)}$ denote the set of all traces of system $\mathfrak{S}$ under the labeling map $\mathcal{L}$ and controller κ. For convenience, when U is singleton, we use $\mathfrak{S}_{dyn} = (\mathcal{X}, \mathcal{X}_0, f)$, to denote a dynamical system with constant (or no) input, i.e., $f : \mathcal{X} \to \mathcal{X}$ is the state transition function. To motivate the use of closure certificates to synthesize controllers for ω-regular specifications, we first draw an analogy to the use of control barrier certificates to ensure safety.

2.2 Safety Verification and Barrier Certificates

A control system $\mathfrak{S} = (\mathcal{X}, \mathcal{X}_0, U, f)$ is safe with respect to a set of unsafe states $\mathcal{X}_u$, if no state sequence reaches $\mathcal{X}_u$, i.e., for every state sequence $\langle x_0, x_1, \ldots \rangle$, we have $x_i \notin \mathcal{X}_u$ for all $i \in \mathbb{N}$.

Definition 1. *A function $\mathcal{B} : \mathcal{X} \to \mathbb{R}$ is a control barrier certificate for a system $\mathfrak{S}$ with respect to a set of unsafe states $\mathcal{X}_u$ if:*

$$\mathcal{B}(x) \leq 0, \quad \text{for all } x \in \mathcal{X}_0, \tag{1}$$
$$\mathcal{B}(x) > 0, \quad \text{for all } x \in \mathcal{X}_u, \tag{2}$$

and for all $x \in \mathcal{X}$, there exists $u \in U$ such that:

$$\big(\mathcal{B}(x) \leq 0\big) \implies \big(\mathcal{B}(f(x, u)) \leq 0\big) \tag{3}$$

Theorem 1. *Consider a control system $\mathfrak{S} = (\mathcal{X}, \mathcal{X}_0, U, f)$, with a set of unsafe states $\mathcal{X}_u$. The existence of a function $\mathcal{B} : \mathcal{X} \to \mathbb{R}$ satisfying conditions (1)–(3) implies that there exists a controller κ to ensure that the system is safe.*

---

[1] We should add that in the case of ω-regular specifications, we consider controllers that are state feedback over the product of the system and the desired automaton, as well as controllers with a finite amount of memory.

2.3 Büchi and Parity Automata

We now discuss some classes of ω-regular automata to capture our specifications of interest. An ω-regular automaton $\mathcal{A}$ is a tuple $(\Sigma, Q, Q_0, \delta, Acc)$, where Σ denotes a finite alphabet, Q a finite set of states, $Q_0 \subseteq Q$ an initial set of states, $\delta \subseteq Q \times \Sigma \times Q$ the transition relation, and Acc denotes its accepting condition. If the accepting condition is Büchi, then we call that automaton a nondeterministic Büchi automaton (NBA), and we have $Acc \subseteq Q$. An automaton is a nondeterministic parity automaton (NPA) if the accepting condition $Acc : Q \to \{1, \ldots, c\}$ maps each state $q \in Q$ to some color (denoted by a natural number). A run of the automaton $\mathcal{A} = (\Sigma, Q, q_0, \delta, Acc)$ over a word $w = \langle \sigma_0, \sigma_1, \sigma_2 \ldots \rangle \in \Sigma^\omega$, is an infinite sequence of states $\rho = \langle q_0, q_1, q_2, \ldots \rangle \in Q^\omega$ with $q_0 \in Q_0$ and $q_{i+1} \in \delta(q_i, \sigma_i)$. An NBA $\mathcal{A} = (\Sigma, Q, Q_0, \delta, Acc)$ is said to accept a word w, if there exists a run ρ on w where $\mathsf{Inf}(\rho) \cap Acc \neq \emptyset$. An NPA $\mathcal{A} = (\Sigma, Q, Q_0, \delta, Acc)$ is said to accept a word w, if there exists a run ρ on w if we have the minimum priority seen infinitely often in ρ is even (equivalently one may consider maximum priorities, or colors that are odd). We denote the set of words accepted by an automaton $\mathcal{A}$ (the language of the automaton) as $L(\mathcal{A})$. Finally, we say that an automaton is *deterministic* if $|Q_0| = 1$ and for all $q \in Q$, and $\sigma \in \Sigma$, we have $|\delta(q, \sigma)| \leq 1$. We use DBA or DPA to denote deterministic Büchi or deterministic parity automata, respectively. As $|Q_0| = 1$, we use q_0 to denote the initial state for a DPA or DBA in the tuple, i.e., a DPA is of the form $\mathcal{A} = (\Sigma, Q, q_0, \delta, Acc)$. Note that both NBAs and DPAs are closed under complementation [27]: given an NBA (resp. DPA) $\mathcal{A} = (\Sigma, Q, Q_0, \delta, Acc)$, there exists an NBA (resp. DPA) $\mathcal{A}' = (\Sigma, Q', Q'_0, \delta', Acc)$ such that $L(\mathcal{A}') = \overline{L(\mathcal{A})}$.

2.4 Problem Statement

The key problem we consider is as follows: Given a control system $\mathfrak{S} = (\mathcal{X}, \mathcal{X}_0, U, f)$, a deterministic parity automaton $\mathcal{A} = (\Sigma, Q, Q_0, \delta, Acc)$, and a labeling map $\mathcal{L} : \mathcal{X} \to \Sigma$, find a controller $\kappa : \mathcal{X} \times Q \to 2^U$ such that $\mathsf{Tr}_{(\mathfrak{S}, \mathcal{L}, \kappa)} \subseteq L(\mathcal{A})$. To tackle this problem we introduce a notion of control closure certificates.

3 Control Closure Certificates (C³s)

Typical inductive state invariants seek to overapproximate the reachable states of a system. Transition invariants [23], on the other hand, seek to to overapproximate the reachable transitions of a system. Such invariants can be inductively characterized as follows. Given a dynamical system $\mathfrak{S}_{dyn} = (\mathcal{X}, \mathcal{X}_0, f)$, a relation $R \subseteq \mathcal{X} \times \mathcal{X}$ is a transition invariant if:

$$(x, f(x)) \in R \qquad \text{for all } x \in \mathcal{X}, \text{ and}$$
$$((f(x), y) \in R) \implies (x, y) \in R \qquad \text{for all } x, y \in \mathcal{X}.$$

Building on this intuition, the results in [19] considered a notion of closure certificates that act as functional transition invariants. It was demonstrated that such functions can be used to verify ω-regular properties as well as provide simpler templates of functions compared to existing approaches. In the following sections, we describe how closure certificates can be used to design controllers to ensure a set is visited either only finitely often or infinitely often. We then demonstrate how one may combine these conditions to design controllers to satisfy objectives specified by parity automata. We should add that as parity, Rabin, and Streett are equally expressive, one can effectively consider alternate conditions for Rabin or Streett automata. We omit these conditions but note that one might combine certificates in a similar fashion as parity automata. We first start with designing C^3s to synthesize controllers that ensure a given set is visited only finitely often.

3.1 C^3s for Finite Visits

In this section, our objective is to design a controller to ensure that a system visits a set $\mathcal{X}_{VF} \subseteq \mathcal{X}$ only finitely often via C^3s. First, we discuss how one may leverage disjunctive well-foundedness to verify such a condition as follows.

Definition 2. *Consider a dynamical system $\mathfrak{S}_{dyn} = (\mathcal{X}, \mathcal{X}_0, f)$ and a set of states $\mathcal{X}_{VF} \subseteq \mathcal{X}$ that must be visited only finitely often. Let $\mathcal{X}_{VF}$ be partitioned into sets $\mathcal{X}_{VF_1}, \ldots, \mathcal{X}_{VF_p}$, i.e., $\mathcal{X}_{VF} = \bigcup_{0 \leq i \leq p} \mathcal{X}_{VF_i}$ for some $p \in \mathbb{N}$. Then, function $\mathcal{T} : \mathcal{X} \times \mathcal{X} \to \mathbb{R}$, and bounded (from below) functions $\mathcal{V}_i : \mathcal{X} \to \mathbb{R}_{\geq 0}$ for all $0 \leq i \leq p$ are a disjunctive closure certificate if for all $x, y \in \mathcal{X}$:*

$$(\mathcal{T}(x, f(x)) \geq 0), \tag{4}$$

$$(\mathcal{T}(f(x), y) \geq 0) \implies (\mathcal{T}(x, y) \geq 0), \tag{5}$$

and for all $x_0 \in \mathcal{X}_0$, and any $0 \leq i \leq p$, there exists $\xi_i \in \mathbb{R}_{>0}$ such that for all $z, z' \in \mathcal{X}_{VF_i}$, we have:

$$(\mathcal{T}(x_0, z) \geq 0) \wedge (\mathcal{T}(z, z') \geq 0) \implies (\mathcal{V}_i(x_0, z') \leq \mathcal{V}_i(x_0, z) - \xi_i). \tag{6}$$

Lemma 1. *Consider a dynamical system $\mathfrak{S}_{dyn} = (\mathcal{X}, \mathcal{X}_0, f)$ and a set $\mathcal{X}_{VF}$ that must be visited only finitely often. The existence of functions $\mathcal{T}$ and $\mathcal{V}$ as in Definition 4 guarantees that $\mathcal{X}_{VF}$ is visited only finitely often.*

The proof of Lemma 1 can be found in [18, Appendix A].

A direct approach to consider a notion of control closure certificates is to add an existentially quantified control input to conditions (4) and (5) as follows.

Definition 3. *Consider a control system $\mathfrak{S} = (\mathcal{X}, \mathcal{X}_0, U, f)$ and a set of states $\mathcal{X}_{VF}$ that must be visited only finitely often. Let $\mathcal{X}_{VF}$ be partitioned into sets $\mathcal{X}_{VF_1}, \ldots, \mathcal{X}_{VF_p}$, i.e., $\mathcal{X}_{VF} = \bigcup_{0 \leq i \leq p} \mathcal{X}_{VF_i}$ for some $p \in \mathbb{N}$. Then, function $\mathcal{T} : \mathcal{X} \times \mathcal{X} \to \mathbb{R}$, and bounded (from below) functions $\mathcal{V}_i : \mathcal{X} \times \mathcal{X} \to \mathbb{R}_{\geq 0}$ for all*

$0 \leq i \leq p$ are a control closure certificate if for all $x \in \mathcal{X}$ there exists $u \in U$ such that for all $y \in Y$ we have:

$$(\mathcal{T}(x, f(x, u)) \geq 0), \qquad (7)$$
$$(\mathcal{T}(f(x, u), y) \geq 0) \implies (\mathcal{T}(x, y) \geq 0), \qquad (8)$$

and for all $x_0 \in \mathcal{X}_0$, $0 \leq i \leq p$, and for all $z, z' \in \mathcal{X}_{VF_i}$, there exists $\xi_i \in \mathbb{R}_{>0}$ such that:

$$(\mathcal{T}(x_0, z) \geq 0) \wedge (\mathcal{T}(z, z') \geq 0) \implies (\mathcal{V}_i(x_0, z') \leq \mathcal{V}_i(x_0, z) - \xi_i). \qquad (9)$$

Observe that the conditions above rely on two quantifier alternations over the state set and input set (between x and u, and u and y) rather than one. We now show how one can avoid this alternation by considering an alternative paradigm where we define C^{3}s as follows.

Definition 4. *Consider a control system $\mathfrak{S} = (\mathcal{X}, \mathcal{X}_0, U, f)$ and a set of states $\mathcal{X}_{VF}$ that must be visited only finitely often. Let $\mathcal{X}_{VF}$ be partitioned into sets $\mathcal{X}_{VF_1}, \ldots, \mathcal{X}_{VF_p}$, i.e., $\mathcal{X}_{VF} = \bigcup_{0 \leq i \leq p} \mathcal{X}_{VF_i}$ for some $p \in \mathbb{N}$. Then, function $\mathcal{T} : \mathcal{X} \times \mathcal{X} \to \mathbb{R}$, and bounded (from below) functions $\mathcal{V}_i : \mathcal{X} \to \mathbb{R}_{\geq 0}$ for all $0 \leq i \leq p$ are a C^3 if for all $x \in \mathcal{X}$ there exists $u \in U$ such that:*

$$(\mathcal{T}(x, f(x, u)) \geq 0), \qquad (10)$$

and for all $x, y \in \mathcal{X}$, for all $u \in U$, we have:

$$(\mathcal{T}(x, f(x, u)) \geq 0) \implies \Big((\mathcal{T}(f(x, u), y) \geq 0) \implies (\mathcal{T}(x, y) \geq 0)\Big), \qquad (11)$$

and for all $x_0 \in \mathcal{X}_0$, $0 \leq i \leq p$, and for all $z, z' \in \mathcal{X}_{VF_i}$, there exists $\xi_i \in \mathbb{R}_{>0}$ such that:

$$(\mathcal{T}(x_0, z) \geq 0) \wedge (\mathcal{T}(z, z') \geq 0) \implies (\mathcal{V}_i(x_0, z') \leq \mathcal{V}_i(x_0, z) - \xi_i). \qquad (12)$$

Theorem 2. *Consider a control system $\mathfrak{S} = (\mathcal{X}, \mathcal{X}_0, U, f)$ and a set $\mathcal{X}_{VF}$ that must be visited only finitely often. The existence of functions $\mathcal{T}$ and $\mathcal{V}$ as in Definition 4 guarantees that there exists a controller κ to ensure that $\mathcal{X}_{VF}$ is visited only finitely often.*

Proof. We prove Theorem 2 via contradiction. To do so, assume that there exists an initial state $x_0 \in \mathcal{X}_0$, such that for all input sequences $\boldsymbol{u} = \langle u_0, u_1, \ldots \rangle$, we have the corresponding state sequence $\boldsymbol{x_u} = \langle x_0, x_1, \ldots \rangle$ to visit the set $\mathcal{X}_{VF}$ infinitely often. Consider the control input sequence selected such that $\mathcal{T}(x_i, f(x_i, u_i)) \geq 0$ for all $i \in \mathbb{N}$. As condition (10) holds, this is true for any x_i in the state sequence. Following conditions (11) and (10) and via induction, we have $\mathcal{T}(x_0, x_i) \geq 0$ and $\mathcal{T}(x_i, x_j) \geq 0$ for all $i \in \mathbb{N}$, and all $j \geq (i+1)$. Let $\langle y_0, y_1, \ldots \rangle$ be the subsequence that visits $\mathcal{X}_{VF}$ only finitely often. That is the state sequence is of the form $\boldsymbol{x_u} = \langle x_0, x_1, \ldots, y_0, \ldots, y_1, \ldots \rangle$. Via Ramsey's theorem [26], there exists a subsequence $\langle z_0, z_1, \ldots \rangle \in \mathcal{X}_{VF_i}$ that visits $\mathcal{X}_{VF_i}$ infinitely often for some $0 \leq i \leq p$. From the previous results, we know that $\mathcal{T}(x_0, z_i) \geq 0$ and $\mathcal{T}(z_i, z_j) \geq 0$ for all $i \in \mathbb{N}$, and all $j \geq (i+1)$. Let $\mathcal{V}_i^* := \mathcal{V}_i(x_0, z_0)$ and as function $\mathcal{V}_i$ is bounded from below let the lower bound be $\mathcal{V}_i^\dagger$. Following condition (12) and via induction, we have $\mathcal{V}_i(x_0, z_j) \leq \mathcal{V}_i(x_0, z_0) - j\xi_i$ for all $j \in \mathbb{N}_{\geq 1}$. Thus there exists some $j \in \mathbb{N}$, such that $\mathcal{V}_i(z_j) \leq \mathcal{V}_i^* - j\xi_i < \mathcal{V}_i^\dagger$ which is a contradiction. □

Observe that one may consider the set $\mathcal{X}_{VF}$ to not be partitioned, in which case one recovers the standard conditions of well-foundedness as in [19, Definition 3.2]. In the following section, we define C³s to synthesize a controller for a control system $\mathfrak{S} = (\mathcal{X}, \mathcal{X}_0, U, f)$ to show a set is visited infinitely often.

3.2 C³s for Infinite Visits

In this section, our objective is to design a controller to ensure that the system visits a set $\mathcal{X}_{INF} \subseteq \mathcal{X}$ infinitely often via C³s. We discuss a few approaches to do so, and motivate the use of each successive approach by discussing how they tackle issues with respect to the other. Overall, the three approaches we consider are as follows:

1. We first consider a standard ranking function over transition invariants (Definition 5 following [31]) .
2. Unfortunately, a standard ranking function is not disjunctively well-founded. Thus we introduce proofs that are disjunctive (Definition 6) but this relies on lookaheads.
3. We introduce conditions dependent on counters rather than lookaheads in Definition 7, when the number of states that are not in $\mathcal{X}_{INF}$ between successive visits to $\mathcal{X}_{INF}$ increases.
4. When the number of states that are not in $\mathcal{X}_{INF}$ between successive visits to $\mathcal{X}_{INF}$ increases up to a threshold, and then remains bounded, one can use an approach similar to bounded model checking (Definition 8).

An initial approach to design controllers is to modify the notion of closure certificates for recurrence used in [31] by considering the control input as follows.

Definition 5. *Consider a control system $\mathfrak{S} = (\mathcal{X}, \mathcal{X}_0, U, f)$ and a set of states $\mathcal{X}_{INF}$ that must be visited infinitely often. Then a bounded function $\mathcal{T} : \mathcal{X} \times \mathcal{X} \to \mathbb{R}$, is a control closure certificate for recurrence, if there exists $\xi \in \mathbb{R}_{>0}$ such that for all $x \in \mathcal{X}$ there exists $u \in U$ such that:*

$$\big(\mathcal{T}(x, f(x,u)) \geq 0\big), \tag{13}$$

and for all $x, y \in \mathcal{X}$, and for all $u \in U$, we have:

$$\big(\mathcal{T}(x, f(x,u)) \geq 0\big) \implies \Big(\big(\mathcal{T}(f(x,u), y) \geq 0\big) \implies \big(\mathcal{T}(x,y) \geq 0\big)\Big), \tag{14}$$

and for all $x_0 \in \mathcal{X}_0$, $y \in \mathcal{X} \setminus \mathcal{X}_{INF}$, and $u \in U$ we have:

$$\big(\mathcal{T}(x_0, y) \geq 0\big) \wedge \big(\mathcal{T}(y, f(y,u)) \geq 0\big)\big) \implies \big(\mathcal{T}(x_0, f(y,u)) \geq \mathcal{T}(x_0, y) + \xi\big). \tag{15}$$

Theorem 3. *Consider a control system $\mathfrak{S} = (\mathcal{X}, \mathcal{X}_0, U, f)$ and a set $\mathcal{X}_{INF}$ that must be visited infinitely often. The existence of a function $\mathcal{T}$ as in Definition 5 guarantees that there exists a controller κ to ensure that the set $\mathcal{X}_{INF}$ is visited infinitely often.*

We omit the proof of Theorem 3 as it follows in a similar fashion as the proof of [31, Theorem 2]. While C^3s as in Definition 5 provide an effective automated approach to synthesize a controller that ensures a set is visited infinitely often, they unfortunately face two drawbacks. First, there are some systems for which one is unable to satisfy conditions (13)–(15) even though the set $\mathcal{X}_{INF}$ is visited infinitely often. Second, the above does not rely on transition invariants to provide well-founded arguments and thus one may provide a similar argument with other invariants such as barrier certificates as illustrated in [7]. The key benefit of this approach then relies on the expressivity of the transition invariant, compared to the state invariant. To illustrate the first drawback we consider the following Lemma.

Lemma 2. *There exists a dynamical system $\mathfrak{S}_{dis} = (\mathcal{X}, \mathcal{X}_0, f)$, that visits a region $\mathcal{X}_{INF} \subseteq \mathcal{X}$ infinitely often, however one is unable to find a control closure certificate for recurrence as in Definition 5.*

The proof for Lemma 2 is found in [18, Appendix B] but this relies on systems whose state sequence is similar to the one described in Fig. 1. The key issue is that we cannot assume the function $\mathcal{T}$ to be bounded both from above and below. To provide a (relatively)-complete proof rule, one can only assume the function to be bounded in one direction as in [7]. An easy remedy to the above problem is to change condition (15) by considering a function $\mathcal{V}$ to denote a ranking function and ensure it is only bounded from below.

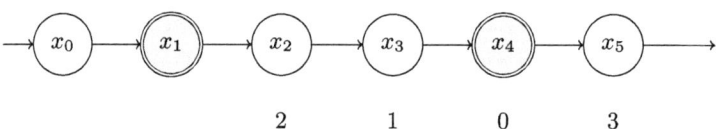

Fig. 1. An infinite chain that visits $\mathcal{X}_{INF}$ infinitely often. However in such a chain, the distance between successive visits to this set increases. We annotate the least possible value of $\mathcal{T}(x_0, x_i)$ below each state x_i in this example, when $\xi = 1$. Observe that the value of $\mathcal{T}(x_0, x_i)$ needs to increase (unboundedly) as the sequence grows.

One benefit of C^3s is that one may still find a bounded function for the above example, even when the distance between successive visits to the set $\mathcal{X}_{INF}$ increases. To do so, we need to modify the conditions in Definition 5 and rely on the following insight. The key issue with the above example is that the value of ξ needs to be fixed. While we cannot arbitrarily change ξ at every step, we note that one can select the value ξ as a parameter for each subsequence between states in $\mathcal{X}_{INF}$. Allowing this value to be a function of the possible state in $\mathcal{X}_{INF}$ that may be visited in the future ensures that one may still find a bounded function to act as a proof of well-foundedness. We rely on this to consider a notion of C³s which allows for the value of ξ to be dependent on a state as defined below.

Definition 6. *Consider a control system $\mathfrak{S} = (\mathcal{X}, \mathcal{X}_0, U, f)$ and a set of states $\mathcal{X}_{INF}$ that must be visited infinitely often. Then, function $\mathcal{T} : \mathcal{X} \times \mathcal{X} \to \mathbb{R}$, and bounded (from below) function $\mathcal{V} : \mathcal{X} \times \mathcal{X} \times \mathcal{X} \to \mathbb{R}_{\geq 0}$ are a control closure certificate, if, for all $x \in \mathcal{X}$ there exists $u \in U$ such that:*

$$\bigl(\mathcal{T}(x, f(x,u)) \geq 0\bigr), \tag{16}$$

and for all $x, y \in \mathcal{X}$, for all $u \in U$, we have:

$$\bigl(\mathcal{T}(x, f(x,u)) \geq 0\bigr) \implies \Bigl(\bigl(\mathcal{T}(f(x,u), y) \geq 0\bigr) \implies \bigl(\mathcal{T}(x,y) \geq 0\bigr)\Bigr), \tag{17}$$

and for all $x_0 \in \mathcal{X}_0$, and all $y \in \mathcal{X} \setminus \mathcal{X}_{INF}$, there exists $w \in \mathcal{X}_{INF}$ and $\xi \in \mathbb{R}_{>0}$, such that for all $z, z' \in \mathcal{X} \setminus \mathcal{X}_{INF}$ we have:

$$\bigl(\mathcal{T}(x_0, y) \geq 0\bigr) \wedge \bigl(\mathcal{T}(y, z) \geq 0\bigr) \wedge \bigl(\mathcal{T}(z, z') \geq 0\bigr) \implies$$
$$\bigl(\mathcal{V}(y, z', w) \leq \mathcal{V}(y, z, w) - \xi\bigr). \tag{18}$$

Note, however, that such a strategy introduces an additional quantifier alternation in condition (18) between y and w, and w and z, respectively and that the positive real ξ depends on the universally quantified value y. Intuitively, one seeks to select the value of ξ such that state w that is reachable from both states z, and z' with a ranking function argument that decreases with ξ. Second, we need to consider every state z, and z' even if there might be accepting states that are visited in between. Returning to the example from Fig. 1, one needs to provide a ranking function argument between states x_5 and x_3, even though there exists an accepting state between them. Typically, existing approaches such as in [2,6] avoid this issue by allowing for the ranking function to increase over the accepting states. The issue one faces is that in examples such as in Fig. 1 where one jumps to, and out of, the set $\mathcal{X}_{INF}$ without significant dwell time, one require values of function $\mathcal{V}$ to change significantly. Such an increase condition is not immediately obvious for closure certificates without considering one step successors as in Definition 5. Due to these challenges, we consider another set of conditions for control closure certificates. Given a state sequence of a system that visits $\mathcal{X}_{INF}$ infinitely often, consider a partitioning of the state sequence into subsequences in between successive visits. For example, consider the infinite chain in Fig. 1, and consider the subsequences $\langle x_0, x_1 \rangle$, $\langle x_2, x_3, x_4 \rangle$, and so on. Observe that if one were able to find ranking functions for each of these subsequences, then one is able to provide a proof that the system visits the set $\mathcal{X}_{INF}$ infinitely often. Formally, consider the control system defined as $\hat{\mathfrak{S}} = \{\hat{\mathcal{X}}, \hat{\mathcal{X}}_0, U, \hat{f}\}$, where $\hat{\mathcal{X}} = \mathcal{X} \times \mathbb{R}$ denotes the set of states, $\hat{\mathcal{X}}_0 = \mathcal{X}_0 \times \{0\}$ denotes the set of initial states, and the transition function $\hat{f}((x,j), u) = \{(f(x,u), k)\}$, where $k = j+1$

if $x \in \mathcal{X}_{INF}$ and $k = j$ otherwise[2]. An illustration of this construction on the infinite sequence in Fig. 1 can be found in [18, Appendix C]. Intuitively, this modified system consists of the states of original system appended with a counter. The value of this counter increments every time one visits the set $\mathcal{X}_{INF}$. Then one may find different ranking function $\mathcal{V}_j$ that show states in $\mathcal{X} \setminus \mathcal{X}_{INF}$ are visited only finitely often for every counter value j. In the next definition, we consider how one may find certificates over this modified system to ensure that the set $\mathcal{X}_{INF}$ is visited infinitely often.

Definition 7. *Consider a control system* $\mathfrak{S} = (\mathcal{X}, \mathcal{X}_0, U, f)$ *and a set of states* $\mathcal{X}_{INF}$ *that must be visited infinitely often. Then, function* $\mathcal{T} : (\mathcal{X} \times \mathbb{R}) \times (\mathcal{X} \times \mathbb{R}) \to \mathbb{R}$, *and a function* $\mathcal{V} : \mathcal{X} \times \mathcal{X} \times \mathbb{R} \to \mathbb{R}_{\geq 0}$ *that is bounded from below in* $\mathcal{X} \times \mathcal{X}$ *for every* $\mathbb{R}$, *are a control closure certificate, if for all* $x \in \mathcal{X}$, *there exists* $u \in U$ *such that for all* $j \in \mathbb{R}$:

$$\bigl(\mathcal{T}((x,j), (f(x,u), k)) \geq 0\bigr), \tag{19}$$

where $k = j+1$ *if* $x \in \mathcal{X}_{INF}$, *and* $k = j$ *otherwise. And for all* $x, y \in \mathcal{X}$, $j \in \mathbb{R}$, $\ell \geq (j+1)$, *and for all* $u \in U$, *we have:*

$$\bigl(\mathcal{T}((x,j), (f(x,u), k)) \geq 0\bigr) \implies \\ \Bigl(\bigl(\mathcal{T}((f(x,u), k), (y, \ell)) \geq 0\bigr) \implies \bigl(\mathcal{T}((x,j), (y, \ell)) \geq 0\bigr)\Bigr), \tag{20}$$

where $k = j+1$ *if* $x \in \mathcal{X}_{INF}$, *and* $k = j$ *otherwise. And for all* $j \in \mathbb{R}$, *there exists* $\xi_j \in \mathbb{R}_{>0}$ *such that for all* $x_0 \in \mathcal{X}_0$, *and for all* $z, z' \in \mathcal{X} \setminus \mathcal{X}_{INF}$, *we have:*

$$\bigl(\mathcal{T}((x_0, 0), (z, j)) \geq 0\bigr) \wedge \bigl(\mathcal{T}((z, j), (z', j)) \geq 0\bigr) \implies \\ \bigl(\mathcal{V}(x_0, z', j) \leq \mathcal{V}(x_0, z, j) - \xi_j\bigr). \tag{21}$$

Theorem 4. *Consider a control system* $\mathfrak{S} = (\mathcal{X}, \mathcal{X}_0, U, f)$ *and a set* $\mathcal{X}_{INF}$ *that must be visited infinitely often. The existence of functions* $\mathcal{T}$ *and* $\mathcal{V}$ *as in Definition 7 guarantees that there exists a controller* κ *to ensure that* $\mathcal{X}_{INF}$ *is visited infinitely often.*

The proof of Theorem 4 can be found in [18, Appendix D]. Observe that while the above definition still has a quantifier alternation, the existential quantifier is no longer over the states of the system or the set of control inputs, but rather over the selection of the real value ξ for each choice of counter value j. Intuitively, the goal of the function $\mathcal{V}$ is to prove that only finitely many states are visited with a counter value j for any real value $j \in \mathbb{R}$. Observe that each of these proofs for the counter value j corresponds to a proof where the goal is to show a set of states is visited only finitely often. Thus, one may adapt the approach considered in Definition 4 to provide disjunctive well-founded proofs for each counter value. Here, we may replace condition (21) by combining it with condition (12). We

---

[2] This construction is similar to the counter construction to degeneralize a generalized Büchi automaton [28], except here we consider the counter to be unbounded.

describe these conditions in [18, Appendix E]. To avoid considering all real values for the counter j, one may adopt a strategy similar to bounded model checking where we first fix a bound (say $j_{\max}$) on the value j. Then we consider piecewise functions for conditions (19) to (21) for all $0 \leq j \leq j_{\max}$. The benefit of this approach lies in the fact that the control input u can now depend on the value of the counter j. If we changed the alternation in condition (19), then we would need an infinite memory policy as the value u could depend on the value of the unbounded counter j. In particular, if we are able to show that we have that $\mathcal{T}((x_0,0),(z,j_{\max}+1)) \geq 0 \implies \mathcal{T}((x_0,0),(z,j_{\max})) \geq 0$ for any $x_0 \in \mathcal{X}_0$ and $z \in \mathcal{X}$, we note that one may use the same function $\mathcal{V}_{j_{\max}}$ and the same control inputs u as that of counter $j_{\max}$. In such a case, the set of states z that satisfy the above conditions represent an overapproximation of the states that can be reached infinitely often. In particular, this provides guarantees for systems which see both accepting and non-accepting states infinitely often. We described the conditions for such a certificate below.

Definition 8. *Consider a control system $\mathfrak{S} = (\mathcal{X}, \mathcal{X}_0, U, f)$, a set of states $\mathcal{X}_{INF}$ that must be visited infinitely often and $j_{\max} \in \mathbb{N}$ denote a bound on the counter value. Then, functions $\mathcal{T}_{j,\ell} : \mathcal{X} \times \mathcal{X} \to \mathbb{R}$, and functions $\mathcal{V}_j : \mathcal{X} \times \mathcal{X} \to \mathbb{R}_{\geq 0}$ for all $0 \leq j \leq \ell \leq j_{\max}$, that are bounded from below in $\mathcal{X} \times \mathcal{X}$, constitute a control closure certificate, if for all $0 \leq j \leq j_{\max}$, and for all $x \in \mathcal{X}$, there exists $u \in U$ such that:*

$$\bigl(\mathcal{T}_{j,k}(x, f(x,u)) \geq 0\bigr), \tag{22}$$

where $k = j+1$ if $x \in \mathcal{X}_{INF}$, and $k = j$ otherwise. And for all $0 \leq j < \ell \leq (j_{\max}+1)$, and for all $x, y \in \mathcal{X}$, and for all $u \in U$, we have:

$$\bigl(\mathcal{T}_{j,k}(x, f(x,u))) \geq 0\bigr) \implies \Bigl(\bigl(\mathcal{T}_{k,\ell}(f(x,u), y) \geq 0\bigr) \implies \bigl(\mathcal{T}_{j,\ell}(x,y) \geq 0\bigr)\Bigr), \tag{23}$$

where $k = (j+1)$ if $x \in \mathcal{X}_{INF}$, and $k = j$ otherwise. And for all $x_0 \in \mathcal{X}_0$, and $z, z' \in \mathcal{X}$ we have:

$$\bigl(\mathcal{T}_{0,(j_{\max}+1)}(x_0,z)) \geq 0\bigr) \implies \bigl(\mathcal{T}_{0,j_{\max}}(x_0,z) \geq 0\bigr), \text{ and} \tag{24}$$

And for all $0 \leq j \leq j_{\max}$, there exists $\xi_j \in \mathbb{R}_{>0}$ such that for all $x_0 \in \mathcal{X}_0$, for all $z, z' \in \mathcal{X} \setminus \mathcal{X}_{INF}$, we have:

$$\bigl(\mathcal{T}_{0,j}(x_0,z) \geq 0\bigr) \wedge \bigl(\mathcal{T}_{j,j}(z,z') \geq 0\bigr) \implies \bigl(\mathcal{V}_j(x_0, z') \leq \mathcal{V}_j(x_0, z) - \xi_j\bigr). \tag{25}$$

Theorem 5. *Consider a control system $\mathfrak{S} = (\mathcal{X}, \mathcal{X}_0, U, f)$, a set $\mathcal{X}_{INF}$ that must be visited infinitely often and $j_{\max} \in \mathbb{N}$ denote a bound on the counter value. The existence of functions $\mathcal{T}_{j,\ell}$ and $\mathcal{V}_j$ for all $0 \leq i, j \leq (j_{\max}+1)$ as in Definition 8 guarantees that there exists a controller κ to ensure that $\mathcal{X}_{INF}$ is visited infinitely often.*

Proof. Consider the finite memory control strategy $\kappa : \mathcal{X} \times \{0, \ldots, j_{\max}\}$ such that we use controller $\kappa(x_i, j)$ for any $j \leq j_{\max}$, if j states in the set $\mathcal{X}_{INF}$

are visited, and $\kappa(x_i, j_{max})$ otherwise. Let $\kappa(x_i, j) = \{u \mid \mathcal{T}_{j,k}(x_i, f(x_i, u)) \geq 0\}$, where $k = j+1$ if $x_i \in \mathcal{X}_{VF}$ and $k = j$ otherwise, when $j \leq j_{max}$. Assume that the system visits the set $\mathcal{X}_{INF}$ only finitely often under this control strategy. That is, let the corresponding sequence be $\boldsymbol{x} = \langle x_0, x_1, \ldots \rangle$. Let this correspond to the sequence $\hat{\boldsymbol{x}} = \langle (x_0, \ell_0), (x_1, \ell_1), \ldots \rangle$ in the system $\hat{\mathfrak{S}}$, where $x_{i+1} = \kappa(x_i, \ell_i)$, and $\ell_{i+1} = \ell_i + 1$ if $x_i \in \mathcal{X}_{INF}$ and $\ell_{i+1} = \ell_i$ otherwise. Observe that $\ell_0 = 0$. Thus there exists some $k \in \mathbb{N}$ such that for all $i \geq k$, we have $\ell_i = \ell_k$. Following the results of Theorems 2 and 4, we cannot have $k \leq j_{max}$. Let $k \geq (j_{max}+1)$, and consider state x_v such that $\ell_v = j_{max}$, and $\ell_{v+1} = (j_{max}+1)$. Following condition (22), we must have $\mathcal{T}_{\ell_{(v-1)}, \ell_v}(x_{v-1}, x_v) \geq 0$ and $\mathcal{T}_{\ell_v, \ell_{(j_{max}+1)}}(x_v, x_{v+1}) \geq 0$. Thus via condition (23), we must have $\mathcal{T}_{\ell_{(v-1)}, (j_{max}+1)}(x_{v-1}, x_{v+1}) \geq 0$. Inducting on conditions (22) and (23), we get $\mathcal{T}_{0, (j_{max}+1)}(x_0, x_{v+1}) \geq 0$ and so following condition (24), we must have $\mathcal{T}_{0, j_{max}}(x_0, x_{v+1}) \geq 0$. Observe that one may select a control input u as in condition (22) to ensure $\mathcal{T}_{j_{max}, j_{max}+1}(x_{v+1}, x_{v+2})$, and thus we have an inductive argument that for any $r \in \mathbb{N}_{\geq 1}$, we have $\mathcal{T}_{0, j_{max}}(x_0, x_{v+r}) \geq 0$. Thus, we observe that the antecedent of condition (25) holds and so the ranking function must decrease. In a similar manner as earlier proofs we can conclude that this creates a contradiction.

Now, we describe how one may use the above conditions to design controllers against ω-regular specifications.

3.3 C^3s for ω-Regular Specifications

To synthesize controllers against ω-regular specifications via C^3s, let the DPA $\mathcal{A} = (\Sigma, Q, q_0, \delta, Acc)$ denote the desired specification and the set $\{1, \ldots, c\}$ denote the set of priorities or colors, i.e., $Acc : Q \to \{1, \ldots c\}$. Then the system $\mathfrak{S}$ under labeling map $\mathcal{L}$ and controller κ satisfies the ω-regular specification if $\text{Tr}_{(\mathfrak{S}, \mathcal{L}, \kappa)} \subseteq L(\mathcal{A})$, i.e., every trace of the system under the labeling map and controller κ is accepted by $\mathcal{A}$. To synthesize controller κ, we first construct the product $\mathfrak{S} \otimes \mathcal{A} = (\mathcal{X}', \mathcal{X}'_0, U, f')$ of the system $\mathfrak{S} = (\mathcal{X}, \mathcal{X}_0, U, f)$ with the DPA $\mathcal{A}$ representing the the specification, where $\mathcal{X}' = \mathcal{X} \times Q$ indicates the state set, and $\mathcal{X}'_0 = \mathcal{X}_0 \times q_0$ are the initial set of states. We define the state transition relation $f' : \mathcal{X} \times Q \times U \to \mathcal{X} \times Q$ as :

$$f'((x, q_i), u) = \{(f(x, u), q_j) \mid q_j \in \delta(q_i, \mathcal{L}(x))\}.$$

We note that ensuring the specification is satisfied is equivalent to showing that the minimum priority seen infinitely often is even. That is, we need to show that for every sequence $\boldsymbol{s}' = \langle x'_0, x'_1, \ldots \rangle$, under controller κ, if $x'_j = (x_j, q_i)$ where $Acc(q_i)$ is odd, either:

1. There exists some $\ell_1 \in \mathbb{N}$ such that for all $\ell_2 \geq \ell_1$, we have $\pi_2(x'_{\ell_2}) \neq q_i$, or
2. There exists some q_j, where $Acc(q_j)$ is even, $Acc(q_j) < Acc(q_i)$, and for all $\ell_1 \in \mathbb{N}$, there exists $\ell_2 \geq \ell_1$, such that we have $\pi_2(x'_{\ell_2}) = q_J$.

These correspond to showing that either we see automata states with priority $Acc(q_j)$ only finitely often or we see some automaton state q_i which as an even priority that is less than $Acc(q_j)$ infinitely often. We observe that the first two conditions for building invariants are the same for all the conditions. To do so, let us assume sets $\mathcal{X}_{VF}$ and $\mathcal{X}_{INF}$ are sets that must be visited finitely often and infinitely often. Then one may search for certificates to prove both of the above as follows:

Definition 9. *Consider a control system $\mathfrak{S} = (\mathcal{X}, \mathcal{X}_0, U, f)$, a set of states $\mathcal{X}_{VF} = \bigcup_{1 \leq r \leq p} \mathcal{X}_{VF_r}$ that must be visited finitely often, and a set of states $\mathcal{X}_{INF}$ that must be visited infinitely often. Then, function $\mathcal{T}_{i,j} : \mathcal{X} \times \mathcal{X} \to \mathbb{R}$, functions $\mathcal{Z}_r : \mathcal{X} \times \mathcal{X} \to \mathbb{R}_{\geq 0}$ that are bounded from below, and functions $\mathcal{V}_i : \mathcal{X} \times \mathcal{X} \to \mathbb{R}_{\geq 0}$ that are bounded from below and defined for all $1 \leq r \leq p$, and all $0 \leq i, j \leq j_{\max}$ are a control closure certificate, if for all $x \in \mathcal{X}$, and all $0 \leq j \leq j_{\max}$, there exists $u \in U$ such that:*

$$\bigl(\mathcal{T}_{j,k}(x, f(x,u)) \geq 0\bigr), \tag{26}$$

where $k = j+1$ if $x \in \mathcal{X}_{INF}$, and $k = j$ otherwise. And for all $x, y \in \mathcal{X}$, and all $0 \leq j < \ell \leq (j+1)$, and for all $u \in U$, we have:

$$\bigl(\mathcal{T}_{j,k}(x, f(x,u))) \geq 0\bigr) \implies \Bigl(\bigl(\mathcal{T}_{k,\ell}((f(x,u), y) \geq 0\bigr) \implies \bigl(\mathcal{T}_{j,\ell}(x, y) \geq 0\bigr)\Bigr), \tag{27}$$

where $k = j+1$ if $x \in \mathcal{X}_{INF}$, and $k = j$ otherwise. And for all $x_0 \in \mathcal{X}_0$, and $z, z' \in \mathcal{X}$ we have:

$$\bigl(\mathcal{T}_{0,(j_{\max}+1)}(x_0, z)) \geq 0\bigr) \implies \bigl(\mathcal{T}_{0,j_{\max}}(x_0, z) \geq 0\bigr). \tag{28}$$

And for all $x_0 \in \mathcal{X}_0$, and all $1 \leq r \leq p$, and all $0 \leq \ell_1 \leq \ell_2 \leq (j_{\max}+1)$, there exists $\xi_r \in \mathbb{R}_{>0}$ such that for all $z, z' \in \mathcal{X}_{VF_r}$,:

$$\bigl(\mathcal{T}_{0,\ell_1}(x_0, z) \geq 0\bigr) \wedge \bigl(\mathcal{T}_{\ell_1,\ell_2}(z, z') \geq 0\bigr) \implies \bigl(\mathcal{Z}_r(x_0, z') \leq \mathcal{Z}_r(x_0, z) - \xi_r\bigr). \tag{29}$$

And for all $0 \leq j \leq j_{\max}$, there exists $\xi_j \in \mathbb{R}_{>0}$ such that for all $x_0 \in \mathcal{X}_0$, for all $z, z' \in \mathcal{X} \setminus \mathcal{X}_{INF}$, we have:

$$\bigl(\mathcal{T}_{0,j}(x_0, z) \geq 0\bigr) \wedge \bigl(\mathcal{T}_{j,j}(z, z')\bigr) \geq 0\bigr) \implies \bigl(\mathcal{V}_j(x_0, z') \leq \mathcal{V}_j(x_0, z) - \xi_j\bigr). \tag{30}$$

Theorem 6. *Consider a control system $\mathfrak{S} = (\mathcal{X}, \mathcal{X}_0, U, f)$ and a set $\mathcal{X}_{INF}$ that must be visited infinitely often and a set $\mathcal{X}_{VF} = \bigcup_{1 \leq i \leq r} \mathcal{X}_{VF_r}$ that must be visited only finitely often. Let $j_{\max} \in \mathbb{N}$ denote a threshold for the counter value. Then, the existence of functions $\mathcal{T}_{j,\ell}$, $\mathcal{V}_j$, and $\mathcal{Z}_r$ for all $1 \leq i \leq r$, and $0 \leq j, \ell \leq (j_{\max}+1)$ as in Definition 9 guarantees that there exists a controller κ to ensure that $\mathcal{X}_{INF}$ is visited infinitely often and $\mathcal{X}_{VF}$ only finitely often.*

The proof of Theorem 6 follows from the proof of Theorem 2 and Theorem 5. Note that one may equivalently consider other conditions for finite and infinite visits as discussed earlier. We now show how one may use certificates as in Definition 9 to design controllers for ω-regular specifications. First, we search for a C^3 over $\mathfrak{S} \otimes \mathcal{A}$ to ensure that the set $\mathcal{X}'_{VF} = \mathcal{X} \times \{q_i \mid Acc(q_i) = 1\}$ is visited only finitely often. If we fail to do so, then we do not have an even priority that is smaller than 1 as the set of colors we consider are $\{1, \ldots c\}$ and thus we need to change the template of certificates. If we are successful, we then try to find a certificate to ensure that the set $\mathcal{X}'_{VF} = \mathcal{X} \times \{q_i \mid Acc(q_i) = 1\} \cup \mathcal{X} \times \{q_i \mid Acc(q_i) = 3\}$ is visited only finitely often. If we fail to do so we instead seek to find two certificates to show that $\mathfrak{S} \otimes \mathcal{A}$ visits $\mathcal{X}'_{VF} = \mathcal{X} \times \{q_i \mid Acc(q_i) = 1\}$ only finitely often and visits the set $\mathcal{X}'_{INF} = \mathcal{X} \times \{q_i \mid Acc(q_i) = 2\}$ infinitely often. If we succeed, we continue till we fail for some state with odd parity q_j, we then set $\mathcal{X}_{INF} = \mathcal{X}_{INF} \cup \mathcal{X} \times \{q_\ell\}$ where $Acc(q_\ell) < Acc(q_j)$ and ℓ is even. We continue this process until we either find a certificate satisfying the above conditions for all odd automaton states, or we conclude that we do not have a proof with the desired template. We should note that we need to search independently over these different combinations of priorities as we consider different sets for $\mathcal{X}_{INF}$ and $\mathcal{X}_{VF}$ respectively.

4 Computation of C^{3}s

To find control closure certificates, we make use of a semidefinite programming approach [22] via sum-of-squares (SOS) similar to the automated search for standard barrier certificates [24]. A set $A \subseteq \mathbb{R}^n$ is semi-algebraic if it can be defined with the help of a vector of polynomial inequalities $h(x)$ as $A = \{x \mid h(x) \geq 0\}$, where the inequalities is interpreted component-wise.

To adopt an SOS approach to find C^{3}s, we consider the sets $\mathcal{X}$, $\mathcal{X}_0$, $\mathcal{X}_{VF}$, $\mathcal{X}_{INF}$, $\mathcal{X} \setminus \mathcal{X}_{INF}$ and U to be semi-algebraic sets defined with the help of vectors of polynomial inequalities g, g_0, g_{VF}, g_{INF}, g_{CINF}, and g_u, respectively. When dealing with finite partitions such as in condition (10), we also assume that each partition $\mathcal{X}_{VF_i}$ is represented by polynomial inequalities g_{VF_i} respectively. As these sets are semi-algebraic, we know that sets $\mathcal{X} \times \mathcal{X} \times U$, $\mathcal{X}_0 \times \mathcal{X}$, $\mathcal{X}_0 \times \mathcal{X}_{VF_i} \times \mathcal{X}_{VF_i}$ and $\mathcal{X}_0 \times (\mathcal{X} \setminus \mathcal{X}_{INF}) \times (\mathcal{X} \setminus \mathcal{X}_{INF})$ are semi-algebraic as well, with their corresponding vectors denoted by g_A, g_B, $g_{C,i}$ and g_D respectively. Furthermore, we assume that the function f is polynomial. To deal with constraints with implications, we rewrite them in the form of sufficient conditions. We strengthen implication-based conditions into ones that are compatible with SOS optimization via S-procedure [32]. For example, condition (8) can be rewritten as $\mathcal{T}(x,y) - \tau \mathcal{T}(f(x,u),y) \geq 0$, where $\tau \in \mathbb{R}_{>0}$. Observe that if the above holds, then so does condition (8). Observe that if one satisfies this inequality, then condition (8) holds. To find C^{3}s, we fix the template to be a linear combination of user-defined basis functions of the form: $\mathcal{T}(x,y) = \mathbf{c}_\mathcal{T}^T \mathbf{b}(x,y) = \sum_{i=1}^n c_i b_i(x,y)$, $\mathcal{V}(x) = \mathbf{c}_\mathcal{V}^T \mathbf{b}(x) = \sum_{m=1}^n \bar{c}_m b_m(x)$, and $\mathcal{Z}_i(x) = \mathbf{c}_{\mathcal{Z},i}^T \mathbf{b}(x) = \sum_{m=1}^n \underline{c}_{m,i} b_m(x)$, where functions $b_i(x,y)$ are monomials over the state variables x and y, and $b_m(x)$ are monomials over the state variable x, and $c_1, \ldots, c_n$, $\bar{c}_1, \ldots, \bar{c}_n$, and $\underline{c}_{1,i}, \ldots, \underline{c}_{n,i}$ are real coefficients. We then restrict the input set $U_d = \{u_1, \ldots, u_m\}$ to consist of a set of finite inputs. One can then rewrite condition (10) as $\sum_{i=1}^{m} \mu_i \mathcal{T}(x, f(x, u_i)) \geq 0$ where $\mu_i \in \mathbb{R}_{>0}$. Observe that satisfying this implies condition (10). Now we illustrate how one can encode conditions (26)-(30) of Definition 9 into SOS program. To ensure functions $\mathcal{V}_j$ and $\mathcal{Z}_r$ are bounded from below, we assume them to be SOS over the relevant sets. One can reduce the search for a C³ to showing that the following polynomials are SOS for all states $x, y \in \mathcal{X}$, $x_0 \in \mathcal{X}_0$, $w_r, w'_r \in \mathcal{X}_{VF_r}$ for any $0 \leq r \leq p$, and all $z, z' \in \mathcal{X} \setminus \mathcal{X}_{INF}$, and all inputs $u \in U$, and finite inputs $u_t \in U_d$, and constants $j, \ell_1 \in \{1, \cdots, j_{max}\}$, $\ell \geq (j+1)$, $\ell_2 \geq (\ell_1 + 1)$, where $k = (j+1)$ if $x \in \mathcal{X}_{INF}$, and $k = j$ otherwise:

$$\mathcal{T}_{j,k}(x, f(x, u_m)) + \sum_{t=1}^{m-1} \left(\mu_t \mathcal{T}_{j,k}(x, f(x, u_t))\right) - \lambda_0^T(x)g(x), \tag{31}$$

$$\mathcal{T}_{j,\ell}(x, y) - \tau_1 \mathcal{T}_{k,\ell}(f(x, u), y) - \tau_2 \mathcal{T}_{j,k}(x, f(x, u)) - \lambda_A^T(x, y, u)g_A(x, y, u), \tag{32}$$

$$\mathcal{T}_{0, j_{\max}}(x_0, y) - \tau_3(\mathcal{T}_{0, (j_{\max}+1)}(x_0, y)) - \lambda_B^T(x_0, y)g_B(x_0, y), \tag{33}$$

$$\mathcal{Z}_r(x) - \lambda_1^T(x)g(x), \tag{34}$$

$$\mathcal{Z}_r(w_r) - \mathcal{Z}_r(w'_r) - \tau_4 \mathcal{T}_{0, \ell_1}(x_0, w_r) - \tau_5 \mathcal{T}_{\ell_1, \ell_2}(w_r, w'_r) - \xi_i$$
$$- \lambda_{C,r}^T(x_0, w_r, w'_r)g_{C,r}(x_0, w_r, w'_r), \tag{35}$$

$$\mathcal{V}_j(x) - \lambda_{2,j}^T(x)g(x), \tag{36}$$

$$\mathcal{V}_j(z) - \mathcal{V}_j(z') - \tau_6 \mathcal{T}_{0,j}(x_0, z) - \tau_7 \mathcal{T}_{j,j}(z, z') - \xi_D - \lambda_D^T(x_0, z, z')g_D(x_0, z, z'), \tag{37}$$

where $\mu_i, \tau_i, \xi_i \in \mathbb{R}_{>0}$ are some positive values, and the multipliers $\lambda_A, \lambda_B, \lambda_{C,r}, \lambda_D$ are arbitrary sum-of-squares polynomials in their respective state variables over the regions $\mathcal{X} \times \mathcal{X} \times U$, $\mathcal{X}_0 \times \mathcal{X}$, $\mathcal{X}_0 \times \mathcal{X}_{VF_r} \times \mathcal{X}_{VF_r}$, and $\mathcal{X}_0 \times (\mathcal{X} \setminus \mathcal{X}_{INF}) \times (\mathcal{X} \setminus \mathcal{X}_{INF})$, respectively. Similarly, λ_0, λ_1, and $\lambda_{2,j}$ are arbitrary sum-of-squares polynomials over the region $\mathcal{X}$. For ω-regular specifications, one can take the product of the system with the corresponding DPA and employ the techniques discussed in [19, Section 4.2]. We omit these details due to lack of space, and for simpler readability, but we use these in our case studies for the next section.

5 Case Studies

We experimentally demonstrate the utility of C³s on a control dynamical system that describes an instance of Hopf bifurcation that under certain control inputs can either exhibit periodic orbits or die out over time [14]. Wind-induced oscillations for an overhead line [20] are an example of such system where the states x_1 and x_2 represent the displacement of the suspended conductor from its equilibrium position. The control input is used to regulate the value of these states so that they stay within a predetermined bound, which is denoted by the set of states that should be visited infinitely often. If the system were to start outside the bounds, a control input will be applied to push the states to be within bounds. The set of states outside the bounds (or its subset) is then designated as a set that should be visited only finitely often. The definition of our system is given below. Given a state $x = x(t)$, we use x' to denote $x(t+1)$.

$$x_1' = x_1 + T(ux_1 - x_2 - x_1(x_1^2 + x_2^2)), \quad (38)$$
$$x_2' = x_2 + T(x_1 - ux_2 - x_2(x_1^2 + x_2^2)), \quad (39)$$

where $T = 0.1s$ is the sampling time, $x^T = [x_1, x_2]$ is the state of the system, and u is the control input. We first start with a linear function in two variables and in a single variable as our parametric template for $\mathcal{T}(x,y)$ and $\mathcal{V}(x)$ (or $\mathcal{Z}(x)$), respectively. We increase the degree of both template functions until we find the polynomials satisfying the C^3 conditions for finite visit only, infinite visit only and both finite and infinite visits. We continue to increment the degree of the polynomial template up to $degree_{max} = 4$, above which the SOS fails to compute due to device memory constraints. To solve these SOS constraints, we make use of JuMP [15] and TSSOS [30] in Julia. Our code is available online.[3]

5.1 Without DPA

For the system given above, the state set, the set of initial states, finite visit states, infinite visit states, and the input set are given by $\mathcal{X} = [-0.75, 1] \times [-0.75, 0.75]$, $\mathcal{X}_0 = [0.8, 1] \times [-0.2, 0.2]$, $\mathcal{X}_{VF} = [0.8, 1] \times [0, 0.75]$, $\mathcal{X}_{INF} = [-0.75, 0.75]^2$, and $U = [-3, 0.5]$, respectively. Using constants $\mu_i = 0.5$, $\tau_i = 1$ and $\xi_i = 0.1$, we were able to obtain cubic polynomial C^3s. Figure 2 displays sample trajectories generated for the system along with the relevant state sets under consideration. The successful search results of our SOS program are included in [18, Appendix F.1].

5.2 With DPA

To demonstrate our approach for designing controllers for DPA objectives, we consider the DPA $\mathcal{A} = (\Sigma, Q, Q_0, \delta, Acc)$ in Fig. 3, where $\Sigma = \{a, b\}$ $Q = q_1, q_2, q_3$, $Q_0 = q_1$, $Acc : Q \to \{1, \ldots, 4\}$ such that $Acc(q_1) = 1$, $Acc(q_2) = 3$, and $Acc(q_3) = 4$. The specification is to show that eventually, the system only witnesses states with label a. This specification cannot be captured via a DBA [29]. To find a C^3, we consider the product of the system with the DPA. Here q_1 is the initial state, q_2 is the state that must be visited only finitely often, and q_3 only infinitely often. We consider a control system $\mathfrak{S} = (\mathcal{X}, \mathcal{X}_0, U, f)$ where $\mathcal{X} = [-0.75, 1] \times [0, 0.75]$, $\mathcal{X}_0 = [0.8, 1] \times [0, 0.2]$, and $U = [-3, 0.5]$. We consider a labeling map $\mathcal{L} : \mathcal{X} \to \Sigma$, such that $\mathcal{L}(x) = a$ if $x \in \mathcal{X}_{INF} = [-0.75, 0.75] \times [0, 0.75]$, and $\mathcal{L}(x) = b$ if $x \in \mathcal{X}_{VF} = [0.75, 1] \times [0, 0.75]$. The dynamic f is given in equations (38)–(39). Using constants $\mu_i = 0.5$, $\tau_i = 1$ and $\xi_i = 0.01$, we were able to obtain cubic polynomial C^3s. The successful search results of our SOS program are included in [18, Appendix F.2].

---

[3] [Online]. Available: https://github.com/maoumer/CCC.

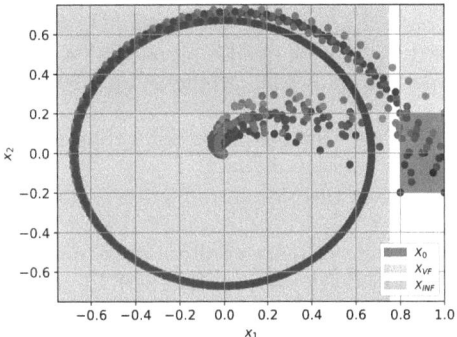

Fig. 2. Sample trajectories of the system along with relevant regions shaded.

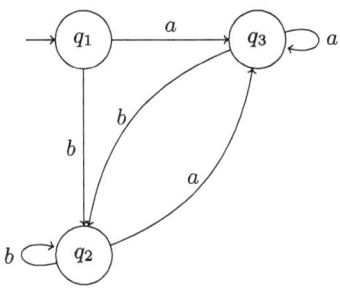

Fig. 3. A DPA $\mathcal{A}$ representing the LTL formula $\mathsf{FG}a$.

6 Conclusion

We introduced a notion of control closure certificates to synthesize controllers against ω-regular specifications. We discussed different conditions to show a set is visited finitely and infinitely often and demonstrated how one may combine them for ω-regular specifications and demonstrated their efficacy over relevant case studies. As future work, we plan to investigate their use in verifying more general hyperproperties as well as possible modifications via property-directed techniques such as IC3 [5].

References

1. Abate, A., Ahmed, D., Edwards, A., Giacobbe, M., Peruffo, A.: Fossil: a software tool for the formal synthesis of lyapunov functions and barrier certificates using neural networks. In: Proceedings of the 24th International Conference on Hybrid Systems: Computation and Control, pp. 1–11 (2021)
2. Abate, A., Giacobbe, M., Roy, D.: Stochastic omega-regular verification and control with supermartingales. In: International Conference on Computer Aided Verification, pp. 395–419. Springer (2024)
3. Abate, A., Giacobbe, M., Roy, D.: Quantitative supermartingale certificates. In: International Conference on Computer Aided Verification, pp. 3–28. Springer (2025)
4. Alur, R., Henzinger, T.A., Kupferman, O.: Alternating-time temporal logic. J. ACM (JACM) **49**(5), 672–713 (2002)
5. Bradley, A.R.: Sat-based model checking without unrolling. In: International Workshop on Verification, Model Checking, and Abstract Interpretation, pp. 70–87. Springer (2011)
6. Chatterjee, K., Fu, H., Goharshady, A.K., Goharshady, E.K.: Polynomial invariant generation for non-deterministic recursive programs. In: Proceedings of the 41st ACM SIGPLAN Conference on Programming Language Design and Implementation, pp. 672–687 (2020)

7. Chatterjee, K., Goharshady, A., Goharshady, E., Karrabi, M., Zikelic, D.: Sound and complete witnesses for template-based verification of LTL properties on polynomial programs. In: International Symposium on Formal Methods, pp. 600–619. Springer (2024)
8. Cook, B.: Priciples of program termination. Eng. Methods Tools Softw. Saf. Secur. **22**(161), 125 (2009)
9. De Moura, L., Bjørner, N.: Satisfiability modulo theories: introduction and applications. Commun. ACM 69–77 (2011)
10. Dimitrova, R., Majumdar, R.: Deductive control synthesis for alternating-time logics. In: 2014 International Conference on Embedded Software (EMSOFT), pp. 1–10. IEEE (2014)
11. Gao, S., Kong, S., Clarke, E.M.: dReal: an SMT solver for nonlinear theories over the reals. In: Automated Deduction – CADE-24, pp. 208–214. Lecture Notes in Computer Science, Springer (2013)
12. Heim, P., Dimitrova, R.: Solving infinite-state games via acceleration. Proc. ACM Program. Lang. **8**(POPL), 1696–1726 (2024)
13. Henzinger, T.A., Mallik, K., Sadeghi, P., Žikelić, D.: Supermartingale certificates for quantitative omega-regular verification and control. In: International Conference on Computer Aided Verification, pp. 29–55. Springer (2025)
14. Herman, R.L.: A second course in ordinary differential equations of dynamical systems and boundary value problems (2008)
15. Lubin, M., Dowson, O., Dias Garcia, J., Huchette, J., Legat, B., Vielma, J.P.: JuMP 1.0: recent improvements to a modeling language for mathematical optimization. Math. Program. Comput. (2023). https://doi.org/10.1007/s12532-023-00239-3
16. Majumdar, R., Sathiyanarayana, V., Soudjani, S.: Necessary and sufficient certificates for almost sure reachability. IEEE Control Syst. Lett. (2024)
17. Moura, L.d., Bjørner, N.: Z3: An efficient smt solver. In: International conference on Tools and Algorithms for the Construction and Analysis of Systems, pp. 337–340 (2008)
18. Murali, V., Oumer, M.A., Zamani, M.: Control closure certificates. arXiv preprint arXiv:2508.03947 (2025)
19. Murali, V., Trivedi, A., Zamani, M.: Closure certificates. In: Proceedings of the 27th ACM International Conference on Hybrid Systems: Computation and Control, pp. 1–11 (2024)
20. Myerscough, C.: A simple model of the growth of wind-induced oscillations in overhead lines. J. Sound Vib. **28**(4), 699–713 (1973)
21. Nadali, A., Murali, V., Trivedi, A., Zamani, M.: Neural closure certificates. In: Proceedings of the AAAI Conference on Artificial Intelligence, vol. 38, pp. 21446–21453 (2024)
22. Parrilo, P.A.: Semidefinite programming relaxations for semialgebraic problems. Math. Program. **96**, 293–320 (2003)
23. Podelski, A., Rybalchenko, A.: Transition invariants. In: Proceedings of the 19th Annual IEEE Symposium on Logic in Computer Science, 2004, pp. 32–41. IEEE (2004)
24. Prajna, S., Jadbabaie, A.: Safety verification of hybrid systems using barrier certificates. In: International Workshop on Hybrid Systems: Computation and Control, pp. 477–492. Springer (2004)
25. Putinar, M.: Positive polynomials on compact semi-algebraic sets. Indiana Univ. Math. J. **42**(3), 969–984 (1993)
26. Ramsey, F.P.: On a problem of formal logic. In: Classic Papers in Combinatorics, pp. 1–24. Springer (1987)

27. Safra, S.: On the complexity of ω-automata. In: Proc. 29th IEEE Symp. Found. of Comp. Sci., pp. 319–327. IEEE (1988)
28. Mazala, R.: Infinite games. In: Grädel, E., Thomas, W., Wilke, T. (eds.) Automata Logics, and Infinite Games. LNCS, vol. 2500, pp. 23–38. Springer, Heidelberg (2002). https://doi.org/10.1007/3-540-36387-4_2
29. Vardi, M.Y.: An automata-theoretic approach to linear temporal logic. Logics for concurrency: structure versus automata pp. 238–266 (2005)
30. Wang, J., Magron, V., Lasserre, J.B.: Tssos: a moment-SOS hierarchy that exploits term sparsity. SIAM J. Optim. **31**(1), 30–58 (2021)
31. Wang, P., Bai, J., Zhi, D., Zhang, M., Ong, L.: Verifying omega-regular properties of neural network-controlled systems via proof certificates. In: ICLR 2025 Workshop: VerifAI: AI Verification in the Wild (2025)
32. Yakubovich, V.A.: S-procedure in nolinear control theory. Vestnik Leninggradskogo Universiteta, Ser. Matematika pp. 62–77 (1971)

Verification

PolyQEnt: A Polynomial Quantified Entailment Solver

Krishnendu Chatterjee[1], Amir Kafshdar Goharshady[2],
Ehsan Kafshdar Goharshady[1], Mehrdad Karrabi[1(✉)], Milad Saadat[3],
Maximilian Seeliger[4], and Đorđe Žikelić[5]

[1] Institute of Science and Technology Austria, Klosterneuburg, Austria
{krishnendu.chatterjee,ehsan.goharshady,mehrdad.karrabi}@ist.ac.at
[2] University of Oxford, Oxford, England
[3] Sharif University of Technology, Tehran, Iran
Milad.Saadat@sharif.edu
[4] Vienna University of Technology, Vienna, Austria
maximilian.seeliger@tuwien.ac.at
[5] Singapore Management University, Singapore, Singapore
dzikelic@smu.edu.sg

Abstract. Polynomial quantified entailments with existentially and universally quantified variables arise in many problems of verification and program analysis. We present PolyQEnt which is a tool for solving polynomial quantified entailments in which variables on both sides of the implication are real valued or unbounded integers. Our tool provides a unified framework for polynomial quantified entailment problems that arise in several papers in the literature. Our experimental evaluation over a wide range of benchmarks shows the applicability of the tool as well as its benefits as opposed to simply using existing SMT solvers to solve such constraints.

Keywords: Polynomial Quantified Entailments · Constraint Solving · Positivity Theorems · Program Analysis

1 Introduction

Polynomial Constraint Solving in Verification. A fundamental computational task that arises in several contexts of verification and static analysis of programs is constraint solving over polynomials. The most prominent example of an application in program analysis is *template-based synthesis* [27]. Given a program and a property, a classical approach to proving that the program satisfies the property is to compute a certificate (i.e. a formal proof) of the property [22]. This can be achieved by fixing a suitable *symbolic template* for the certificate, which allows reducing the program verification problem to computing values of symbolic template variables that together give rise to a correct certificate [42]. Such an approach with symbolic templates being linear or polynomial functions has found extensive applications in static analysis of programs with linear or polynomial arithmetic, including termination analysis [6,14,37], invariant generation [7,13,21], reachability [2], cost analysis [28,32,45], program synthesis [24,26] and probabilistic program analysis [5,6,11]. This approach has also found extensive applications in other domains of computer science, e.g. controller verification and synthesis [1,38,39].

Polynomial Quantified Entailments. In all cases mentioned above, the goal of template-based synthesis is to compute a certificate for the property of interest, where the certificate is computed in the form of a symbolic linear or polynomial function. The computation is achieved by a reduction to solving a system of *polynomial entailments*, i.e. a system of $K \in \mathbb{N}$ constraints of the form

$$\exists t \in \mathbb{R}^m. \bigwedge_{i=1}^{K} \Big(\forall x \in \mathbb{R}^n. \, \Phi^i(x,t) \implies \Psi^i(x,t) \Big).$$

Here, the variables $t \in \mathbb{R}^m$ present real-valued *template coefficients* of the symbolic linear or polynomial function that together define the certificate, and each Φ^i and Ψ^i is a *boolean combination of polynomial inequalities* over a vector $x \in \mathbb{R}^n$ of program variables. The entailments $\forall x \in \mathbb{R}^n. \, \Phi^i(x,t) \implies \Psi^i(x,t)$ together encode the necessary properties for the symbolic template polynomial to define a correct certificate. Hence, any valuation of the variables $t \in \mathbb{R}^m$ that gives rise to a solution to the system of constraints above also gives rise to a concrete instance of the correct certificate. We refer to each entailment $\forall x \in \mathbb{R}^n. \, \Phi^i(x,t) \implies \Psi^i(x,t)$ as a *polynomial quantified entailment (PQE)*, and to the problem of solving a system of PQEs in eq. (1) as *PQE solving*.

Solving PQEs via Positivity Theorems. Initial work on template-based synthesis has focused on linear programs and linear certificate templates. A classical approach to solving this problem is to use Farkas' lemma that considers implications over linear expressions [18], which has been applied in several works related to program analysis, e.g. [5,8,13,31]. However, this method was insufficient for analyzing programs described by polynomials, e.g. programs that may contain program variable multiplication. A generalization of Farkas' lemma-style reasoning to the setting of polynomial constraints and PQEs is achieved by using *positivity theorems*, such as Handelman's [30] and Putinar's theorem [40]. It was shown in [2,6] that they can be applied towards effectively solving systems of PQEs, with applications in static analysis of polynomial programs for termination [6], reachability [2], invariant generation [7], non-termination [10] properties and for probabilistic program analysis [11,43].

POLYQENT. PQE solving via positivity theorems is becoming increasingly popular in static program analysis, however tool support for its integration into these analyses is non-existent and researchers have relied on their own implementations. In this work, we present our tool POLYQENT which implements methods for solving systems of PQEs over the theories of polynomial real or unbounded integer arithmetic, based on Handelman's theorem, Putinar's theorem and Farkas' lemma. We provide efficient implementations of each of these methods together with practical heuristics that we observed to improve their performance. At the same time, our tool preserves soundness and relative completeness guarantees of these translations as established in the previous results in the literature [2,7]. We envision that PolyQEnt will allow future research to focus on the design of appropriate certificate templates, whereas the constraint solving part can be fully delegated to our tool. PolyQEnt is implemented in Python and publicly available on GitHub[1]. It allows users to provide constraints as input in the SMT-LIB syntax [4], which is a standard and widely used input format. PolyQEnt also automates the selection of the positivity theorem to be used (Handelman's theorem, Putinar's theorem or Farkas' lemma) in order to achieve most efficient constraint solving while providing the soundness and relative completeness guarantees.

Experimental Evaluation. We experimentally evaluate PolyQEnt on several benchmarks collected from the literature on termination and non-termination analysis in polynomial programs, termination of probabilistic programs and polynomial program synthesis. While all these problems could also be directly solved using off-the-shelf SMT solvers that support quantifier elimination, e.g. Z3 [15], our experimental results show *significant improvements in runtime* when positivity theorems are used to eliminate quantifier alternation.

Comparison to Constrained Horn Clauses. The problem of PQE solving syntactically resembles the more studied problem of constrained Horn clause (CHC) solving. CHC solving is a classical approach to program verification [25] with many readily available tools, e.g. [16,19,29,33,34]. However, the goal of the PQE solving problem is fundamentally different from CHC solving, and methods for one problem are not readily applicable to the other problem. In CHC solving, the focus is on computing boolean predicates that together make the CHC valid. In contrast, template-based synthesis applications discussed above require computing *values of template variables* that together define a certificate conforming to a given template, where the template is specified as a boolean combination of symbolic linear or polynomial inequalities over program variables. Hence, what would be viewed as an uninterpreted predicate in CHC solving, becomes a fixed boolean combination of polynomial inequalities of a specified maximal polynomial degree in PQE solving. The existing CHC solvers are thus not applicable to the problem of PQE solving.

Finally, FreqHorn [20] is a CHC solver that is able to generate interpretations for uninterpreted predicates in the form of polynomial inequalities. Once predicate interpretations are generated, the satisfiability of the resulting interpreted formula is checked by performing quantifier elimination via a technique based on Model-Based Projections [19], after which the resulting quantifier-free formula is solved via Gauss-Jordan elimination. Hence, the last step of FreqHorn's methodology is also applicable to our problem. The novelty provided by our PolyQEnt is twofold. First, our quantifier elimination procedure is based on positivity theorems, which have recently been extensively utilized in program

---

[1] https://github.com/ChatterjeeGroup-ISTA/polyqent.

analysis and verification but for which tooling support is inexistent. Second, while the methodology of FreqHorn is in principle applicable to our problem setting, the tool itself only supports CHC solving over uninterpreted predicates. Hence, we could not perform a direct comparison.

2 Tool Overview

In this section we provide an overview of our tool and discuss details of the considered problem, the tool's architecture and its backend design.

2.1 Problem Statement

The problem of *polynomial quantified entailment (PQE) solving* is concerned with computing a valuation of existentially quantified variables $t_1, \ldots, t_m$ that make the following logical formula true

$$\exists t \in \mathbb{R}^m. \bigwedge_{i=1}^{K} \Big(\forall x \in \mathbb{R}^n.\ \Phi^i(x,t) \implies \Psi^i(x,t) \Big). \tag{1}$$

Here, each Φ^i and Ψ^i is a boolean combination of polynomial inequalities of the form $p(t_1, \ldots, t_m, x_1, \ldots, x_n) \bowtie 0$, with p a polynomial function and $\bowtie \in \{\geq, >\}$. We refer to each entailment $\forall x \in \mathbb{R}^n.\ \Phi^i(x,t) \implies \Psi^i(x,t)$ as a *polynomial quantified entailment (PQE)*, and to the formula in eq. (1) as a *system of PQEs*.

In what follows, we consider systems of PQEs defined over the background theory of *real arithmetic*. However, our POLYQENT is also applicable to PQEs defined over *unbounded integer arithmetic* (i.e. mathematical integers). While our presentation will mostly focus on PQEs defined over real arithmetic, in Sect. 2.3 we discuss differences that arise in considering unbounded integer arithmetic and how POLYQENT addresses them.

Canonical form of PQEs. We say that a PQE $\forall x \in \mathbb{R}^n.\ \Phi(x,t) \implies \Psi(x,t)$ is in the *canonical form*, if Φ is a conjunction of finitely many polynomial inequalities and Ψ is a single polynomial inequality, i.e. if $\Phi \equiv \bigwedge_{j=1}^{k} \Big(p_j(t_1, \ldots, t_m, x_1, \ldots, x_n) \bowtie 0 \Big)$ and $\Psi \equiv p(t_1, \ldots, t_m, x_1, \ldots, x_n) \bowtie 0$. Each PQE can be translated into an equisatisfiable PQE in the canonical form, defined over the same set of free variables $t \in \mathbb{R}^m$ and universally quantified variables $x \in \mathbb{R}^n$. This translation presents the preprocessing step of our POLYQENT. We formally state and prove this result in the extended version of the paper [9].

Example 1. To illustrate how the problem of solving a system of PQEs arises in template-based synthesis for program analysis, we consider an example of proving termination of programs by computing ranking functions. Consider the program in Fig. 1 (left) and termination as a specification. We describe the three steps of the classical template-based method for synthesizing linear ranking functions [13]. We consider linear programs and ranking functions for simplicity of

```
Invariant:
  -1024 ≤ x ≤ 1023
l₁: while x ≥ 1 do
      x := x-1
    done
lₜ:
```

$$\exists t_1, t_2, t_3, t_4 \in \mathbb{R} \begin{cases} \forall x \in \mathbb{R}, \left(-1024 \leq x \leq 1023 \Rightarrow t_1 x + t_2 \geq 0\right) \\ \forall x \in \mathbb{R}, \left(-1024 \leq x \leq 1023 \land x \geq 1 \right. \\ \left. \Rightarrow t_1(x-1) + t_2 \geq 0 \land t_1(x-1) + t_2 \leq t_1 x + t_2 - 1\right) \\ \forall x \in \mathbb{R}, \left(-1024 \leq x \leq 1023 \land x < 1 \right. \\ \left. \Rightarrow t_3 x + t_4 \geq 0 \land t_3 x + t_4 \leq t_1 x + t_2 - 1\right) \end{cases}$$

Fig. 1. A simple program (left) and the corresponding system of polynomial Horn clauses for computing ranking function that proves termination (right).

the example, however this method was extended to the setting of polynomial programs and ranking functions in [6] and is supported in POLYQENT:

1. To find a linear ranking function, we first fix a symbolic linear expression template for each cutpoint location in the program: $T_{l_1}(x) = t_1 x + t_2$ and $T_{l_t}(x) = t_3 x + t_4$, where t_1, t_2, t_3 and t_4 are the symbolic template variables.
2. A system of PQEs in Fig. 1 (right) encodes that T is a ranking function. Intuitively, the value of the ranking function should be non-negative at the beginning (the first PQE), and it should decrease in every step while staying non-negative until termination is reached (the second and third PQEs).
3. Hence, any valuation of template variables t_1, t_2, t_3, t_4 that makes all PQEs valid gives rise to a correct ranking function for the program in Fig. 1 (left).

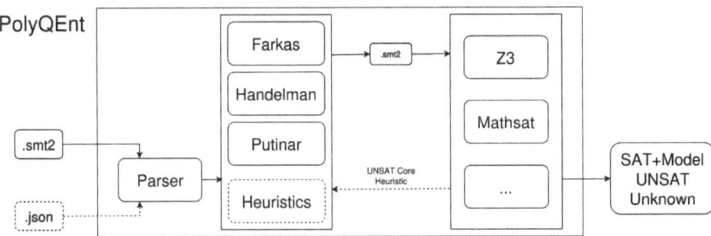

Fig. 2. Overview of the tool architecture.

2.2 Tool Architecture

Architecture. An overview of the architecture of POLYQENT is shown in Fig. 2. The tool takes as input a system of PQEs in the form as in eq. (1). The input is provided in the SMT-LIB format [4], alongside with an optional config file in the .json format (see the following paragraph for details). Examples are provided in the tool's repository. Note that we do not assume any logical structure of the polynomial inequalities in the PQEs, i.e. polynomial predicates in each PQE can have arbitrary and/or logical connectives.

The input files are then parsed and the PQEs are translated to their equi-satisfiable canonical forms. POLYQENT then applies the appropriate positivity theorem to reduce the problem of PQE solving to solving a fully existentially quantified system of polynomial constraints (see Sect. 2.3 for details). The resulting fully existentially quantified system of polynomial constraints is then fed to an SMT-solver. In case when the "UNSAT Core" heuristic is used, POLYQENT will further process the output of the SMT-solver (see Sect. 2.3 for details). Finally, the output of POLYQENT is either (1) SAT with a valuation of existentially quantified variables for which the system of PQEs is valid, (2) UNSAT if the SMT-solver proves unsatisfiability, or (3) Unknown if the SMT-solver returns unknown.

Configuration File (Optional). POLYQENT has a default (and recommended) configuration, which does not require the user to provide the config file. However, we also allow the user to change some of the parameter values used by POLYQENT and the set of heuristics used by providing a .json config file:

1. Positivity theorem to be used (farkas, handelman or putinar). The default configuration of POLYQENT automatically chooses the most efficient positivity theorem to be applied while preserving soundness and relative completeness guarantees (see Sect. 2.3 for details). However, this optional parameter allows the user to opt for a different positivity theorem whose application is sound but not relatively complete, but may sometime lead to a more efficient constraint solving.
2. Parameters of the positivity theorem to be used. See the extended version [9] for details. The default parameter values are also specified in the extended version [9].
3. The set of heuristics (if any) to be applied. The default configuration applies the Assume-SAT heuristic (see Sect. 2.3 for details).
4. An SMT-solver to be used to solve the fully existentially quantified system of polynomial constraints from applying the positivity theorem. The default configuration uses z3 [15], however POLYQENT also supports mathsat [12].
5. Background theory to be considered. The default is real arithmetic, however the config file allows the user to choose unbounded integer arithmetic.

Remark 1. We integrated the commands for running Z3 and MathSAT5 into POLYQENT. However, POLYQENT also stores the obtained system of existentially quantified polynomial inequalities in an SMTLIB format output file which can then be fed to other SMT-solvers.

2.3 Backend Algorithms and Heuristics

We now overview the backend of our tool. Observe that the system of PQEs in eq. (1) contains quantifier alternation with existential quantification preceding universal quantification. As mentioned in Sect. 1, constraints involving such quantifier alternation can in principle be solved directly by using an off-the-shelf SMT solver that supports quantifier elimination, e.g. Z3 [15]. However, decision procedures for solving such constraints are known to be highly unscalable and a major source of inefficiency [41]. PQE solving can be made *significantly more efficient* by first using positivity theorems to eliminate universal quantification and reduce the problem to solving a purely existentially quantified system of polynomial constraints. Our experiments in Sect. 3 support this claim. In what follows, we describe an overview of positivity theorems and also how POLYQENT uses them for quantifier elimination.

Overview of Positivity Theorems. All three positivity theorems implemented in POLYQENT, namely Handelman's theorem, Putinar's theorem and Farkas' lemma, consider constraints of the form

$$\forall x \in \mathbb{R}^n. \Big(f_1(x) \bowtie 0 \wedge \cdots \wedge f_m(x) \bowtie 0 \Longrightarrow g(x) \bowtie 0 \Big), \tag{2}$$

where $f_1, \ldots, f_m, g$ are polynomials over real-valued variables $x_1, \ldots, x_n$ and each $\bowtie \in \{\geq, >\}$ (we discuss the unbounded integer variables case in the following paragraph). These theorems provide *sound* translations of the implication in eq. (2) into a purely existentially quantified system of polynomial inequalities over newly introduced auxiliary symbolic variables. Translations are sound in the sense that, if the obtained purely existentially quantified system of constraints is satisfiable, then the implication in eq. (2) is valid. Moreover, these theorems provide additional sufficient conditions under which the translation is also *complete*, i.e. the implication in eq. (2) and the resulting existentially quantified system are equisatisfiable:

- **Farkas' lemma.** Farkas' lemma [18,36] provides a sound and complete translation if all f_i's and g are linear expressions.
- **Handelman's theorem.** Handelman's theorem [30] provides a sound translation if all f_i's are linear expressions and g is a polynomial expression. Moreover, the translation can be made complete if in addition all inequalities $f_i(x_1, \ldots, x_n) \bowtie 0$ are non-strict, the inequality $g(x_1, \ldots, x_n) \bowtie 0$ is strict and the set $\{(x_1, \ldots, x_n) \mid \forall 1 \leq i \leq n. f_i(x_1, \ldots, x_n) \geq 0\} \subseteq \mathbb{R}^n$ is bounded.
- **Putinar's Theorem.** Putinar's theorem [40] provides a sound translation if all f_i's and g are polynomial expressions. Moreover, the translation can be made complete if in addition all inequalities $f_i(x_1, \ldots, x_n) \bowtie 0$ are non-strict, the inequality $g(x_1, \ldots, x_n) \bowtie 0$ is strict and the set $\{(x_1, \ldots, x_n) \mid \forall 1 \leq i \leq n. f_i(x_1, \ldots, x_n) \geq 0\} \subseteq \mathbb{R}^n$ is bounded.

In the extended version of the paper [9], we provide formal statements of each positivity theorem. When invoked in POLYQENT each theorem has some input parameters which are set to default values, that can be modified in the config file.

Automatic Choice of Theorems. If none of the theories above are specified in the configuration file, POLYQENT automatically chooses the most efficient positivity theorem that preserves the relative completeness guarantees. This is done by analyzing the degree of LHS and RHS of the entailments. Specifically, for a given entailment, it chooses Farkas' lemma if both sides are linear, Handelman's if the LHS is linear and the RHS is non-linear, and Putinar's if both sides are non-linear.

Polynomial Unbounded Integer Arithmetic. While positivity theorems consider polynomials over real-valued variables, the resulting translations remain sound under unbounded integer arithmetic. In this case, strict inequalities can always be treated as non-strict by incrementing the appropriate side of the inequality by 1, and the above yield sound but incomplete translations. Usage of positivity theorems in polynomial unbounded integer arithmetic was discussed in [10]. PolyQEnt provides support for unbounded integer arithmetic PQEs.

Heuristics. We conclude by outlining two heuristics that we implemented in PolyQEnt and that we observed to improve the tool's performance. The effect of each heuristic is studied in our experimental evaluation in Sect. 3:

1. *Assume-SAT.* For a PQE $[\forall x.P(x) \Rightarrow Q(x)]$ to be valid, either (i) $P(x)$ needs to be satisfiable and to imply $Q(x)$ at all satisfying points, which is captured by e.g. the condition (F1) in Farkas lemma (Theorem 1 in the extended version [9]), or (ii) $P(x)$ needs to be unsatisfiable, which is captured bt e.g. the conditions (F2) and (F3) in Farkas lemma. In order to guarantee completeness, the system of inequalities generated by PolyQEnt has a disjunction that states either (i) or (ii) should be true. The Assume-SAT heuristic instead collects a system of constraints whose satisfiability only implies (i). This heuristic is sound but it leads to incompleteness, as (ii) also implies that the system of PQEs is satisfiable. However, we observed that the Assume-SAT heuristic can sometimes considerably reduce the size of the obtained system of constraints, which can make the subsequent SMT solving step significantly more efficient.
2. *UNSAT core.* This heuristic was proposed in [24], a work which uses positivity theorems for program synthesis. Since the positivity theorem translations introduce a large number of fresh symbolic variables that are now existentially quantified, the idea behind the heuristic is to first try to solve the resulting system of constraints while adding additional constraints that set the values of some of these newly introduced symbolic variables to 0. If the SMT-solver returns SAT, then the original system is satisfiable as well. Otherwise, SMT solvers such as Z3 [15] and MathSAT [12] can return an unsatisfiability core, a subset of constraints that are unsatisfiable themselves. If the core contains none of the newly added constraints, it implies that the original system was unsatifiable. Otherwise, PolyQEnt removes the newly added $t = 0$ constraints that are in the core and repeats this procedure.

3 Experimental Evaluation

We evaluate the performance of our tool on three benchmark sets in the following three subsections. The goal of our experiments is to illustrate (1) soundness of the tool, (2) its ability to solve PQEs that arise in program analysis literature, (3) the necessity of using positivity theorems for quantifier elimination as opposed to feeding PQEs to an SMT solver directly, and (4) to study the performance of different combinations of our two heuristics and different SMT solvers. Benchmarks are provided in the .smt2 format. All the experiments were conducted on a Debian 11 machine with AMD EPYC 9654 2.40 GHz CPU and 6 GB RAM with a timeout of 180 s.

Baselines. To illustrate the necessity of using positivity theorems for quantifier elimination, on all three benchmark sets we compare POLYQENT against baseline method which directly uses Z3(v4.13.4) [15] to solve the system of PQEs, i.e. without applying positivity theorems.

Moreover, we executed CVC5(v1.2.0) [3], Mathematica [44] and Redlog [17] on all our benchmarks and they could solve 18, 3 and 32 instances, respectively. We do not include this result in our tables as other methods outperform them significantly.

3.1 Termination and Non-termination

The first benchmark set consists of systems of PQEs that arise in termination analysis of programs. We consider TermComp'23 [23], C-Integer category, benchmark suite that consists of 335 non-recursive programs written in C. Initial value of every program variable is assumed to be in the range $[-1024, 1023]$. The goal is to either prove termination or non-termination of each program. More details of PQE extraction from benchmarks is presented in the extended version [9].

Results. Table 1 shows a summary of our results on POLYQENT's performance on PQEs coming from termination analysis. Clearly, POLYQENT performs far better than using Z3 directly for quantifier elimination. Comparing performance of different heuristics, we observe several interesting points:

- Applying heuristic H1 (Assume-SAT) helps POLYQENT greatly, especially when using MathSAT as the backend solver. Specifically, MathSAT solves only 44 instances of the termination benchmarks in the base case and solves 148 when equipped with H1. On the other hand, Z3's performance is improved, both in terms of runtime and number of solved instances, on the non-termination benchmarks when the H1 heuristic is turned on.
- Applying heuristic H2 (UNSAT Core) does not prove any unique cases that other configurations of POLYQENT could not prove. However, Z3 solves more instances than MathSAT when both are equipped with this heuristic.
- While Z3 solves more termination analysis instances, MathSAT outperforms it in solving PQEs coming from non-termination analysis. This suggests running several SMT solvers in parallel in order to achieve the best results.

Runtime Comparison. Figure 3 plots the number of instances solved by each tool against runtime. For several benchmarks the direct-Z3 method terminates nearly instantly. Apart from them, it can be seen that Z3 is faster than MathSAT in settings where H1 heuristic is not applied, but applying H1 makes MathSAT slightly more efficient than Z3. Moreover, compared to not using any heuristics, applying H1 and H2 results in a speed-up in 220 and 32 benchmarks, respectively.

Table 1. Summary of results on TermComp benchmarks. The **Base** column shows the results of PolyQEnt without any heuristics. The next 3 columns enable heuristics H1 and H2. The 'Dir. Z3' column summarize the results obtained by applying Z3 directly. For each setting, we show the number of instances solved by MathSAT 5 (**MS 5**), Z3 and their union (**U.**).

Specification	Base			Base+H1			Base+H2			Base+H1+H2			Dir. Z3
	MS 5	Z3	U.	MS 5	Z3	U.	MS 5	Z3	U.	MS 5	Z3	U.	
Termination	44	154	154	148	153	153	43	109	113	125	132	145	103
Non-Termination	72	76	78	101	87	103	61	75	76	81	82	89	39
Avg. Time (s)	4.4	3.9	1.6	0.5	2.5	0.5	4.3	3.5	3.4	2.7	3.7	3.6	1.6

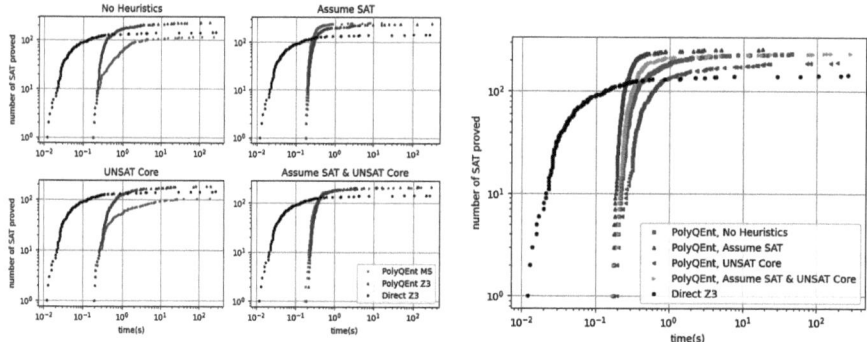

Fig. 3. Performance of PolyQEnt with different settings in comparison to baselines. Both axes are scaled logarithmically for better visualization. The leftmost four plots demonstrate the effect of using different solvers and heuristic settings, and the rightmost plot unionizes solvers to just compare heuristics.

3.2 Almost-Sure Termination

The second benchmark set comes from almost-sure termination proving in probabilistic programs. We collected benchmarks from two sources: i) 10 benchmarks from [43] (Table 3) and ii) 7 benchmarks from [35]. We choose these benchmarks because both works consider probabilistic program models of different applications which are required to be almost-surely terminating. More details of PQE extraction from benchmarks are presented in the extended version [9].

Results. Table 2 shows a summary of our results on PolyQEnt's performance on PQEs coming from almost-sure termination analysis. Applying Z3 directly is not successful on any of the benchmarks. On the other hand, PolyQEnt successfully solves 13 out of 17 instances. Moreover, it can be seen that in most of the settings, running one SMT-solver alone does not provide the best results. This again suggests running several SMT solvers in parallel.

Table 2. Results on the second benchmark set

Benchmark set	Base			Base+H1			Base+H2			Base+H1+H2			Dir. Z3
	MS 5	Z3	U.	MS 5	Z3	U.	MS 5	Z3	U.	MS 5	Z3	U.	
From [43]	7	6	7	7	6	7	7	6	7	7	5	7	0
From [35]	6	5	6	5	6	6	5	4	5	6	4	6	0
Avg. Time (s)	10.4	6.1	10.4	9.5	3.5	9.7	10.1	3.4	10.1	10.9	2.0	10.9	NA

3.3 Synthesis

The third benchmark set comes from polynomial program synthesis, where we collect 32 benchmarks from *PolySynth* [24]. Each benchmark is a non-deterministic program that contains holes and a desired specification. PolySynth uses a template-based technique to synthesize suitable polynomial expressions for the holes such that the specification is satisfied. More details of PQE extraction from benchmarks are presented in the extended version [9].

Results. Table 3 shows a summary of our results on PolyQEnt's performance on PQEs coming from program synthesis. We note that for two benchmarks (namely, positive_square_with_holes and positive_square_with_number_holes) the Direct Z3 method could find a solution while PolyQEnt equipped with Farkas and Handelman could not. However, using Putinar with polynomial degree 2, PolyQEnt can solve those instances as well. Other than that, PolyQEnt outperforms the Direct Z3 approach both in terms of the number of solved instances and runtime. Comparing the performance of heuristics, it can be seen that the UNSAT Core heuristic slightly outperforms the Assume-SAT heuristic.

Table 3. Results on the third benchmark set

Benchmark Set	Base			Base+H1			Base+H2			Base+H1+H2			Dir. Z3
	MS 5	Z3	U.	MS 5	Z3	U.	MS 5	Z3	U.	MS 5	Z3	U.	
From [24]	28	30	30	28	29	29	28	30	30	28	29	29	24
Avg. Time (s)	3.2	2.6	2.6	2.4	2.4	2.4	2.9	2.7	2.6	2.6	2.5	2.5	14.0

Concluding Remarks. We presented our tool POLYQENT for solving systems of polynomial quantified entailments, a problem that arises in many template-based synthesis methods for program analysis and verification. The significance of POLYQENT is that, for template-based synthesis, it separates the task of certificate design, which future research can focus on, and the task of polynomial constraint solving, for which POLYQENT provides an efficient tool support. Future work includes studying further heuristics towards making POLYQENT even more efficient for solving systems of polynomial quantified entailments.

Acknowledgments. This work was supported by the following grants: ERC CoG 863818 (ForM-SMArt), Austrian Science Fund (FWF) 10.55776/COE12, ERC StG 101222524 (SPES), the Ethereum Foundation Research Grant FY24-1793, and the Singapore Ministry of Education (MOE) Academic Research Fund (AcRF) Tier 1 grant (Project ID:22-SISSMU-100).

Disclosure of Interests. The authors have no competing interests to declare that are relevant to the content of this article.

References

1. Ahmadi, A.A., Majumdar, A.: Some applications of polynomial optimization in operations research and real-time decision making. Optim. Lett. **10**(4), 709–729 (2016)
2. Asadi, A., Chatterjee, K., Fu, H., Goharshady, A.K., Mahdavi, M.: Polynomial reachability witnesses via stellensätze. In: PLDI, pp. 772–787. ACM (2021)
3. Barbosa, H., et al.: cvc5: a versatile and industrial-strength SMT solver. In: TACAS 2022. LNCS, vol. 13243, pp. 415–442. Springer, Cham (2022). https://doi.org/10.1007/978-3-030-99524-9_24
4. Barrett, C., Fontaine, P., Tinelli, C.: The Satisfiability Modulo Theories Library (SMT-LIB). www.SMT-LIB.org (2016)
5. Chakarov, A., Sankaranarayanan, S.: Probabilistic program analysis with martingales. In: Sharygina, N., Veith, H. (eds.) CAV 2013. LNCS, vol. 8044, pp. 511–526. Springer, Heidelberg (2013). https://doi.org/10.1007/978-3-642-39799-8_34
6. Chatterjee, K., Fu, H., Goharshady, A.K.: Termination analysis of probabilistic programs through Positivstellensatz's. In: Chaudhuri, S., Farzan, A. (eds.) CAV 2016. LNCS, vol. 9779, pp. 3–22. Springer, Cham (2016). https://doi.org/10.1007/978-3-319-41528-4_1
7. Chatterjee, K., Fu, H., Goharshady, A.K., Goharshady, E.K.: Polynomial invariant generation for non-deterministic recursive programs. In: PLDI, pp. 672–687. ACM (2020)
8. Chatterjee, K., Fu, H., Novotný, P., Hasheminezhad, R.: Algorithmic analysis of qualitative and quantitative termination problems for affine probabilistic programs. ACM Trans. Program. Lang. Syst. **40**(2), 7:1–7:45 (2018)
9. Chatterjee, K., et al.: Polyqent: a polynomial quantified entailment solver. arXiv preprint arXiv:2408.03796 (2024)
10. Chatterjee, K., Goharshady, E.K., Novotný, P., Zikelic, D.: Proving non-termination by program reversal. In: PLDI, pp. 1033–1048. ACM (2021)
11. Chatterjee, K., Novotný, P., Zikelic, D.: Stochastic invariants for probabilistic termination. In: POPL, pp. 145–160. ACM (2017)

12. Cimatti, A., Griggio, A., Schaafsma, B.J., Sebastiani, R.: The mathsat5 SMT solver. In: International Conference on Tools and Algorithms for the Construction and Analysis of Systems, pp. 93–107. Springer (2013)
13. Colón, M.A., Sankaranarayanan, S., Sipma, H.B.: Linear invariant generation using non-linear constraint solving. In: Hunt, W.A., Somenzi, F. (eds.) CAV 2003. LNCS, vol. 2725, pp. 420–432. Springer, Heidelberg (2003). https://doi.org/10.1007/978-3-540-45069-6_39
14. Colón, M., Sipma, H.: Synthesis of linear ranking functions. In: TACAS. Lecture Notes in Computer Science, vol. 2031, pp. 67–81. Springer (2001)
15. De Moura, L., Bjørner, N.: Z3: An efficient smt solver. In: International Conference on Tools and Algorithms for the Construction and Analysis of Systems, pp. 337–340. Springer (2008)
16. Dietsch, D., Heizmann, M., Hoenicke, J., Nutz, A., Podelski, A.: Ultimate treeautomizer (CHC-COMP tool description). In: HCVS/PERR@ETAPS. EPTCS, vol. 296, pp. 42–47 (2019)
17. Dolzmann, A., Sturm, T.: Redlog: computer algebra meets computer logic. ACM Sigsam Bulletin **31**(2), 2–9 (1997)
18. Farkas, J.: Theorie der einfachen ungleichungen. J. für die reine und angewandte Mathematik (Crelles Journal) **1902**(124), 1–27 (1902)
19. Fedyukovich, G., Prabhu, S., Madhukar, K., Gupta, A.: Solving constrained horn clauses using syntax and data. In: FMCAD, pp. 1–9. IEEE (2018)
20. Fedyukovich, G., Prabhu, S., Madhukar, K., Gupta, A.: Quantified invariants via syntax-guided synthesis. In: Dillig, I., Tasiran, S. (eds.) CAV 2019. LNCS, vol. 11561, pp. 259–277. Springer, Cham (2019). https://doi.org/10.1007/978-3-030-25540-4_14
21. Feng, Y., Zhang, L., Jansen, D.N., Zhan, N., Xia, B.: Finding polynomial loop invariants for probabilistic programs. In: D'Souza, D., Narayan Kumar, K. (eds.) ATVA 2017. LNCS, vol. 10482, pp. 400–416. Springer, Cham (2017). https://doi.org/10.1007/978-3-319-68167-2_26
22. Floyd, R.W.: Assigning meanings to programs. In: Program Verification: Fundamental Issues in Computer Science, pp. 65–81. Springer (1993)
23. Frohn, F., Giesl, J., Moser, G., Rubio, A., Yamada, A., et al.: Termination competition 2023 (2023). https://termination-portal.org/wiki/Termination_Competition_2023
24. Goharshady, A.K., Hitarth, S., Mohammadi, F., Motwani, H.J.: Algebro-geometric algorithms for template-based synthesis of polynomial programs. Proc. ACM Program. Lang. **7**(OOPSLA1), 727–756 (2023)
25. Grebenshchikov, S., Lopes, N.P., Popeea, C., Rybalchenko, A.: Synthesizing software verifiers from proof rules. In: PLDI, pp. 405–416. ACM (2012)
26. Gulwani, S., Jha, S., Tiwari, A., Venkatesan, R.: Synthesis of loop-free programs. In: PLDI, pp. 62–73. ACM (2011)
27. Gulwani, S., Srivastava, S., Venkatesan, R.: Program analysis as constraint solving. In: PLDI, pp. 281–292. ACM (2008)
28. Gulwani, S., Zuleger, F.: The reachability-bound problem. In: PLDI, pp. 292–304. ACM (2010)
29. Gurfinkel, A., Kahsai, T., Komuravelli, A., Navas, J.A.: The SeaHorn verification framework. In: Kroening, D., Păsăreanu, C.S. (eds.) CAV 2015. LNCS, vol. 9206, pp. 343–361. Springer, Cham (2015). https://doi.org/10.1007/978-3-319-21690-4_20
30. Handelman, D.: Representing polynomials by positive linear functions on compact convex Polyhedra. Pac. J. Math. **132**(1), 35–62 (1988)

31. Heizmann, M., Hoenicke, J., Leike, J., Podelski, A.: Linear ranking for linear lasso programs. CoRR abs/1401.5347 (2014)
32. Hoffmann, J., Aehlig, K., Hofmann, M.: Multivariate amortized resource analysis. ACM Trans. Program. Lang. Syst. **34**(3), 14:1–14:62 (2012)
33. Hojjat, H., Rümmer, P.: The ELDARICA horn solver. In: FMCAD, pp. 1–7. IEEE (2018)
34. Komuravelli, A., Gurfinkel, A., Chaki, S.: SMT-based model checking for recursive programs. Formal Methods Syst. Des. **48**(3), 175–205 (2016)
35. Kura, S., Urabe, N., Hasuo, I.: Tail probabilities for randomized program runtimes via martingales for higher moments. In: Vojnar, T., Zhang, L. (eds.) TACAS 2019. LNCS, vol. 11428, pp. 135–153. Springer, Cham (2019). https://doi.org/10.1007/978-3-030-17465-1_8
36. Matoušek, J., Gärtner, B.: Understanding and using linear programming, vol. 1. Springer (2007)
37. Podelski, A., Rybalchenko, A.: A complete method for the synthesis of linear ranking functions. In: Steffen, B., Levi, G. (eds.) VMCAI 2004. LNCS, vol. 2937, pp. 239–251. Springer, Heidelberg (2004). https://doi.org/10.1007/978-3-540-24622-0_20
38. Prajna, S., Jadbabaie, A.: Safety verification of hybrid systems using barrier certificates. In: Alur, R., Pappas, G.J. (eds.) HSCC 2004. LNCS, vol. 2993, pp. 477–492. Springer, Heidelberg (2004). https://doi.org/10.1007/978-3-540-24743-2_32
39. Prajna, S., Papachristodoulou, A., Parrilo, P.A.: Introducing sostools: a general purpose sum of squares programming solver. In: Proceedings of the 41st IEEE Conference on Decision and Control, 2002, vol. 1, pp. 741–746. IEEE (2002)
40. Putinar, M.: Positive polynomials on compact semi-algebraic sets. Indiana Univ. Math. J. **42**(3), 969–984 (1993)
41. Renegar, J.: On the computational complexity and geometry of the first-order theory of the reals. part iii: Quantifier elimination. J. Symbolic Comput. **13**(3), 329–352 (1992).https://doi.org/10.1016/S0747-7171(10)80005-7
42. Srivastava, S., Gulwani, S., Foster, J.S.: Template-based program verification and program synthesis. Int. J. Softw. Tools Technol. Transf. **15**(5–6), 497–518 (2013)
43. Wang, P., Fu, H., Goharshady, A.K., Chatterjee, K., Qin, X., Shi, W.: Cost analysis of nondeterministic probabilistic programs. In: PLDI, pp. 204–220. ACM (2019)
44. Wolfram, S.: The Mathematica Book. Inc. Wolfram Research, Champaign (2003)
45. Zikelic, D., Chang, B.E., Bolignano, P., Raimondi, F.: Differential cost analysis with simultaneous potentials and anti-potentials. In: PLDI, pp. 442–457. ACM (2022)

Data Structures for Finite Downsets of Natural Vectors: Theory and Practice

Michaël Cadilhac[1](✉), Vanessa Flügel[2], Guillermo A. Pérez[2], and Shrisha Rao[2]

[1] DePaul University, Chicago, USA
michael@cadilhac.name
[2] University of Antwerp – Flanders Make, Antwerp, Belgium
{vanessa.flugel,guillermo.perez,shrisha.rao}@uantwerpen.be

Abstract. Manipulating downward-closed sets of vectors forms the basis of so-called antichain-based algorithms in verification. In that context, the dimension of the vectors is intimately tied to the size of the input structure to be verified. In this work, we formally analyze the complexity of classical list-based algorithms to manipulate antichains as well as that of Zampuniéris's sharing trees and traditional and novel k-d-tree-based antichain algorithms. In contrast to the existing literature, and to better address the needs of formal verification, our analysis of k-d tree algorithms does not assume that the dimension of the vectors is fixed. Our theoretical results show that k-d trees are asymptotically better than both list- and sharing-tree-based algorithms, as an antichain data structure, when the antichains become exponentially larger than the dimension of the vectors. We evaluate this on applications in the synthesis of reactive systems from linear-temporal logic and parity-objective specifications, and establish empirically that current benchmarks for these computational tasks do not lead to a favorable situation for current implementations of k-d trees.

Keywords: Antichain algorithms · Data structures

1 Introduction

The efficiency and scalability of verification techniques such as model checking and temporal synthesis largely depend on the size and complexity of the input. One way to mitigate this consists in making use of (symbolic) data structures to represent the model implicitly [9]. For instance, when the states of a model admit some partial order and sets of states satisfying properties of interest are downward-closed with respect to the partial order, verification algorithms can manipulate sets of states by storing their (antichain of) maximal states only.

Antichain-based algorithms exist for various verification problems. There are antichain-based algorithms for stable failures refinement checking, for failures-divergence refinement checking, and for probabilistic refinement checking [27,30].

This work was supported by the FWO "SynthEx" project (G0AH524N).

© The Author(s), under exclusive license to Springer Nature Switzerland AG 2026
M. D'Souza et al. (Eds.): ATVA 2025, LNCS 16245, pp. 425–446, 2026.
https://doi.org/10.1007/978-3-032-08707-2_20

Antichains have also been used in algorithms to check the inclusion between the sets of traces (i.e. data languages) recognized by generic register automata—this is undecidable, but there is a semi-algorithm based on abstraction refinement and antichains that is known to be sound and complete [22]. There are also antichain algorithms to solve universality and language inclusion problems for nondeterministic Büchi automata, and the emptiness problem for alternating Büchi automata [16]. As a final example, there are antichains algorithms for the inclusion problem between infinite-word visibly pushdown languages [15].

It is important to note that there is no easy template for antichain-based algorithms. Each algorithm mentioned above exploits a slightly different partial order and must argue that different operations preserve closure of the sets to be able to manipulate antichains only. In this work, we are primarily interested in state spaces that can be encoded as vectors of natural numbers in $\mathbb{N}^k$. The partial order we consider is the product order, that is, the component-wise order. There are a number of antichain-based algorithms where such an encoding into natural vectors arises naturally. They appear, for example, in checking safety properties for Petri net markings, such as mutual exclusion and coverability [12] and in antichain algorithms to solve parity and mean-payoff games with imperfect information [4,17,24], where the vectors keep track of visits to vertices with "bad priorities" and running sums of weights, respectively. Finally, in antichain algorithms for the synthesis of reactive systems [7,19], the vectors keep track of visits to rejecting states (in universal co-Büchi automata).

Despite the abundance of antichain-based algorithms, there seems to be no systematic study of the complexity of antichain-manipulating operations. There are two notable exceptions: First, there are algorithms and upper bounds for the computation of the antichain of maximal elements given a downward-closed set [11, Sec. 4]. Second, a result from [19] implies that computing the intersection of a given set of antichains cannot be done in polynomial time unless **NP** = **P**.

Similarly, the body of work focusing on data structures to support the manipulation of antichains is surprisingly slim. Delzanno et al. [12,21] propose a representation of downward-closed sets based on sharing trees, an extension of binary decision diagrams (BDDs) for natural vectors proposed by Zampuniéris [31]. However, the work of Zampuniéris focuses on general sets of vectors instead of downward-closed sets and the works by Delzanno et al. do not reduce downward-closed sets to antichains of maximal elements but instead use approximate reductions. In [7], it is suggested that some version of k-d trees may work well for closed sets of natural vectors. These are classic data structures used in computational geometry to implement efficient range-search algorithms [2]. In particular, they support fast dominance queries, which can be used to implement membership of a vector in a downward-closed set. Unfortunately, in [7] it is also reported that a simple textbook implementation of k-d trees does not outperform their list-based versions of antichain operations. We postulate that this is due to the fact that the algorithm analyses and optimizations for k-d trees described in the computational geometry literature make the assumption that the dimension k of the vectors is fixed or at least logarithmically small with respect to the rest of the input [8]. In contrast, for antichain-based algorithms, the dimension is a crucial part of the input. For instance, in the reactive-system synthesis application, k corresponds to the number of states of a (co-)Büchi automaton, which is typically large, while small sets of vectors with small entries are not uncommon.

Our Contributions. In this work, we formally compare the worst-case running times of classic list-based, novel (antichain-ensuring) sharing-tree-based, and novel k-d-tree-based antichain algorithms. On the way, we re-examine classic tree-building and searching algorithms for k-d trees. These lead to a more efficient implementation of k-d trees than the simple textbook one used in [7]. We have implemented optimized versions of list-, sharing-tree-, and k-d-tree-based algorithms in a library written in C++20, enabling an empirical evaluation of the algorithms. This evaluation is carried out on applications to synthesis of reactive systems inside Acacia-Bonsai [7] and Oink [13,14].

2 Preliminaries

We write $\mathbb{N}$ for the set of all nonnegative integers, including 0. When we need to exclude 0, we instead write $\mathbb{N}_{>0}$. Let $k \in \mathbb{N}_{>0}$ and consider vectors $\boldsymbol{u}, \boldsymbol{v} \in \mathbb{N}^k$. Then, $\boldsymbol{u}$ is *smaller* than $\boldsymbol{v}$ (equivalently, $\boldsymbol{v}$ is *larger* than $\boldsymbol{u}$), denoted by $\boldsymbol{u} \leq \boldsymbol{v}$, if each component of $\boldsymbol{v}$ is greater than or equal to that component of $\boldsymbol{u}$ and the inequality is strict if the relation is strict for at least one component. If $\boldsymbol{u}$ is neither larger, nor smaller than $\boldsymbol{v}$, then they are said to be *incomparable*.

Definition 1 (Downset). *Let $k \in \mathbb{N}_{>0}$. A set $V \subset \mathbb{N}^k$ is a* downset *if all vectors smaller than any vector in the set are also in the set, i.e. if for all $\boldsymbol{u} \in \mathbb{N}^k$ and $\boldsymbol{v} \in V$ we have that $\boldsymbol{u} \leq \boldsymbol{v}$ implies $\boldsymbol{u} \in V$.*

For any $V \subset \mathbb{N}^k$, we use $V{\downarrow}$ to denote the *downward closure of V*, i.e. the set obtained by adding to V all the vectors smaller than the vectors in V. In symbols, $V{\downarrow} = \{\boldsymbol{u} \in \mathbb{N}^k \mid \exists \boldsymbol{v} \in V, \boldsymbol{u} \leq \boldsymbol{v}\}$. Note that the downward closure of any set of vectors is a downset.

Next, we define *antichains* of natural vectors. These arise, for instance, when considering the maximal elements of a downset.

Definition 2 (Antichain). *Let $k \in \mathbb{N}_{>0}$. A set $V \subset \mathbb{N}^k$ is an* antichain *if it consists only of pairwise incomparable vectors, i.e. for all $\boldsymbol{u}, \boldsymbol{v} \in V$ we have neither $\boldsymbol{u} \leq \boldsymbol{v}$ nor $\boldsymbol{u} \leq \boldsymbol{v}$ (i.e. they are incomparable).*

It follows from Dickson's lemma that any antichain (of natural vectors) is finite.

For a finite set $V \subset \mathbb{N}^k$, we write $\lceil V \rceil$ to denote the *antichain of maximal elements from V*. In symbols, $\lceil V \rceil = \{\boldsymbol{v} \in V \mid \forall \boldsymbol{u} \in V, \boldsymbol{v} \not< \boldsymbol{u}\}$.

Antichain Algorithms. We are interested in efficient algorithms to manipulate k-dimensional downsets, for $k \in \mathbb{N}_{>0}$. Note that for any finite downset $V \subset \mathbb{N}^k$, we have that $V = \lceil V \rceil{\downarrow}$. This follows from the result below, which is itself a simple consequence of the transitivity of the partial order on vectors.

Proposition 1. *Let $k \in \mathbb{N}_{>0}$, $u \in \mathbb{N}^k$, and a finite set $V \subset \mathbb{N}^k$. Then, $\boldsymbol{u} \in V{\downarrow}$ if and only if $\boldsymbol{u} \leq \boldsymbol{v}$ for some $\boldsymbol{v} \in \lceil V \rceil$.*

Hence, one can store the antichain $A = \lceil V \rceil$ as a representation of $V = A{\downarrow}$.

To realize (binary) operations on downsets represented by the antichains A and B, an algorithm can avoid (as much as possible) to explicitly compute the downward closures of the antichains. Further, the result of the operation should also be output by the algorithm represented as antichains. Since, we focus on union and intersection, the following result implies that a single antichain suffices as output of such an algorithm.

Proposition 2. *Let $k \in \mathbb{N}_{>0}$ and $U, V \subset \mathbb{N}^k$. If U and V are both downsets, then $U \cup V$ and $U \cap V$ are also downsets.*

Concretely then, given $A = \lceil U \rceil$ and $B = \lceil V \rceil$, we are looking for efficient algorithms to compute $\lceil A{\downarrow} \cup B{\downarrow} \rceil$ and $\lceil A{\downarrow} \cap B{\downarrow} \rceil$. In the rest of this paper we consider data structures to encode A, B, and their union or intersection.

Finally, there is a decision problem whose complexity is related to that of (all variations) of the union and intersection algorithms present in this paper. Namely, given a k-dimensional vector $\boldsymbol{v}$ and an antichain $A \subset \mathbb{N}^k$ representing a downset, determine whether $\boldsymbol{v} \in A{\downarrow}$. We call this the *membership problem*.

Algorithm Analysis. For all our analyses, our working computational model is that of a random-access machine instead of a Turing machine. In particular, this means we assume indirect addressing takes constant time. Furthermore, we assume comparing two natural numbers $a, b \in \mathbb{N}$ takes constant time. That is, all of the following constitute atomic operations: $a \leq b$, $a < b$, and $a = b$.

3 List-Based Antichain Algorithms

Fix $k \in \mathbb{N}_{>0}$ and a finite k-dimensional downset represented by the antichain $A \subset \mathbb{N}^k$ of its maximal elements. Write m for the cardinality of A, i.e. $|A| = m$.

Example 1. To illustrate the data structures, we use the following antichain as a running example:

$$E = \{(5,2,6,1), (4,3,6,1), (5,1,7,2), (4,3,5,5)\}$$

3.1 The Membership Problem

The naïve approach to check whether a vector $\boldsymbol{v} \in \mathbb{N}^k$ is in the downset $A{\downarrow}$ consists in comparing it, component by component, with each vector in A. Correctness of this approach follows from Proposition 1. This requires km time in the worst case since checking whether a vector is smaller than another vector can be done in k comparisons of numbers.

Proposition 3. *List-based algorithms solve membership in time $O(km)$.*

3.2 The Union Operation

Henceforth, let us fix a second antichain $B \subset \mathbb{N}^k$ representing a k-dimensional downset. Further, write $|B| = n$ for the cardinality of B.

To compute the antichain corresponding to $\lceil A{\downarrow} \cup B{\downarrow} \rceil$, we first note that this antichain will be a subset of vectors in A and B.

Lemma 1 ([19, **Prop. 2, (i)**]). *Let $C = \lceil A{\downarrow} \cup B{\downarrow} \rceil$. Then, $C \subseteq A \cup B$. Moreover, for all $\boldsymbol{u} \in A$, we have $\boldsymbol{u} \notin C$ if and only if $\boldsymbol{u} < \boldsymbol{v}$ for some $\boldsymbol{v} \in B$.*

Based on this, we can check, for each vector in the antichain A, whether it is in the downward closure of B using the membership algorithm described earlier. If the answer is yes, the vector from A is discarded, if not, it is kept for the resulting antichain. We repeat the process once again but now checking, for each vector in the antichian B, whether some vector in the downward closure of A is strictly larger than it. (This can be done with a minimally modified membership algorithm.) Both of these checks take kmn time in the worst case: when the new antichain is $A \cup B$.

Proposition 4. *List-based algorithms for union run in time $O(kmn)$.*

We describe a small optimization for the union algorithm that halves the number of comparisons required. Instead of comparing each element of A with each element of B twice, when comparing the components of a vector $\boldsymbol{u} \in A$ with those of $\boldsymbol{v} \in B$, we check for equality until we find a dimension $1 \leq i \leq k$ such that $u_i \neq v_i$. Let us assume, without loss of generality, $u_i > v_i$. We can now conclude that $\boldsymbol{u} \not< \boldsymbol{v}$. Thus, for the remaining components $i < p \leq k$, we only need to check whether $u_p > v_p$, to determine whether $\boldsymbol{u} > \boldsymbol{v}$. In total, these are $k+1$ comparisons for each pair of vectors instead of $2k$.

3.3 The Intersection Operation

For the intersection, we note that $\lceil A{\downarrow} \cap B{\downarrow} \rceil$ will be a subset of the *meets* of vectors in A and B, i.e. their component-wise minimum. Formally, the meet of two vectors $\boldsymbol{u}, \boldsymbol{v} \in \mathbb{N}^k$ is defined as $\boldsymbol{u} \sqcap \boldsymbol{v} = (\min(u_1, v_1), \ldots, \min(u_k, v_k))$. The notion is extended to sets: $U \sqcap V$ of $U, V \subset \mathbb{N}^k$ is the set $\{\boldsymbol{u} \sqcap \boldsymbol{v} \mid \boldsymbol{u} \in U, \boldsymbol{v} \in V\}$.

Lemma 2 ([19, **Prop. 2, (ii)**]). *Let $C = \lceil A{\downarrow} \cap B{\downarrow} \rceil$. Then, $C = \lceil A \sqcap B \rceil$.*

The cardinality of $A \sqcap B$ is at most mn. Now, to compute its antichain of maximal elements, we check the membership of each vector in $A \sqcap B$ within the downward closure of the other vectors using the membership algorithm introduced earlier. This results in a quadratic worst-case running time.

Proposition 5. *List-based algorithms for intersection run in time $O(km^2n^2)$.*

Observe that intersection is much more costly than union even when working with antichains as a representation of downsets. There is no known approach to computing intersection that avoids the explicit computation of the set of meets of both antichains. The proof of [19, Proposition 5] establishes that all independent sets of a graph can be obtained as the intersection of linearly many downsets. The authors use a different partially ordered set, but the argument can be adapted to use Boolean vectors whose dimension is the number of vertices in the graph. Hence, unless $\mathbf{P} = \mathbf{NP}$, no algorithm for polyadic intersection runs in polynomial time, and therefore we cannot implement binary intersections in $O(kn + km)$.

As a small optimization, we observe that a vector $\boldsymbol{v} \in A$ can be excluded from the computation of all meets if the membership check $\boldsymbol{v} \in B{\downarrow}$ is positive, i.e. there is some $\boldsymbol{w} \in B$ such that $\boldsymbol{v} \leq \boldsymbol{w}$. This is because all elements in $\{\boldsymbol{u} \sqcap \boldsymbol{v} \mid \boldsymbol{u} \in B\}$ will be smaller than $\boldsymbol{v} \sqcap \boldsymbol{w} = \boldsymbol{v}$. This can be used to reduce the number of meets that must be considered. To conclude, one could also follow the analysis from [11, Theorem 11] to establish a bound which replaces one of the mn factors in Proposition 5 by the *width*, i.e. the largest antichain over $A{\downarrow} \cap B{\downarrow}$.

4 Sharing-Tree-Based Antichain Algorithms

As before, let us fix $k \in \mathbb{N}_{>0}$ and a finite k-dimensional downset represented by the antichain $A \subset \mathbb{N}^k$ of its m maximal elements. An additional parameter of interest is $W = \max_{\boldsymbol{v} \in A} \|\boldsymbol{v}\|_\infty$, the maximal norm over elements in A.

In this section, instead of encoding A as a plain list, we construct a *sharing tree* [31] for it. One can look at each vector $v \in V$ as a word over $\mathbb{N}$ of length k. Hence, A is a (finite) regular language. The sharing tree of A is nothing more than its minimal deterministic *acyclic* finite-state automaton (DFA) [5,10].

Definition 3 (Sharing tree). *A sharing tree[1] $(N, r, \mathrm{val}, \mathrm{succ})$ is a rooted acyclic graph where $N = N_0 \uplus \cdots \uplus N_k$ is a set of nodes, partitioned into $k+1$ layers, $N_0 = \{r\}$ is the root, $\mathrm{val} \colon N \to \mathbb{N} \cup \{\top\}$ is a value-labeling function that satisfies $\mathrm{val}(r) = \top$, and $\mathrm{succ} \colon N \to 2^N$ is the successor function. Additionally:*

1. *For all $0 \leq i < k$ and $n \in N_i$, $\mathrm{succ}(n) \subseteq N_{i+1}$, i.e., nodes can only have edges to the next layer;*
2. *For all $n \in N$ and $s_1 \neq s_2 \in \mathrm{succ}(n)$, it holds that $\mathrm{val}(s_1) \neq \mathrm{val}(s_2)$, i.e., two successors cannot have the same value;*
3. *For all $0 \leq i < k$ and $n_1 \neq n_2 \in N_i$, $\mathrm{val}(n_1) = \mathrm{val}(n_2) \implies \mathrm{succ}(n_1) \neq \mathrm{succ}(n_2)$, i.e., same-layer nodes cannot have the same label and successors;*
4. *For all $n \in N_k$, $\mathrm{succ}(n) = \emptyset$, i.e., nodes on the last layer have no successors;*
5. *If $n \in N_1 \cup \cdots \cup N_{k-1}$, then $\mathrm{succ}(n) \neq \emptyset$, that is, each node which is not r or in N_k must have at least one successor.*

Note that we label nodes of the graph and not the edges for ease of notation. Equivalently, one can label all the incoming edges of a node by the value of that node to obtain a DFA in the usual sense.

---
[1] It is a directed acyclic graph, not a tree, but it was thus named in earlier literature.

Example 2. Returning to the antichain E from Example 1, we now represent it as a sharing tree. The result is shown in Fig. 1. The vectors can be obtained by following all possible paths through the tree starting in the root $\top$ and ending in the final node $\bot$.

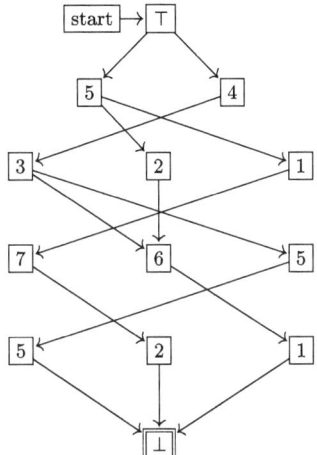

Fig. 1. A sharing tree encoding $\{(5,2,6,1),(4,3,6,1),(5,1,7,2),(4,3,5,5)\}$

4.1 Growing Sharing Trees

Our algorithm for building a sharing tree is given in Algorithm 1, where $j = 0$ initially and (for technical convenience) $v_0 = \top$ for all $v \in A$. Intuitively, one builds an (implicit) trie for A and then minimizes the resulting DFA in a bottom-up fashion. Minimization, i.e. merging of the (language-)equivalent nodes, is then handled à la Revuz [29] by giving unique identifiers to the nodes based on their label and the indices of their successors in their layer.[2]

Example 3. To build the sharing tree storing the four vectors in Fig. 1, the procedure is called with the arguments $(E, 0)$. The vertices are bucketed based on the first dimension (lines 3 and 4), and the root node with the special value $\top$ is created. In the recursive call, the buckets $\{(5,2,6,1),(5,1,7,2)\}$ and $\{(4,3,6,1),(4,3,5,5)\}$ respectively, and 1 are used as arguments, as all vectors passed to the procedure share the value at position $j = 1$. Consequently, the two new nodes with labels 5 and 4 can be created and, after recursively adding their successors, set as successors of $\top$. This process is repeated until dimension $j = 5$ is reached, which calls line 1 of the algorithm. By definition, the antichain passed as argument to the procedure here contains a single element $\bot$. Otherwise, multiple vectors would have been placed in the same bucket in every recursive call,

---
[2] By Item 4 this combination is indeed unique per layer.

Algorithm 1. BuildSharingTree(A, j)

1: **if** $j = k$ **then**
2:   Return (cached) leaf T with label v_k, where $A = \{v\}$
3: **for all** $v \in A$ **do**
4:   add v to bucket$[v_{j+1}]$
5: $T \leftarrow$ tree node with label v_j
6: **for all** $a \in \mathbb{N}$ such that bucket$[a] \neq \emptyset$, in decreasing order **do**
7:   $T_a, \mathrm{idx}_{j+1}(a) \leftarrow$ BuildSharingTree(bucket$[a], j+1$) ▷ New node & its index
8:   add T_a as successor of T
9: Set id of T to $(j, v_j, \mathrm{idx}_{j+1}(0), \mathrm{idx}_{j+1}(1)\ldots)$ ▷ Uniquely identifies this subtree
10: Return (cached) (sub)tree root T
---

making them identical, contradicting the definition of an antichain (lines 9 and 10).

Note that every layer of the trie will have at most m nodes. Then, since we have k layers, and every recursive call of the algorithm runs in $O(W)$ time (initializing the buckets to empty already costs that much), we get that the tree can be computed in time $O(kmW)$. Observe that if $W > m$ one can "compress" the vectors by sorting them per dimension (in time $O(km \log m)$) and keeping only their position in the corresponding sorted list. This ensures $W \leq m$ and one can store the sorted lists as an $m \times k$ matrix to keep the original values (the components of which can be accessed in constant time via the stored indices).

Lemma 3. *A sharing tree, with $O(km)$ nodes and edges, for a set of m vectors in dimension k with max norm W can be constructed in time $O(km \min(m, W))$.*

To avoid wasting memory due to sparse successor arrays, the trie can be built by first sorting the vectors based on the relevant component and using a linked list instead of an array with $\{0, 1, \ldots, W\}$ as indices. This also means we can conveniently store all successors in decreasing order of their labels. Additionally, instead of an exact cache for nodes, one can use a hash table.

Although building a sharing tree for A is more costly than storing it as a list, it may result in exponential savings in terms of space and subsequent membership queries. Indeed, due to sharing, the constructed sharing tree could be exponentially smaller than the starting set. For example, the antichain represented by the language $\{01 + 10\}^n$ has size exponential in n, but can be represented as a sharing tree of size $O(n)$ (cf. [31, Sec. 1.3.3] and [12, Prop. 2]).

4.2 The Membership Problem

To determine whether a vector $\boldsymbol{u} \in \mathbb{N}^k$ is part of the downset $A{\downarrow}$, we can use a depth-first search (DFS). Starting from the root, the values of the successors are compared to the corresponding component of $\boldsymbol{u}$ at every layer. If the value of the node is greater than or equal to the component, the branch is followed further down or membership is confirmed, if it is the last layer, otherwise it is discarded. Based on the linear-time complexity of DFS and Lemma 3, we get:

Proposition 6. *Sharing-tree-based algorithms solve membership in time $O(km)$.*

We again remark that the sharing tree may be of logarithmic size with respect to A. Hence, the DFS may in fact be much more efficient than a search over A, even if the conclusion is that the given vector is not a member of $A\downarrow$.

As a small optimization, we note that having stored the successors of every node in decreasing label order allows for early exits. Indeed, if during the DFS we encounter a node whose first successor has a smaller label than the corresponding component of $\boldsymbol{u}$, there is no need to check the remaining branches following the remaining successors. Similarly, when searching at the second-to-last layer of the sharing tree, a dominating vector is encoded by some branch only if the label of the last successor is larger than the last component of $\boldsymbol{u}$.

Covering Sharing Trees. We are using Zampuniéris' version of sharing trees [31] while ensuring we encode an antichain. This is in contrast to *covering sharing trees*, as proposed in [12], which do not encode the antichain of maximal elements only. Due to the usage of an *approximate* domination check, covering sharing trees could be much larger than the sharing tree of the antichain of maximal elements. Moreover, the union and intersection algorithms for covering sharing trees are more graph-based and reminiscent of BDD operations than the ones we give below. These facts make complexity comparisons with the other approaches in this work more difficult and less interesting. In Sect. 6 we do present some empirical evidence showing that ensuring that the encoded set is an antichain results in size and time gains.

4.3 The Union and Intersection Operations

As before, for the binary operations, we shall fix a second antichain $B \subset \mathbb{N}^k$ with n vectors representing a k-dimensional downset. We also extend our bound on the maximal norm so that $W = \max_{v \in A \cup B} \|\boldsymbol{v}\|_\infty$. Our sharing-tree-based algorithms for the binary operations are mostly identical to the list-based ones. However, their complexity is higher due to the added cost of building sharing trees compared to just keeping a list of vectors.

Recall that the antichain $C = \lceil A\downarrow \cup B\downarrow \rceil$ is a subset of both A and B, see Lemma 1. Moreover, for both A and B, the vectors are added to C if they are not in the closure of the respective other set, so if there is no strictly larger vector. As shown, these checks can be realized using a DFS in time $O(kmn)$. Finally, constructing the sharing tree for C takes time $O(k(m+n)\min(m+n,W))$.

Theorem 1. *There is a sharing-tree-based algorithm for the union operation that runs in time $O(kn(m + \min(n, W))$ assuming (w.l.o.g.) that $m \leq n$.*

For intersection, our starting point is the set $A \sqcap B$, as per Lemma 2. To compute the antichain $C = \lceil A \sqcap B \rceil$, we first construct a sharing tree for the set $A \sqcap B$. Then, we use the sharing tree to check, for each vector in the set, whether it is strictly smaller than some other vector. Finally, we construct a second sharing tree for the vectors for which the result of the previous check was negative (i.e. the maximal elements from $A \sqcap B$). The number of possible meets $A \sqcap B$ is at most mn and can be enumerated in time $O(kmn)$. Conveniently, constructing the sharing tree removes duplicates due to the minimization step. So constructing a sharing tree for $A \sqcap B$ is as simple as enumerating all the meets and constructing a sharing tree, the latter in time $O(kmn \min(mn, W))$. Hence, building the first sharing tree can be done in time $O(kmn \min(mn, W))$. Then, for each vector in the set, the strict membership takes time $O(kmn)$, yielding a total time of $O(k(mn)^2)$. To conclude, we note that, in the worst case, constructing the second tree is just as costly as constructing the first one.

Theorem 2. *There is a sharing-tree-based algorithm for the intersection operation that runs in time $O(km^2n^2)$.*

5 k-d-Tree-Based Antichain Algorithms

One final time, let us fix $k \in \mathbb{N}_{>0}$ and a finite k-dimensional downset represented by the antichain $A \subset \mathbb{N}^k$ of its m maximal elements. In this section, we encode A using a (real) tree structure that generalizes binary search trees to higher dimensions. In fact, we will make use of k-d trees.

We closely follow the presentation from [2, Ch. 5.2]. To present the theory as close as possible to what we implement for the forthcoming experiments, we introduce some additional notation. Mainly, we need a clear definition of the median of a sorted list with repeated elements and a total strict order on the elements of the list (cf. [2, Ch. 5.5]).

Consider a sequence $x_1, x_2, \ldots, x_p$ of natural numbers. Let us write $x_i \prec x_j$ if and only if $x_i < x_j$ or $x_i = x_j$ and $i < j$. That is, $\prec$ is the lexicographic order obtained from the order on the elements in the sequence and their indices. Now, the $\prec$-median of the sequence is the $\lceil p/2 \rceil$-th $\prec$-largest number in the sequence.

Example 4. Once again, we return to the antichain E used in Examples 1 and 2. The representation as a k-d tree can be seen in Fig. 2.

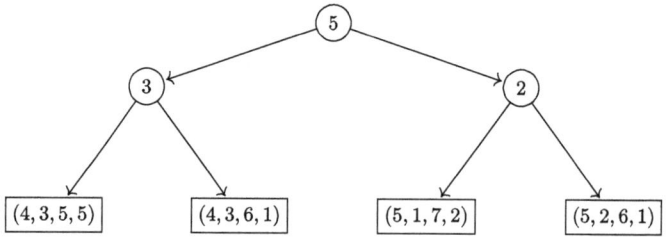

Fig. 2. An example for a k-d tree.

5.1 Growing k-d Tree

Intuitively, a k-d tree is the natural generalization of a binary search tree from 1 to multiple dimensions. When going down a branch of the tree by j levels, the remaining set of vectors is partitioned based on the $(j+1)$-th coordinate. The algorithm to build a k-d tree is given in Algorithm 2, where $j=0$ initially.

Algorithm 2. BuildKDTree(A, j)

1: **if** $A = \{v\}$ **then**
2:     Return leaf storing v
3: $i \leftarrow (j \bmod k) + 1$ ▷ The current dimension
4: $\mu \leftarrow$ the $\prec$-median of A with respect to the i-th coordinate
5: $B_\prec \leftarrow \{v \in A \mid v_i \prec \mu_i\}$
6: $B_\succ \leftarrow \{v \in A \mid v_i \succ \mu_i\} \cup \{\mu\}$
7: $T_\prec \leftarrow$ BuildKDTree($B_\prec, j+1$)
8: $T_\succ \leftarrow$ BuildKDTree($B_\succ, j+1$)
9: Return tree T with children $T_\prec$ and $T_\succ$ and label μ_i

---

In Algorithm 2, the set of vectors is first split on the median value in dimension i in lines 4 through 6. These two sets are now further split recursively on dimension $i \bmod k$ in lines 7 and 8.

Note that when k is small, e.g. 2, then we need to make sure we are still partitioning the vectors according to valid dimensions even after the second layer of the tree. This is why Algorithm 2 requires a modulo operator.

It is instructive to consider the case where all elements of A are unique with respect to all coordinates. Here, one can think of each step of the algorithm as computing the median of the vectors according to dimension i, splitting the space $\mathbb{N}^k$ into two on the i-th coordinate: the left subtree encodes the region of space consisting of all the vectors whose i-component is strictly less than that of the median; the right one, all those greater than or equal to it. The use of $\prec$ is really only a technicality useful to ensure the tree is balanced.

Lemma 4 ([2, Lemma 5.3]). *A k-d tree for a set of m vectors in k dimensions can be constructed in time $O(m \log m)$.*

We highlight a discrepancy between k-d trees in fixed dimension and those where k is part of the input. In most presentations of k-d trees (e.g. [2,6]) it is suggested that computing the median on every recursive call of the algorithm to build the tree can be avoided by doing some preprocessing: compute a sorted version of the initial list for each dimension and split these into sorted sublists for the recursive calls. Note that even the presorting introduces a dependency on k as sorting k lists costs us $O(km \log m)$ if the dimension is part of the input. Hence, computing the median in each recursive call does seem better in our case.

5.2 The Membership Problem

Let $u \in \mathbb{N}^k$. Now, given a k-d tree T encoding the antichain A, we will appeal to Proposition 1 and use T to determine whether $u \in A\!\downarrow$ by searching the tree to find some $v \in A$ such that $u \leq v$. First, we introduce some additional notation.

To each internal node T we associate a region[3] $\mathrm{Reg}(T) \subseteq \mathbb{N}^k$ inductively. We start with the entirety of $\mathbb{N}^k$ at the root. Then, for a node T at depth j and with μ the $\prec$-median used to build it, to its right child $T_\succ$, we associate $\{v \in \mathrm{Reg}(T) \mid v_i \geq \mu_i, i = (j \bmod k) + 1\}$; to its left child $T_\prec$, the region $\{v \in \mathrm{Reg}(T) \mid v_i < \mu_i, i = (j \bmod k)+1\} \cup M$, where M is the set of all vectors $v \in \mathrm{Reg}(T)$ with $v_i = \mu_i$ if $B_\prec$ (as defined in Algorithm 2) contains any such vector and $\emptyset$ otherwise. We also write $\mathrm{Reg}(u)$ for the region $\{v \in \mathbb{N}^k \mid u \leq v\}$, i.e. the *upward closure* of u. The following is our search algorithm:

Algorithm 3. SearchKDTree(T, u)

1: **if** T is a leaf storing v **then**
2:     Return whether $u \leq v$
3: **if** $\mathrm{Reg}(T_\succ) \subseteq \mathrm{Reg}(u)$ **then**
4:     Return true
5: $R_\succ \leftarrow$ SearchKDTree($T_\succ, u$), $R_\prec \leftarrow$ false
6: **if** $\mathrm{Reg}(T_\prec) \cap \mathrm{Reg}(u) \neq \emptyset$ **then**
7:     $R_\prec \leftarrow$ SearchKDTree($T_\prec, u$)
8: Return $R_\succ \vee R_\prec$

By construction of a k-d tree T, if $\mathrm{Reg}(T) \subseteq \mathrm{Reg}(u)$, all vectors v stored at the leaves of T are such that $u \leq v$. There are no empty k-d trees, so this instance of the membership problem is positive. Conversely, if $\mathrm{Reg}(T) \cap \mathrm{Reg}(u) = \emptyset$, for all vectors v stored at its leaves we have $u \not\leq v$. Since $\mathrm{Reg}(u)$ is upward closed:

- $\mathrm{Reg}(T_\succ) \cap \mathrm{Reg}(u) \neq \emptyset$ if $\mathrm{Reg}(T) \cap \mathrm{Reg}(u) \neq \emptyset$, and
- $\mathrm{Reg}(T_\prec) \subseteq \mathrm{Reg}(u)$ only if $\mathrm{Reg}(T) \subseteq \mathrm{Reg}(u)$.

It follows that Algorithm 3 returns true if and only if the instance is positive. It remains to study its complexity.[4]

Theorem 3. *There is a k-d tree algorithm that solves membership in time $O(\min(km, k^2 m^{1-1/k}))$.*

Proof. The first term in the minimum comes from the fact that the tree has at most $2m$ nodes. The second term will follow from bounding the number of nodes

---
[3] Technically, we are dealing with the natural vectors contained in the region. We find that the name region still conveys the right intuition.
[4] It is interesting to compare the k^2 factor in the bound with the linear one k informally claimed by Chan in the introduction of [8]. We did not find a reference for the claimed $O(km^{1-1/k})$ bound, nor were we able to re-prove it ourselves.

the algorithm treats by $O(km^{1-1/k})$. For the remaining k factor in both terms, we observe that, on leaves, one does need to compare k numbers against each other. However, on internal nodes of the tree, a recursive call can be made to do only a constant amount of work. It is easy to see that checking whether the intersection of the regions is empty can be done in constant time: we only need to see how μ_i and u_i compare, where $\boldsymbol{\mu}$ is the median used to split at this node of the tree and $i = (j \mod k) + 1$ with j the depth. Slightly less obvious is the fact that one can determine the region inclusions from line 3 in constant time. This can be done by keeping track of k variables which store the lower bounds of the region of the current node and a counter c initially set to the number of strictly positive components of $\boldsymbol{u}$. On each recursive call, only one variable needs to be updated and if it becomes larger than the corresponding component of $\boldsymbol{u}$ we decrement c, i.e. $c \leftarrow c - 1$. Clearly, the inclusion holds if and only if $c = 0$.

It remains to argue that the number of nodes treated is indeed $O(km^{1-1/k})$. Say a region $\text{Reg}(T)$ is i-interesting, for $1 \leq i \leq k$, if there are $\boldsymbol{v}, \boldsymbol{w} \in \text{Reg}(T)$ such that $v_i < u_i \leq w_i$. Essentially, not all vectors stored in T are guaranteed to be larger than $\boldsymbol{u}$, with respect to the i-th coordinate, but neither are they all strictly smaller. The algorithm makes a recursive call on T only if $\text{Reg}(T)$ is i-interesting for some i. Hence, if for all i we can bound the number of nodes of the tree with an i-interesting region by $O(m^{1-1/k})$, the bound will follow. From here on, our argument follows [6, Ch. 4.10].

Let $1 \leq i \leq k$ be arbitrary and consider a node T at depth $(i-1)$ from the root. Since $B_\prec$ and $B_\succ$ are constructed based on the i-th coordinate, we have that at most one subtree among $\text{Reg}(T_\prec)$ and $\text{Reg}(T_\succ)$ is i-interesting. This dichotomy holds again for the subtrees rooted k levels down since, once more, the vectors are split based on the i-th coordinate. Now let a_j be the number of nodes at level $0 \leq j \leq \log m$ from the root with an i-interesting region. From the analysis above we have that $a_j \leq 2^{\lfloor (1-1/k)j \rfloor}$ since we double the number of nodes at every level except when $i = (j \mod k) + 1$. For the total number of nodes (across all levels) with i-interesting regions we get the following.

$$a_0 + a_1 + \cdots + a_{\log m} \leq 2(2^{(1-1/k)(\log m)}) = 2\, m^{1-1/k}$$

Intuitively, every k layers, the doubling does not happen, so we lose a factor of $m^{\frac{1}{k}}$ nodes out of the total $2m$ nodes. Since the right-hand side of the equation above is $O(m^{1-1/k})$, as required, this concludes the proof. □

Note that the bound from Theorem 3 simplifies to $O(k^2 m^{1-1/k})$ if $m \geq 2^{k \log k}$. Henceforth, to simplify our analysis, we will assume this inequality holds. Nevertheless, for the claims, we state the bounds in their full generality.

5.3 The Union Operation

Let $B \in \mathbb{N}^k$ be a second antichain with n vectors representing a k-dimensional downset. Our k-d-tree-based algorithm for the union operation follows the one proposed in Sect. 3.2. The main difference is that we leverage the complexity of the k-d-tree-based membership problem to obtain a different complexity bound.

By Lemma 1, to compute $C = \lceil A{\downarrow} \cup B{\downarrow} \rceil$ it suffices to remove from A those elements dominated by some element in B and to union them with the elements of B that are not (strictly) dominated by some element in A. The strict domination check can be realized with a modification of our membership algorithm. The checks take time $O(k^2 mn^{1-1/k})$ and $O(k^2 m^{1-1/k}n)$, respectively. Finally, constructing the k-d tree for C takes time $O((m+n)\log(m+n))$.

Theorem 4. *There is a k-d-tree-based algorithm for the union operation that runs in time $O(kn \min(m, km^{1-1/k}) + n \log n)$ assuming (w.l.o.g.) that $m \leq n$.*

Observe that, even if $2^{k \log k} \leq m, n$, this bound is *not always* better than the one we get for our list-based algorithm. Indeed, when $\log(m+n)$ is larger than km or kn, the last summand is already worse than kmn. If $m \leq n$, then this cannot happen when, for instance, $n \leq 2^m$.

5.4 The Intersection Operation

For intersection, we follow Sect. 3.3 except that we use our k-d-tree-based membership algorithm. To compute $C = \lceil A \sqcap B \rceil$, we first construct a k-d tree for the collection of meets obtained from A and B. Note that this may not be a set. Nevertheless, the collection has size at most mn. Next, we use the tree to check, for all vectors it encodes, whether they are strictly smaller than some other vector in the tree. If the answer is negative, we add them to a new collection of nondominated meets. Now, to remove duplicates, we sort the collection lexicographically, this can be done in time $O(kmn \log(mn))$, and traverse it in search for consecutive copies of the same vector, this can be done in time $O(kmn)$. Finally, we construct a second k-d tree for the set of vectors.

Building the first k-d tree can be done in time $O(kmn + mn \log(mn))$. For each vector in the set, the (strict) membership checks can be done in time $O(k^2 (mn)^{1-1/k})$, yielding a total of $O(k^2 (mn)^{2-1/k})$ checks. After removing duplicates in time $O(kmn \log(mn))$, we construct the second k-d tree in time $O(mn \log(mn))$. The total complexity is summarized in the result below.

Theorem 5. *There is a k-d-tree-based algorithm for the intersection operation that runs in time $O(kmn \min(mn, k(mn)^{1-1/k}))$.*

This is better than our list-based algorithm, assuming $2^{k \log k} \leq m, n$.

A complementary behavior of k-d trees and sharing trees emerges from the fact that k-d trees perform better when a number does not occur in several vectors in the same dimension, whereas in sharing trees, repetition of a number in a dimension enables "sharing", and hence decreases the size of the tree.

5.5 Discussion: Theory

The following table summarizes the complexity bounds of the list and k-d-tree-based algorithms from the previous sections. To recall, m and n are the sizes of

Operation	Lists	k-d trees	Sharing trees
Membership	$O(km)$	$O(\min(km, k^2 m^{1-1/k}))$	$O(km)$
Union	$O(kmn)$	$O(kn \min(m, km^{1-1/k}) + n \log n)$	$O(kn(m + \min(n, W)))$
Intersection	$O(k m^2 n^2)$	$O(kmn \min(mn, k(mn)^{1-1/k}))$	$O(k m^2 n^2)$

antichains A and B, respectively, of dimension k, and W is the largest integer occurring among all vectors in A and B. To simplify, we assume $m \leq n$.

Our analysis confirms the empirical findings of [7]: k-d trees are not always a better data structure than lists when manipulating antichains. However, based on the remarks at the end of Sect. 5.3, one could conclude that dynamically switching from lists to k-d trees when $2^{k \log k} \leq m \leq n \leq 2^m$ can result in a good tradeoff. We implemented this, but unfortunately the size-to-dimension ratio of most antichains in our experiments does not trigger a switch to k-d trees.

6 Experiments

We implemented several variations of the list-, k-d-tree-, and sharing-tree-based algorithms using a generic library for partially-ordered sets of vectors [28]. Tests "in a vacuum", where the data structure operations are benchmarked on random data, exhibit the expected behavior dictated by their theoretical complexity. We do not report on these unsurprising conclusions. Our main interest lies in tests "in the field", that is, in applications that rely on antichains; one specific aim is to establish whether the conditions for k-d trees or sharing trees to outperform list-based downsets are met in practice. We focus on two such applications: LTL-realizability and parity game solving, relying on benchmark sets used in authoritative competitions. For both applications, we formally present the computational task at hand, the downset-based algorithm to solve it, and experimental results. We also study the ratio of size vs. dimension within the benchmark sets used in these applications.

All the following experiments were carried on an Intel® Core™ i7-8700 CPU @ 3.20 GHz paired with 16 GiB of memory.

6.1 LTL-Realizability

The Task. Let I and O be disjoint and finite sets of *input* and *output propositions*. A *linear-temporal-logic* (LTL) formula over $P = I \cup O$ specifies temporal dependencies between truth values of the propositions. Formulas in LTL are constructed from the propositions, the usual Boolean connectives, and temporal operators "next", "eventually", "always", and "until", with their intuitive semantics. (We refer the reader to [1] for the formal syntax and semantics of LTL.) It is well known that the set Words(φ) of all words, over valuations 2^P of the propositions, that satisfy a given LTL formula φ can be "compiled" into an infinite-word automaton. In particular, one can construct a non-deterministic automaton $\mathcal{N}$ with a *Büchi acceptance condition* such that its language is exactly Words(φ).

The Büchi acceptance condition stipulates that infinite runs of the automaton are accepting if they visit accepting states infinitely often.

LTL realizability can be defined in terms of the aforementioned automaton. Namely, given the nondeterministic Büchi automaton $\mathcal{N}$ constructed from an input LTL formula φ over P, we have an *input player* and an *output player* take turns choosing truth values for I and O. This induces an infinite word over 2^P. The winner of the game depends on whether the word is in the language of $\mathcal{N}$: the input player wins if it is *not* in the language, otherwise the output player wins. The computational task lies in determining if the input player has a winning strategy for this game.

The Algorithm. We succinctly present the downset-based approach of Filiot et al. [19] to solving the task at hand. Fix a *Büchi automaton* $\mathcal{N} = (Q, q_0, \delta, B)$ with Q a set of states, q_0 the initial state, δ the transition relation that uses valuations 2^P as labels, and $B \subseteq Q$ the set of Büchi states. We will be interested in *vectors over* Q, i.e. elements in $\mathbb{Z}^Q$ mapping states to integers, to encode the number of visits to Büchi states—recall the input player wants to avoid there being a run that visits these infinitely often. We will write $\boldsymbol{v}$ for such vectors, and v_q for its value for state q. In practice, these vectors will range into a finite subset of $\mathbb{Z}$, with -1 as an implicit minimum value (i.e. $(-1) - 1$ is still -1) and an upper bound k that can be thought of as a hyperparameter of the algorithm.

For a vector $\boldsymbol{v}$ over Q and a valuation x, we define a function that takes one step back in the automaton, decreasing components that have seen Büchi states. Write $\chi_B(q)$ for the function mapping a state q to 1 if $q \in B$, and 0 otherwise. We then define $\mathrm{bwd}(\boldsymbol{v}, x)$ as the vector over Q that maps each state $p \in Q$ to $\min_{(p,x,q) \in \delta} (v_q - \chi_B(q))$, and generalize it to sets: $\mathrm{bwd}(S, x) = \{\mathrm{bwd}(\boldsymbol{v}, x) \mid \boldsymbol{v} \in S\}$. For a set S of vectors over Q and a valuation $i \in 2^I$ of the inputs, define:

$$\mathrm{CPre}_i(S) = S \cap \bigcup_{o \in 2^O} \mathrm{bwd}(S, i \cup o) .$$

It is proved in [19] that iterating CPre converges to a fixed point that is independent from the order in which the valuation of the inputs is selected. We define $\mathrm{CPre}^*(S)$ to be that set.

All the sets that we manipulate above are *downsets*. Now, for any $k > 0$, if there is a $\boldsymbol{v} \in \mathrm{CPre}^*(\{i \in \mathbb{N} \mid i \leq k\}^Q)$ with $v_{q_0} \geq 0$ then the input player has a winning strategy. Conversely, there is a large enough value of k such that if the condition does not hold then the output player has a winning strategy.

Experimental Results. The above algorithm was implemented as the tool Acacia-Bonsai [7], relying on our generic library for partially-ordered sets. We considered the benchmarks used in the yearly competition in LTL-realizability, SYNTCOMP [25]. These consist in 1048 LTL formulas, of which the best LTL tools solve 90% in under a second. We present the experimental results as a survival plot, indicating how many tests are solved (x-axis) within a time limit (y-axis, time per test). In particular, the lower the curve, the better. To reduce clutter, we focus on the benchmarks that took the longest: 500 benchmarks are not shown, with all implementations solving each of them in less than 0.1 s. The tests were executed with a 60-second timeout. We observe, crucially, that the dynamic switching between the two data structures follows closely the list-based implementation, witnessing the fact that the threshold provided by the theory at which k-d trees are more advantageous (see Sect. 5.5) is rarely crossed. To illustrate this, we studied the *ratio* of set size vs. dimension; it is also displayed here as a survival plot, indicating how many sets (x-axis) have a ratio below a certain value (y-axis). The sets we considered are all the different values of CPre, which, over all the benchmarks, amounts to 67,143 sets.

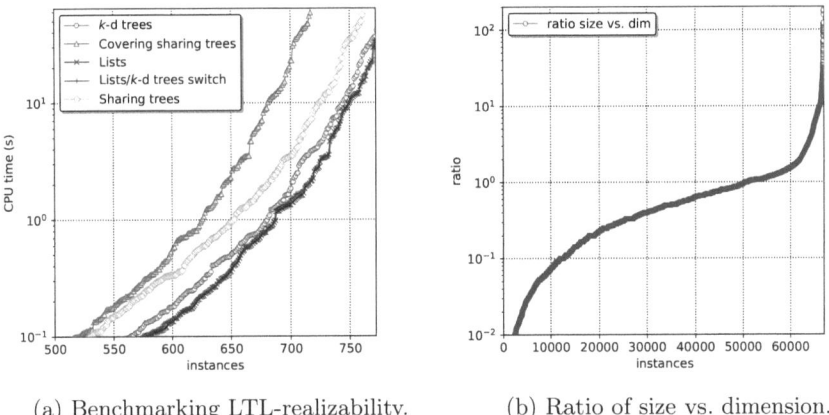

(a) Benchmarking LTL-realizability. (b) Ratio of size vs. dimension.

Fig. 3. Survival plots of downset-based LTL-realizability.

The k-d tree implementation solved 779 test cases, while the list implementations solved a strict superset of 787 cases. Sharing tree implementations performed uniformly worse than all the others, solving 717 test cases for covering sharing trees, and 761 for sharing trees. These are in turn subsets of the ones solved by k-d tree, except for one case.

These results indicate that the size of the antichains and their dimensions are too low to translate into an edge for the k-d tree structure, but that they nonetheless achieve similar performances. This is clearly indicated by Fig. 3b: roughly 95% of sets that are created in the algorithm are of size that is bounded by twice the dimension. Larger ratios are only found in 161 of the 787 solved cases.

When introduced in 2023, Acacia-Bonsai also included an implementation of k-d trees. On the set of benchmarks presented in the next subsection, optimized algorithms based on the theoretical insights presented in this paper have led to half an order of magnitude improvement in the performance of the data structure. We speculate that similar improvements are still possible for our implementation of (covering) sharing trees.

6.2 Parity Game Solving

The Task. A *parity game* $\mathcal{G}$ is a tuple (V_0, V_1, E, p) where V_0 and V_1 are disjoint sets of vertices with $V = V_0 \cup V_1$, $E \subseteq V \times V$ is a set of directed edges, and $p \colon V \to \mathbb{N}$ assigns a *priority* to each vertex.

In such games, we usually assume an *even player* controls V_0 while an *odd player* controls V_1. The players select outgoing edges from their vertices, and it induces an infinite path from a given starting vertex. The winner of the game depends on the maximal vertex priority appearing infinitely often along the path: the even player wins if it is even, otherwise the odd player wins. The computational task of parity game solving is to determine for each vertex v if the controller of the vertex has a winning strategy in the game starting in v.

The Algorithm. We present an algorithm, based on a construction of Bernet et al. [3], to determine the winner of a parity game via manipulation of downsets. Our presentation follows the vocabulary of [17, Ch. 6]. Let us fix a parity game (V_0, V_1, E, p) and an initial vertex v_0. Also, write $d = \lceil \max_{v \in V} p(v)/2 \rceil$ and $p^{-1} \colon \{0, 1, \ldots, 2d\} \to 2^V$ for the mapping from every priority to the set of all vertices labelled by it. We use vectors $\mathbf{c} \in \mathbb{N}^d$ to keep track of the number of visits to odd-priority vertices. More precisely, we consider $\mathbf{c} \in \mathbb{Z}^d$ such that $-1 \leq c_i \leq n_i$ for all $1 \leq i \leq d$, where $n_i = |p^{-1}(2i-1)|$. We adopt the convention that $c_i - a = -1$ for all $a \geq 1 + c_i$ or if $c_i = -1$, and $c_i + b = n_i$ for all $b \geq n_i - c_i$. The intuition is that c_i keeps track of the number of visits to vertices with odd priority $2i - 1$ and having a value of -1 means that reaching a value of n_i, hence a simple cycle with that odd priority, is unavoidable.

For a vector $\mathbf{c}$ and a vertex $v \in V$, we define an operator to obtain a predecessor vector (recall that we are counting visits to odd-priority vertices). Formally,

$$\mathrm{bwd}(\mathbf{c}, v) = \begin{cases} \mathbf{c} - \mathbf{e}_i & \text{if } p(v) = 2i - 1 \\ \mathbf{c} + \sum_{j=1}^{i} n_j \mathbf{e}_j & \text{if } p(v) = 2i \end{cases}$$

where $\mathbf{e}_i$ is a vector with 1 as its i-th component and zeros elsewhere. We lift the operator to sets C of vectors as follows: $\mathrm{bwd}(C, v) = \{\mathrm{bwd}(\mathbf{c}, v) \mid \mathbf{c} \in C\}$.

Consider a mapping $\mu \colon V \to 2^{\mathbb{N}^d}$ from vertices to sets of vectors. We introduce an update operation on such mappings to compute over-approximations of the states from which the even player wins. The initial mapping μ_0 is the closure of the vector of n_i, i.e. it assigns the following set to all vertices $v \in V$:

$$\mu_0(v) = \{(n_1, n_3, \ldots, n_{2i+1}, \ldots)\}{\downarrow}.$$

Intuitively, this is the worst possible situation for the even player without having reached the maximal number of visits to some odd-priority vertex. The update operation CPre, for a given mapping μ, outputs a new mapping ν such that:

$$\nu(u) = \mu(u) \cap C \ , \text{ where } \quad C = \begin{cases} \bigcup_{(u,v) \in E} \mathrm{bwd}(\mu(v), u){\downarrow} & \text{if } u \in V_0 \\ \bigcap_{(u,v) \in E} \mathrm{bwd}(\mu(v), u){\downarrow} & \text{if } u \in V_1. \end{cases}$$

It can be shown that the mappings obtained by iterating CPre starting from μ_0 converge. We write CPre* for that fixpoint. We have that for all $v \in V$, there is some $\boldsymbol{c} \in \mathrm{CPre}^*(v)$ such that $0 \leq c_i \leq n_i$ for all $1 \leq i \leq d$ if and only if the even player wins the parity game when starting from v. To prove this, one can follow the argument used to establish [17, Lemma 6.4] or [3, Corollary 6.4].

Experimental Results. We again rely on the SYNTCOMP24 benchmarks, which has a competition track for parity game solvers, and augment these benchmarks with the ones provided by Keiren [26]. We implemented our downset-based algorithm in the tool Oink [13]. The implementation is agnostic to the downset implementation, allowing for easy comparison of the underlying data structure. The 779 benchmarks were each executed with a 60-s timeout and 10 GB memory limitation. The survival plot appears below in the form of Fig. 4.

We studied the ratio of set size vs. dimension, listing the size of the set C (as used in the definition of ν above) every time it is computed; this is a grand total of 1,106,234,004 sets. For 98% of them, the ratio was smaller than 0.03; in fact, out of the billion sets processed by our algorithm, only 746,139 are of size greater or equal to 3. These are concentrated on only 22 out of 1024 benchmarks and we also display the survival plot corresponding to these tests only, since they are more likely to favor implementations that perform well with large-sized sets.

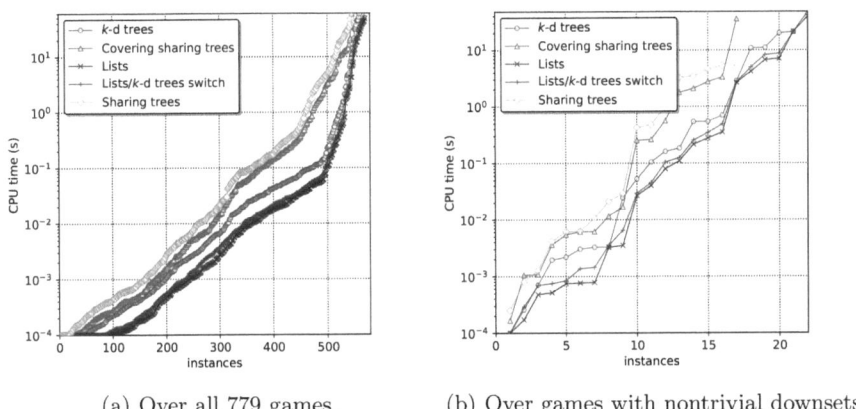

(a) Over all 779 games.   (b) Over games with nontrivial downsets.

Fig. 4. Survival plots of downset-based parity-game solving.

On these smaller downsets, covering sharing trees does better than sharing trees. It would seem that when the size of the antichain of maximal elements is not much smaller than the downset itself, the approximate domination check of covering sharing trees shines through. However, list-based algorithms are also best for the use case of parity games: over all 779 games, they solve 569 test cases, while k-d trees solve 559, and (covering) sharing trees 544.

7 Conclusion

We provided a theoretical analysis of two data structures for downsets of natural vectors: list-, sharing-tree-, and k-d-tree-based. We identified when k-d trees should outperform the others and provided experiments showing that uses "in the field" are not conducive to cases where k-d trees outperform the humble list-based implementation. We posit other antichain-based tools like the Petri-net safety-checking tool MIST [20] may benefit from using list-based antichains.

For future work, it would be interesting to provide average-case complexity bounds for the operations we have studied. Most naive approaches for an average-case analysis of antichain-manipulations seem to require tighter bounds on *Dedekind numbers* than the ones we found in the literature (see, e.g. [18]). Additionally, our study of antichain size vs. dimension may indicate sharing-tree based antichains benefit from radix-tree like compression [23].

Acknowledgements. We would like to thank Jean Cardinal and Gwenaël Joret for useful discussions on the topic of orthogonal range searching and k-d trees, and Marcin Jurdzinski for helping us navigate the landscape of parity-game algorithms.

References

1. Baier, C., Katoen, J.: Principles of Model Checking. MIT Press (2008)
2. de Berg, M., Cheong, O., van Kreveld, M.J., Overmars, M.H.: Computational Geometry: Algorithms and Applications, 3rd edn. Springer (2008). https://www.worldcat.org/oclc/227584184
3. Bernet, J., Janin, D., Walukiewicz, I.: Permissive strategies: from parity games to safety games. RAIRO Theor. Informatics Appl. **36**(3), 261–275 (2002). https://doi.org/10.1051/ITA:2002013
4. Berwanger, D., Chatterjee, K., Wulf, M.D., Doyen, L., Henzinger, T.A.: Strategy construction for parity games with imperfect information. Inf. Comput. **208**(10), 1206–1220 (2010)
5. Blumer, A., Blumer, J., Ehrenfeucht, A., Haussler, D., McConnell, R.M.: Linear size finite automata for the set of all subwords of a word - an outline of results. Bull. EATCS **21**, 12–20 (1983)
6. Brass, P.: Advanced Data Structures. Cambridge University Press (2008). https://doi.org/10.1017/CBO9780511800191
7. Cadilhac, M., Pérez, G.A.: Acacia-bonsai: a modern implementation of downset-based LTL realizability. In: Sankaranarayanan, S., Sharygina, N. (eds.) TACAS 2023. LNCS, vol. 13994, pp. 192–207. Springer, Cham (2023). https://doi.org/10.1007/978-3-031-30820-8_14
8. Chan, T.M.: Orthogonal range searching in moderate dimensions: k-d trees and range trees strike back. Discret. Comput. Geom. **61**(4), 899–922 (2019). https://doi.org/10.1007/S00454-019-00062-5
9. Clarke, E.M., Henzinger, T.A., Veith, H., Bloem, R. (eds.): Handbook of Model Checking. Springer, Cham (2018). https://doi.org/10.1007/978-3-319-10575-8
10. Daciuk, J., Mihov, S., Watson, B.W., Watson, R.E.: Incremental construction of minimal acyclic finite state automata. Comput. Linguist. **26**(1), 3–16 (2000). https://doi.org/10.1162/089120100561601

11. Daskalakis, C., Karp, R.M., Mossel, E., Riesenfeld, S.J., Verbin, E.: Sorting and selection in posets. SIAM J. Comput. **40**(3), 597–622 (2011). https://doi.org/10.1137/070697720
12. Delzanno, G., Raskin, J., Begin, L.V.: Covering sharing trees: a compact data structure for parameterized verification. Int. J. Softw. Tools Technol. Transf. **5**(2-3), 268–297 (2004). https://doi.org/10.1007/S10009-003-0110-0
13. Dijk, T.: Oink: an implementation and evaluation of modern parity game solvers. In: Beyer, D., Huisman, M. (eds.) TACAS 2018. LNCS, vol. 10805, pp. 291–308. Springer, Cham (2018). https://doi.org/10.1007/978-3-319-89960-2_16
14. Dijk, T., Abbema, F., Tomov, N.: Knor: reactive synthesis using oink. In: Finkbeiner, B., Kovács, L. (eds.) TACAS 2024, Part I. LNCS, vol. 14570, pp. 103–122. Springer, Cham (2024). https://doi.org/10.1007/978-3-031-57246-3_7
15. Doveri, K., Ganty, P., Hadzi-Dokic, L.: Antichains algorithms for the inclusion problem between omega-VPL. In: Sankaranarayanan, S., Sharygina, N. (eds.) TACAS 2023. LNCS, vol. 13993, pp. 290–307. Springer, Cham (2023). https://doi.org/10.1007/978-3-031-30823-9_15
16. Doyen, L., Raskin, J.: Antichains for the automata-based approach to model-checking. Log. Methods Comput. Sci. **5**(1) (2009)
17. Doyen, L., Raskin, J.: Games with imperfect information: theory and algorithms. In: Lectures in Game Theory for Computer Scientists, pp. 185–212. Cambridge University Press (2011)
18. Falgas-Ravry, V., Räty, E., Tomon, I.: Dedekind's problem in the hypergrid (2023). https://arxiv.org/abs/2310.12946
19. Filiot, E., Jin, N., Raskin, J.: Antichains and compositional algorithms for LTL synthesis. Formal Methods Syst. Des. **39**(3), 261–296 (2011)
20. Ganty, P.: Algorithmes et structures de données efficaces pour la manipulation de contraintes sur les intervalles (in French). Master's thesis, Université Libre de Bruxelles, Belgium (2002)
21. Ganty, P., Meuter, C., Delzanno, G., Kalyon, G., Raskin, J., Van Begin, L.: Symbolic data structure for sets of k-uples. Technical report 570, Université Libre de Bruxelles, Belgium (2007)
22. Holík, L., Iosif, R., Rogalewicz, A., Vojnar, T.: Abstraction refinement and antichains for trace inclusion of infinite state systems. Formal Methods Syst. Design **55**(3), 137–170 (2020). https://doi.org/10.1007/s10703-020-00345-1
23. Holub, J., Crochemore, M.: On the implementation of compact DAWG's. In: Champarnaud, J.-M., Maurel, D. (eds.) CIAA 2002. LNCS, vol. 2608, pp. 289–294. Springer, Heidelberg (2003). https://doi.org/10.1007/3-540-44977-9_31
24. Hunter, P., Pérez, G.A., Raskin, J.: Looking at mean payoff through foggy windows. Acta Inform. **55**(8), 627–647 (2018)
25. Jacobs, S., et al.: The reactive synthesis competition (SYNTCOMP): 2018–2021. Int. J. Softw. Tools Technol. Transf. **26**(5), 551–567 (2024). https://doi.org/10.1007/S10009-024-00754-1
26. Keiren, J.J.A.: Benchmarks for parity games. In: Dastani, M., Sirjani, M. (eds.) FSEN 2015. LNCS, vol. 9392, pp. 127–142. Springer, Cham (2015). https://doi.org/10.1007/978-3-319-24644-4_9
27. Laveaux, M., Groote, J.F., Willemse, T.A.C.: Correct and efficient antichain algorithms for refinement checking. Log. Methods Comput. Sci. **17**(1) (2021). https://lmcs.episciences.org/7143
28. Michaël Cadilhac, Vanessa Flügel, G.A.P.: Code for data structures for finite downsets of natural vectors (2025). https://doi.org/10.5281/zenodo.15837722

29. Revuz, D.: Minimisation of acyclic deterministic automata in linear time. Theor. Comput. Sci. **92**(1), 181–189 (1992). https://doi.org/10.1016/0304-3975(92)90142-3
30. Wang, T., et al.: More anti-chain based refinement checking. In: Aoki, T., Taguchi, K. (eds.) ICFEM 2012. LNCS, vol. 7635, pp. 364–380. Springer, Heidelberg (2012). https://doi.org/10.1007/978-3-642-34281-3_26
31. Zampuniéris, D.: The sharing tree data structure, theory and applications in formal verification. Ph.D. thesis, Department of Computer Science, University of Namur, Belgium (1997)

Antarbhukti: Verifying Correctness of PLC Software During System Evolution

Soumyadip Bandyopadhyay[1] and Santonu Sarkar[2](✉)

[1] Goa, India
soumyadip.bandyopadhyay@gmail.com
[2] BITS Pilani Goa K K Birla Goa Campus, Goa, India
santonus@goa.bits-pilani.ac.in

Abstract. Upgradation of Programmable Logic Controller (PLC) software is quite common to accommodate evolving industrial requirements. Verifying the correctness of such upgrades remains a significant challenge. In this paper, we propose a verification-based approach to ensure the correctness of the existing functionality in the upgraded version of a PLC software. The method converts the older and the newer versions of the sequential function chart (SFC) into two Petri net models. We then verify whether one model is contained within another, based on a novel containment checking algorithm grounded in symbolic path equivalence. For this purpose, we have developed a home-grown Petri net-based containment checker. Experimental evaluation on 80 real-world benchmarks from the OSCAT library highlights the scalability and effectiveness of the framework. We have compared our approach with `verifAPS`, a popular tool used for software upgradation, and observed nearly 4x performance improvement.

Keywords: Petri net · PLC software verification · industrial automation · Sequential Function Chart (SFC) · containment checking · software evolution

1 Introduction

A modern automation system is driven by process control software written in various programmable logic controller (PLC) languages. To remain efficient, reliable, and sustainable, existing software must be continually upgraded to meet evolving market demands and new safety regulations. However, modifying PLC software carries far more risks, particularly unintended regressions may disrupt existing process operations, leading to disastrous consequences. Therefore, ensuring the correctness of upgraded PLC software is extremely critical.

Traditional approaches to PLC software regression testing primarily rely on simulation and regression tests, which can be time-consuming, incomplete, and

S. Bandyopadhyay—ACM Member.

dependent on domain-specific expertise. While regression testing is commonly employed to compare outputs before and after software modifications, it may not always capture behavioral discrepancies introduced during upgrades.

In this paper, we propose a novel verification-based approach that formally ensures the correctness of existing functionality in the upgraded PLC software. Here, we consider a popular IEC 61131-3 compliant PLC language known as the Sequence Function Chart (SFC). We transform both the older and newer versions of the SFC into Petri net models and verify whether one model is contained in the other. This containment check is based on the notion of behavioral equivalence, ensuring that the upgraded version preserves the expected execution behavior of the previous version. The contributions of our paper are as follows.

1. Model Enhancement – We present an improved version of the Petri net model, where a place can have a sequence of functions (instead of a single function in [1,2]), while transitions are now limited to guard conditions only. This refinement leads to a more compact model representation. We further propose the notion of *execution cut point* to handle PLC tick semantics.
2. Petri Net-based Model Construction – We introduce a model transformation process that converts an SFC program into a Petri net in order to compare behaviors across versions. The transformation process handles synchronous execution semantics through tick labeling, which is crucial for PLC verification but not addressed in general Petri net approaches.
3. Containment Checking Tool – We defined a new theoretical foundation of *containment* and proposed an algorithm to check containment of one Petri net in another. This, in turn, verifies behavioral consistency between different software versions.
4. Scalability and Practical Evaluation – We validate our approach on a diverse set of eighty benchmarks from the open-source OSCAT library, demonstrating its effectiveness in real-world PLC software evolution scenarios. We have also compared our approach with the popular open-source `verifAPS` tool.

The paper has been organized as follows. Section 2 introduces a motivating use-case as a running example in the paper. Section 3 describes the functional architecture of the proposed tool. Section 4 illustrates the construction of a Petri net model. We describe the containment checking process in Sect. 5. We report the experimental evaluation of the tool in Sect. 6. We discuss the utility and limitations of our approach in Sect. 7. Section 8 discusses several important relevant contributions in this area. Finally, we conclude our paper.

2 Motivating Example

Within this paper, we employ a widely recognized "Pick and Place system" [3] as an ongoing example. The system outlined is a simplified representation of a complex industrial process where items are initially placed on Conveyor A. A robotic arm then simultaneously transfers two items from Conveyor A to Conveyor B. Conveyor B is equipped with a scaling sensor that verifies the

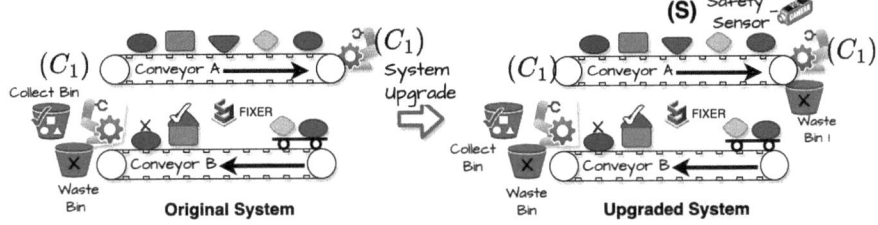

Fig. 1. Pick and Place System- original and upgraded version with safety features

scaling parameters of these items, denoted as a and b. When these parameters are positive, a fixer combines them, and a second robotic arm deposits the composite item into the green *Collect Bin*. Conversely, if the parameters fail to meet a positive value, the items are put to the red *Waste Bin*. The fixing process hinges on intricate calculations adjusting individual scaling factors of items a and b to derive an integrated, custom scaling metric.

In its upgraded version, the system includes a newly installed safety guard sensor, complying with the latest safety protocol (ISO 10218-1)[1]. This sensor oversees the overall system operation and ensures that, without the safety guard being active, the robotic arm on Conveyor A remains immobilized, preventing any object transfer from Conveyor A to B due to breach of safety norms. If the safety guard is *in place*, the robot will place the objects on the conveyor belt B, and the scaling sensor will check the scaling parameters as in the original version. Furthermore, the upgraded version computes the fine-tuning of the individual scaling factors (for a and b) concurrently. The classical testing method is not useful for two reasons.

1. An SFC software testing generally takes 3 to 5 min by an expert engineer in a testing environment.
2. The older version is purely sequential, whereas the upgraded version has parallelism, as it performs the scaling computation concurrently.

The entire control logic is implemented in SFC. The SFC for Fig. 3(a) is in Fig. 4(c), and for the upgraded version in Fig. 3(b), it is shown in Fig. 4(d).

3 Containment Checking Software

The containment verification tool illustrated in Fig. 2 includes three key components: the Petri net model constructor, the Model Analyzer, and the Report Generator. As detailed in Sect. 4, the Petri net model constructor transforms an SFC program into a Petri net model. *Petri nets are selected as the formal model due to their semantics being well-aligned with those of Sequential Function Charts (SFC)* [4], *facilitating a more intuitive and precise translation. Conversely, converting SFC to a Control Data Flow Graph (CDFG) entails multiple intermediate*

---

[1] https://www.iso.org/standard/73933.html.

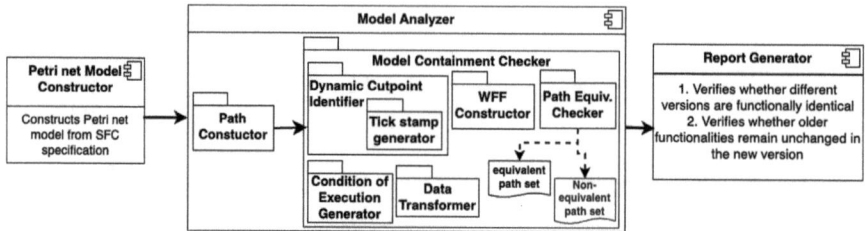

Fig. 2. Functional Block Diagram

transformations [5], *increasing the modeling complexity*. The Path constructor component generates an array of paths derived from a set of cut-points to a cut-point without any intermediary cut-points. The Model Containment Checker component takes two Petri net models—one for the original SFC code and the other for the updated SFC code—to determine if the updated SFC retains the original SFC's functionality. This process is referred to as model containment checking (Definitions 7 and 6). This component leverages data transformation and an execution condition checker to assess model containment. We incorporate the concept of path equivalence checking [1] for this purpose. The report generator module delivers a comprehensive textual explanation of how two SFC codes meet the containment requirements, and if there is a violation, it explains why the containment relationship does not hold.

4 Petri Net Based Containment Checking

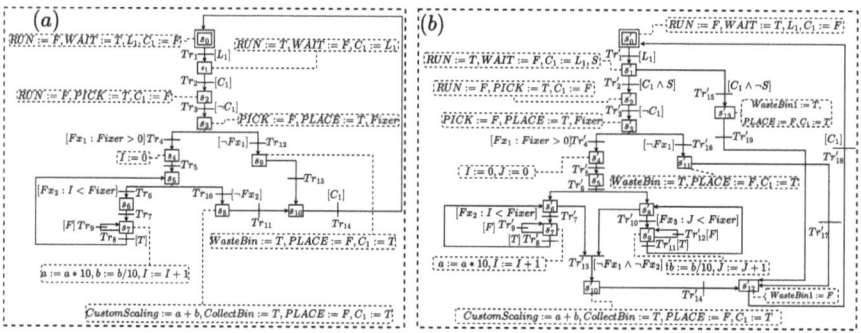

Fig. 3. Two versions of Pick and Place, (a) Original SFC (b) Upgraded SFC (changes shown in blue color) (Color figure online)

An SFC code is comparable to a Petri net; formally described in [6]. We reproduce the definition for brevity.

Definition 1. *A sequential function chart (SFC)* $\mathcal{S} = \langle S, X, A, T_S, s_0 \rangle$, *is a structure where S is a finite set of steps, X is a finite set of variables, A is a finite set of actions, T_S is a finite set of transitions for SFC, and s_0 is the initial step.*

Let Σ_{SFC} be the all possible states for variable in X, i.e., $\Sigma_{SFC} = \{\sigma | \sigma : X \rightarrow Value\}$ where σ assigns a $val \in Value$ to each variable in X. Next, $a_N \in A$ is an action, modeled as a state transformation function $\mathcal{T} : \Sigma_{SFC} \rightarrow \Sigma_{SFC}$.

A `block` is an action labeling function that assigns to each step a collection of pairs $\langle a_N, q \rangle$, referred to as an action block, where a_N is an action and $q \in \{entry, active, exit\}$ denotes an action qualifier. We consider the qualifiers *entry:* to indicate computation during the entry of the step, *exit:* to indicate computation during the exit of the step, and *active:* to indicate computation when the step is active. There is a flow relation between a *step* to a *transition* and a *transition* to a *step*. Each transition $t \in T_S$ is associated with a *guard condition* g_s which is a boolean function over a subset of the variables in X.

SFC semantics contains a global time, modeled by a *tick*[2]. Computation in the *active* step happens at each *tick* value. After the computation, the *tick* value is incremented. We do not consider hierarchical SFCs in this work, where actions may also contain another SFC.

Example 1. Figures 3(a) and 3(b) are SFC programs for the original and the upgraded version of the pick and place system (Fig. 1), respectively. In Fig. 3(a), $S = \{s_0, \cdots, s_{10}\}$, $T_S = \{Tr_1, \cdots, Tr_{14}\}$. Every step $s \in S$ is associated with an action sequence. The action sequence for s_7 is a= a*10, followed by b=b/10 and then I++. Every transition has a guard condition. In Fig. 3(a), the guard condition associated with Tr_4 is F_{x_1} and Tr_{12} is $\neg F_{x_1}$. Here F_{x_1} denotes the expression $Fixer > 0$. If no guard condition is explicitly associated with a transition, it is treated as *true*.

In Fig. 3(a), the SFC starts from step s_0, with the action WAIT=T, while all other actions are false. The sensor L_1 represents a load sensor on conveyor belt A. When an object is detected on this conveyor, L_1 becomes true, enabling transition Tr_1 and progressing to s_1, with update actions RUN=T, WAIT=F, and $C_1 = T$.

Next, with the activation of the guard condition $C_1 = T$, transition Tr_2 is enabled, leading to s_2. Here, the robotic arm picks the object from conveyor belt A, and C_1 is set to false (RUN=F, PICK=T, and $C_1 = F$).

When the guard condition for transition Tr_3 is true, the system enters s_3 where the object is transferred from conveyor belt A to B, and the action PLACE=T is set. During this placement, the robotic arm also checks the scaling parameter value using a sensor attached to the arm. If the scaling parameter is positive, they are fixed by a fixer, via step s_4 and the object is placed in the collection bin at s_8. Otherwise, the object is sent to the waste bin through step s_9.

---

[2] https://control.com/technical-articles/an-overview-of-iec-61131-3-Industrial-Automation-Systems/.

In the upgraded version shown in Fig. 3(b), an additional safety sensor (S) monitors the system's status. If the safety guard is *false*, the robot arm of Conveyor A remains locked, preventing the robot from transferring any object from Conveyor A to B. Instead, all objects are redirected to the waste bin via step s'_{13}. Additionally, the custom scaling process is now carried out in parallel. The blue-colored portion in Fig. 3(b) indicate the upgraded portions of the SFC. ∎

Definition 2. *A Petri net model is $N = \langle P, V, F, T, I, O, P_{M_0}, \texttt{tick} \rangle$, where P is a finite non-empty set of places, V is a set of variables, F be set of all update functions, T is a finite non-empty set of transitions, $I \subset P \times T$ is a finite non-empty set of input arcs which define the flow relation between places and transitions, $O \subset T \times P$ is a finite non-empty set of output arcs which define the flow relation between transitions and places and P_{M_0} is the initial set of place marking. Finally, $\texttt{tick}{:}T \rightarrow \mathbb{N}$ is a tick function that assigns a non-zero integer value to a transition.*

Each place is associated with a set of variables using the function $\phi : P \rightarrow 2^V$. Each element of V belongs to one of two disjoint subsets, namely the set of changed variables (V_c) or the set of unchanged variables (V_u). Here we only consider integer and boolean types. Each place is associated with a sequence of update functions $F_p \subseteq F$ for the variables in V where each function is of the form $\Sigma_{PN} \rightarrow \Sigma_{PN}$ such that Σ_{PN} represents set of all possible states of variable in V.

A place can hold a *token*. A place with a token is called a *marked place*. When a place is *marked*, it computes a sequence of functions associated with it. The corresponding values of the variables, as defined by these functions, are updated.

Each transition t is associated with a *guard condition* g_t, a boolean function over a subset of the variables. A transition t is said to be *enabled* when all its pre-place(s) have token(s), and they are associated with the set(s) of values of the variable which satisfy g_t. All the enabled transitions can fire simultaneously, which in turn models parallel execution. A transition $t_s \in T$ is said to be a *synchronizing transition* if its post-places are all the initial marked places. Our Petri net model is deterministic and one-safe (at any point in time, a place contains at most one token).

Tick Function: In PLC systems, the notion of a tick is a fundamental concept that captures the idea of synchronous execution. A tick represents a discrete scan cycle during which all enabled transitions are executed simultaneously, reflecting the cyclic nature of PLC operation. In our Petri net model, each transition t is associated with a tick value through the function tick(t), which indicates the specific execution cycle in which t fires. To ensure synchronous behavior, we enforce the constraint that all enabled transitions within a cycle must share the same tick value. If a transition t is enabled at multiple markings, its execution tick must reflect the latest logical time among its enabling pre-transitions. To ensure that all transitions occurring at the same logical time are executed simultaneously, the tick value of t is computed as the maximum of the tick values of its enabling pre-transitions. Formally, this is defined as:

$$\text{tick}(t) = \max\left(\text{tick}(t_1), \text{tick}(t_2), \ldots, \text{tick}(t_n)\right)$$

This guarantees causality preservation and enforces proper synchronization among concurrently enabled transitions.

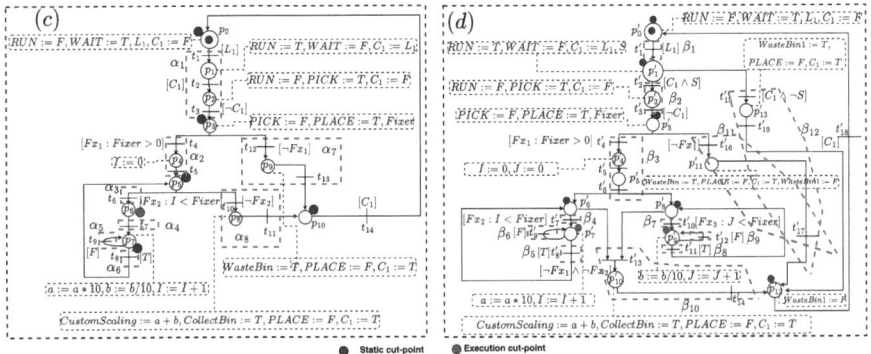

Fig. 4. Two versions of Petri nets

4.1 SFC to Petri Net Translation

Translating an SFC into a Petri net is syntactic and straightforward, where one can generate a Petri net in a single pass over the SFC structure. The Petri net model's entities I and O correspond to the SFC's flow relation. The mapping of SFC entities to Petri net entities is $S \to P$, $X \to V$, $T_s \to T$, $g_s \to g_t$, $s_0 \to P_{M_0}$, and $A \to F$. Note that the action names for each action block in the SFC are executed in the same order as the functions in F_p in the Petri net, with both following the ordering defined by the action qualifier in the order of *entry*, *active*, and *exit* for the particular action block.

For any *state-modifying action* (e.g., incrementing a variable) associated with a step in a Sequential Function Chart (SFC), the corresponding Petri net sub-net can be modeled as follows:

1. A *place p* represents the corresponding *SFC step* in the Petri net.
2. This place is connected to two *mutually exclusive transitions*.
3. One of these transitions, denoted t_u, models the execution of the state-modifying action. It forms a self-loop with p, represented by the flow relations (p, t_u) and (t_u, p).
4. The transition t_u is enabled under the *negation of the condition* that enables the alternative transition.

4.2 Computation and Containment of Petri Net Model

Before describing the containment checking in this subsection, we describe the prerequisites of the Petri net model related to computational equivalence.

Definition 3 (Successor marking). *A set of marked places P_{M+} is said to be a successor place marking of P_M, if P_{M+} includes all post-places of transitions T_M enabled by P_M. and also all the places of P_M whose post-transitions are not enabled; symbolically, $P_{M+} = \{p \mid p \in t^\circ \text{ and } t \in T_M\} \cup \{p \mid p \in P_M \text{ and } p \notin {}^\circ T_M\}$.*

Definition 4 (Computation). *In a Petri net model N with initial marked places P_{M_0}, a computation μ_p of an out-port p (place having a synchronizing transition) is a sequence $\langle T_1, T_2, \ldots, T_i, \ldots, T_l \rangle$ of sets of maximally parallelizable transitions [1] satisfying the following properties:*

1. *There exists a sequence of markings of places $\langle P_{M_0}, P_{M_1}, \ldots, P_{M_{l-1}} \rangle$ such that*
   (a) *P_{M_0} be the set of initial marked places*
   (b) *$\forall i, 1 \leq i < l$, P_{M_i} is a successor place marking of $P_{M_{i-1}}$, ${}^\circ T_i \subseteq P_{M_{i-1}}$ and $T_i^\circ \subseteq P_{M_i}$.*
2. *$p \in T_l^\circ$.*

There are two entities associated with every computation: (1) the condition of execution denoted as R_{μ_p} which is the boolean constraint that must hold for the computation path to be taken and (2) the data transformation denoted as r_{μ_p} which is the sequence of variable updates performed along the computation path; both are expressed in normalized form [8].

Definition 5 (Equivalence of a Computation). *Let N_0 and N_1 be two Petri net models with their set of initial place marking bijection f_{in} and out-port bijection f_{out}. A computation μ_p of a model N_0 having an out-port p is said to be equivalent to a computation $\mu_{p'}$ of another model N_1 having an out-port p' such that $f_{out}(p) = p'$, symbolically denoted as $\mu_p \simeq_c \mu_{p'}$, if $R_{\mu_p} \equiv R_{\mu_{p'}}$ and $r_{\mu_p} = r_{\mu_{p'}}$.*

Definition 6 (Containment of two models). *The Petri net model N_0 is said to be contained in the Petri net model N_1, represented as $N_0 \sqsubseteq N_1$, if, $\forall p \in$ out-port of N_0, for any computation μ_p of p, $\exists$ a computation $\mu_{p'}$ of an out-port $p' = f_{out}(p)$ of N_1 such that $\mu_p \simeq_c \mu_{p'}$.*

Definition 7 (Equivalence of two models). *A model N_0 is said to be computationally equivalent to a model N_1, symbolically denoted as $N_0 \simeq N_1$, if $N_0 \sqsubseteq N_1$ and $N_1 \sqsubseteq N_0$.*

In symbolic computation-based program equivalence checking, a loop is cut to create a cut-point. Then, a path α is constructed from one cut-point to another without any intermediary cut-points such that *any computation can be represented as a concatenation of paths* [9–12].

The notion of cut-points and paths has been adopted in Petri-net based models [1,2] as *static cut-points* for program equivalence checking. We revisit these concepts here since our approach is also built upon the general notion of cut-points and paths. Static cut-points are introduced in initial marked places, places with multiple post-transitions, places containing back edges, and out-ports. This enables us to break the model into a finite set of paths between these cut-points. The symbol $°\alpha$ denotes the set of places where the path α originates.

Like computation (Definition 4), every path α is associated with two entities: 1) the condition of execution along the path, denoted as R_α and 2) the data transformation along the path r_α. For example, consider Fig. 4(c). For the path α_1, $R_{\alpha_1} = L_1 \leadsto C_1 \leadsto \neg C_1$, and $r_{\alpha_1} = \{$RUN=F, PICK=F, PLACE=T, WAIT=F, $C_1 = F$,Fixer$\}$. The WFF constructor component (Fig. 1) stores these expressions in the normalized form [8].

While a static cut-point is a handy tool to model a computation, it is not sufficient when a computation involves an unknown number of loop traversals, as explained Example 2.

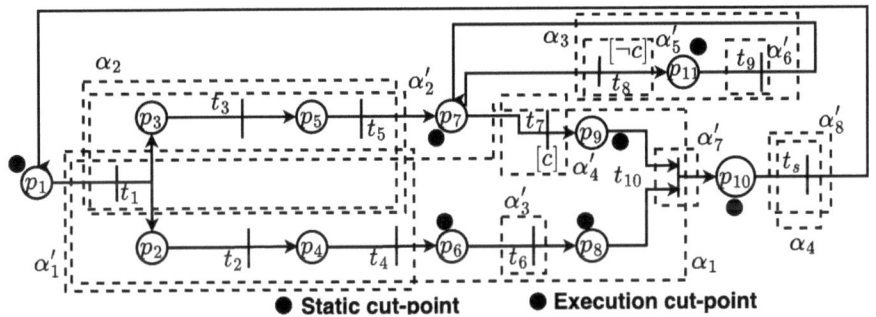

Fig. 5. A Petri net model of a computation involving loops

Example 2. Let us consider the computation in Fig. 5. The set of static cut-points is $\{p_1, p_7, p_{10}\}$ and the paths will be $\alpha_1 = \langle \{t_1\}, \{t_2\}, \{t_4\}, \{t_6\}, \{t_7\}\rangle$, $\alpha_2 = \langle\{t_1\}, \{t_3\}, \{t_5\}\rangle$, $\alpha_3 = \langle\{t_8\}, \{t_9\}\rangle$ and $\alpha_4 = \langle\{t_s\}\rangle$. Let us consider a computation μ of the out-port p_{10}, where $\mu = \langle T_1 = \{t_1\}, T_2 = \{t_2, t_3\}, T_3 = \{t_4, t_5\}, T_4 = \{t_6, t_8\}, (T_5 = \{t_9\}, T_6 = \{t_8\}, T_5 = \{t_9\})^n, T_7 = \{t_7\}, T_8 = \{t_{10}\}\rangle$. Since t_{10} (in α_1) and t_8 (in α_3) are mutually exclusive transitions and can't execute in parallel, α_1 and α_3 need to be concatenated in any computation, hence in μ as well. However, *There does not exist any concatenation of paths $\{\alpha_1, \alpha_2, \alpha_3\}$ that can express this computation μ due to the transition group T_4.* T_4 has transitions $\{t_6, t_8\}$ which execute in parallel. However, t_6 is a part of the path α_1, and t_8 belongs to α_3. As a result, α_1, α_3 cannot be concatenated in any order.

However, if we had p_6, p_7, p_8, p_9 and p_{11} also as cut-points (which we define as *Execution cut points* later in this paper), the path-set would have been $\alpha'_1 = \langle\{t_1\},\{t_2\},\{t_4\}\rangle$, $\alpha'_2 = \langle\{t_1\}.\{t_3\}.\{t_5\}\rangle$, $\alpha'_3 = \langle\{t_6\}\rangle$, $\alpha'_4 = \langle\{t_7\}\rangle$, $\alpha'_5 = \langle\{t_8\}\rangle$, $\alpha'_6 = \langle\{t_9\}\rangle$ and $\alpha'_7 = \langle\{t_{10}\}\rangle$ (green boundaries in Fig. 5). Now, intuitively, the computation μ can be depicted as the sequence $(\alpha'_1 \parallel \alpha'_2).(\alpha'_3 \parallel \alpha'_5).(\alpha'_6.\alpha'_5)^n.\alpha'_4.\alpha'_7$ of concatenation of parallelizable paths from the set $\{\alpha'_1, \alpha'_2, \alpha'_3, \alpha'_4, \alpha'_5, \alpha'_6, \alpha'_7\}$, where $(\alpha_1 \parallel \alpha_2)$ means parallel execution of α_1 and α_2 and $(\alpha_1.\alpha_2)$ means sequential execution α_1 followed by α_2. ∎

Definition 8 (Execution cut-point). *A place p is designated as a Execution cut-point if, during a token tracking execution of the model [13] (with static cut-points already incorporated), a place marking P_M containing p is encountered such that one of the following conditions is satisfied:*

1. P_M contains at least one cut-point; or
2. P_M contains more places than its pre-transitions T_M whose tick values are identical, i.e., $|P_M| > |{}^\circ P_M| \wedge {}^\circ P_M = \{t \in T_M \mid tick(t) = v\}$, where v is a fixed tick value common to all $t \in T_M$; this indicates that P_M contains more places than its pre-transitions whose tick values are identical, indicating parallel thread creation.

The concept of an *execution cut point* is similar to the *dynamic cut point*, introduced in [2] to address limitations of static cut-point computation, as shown in Example 2. The key distinction lies in their approach to timing and synchronization. Dynamic cut points, for Petri nets from C programs, focus on syntactic division into parallel branches without considering time. They disregard execution ticks and concurrency. Conversely, execution cut points accurately capture synchronous PLC semantics, such as in SFC, by showing enabled transitions and pre-places per tick, maintaining both timing and concurrency. Events within a tick are viewed as atomic and simultaneous, offering precise modeling of synchronized parallelism, reflecting true PLC execution. Henceforth, both static and execution cut-points will be collectively referred to as cut-points for simplicity.

Definition 9 (Path cover). *A finite set of paths $\Pi = \{\alpha_0, \alpha_1, \ldots, \alpha_k\}$ is said to be a path cover of a Petri net model N if any computation μ of an out-port of N can be represented as a sequence of concatenations of parallelizable paths from Π.*

The definition of the parallelizable path and the concatenation of a path, along with its characteristic, is reported in [2].

Definition 10 (Place, Transition and Variable correspondence). *Let N_0 and N_1 be two Petri net models with their initial marked places bijection f_{in} and out-port bijection f_{out}. Equivalence of paths of N_0 and N_1, a transition correspondence relation, denoted as $\eta_t \subseteq T_0 \times T_1$, and a place correspondence relation, denoted as $\eta_p \subseteq P_0 \times P_1$, are defined as follows:*

1. $f_{in} \subseteq \eta_p$,

2. Two paths α of N_0 and β of N_1 are said to be equivalent, denoted as $\alpha \simeq \beta$, if $\forall p \subseteq {}^\circ \alpha$, there exists exactly one $p' \subseteq {}^\circ \beta$ such that $\phi^0(p) = \phi^1(p')$, $\langle p, p' \rangle \in \eta_p$, $R_\alpha(\phi^0({}^\circ\alpha)) \equiv R_\beta(\phi^1({}^\circ\beta))$, $r_\alpha(\phi^0({}^\circ\alpha)) = r_\beta(\phi^1({}^\circ\beta))$ and TickStamp(last(α))= TickStamp(last(β)). Note that last(α) indicates the last member of the path α.
3. For any two equivalent paths α, β, $\langle$ last(α), last(β) $\rangle \in \eta_t$ if their TickStamps are identical.
4. Let V_0 and V_1 be the set of variables for N_0 and N_1 respectively, and the variable correspondence relation η_v is defined as $\eta_v \subseteq ((V_0 - V_1) \times V_1) \cup (V_0 \times (V_1 - V_0))$; thus, if $\langle v, v' \rangle \in \eta_v$ then either $(v \in V_0) \wedge (v \notin V_1)$ or, $(v' \in V_1) \wedge (v' \notin V_0)$. Furthermore, for any two equivalent paths α of N_0 and β of N_1, for any two places $p \in$ post place of $\alpha, p' \in$ post place of path $\beta, \langle p, p' \rangle \in \eta_p$ if
   (a) $\phi^0(p) = \phi^1(p')$ or
   (b) if $\phi^0(p) \in V_0 - V_1$ or $\phi^1(p') \in V_1 - V_0$ then
      i. either $\langle \phi^0(p), \phi^1(p') \rangle$ have already been associated with each other in η_v, or
      ii. they have not yet been associated with any other variables and can now be associated associated in η_v; also $\langle p, p' \rangle$ is put in η_p;

Validity of Equivalence Checking Calculus:

Proof (Proof sketch). We aim to show that any computation of an out-port in the original Petri net model N_0 has a behaviorally equivalent counterpart in the upgraded Petri net N_1.

Since our Petri net models (N_0 and N_1) is one-safe and deterministic, it admits at least one computation. A computation μ_p of an out-port (p) of N_0 is a sequence of sets of maximally parallelizable transitions, having a path cover Π (refer to Definition 9). This path cover can be decomposed into a sequence of parallel paths grouped by execution stages. The last group contains a single path because of a synchronizing transition.

Using the correspondence between places and transitions of N_0 and N_1, we replace each path in N_0 with an equivalent path in N_1. This produces a new sequence of grouped parallel paths in N_1, maintaining structural and behavioral similarity.

We then flatten each group by aligning the transitions across the paths into maximally parallelizable sets of transition, forming a complete sequence for N_1. To verify that this sequence is a valid computation, we check whether tokens are either produced by firing transitions or carried forward unchanged. This satisfies the marking update rule.

Thus, the sequence constructed in N_1 is a valid computation, which shows that every computation in N_0 has a behaviorally equivalent one in N_1. ∎

Algorithm 1: ContainmentChecker(N_0, N_1)

Input: Petri net models N_0 and N_1
Output: A six-tuple: (1) Π_0: path cover of N_0, (2) Π_1: path cover of N_1 matching Π_0, (3) E: set of $\langle \alpha, \beta \rangle$ such that $\alpha \simeq \beta$, (4) η_t: matched transition pairs, (5) $\Pi_{n,0}$: unmatched paths from N_0, (6) $\Pi_{n,1}$: unmatched paths from N_1

1:   $\eta_p \leftarrow \{\langle p, p' \rangle \mid p \in P_{M_0} \wedge p' \in P'_{M_0} \wedge p' = f_{in}(p)\}; \quad \eta_t \leftarrow \emptyset$
2:   $\Pi'_0 \leftarrow$ **PathConstructor**$(N_0); \quad \Pi'_1 \leftarrow$ **PathConstructor**(N_1)
3:   Initialize $\Pi_0, \Pi_1, \Pi_{n,0}, \Pi_{n,1}, E$ to $\emptyset$
4:   **for all** $\alpha \in \Pi'_0$ **do**
5:     Compute R_α and r_α
6:     $\Gamma' =$ **SelectedPathForCheckingEquivalence**$(\alpha, \Pi'_1, \eta_t, f_{in})$
7:     **for all** $\beta \in \Gamma'$ **do**
8:       Remove all uncommon variables and then Compute R_β and r_β
9:       **if** $(R_\alpha \simeq R_\beta) \wedge (r_\alpha == r_\beta) \wedge ($TickStamp$($last$(\alpha)) ==$ TickStamp$($last$(\beta)))$ **then**
10:         $\eta_t = \eta_t \cup \{\langle$last$(\alpha),$ last$(\beta)\rangle\}$
11:         $E = E \cup \{\langle \alpha, \beta \rangle\}$
12:         $\Pi_0 = \Pi_0 \cup \{\alpha\}; \Pi'_0 = \Pi'_0 \setminus \{\alpha\}$
13:         $\Pi_1 = \Pi_1 \cup \{\beta\}; \Pi'_1 = \Pi'_1 \setminus \{\beta\}$
14:         $\eta_p = \eta_p \cup \{\alpha^\circ, \beta^\circ\} \{\beta \simeq \alpha\}$
15:       **else if** $((R_{\alpha_1} \lesssim R_{\beta_1}) \wedge ($TickStamp$($last$(\alpha)) <$TickStamp$($last$(\beta))) \vee (r_\alpha = \emptyset))$ **then**
16:         $\Pi_0 =$ **prepareForExtension**$(\alpha, \Pi_0, \Pi_{n,0}, \eta_t, E)$ // extend α
17:       **else if** $((R_{\beta_1} \lesssim R_{\alpha_1}) \wedge ($TickStamp$($last$(\alpha)) >$ TickStamp$($last$(\beta))) \vee (r_\beta = \emptyset))$ **then**
18:         $\Pi_1 =$ **prepareForExtension**$(\beta, \Pi_1, \Pi_{n,1}, \eta_t, E)$ // extend β
19:       **else if** $(R_\beta \simeq R_\alpha) \wedge ($TickStamp$($last$(\alpha)) \neq$ TickStamp$($last$(\beta))) \wedge (r_{\alpha^\neg} = r_\beta)$ **then**
20:         $\Pi'_0 =$ **prepareForMerging**(Γ)
           //merging operation through N_0 or N_1
21:       **else if** $(R_{\alpha^\neg} \simeq R_\beta)$ **then**
22:         $\Pi_{n,0} = \Pi_{n,0} \cup \{\alpha\}$
23:         $\Pi_{n,1} = \Pi_{n,1} \cup \{\beta\}$
24:         $\Pi'_0 = \Pi_0 \setminus \{\alpha\}$ //Non-equivalent
25:         $\Pi'_1 = \Pi_1 \setminus \{\beta\}$ //Non-equivalent
26:       **end if**
27:     **end for**
28:   **end for**
29:   **if** $\Pi_{n,0} = \emptyset \wedge \Pi_{n,1} = \emptyset$ **then**
30:     Report "N_0 and N_1 are equivalent models."
31:   **else if** $\Pi_{n,0} = \emptyset \wedge \Pi_{n,1} \neq \emptyset$ **then**
32:     Report "$N_0 \sqsubseteq N_1$ and $N_1 \not\sqsubseteq N_0$."
33:   **else if** $\Pi_{n,0} \neq \emptyset \wedge \Pi_{n,1} = \emptyset$ **then**
34:     Report "$N_1 \sqsubseteq N_0$ and $N_0 \not\sqsubseteq N_1$."
35:   **else**
36:     Report "Two models may not be equivalent."
37:   **end if**
38:   **return** $\langle \Pi_0, \Pi_1, E, \eta_t, \Pi_{n,0}, \Pi_{n,1} \rangle$

5 Containment Checking Method

We describe the containment checking approach in Algorithm 1. The functionalities of the functions used in Algorithm 1 are described in Table 1. We demonstrate the containment checking between two Petri nets N_0 and N_1 shown in Figs. 4(c) and (d), respectively.

1. Step 1 of ContainmentChecker (Algorithm 1) accepts the user supplied place correspondence between the place p_0 of N_0 and the place p'_0 of N_1 to start the process.

2. Step 2 of Algorithm 1 invokes PathConstructor method(given in Table 1) to generate the set of paths for both N_0 and N_1 as $\{\alpha_1, \alpha_2, \ldots, \alpha_8\}$ and $\{\beta_1, \beta_2, \ldots, \beta_{12}\}$, respectively. The dotted boundaries for N_0 and N_1 represent these paths. The PathConstructor method invokes *getPathsForexecutionCutPt(* detailed functionalities is in Table 1) to generate execution cut-points and paths corresponding to these cut-points. For instance, the function *getPathsForexecutionCutPt* marked the place p_6 of N_0 and the places p'_7 and p'_9 of N_1 as *execution cut-points*.

3. *(Path Extension)*: Step 6 of Algorithm 1 identifies a set of candidate paths in N_1 for a path α in N_0. To begin with, the place correspondence between p_0 of N_0 and p'_0 of N_1 is considered. Accordingly, the path α_1 of N_0 is selected as the candidate path for β_1 of N_1 for equivalence checking. Since $R_{\alpha_1} \equiv L_1 \leadsto C_1 \leadsto \neg C_1$, and $R_{\beta_1} \equiv L_1$, $R_{\beta_1} \lesssim R_{\alpha_1}$ This is evaluated in step 17 of Algorithm 1 and *prepareForExtension* method (the detailed functionality is given in Table 1) is called to extend β_1.

The function *prepareForExtension* computes the set of post paths, i.e., the successor path of β_1 to be β_2. The execution condition of the concatenated path $(\beta_1.\beta_2)$ is $L_1 \leadsto C_1 \leadsto S \leadsto \neg C_1$. Since S is an uncommon variable, it is dropped and the resulting $R_{\beta_1.\beta_2} \equiv L_1 \leadsto C_1 \leadsto \neg C_1$. Now $R_{\alpha_1} \simeq R_{(\beta_1.\beta_2)}$ and $r_{\alpha_1} = r_{(\beta_1.\beta_2)}$. In the next iteration, step 9 of Algorithm 1 ensures $\alpha_1 \simeq (\beta_1.\beta_2)$, and the place correspondence between p_3 and p'_3 is established.

Similarly for the path α_2, step 6 of Algorithm 1 selects the candidate path β_3. In β_3, both variables I and J are initialized to 0. Therefore, variable I corresponds to variable J. As a result, their execution conditions are equivalent, and the data transformations are the same. Hence, $\alpha_2 \simeq \beta_3$, and p_5 of N_0 corresponds to both p'_6 and p'_8 of N_1 (step 9 of Algorithm 1).

4. *(Path Merging)*: The data transformation r_α is empty for the path α_3 in N_0. Therefore, step 27 of Algorithm 1 asserts that it is necessary to extend α_3 until the data transformation becomes non empty. The post-path of α_3 is α_4. The data transformation of the concatenated path $\alpha_e = (\alpha_3.\alpha_4)$ is r_{α_e} =(a=a*10,b=b/10,I++). Recall that the WFF constructor component (Fig. 1) the normalized form [8].

In the next iteration, step 6 selects candidate paths (from N_1) for this new path α_e, to be β_4 and β_7. For the path β_4, the execution condition matches; however, the data transformation does not, resulting in path merging (step 20 of Algorithm 1). We now explain how path merging works.

The function **prepareForMerging** first computes the pre-path of β_4 which is β_3, and identifies the post-path of β_3 as β_7. Recall, that β_7 is also a candidate for α_3. Therefore, β_4 merges with β_7, forming $\beta_m = (\beta_4 \curlyvee \beta_7)$. This process continues extending non-equivalent paths until another valid candidate path is found. Now, $r_{\alpha_e} = r_{\beta_m}$ and $\alpha_e \simeq \beta_m$. Therefore, place p_7 of N_0 corresponds to places p'_7 and p'_9 of N_1.

Using the same approach, the path α_5 is equivalent to the merged path $\beta_6 \curlyvee \beta_9$ and α_6 is equivalent to the merged path $\beta_5 \curlyvee \beta_8$. With this informal explanation, we now formally define path merging.

Definition 11 (Merge path). *A path α is said to be a Merge path, obtained by merging a set $Q_P = \{\alpha_1, \ldots, \alpha_k\}$ of parallelizable paths [2], if there exists a common transition t such that $t \in {}^\circ({}^\circ\alpha_i)$ for all i, $1 \leq i \leq k$. The path α is* denoted as $(\alpha_1 \curlyvee \ldots \curlyvee \alpha_k)$. The set of pre-places of α is equal to the union of the pre-places of the paths $\alpha_1, \ldots, \alpha_k$, i.e., $°\alpha = \bigcup_{i=1}^{k} °\alpha_i$.

5. *(One-to-one equivalence)*: The step 9 of Algorithm 1 asserts that the path α_7 of N_0 are equivalent to β_{11} because their data transformations and execution conditions are equivalent. Since `WasteBin1` is uncommon in β_{10}, it is dropped, after which step 9 also asserts that α_8 is equivalent to β_{10}.

6. *(Non-equivalence)*: The path β_{12} has no equivalent path in N_0, and its execution condition contains the uncommon variable S, causing $(R_\alpha \neg \simeq R_\beta)$. Therefore, the path β_{12} is put in Π'_1 in step 25 of Algorithm 1.

7. *(Termination)*: Finally, the method identifies that the non-equivalent path sets of N_1 are not empty in step 30 and accordingly declares that $N_0 \sqsubseteq N_1$ (step 32), i.e., the Petri net N_0 is contained in N_1.

Table 1. Summary of Functions with their main tasks which are used in Algorithm 1

Function Name	Functionalities
`PathConstructor(N)`	Constructs the set of paths from a Petri net N using the initial marking.
`getPathsFor` `executionCutPt` $(M_h, T_e, T_{sh}, \text{tick}, N)$	Given a Petri net N, the algorithm constructs the set of paths Q from marking M_h by firing concurrent transitions T_e, updating T_{sh} and $tick$, detecting cut-points when back-edges exist or $|T_e^\circ| > |T_e|$, invoking `constOnePath` on M_h, and recursively over new sets from `computeAllConcurTrans`.
`prepareForExtension` $(\gamma, \Pi', \Pi_n, \eta_t, E)$	Given a path γ, the algorithm updates Π' by identifying post-paths Γ_E^+, computing the set of pre-path χ_γ, trimming via `trimPrePaths` to update Π_n, and extending γ to γ_e using `extend`, guided by η_t and equivalence set E.
`prepareForMerging`(Γ)	Given $\Gamma \subseteq \Pi_0$ or Π_1, the algorithm merges a subset into γ_m if paths in $\mathcal{G} \subseteq \mathcal{P}$ end at the same transition τ and start from a common t (i.e., $P_G \subseteq t^\circ$); otherwise, it returns $\emptyset$.

Correctness and Complexity: The containment checker (Algorithm 1 is iterative over a set of finite paths. At each iteration, the number of paths to be compared is reduced. Therefore, its termination is guaranteed. All the functions which are called by the Algorithm 1 are also terminated. The worst-case time complexity of the containment checking algorithm is exponential because Algorithm 1 invokes the WFF constructor [8] at steps 9, 15, 17, 20, and 21. This constructor checks the equivalence between two expressions, a process that can be exponential in the worst case. The proof of the soundness of Algorithm 1 is given below.

Proof of the Soundness of Algorithm 1:

Proof (Proof sketch). We consider a computation of an out-port $p \in outP_0$ in the original Petri net N_0, represented as a sequence of sets of parallel paths from a path cover Π_0. Using the mapping E, which records the equivalence between the paths of N_0 and N_1 (constructed in Algorithm 1), we build a corresponding computation in N_1 by replacing each path in Π_0 with its equivalent path in N_1.

To show this forms a valid computation in N_1, we verify that each marking update respects Petri net semantics: post places of transitions in one step match pre places of the next, newly produced or retained places evolve the marking correctly.

For behavioral equivalence, we inductively prove that at each step, the corresponding paths in N_0 and N_1 preserve the condition of execution, data transformations, and tick value. This is ensured by the equivalence checks in the algorithm. Thus, the constructed computation in N_1 is both valid and semantically equivalent to that in N_0. ∎

6 Experimental Results

We tested our *'Antarbhukti*[3] tool on the open-source OSCAT library[4]. The OSCAT library comprises 1,000 applications, organized into 55 clusters according to their complexity. From this library, we selected 80 applications, each of which belongs to at least one of the 55 clusters. These 80 applications were then classified into four classes, classified on their Lines of Code (LOC) and complexity. The control programs are generally contained within 200 LOC.

6.1 Benchmark Preparation

Table 2 provides an overview of the applications considered for our experimental study. We have considered 80 applications from the OSCAT library and divided them into four classes based on their complexity.

Table 2. Description of various types of benchmarks from OSCAT library

Type	Description
Basic	Average 20 lines of program with one loop and two IF THEN ELSE
Simple	Avg. 40 lines of program with one level nested loop and three IF THEN ELSE
Medium	Average 60 lines with two level nested loops and there data independent loops
Complex	Average 90 lines with two or more data independent loops and two or more level nested IF THEN ELSE

---

[3] https://doi.org/10.5281/zenodo.15825113.
[4] http://www.oscat.de/images/OSCATBasic/oscat_basic333_en.pdf.

Next, for each of the SFC programs in Table 2, we have taken their upgraded versions from the OSCAT library. These upgradations are essentially the addition of sensors and actuators in the system, as well as some code improvement rules such as loop parallelization, thread-level parallelism, and code motion across the loop, to name a few.

6.2 Experimental Evaluation

We used only a single core of a 2.0GHz Intel® Core™2 machine to run these benchmarks. For both cases, we have performed the following steps systematically.

Tool Verification: We feed the original and the upgraded version of each benchmark as inputs to our tool. We evaluate the tool's performance when the original program is contained to the upgraded program and when the upgrade is faulty (i.e., the upgraded version does not retain the original functionality).

Performance: In Table 3, we report the average number of paths for both Petri net models as well as average containment checking time. The 4th column of Table 3 depicts whether the containment checker performed path merging (PM) to establish the containment between two models. As explained in Sect. 5, the containment checker may have to perform path merging in the case of either loop distribution followed or thread-level parallelism or both. Here we observe that path merging takes place in the Medium and Complex classes of OSCAT benchmarks. The 5th column of Table 3 depicts whether the containment checker performed path extension (PE) to establish the containment between two models. As explained in Sect. 5, the containment checker may have to perform path extension in the case of either non-uniform code transformations. Here, we observe that path extension occurs in the Simple and Complex classes of OSCAT benchmarks.

Comparison: We compare our approach with a popular state-of-the-art tool verifAPS[5], which is often used for software upgrades. This tool takes two SFCs as input and translates them into a subset of Structured Text. During this process, it eliminates all uncommon variables from the two SFCs, similar to our approach. Then they are converted to SMV models [14] and these two SMV models are verified for equivalence using NuXMV[6]. Unlike ours, verifAPS employs an inductive inference-based technique [15]. We compare our results with those produced by verifAPS in the last column of Table 3. Our method is approximately $\approx 4X$ faster than verifAPS because it translates the SFC to a Petri net in a syntactic way and uses path-based containment checking. This approach eliminates the need for invariant computation at each state, unlike verifAPS, which translates the SFC into two intermediate representations and computes the invariant during equivalence checking.

---

[5] https://formal.kastel.kit.edu/~weigl/verifaps/stvs/.
[6] https://nuxmv.fbk.eu/.

6.3 Fault Injection

In order to experimentally evaluate the performance of the tool in the presence of faulty code upgradation, we inject some errors in the SFC and observe the time it takes to detect these errors during the containment checking process. We have introduced the following types of (both control level and thread level) erroneous code upgradation.

1. **Type 1:** non-uniform boosting up assignment statement motions from one branch of step to the step preceding it, which introduces false-data dependencies; this has been injected into the `Medium` and `Simple` benchmarks.
2. **Type 2:** non-uniform duplicating down assignment statement motions from the step where bifurcation takes place to one branch that removes data dependency in the other branch; this has been injected in the `Complex` and `Basic` benchmarks.
3. **Type 3:** data-locality transformations which introduce false data-locality in the body of the loop in `Medium` and `Complex` benchmarks.

Table 3. Containment checking results

Benchmarks	# Paths from Original SFC	# Paths from Upgraded SFC	PM	PE	Time (Sec)	verifAPS Time (sec)
Basic	7	7	NO	NO	1.43	5.45
Simple	9	9	NO	YES	1.54	7.2
Medium	9	12	YES	NO	3.01	11.23
Complex	17	19	YES	YES	6.12	28.3

Table 4. Non-Equivalence checking times for faulty upgradation

Types	Benchmarks	Time (Sec)	1-BisimDegree	verifAPS Time (Sec)
Type 1	Medium	12.12	20 %	55.4
	Simple	1.27	10%	12.2
Type 2	Complex	14.11	22%	–
	Basic	1.23	8%	–
Type 3	Medium	2.43	14%	10.43
	Complex	5.32	21%	24.31

The third column of Table 4 shows the non-equivalence detection time in seconds. For OSCAT benchmarks, we have taken the average non-equivalence checking time for the "no" answer. The fourth column computes the fraction of non-equivalent paths for the two programs, expressed as $1 - \text{BisimDegree}$

(Definition 12). Here, the non-equivalence arises due to the injection of faults during upgradation.

Definition 12 (Degree of Bisimilarity). *The Degree of Bisimilarity (BisimDegree) between two models N_0 and N_1 comprising path sets Π_0 and Π_1 respectively, is defined as $BisimDegree = \frac{|\Pi_0 \cap \Pi_1|}{|\Pi_0 \cup \Pi_1|}$ where $\Pi_0 \cap \Pi_1$ comprises all pairs $\alpha \in \Pi_0, \beta \in \Pi_1$, such that $\alpha \simeq \beta$, as defined in Definition 10.*

The last column depicts the non-equivalence detection time for verifAPS tool. Here we observe that the tool verifAPS takes more time to detect equivalence than our tool because of checking the invariant in each state of the translated ST code from SFC. It is also to be noted that the **Type 2** error cannot be detected by verifAPS tool.

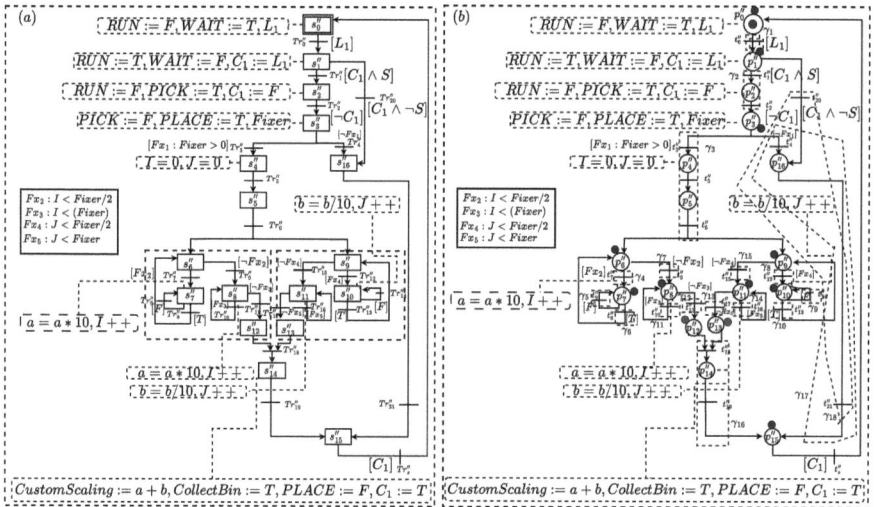

Fig. 6. Limitations of our method

7 Discussion

In light of the experimental results, we highlight several usage scenarios of the tool and mention a few limitations.

7.1 Utility of the Tool

Efficiency in Regression Testing: Since our tool relies on symbolic containment checking, an "yes" answer from the tool (the original code is contained in the upgraded code) completely eliminates any further testing. However, the tool is not *complete*, therefore, it is always possible that the tool falsely declares two containment programs as *non-equivalent*. In such a case, the testing team needs to manually investigate if the migration process is indeed correct. Thus, the tool offers an assistive approach as it does not completely automate verification. An objective evaluation of effort reduction requires rigorous field testing, which will be taken up by the engineering team. We have currently conducted a controlled field trial with a selected set of open-source SFC experts. A ballpark comparison revealed that our verification approach is $\approx 10X$ faster than manual testing; an SFC testing generally takes 3 to 5 min by a domain expert in a testing environment. The expert team has reported an effort reduction of the order of 60–80% in most cases. Furthermore, we have observed that our tool has been able to successfully detect containment of nearly 90% of software upgradation use cases.

Upgradation Assistance: The Developer Assistance component shown in Fig. 1 currently generates an elaborate report of equivalent and non-equivalent paths for the old and upgraded versions with the corresponding source code. This can be easily extended, where the tool is a plugin to a popular IDE (VSCode, Eclipse) and can provide real-time feedback by highlighting the portion of the source codes that are found to be non-equivalent. The user can then decide to accept or reject the suggestion given by the tool.

Noteworthy Capabilities: Our tool can handle various syntactic upgradations, including upgradation of data type, control structures, and more. Additionally, it captures several types of semantic-level upgradation, such as uniform and non-uniform code movement, loop-invariant code translation, code motion across loops, and thread-level parallelizing transformations.

7.2 Limitations

We illustrate an important limitation by manually creating a new version of the SFC (Fig. 6(a)) that is functionally equivalent to the original SFC code as shown in Fig. 3(a), but non-bisimilar. We took the help of open source SFC experts to ensure that this new version of the SFC, the original SFC (Fig. 3(a)), and the upgraded SFC (Fig. 3(b)) are all functionally equivalent. Figure 6(b) is the corresponding Petri net model generated by the proposed tool. Our method cannot establish containment between the Petri net in Fig. 6(b)) and the Petri net model of the SFC code in Fig. 4(c) because they are non-bisimilar.

The SFC code Fig. 3(a) has two parallel loop containing two independent operations. The variable *Fixer* determines how many times the loop will run. In the hand-crafted SFC in Fig. 6(a), the operations (multiplying a and dividing b) are split into two separate loops for parallelism, and the loop is also split in half. The first loop runs for Fixer/2 iterations, and then the second loop continues until the variable reaches Fixer. Since the loop iterations differ between SFC in Fig. 3(a) and the hand-crafted SFC in Fig. 6(a), the programs are considered non-bisimilar. In Fig. 6(a), the red boundaries show the non-bisimilar portions. The containment checker can not find paths in Fig. 4(c) that are equivalent to the paths $\gamma_4, \ldots \gamma_{16}$ in the Petri net shown in Fig. 6(b). In this example, the percentage of non-bisimilarity $(1 - \text{BisimDegree}) = 72.2\%$.

Another type of non-bisimilarity can arise if arithmetic expressions are modified without changing the functionality. For instance, if the multiplication operation is replaced with addition and shift operations, our current version of the tool will fail to establish their equivalence.

8 Related Work

Verifying safety-critical systems has gained prominence since 2000 and has emerged as a serious concern across various industries. Numerous literature sources [16–28] have recognized this problem and reported various verification schemes. A detailed survey [29] reported different verification approaches for IEC 61131-3 languages. Simon et al. [30] introduced test case generation for PLC software using a model checker that iteratively created program traces, trying to increase coverage metrics.

There have been two distinct approaches for verifying SFCs: model checking and theorem proving, both stemming from the SFC's ancestor standard Grafcet [31]. The model-checking approach translates SFCs into transition systems utilizing various models such as timed automata, hybrid automata, or state machines. Several property verification techniques for PLC programs are reported in [5,21,22,27,32–41]. These approaches primarily focus on verifying safety or liveness properties of subsets of IEC 61131-3 languages or language features. On the other hand, the theorem-proving method attempts to certify the properties of SFC-based system specifications, as reported in several studies [42–45].

Unlike these approaches, our focus is on the behavioural verification of the upgradation process, where our tool checks whether the original code is behaviourally contained to the upgraded code. The tool verifAPS reported in [5] describes an inductive inference-based approach for checking equivalence between two versions of SFCs. Behavioural verification and its applications have been well studied; several techniques for code-level verification are reported in [1,10–12,15,46–56]. A comprehensive and exhaustive set of benchmarks for various behavioural verification techniques is reported in [57]. In addition, several model-based behavioural verification methods are discussed in [58–63]. However, to the best of our knowledge, there has been *no reported work* on path based behavioral verification in the context of *software upgradration of PLC programs*.

9 Conclusion

In this work, we proposed a formally grounded verification framework to validate whether behavioral correctness is preserved during software upgrades of PLC software. Our approach introduces a novel technique that checks for behavioral containment through symbolic path equivalence of two Petri net models. Experimental evaluation on a diverse suite of benchmarks from the OSCAT library demonstrates the scalability and efficacy of our tool, with significant performance gains over the state-of-the-art *verifAPS* system. Our method is reliable, it does not give any false positive results. Our approach is language-agnostic; it can be extended to verify equivalence between any two control programs, as long as they are mapped to Petri nets.

An important limitation of our method is, its inability to handle hierarchical SFC as well as non-bisimilar SFCs. This is due to the restriction of traversing each loop exactly once. Furthermore, our method cannot accommodate timing behaviour (like TON construct), writable shared variables, and only operates on integer and boolean type variables. Overcoming these limitations will be key focus areas for our *future work*.

Acknowledgment. We are sincerely grateful to the reviewer for their valuable feedback, which greatly improved the presentation of this work. We also extend our heartfelt thanks to Mattias Ulbrich from KIT, Germany, for the valuable discussions that significantly enhanced this work.

References

1. Bandyopadhyay, S., Sarkar, D., Mandal, C.: Equivalence checking of petri net models of programs using static and dynamic cut-points. Acta Informatica **56**(4), 321–383 (2019)
2. Bandyopadhyay, S., Sarkar, D., Mandal, C., Banerjee, K., Duddu, K.R.: A path construction algorithm for translation validation using PRES+ models. Parallel Process. Lett. **26**(2), 1650010:1–1650010:18 (2016)
3. Vogel-Heuser, B., Legat, C., Folmer, J., Feldmann, S.: Researching evolution in industrial plant automation: scenarios and documentation of the pick and place unit (2014)
4. David, R.: Grafcet: a powerful tool for specification of logic controllers. IEEE Trans. Control Syst. Technol. **3**(3), 253–268 (1995)
5. Ulewicz, S., Vogel-Heuser, B., Ulbrich, M., Weigl, A., Beckert, B.: Proving equivalence between control software variants for programmable logic controllers. In: 20th IEEE Conference on Emerging Technologies & Factory Automation, ETFA 2015, Luxembourg, 8–11 September 2015, pp. 1–5. IEEE (2015)
6. Bauer, N., Huuck, R., Lukoschus, B., Engell, S.: A unifying semantics for sequential function charts. In: Ehrig, H., et al. (eds.) Integration of Software Specification Techniques for Applications in Engineering. LNCS, vol. 3147, pp. 400–418. Springer, Heidelberg (2004). https://doi.org/10.1007/978-3-540-27863-4_22
7. Lee, J., Bae, K.: Formal semantics and analysis of multitask PLC ST programs with preemption. In: Platzer, A., Rozier, K.Y., Pradella, M., Rossi, M. (eds.) Formal Methods - 26th International Symposium, FM 2024, Milan, Italy, 9–13 September 2024, Proceedings, Part I. Lecture Notes in Computer Science, vol. 14933, pp. 425–442. Springer (2024)
8. Sarkar, D., Sarkar, S.C.: A theorem prover for verifying iterative programs over integers. IEEE Trans. Software Eng. **15**(12), 1550–1566 (1989)
9. Manna, Z.: Mathematical theory of partial correctness. In: Engeler, E. (ed.) Symposium on Semantics of Algorithmic Languages. Lecture Notes in Mathematics, vol. 188, pp. 252–269. Springer (1971)

10. Necula, G.C.: Translation validation for an optimizing compiler. In: PLDI, pp. 83–94 (2000)
11. Barrett, C.W., Fang, Y., Goldberg, B., Hu, Y., Pnueli, A., Zuck, L.D.: Tvoc: a translation validator for optimizing compilers. In: CAV, pp. 291–295 (2005)
12. Rinard, M., Diniz, P.: Credible compilation. Technical Report MIT-LCS-TR-776, MIT (1999)
13. Wisniewski, R., Grobelna, I., Karatkevich, A.: Determinism in cyber-physical systems specified by interpreted petri nets. Sensors **20**(19), 5565 (2020)
14. McMillan, K.L.: Symbolic model checking. Kluwer (1993)
15. Beckert, B., Ulbrich, M., Vogel-Heuser, B., Weigl, A.: Regression verification for programmable logic controller software. In: Butler, M., Conchon, S., Zaïdi, F. (eds.) ICFEM 2015. LNCS, vol. 9407, pp. 234–251. Springer, Cham (2015). https://doi.org/10.1007/978-3-319-25423-4_15
16. Mitra, S., Wang, Y., Lynch, N., Feron, E.: Safety verification of model helicopter controller using hybrid input/output automata. In: Maler, O., Pnueli, A. (eds.) HSCC 2003. LNCS, vol. 2623, pp. 343–358. Springer, Heidelberg (2003). https://doi.org/10.1007/3-540-36580-X_26
17. Hsiung, P.-A., Lin, Y.-H.: Modeling and verification of safety-critical systems using safecharts. In: Wang, F. (ed.) FORTE 2005. LNCS, vol. 3731, pp. 290–304. Springer, Heidelberg (2005). https://doi.org/10.1007/11562436_22
18. Moser, L.E., Melliar-Smith, P.M.: Formal verification of safety-critical systems. Softw. Pract. Exper. **20**(9), 799–811 (1990)
19. Fan, C., Qin, Z., Mathur, U., Ning, Q., Mitra, S., Viswanathan, M.: Controller synthesis for linear system with reach-avoid specifications. IEEE Trans. Autom. Control **67**(4), 1713–1727 (2022)
20. Sibai, H., Mokhlesi, N., Fan, C., Mitra, S.: Multi-agent safety verification using symmetry transformations. In: TACAS 2020. LNCS, vol. 12078, pp. 173–190. Springer, Cham (2020). https://doi.org/10.1007/978-3-030-45190-5_10
21. Bornot, S., Huuck, R., Lukoschus, B.: Verification of sequential function charts using SMV. In: Arabnia, H.R. (ed.) Proceedings of the International Conference on Parallel and Distributed Processing Techniques and Applications, PDPTA 2000, 24–29 June 2000, Las Vegas, Nevada, USA. CSREA Press (2000)
22. Niang, M., Riera, B., Philippot, A., Zaytoon, J., Gellot, F., Coupat, R.: A methodology for automatic generation, formal verification and implementation of safe plc programs for power supply equipment of the electric lines of railway control systems. Comput. Ind. **123**, 103328 (2020)
23. Klikovits, S., Lawrence, D.P.Y., Gonzalez-Berges, M., Buchs, D.: Automated test case generation for the CTRL programming language using pex: lessons learned. In: Crnkovic, I., Troubitsyna, E. (eds.) SERENE 2016. LNCS, vol. 9823, pp. 117–132. Springer, Cham (2016). https://doi.org/10.1007/978-3-319-45892-2_9
24. Hansen, S.T., Thule, C., Gomes, C.: An FMI-based initialization plugin for INTO-CPS maestro 2. In: Cleophas, L., Massink, M. (eds.) SEFM 2020. LNCS, vol. 12524, pp. 295–310. Springer, Cham (2021). https://doi.org/10.1007/978-3-030-67220-1_22
25. Gomes, C., Meyers, B., Denil, J., Thule, C., Lausdahl, K., Vangheluwe, H., Meulenaere, P.: Semantic adaptation for FMI co-simulation with hierarchical simulators. Simulation **95**(3), 241–269 (2019)
26. Gomes, C.G.: Property preservation in co-simulation. Ph.D. thesis, University of Antwerp, Belgium (2019)

27. Bauer, N., et al.: Verification of PLC programs given as sequential function charts. In: Ehrig, H., et al. (eds.) Integration of Software Specification Techniques for Applications in Engineering. LNCS, vol. 3147, pp. 517–540. Springer, Heidelberg (2004). https://doi.org/10.1007/978-3-540-27863-4_28
28. Sarkar, S., Schoch, N., Hoernicke, M.: Modeling error propagation in a modular plant. In: 27th IEEE International Conference on Emerging Technologies and Factory Automation, ETFA 2022, Stuttgart, Germany, 6–9 September 2022, pp. 1–4. IEEE (2022)
29. Rossi, O., Lesage, J.-J., Roussel, J.-M.: Formal validation of PLC programs: a survey. In: European Control Conference, ECC 1999 - Conference Proceedings (1999)
30. Simon, H., Friedrich, N., Biallas, S., Hauck-Stattelmann, S., Schlich, B., Kowalewski, S.: Automatic test case generation for plc programs using coverage metrics. In: 2015 IEEE 20th Conference on Emerging Technologies & Factory Automation (ETFA), pp. 1–4 (2015)
31. British Standards Institute Staff. GRAFCET Specification Language for Sequential Function Charts. B S I Standards (2002)
32. Tournier, J.-C., Adiego, B.F., Lopez-Miguel, I.D.: PLCverif: status of a formal verification tool for programmable logic controller. In: Proceedings of ICALEPCS 2021, number 18 in International Conference on Accelerator and Large Experimental Physics Control Systems, pp. 248–252. JACoW Publishing, Geneva, Switzerland (2022)
33. He, N., Oke, V., Allen, G.: Model-based verification of plc programs using simulink design. In: 2016 IEEE International Conference on Electro Information Technology (EIT), pp. 0211–0216 (2016)
34. Ukegbu, C., Mehrpouyan, H.: Cooperative verification of plc programs using coveriteam: towards a reliable and secure industrial control systems. In: Proceedings of Cyber-Physical Systems and Internet of Things Week 2023, CPS-IoT Week 2023, pp. 37–42. Association for Computing Machinery, New York (2023)
35. Filkorn, Th., Hölzlein, M., Warkentin, P., Wei, M.: Formal verification of PLC-programs. IFAC Proc. Vol. **32**(2), 1513–1518 (1999). 14th IFAC World Congress 1999, Beijing, Chia, 5-9 July
36. Xiao, L., Li, M., Gu, M., Sun, J.: Combinational model-checking of plc programs' verification based on instructions. In: 2014 IEEE International Conference on Mechatronics and Automation, pp. 1335–1340 (2014)
37. Ovatman, T., Aral, A., Polat, D., Ünver, A.O.: An overview of model checking practices on verification of PLC software. Softw. Syst. Model. **15**(4), 937–960 (2016)
38. Ravakambinintsoa, J., Dumitrescu, E., Zamaï, E., Chalon, D.: Work in progress - model-check PLC programs: towards a efficient formalization approach. In: 29th IEEE International Conference on Emerging Technologies and Factory Automation, ETFA 2024, Padova, Italy, 10–13 September 2024, pp. 1–4. IEEE (2024)
39. De Smet, O., et al.: Safe programming of plc using formal verification methods (2007)
40. Ukegbu, C., Mehrpouyan, H.: Cooperative verification of PLC programs using coveriteam: towards a reliable and secure industrial control systems. In: Proceedings of Cyber-Physical Systems and Internet of Things Week 2023, CPS-IoT Week 2023 Workshops, San Antonio, TX, USA, 9–12 May 2023, pp. 37–42. ACM (2023)
41. Beckert, B., Cha, S., Ulbrich, M., Vogel-Heuser, B., Weigl, A.: Generalised test tables: a practical specification language for reactive systems. In: Polikarpova, N., Schneider, S. (eds.) IFM 2017. LNCS, vol. 10510, pp. 129–144. Springer, Cham (2017). https://doi.org/10.1007/978-3-319-66845-1_9

42. Blech, J.O.: A tool for the certification of PLCs based on a coq semantics for sequential function charts. CoRR, abs/1102.3529 (2011)
43. Blech, J.O., Ould Biha, S.: Verification of PLC properties based on formal semantics in Coq. In: Barthe, G., Pardo, A., Schneider, G. (eds.) SEFM 2011. LNCS, vol. 7041, pp. 58–73. Springer, Heidelberg (2011). https://doi.org/10.1007/978-3-642-24690-6_6
44. Blech, J.O., Biha, S.O.: On formal reasoning on the semantics of PLC using Coq. CoRR, abs/1301.3047 (2013)
45. Bornot, S., Huuck, R., Lakhnech, Y., Lukoschus, B.: An Abstract Model for Sequential Function Charts, pp. 255–264. Springer, Boston (2000)
46. Verdoolaege, S., Janssens, G., Bruynooghe, M.: Equivalence checking of static affine programs using widening to handle recurrences. In: Proceedings of CAV 2009, pp. 599–613 (2009)
47. Dahiya, M., Bansal, S.: Black-box equivalence checking across compiler optimizations. In: Chang, B.-Y.E. (ed.) APLAS 2017. LNCS, vol. 10695, pp. 127–147. Springer, Cham (2017). https://doi.org/10.1007/978-3-319-71237-6_7
48. Kurhe, V.K., Karia, P., Gupta, S., Rose, A., Bansal, S.: Automatic generation of debug headers through blackbox equivalence checking. In: Lee, J.W., Hack, S., Shpeisman, T. (eds.) IEEE/ACM International Symposium on Code Generation and Optimization, CGO 2022, Seoul, Korea, Republic of, 2–6 April 2022, pp. 144–154. IEEE (2022)
49. Kundu, S., Lerner, S., Gupta, R.: Validating high-level synthesis. In: Gupta, A., Malik, S. (eds.) CAV 2008. LNCS, vol. 5123, pp. 459–472. Springer, Heidelberg (2008). https://doi.org/10.1007/978-3-540-70545-1_44
50. Kundu, S., Lerner, S., Gupta, R.K.: Translation validation of high-level synthesis. IEEE Trans. CAD Integr. Circ. Syst. **29**(4), 566–579 (2010)
51. Badihi, S., Akinotcho, F., Li, Y., Rubin, J.: Ardiff: scaling program equivalence checking via iterative abstraction and refinement of common code. In: Proceedings of the 28th ACM Joint Meeting on European Software Engineering Conference and Symposium on the Foundations of Software Engineering, ESEC/FSE 2020, pp. 13–24. Association for Computing Machinery, New York (2020)
52. Pailoor, S., Wang, Y., Dillig, I.: Semantic code refactoring for abstract data types. Proc. ACM Program. Lang. **8**(POPL) (2024)
53. Sharma, R., Schkufza, E., Churchill, B., Aiken, A.: Data-driven equivalence checking. SIGPLAN Not. **48**(10), 391–406 (2013)
54. Gupta, S., Saxena, A., Mahajan, A., Bansal, S.: Effective use of SMT solvers for program equivalence checking through invariant-sketching and query-decomposition. In: Beyersdorff, O., Wintersteiger, C.M. (eds.) SAT 2018. LNCS, vol. 10929, pp. 365–382. Springer, Cham (2018). https://doi.org/10.1007/978-3-319-94144-8_22
55. Mora, F., Li, Y., Rubin, J., Chechik, M.: Client-specific equivalence checking. In: Proceedings of the 33rd ACM/IEEE International Conference on Automated Software Engineering, ASE 2018, pp. 441–451. Association for Computing Machinery, New York (2018)
56. Churchill, B., Padon, O., Sharma, R., Aiken, A.: Semantic program alignment for equivalence checking. In: Proceedings of the 40th ACM SIGPLAN Conference on Programming Language Design and Implementation, PLDI 2019, pp. 1027–1040. Association for Computing Machinery, New York (2019)
57. Badihi, S., Li, Y., Rubin, J.: Eqbench: a dataset of equivalent and non-equivalent program pairs. In: 2021 IEEE/ACM 18th International Conference on Mining Software Repositories (MSR), pp. 610–614 (2021)

58. Truong, N.-T., Souquieres, J.: Verification of behavioural elements of UML models using B. In: Proceedings of the 2005 ACM Symposium on Applied Computing, SAC 2005, pp. 1546–1552. Association for Computing Machinery, New York (2005)
59. Ossami, D.D.O., Jacquot, J.-P., Souquières, J.: Consistency in UML and B multi-view specifications. In: Romijn, J., Smith, G., van de Pol, J. (eds.) IFM 2005. LNCS, vol. 3771, pp. 386–405. Springer, Heidelberg (2005). https://doi.org/10.1007/11589976_22
60. Molnár, V., et al.: Towards the formal verification of SysML v2 models. In: Proceedings of the ACM/IEEE 27th International Conference on Model Driven Engineering Languages and Systems, MODELS Companion 2024, pp. 1086–1095. Association for Computing Machinery, New York (2024)
61. Grobelny, M., Grobelna, I., Adamski, M.: Hardware behavioural modelling, verification and synthesis with UML 2.x activity diagrams. IFAC Proc. Vol. **45**(7), 134–139 (2012). 11th IFAC, IEEE International Conference on Programmable Devices and Embedded Systems
62. Ding, J., Reniers, M., Lu, J., Wang, G., Feng, L., Kiritsis, D.: Integration of modeling and verification for system model based on karma language. In: Proceedings of the 18th ACM SIGPLAN International Workshop on Domain-Specific Modeling, DSM 2021, pp. 41–50. Association for Computing Machinery, New York (2021)
63. Gu, C., Ma, Z., Li, Z., Giua, A.: Verification of nonblockingness in bounded petri nets with a semi-structural approach. In: 2019 IEEE 58th Conference on Decision and Control (CDC), pp. 6718–6723 (2019)

Author Index

A
Akshay, S. 321
An, Jie 3
Anand, Ashwani 65
Anand, Ayush 135
Aryaman, Shaan 299

B
Bandyopadhyay, Soumyadip 447
Bansal, Suguman 277
Battista, Ludovico 363
Brand, Sebastiaan 260

C
Cadilhac, Michaël 425
Cardelli, Luca 345
Chakraborty, Supratik 321
Chatterjee, Krishnendu 411
Corsi, Davide 157

F
Flügel, Vanessa 425
Fujinami, Hiroya 3

G
Genest, Blaise 299
Germerie Guizouarn, Loïc 135
Goharshady, Amir Kafshdar 411
Goharshady, Ehsan Kafshdar 411
Gonzalez, Bruno Maria René 49

H
Halevy, Naama Shamash 87
Hasuo, Ichiro 3, 109
Heck, Linus 207

I
Iseri, Hiroki 3

J
Jensen, Peter Gjøl 49
Jéron, Thierry 135
Joshi, Aniruddha 321
Junges, Sebastian 180, 207

K
Karrabi, Mehrdad 411
Katoen, Joost-Pieter 207
Kupferman, Orna 87
Kushwah, Rohit 277

L
Laarman, Alfons 260
Liao, Yuke 299

M
Majumdar, Anirban 27
Mallik, Kaushik 157
Meel, Kuldeep 299
Miao, Yan 231
Mitra, Sayan 231
Mukherjee, Sayan 27, 135
Murali, Vishnu 387

N
Nayak, Satya Prakash 65

O
Oumer, Mohammed Adib 387

P
Peper, Jordan 231
Pérez, Guillermo A. 425
Phalakarn, Kittiphon 109
Pinisetty, Srinivas 135

Q
Quatmann, Tim 207

R

Raha, Ritam 65
Rao, Shrisha 425
Raskin, Jean-François 27
Rodríguez, Andoni 157
Roy, Subhajit 277
Ruchkin, Ivan 231

S

Saadat, Milad 411
Sağlam, Irmak 65
Sánchez, César 157
Sankur, Ocan 135
Sarkar, Santonu 447
Schmid, Stefan 49
Schmuck, Anne-Kathrin 65
Seeliger, Maximilian 411
Seshia, Sanjit 321
Shah, Shetal 321
Spel, Jip 207
Squillace, Giuseppe 345
Srba, Jiří 49
Subramanian, Vignesh 277

Suenaga, Kohei 3

T

Tonetta, Stefano 363
Torfah, Hazem 321
Tribastone, Mirco 345
Tsai, Yun Chen 109
Tschaikowski, Max 345

V

van der Maas, Luko 180
Vandin, Andrea 345

W

Waga, Masaki 3

Y

Yanagisawa, Nayuta 3

Z

Zamani, Majid 387
Zimmermann, Martin 49
Žikelić, Đorđe 411

MIX
Papier aus verantwortungsvollen Quellen
Paper from responsible sources
FSC® C105338

If you have any concerns about our products,
you can contact us on
ProductSafety@springernature.com

In case Publisher is established outside the EU,
the EU authorized representative is:
**Springer Nature Customer Service Center GmbH
Europaplatz 3, 69115 Heidelberg, Germany**

Printed by Libri Plureos GmbH
in Hamburg, Germany